Civil Justice in Renaissance Scotland

Medieval Law and Its Practice

VOLUME 4

Civil Justice in Renaissance Scotland

The Origins of a Central Court

By

A.M. Godfrey

BRILL

LEIDEN • BOSTON
2009

Cover illustration: Detail from a page from the Books of Council recording the sitting of the Session on 27 May 1532, following the Parliament which legislated for the College of Justice in the same month: NAS CS 6/1, fol. 1. ScotlandsImages.com. Crown Copyright 2007, The National Archives of Scotland, CS 6/1 Acta Dominorum Concilii et Sessionis.

This book is printed on acid-free paper.

Library of Congress Cataloging-in-Publication Data

Godfrey, A.M. (Andrew Mark)
Civil justice in Renaissance Scotland : the origins of a central court / by A.M. Godfrey
Brill.
p. cm. — (Medieval law and its practice ; 4)
Includes bibliographical references (p.) and an index.
ISBN 978-90-04-17466-5 (hardback : alk. paper)
1. Scotland. Court of Session—History—To 1500. 2. Scotland. Court of Session—History—16th century. 3. Courts—Scotland—History—To 1500. 4. Courts—Scotland—History—16th century. I. Title. II. Series.

KDC844.G63 2009
347.411'023—dc22

2009002161

ISSN 1873-8176
ISBN 978 90 04 17466 5

PRINTED IN THE NETHERLANDS

CONTENTS

PREFACE

This book expores the nature of civil justice in Renaissance Scotland through a reconsideration of the foundation of the College of Justice in 1532. The main argument to be advanced is that this was the culmination of the development of the Court of Session ("the Session") as a central court. The institutional history of central justice is assessed from the thirteenth-century Parliament onwards, against the background of jurisdictional change in late medieval Scotland. This provides the basis for a discussion of litigation in the Session and the nature of its jurisdiction in 1532. The book is primarily concerned with the origins of a central court, and the implications of this for governance, the legal order and society in terms of both legal development and dispute resolution. Although mostly based upon archival research concerned to trace the development of a Scottish central court out of the medieval King's Council, this exercise should be regarded in part as a detailed case-study of a common European development. It is not itself comparative history, but it does address themes of comparative relevance to the study of central courts, centralisation, increasing reliance on central authority, and the development of the state in the early modern period. Such themes include jurisdictional change and its relationship with central authority, how such change was embodied in a new generation of law courts associated with royal councils, related shifts in the structures of jurisdictional competence and judicial remedies, the relationship between forms of remedy and conceptual frameworks for legal liability in private law, the effect of this upon substantive rules of private law, and relations between private and public justice.

Other aspects of the book are not only of comparative relevance but also have a special relevance to Scottish historical debate. These involve examining the changing role which a central court, and legal culture in general, played in sixteenth century Scotland. Recent scholarship has done much to illuminate understanding of how law was understood in seventeenth-century Scotland, above all in J.D. Ford's hugely important and ground-breaking study, *Law and Opinion in Scotland during the Seventeenth Century* (Oxford, 2007). This book aims to bring into clearer focus our understanding of some central features of the sixteenth-century legal order which lay behind such later developments in juristic thought. An appreciation of the origins of a central court is the essential starting point for a wider understanding of the sixteenth-century legal system. Assessing the role of law and litigation in patterns of dispute resolution is also essential to understanding the wider changes in sixteenth century society, which resulted in a "feuding society" giving way to one which relied more fundamentally on the observation of legal norms, protected and applied through court remedies.

The Session ultimately evolved as a function of the King's Council exercising a judicial role inherited from the medieval Parliament, embodied in 1532 in a newly instituted College of Justice. To that extent this book relates to four distinct but connected institutions: Parliament, Council, Session, and the College of Justice. The book offers a new perspective as the first study of the sixteenth-century Session to evaluate its role as a court of law. It is the first to systematically examine its jurisdiction and litigation with reference to the manuscript record of its business. It is also the first to examine and reassess the foundation of the College of Justice since the classic account by R.K. Hannay was published in 1933. In doing so it has greatly benefited from following upon recent pioneering and foundational works, above all Hector MacQueen's *Common Law and Feudal Society in Medieval Scotland* (Edinburgh, 1993). Although the focus of the book lies in the early to mid-sixteenth century, the whole prior history of central justice in Scotland is taken as the framework for evaluating developments within that more specific period. This has only been possible through reliance on a series of extremely important but unpublished Ph.D. theses by Alison McQueen, Alan Borthwick, Trevor Chalmers, and Kenneth Emond. These unpublished works afford fundamental new insights into the early judicial role of Parliament (McQueen), the fifteenth-century King's Council (Borthwick and Chalmers) and the administration of central justice during the minority of James V from 1513 to 1528 (Emond). The account presented here is greatly indebted to these studies.

The first two chapters are preliminary ones which critically examine the history of a central court in Scotland before the foundation of the College of Justice in 1532. They set out developments in the medieval Parliament and the fifteenth and early sixteenth-century Session so as to provide a clear account which incorporates the fruits of recent scholarship for the first time since Hannay's works were published between seventy-five and a hundred years ago. The stages in the evolution of the Session are presented chronologically so as to present the clearest possible picture of each separate development, since the more discursive nature of Hannay's analysis sometimes led to this being obscured. The main thesis of the book is presented in chapter 3, in which the foundation of the College of Justice in 1532 and its significance is re-assessed. Thereafter, a series of chapters examine the procedure, judicial business and jurisdiction of the Session, and the light which they shed upon the significance of 1532. Finally, the last two chapters seek to place the Session in the wider context of dispute resolution in Scottish society more generally. They examine alternative "private" methods of conducting disputes, with a focus on arbitration in particular, but they also evaluate the relationship between private methods and the public justice of the courts.

Apart from the specific enquiries with which the book is concerned, it is hoped that it will provide many new points of departure for further research on sixteenth century Scottish legal history as well as suggest themes which may have application to legal development and central justice in other European jurisdictions too. The sixteenth century remains a neglected period in terms of Scottish legal history. The prevalence of juristic accounts of the law written in the seventeenth century, such as most famously Lord Stair's *Institutions of the Law of Scotland* (1681), and the increasing accessibility of other source materials around this time, have presented a mature vision of early modern Scots law which has tended to disguise from modern eyes the significance of the transitional and formative period constituted by the sixteenth century. As this book shows, the sixteenth century was of particular significance because it witnessed a fundamental transition between the late medieval legal order in Scotland and the contrasting legal order of a recognisably early modern state. Jurisdictional change is one measure of that transition, but many other strands of legal change flowed from it in turn. The starting point for most if not all of the changes in question is the history of the Session, and the way it exercised its role as a central court. The central argument of this book is that the Session became a central court in 1532 with the foundation of the College of Justice. The foundation was the final and decisive step in a series of developments which saw the Session come to function and be constituted as a central court. A better understanding of these developments should therefore help illuminate legal development in the century as a whole and suggest new directions for research. It should be noted, however, that this book is not intended to be a general institutional history of the Court of Session. It traces the main features of institutional development but otherwise is concerned with its jurisdiction and litigation from a legal perspective, but not personnel, judges, advocates, or litigants themselves. On some of these aspects, however, an authoritative treatment can be found in John Finlay's *Men of Law in Pre-Reformation Scotland* (East Linton, 2000).

The treatment of many subjects in the book is naturally constrained by the methodology I have used and the selection of sources I have made. It goes without saying that many of these will undoubtedly benefit from the labour of further research and that more can and should be added to the account given here. The new perspective in the book has been afforded primarily by the exploitation of the manuscript record of the acts and decreets of the Lords of Council and Session. Until 1540 there are few if any other substantial sources concerning litigation which could be systematically exploited. From 1540 there begins to survive a series of judicial notebooks of which the first we currently know about is the "Practicks" of John Sinclair, covering the 1540s. However, my study of the manuscript record is to 1534, because it was intended to illuminate the position around 1532. I have therefore not attempted to incorporate reference to later sources such as Sinclair except in particular isolated instances.

In an earlier form, I have previously published some of the material presented in the book (in chapters 4, 6 and 8, and appendices 1 and 2 in particular) in a number of articles. The main instances are:

> "Jurisdiction over rights in land in later medieval Scotland", *Juridical Review* (2000), 243–263
> "Arbitration and dispute resolution in sixteenth century Scotland", *Tijdschrift voor Rechtsgeschiedenis* 70 (2002), 109–135
> "*Ius Commune*, Practick and Civil Procedure in the Sixteenth-Century Court of Session", *Tijdschrift voor Rechtsgeschiedenis* 72 (2004), 283–295
> "Arbitration in the *Ius Commune* and Scots Law", *Roman Legal Tradition* 2 (2004), 122–135.

In substance, these articles will now be superseded by the contents of this book.

It should be noted that the text of the book was first completed in November 2007, prior to the publication in online form of *The Records of the Parliaments of Scotland to 1707*, ed. K.M. Brown et al. (St Andrews, 2007) (*RPS*). This is now the authoritative scholarly edition of the legislation and other records of the Parliament of Scotland within an independent kingdom and includes all legislation from 1235 to 1707. The edition has the advantage of being constructed as a searchable database which presents the original manuscript text together with a translation into modern English. It supersedes the massive nineteenth-century Record Commission edition of *The Acts of the Parliaments of Scotland* (Edinburgh 1814–1875) (*APS*). Scholarship published to date obviously refers to *APS* and inevitably this book does so too. However, from now on scholars will work from *RPS* using its website (http://www.rps.ac.uk/). Its edition of the text of some of the sources relevant to this book differs in some details from that of *APS*. It is also distinguished by a detailed critical apparatus which refers very informatively to the complex manuscript tradition and variant readings. Readings of the fifteenth century legislation on the Session is particularly affected in this way and therefore, in the course of revising the text of the book in 2008, I made the decision to incorporate reference to the *RPS* edition in relation to the most significant statutes, even though the book as a whole relies on *APS*. Of course, all legislation referred to in the book from *APS* can also be consulted in the *RPS* edition online. However, I have only consulted it in the more limited way described. When I have done so will be apparent from the form of reference given in the text.

I have become happily indebted to many people over a long period of time in pursuing the research which led to this book. However, the inspiration to undertake research on Scottish history in the first place can be pinpointed in almost uncanny fashion. It came quite serendipitously from attending Jenny Wormald's brilliantly memorable O'Donnell Lectures on "The Conception of Scottish Kingship and the Rebirth of Britain" in Oxford on 8 and 9 May 1990. Equally serendipitously, I was soon afterwards a member of Dr Wormald's special subject seminar on sixteenth-century Tudor government and society, run jointly with C.S.L. Davies, and able to benefit from its lively debates. These helped introduce me to themes, sources and institutions which were to prompt my subsequent interest in research in Scottish history. Furthermore, in that context, Dr Wormald's writings on Scottish governance, dispute settlement and kinship provided and continue to provide a richly suggestive source for my own research. These things have shaped the foundation for everything that follows, and for that I am deeply grateful. At a crucial and uncertain stage I also received early encouragement and advice in Oxford from Dr Wormald, Dr Davies and Professor Laurence Brockliss about historical study and embarking upon my research. This was immensely helpful and supportive and proved to be of decisive importance. That I had come to feel enthusiasm and dedication about pursuing historical research also derived in large measure from the stimulating experience of having undergraduate tutorials on medieval and early modern European and British history with Laurence Brockliss, Gerald Harriss, Maurice Keen and Penry Williams and the encouragement that each of them gave to me. Again, I cannot thank them enough.

I owe a very great debt to the Faculty of Law (now School of Law) of the University of Edinburgh for awarding a Gray scholarship and a research studentship which allowed me to complete the Ph.D. thesis from which this book ultimately derives. Similar debts for supporting my research are also owed respectively to the Schools of Law at the University of Aberdeen, where I was a lecturer from 1999 to 2002, and at the University of Glasgow, where I have been a lecturer since 2002. Support included the grant of one semester of sabbatical research leave from Glasgow in 2006. Similarly, I am very grateful to the Royal Society of Edinburgh and the Caledonian Research Foundation, who awarded me a six-month European Visiting Research Fellowship in 2006, and to the Max Planck Institute for European Legal History in Frankfurt am Main, who accepted me as a Visiting Research Fellow for six months in 2006 and for a further two months on a return visit in 2007. The primary research for this book was undertaken at the National Archives of Scotland and I am grateful to the staff there for their assistance over many years. In relation to preparing the book for publication I am very grateful to John Hudson as General Editor of the series for his advice and patience, to an anonymous reader for comments on the manuscript of the book, and to the staff at Brill.

A great many colleagues and friends have contributed support, assistance, advice, discussion and encouragement over a long period of time. Here is not the place to identify them all. Collectively, however, I would like to thank the members of the Scottish Legal History Group, the Conference of Scottish Medievalists, the Scottish Parliament Project at the University of St Andrews, the British Legal History Conference, the London Legal History Seminar, the Ius Commune Research School of the Universities of Maastricht, Leuven, Utrecht and Amsterdam, the Gerda Henkel Stiftung Research Group on the History of Delay in Civil Procedure, and the Max Planck Institute for European Legal History. All have given me the opportunity to present my research over the years in a way which has been invaluable. More particularly I would specially like to thank John Cairns, Julian Goodare, Bill Gordon, Alan Harding, Gerald Harriss, David Ibbetson, Hector MacQueen, Athol Murray, Douglas Osler, Remco van Rhee, and David Sellar for their encouragement and assistance over a long period of time. I owe a particularly important debt to Athol Murray, who has shown generosity over many years in giving advice, sharing expertise, answering questions, engaging in discussions, and reading and commenting on my work. However, even greater debts are owed without doubt to John Cairns, Hector MacQueen, and David Sellar in the Centre for Legal History at the University of Edinburgh, and I would like to express my very deep thanks to all three. David Sellar and Hector MacQueen supervised my Ph.D. thesis and John Cairns examined it with Bill Gordon. They have continued to provide me with unfailing encouragement and support in my research. They have given advice and many suggestions over a long period of time. Their own work has provided a wonderfully rich source of ideas for me to draw upon, and they have been generous with their time over the years in reading, commenting upon and discussing mine. Our discussions have stimulated a great deal of my thinking about legal history and have helped guide my research immeasurably. Without their scholarly contribution to Scottish legal history, it would have been scarcely imaginable to embark upon that research in the first place. My sense of gratitude to them could therefore hardly be greater. Finally, beyond the academic sphere, it simply remains to thank my parents for their very great support and encouragement, all of which has contributed to my writing this book.

Mark Godfrey
Glasgow
September 2008

ABBREVIATIONS

APS — *The Acts of the Parliaments of Scotland*, ed. T. Thomson and C. Innes. 12 vols. Edinburgh, 1814–1875.

ADA — *Acts of the Lords Auditors of Causes and Complaints*, ed. T. Thomson. Edinburgh, 1839.

ADC i — *Acts of the Lords of Council in Civil Causes*, ed. T. Thomson. Edinburgh, 1839.

ADC ii — *Acts of the Lords of Council in Civil Causes Volume II, 1496–1501*, ed. G. Neilson and H. Paton. Edinburgh, 1918.

ADC iii — *Acts of the Lords of Council Volume III, 1501–1503*, ed. A.B. Calderwood. Edinburgh, 1993.

ADCP — *Acts of the Lords of Council in Public Affairs 1501–1554: Selections from the Acta Dominorum Concilii introductory to the Register of the Privy Council of Scotland*, ed. R.K. Hannay. Edinburgh, 1932. [i.e. *Acta Dominorum Concilii (Public)*].

NAS — National Archives of Scotland, Edinburgh.

RPS — *The Records of the Parliaments of Scotland to 1707*, ed. K.M. Brown et al. St Andrews, 2007 [http://www.rps.ac.uk/]

INTRODUCTION

Jurisdiction and central courts in later medieval Europe

Jurisdiction means power to decide. A law court is a formal expression and instrument of such power. In medieval society, however, jurisdiction was far more than a technical statement of the limits of judicial competence. It was the primary constituent of the legal order and of governance more generally. The impersonal concept of the state could not yet provide the authority in terms of which such a legal and governmental order could be rationalised and explained. It was jurisdiction itself which provided the basic measure of authority. Alan Harding has noted this when commenting upon "the medieval preoccupation with jurisdiction as the form of political power and with courts as the framework of government" and how "it was in terms of jurisdiction that power was measured in medieval societies".[1] In modern times, it is generally the state which has become the fundamental unit of jurisdiction as well as the formal constitutional source of the legal order. In medieval Europe, by contrast, the significance of jurisdiction was more commonly localised and personal, and was related closely to the feudal concept of tenurial lordship. Jurisdiction is naturally understood in territorial terms. Its grant or transfer implied, and usually conferred explicitly, the power to determine disputes within a particular territory. In medieval Europe, however, the structure of jurisdiction was also fragmented and layered with the result that its content was typically differentiated according to subject matter and personal status as well as territory. This was most evident in relation to ecclesiastical jurisdiction, which all European secular legal orders recognised as possessing authority over some aspects of secular affairs. Karl Leyser's description of later twelfth century Germany as "a teeming welter of developing princely and aristocratic lordships, lay and clerical, [and] a bewildering variety of substructures like counties, advocacies, immunities, burgraviates, *banni*, and *mundeburdia*" with "no common underlying grid or shared

[1] A. Harding, "*Regiam Majestatem* Amongst Medieval Law Books", *Juridical Review* (1984), 97–111, at pp. 105, 102.

development" typifies one extreme.[2] In Scotland the medieval structure of jurisdiction was more unified than this, because of the early dynastic and territorial coalescence of the kingdom in the twelfth and thirteenth centuries. Nevertheless it was also highly differentiated and localised in its distribution. One unifying feature, however, was the manner in which it came to be defined by the thirteenth century through rules embedded in a Scottish common law, embracing a variety of royal and feudal courts, the church courts, and Parliament itself.

Against this background, any substantial alteration in the pattern of jurisdiction within a medieval state is of great potential significance as a possible sign of political, constitutional, governmental or legal change and development. Arguably the most striking alteration of this kind in medieval Europe can be seen to relate to a process of jurisdictional centralisation which accompanied an increase in the role of central authority in the fifteenth and sixteenth centuries. This was evident in the development of a new generation of royal central courts across Europe. In jurisdictional terms, the significance of this is that it seems to indicate that European societies were looking increasingly towards central forms of authority to settle disputes and underwrite the stability of the legal order, even in matters previously reserved to more local manifestations of jurisdiction. Whether by way of response to such pressure, or for other reasons, a new form of central court developed in many European jurisdictions. Alongside this centralisation went institutional and procedural innovation, as central courts took more definite form and formulated procedures to regulate the litigation transacted before them. This jurisdictional shift towards central authority is merely one facet of the general centralisation which accompanied the growth in the authority of rulers in the later medieval period and which "replaced the local independence of the early Middle Ages".[3] R.C. van Caenegem has gone as far as to suggest that "the decisive element in this development for both church and state was the establishment of a central court with jurisdiction over the whole of a community or principality".[4]

In this light, the judicial activity of the King's Council in fifteenth and early sixteenth-century Scotland can be seen as part of a Euro-

[2] Quoted in A. Harding, *Medieval Law and the Foundations of the State* (Oxford, 2002), p. 94.

[3] R.C. van Caenegem, *An Historical Introduction to Private Law* (Cambridge, 1992), p. 100.

[4] Van Caenegem, *An Historical Introduction to Private Law*, p. 100.

pean pattern of development. At its widest, this European pattern was leading to the creation of centralised royal administrations which were increasingly functioning so as to direct and sustain wider aspects of governance in the early modern state.[5] Indeed, in this wider context, it is worth noting the view of Bernard Guenée that by the closing years of the fifteenth century, and particularly during the sixteenth century, the word "state" was "undoubtedly beginning to acquire its present meaning... of a political body subject to a government and to common laws".[6] This period therefore marked a new phase, one we tend to associate with the development of state bureaucracies, central taxation, royal armies, and a public ideology of royal authority rooted in notions of sovereignty, all leading to a transformation across Europe towards a different kind of state.

One fundamental aspect of this transformation related to the legal order. As already noted above, authority had previously tended to be mediated through a complex, devolved pattern of jurisdiction. In Scotland, for example, the principal remedies of the medieval common law could only be granted following legal process in the locally constituted courts of the sheriff, justiciar and burgh. The basis for the exercise of such remedies was usually concealed behind the determinations of local juries. Forms of appeal were narrowly understood and the possibility of review limited. Even in England, with its precociously early development of central courts in the thirteenth century, J.H. Baker has commented upon how "the centralisation of royal justice was reconciled with the need for local investigation and trial", with judges out on circuit under commission in the system of assizes.[7] The expansion of centralised royal administrations at the end of the medieval period across Europe had a significant impact on the legal orders of the various states, and on the patterns of jurisdiction, with the role of royal councils gaining in importance markedly.[8] It was indeed the exercise of jurisdiction by royal councils across Europe which created new central courts. Bernard Guenée has tellingly analysed the wider administrative background to these conciliar developments, contrasting "the period of the court and the great officers" in royal administration in the eleventh and twelfth

---

[5] See especially J. Goodare, *State and Society in Early Modern Scotland* (Oxford, 1999); J. Goodare, *The Government of Scotland 1560–1625* (Oxford, 2004).

[6] B. Guenée, *States and Rulers in Later Medieval Europe* (Oxford, 1985), p. 5.

[7] J.H. Baker, *An Introduction to English Legal History*, 4th ed. (London, 2002), p. 20.

[8] Guenée, *States and Rulers in Later Medieval Europe*, p. 122.

centuries with "the age of the Chancellor and the Council" in the fourteenth and fifteenth centuries.[9]

Guenée's model points to a fundamental differentiation of the functions of what at one time was a single institution, i.e. the royal court—the *curia regis*—so that its various functions could be exercised separately within the royal council and the royal household. One such function was, of course, judicial. In the course of the fifteenth and sixteenth centuries, the functions of royal councils themselves would be further differentiated, meaning that "the judicial activity of the council gave way to a new generation of courts of justice".[10] Of course, central courts in one form or another were already to be found in countries such as England and France by the thirteenth and fourteenth centuries, as well as within the supranational legal order of the church. The English courts of King's Bench and Common Pleas, the Parlement of Paris, and the *Sacra Rota Romana* provide the most obvious examples. Even within these countries or jurisdictions, supplementary development also occurred in the later Middle Ages through royal councils where they existed. The English Chancery is a case in point. By the 1480s the English bill jurisdiction of the English Chancery had become a "routine feature of the legal system".[11] But in other countries or legal orders it was principally through the development of royal councils that a central court was created. One example would be the Great Council of Malines in the Burgundian Netherlands, which dated from the 1430s and 1440s. Famously, in 1495 the Reichskammergericht of the Holy Roman Empire was instituted as a form of central court. In Scotland the College of Justice was founded in 1532, sealing the primacy of conciliar jurisdiction in place of that of the medieval parliament. Therefore, it is notable how even those countries or institutions which already possessed central courts clearly witnessed further developments in their central conciliar courts in the fifteenth and sixteenth centuries. Correspondingly, the residual royal councils tended thereafter to exercise a wide governmental competence, but one which was essentially political and lacking a general judicial role (though usually some residual jurisdiction was retained). This course was reflected in developments in Scotland. The medieval Parliament was gradually superseded in its judicial role

[9] Guenée, *States and Rulers in Later Medieval Europe*, p. 122.
[10] Guenée, *States and Rulers in Later Medieval Europe*, p. 125.
[11] J.H. Baker, *The Oxford History of the Laws of England, Volume VI, 1483–1558* (Oxford, 2003), p. 173.

by the King's Council, which in the fifteenth century came to act as a form of central law court when sitting as "the Session", culminating in the foundation of the College of Justice in 1532. Scotland was to develop an essentially political Privy Council from the 1540s, Professor Donaldson remarking that "the differentiation of institutions was complete by the middle of the sixteenth century".[12]

It was not only in the jurisdiction which they exercised that central courts were significant. They also required and provided a focus for professional pleaders and judges with legal education, thus enabling the law to develop through pleading and judicial decisions together with borrowings and argumentation from sources such as Roman and canon law, and the wider medieval *ius commune*. In some parts of Europe they could also serve a more overtly political purpose in promoting legal assimilation in various lands under a common jurisdiction. Scotland had already developed its common law, dating from the thirteenth century, but there were still political implications to the establishment of a central court within that common jurisdiction. As John Cairns, David Fergus and Hector MacQueen noted, "by the end of the fifteenth century... a central court, the Session, was emerging from the regularisation of the judicial business of the king's council, and its reconstitution in 1532 gave it jurisdiction in all civil matters, contrasting with its earlier, relatively limited powers".[13] Examination of the precise nature of the jurisdiction of the Session in 1532 will form a substantial element of this book. Clearly, however, it can already be seen that the political influence and control traditionally asserted in medieval Scotland through the exercise of jurisdiction in the locality was subject by 1532 to an intensified form of central authority. This was exercised through the jurisdiction of the Session in its role as a central court. It is the nature of the institutional developments and jurisdictional change which lay behind the realisation of such a central court in Scotland which form the subject-matter of the chapters which follow.

---

[12] G. Donaldson, *Scotland: James V to James VII* (Edinburgh, 1965), p. 288.

[13] J.W. Cairns, T.D. Fergus and H.L. MacQueen, "Legal Humanism in Renaissance Scotland", *Journal of Legal History* 11 (1990), 40–69 at p. 42.

CHAPTER ONE

THE MEDIEVAL SCOTTISH PARLIAMENT AS A CENTRAL COURT

Introduction—the pattern of development to 1600

The development of a central civil court in Scotland arose principally from the evolution of the judicial functions of the King's Council in the fifteenth century. However, its origins lie much further back. They can be traced in the history of the medieval parliament of Scotland. This demonstrates that a form of central court was already in existence by the last decade of the thirteenth century. It was at this time that great royal councils were first routinely described by the term "parliament", though evidence also survives of similar forms of assembly meeting earlier in the century.

It is clear that parliaments adjudicated upon disputes. Moreover their authority to do so was already understood in terms of jurisdiction, structured according to what was recognised as the common law of Scotland. This common law had developed since the twelfth century, when, following the accession of David I (1124–1153), new influences had begun to transform the earlier Celtic legal inheritance.[1] What little is documented of the character of the thirteenth-century parliament suggests that from the very beginning its business and constitution were fundamentally rooted in the maintenance of the law and the administration of royal justice. The letter of summons to the parliament of 1293 invited "everyone with a complaint... to show the injuries and trespasses done to them by whatsoever ill-doers... and to receive from them what justice demands".[2] Another description from around 1292 emphasised that the purpose of the "common assembly" which the King should have with the prelates, earls and barons of the realm was to demonstrate the King's willingness to govern "according

---

[1] W.D.H. Sellar, "Celtic law and Scots law: survival and integration", *Scottish Studies* 29 (1989), 1–27.

[2] A.A.M. Duncan, "The early parliaments of Scotland", *Scottish Historical Review* 45 (1966), 36–58 at p. 46.

to the ancient laws and usages of the land in all points".[3] In giving guidance on where certain disputes should be entertained, a distinction was drawn in this account between a "full parliament" and a "lesser council". The holding of a parliament was therefore seen to possess a special significance in judicial terms.

Of course, the judicial determination of disputes, as well as the issuing of laws, were activities long associated with Scottish kingship and had a history which pre-dated the first appearance of Parliament.[4] The parliaments of the 1290s were successors to more loosely defined *colloquia*, first described as such in the 1230s.[5] Less formal assemblies of notables around the King can be traced back at least as far as David I. The personal role of the King in dispensing justice is captured in Ailred of Rievaulx's almost mythic description telling us how David "was accustomed to sit at the entrance of the royal hall and diligently to hear the cases of poor men and old women who on certain days were called to him singly in whatever district he came to and often with much labour to satisfy each".[6] In the development of an interlinked structure of formal assemblies with legal functions in medieval Scotland, the role of kingship provided the common thread of development.

The relationship between kingship, government and law in Scotland reflected wider European developments. As Susan Reynolds has stated, "there can be no doubt that the twelfth and thirteenth centuries began to bring important changes to the ideas and practices of law". Reynolds has emphasised two developments in particular. First, the "strengthening of government began to transform the law by emphasizing one source of its authority and enforcement among others". Secondly, she noted

---

[3] "The Scottish king's household and other fragments", ed. M. Bateson, in *Miscellany of the Scottish History Society (Second Volume)*, Scottish History Society First Series 44 (Edinburgh, 1904), pp. 3–43 at pp. 31, 37–38. Note that, although reliance on this source was cautioned against in Duncan, "The early parliaments of Scotland", p. 36, owing to doubt over its dating, it has subsequently come to be discussed as dating from "probably about 1292" in A.A.M. Duncan, *Scotland: The Making of the Kingdom* (Edinburgh, 1975), p. 595.

[4] A.A.B. McQueen, "The origins and development of the Scottish parliament, 1249–1329" (University of St Andrews, unpublished Ph.D. thesis, 2002), p. 30.

[5] Duncan, *Scotland: The Making of the Kingdom*, p. 610. There is some evidence suggesting that the term "parliament" was used intermittently after 1249: McQueen, "The origins and development of the Scottish parliament", p. 35.

[6] A.A.M. Duncan, "The Central Courts before 1532" in *An Introduction to Scottish Legal History*, ed. G.C.H. Paton, Stair Society 20 (Edinburgh, 1958), pp. 321–340 at p. 321; A.O. Anderson (ed.), *Scottish Annals from English Chroniclers AD 500 to 1286* (London, 1908), p. 233.

how "the old amorphous assemblies were replaced by something more like defined jurisdictions, and these gradually began to be organized into hierarchies of superior and inferior authority".[7] Alan Harding has applied a similar analysis in considering the implications of legal change for the development of medieval states, observing that "by the second half of the thirteenth century there existed an idea of the territorial state structured by law which could be used by practical administrators as well as theologians". He has argued persuasively that in Western Europe it is possible to:

> trace the building of a model of the State out of the systems of legal procedures and law-courts, acts of legislation, and definitions of public crime, private property and injury, which had begun to appear in the Germanic kingdoms that succeeded the Roman Empire in the West; and show how it reached completion as an arrangement of legally differentiated estates that included the king and embedded the regime in the commonwealth.[8]

In Scotland, the growing emphasis upon the authority of the King above other lords followed the jurisdictional form identified by Reynolds and resulted in the institutional model described by Harding. The legal transformation in question was the emergence from the King's jurisdiction of a Scottish "common law", gradually taking its place as the basis for a distinct national system of law and a framework for the administration of justice. The key to this was indeed the authority of the King, since this could justify and compel the application of the common law in precedence to the customs of local jurisdictions under the authority of inferior lords. The common law can be said to have come clearly into being in the thirteenth century, and by the end of the century it seems that meetings of the King in Parliament were formally at its heart.

The common law arose from two related developments in particular—the evolution of courts held in the King's name, and the development of a system of remedies administered by them. Parliament naturally assumed the role of the highest court, being at one level simply the court of the King himself, in which he sat in person with his

---

[7] S. Reynolds, *Kingdoms and Communities in Western Europe 900–1300* (Oxford, 1984), p. 39.

[8] A. Harding, *Medieval Law and the Foundations of the State* (Oxford, 2002), p. 9.

council at its fullest extent.[9] Its role was therefore necessarily judicial. Though essentially the most important political form of assembly of notable magnates and lords, including ecclesiastics, Parliament was also the primary forum for the King and his council to transact legal business, especially to pronounce upon or mediate disputes and to confirm other matters which required a ruling.

The judicial role of Parliament placed it during the medieval period at the apex of a structure of royal courts providing litigants with remedies.[10] The common law resulted from what proved to be an irreversible emphasis upon the superior jurisdiction of such royal courts, in a land-holding society structured generally around the exercise of jurisdiction by feudal lords. This royal jurisdictional structure was unified in Parliament, since all legal process could ultimately be challenged there. Indeed, Parliament's most commonly recorded business was not legislation, ratification of treaties or charters but rather the determination of legal disputes.[11]

Parliament's legal concerns were predominantly judicial at first, with an important but less prominent concern with legislation. This emphasis came to be wholly reversed over time, however, as Parliament found itself increasingly unable to function effectively as a central court. Indeed, it could be argued that the coalescence of the common law had by the end of the thirteenth century thrust onto Parliament a routine judicial role which it was never able properly to fulfil. Its functioning as a court during the fourteenth century is hard to assess, and uncertainty exists over the extent of the records which survive from this time for its judicial business. In many ways, the extant fourteenth-century parliamentary record suggests relatively little judicial business

---

[9] A view prominently expressed by the seventeenth century: See King James VI, *The Trew Law of Free Monarchies*, in J.P. Sommerville, ed., *King James VI and I, Political Writings* (Cambridge, 1994), p. 74. See also King James' *Basilicon Doron*, in *King James VI and I, Political Writings*, p. 21; K.M. Brown and A.J. Mann, "Introduction", in *The History of the Scottish Parliament, Volume II. Parliament and Politics in Scotland 1567–1707*, ed. K.M. Brown and A.J. Mann (Edinburgh, 2005), pp. 1–56 at p. 18; Sir George Mackenzie, *The Institutions of the Law of Scotland* (1684) Book 1: Title 3, quoted in H.L. MacQueen, "Mackenzie's *Institutions* in Scottish legal history", *Journal of the Law Society of Scotland* (1984), 498–501 at p. 500. See *The Works of that Eminent and Learned Lawyer, Sir George Mackenzie of Rosehaugh*, (Edinburgh, 1722), vol. 2, p. 281.

[10] The seminal and most authoritative discussion of the history of parliament as a central court, based on evaluation of many primary sources, remains Duncan, "The Central Courts before 1532", though it must now be read subject to H.L. MacQueen, *Common Law and Feudal Society in Medieval Scotland* (Edinburgh, 1993), chap. 8.

[11] G.W.S. Barrow, *Kingship and Unity: Scotland 1000–1306* (Edinburgh, 1981), p. 127.

was transacted, but it would be unsafe to draw firm conclusions given the incomplete survival of the evidence—it is only from as late as 1466 that a complete contemporary record of Parliament survives.[12]

By the fifteenth century, however, Parliament seems to have struggled to meet the expectations of litigants. At the same time, new priorities seem to have arisen so that the relatively short periods during which a parliament sat were increasingly inadequate to transact the full range of business expected of a parliament, especially in the field of legislation. This may be inferred from fifteenth-century experiments to channel its judicial business elsewhere, to specially devised or alternative bodies. These experiments may have functioned both to relieve Parliament of some of its work, as well as having been intended to improve the administration of justice. The insistent demand for justice, which ultimately, as the highest court of law, only Parliament could provide, was to lead in 1426 to the establishment of a new tribunal which was to function through a separate structure of itinerant sittings. These came to be referred to as "sessions". The new tribunal represented a form of delegation to a specially constituted body wholly unconnected with meetings of Parliament. The Session sat with specially appointed parliamentary judges sitting independently from Parliament for the determination of judicial business. Its significance is that it represented the first attempt in Scotland to establish a central structure to administer justice separately from Parliament, and the beginning of a century of experimentation which culminated in the foundation of the College of Justice in 1532.

The 1426 expedient appears to have fulfilled its role, since it was renewed during subsequent decades and repeated until the 1460s. However, by the later fifteenth century a further transition occurred which resulted both in the abandonment of the statutory Session and the withering away of Parliament's general judicial functions completely. Instead, between the 1460s and the 1490s the King's Council inherited the functions of both. The Council had always exercised a residual jurisdiction outside the normal course of the common law. It was a smaller, less formal and more flexible body which could ordain its own sittings and did not require formal summons on forty days' notice like a parliament. Its meetings for judicial business were also known as "sessions" by the later fifteenth century. Parliament seems by

[12] B. Webster, *Scotland from the Eleventh Century to 1603* (London, 1975), pp. 128–130.

the 1470s and 1480s to have been transacting a great deal of judicial business alongside the Council, but by the 1490s the judicial sessions of Council absorbed that work and left the parliamentary Auditors of Causes and Complaints redundant in practical institutional terms. By the 1520s, however, tensions had developed between the Council's narrower judicial role, when sitting as the Session, and its political character as the King's Council. Finally, in 1532 a major institutional reform saw these judicial functions of the Council bestowed upon a new College of Justice. This was typical of the European pattern of development described by Bernard Guenée as "the appearance of new administrative bodies that were gradually detached from the rudimentary Council".[13] In Scotland there was still great institutional continuity since the judges of the college retained the technical status and authority of Lords of Council *and* Session. Such was the nature of sixteenth-century governance that most continued to function outside the Session as Lords of Council as well—remaining active in Guenée's "rudimentary Council". Meanwhile, Parliament's judicial functions had become effectively confined to treason cases. These institutional developments will form the subject of subsequent chapters.

Parliament's original predominant concern with judging legal disputes had therefore given way by the sixteenth century to its legislative role. The principal exceptions were its treason jurisdiction and the issue of whether it retained some residual appellate function. Legislative activity developed considerably in the fifteenth century and especially during the later sixteenth century. This reflected changing ideas of kingship, governance, the role of parliaments and of legislation, as well as the practice of kingship by successive monarchs. The fifteenth century saw almost annual meetings of Parliament, often concerned with legislative programmes which were ambitious by medieval standards.[14] Although the medieval parliament's judicial functions were exclusive to it by comparison with lesser councils, this was not true of its legislative powers. The King in Council could legislate outside Parliament. The power to legislate therefore did not as a matter of principle distinguish Parliament from lesser meetings of the King and Council.[15] By the

[13] B. Guenée, *States and Rulers in Later Medieval Europe* (Oxford, 1985), p. 122.

[14] R. Tanner, *The Late Medieval Scottish Parliament: Politics and the Three Estates, 1424–1488* (East Linton, 2001), p. 7.

[15] See the seminal work of R.K. Hannay: "On 'parliament' and 'general council'," *Scottish Historical Review* 18 (1921), 158–170; "General council and convention of estates",

sixteenth century, however, Parliament's legislative function was becoming increasingly its exclusive preserve.[16] Large "general councils" in the fourteenth and fifteenth centuries had issued legislation alongside parliaments. However, by the sixteenth-century, the similar gatherings known as "conventions of the estates" did not normally issue permanent legislation.[17] The fifteenth and sixteenth centuries generally witnessed a new consciousness of the importance of statute law, and the reservation of its enactment to Parliament is consistent with this change. Following these developments, the one branch of the medieval *curia regis* which was left to exercise judicially the jurisdiction of King and Council was embodied from 1532 in the College of Justice.

The origins of Parliament's judicial functions

As we have seen, the judicial functions of the medieval parliament were to be its distinguishing feature far more than any others in terms of its formal constitution. Though a vehicle for a range of political and administrative business, in terms of its formal ordering the medieval Scottish parliament emerged as a court of law—and was perceived as such from the beginning. It was for this reason that, like other law courts, it was required to be summoned upon a full forty days' notice.[18] Of course, to classify adjudication as a judicial function clearly distinguishable from that of making legislation is to some extent anachronistic for the medieval period. As Susan Reynolds has stated more generally in relation to legal change across Europe at this time, "the boundary between legislation and judgement everywhere continued in practice to be vague and the power to legislate was still diffused".[19] Nevertheless, by the late thirteenth century, the parliament we see in operation was the King's Council at its fullest extent sitting with what seems to

Scottish Historical Review 20 (1923), 98–115; "General council of estates", *Scottish Historical Review* 20 (1923), 263–284. All are reprinted in *The College of Justice: Essays by R.K. Hannay*, ed. H.L. MacQueen, Stair Society Supplementary Series 1 (Edinburgh, 1990).

[16] I.E. O'Brien, "The Scottish parliament in the fifteenth and sixteenth centuries", (University of Glasgow, unpublished Ph.D. thesis, 1981), p. 149.

[17] See generally J. Goodare, "The Scottish parliament and its early modern 'rivals'," *Parliaments, Estates and Representation* 24 (2004), 147–172; J. Goodare, *The Government of Scotland 1560–1625* (Oxford, 2004), p. 86.

[18] Hannay, "General council and convention of estates", p. 112; Hannay, "On 'parliament' and 'general council'," pp. 157–166.

[19] Reynolds, *Kingdoms and Communities*, p. 51.

be a special *judicial* competence denied to the King personally or to other forms of meeting between King and Council. By this time only a parliament could exercise the full authority vested in the King to dispense justice. This might have been at first a mere expectation, perhaps hardening over time into a convention, but certainly must have been an established legal rule by the fourteenth century.

In considering the origins of Parliament's judicial role, we have already noted the personal involvement of kings such as David I in hearing certain cases.[20] As the fount of justice, the opportunity for personal involvement by the King in the hearing of pleas continued into the sixteenth century, as demonstrated by both James IV's and James V's occasional participation in judicial business in Council. Under James V, on rare occasions litigants still even referred disputes to the King in person. Such a procedure might appear to be an "extra-judicial" form of resolution, but could nevertheless result in a decree given by the King personally, stated to be merely with the advice of his Lords of Council.[21] However, the dispensing of justice with any regularity requires the organisation of formal opportunities for the hearing of complaints. In relation to the King, this process came to be conceived by at least the end of the twelfth century as requiring the holding of something like a court. This marked the development of an institution in which the King gave judgement with the advice, or at least tacit acceptance or support, of his counsellors. Whatever the technical role of those notables who made up the King's "Council" in giving such judgements, their involvement emphasised the collective nature of judgement (as opposed to the personal decision of the King) and promoted the development of a more regular institution within which the King's authority was exercised. There had to be a separation between the exercise of a jurisdiction and the individual who was the source of its authority before a system of administration of justice could develop,

---

[20] Duncan, "The Central Courts before 1532", p. 321; Anderson, *Scottish Annals from English Chroniclers*, p. 233.

[21] A.M. Godfrey, "Arbitration and dispute resolution in sixteenth century Scotland", *Tijdschrift voor Rechtsgeschiedenis* 70 (2002), 109–135 at p. 130; *Acts of the Lords of Council in Public Affairs 1501–1554: Selections from the Acta Dominorum Concilii introductory to the Register of the Privy Council of Scotland*, ed. R.K. Hannay (Edinburgh, 1932), p. 309 [hereafter *ADCP*]; Edinburgh, National Archives of Scotland [hereafter NAS], CS 5/40, fols. 23, 51. The matter was "to be decidit by his grace and he to tak quhat lordis his grace plesis to be counselaris to his grace" (fol. 23).

capable of extending over the whole kingdom. As a feudal lord, a king such as David I certainly held court for his vassals,[22] and Professor Rait long ago pointed to the appearance of the "technical term" *curia regis* in the reign of William the Lion (1165–1214).[23] Professor A.A.M. Duncan suggested that, although this would not have denoted a formal tribunal in the later sense of a "court", the King may have already been relying in the *curia regis* on advisers trained in the law.[24] But alongside the development of some central institutional structure, the King also delegated authority to determine disputes when he made grants of jurisdiction with land, as illustrated by the extensive jurisdiction granted between 1165 and 1170 in the charter from King William to Robert Bruce of Annandale.[25]

Some form of regularisation of the royal justice handed out in the twelfth century *curia regis* lies behind the thirteenth-century judicial activity of the King and Council meeting *in colloquia*. We can note in Duncan's words how "occasions of consultations between king and barons were already occasions for hearing pleas in Alexander II's reign" (1214–1249).[26] This is recognisably the institution which was to become known as Parliament. In 1256 a dispute between the sheriff of Perth and Dunfermline Abbey appears to have been finally resolved "*in pleno colloquio domini regis*", though involving what seems to have been a rather *ad hoc* legal procedure.[27] In the most detailed analysis of early assemblies around the King and Council to date, Dr Alison McQueen has observed that "justice was certainly one of the earliest factors to have featured within augmented meetings held across the twelfth and thirteenth centuries".[28] At the core of the *curia regis* would naturally have been the King's Council, a "recognised institution" since the early

[22] MacQueen, *Common Law and Feudal Society in Medieval Scotland*, pp. 47–48.

[23] R.S. Rait, *The Parliaments of Scotland* (Glasgow, 1924), p. 2; See also H.L. MacQueen, "Canon Law, Custom and Legislation: Law in the Reign of Alexander II", in *The Reign of Alexander II, 1214–1249*, ed. R.D. Oram (Leiden, 2005), pp. 221–251 at p. 232.

[24] Duncan, "The Central Courts before 1532", p. 321.

[25] H.L. MacQueen, "Tears of a legal historian: Scottish feudalism and the *Ius Commune*", *Juridical Review* (2003), 1–28 at p. 8.

[26] Duncan, "The Central Courts before 1532", p. 322.

[27] A.A.B. McQueen, "Parliament, the Guardians and John Balliol, 1284–1296", in *The History of the Scottish Parliament, Volume I. Parliament and Politics in Scotland, 1235–1560*, ed. K.M. Brown and R.J. Tanner (Edinburgh, 2004), pp. 29–49 at pp. 30–31.

[28] McQueen, "The origins and development of the Scottish parliament", pp. 30, 52.

twelfth century.[29] By the 1290s we find *colloquia* now described by the term *parliamentum*. From this point, parliaments must have been regular types of assembly.[30] The evidence of this decade certainly suggests that "the dispensing of justice was a usual function of parliament", perhaps even the primary one.[31] In King John's parliament of February, 1293, at Scone, for example, seven of the thirteen items of business related to providing justice, and seem to have been dealt with under an established procedure which allowed for the continuation of cases to subsequent sittings of Parliament.[32] The scale of this petitionary business may have been comparatively small, but, as Dr Gwilym Dodd has argued, this would be consistent with the general structure of the legal system in late thirteenth-century Scotland.[33] In these early parliaments it was the King and Council which seem to have played the critical role in determining pleas and dispensing justice, albeit doing so within the duly constituted meeting of Parliament, being itself an afforced sitting of Council. It is from these years that rolls of pleas before the King and Council in Parliament first survive.[34] We should be careful, of course, to avoid assuming a view of the origins of Parliament's judicial role as a story of conscious progression, when it is likely to have been simply the contingent needs of the time and pragmatic responses to them which underlay developments. Those who wished to air a grievance before the King were probably afforded the best opportunities of doing so when he gathered formally with his council, especially at its most extended form in Parliament after a significant period of notice. No doubt that state of affairs underlay the development of the jurisdictional ideas defining and limiting the scope of those matters Parliament could entertain. Parliament was after all "less of an institution than an irregular

[29] Duncan, "The Central Courts before 1532", p. 322.

[30] McQueen, "Parliament, the Guardians and John Balliol", p. 30.

[31] Duncan, "Early parliaments", p. 47; Duncan, *Scotland: the Making of the Kingdom*, p. 610; McQueen, "Parliament, the Guardians and John Balliol", pp. 38, 40; McQueen, "The origins and development of the Scottish parliament", p. 177.

[32] McQueen, "Parliament, the Guardians and John Balliol", pp. 40–41; McQueen, "The Origins and Development of the Scottish Parliament", pp. 148–149, 152, 158, 160.

[33] G. Dodd, "Sovereignty, Diplomacy and Petitioning: Scotland and the English Parliament in the First Half of the Fourteenth Century", in *England and Scotland in the Fourteenth Century: New Perspectives*, ed. A. King and M. Penman (Woodbridge, 2007), pp. 172–195 at pp. 181–182.

[34] Duncan, "Early parliaments", pp. 40, 41; R. Nicholson, *Scotland: the Later Middle Ages*, (Edinburgh, 1974), p. 20.

and short-lived event".[35] However, it also seems by 1293 to have been "a court with settled procedure and periodical Sessions".[36]

Though the judicial processes of the thirteenth-century parliament must have been concerned largely with the rights of the King himself, his magnates and the church, the potentially unlimited scope of judicial redress given by the King and Council in Parliament is illustrated by the letter of summons to the parliament of 1293 already discussed, which talked of the doing of "what justice demands" in relation to "everyone with a complaint".[37] The account from around 1292 also provides a suggestion of the type of supreme jurisdiction exercised by Parliament. As we have seen, although not mentioning Parliament by name at this point, its opening lines refer to the desirability of the King having "common assembly" with earls and other notables.[38] However, at the end of the text, and having described royal officials from chancellor, auditors of exchequer, constable, justices and sheriffs through to clerks of the wardrobe and kitchen, it is stated that claims to heritable offices in fee from the King can only be judged "en plein parlement & noun pas par meindre counsail", i.e. in full Parliament and not by a lesser Council.[39] This does imply that by the 1290s some jurisdictional rules had emerged to govern, as a matter of law, what complaints could or must only be put forward in the "court" of Parliament. This might explain why important assemblies such as that in Dunfermline in February 1296 did not require to be constituted as parliaments, since there was no judicial business.[40] By this time, therefore, the regularisation of royal justice in Parliament requires to be placed in the wider context of Parliament's jurisdictional relationship with other courts.

---

[35] K.M. Brown, *Kingdom or Province? Scotland and the Regal Union, 1603–1715* (London, 1992), p. 13; Brown applies this characterisation to the Scottish Parliament all the way through to 1689, with the possible exception of 1638–1651. It has become a widely used description of a medieval parliament. Helen Cam described the English medieval parliament in the same terms as 'not an institution but an event' in her 'Introduction' to F.W. Maitland, *Selected Historical Essays of F.W. Maitland*, ed. H. Cam (Cambridge, 1957), p. xviii.

[36] H.G. Richardson and G.O. Sayles, "The Scottish parliaments of Edward I", *Scottish Historical Review* 25 (1928), 300–317 at p. 303; Duncan, "The Central Courts before 1532", p. 323; supported by McQueen, "The origins and development of the Scottish parliament", pp. 148–149, 152, 158, 160, and by McQueen, "Parliament, the Guardians and John Balliol", p. 41.

[37] Duncan, "Early parliaments", p. 46.

[38] "The Scottish king's household", pp. 31, 37–38.

[39] "The Scottish king's household", pp. 37, 43.

[40] McQueen, "Parliament, the Guardians and John Balliol", p. 49.

The jurisdiction of Parliament under the common law

The development of Parliament as a court reflects the development of procedures that allowed for the dispensation of justice by the King to be carried out in a regularised form. However, the regularisation of Parliament's judicial functions did not occur in a vacuum but as part of the development by the thirteenth century of a Scottish common law administered principally by the King's justiciars and sheriffs. These offices would of course be held by nobles, who would hold their courts and grant remedies in the name of the King. The most formal remedies would follow the issuing of a royal letter known as a brieve out of chancery, in which a command was issued in the King's name that action be taken in the light of a complaint. It was a royal brieve of 1264 which contained the first known reference to "common law" (here meaning native Scottish customs as opposed to the medieval Roman and canon law *ius commune*). The text alluded to usage over the kingdom of Scotland "according to ancient approved custom and common law". This has led David Sellar to argue that "thirteenth-century Scotland...was a land of the Common law" and that the continuing existence of a distinctively Scottish common law was the main "guiding thread" explaining the underlying continuity of development in Scots law throughout the Middle Ages.[41] It became natural in later centuries to think of Parliament as primarily deliberating upon the creation of statutes, but Sellar's analysis reminds us that by 1300 it was the repository of a supreme jurisdiction to apply the customs of the realm, which by this time amounted to a common law.

The structure of royal courts which had emerged by the thirteenth century saw the jurisdiction of the offices of sheriff and justiciar (based originally in the twelfth century upon Anglo-Norman models) exercised routinely through the holding of courts and ayres (an ayre being the

[41] W.D.H. Sellar, "The resilience of the Scottish common law", in *The Civilian Tradition and Scots Law*, ed. D.L. Carey Miller and R. Zimmermann (Berlin, 1997), pp. 149–164 at p. 151; W.D.H. Sellar, "The common law of Scotland and the common law of England", in *The British Isles 1100–1500*, ed. R.R. Davies (Edinburgh, 1988), pp. 82–99 at pp. 86, 87. For the later history of the concept of common law see Sellar, "The resilience of the common law", p. 149; Sellar, "The common law of Scotland', p. 91. It should be noted that Sellar's analysis of post-medieval developments is partially contested in J.W. Cairns, "Attitudes to Codification and the Scottish Science of Legislation, 1600–1830", *Tulane European and Civil Law Forum* 22 (2007), pp. 1–78 at p. 23, note 96.

holding and concomitant progression of a justiciar's court along its chosen geographical route). The justiciar was "the highest officer under the Crown responsible, in the thirteenth and fourteenth centuries, for the administration of justice and also in some degree, at least in the earlier part of this period, for overseeing royal government generally...".[42] In contrast, the sheriff exercised a local and territorially limited jurisdiction.[43] But commonly lords would exercise a jurisdiction over their own tenants as well, since jurisdiction was conventionally granted with land.[44] Thus, below the royal courts, there lay the local jurisdictions of feudal lords, and by the fourteenth century many hundreds of the particularly extensive grants known as "barony" or "regality" jurisdiction had occurred.[45] The privileges of urban settlements also included such jurisdictional grants if they were incorporated as a burgh. Consequently, it is possible to trace from the early thirteenth century the existence and jurisdiction of the burgh court.[46]

Questions of legal jurisdiction were inherently political in this period, since, as already noted in the Introduction, jurisdiction can be seen as the measure of authority and power in medieval society.[47] By the end of the thirteenth century, a complex network of jurisdiction had emerged in Scotland. The sheriff had been first introduced by David I. By the end of the reign of Malcom IV (1153–1165) there seem to have been as many as twelve identifiable sheriffdoms, and by 1214 there were nineteen in total. Gradually more and more of the kingdom was included within this structure of authority so that "by the mid-thirteenth

---

[42] G.W.S. Barrow, *The Kingdom of the Scots: Government, Church and Society from the Eleventh to the Fourteenth Century* (London, 1973), p. 83.

[43] See W.C. Dickinson, "Introduction" to *The Sheriff Court Book of Fife 1515–1522*, ed. W.C. Dickinson, Scottish History Society Third Series 12 (Edinburgh, 1928) pp. xi–cv.

[44] J.W. Cairns, "Historical introduction", *A History of Private Law in Scotland*, ed. K. Reid and R. Zimmermann (Oxford, 2000), vol. 1, pp. 14–184 at p. 24.

[45] A. Grant, *Independence and Nationhood: Scotland 1306–1469* (London, 1984), p. 125; see generally W.C. Dickinson, "Introduction" to *The Court Book of the Barony of Carnwath 1523–1542*, ed. W.C. Dickinson, Scottish History Society Third Series 29 (Edinburgh, 1937), pp. xi–cxii.

[46] See H.L. MacQueen and W.J. Windram, "Law and courts in the burghs", in *The Scottish Medieval Town*, ed. M. Lynch, M. Spearman and G. Stell (Edinburgh, 1988), pp. 208–227; W.C. Dickinson, "Introduction" to *Early Records of the Burgh of Aberdeen 1317, 1398–1407*, ed. W.C. Dickinson, Scottish History Society Third Series 49 (Edinburgh, 1957), pp. xvii–cli.

[47] A. Harding, "Regiam Majestatem amongst medieval law-books", *Juridical Review* 29 (1984), 97–111 at p. 105.

century, most of Scotland had been divided up into sheriffdoms".[48] By 1300 there were over thirty of them.[49] Amongst their other functions, sheriffs seem to have been holding formal courts by the early thirteenth century.[50] Procedure in these royal courts followed the English model of writ and inquest for the most formal remedies, though John Cairns has observed that "most suits... will not have been initiated by brieve" but by simple complaint, orally or by bill, as a suit of "wrang and unlaw".[51] Indeed, the fourteenth-century manual concerning feudal courts, *Quoniam Attachiamenta*, begins with a discussion relating to "the foundation and commencement of pleas of wrang and unlaw".[52] However, the most significant patrimonial interests arising out of land tenure and succession received protection through royal brieves purchased from the chancery (i.e. royal letters or "writs" authenticated by royal clerks in the King's chapel) and addressed in the form of commands to sheriff, justiciar or burgh court to instigate lawful process and summon a jury to determine the facts necessary to resolve the dispute.[53] The brieve of novel dissasine was almost certainly introduced by statute in 1230,[54] and the brieves of mortancestor and of right are in evidence within the following few decades. All three were based on equivalent English models. Other standard form or "coursable" brieves such as the brieve of succession are also apparent by the 1260s.[55]

The availability of these brieves demanded at least the simplest of jurisdictional rules to determine which court was the appropriate forum in which to seek a particular remedy. Whereas dissasine could initially be brought before sheriff or justiciar according to the statute of 1230,

---

[48] MacQueen, *Common Law and Feudal Society in Medieval Scotland*, p. 49.

[49] These figures are given in *The Sheriffs of Scotland: An Interim List to c. 1306*, ed. N.H. Reid and G.W.S. Barrow (St. Andrews, 2002), p. xv.

[50] MacQueen, *Common Law and Feudal Society in Medieval Scotland*, p. 49.

[51] Cairns, "Historical introduction", pp. 23, 27; see the important article by A. Harding, "Rights, Wrongs and Remedies in Late Medieval English and Scots Law", in *Miscellany Four*, ed. H.L. MacQueen, Stair Society 49 (Edinburgh, 2002), pp. 1–8; see also H.L. MacQueen, "Some Notes on Wrang and Unlaw", in *Miscellany Five*, ed. H.L. MacQueen, Stair Society 52 (Edinburgh, 2006), pp. 13–26.

[52] *Quoniam Attachiamenta*, ed. T.D. Fergus, Stair Society 44 (Edinburgh, 1996), p. 117.

[53] A.L. Murray, "The Scottish Chancery in the Fourteenth and Fifteenth Centuries", in *Écrit et Pouvoir dans les Chancelleries Médiévales: Espace Français, Espace Anglais*, ed. K. Fianu and D.J. Guth, Fédération Internationale des Instituts d'Études Médiévales Textes et Études du Moyen Âge 6 (Louvain-La-Neuve, 1997), pp. 133–151.

[54] MacQueen, *Common Law and Feudal Society*, pp. 137–140.

[55] MacQueen, "Canon Law, Custom and Legislation", pp. 243–249; Sellar, "The common law of Scotland", p. 88.

this brieve was always addressed to the justiciar by the fourteenth century.[56] Equally, Parliament was never the forum in which to raise such an action. Being in the King's name and requiring local process in a particular area of the country, no "coursable" brieve (i.e. those in standard form relating to established forms of remedy) could be addressed to King and Council directly, in Parliament or otherwise. The very structure of the procedure presupposed the direction of a brieve to a local (albeit royal) judge who could carry out the royal instructions on the ground. Above and beyond this level of jurisdictional development, the tiers of jurisdiction were linked by a procedure of "falsing the doom". This developed so as to allow the review of judgments of lower courts, and it was here that Parliament had a special role since it was Parliament that functioned as the final court of review above all others. *Quoniam Attachiamenta* instructively describes procedural aspects of falsing the doom of a baron court before the sheriff, and of the sheriff before the justiciar.[57] The (probably) fourteenth century *Regiam Majestatem* does not discuss the procedure of falsing in these courts, and neither manual does so in relation to Parliament. But following the falsing of a doom in the court of the justiciar (or in a distinct "court of the four burghs", for appeals relating to pleas which arose within burgh jurisdiction) it could then be falsed in Parliament.

The procedure of falsing has been little studied since the work of Sir Philip Hamilton-Grierson in the 1920s and precisely how it operated remains obscure. A proper understanding must await further research. Hamilton-Grierson described how the judges of the lower court would be summoned to the court of review, since falsing was a form of complaint against them personally. This understanding of an appeal in the context of Parliament remained influential right up to the union between England and Scotland in 1707. In the words of a fifteenth-century statute of James I, the judges would have their judgment declared by the falser to be "falss stinkand and rottyn in the self".[58] The higher court would then pronounce its own judgment whether the doom was "wele gevin and evil againsaid" or "evil gevin

[56] MacQueen, *Common Law and Feudal Society*, p. 153.

[57] *Quoniam Attachiamenta*, p. 147.

[58] P.J. Hamilton-Grierson, "Falsing the doom", *Scottish Historical Review* 24 (1926), 1–18 at p. 16; *The Acts of the Parliaments of Scotland*, ed. T. Thomson and C. Innes [hereafter *APS*], 12 vols (Edinburgh, 1814–1875), vol. 2, p. 18, c. 6 (i.e. 1429–1430).

and wele againsaid".[59] If falsed, the judges were fined and the doom revoked. The basis of falsing may be contrasted with the development within medieval canon law of an appeal which was explicitly related to the substantive legal correctness of a decision.[60] Even so, though not necessarily identical to a modern appeal, falsing allowed the operation of an appeal structure of sorts which was unified by Parliament at its head and was active throughout the fourteenth and fifteenth centuries. In a parliament of James III (1460–1488) the doom of a justice ayre was successfully falsed and "ilk soytour of the said dome and thar lordis ilk man be himself is in ane amerciament [i.e. a fine] of the court of parliament".[61] The procedure of falsing was still being regulated by statute as late as the early sixteenth century at a time when Parliament had all but given up its general judicial role.[62]

Parliament did not just unify the structure of royal courts administering the common law, and determine the falsing of dooms, however. It also heard petitions and pleas at first instance. The scope for such business must have been strictly limited by the procedural requirement to seek process by brieve and inquest for certain types of dispute, but nevertheless it seems to have remained important during the fourteenth century. Parliaments of the 1320s are known to have dealt with disputes arising from the disinheritance of magnates unreconciled to Robert Bruce in the Cambuskenneth parliament of 1314, for example.[63] This followed Robert's success in asserting his kingship and defeating the English invading army of Edward II at Bannockburn, earlier in 1314. In relation to a lost roll of thirty-five documents concerning parliaments held between 1323 and 1331, Professor Duncan has argued that "the judicial and remedial work of council in parliament...was now so important a function as to justify the keeping of some 'papers' connected with it".[64] The roll included a series of "petitions, bills of complaint, memoranda of agreements, [and] judgments". What must be

---

[59] Hamilton-Grierson, "Falsing the doom", pp. 1–2.

[60] O.F. Robinson, T.D. Fergus, W.M. Gordon, *European Legal History* (3rd ed., London, 2000), p. 193; G.R. Evans, *Law and Theology in the Middle Ages* (London, 2002), pp. 159–161.

[61] P.J. Hamilton-Grierson, "The appellate jurisdiction of the Scottish parliament", *Scottish Historical Review* 15 (1918), 205–222 at p. 217; *APS* ii, p. 114.

[62] Hamilton-Grierson, "Falsing the doom", p. 6; *APS* ii, p. 254, c. 41.

[63] E.g. Scone, 1323, Cambuskenneth, 1326: McQueen, "The origins and development of the Scottish parliament", pp. 283, 293–294; G.W.S. Barrow, *Robert Bruce and the Community of the Realm of Scotland* (4th ed., Edinburgh, 2005), p. 388.

[64] Duncan, "Early parliaments", p. 50.

supposed to have been pressure of judicial business led to the development of a system of delegation of parliamentary business on judicial matters to committees of auditors, evidence of which survives from 1341 onwards. Duncan has shown that there were precursors to these fourteenth-century auditorial committees in the hearing of appeals by auditors of pleas appointed by Edward I in the parliament of June 1291. He has also shown that this in turn appears to have been an extension of a set of arrangements derived from the English parliament.[65] Alan Harding has taken the argument further still, seeing this as not just a question of borrowed institutional mechanisms, but also as providing significant momentum in the development of new remedies outside the system of brieves, through complaints of "wrang and unlaw".[66] As already noted, the scale of judicial activity in the fourteenth century parliament may remain impossible to accurately determine because of the insufficiency of extant records. However, its judicial role remained and was certainly exercised.

The auditorial committees of Parliament

The fourteenth century reveals signs of institutional innovation to help order Parliament's judicial business. David II (1329–71) succeeded to the throne as a five-year old child following the death of Robert I (1306–29). Internal political challenges forced David into exile in France in 1334.[67] In 1341, following David's return after a seven-year absence, we have the first extant record of the delegation of judicial work by Parliament to a smaller group of auditors, and the beginnings of a more elaborate system of transacting Parliament's judicial business. Few records of this system survive before 1466, when the decisions of the two sets of parliamentary auditors—the Auditors of Causes and Complaints and of Falsed Dooms—become extant in a continuous parliamentary register.[68] It was one aspect of a more general delegation of business

[65] Duncan, "Early parliaments", p. 39; see also Dodd, "Sovereignty, Diplomacy and Petitioning: Scotland and the English Parliament in the First Half of the Fourteenth Century", pp. 176–177.

[66] A. Harding, "Rights, Wrongs and Remedies", p. 3.

[67] M.A. Penman, *David II, 1329–1371* (East Linton, 2004), p. 51.

[68] The proceedings of the auditors were part of the main parliamentary register, though the first modern edition of 1839 obscures this by its publication as a separate volume of *Acts of the Lords Auditors of Causes and Complaints*, ed. T. Thomson (Edinburgh, 1839). The modern *The Records of the Parliaments of Scotland to 1707*, ed. K.M. Brown

by Parliament to committees, seen also in relation to legislation.[69] A surviving decree of 1341 resulted from delegation by Parliament to two auditors of a number of supplications and complaints which had yet to be determined by Parliament as a whole.[70] Political, administrative and legal expediency may all have come together in prompting this development. It has been regarded, for example, as a sign of David II's "commitment to restore the machinery of everyday administration".[71] From 1346 to 1357, David was absent again from Scotland, this time in captivity in England. Parliaments could therefore not readily be held, though exceptionally David summoned one by proxy in 1351, and attended another during a temporary return in 1352.[72] Thereafter the evidence of delegation of judicial work to committees continues only from 1367 onwards.[73] Two committees were appointed in the 1370 parliament, for example, one to determine causes and complaints (i.e. first instance complaints) and the other falsed dooms.[74] The importance of Parliament's judicial role by the end of the fourteenth century is signified by the 1399 statute in which it "is ordanyt that ilke yhere the kyng sal halde a parlement swa that his subjectis be servit of the law".[75] Curiously, after named appointments in 1370 and 1372, there is no extant record of appointments of Auditors of Falsed Dooms from 1372 to 1467, though such appointments must presumably have been made. They re-appear in the record thereafter and were appointed up until the 1540s, the last instances being in two of the early parliaments of the infant Queen Mary (1542–1567), in 1543 and 1544.[76] Thereafter,

---

et al. (St Andrews, 2007) has integrated the judicial record back into the legislative one. Note also that Harding has suggested that a greater volume of business caused by legislation of 1458 concerning spuilzie may lie behind such a record beginning to be kept in the 1460s: A. Harding, "Rights, Wrongs and Remedies", p. 8.

69 R. Tanner, "The lords of the articles before 1540: a reassessment", *Scottish Historical Review* 79 (2000), 189–212 at p. 190.

70 *APS* i, p. 513 (24 September, 1341).

71 Penman, *David II*, p. 80.

72 A.A.M. Duncan, "*Honi soit qui mal y pens*: David II and Edward III, 1346–52", *Scottish Historical Review* 67 (1988), 113–141 at pp. 124, 132; Penman, *David II*, pp. 162, 170.

73 M. Penman, "Parliament Lost—Parliament Regained? The Three Estates in the Reign of David II, 1329–71", in Brown and Tanner, *Parliament and Politics in Scotland, 1235–1560*, pp. 74–101 at p. 99; Penman, *David II*, pp. 359, 380, 394, 431. See the useful calendar in *Acts of the Lords of Council in Civil Causes Volume II, 1496–1501*, ed. G. Neilson and H. Paton (Edinburgh, 1918), pp. xi–xii [hereafter *ADC* ii].

74 *APS* i, pp. 507–508, 534.

75 *APS* i, p. 573.

76 Duncan, 'The Central Courts before 1532', 328–329; *APS* ii, 428, 446.

Parliament's role in falsing dooms lapsed entirely. November 1544 also saw the final appointment of parliamentary auditors to consider causes and complaints. However, by this stage the auditors were named simply as the Lords of Session and the College of Justice, so that, in substance, Parliament was doing little more than preserving the institutional form of the auditorial committees in a purely technical sense. Therefore, although committees for remeid of law, consideration of causes and occasionally falsing of dooms were all appointed at times in the sixteenth century until 1544, there is no record of any specifically judicial proceedings (other than for treason) in the parliamentary record after 1504.[77] There was a limited and unique exception in the parliament of 1661 as the period of the Interregnum came to a close. At this point Parliament resumed sitting some time in advance of the Court of Session, and one of its committees appears to have been reponsible for handling some ordinary judicial business in the intervening months.[78] Very occasionally, *ad hoc* bodies with a parliamentary component are recorded as conducting judicial business: in 1541 the "lordis of articulis, counsale and Sessionis" were "convenit for decisionis" of an action and plea.[79] Though rare, such examples remind us that there continued to be a degree of flux and flexibility in the institutional mechanisms for disposing of judicial business centrally.

Even by the later fifteenth century, the number of falsed dooms in Parliament was remarkably few. This was at a time when its first instance business in causes and complaints was relatively heavy. But by this stage a decree from the King's Council had acquired its popularity as a remedy and contrasted with the problematic features of procedure by falsing a doom first obtained in a lower court. Since the procedure of falsing depended on the summoning of a parliament in the first place, its use could become infrequent or simply unfeasible during royal absences such as occurred during 1346–1357 under David II and 1406–1424, when James I (1406–1437) was a prisoner in England.

[77] *ADC* ii, p. 247. An understanding of how the manuscript record was re-ordered in the 19th century so that judicial proceedings in Parliament were divided from the main parliamentary record is essential. See A.L. Murray, "Introduction", in *Acts of the Lords of Council Volume III, 1501–1503*, ed. A.B. Calderwood (Edinburgh, 1993), pp. xiii–xliv. See also J. Goodare, "The Scottish parliamentary records 1560–1603", *Historical Research* 72 (1999), 244–267.

[78] On the 1661 parliamentary committee see J.D. Ford, *Law and Opinion in Scotland during the Seventeenth Century* (Oxford, 2007), pp. 320, 415.

[79] NAS, CS 6/14, fol. 181. See also *ADCP*, p. 501.

However, the main problem must simply have been that it was an extremely protracted way of negating a judgment originally delivered in the locality but which could require falsing through several tiers of jurisdiction before reaching Parliament. Only once considered in Parliament could a doom be regarded as final or otherwise. Meanwhile, the growing fourteenth and fifteenth-century demand for a remedy at first instance in Parliament, dealt with by Auditors of Causes and Complaints, seems to have continued, if anything, to increase, though this remains a matter of speculation. Whether or not there was a burgeoning of judicial business, it seems likely that there was by this time a feeling that Parliament was inadequate to fulfil the perceived need for central adjudication of disputes, or else that for it to do so would distract it from more important deliberations and the need to make legislation in particular. For whatever reason, the situation led to the experimental statutory sessions introduced by James I in 1426.

Parliament, the Session and the College of Justice

The central judicial role in the law that the Scottish parliament developed in the thirteenth, fourteenth and fifteenth centuries had disappeared by 1500, though, as already noted, competence in criminal matters remained in its jurisdiction over treason.[80] This anticipated the great and fundamental development of the sixteenth century, the transformation of the Session into a supreme central civil court following the foundation of the College of Justice in 1532. In this way Scotland acquired one of the most typical institutions of the early modern European state—a central court, promoting unity, consistency and central supervision in the administration of civil justice.[81] As Julian Goodare has observed in the context of a wider study of the development of governance in sixteenth and early seventeenth century Scotland, "the court of session became a flagship institution of central government".[82] Its effectiveness had implications for governance as a whole. Goodare argues that, looking back from the significant changes seen in govern-

[80] Parliament's jurisdiction in treason matters is described in an account of 1560: "Discours particulier D'Escosse, 1559/60", ed. P.G.B. McNeill in *Miscellany Two*, ed. W.D.H. Sellar, Stair Society 35 (Edinburgh, 1984), pp. 117–119.

[81] For the development of a legal profession, see J. Finlay, *Men of Law in Pre-Reformation Scotland* (East Linton, 2000).

[82] Goodare, *The Government of Scotland*, p. 161.

ment generally by 1625, "the momentum for change had begun in the 1530s, with the establishment of the court of session as a college of justice".[83] From 1532, the College of Justice acted to intensify a differentiation of function between Session and Council, as well as a new and decisive degree of institutional separation between the two. After 1532 the Session contained a defined number of named Lords of Council and Session. It was thereby distinguished from the general body of Lords of Council who constituted the residual Privy Council, which also maintained its own separate register from the 1540s.[84] The institutional separation was clear, even though many of the same lords were active in both bodies. Moreover, since the common source of authority was ultimately that of the King's Council, some degree of overlap and sharing of functions remained inevitable throughout the sixteenth century despite the institutional separation of 1532.

The demand for central determination of complaints by King and Council was one that even annual parliaments in the fifteenth century had apparently not satisfied. The fifteenth-century parliament sat for only short periods and did not possess the administrative structure which would have allowed it to function effectively as a more regular court. As we have seen, it may have been attempts to satisfy the demand for central justice that were behind the famous ordinance of James I in 1426 establishing what was to become the Session.[85] This new body was under the direction of the King, had a jurisdiction associated with the Council, but was constituted by members of the parliamentary estates. Professor Hannay speculated that the jurisdiction of "consal" which was conferred on the tribunal should be broadly construed as encompassing the widest historic jurisdiction of the King sitting in Council in any form, which would therefore include that of Parliament as well as "Council General".[86] That its members should be drawn from the

[83] Goodare, *The Government of Scotland*, p. 172.

[84] Goodare, *The Government of Scotland*, pp. 128–148.

[85] *APS* ii, p. 11. The legislation of 1426 appears to have been revised in about 1430–1431, when the Chancellor was substituted for the Chamberlain. See A.A.M. Duncan, *James I, 1424–1437*, Glasgow University Scottish History Department Occasional Papers (2nd ed., Glasgow, 1984), pp. 1–25 at p. 4; O'Brien, "The Scottish parliament", p. 26. For further discussion, see A.R. Borthwick, "The king, council and councillors in Scotland, c. 1430–1460" (University of Edinburgh, unpublished Ph.D. thesis, 1989), pp. 244–246.

[86] R.K. Hannay, "On the antecedents of the college of justice", *The Book of the Old Edinburgh Club* 11 (1922), 87–123 at p. 90, re-printed in *The College of Justice: Essays by R.K. Hannay*, ed. MacQueen, pp. 179–215 at p. 182.

estates which made up Parliament would indeed have helped equate the jurisdiction with that of Parliament itself. Its hybrid character makes it hard to assess this, however, since it was essentially a committee of auditors appointed to move around the country on behalf not so much of Parliament but of the King, doing the business of his Council. This also makes it hard to determine whether it was intended primarily to liberate the smaller King's Council from receipt of petitions for redress or more broadly to supplement the provision of justice in Parliament. The expedient was continued during the reign of James II (1437–1460) and lasted in one form or another until the 1460s. By the parliament of 1439 these sittings appear to have acquired the name of "sessiounis", though they were by then constituted instead from members of the King's Council rather than the estates.[87] After the late 1460s, the regular King's Council became based in Edinburgh, reflecting the more static nature of government under James III (1460–1488).[88] Thereafter, it gradually took over the business of, and ultimately superseded, the statutory "Session", an institutional innovation that further blurred the previously sharp distinction between the jurisdiction of Parliament and Council. By the 1490s the Council was finally exercising most of Parliament's judicial functions, in particular through assuming competence to transact the business of the parliamentary judicial committee of Lords Auditors of Causes and Complaints. Thereafter, various institutional experiments and reforms were implemented during the reign of James IV (1488–1513) and the minority and early personal rule of James V (1513–1542). In 1532 came the creation of the new institution that finally superseded the judicial functions of Parliament in civil matters: the College of Justice.[89] The College was both an adaptation of the existing workings of Council and Session in judicial business and a new departure in terms of institutional structure, with consequences

[87] *APS* ii, p. 14.

[88] T.M. Chalmers, "The king's council, patronage, and the governance of Scotland 1460–1513" (University of Aberdeen, unpublished Ph.D. thesis, 1982), pp. 212–216, 231.

[89] See later chapters, especially chap. 3. An overview is given in A.M. Godfrey, "The assumption of jurisdiction: parliament, the king's council and the college of justice in sixteenth-century Scotland", *Journal of Legal History* 22 (2001), 21–36. Though now subject to the critique developed in this book, the classic account of the institutional history is traced in R.K. Hannay, *The College of Justice* (Edinburgh, 1933), re-printed in *The College of Justice: Essays by R.K. Hannay*, ed. MacQueen. This should be consulted alongside Hannay, "On the antecedents of the college of justice". See also R.K. Hannay, "Introduction" in *ADCP*, pp. v–lviii.

for related matters such as jurisdiction.[90] These developments will all be examined in more depth in subsequent chapters.

The new College of Justice was established by act of Parliament. Even though Parliament's involvement in judicial business had in practical terms been given up three or four decades earlier, the creation of the College marked formally the discarding by Parliament of executive responsibility for determining pleas, though that did not stop litigants attempting to appeal to Parliament from the College of Justice.[91] An instance of such a litigant announcing that he "appelit to the lordis of parliament" is found in the acts and decreets of the Session on 18 January 1533, though with no corresponding trace in the parliamentary record.[92] The relationship between College of Justice and Parliament was in issue again in a case from 1535 in which there was a protest that the lords were not competent judges because there was "ane decret and determination of the hie parliament of Scotland, quhar it wes fund and decernit that the lordis were na competent jugis to auld infeftments". The Lords ruled that they were competent but did not express a view on the status of any such decree of Parliament.[93] In a case from 1546, it was alleged that "thar was ane act in the mater aboune writtin registrat in the bukis of parliament, and tharfor the lordis of counsale mycht be na competent jugis in the said mater".[94] This could be interpreted as akin to a plea of *res judicata*, whereby a matter already the subject of a court decree cannot be re-opened in a fresh action, or perhaps as a broader claim that a decree of Parliament was in a sense superior to one of the Lords of Council and Session. The Lords rejected the allegation in this case on the more categorical ground that "the said act is na decrete of parliament".[95]

---

[90] See Chs 6 and 7 for this and for the jurisdictional position *before* 1532 being made the subject of debate. See also Godfrey, "The assumption of jurisdiction"; A. Borthwick, "*Montrose v Dundee* and the jurisdiction of parliament and council over fee and heritage in the mid-fifteenth century", in *The Scots and Parliament*, ed. C. Jones (Edinburgh, 1996), pp. 33–53; H.L. MacQueen, *Common Law and Feudal Society*, chap. 8; H.L. MacQueen, "Jurisdiction in heritage and the lords of council and session after 1532", in *Miscellany Two*, ed. Sellar, pp. 61–85.

[91] For a reassessment of the foundation of the College of Justice, see chap. 3.

[92] NAS, CS 6/2 fol. 49.

[93] A.M. Godfrey, "Jurisdiction in heritage and the foundation of the college of justice in 1532", in *Miscellany Four*, ed. MacQueen, pp. 9–36 at pp. 21–22.

[94] *ADCP*, p. 552.

[95] *ADCP*, p. 552.

Parliament's role in relation to the law was, after 1532, largely connected with legislation (other than its criminal jurisdiction over treason), though there is no doubt that its supremacy in this regard gave it at least in some ways a broader primacy over even the College of Justice. In 1535, the senators of the College of Justice felt obliged to refer "to the lordis thre estates of parliament for interpretatioun of certane lawis of the realme schewin and producit befor the saidis lordis of sessioun".[96] The Lords of the Articles responded by making a finding as to what "the use in tymes bigane hes bene", instructing that "the saidis lawis suld be sa interprete and usit in tymes cuming". Arguments that Parliament retained an ordinary role in civil litigation are unconvincing, however.[97] Just as the development of a medieval common law had turned the judicial role of Parliament into a legally-structured jurisdiction, so the sixteenth-century understanding of law and custom may have helped elevate Parliament above the world of mass adjudication in which it had been replaced to a more oracular plane as giver and interpreter of law.

In broader terms, the sixteenth century was also the period when the medieval institutional model of central governance—unified government by King and Council, meeting in Parliament or less formally—begins to look inadequate to describe the practice of government and the roles of Parliament and Council in particular. Whether such changes signal any more fundamental shift in how governance operated before 1600 is a matter of debate.[98] It is also interesting that, despite these developments, an early seventeenth-century account of the Scottish courts still commenced with the statement that "in the Kingdome of Scotland the supreame court of all others ys the court of Parliament".[99]

[96] *APS* ii, pp. 349–350.

[97] W.B. Gray, "The judicial proceedings of the parliaments of Scotland, 1660–1688", *Juridical Review* 36 (1924), 135–151. Gray usefully discusses treason proceedings, but alongside an overstated claim that parliament was still involved in civil judicial business up to 1688. The three examples given are easily distinguishable from ordinary civil proceedings, and all relate to the constitutional upheaval caused by events of the 1640s: *APS* vii, p. 406; *APS* viii, pp. 347, 366.

[98] For an assessment of whether there was a "Stewart revolution in government" see Goodare, *The Government of Scotland*, pp. 276–297.

[99] "Relation of the manner of judicatores of Scotland", ed. J.D. Mackie and W.C. Dickinson, *Scottish Historical Review* 19 (1922), 254–272 at p. 262. Compare this with the recognition in 1498 by the Spanish Ambassador, Don Pedro de Ayala, of the role of what he called General Council, rather than Parliament, in administering justice. It is unclear whether he was meaning to refer to Parliament, General Council or Council. See the discussion in N. Macdougall, *James IV* (Edinburgh, 1989), p. 283.

Even if this reflects little more than a residual perception, or conveys a mark of status rather than function, it also suggests that the structural understanding of the Scottish parliament as a court was powerful enough to outlive by more than a century any routine involvement in adjudicating disputes. A late sixteenth-century account of "the order of the Haldinge of the Court of Parliament in Scotland" noted that, before proceedings could begin, "the Counstable fensesse the Court in like manner as any other Court is fensitt". The jurisdiction over treason may help account for the continuing perception of Parliament as a court—the "order of the Haldinge" describes its procedure "gyft there be any man somoned to compeare in Parliament for treason or othere such like crime".[100] However, treason alone would hardly justify characterising Parliament in jurisdictional terms as "the supreame court of all others", given that it had ceased to exercise such a civil jurisdiction at the end of the fifteenth century.

Following the analysis of Professor R.K. Hannay, there is readily to be identified in the Scottish context a process of differentiation of function which explains the institutional changes to Parliament and King's Council in the later fifteenth and sixteenth centuries.[101] The explanatory power of this approach has continued to be evident in modern studies, the most notable being by Julian Goodare.[102] As Athol Murray has commented in relation to the Council, its "original province was the general administration of the realm, with no real differentiation between its sittings for justice, for finance or for state affairs, except that a special commission was necessary for auditing accounts in exchequer".[103] By the end of the fifteenth century, the Council was not only regularly burdened with its own judicial and financial business, but also exercised what had previously been the ordinary judicial powers of Parliament. By the mid-sixteenth century the Council had yielded to more specialised bodies constituted from Lords of Council, each with relatively distinct

[100] "The Order of the Holding of the Court of Parliament in Scotland", ed. J.D. Mackie, *Scottish Historical Review* 27 (1948) 191–193 at p. 193. "Fencing" was the procedure required to constitute the court: W.C. Dickinson, "Appendix A, The Procedure of the Court" in *The Sheriff Court Book of Fife 1515–1522*, ed. Dickinson, p. 309.

[101] Hannay, "On the antecedents of the college of justice", p. 123; Hannay uses a variety of different expressions referring to differentiation or specialisation of function in the "departmental activities of the royal council". See Hannay, *College of Justice*, p. xi.

[102] Goodare, *The Government of Scotland*, pp. 106, 130, 149–172.

[103] A.L. Murray, "Exchequer, council and session 1513–1542", in *Stewart Style 1513–1542: Essays on the Court of James V*, ed. J. Hadley Williams (East Linton, 1996), pp. 97–117 at p. 108.

functions, and Parliament now existed alongside the Exchequer (from 1584 carrying out its own judicial business on a permanent basis), the College of Justice and the Privy Council.[104]

Nevertheless, there was still an essential overall unity. Julian Goodare has noted this in arguing that "in sixteenth-century Scotland, parliament (legislature), court of session (judiciary), and privy council (executive) all operated in the name of the crown, and cannot be said to have had fully separate spheres of action".[105] In Goodare's view this renders any model drawing on a principle of "separation of powers" particularly inappropriate to explain Scottish development. Goodare's own suggestion is a model based instead on a distinction between making and implementing the law, though perhaps this also struggles to capture the complex reality. Since judges of the new College of Justice were both Lords of Council *and* Session, they continued to issue their decrees in the Session as decrees of the "Lords of Council" after 1532. They had sole authority to exercise this part of the Council's jurisdiction, but it was nevertheless the jurisdiction of the King's Council, and this is where their authority originated. In 1525, we find the *parliamentary* Lords of the Articles giving decree in relation to a dispute, but it was in their general capacity as Lords of Council, thus reflecting again the overall sense of unity across the various manifestations of the King's Council.[106] Even at the end of the sixteenth century this unity remained apparent, with the Lords of Session still exercising on at least one occasion a legislative role quite independently from the Privy Council or Parliament.[107] This occurred on 14 March 1595 when they enacted statutes concerned with crown lands, thirds of benefices and annexed kirklands, legislation subsequently re-enacted in Parliament in 1597.[108] The legislative activity of 1595 was also noted by the early seventeenth century advocate, and lord advocate to Charles I, Sir Thomas Hope, in his *Major Practicks*. He observed that "ther ar ane number of statuts of sessione anent the [i.e. "his majestie's"] propertie quhilk ar enacted in parliament therefter, anno 1597". The one example quoted in the text

[104] A.L. Murray, "Sir John Skene and the exchequer, 1594–1612", *Miscellany One*, Stair Society 26 (Edinburgh, 1971), pp. 125–155 at p. 126.

[105] J. Goodare, *State and Society in Early Modern Scotland* (Oxford, 1999), p. 17. Interestingly, in the sixteenth century the king was often referred to in parliamentary and conciliar records in a literal and personal way as 'our sovereign lord'.

[106] Murray, "Exchequer, council and session 1513–1542", p. 105.

[107] See Murray, "Sir John Skene and the exchequer, 1594–1612", pp. 127, 130.

[108] Books of Sederunt, NAS CS 1/4/1 fols. 168–171; APS iv, pp. 131–133, c. 4–17.

seems more akin to a judicial decision than statute, but carries overtones of an enacting formula, beginning "our soveraigne lord with advyce of the lords of session casses retreits and annulls all and quhatsomever gifts, pensiones, assedations".[109]

It is also the case that up until 1707 it remained technically possible for Parliament to be drawn back into its role as a civil law court in certain ways, however infrequent and exceptional this was in practice. Early relations between Parliament and the College of Justice have already been touched upon. It is not necessary to consider the Cromwellian invasion and English occupation of Scotland in the 1650s here, other than to note that between June 1651 and January 1661 no Scottish parliament was held, and the Court of Session ceased to operate between February 1650 and June 1661.[110] These developments might have had profound consequences for the administration of justice in Scotland, but both Parliament and the Court of Session were restored with the Scottish monarchy after 1660. Later in the seventeenth century, debate about the relationship between the College of Justice and the Parliament was to arise in the context of questioning the competence of the procedure of making a "protest for remeid of law" to Parliament—something which has tended to become confused in modern accounts with the notion of appeal.[111] Its historic judicial role meant that Parliament's relationship with litigation in the College of Justice had remained formally intact (being neither redefined nor explicitly abolished at any technical level) but had, in practical terms, became remote and uncertain after the establishment of the College of Justice. By 1663, it seems to have been accepted in Parliament that an appeal from a decree of the Lords of Session to Parliament was not competent. The parliamentary Lords of the Articles commented upon a case remitted to them that "the reversing of any such decree must needs be upon the iniquitie of the Judges of the supream Judicator of this

[109] *Hope's Major Practicks 1608–1633 Volume I*, ed. J. Clyde, Stair Society 3 (Edinburgh, 1937), p. 51.

[110] The best detailed account of the administration of justice during the Interregnum is Ford, *Law and Opinion in Scotland*, chap. 2. See also G. Donaldson, *Scotland: James V-James VII* (Edinburgh, 1965), chap. 18; F.D. Dow, *Cromwellian Scotland 1651–1660* (Edinburgh, 1979), pp. 270–271; D. Stevenson, "The covenanters and the court of session, 1637–1650", *Juridical Review* (1972), 227–247 at p. 244; J.R. Young, *The Scottish Parliament 1639–1661* (Edinburgh, 1996), pp. 283–288; D. Stevenson, *Revolution and Counter Revolution 1644–1651* (London, 1979), p. 176.

[111] For example, in an otherwise useful survey of the topic, in R.S. Tompson, *Islands of the Law: A Legal History of the British Isles* (New York, 2000), pp. 41–42.

Kingdom in maters civill from whom ther is no appeall be the lawes of this Nation".[112] The concept of reversing a decree is not expressed here in the language of appeal, and appears to preserve something of the medieval notion of falsing the doom, however faintly. This would therefore be distinguishable from a substantive appeal in which the legal basis of a decree were to be open to challenge. The impossibility of appeal from the College of Justice to Parliament had been acknowledged in at least one unofficial but authoritative commentary from the early seventeenth-century.[113] Consistently with this, the Scottish commissioners who were engaged in deliberating union proposals with England in 1670 also stated that "ther was no appeals allowed by our law to our owne parliament from the session".[114]

Nevertheless, a procedure of lodging with Parliament a protest for "remeid of law" against decisions of the Session continued up until 1707. This was an exceptional and rarely sought measure—to call it a remedy might be too elaborate, and wrongly imply that it was predicated upon the availability of defined remedial action. It was specifically mentioned as a "right" of subjects in the constitutional declaration adopted by the Scottish convention of estates meeting in 1689 following the ousting of King James VII (1685–1688), and incorporating the "claim of right". However, it was merely a procedure and does not seem to have constituted a substantive judicial appeal. Little has been added since to the account given by Professor Rait in the 1920s. He pointed out that, unlike an appeal, such a protest did not put a stop on any continuing court process or implementation of the decree protested against. If it permitted any review of decisions by the Session, it seems that it must have operated on the narrowest of grounds concerned with the conduct of the judges in question rather than their decision on purely legal grounds.[115]

The lodging of a protestation in order to formally reserve rights was in any event not a specifically parliamentary device, but had a general currency connected with administrative or legal process in the

---

[112] *APS* vii, p. 500.

[113] "Relation of the manner of judicatores of Scotland", ed. Mackie and Dickinson, pp. 265–266.

[114] J.D. Ford, "The Legal Provisions in the Acts of Union", *Cambridge Law Journal* 66 (2007), pp. 106–141 at p. 123, citing Edinburgh, National Library of Scotland, MS 7004, fols. 161–162.

[115] Rait, *The Parliaments of Scotland*, p. 475; Cairns, "Historical Introduction", pp. 113, 123, 125.

sixteenth century and well before. It is evident not just in Parliament but also in relation to the Session, the Privy Council, and the General Assembly of the reformed church after 1560. In the sixteenth-century Session, for example, a protestation might be lodged when a defender was summoned to court but found that the pursuer was not present and that the action could therefore not proceed. Such a defender would "protest" that they should not have to answer to the summons until "summoned anew" and after refund of their expenses. They would submit that their rights should not be prejudiced since they had duly appeared in court. The protestation did not trigger any further procedural step, and so was not in any way a substantive determination like an appeal, but could simply be "admittit" by the Lords of Session, so that a new summons and repayment of expenses would be required of the pursuer before the defender could be impleaded again.[116] In the case of the Privy Council, we see protests being deployed as a way of formally responding to royal proclamations which were considered to threaten rights which the protest formally asserted and reserved.[117]

In the later seventeenth century, the ordinary procedure of protesting for remeid of law seems, in a parliamentary context, to have become caught up in what now seems a misconceived attempt to assert a full right of appeal in Parliament against decisions of the Session.[118] The safeguarding of protesting for remeid in the "claim of right" of 1689 reflects the unsatisfactory outcome of a heated dispute between 1674 and 1676 over the right to challenge a decree of the College of Justice by a protest to Parliament. Alexander Livingstone, who became second earl of Callendar in March 1674, had initially launched an appeal from the College of Justice to Parliament. He subsequently defied the King's wish that he withdraw the appeal, and his advocate Sir George

[116] NAS CS 5/40, fol. 20.

[117] Examples can be found in D. Stevenson, *The Scottish Revolution 1637–1644* (Newton Abbot, 1973), pp. 80–81 (following proclamations issued by privy council), p. 119 (general assembly), p. 176 (parliament).

[118] For the most detailed available account of protests for remeid in parliament, see G.W. Iredell, "The law, custom and practice of the parliament of Scotland with particular reference to the period 1660–1707", (University of London, unpublished Ph.D. thesis, 1966), pp. 253–259. Useful information is surveyed in E.E.B. Thomson, *The Parliament of Scotland, 1690–1702* (London, 1929), pp. 100–102. See also Gray, "The judicial proceedings of the parliaments of Scotland, 1660–1688"; Tompson, *Islands of the Law*, pp. 40–42. Another valuable perspective is offered in A.R. MacDonald, "Deliberative processes in parliament c. 1567–1639: multicameralism and the lords of the articles", *Scottish Historical Review* 81 (2002), 23–51 at pp. 31–32.

Lockhart of Carnwath justified this stance by arguing that the petition could be characterised as a protest for remeid of law. King Charles II (1660–1685) reacted to the appeal by attempting to ban any challenges to decisions of the Lords of Session by "appeals, protestations, supplications, informations, or any other manner of way".[119] Banning protests was an innovation, however. After Carnwath and three other advocates were disbarred for opposing this, as many as fifty other members of the Faculty of Advocates withdrew from acting in court and walked out in protest.[120] The dispute had a disturbing political aspect for the King's administration in Scotland. Eventually the advocates submitted, but only by January 1676, by which time the dispute had lasted for two years. Moreover the legal threats made by the King against Carnwath and others had to be dropped.[121] Ultimately, however, it was the position established by King Charles which was reversed in the "claim of right" of 1689, after the unseating of King James VII, so as to protect the right of protest to Parliament. Apart from the dispute of 1674–76, the politicisation of the question of protesting for remeid to Parliament also seems to have reflected wider concerns about corruption in the Session in the later seventeenth century, in which context appeals would have a special importance.[122]

Various measures concerning protestations came before Parliament thereafter. For example, there was a draft of an act regulating protestations from Session to Parliament in May 1695, followed by another in 1700, though no statute resulted.[123] In an exceptional case in 1690, a protest did result in Parliament rescinding a decision of the Lords of Session, but the exceptional nature of the remedy given by Parliament was underlined by the statement in the parliamentary record that this was "after much debait how far the protestatione for remeid of law should be regulat to prevent unnecessar and too frequent protestations

[119] Rait, *The Parliaments of Scotland*, pp. 475–476.

[120] J.M. Simpson, "The advocates as Scottish trade union pioneers", in *The Scottish Tradition*, ed. G.W.S. Barrow (Edinburgh, 1974), p. 173. Some further political context is given by Clare Jackson, *Restoration Scotland, 1660–1690: Royalist Politics, Religion and Ideas* (Woodbridge, 2003), pp. 84–86. The most recent and detailed account of the dispute in its wider political context is G.H. MacIntosh, *The Scottish Parliament under Charles II, 1660–1685* (Edinburgh, 2007), pp. 144–149. See also Ford, *Law and Opinion in Scotland*, pp. 318–320.

[121] MacIntosh, *The Scottish Parliament under Charles II*, p. 148.

[122] Ford, "The Legal Provisions in the Acts of Union", p. 123.

[123] *APS* ix, pp. 353, 354; *APS* x, p. 214.

taking off the effect of the sentences".[124] Unease in Parliament about involvement in the ordinary course of litigation is brought out further by its remitting in 1701 a process concerning a protest for remeid of law back to the Lords of Session, but to be determined "summarly with a parliamentary power".[125] This is reminiscent of the referring of parliamentary auditorial business to the Lords of Session and College of Justice upon the occasion of the final appointment of Auditors of Causes and Complaints in 1544. All of this strikes a cautionary note that, when we trace structural relations between institutions which were themselves evolving, we should be prepared to accept that the meaning of the rules and procedures which expressed such relations, and the underlying concepts which informed them, were also likely to experience some change. Against the background of flux in the development of sixteenth and seventeenth-century governance in Scotland, the role of the protest for remeid of law in Parliament almost certainly changed over time, and its contentiousness in the later seventeenth century tells us more about later seventeenth century constitutional politics than about the history and procedure of protesting for remeid. Indeed, prior to this it appears to have had little of the same significance.

In the earlier seventeenth century, the unlimited competence of the Session and the impossibility of appeal from its decisions could be acknowledged (as one would expect in relation to a supreme civil court) whilst at the same time that:

> in some matters of greate ymportance and difficultie (for which there was noe president for a warrant for them to proceede into), they [i.e. the judges of the Session] have bene accustomed (but verie seldome) to remitt these matters to be iudged upon by parliament, that by statute of parliament they may have a warrant for their decision in such like cases thereafter.[126]

This practice represents an interesting parallel with the procedure already discussed from 1535, when the College of Justice referred to Parliament a question of interpretation of laws which had been "producit" in court, following which the Lords of the Articles determined past usage and how the laws in question should be construed for the future.[127]

---

[124] *APS* ix, pp. 175–180; *APS* ix, appendix, p. 160.

[125] *APS* x, p. 339.

[126] "Relation of the manner of judicatores of Scotland", ed. Mackie and Dickinson, p. 266.

[127] *APS* ii, pp. 349–350.

The 1535 example concerned interpretation of the law, presumably a parliamentary statute, whereas the early seventeenth century description seems to envisage the remitting of an actual decision, though this is not clear. However, though the two procedures may have addressed different issues, it is noteworthy that the latter resulted in the formality of a statute, rather than mere informal communing between Parliament and Council such as occurred in 1535. This suggests a greater primacy being given to resort to statute by 1600. By this time Scottish jurists were also beginning to develop more systematic contrasts between the varying sources of law applied in Scotland, particularly civil law (Roman law) and what was usually termed municipal law (native legislation and customs). In describing the municipal law of the state, late sixteenth-century writers such as Thomas Craig naturally gave written law a higher ranking than the customs applied in the courts, and both were to be ranked above Roman law, even though it possessed the authority of being *ius scriptum*.[128]

The creation of the United Kingdom in 1707 and the provision that it be represented by "one and the same parliament" brought the Scottish parliament and its relationship with the law of Scotland to an end. The disappearance of the Scottish parliament had little effect on the administration of justice, however, due to the previous abandonment of its judicial functions in the late fifteenth century, and the subsequent development of a permanent central court and legal system based upon the existence of that court, referred to in the articles of union by its twin identity as the "Court of Session or College of Justice". Famously, as one of the foundations of the union settlement, it was provided that the Court of Session "do after the Union, and notwithstanding thereof, remain in all time coming within Scotland, as it is now constituted by the laws of that Kingdom, and with the same Authority and Privileges as before the Union".[129] Curiously, in relation to judicial matters, the union in one sense promoted a greater role for the parliament of

[128] I acknowledge that these comments on sources risk being extremely simplistic, and cannot do any justice to the complex thesis presented in Ford, *Law and Opinion in Scotland*. See also J.W. Cairns, "The civil law tradition in Scottish legal thought", in *The Civilian Tradition and Scots Law*, ed. Carey Miller and Zimmermann, pp. 191–223 at pp. 200–203. See also J.W. Cairns, "*Ius Civile* in Scotland, ca. 1600", *Roman Legal Tradition* 2 (2004), pp. 136–170; J.W. Cairns, "Attitudes to Codification and the Scottish Science of Legislation, 1600–1830".

[129] The full provisions are more complex. See Cairns, "Historical introduction", pp. 114–116.

Great Britain than the Scottish parliament had recently enjoyed. This was because civil appeals to the House of Lords were not prohibited under the articles of union, and became quickly established.[130] The point has been well made by Dr J.D. Ford that Scottish legal opinion informing the union debates of 1706 would have regarded an appeal to Parliament as limited to reviewing the conduct of the judges, and not the legal substance of their decisions.[131] This was consistent with later seventeenth century views already discussed. Nevertheless, that view of the nature of an appeal was not reflected in the approach of the House of Lords after 1707. The post-union appeal superseded this more limited conception and the even more limited notion of merely lodging with the old Scottish parliament a protest for "remeid of law". This was to be one of the most influential legacies of the union for the development of Scots law.

[130] Cairns, "Historical introduction", p. 123; A.J. MacLean, "The 1707 union: Scots law and the house of lords", *Journal of Legal History* 4 (1983), 50–75.

[131] Ford, "The Legal Provisions in the Acts of Union", pp. 124–125, 140.

CHAPTER TWO

THE EVOLUTION OF THE SESSION 1426–1532

As noted in the previous chapter, the word "session" was used to describe a series of judicial bodies which developed in the century or so after 1426. It described simply a "sitting" of a body with special judicial competence. Though at first a form of tribunal outside the normal structure of courts, the history of the Session charts a process in which it became a permanent court. It continued to be referred to as the Session after the foundation of the College of Justice in 1532, though later it came generally to be referred to more expansively as the "Court of Session". This development in nomenclature seems to reflect nothing of deeper significance. However, within the period 1426–1532 we can categorise three distinguishable institutions which were designated by the word "session". The first could be termed the auditorial Session, composed of members of the three estates of Parliament (nobility, church and burghs) and sitting as a statutory judicial tribunal enabled by successive though intermittent acts of Parliament.[1] The second could be termed the conciliar Session, being sessions of the King's Council which were devoted to judicial work. The third was constituted by the Session as defined within the institutional framework of the College of Justice after its foundation in 1532, conducted by individuals who continued to be Lords of Council *and* Session. The auditorial-type Session of the 1420s was a very different type of body from the conciliar one of the 1490s, and both differed from the Session of the mid-1530s and later. Although all are linked by certain threads of continuity in their evolution, there was no trajectory or path of development which saw the original tribunal of 1426 reshaped and modified as a matter of consistent policy aiming towards the goal of a permanent central civil court. Over the longer term, there was no such goal. The apparent continuity in nomenclature should therefore not disguise the highly contingent nature of the developments.

---

[1] See J. Goodare, "The Estates in the Scottish Parliament, 1286–1707", *Parliamentary History* 15 (1996), 11–32.

The evolution related to changing political circumstances over time rather than to any long-adumbrated goals of policy. It also occurred within a wider institutional framework which was itself evolving—the governmental framework of Parliament and its committees, the institutions of Council, General Council, and Exchequer, as well as the developing roles of individual offices of state. These developments also had implications for the use of royal seals and the arrangement of the associated writing offices, as well as the framework provided by the existing structure of jurisdiction and law courts, secular and ecclesiastical. The Session was a constitutional and judicial novelty when it first appeared in 1426, though to some extent it resembled Parliament's judicial committees, in particular the committee of Auditors of Causes and Complaints. However, the new Session was a body liberated from the structure of a sitting of Parliament or Council. This must have been the main purpose of the 1426 innovation, and suggests that earlier arrangements were considered inadequate, or that by 1426 judicial work was now competing for attention less successfully with other forms of parliamentary business. In our examination of the role of Parliament as a central court in the previous chapter, we noted the improvisations made during the fourteenth century involving the delegation of judicial work to parliamentary committees. This might suggest some increase in central judicial business in the century following the crystallisation of Parliament's judicial role in the 1290s. However, without further research that remains a matter of speculation. At least as plausibly, it might represent simply the establishment of an efficient procedure within Parliament to transact its judicial business in a manner which spared the plenary sessions from being dominated by involved legal hearings. Although the judicial business of the medieval parliament has never been systematically examined, it would appear that by the later fourteenth century there is little such business for which records survive. However, precisely the absence of surviving records makes it difficult to draw any conclusion about the scale of such business. In any event, the effect on central justice of the captivity of James I in England from 1406 to 1424 could have generated a feeling by the time of James's return that institutions of central justice had become damagingly moribund and needed to be revived. For such a purpose, however, Parliament itself would have proved unsuited. However frequently it met, the fifteenth-century parliament nevertheless sat for very short periods and was thereby obstructed from easily transacting any large quantity of business. Furthermore, it did not possess the administrative structure of a regular court, with its ability to determine procedural issues between full hearings for proof or legal debate, or to postpone hearings on a short-term basis. Therefore the demand for central determination of complaints by King, Council and Parliament was to prove one that even annual parliaments in the fifteenth century were unable to satisfy. Consequently, the experimentation which began early in the active reign of James I was never abandoned.

The most important evidence we have for the fifteenth-century Session is contained in acts of Parliament from 1426, and the records of the King's Council which become extant in 1478. Caution is required in interpreting the parliamentary statutes, since usually we know little of their context. Besides, legislation can only provide indirect evidence of the activity of the judicial bodies which were being regulated in this way. It does not provide evidence of how the institution in question functioned thereafter, or whether it functioned at all. To examine these acts in serial fashion may give an impression of continuous development, perhaps even the "rise" of a supreme central court. This would be misleading, conferring upon them what A.A.M. Duncan termed a "spurious air of unity" in the context of his discussion of the legislation of James I generally.[2] The general pattern of development revealed in these statutes is a shift from Parliament being the main central forum for the administration of justice in the fourteenth century to the exercise of this function by the King's Council in the sixteenth century. During the fifteenth century, it appears, various expedients were tried in order to process the flow of complaints which was being directed into Parliament (and perhaps Council). The first Sessions were set up to enable such complaints to be heard independently of sittings of either. As we have already noted, justice was otherwise provided for at common law through procedure by brieve and inquest in the ordinary courts, in particular those of the sheriff and justiciar. Since the emphasis in the fourteenth and fifteenth centuries was on justice administered in the locality, it would seem likely that resort to Parliament must have been exceptional. The transition by the mid-sixteenth century is then all the more extraordinary, since not only had Parliament largely abandoned its judicial functions, but now central justice appeared the dominant form of justice in Scotland, administered through the Session in its new

---

[2] A.A.M. Duncan, *James I, 1424–1437*, Glasgow University Scottish History Department Occasional Papers (2nd ed., Glasgow, 1984), p. 1.

guise from 1532 as the College of Justice. The Session after 1532 also had a wider competence than any of its fifteenth-century predecessors, even asserting exclusive jurisdiction in matters which had been outwith their ordinary remit in terms of the medieval common law.[3]

The Auditorial Session 1426–1468

The act of 1426[4]

The first Sessions are connected with the return of James I to Scotland in 1424 at almost the age of thirty, after eighteen years of captivity in England. As Michael Brown has observed, James' reign "marked a return to active monarchy after almost half a century of weak kings and delegated authority".[5] James was an active king, holding ten parliaments and three general councils in his thirteen-year reign, with a "flurry of legislation" up to 1431.[6] Professor Duncan commented in his study of the reign that "law-making, once an infrequent and limited exercise, becomes suddenly in 1424 a willingness to interfere, to regulate, on almost any subject of concern to the king or his subjects".[7] James returned in April 1424, and by March 1426 Parliament had legislated for "sessions" (although this word was not used in the act), which, as Professor Nicholson put it, "were not intended to displace the jurisdiction of parliament but were to exist alongside it with equal authority and competence".[8] The first Sessions must have represented an attempt to satisfy a demand for central justice which Parliament and Council did not feel capable of meeting or willing to accomodate. The famous statute of James I in 1426 stated (in its earliest extant version):

> Alsua the kyng vyth hall consent of his parlyament hass ordanit that his chaumerlayne and vyth him certane dyscreyt persouns of the thre estatis sall syt xiiij days in ilk quartir of the yhere quhar the kyng lykis to command thaim, the quhilkis sall heyr, knaw and exsamyn and determe all and sindry complanttis that may be decrettyt and determynit befor the kyngis consall. And at tha persons be chossing be the kyng and have

[3] Heritable title is the main example of this and is discussed in Chapters 6 and 7.
[4] *APS* ii, p. 11, c. 19.
[5] M. Brown, *James I* (Edinburgh, 1994), p. xii.
[6] Michael Lynch, *Scotland, A New History* (London, 1991), pp. 144–145.
[7] Duncan, *James I*, p. 3.
[8] R. Nicholson, *Scotland, the Later Middle Ages* (Edinburgh, 1974), p. 311.

> thir expensis of the party fundin in the faut or uthir vays as it plessis to the kyng.[9]

The better known version is contained in a different manuscript tradition and is thought to have been a subsequent re-enactment. It appeared in the older nineteenth-century edition of *The Acts of the Parliaments of Scotland*. The existence of two versions has only received comment following research completed by Dr Irene O'Brien in 1980, and which is discussed below. Both are now published for the first time with an authoritative editorial apparatus in *The Records of the Parliaments of Scotland to 1707* (St. Andrews, 2007). This subsequent re-enactment replaced the Chamberlain with the Chancellor:

> Item oure lorde the king with consent of his parliament has ordanit that his chansleir, and with hym certane discret personis of the thre estatis to be chosyn ande depute be oure lorde the king, sall syt fra hyn forwart thre tymmis in the yere quhare the king likis to commande thaim, quhilk sal knaw, examen, conclude and finally determyn all and sindry complayntis, querallis and causs that may be determynit befor the kingis consal. The quhilk personis sal hafe thare expenss of the partiis fundyn fautyce, and of thar unlawis, or uthir ways as beis plesande to our lorde the king.[10]

Professor Harding has suggested that there may have been a model for the initiative in ordinances of 1423 in England, made whilst James was still captive there and "which provided that bills ordinarily terminable at common law should be heard by the council" in some situations.[11] In Scotland, the new body of 1426 was a hybrid one and not simply coterminous with the King's Council. It was under the direction of the King, had a jurisdiction associated with the Council, but was constituted by members of the parliamentary estates.

As finally revised, the act provided for an unspecified number of men "of the thre estatis" to sit three times a year to determine all

[9] *The Records of the Parliaments of Scotland to 1707*, ed. K.M. Brown et al. (St Andrews, 2007) [*RPS*], 1426/25, Manuscript Group C version.

[10] *RPS*, 1426/25, Manuscript Group D version. The Record Edition version is *APS* ii, p. 11, c. 19. The legislation of 1426 appears to have been revised in about 1430–31, when the Chancellor was substituted for the Chamberlain. See Duncan, *James I*, p. 4; O'Brien, "The Scottish parliament", p. 26; for further discussion, see A.R. Borthwick, "The King, Council and Councillors in Scotland, c. 1430–1460" (University of Edinburgh, unpublished Ph.D. thesis, 1989), pp. 244–246.

[11] A. Harding, "Rights, Wrongs and Remedies in Late Medieval English and Scots Law", in *Miscellany Four*, ed. H.L. MacQueen, Stair Society 49 (Edinburgh, 2002), pp. 1–8 at p. 7.

complaints "that may be determynit befor the kingis consal". A possible motive for the innovation was suggested by Professor Duncan, "namely that the king was anxious to free the council about himself from the weight of judicial business, and to strengthen those whom along with the chancellor he would depute to take this weight".[12] Professor MacQueen has also seen the purpose of the scheme as tending "to enable the work of government to be done efficiently" as a result of the despatch of judicial business through the Session.[13] However, the precise nature of the tribunal is rather unclear. The structure of personnel is usually taken to be based on the auditorial committees of Parliament, since it was composed of "certane discret personis of the thre estatis", but there was no specification as to whether these "persouns" were to be drawn from Parliament generally, more narrowly from its auditorial committees, or more narrowly still from members of the King's Council. Despite the link with the estates, it would seem that these persons were to be chosen by the King, whilst the sittings of the tribunal were to be where the King wished them to be. It is difficult to analyse such matters without making constitutionally anachronistic assumptions, such as that institutional categories must have affected the choice of personnel, but the hybrid character of the tribunal seems to have been innovative.

Furthermore, whilst the structure of the personnel mirrored the structure of the auditorial committees, the *jurisdiction* of the tribunal is stated to be that of the King's Council, not that of the parliamentary Auditors. If invoking Council's jurisdiction was normally restricted to complaints of the poor, widows, churchmen, "strangers" and complaints against royal officers,[14] then it can be imagined that it was the business of Council which was being relieved by the new Session as much as Parliament. This would make the requirement that its members be drawn from the three estates puzzling. As noted in the previous chapter, Hannay assumed that "consal" meant Council in its most "comprehensive" sense, including General Council and Parliament,[15] though he

---

[12] A.A.M. Duncan, "The Central Courts before 1532" in *An Introduction to Scottish Legal History*, ed. G.C.H. Paton, Stair Society 20 (Edinburgh, 1958), pp. 321–340 at p. 330.

[13] H.L. MacQueen, "Pleadable Brieves and Jurisdiction in Heritage in Later Medieval Scotland" (University of Edinburgh, unpublished Ph.D. thesis, 1985), p. 267.

[14] MacQueen, "Pleadable Brieves and Jurisdiction in Heritage", p. 258.

[15] R.K. Hannay, "On the Antecedents of the College of Justice", *The Book of the Old Edinburgh Club* 11 (1922), 87–123 at p. 90.

offered little reasoning on the point or even examples of this usage in other, less ambiguous, contexts. Balfour-Melville suggested that "while it might seem to be an attempt to organise the equitable jurisdiction of the chancellor, as had been done in England, the phrase probably signifies all cases which did not, like treason, require the special competence of parliament" and was directed towards handling "the rush of cases to the council".[16] Dickinson implied that the new body might have relieved both Parliament and Council, referring to "the old difficulty presented by a host of causes and complaints coming before the King in Council and in Parliament".[17] On the other hand, there seems to be no obvious reason not to interpret the act literally, as conferring the customary jurisdiction of the King's Council as distinct from that of Parliament. There is also no evidence that Council was dealing with a wider class of complaints or exercising a wider jurisdiction than normal at this time. The later legislative style of enactment would generally state the jurisdiction of Sessions explicitly when it was wider than that of Council. Nevertheless, it may well be that the *jurisdiction* of the King's Council was little different from that of the parliamentary Auditors of Causes and Complaints other than in particular categories such as heritable title to land (i.e. "fee and heritage"), even though as a matter of practice Council would customarily only entertain complaints within its jurisdiction from a limited *class* of litigants. In this case, the new tribunal could indeed be seen to have been relieving both Parliament and Council.

All of this draws attention to the paucity of our knowledge about the reason for the introduction of these "sessions". Why was there pressure on the central administration of justice which could not be discharged through Parliament's routine sittings? One explanation is of an indirect nature. James held annual parliaments in the first four years of his reign, and a principal motive was to raise taxation because of the £40,000 ransom payment he owed in terms of the 1423 treaty for his release from captivity in England.[18] Of the lesser sum paid in the end, almost all was raised from the burghs.[19] In the light of this, Professor Duncan suggested that the Session was a response to pressure from the burghs,

[16] E.W.M. Balfour-Melville, *James I, King of Scots 1406–1437* (London, 1936), pp. 132, 253.

[17] W.C. Dickinson, *Scotland from the Earliest Times to 1603* (Edinburgh, 1961), p. 213.

[18] Nicholson, *Scotland, the Later Middle Ages*, p. 259.

[19] Brown, *James I*, pp. 121–122.

who may have had an interest in more regular access to justice than the ordinary King's Council could provide.[20] Amongst royal officials, the burghs had a particular connection with the chamberlain, through the annual chamberlain ayres for which he was responsible.[21] Dr Alan MacDonald has noted that "the chamberlain's job was to collect all the king's revenues, which theoretically involved an annual ayre, a tour of the royal estates and the king's burghs", but "in the fifteenth century, his jurisdiction became confined to the burghs".[22]

Duncan was prompted in his analysis by Dr Irene O'Brien's study of the different manuscript sources underlying the legislative tradition. Dr O'Brien demonstrated that the original 1426 act stated that the *chamberlain* would preside over the Session, and that it was a subsequent revision of the act which saw him replaced by the chancellor.[23] However, Dr Alan Borthwick has effectively refuted any argument relying on the role of the chamberlain in 1426 by suggesting that the chamberlain was most likely to have been named rather than the chancellor simply because there was no chancellor in Scotland in 1426.[24] The office was vacant for almost two years between the death of Bishop Lauder in June 1425 and the appointment of Bishop Cameron by May 1427.[25] Moreover, Duncan himself has suggested that only five years or so were to pass before the chamberlain *was* replaced by the chancellor in a revision of the act.[26] Duncan's overall hypothesis about the connection with the burghs may still be correct, but there is no firm evidence to support it. Also, if the Sessions were introduced especially so that the burghs be "servit of the law", it should be noted that the act itself makes no reference to this. Whilst Professor Duncan speculated that "by 1426 the towns were deeply involved in raising money for the King, a process which may have given rise to complaints over assessment and levying taxes there, complaints which the King would be under some obligation to remedy", there is no evidence to demonstrate that this was the basis for establishing the Session. It therefore remains difficult

[20] Duncan, *James I*, p. 4.

[21] Borthwick, "The King, Council and Councillors in Scotland", p. 244.

[22] A.R. MacDonald, *The Burghs and Parliament in Scotland, c. 1550–1651* (Aldershot, 2007), p. 7.

[23] I.E. O'Brien, "The Scottish Parliament in the Fifteenth and Sixteenth Centuries" (University of Glasgow, unpublished Ph.D. thesis, 1980), p. 26.

[24] Borthwick, "The King, Council and Councillors in Scotland", pp. 245–246.

[25] Balfour-Melville, *James I*, pp. 138–140.

[26] Duncan, *James I*, p. 4.

to see the introduction of the the Session as primarily a response to pressure from the burghs, if indeed they were applying any pressure in the first place.

Regardless of who might have seen some advantage in its creation, the nature of the Session was that it was a flexible body, supplementary to Council and Parliament, which could be sent out beyond their geographical range and meet at times unconnected with their sittings. The resort to legislation in 1426 implies that the King wished the jurisdiction of Council to be accessible and actively deployed in determining complaints, or at least that he agreed with those who may have urged that this be so. The act certainly envisaged fairly regular terms being kept by the Session. Whatever the extent to which Council actively continued to determine complaints concurrently with the Session, it seems likely that the business of the Session must have relieved pressure on Council as well as Parliament. The fact that arrangements seem to have been revised in 1431, when sittings were rescheduled to three terms a year instead of four quarters, provides some evidence that the experiment was a valuable one which had served whatever purpose underlay the original 1426 act.[27]

The act of 1439

The next extant piece of evidence about the Session is an act of 1439 ordaining *two* Sessions to be held yearly, upon which the Lord Lieutenant and the King's "chosyn consal" would sit. This was a period of royal minority since the murder of James I in February 1437 had placed James II on the throne aged only six years old.[28] The legislation came exactly two years after the coronation of James II. It stated that:

> Item it was sene spedfull and deliverit that thar suld be twa Cessiounis yerly in the quhilk the lorde lieutenent ande the kyngis chosyn consal [sall sit], the frist begynnande one the morn eftir the Exaltatioune of the Haly Corse next to cum ande the tothir to begyn a poun the frist Monunday of Lentiryn nixt thareftir folowande, etc.[29]

[27] For the terms of the original act, see now *RPS* or Duncan, *James I*, p. 4; *APS* prints only the revised version.

[28] Christine McGladdery, *James II* (Edinburgh, 1990), p. 5.

[29] The version of the statute quoted in full is from *RPS*, A1439/3/2. The superseded Record Edition is *APS* ii, p. 32, c. 1.

The 1439 legislation would seem to confirm the usefulness of the Session thirteen years on from the initial experiment. Hannay noted that the act showed the institution to have become sufficiently familiar to have acquired its technical name of a "session".[30] It is not known whether Sessions had been in abeyance since the abrupt end of James I's reign, or since earlier in the 1430s. It seems improbable that they had simply continued to function into the new reign, since otherwise there would have been no need for new legislation. It was in fact one of only a very few enactments in the first two years of the reign and therefore assumes some prominence. The act was one of a Council General, which was a less formal gathering of the three estates than Parliament. However, except for a few matters within the special competence of Parliament which related to its judicial role (including treason), such councils were until the sixteenth century a simple alternative to meetings of Parliament.[31]

The act of 1450[32]

A further statute of James II requires mention since, as Hannay remarked, it shows that "the enactment of James I was renewed", though it was in fact one of a number of statutes of James I which were reissued in this year.[33] Over ten years had passed since the previous act on Sessions. This was only the third parliament of James II, and the first with a heavy legislative programme—enacting eighteen statutes in all. Moreover, this was effectively the very year of the "entry into politics" of the nineteen year-old king, though he was still faced with the great influence of William, eighth earl of Douglas, who had been appointed Lieutenant General in 1444.[34] Just as it is difficult to speculate about the fate of the Sessions between 1426 and 1439, so too are we faced with a virtual absence of evidence between 1439 and 1450. However, between then and the occasion of the next legislation on the Session in 1456 came political developments with wider

[30] R.K. Hannay, *The College of Justice* (Edinburgh, 1933), p. 7, reprinted in *The College of Justice: Essays by R.K. Hannay*, ed. H.L. MacQueen, Stair Society Supplementary Series 1 (Edinburgh, 1990).

[31] O'Brien, "The Scottish Parliament", pp. 158, 149.

[32] *APS* ii, p. 34, c. 5.

[33] Hannay, "Antecedents", p. 91; Duncan's view was that it "is no more than one among several articles derived from statutes of James I considered for re-enactment by the council": Duncan, "The Central Courts before 1532", p. 331.

[34] Lynch, *Scotland*, p. 148.

implications. In 1452, the eighth earl of Douglas was murdered by James II, and then in 1455 the ninth earl had his estates forfeited, together with the estates of his deceased brothers, the earl of Moray and the earl of Ormond.[35] It seems possible that the effects of the vast forfeitures might have led to an increased demand for the effective resolution of disputes, stimulating the subsequent legislation of 1456 and 1458.[36] It remains unclear, however, to what extent the Session was indeed revived, and if so whether it would have been revived to serve a particular purpose, or would have been functioning continuously all along.

The act of 1456[37]

In 1456 a further statute was passed. Professor Duncan characterised this act of a Council General as engendering a "new scheme" and an "experiment", finding the wealth of detail provided by the subsequent parliamentary statute of 1458 as representing a retrospective confirmation of its success. Duncan also saw the scheme as "much fuller" than its predecessors.[38] Although it did not make mention of the word "session" as such, from its terms it must be taken to be regulating the Session anew, though Neilson and Paton did not include it in their series of excerpts from statutes related to the Session.[39] It ordained named lords to begin and sit to minister justice and decide complaints "efter the tenor of the actis". The act of 1456 is notable as being the first piece of surviving evidence which gives any indication of who sat on the Session, or at least who was intended to. It has been taken to imply that those listed to sit had been chosen by the estates.[40] If this were true it would offer some contrast with the earlier Sessions which appeared to be chosen by the King,[41] or in effect by the lord lieutenant when in 1439 it was ordained that "the kingis chosyn consal sall sit".[42] The 1456 act as printed in *APS* gives no indication of who was responsible for choosing the members of this Session. It simply stated

---

35 Alexander Grant, *Independence and Nationhood* (London, 1984), pp. 191–195.

36 T.M. Chalmers, "The King's Council, Patronage and the Governance of Scotland 1460–1513" (University of Aberdeen, unpublished Ph.D. thesis, 1982), p. 152.

37 *APS* ii, p. 46, c. 8.

38 Duncan, "The Central Courts before 1532", p. 331.

39 *Acts of the Lords of Council 1496–1501*, ed. G. Neilson and H.M. Paton (Edinburgh, 1918), pp. x–xiv [hereafter referred to as *ADC* ii].

40 Borthwick, "King, Council, and Councillors", p. 247.

41 Hannay, "Antecedents", p. 90.

42 *APS* ii, p. 32, c. 1.

who had been chosen. However, the modern *RPS* edition has been emended after reconsideration of the manuscript sources to suggest that the estates did in fact choose the judges.[43]

There is some ambiguity about the timing of these Sessions and therefore how extensive their role was. Three groups of "auditouris" are named to sit and decide complaints, for what are simply described as the first, second and third months, the first presumably beginning on the 8 November 1456 (this date is given in the act as when the named lords in general should begin). However, it is not clear whether the Session is then to sit more or less continuously, changing personnel after each month, or whether after three consecutive months the mandate of this set of Sessions would be exhausted. Since in the past there had been either two, three or four defined "terms" a year, this could suggest that the 1456 act was a special measure designed to last only for three months. If it were to have lasted longer, then it might have been expected to lay down terms more clearly, just as they had been in previous legislation. If it was only envisaged as lasting for three months, then that would imply that the statute represented action by the Council General to meet a special need in providing for the King's justice to be available to his subjects. The fact that all causes which could not "at this tyme" be dealt with by the parliamentary Auditors of Complaints were to be continued to the opening Session may also imply that the Sessions were being deployed as a special device for a three month period to transact business which would otherwise have had to await a parliament. The Council General sat on 19 October, and the Sessions were envisaged as commencing three weeks later.

Following Duncan's analysis, there does seem to be a sense of new departure about the act, albeit one which was effected through a familiar enough institution. This might be inferred from the absence of any reference to previous Sessions from before 1456, an acknowledgement in the record that "the clergy thinkes the artikill is weill maide", and the injunction that they should commence "furthwithe". However, continuity may still be inferred from the statement in the act that justice is to be administered by the Lords after the tenor of the "actes" in the plural, possibly referring back to previous ordinances on the Session. Despite

[43] The annotations in *RPS*, 1456/9 should be consulted in this regard, where the different MS readings are analysed. Before the list of members is narrated, the legislation as edited in *RPS* states that "thir ar the persounis chosyne be the clergy, etc., etc." whereas *APS* omitted "be the clergy, etc., etc."

these ambiguities about the exact purpose and status of this Session, Duncan regarded a decision recorded in Perth a few months later (on 7 February 1456) as proof that this body did sit.[44] The forum was "*in cessione publica*"[45] and Duncan argued that it was not a decision of the parliamentary Auditors of Causes and Complaints because the body was referred to as "*auditores querelarum et ad decisionem causarum specialiter electis*".[46] Although this decreet is printed in *APS* as given *in parliamento*, Hannay showed it to have been most unlikely that the sitting was that of a parliamentary committee.[47] The decreet occured within three months of the first scheduling of the 1456 Sessions. Though it seems that the names of the Auditors do not correspond to any of the three lists in the act, nevertheless individuals from each group do feature. Therefore, despite not conforming to the statutory scheme precisely, it would seem to be a sitting of a Session, demonstrating that the 1456 scheme did operate.

The acts of 1458[48]

A further five acts came just over a year later, beginning:

> as to the artikill of the Sessione, it is seyne speidfull to the king ande the thre estatis that it be contynuit to the nixt parliament in maner as efter followys...

This seems to imply that the Session had functioned during the course of the previous year, as had been intended by the 1456 act, and that it would continue to do so for the foreseeable future until the holding of another parliament. Whereas the 1456 Session was merely to function "efter the tenor of the actes", the 1458 Sessions were regulated afresh in the most detailed manner yet, filling five chapters in the parliamentary register. The statement about continuation of the Session "to the nixt parliament" clearly implies that the Session was to carry on functioning in the interim, and that it was being seen as a substitute for the parliamentary Auditors. If so, this simply emphasises the institutional continuity dating back to 1426. The fifth statute also suggests this, stating that "the saide thre sessiounis endit, our sovirane

---

[44] Duncan, "The Central Courts before 1532", p. 331.
[45] *APS* ii, p. 77.
[46] Duncan, "The Central Courts before 1532", p. 332.
[47] Hannay, "Antecedents", p. 92.
[48] *APS* ii, pp. 47–48, c. 1–5; *RPS*, 1458/3/2–6.

lorde and his daily consale sall ordane and name wthir lordis to syt at tymis and placis sene speidfull [i.e. advantageous or expedient] to him and his saide consale on to the tyme of the nixt parliament with sik power as thai hade of befor".[49] The fourth statute refers to a lord being able to expect not to sit again for seven years, suggesting that there was a structure envisaged which could be maintained even without a parliament meeting during the years ahead. This might even imply that the 1458 Sessions were seen as a permanent feature to be continued beyond the next meeting of Parliament.

What is clear is that this Session no longer exercised only the residual jurisdiction of the King's Council. It was given a new and apparently far wider statutory jurisdiction under the act. How much wider is of course difficult to determine, since we have so little knowledge of the precise jurisdiction of the earlier Sessions which had operated since 1426. The way that the jurisdiction of the Session was to fit in with other existing jurisdictions was also articulated in new depth. A further difference in 1458 was that three terms were specified, lasting forty days each, in Edinburgh, Perth and Aberdeen. The 1426 Sessions had been to sit where the King commanded—wherever that may have been—whilst the 1456 ones were to have sat "quhar the auditoures thinkes maist spedfull". In 1458 "lordis of the Sessione" were named to sit in each specified location, the selection of individual lords perhaps reflecting the relation of their different geographical provenances to these locations. All of these details were set out systematically in the first of the five related statutes.

The first and second statutes turned also to jurisdiction and elaborated the causes that "the lordis of the sessione sall haif full powere to knawe and decide".[50] This might imply that it would not have been enough simply to transfer the jurisdiction of Council again, but that in order to hear the types of action concerned, specific parliamentary authority had to be conferred. It is hard to tell why. Perhaps the sense of such a need raises questions about whether even the Council could have heard the full range of such cases that were now to come before the 1458 Sessions. Previously the jurisdiction of Council had been all that had been conferred upon the Session, and yet this was presumably not sufficient to empower the 1458 Sessions to fulfil their purpose. There

[49] *RPS*, 1458/3/6.
[50] *RPS*, 1458/3/3.

seems to have been a perceived need to declare in precise terms what the jurisdiction of the Session was to be, perhaps simply to establish certainty, given that for Session and Council alike to exercise such a very wide jurisdiction would have been seen as a novelty. Of course, it is still possible that the apparent widening of jurisdiction in 1458 is to some extent illusory and merely reflects a more precise approach to the drafting of the statute. Moreover, the law itself and its remedies were themselves developing during the course of the fifteenth century. In particular the action of "spuilzie" (wrongful dispossession) was a new development, arising outside the structures of the earlier common law and its notions of procedure and jurisdiction. Approaches to framing jurisdiction for a tribunal such as the Session may therefore have simply changed in a very pragmatic way to accommodate this new complexity.

The matters in question in 1458 included possessory actions relating to spuilzie which had occured since 1449. Spuilzie from before 1449 and as far back as the coronation of James II in 1437 could be brought before the Lords during the forthcoming year, after which time it would have to be dealt with by the ordinary judges in the localities. If the spuilzie involved possession of land then there was a special procedure laid down for the sheriff to retour to the Lords a finding as to the "last lauchfull possessoure", whose rights of possession would be protected. Also mentioned as within its jurisdiction were all obligations, contracts and debts, and generally other civil actions, with precisely drafted provisions excepting issues of fee and heritage (i.e. ownership through heritable title to landed property). The jurisdiction of the Session in 1458 therefore included almost everything except the category of fee and heritage, though the method used to frame its jurisdiction was to list the general classes of action, rather than employing some general concept of full jurisdiction, with exceptions listed thereafter. This may have been simply a matter of transparency and certainty, given the complex network of jurisdiction which existed in this period. No one court in fifteenth-century Scotland exercised a wholly unrestricted jurisdiction, and even Parliament would not customarily decide issues of fee and heritage. Such cases continued throughout the fifteenth century to require instead a pleadable brieve served in the locality through local judicial process.

The nature of the jurisdiction conferred on the 1458 Sessions is therefore in many ways remarkable, especially if it is accurate to contrast it with what we can reasonably take as likely to have been the more restricted, conciliar jurisdiction of the earlier Sessions. Part of this relates to the manner in which the jurisdiction was systematically expressed for the first time, and part to the special provisions included in relation to spuilzie and the jurisdiction of other courts. This is the case even if, as was suggested earlier, in practice the jurisdiction of parliamentary Auditors in Causes and Complaints and the King's Council may have been virtually co-extensive in the fifteenth century. It is therefore not possible to wholly discount Professor Duncan's view that "it would be totally false to view this statute of 1458 as committing to the sessions a new jurisdiction, a jurisdiction unshared by the council because the council was not a statutory body".[51] Nevertheless, from 1458 even the class of complaints brought before Parliament might have been equalled or exceeded by that which the Session could now hear. In fact, the legislation explicitly stated that complainers faced a free choice whether to proceed before the judge ordinary (in the locality) or before the Session (in Edinburgh, Perth or Aberdeen). This in itself is a startling innovation, and suggests a conscious policy that this tribunal of the estates should have parity with the ordinary judges in the administration of justice. It also implies a recognition that litigants desired more flexible access to justice as dispensed by the central judicial bodies. Detailed procedures were laid down for the sheriffs to proclaim the commencement of the Session in their sheriffdoms three months in advance, and for summonses to be obtained by complainers from the King's chapel if they wished to raise an action. This represented a conscious expansion of the common law machinery of justice. Professor MacQueen recognised in the act "a liberalisation of the jurisdiction of the central bodies, a shift away from the old position whereby they stood outside the ordinary processes of the common law...After 1458, as the act itself indicated, the Session was an alternative to the judge ordinary rather than a substitute in the event of his default, except in the field of 'fee and heritage'."[52]

The 1461 Parliament

There is no official parliamentary record surviving, but according to the Auchinleck chronicler the first parliament of James III's reign was in February 1461, at which those present "ordanit Sessionis to sit first at

[51] Duncan, "The Central Courts before 1532", p. 333.
[52] MacQueen, "Pleadable Brieves and Jurisdiction in Heritage", p. 270.

aberdene syne at perth syne in Edinburgh".[53] These were presumably to follow the scheme devised in 1458, and this certainly suggests that the Session functioned in these years.

The statutes of 1464 and 1468

Only two further fifteenth-century statutes appear to relate to "auditorial" Sessions, one in 1464, one in 1468. The Session ordained in 1468 was "the last on record which followed the model initiated by James I".[54] Professor Hannay observed that "it cannot be merely accidental that the last 'session' of the old model was ordained for November 1468, and that there was extant in the seventeenth century a volume of decreets which seems to have been the first of the *Acta Dominorum Concilii*, beginning in May 1469".[55] In relation to the earlier statute of 1464, Professor Duncan distinguished "an elaborate statute, apparently from early 1465" from an occasion in 1464 "when an assembly ordered the holding of three Sessions yearly, at Edinburgh, Perth and Aberdeen".[56] There were two assemblies in 1464 but only one statute to which these allusions can refer.[57] The assembly referred to by Duncan—not a parliament but a "congregation of lords spiritual and temporal" with no burgh commissioners mentioned—is recorded as having met on 11 October 1464.[58] Whilst it is stated as having been summoned "for the peace and tranquillity of the realm and doing justice", the record tells only of an act of resumption, nothing of Sessions.[59] Professor Nicholson believed that the parliament which produced the statute on the Session and which was ascribed to early 1465 by Duncan came some months *before* the October 1464 assembly.[60] The statute ordained Sessions for February, April and June "next tocum". Dr Tanner has now dated this parliament to January 1464, on the basis of internal evidence in the

---

53 *The Asloan Manuscript*, ed. W.A. Craigie, Scottish Text Society (Edinburgh, 1923–25), pp. 231–232. See now *RPS* for other unofficial sources confirming the sitting of a parliament.

54 Hannay, "Antecedents", p. 94. There are two related statutes: *APS* ii, p. 92, c. 2, 4.

55 Hannay, "Antecedents", p. 95.

56 Duncan, "The Central Courts before 1532", p. 331.

57 *APS* xii, p. 31.

58 *APS* ii, p. 84; R. Tanner, *The Late Medieval Scottish Parliament: Politics and the Three Estates, 1424–1488* (East Linton, 2001), p. 180.

59 Nicholson, *Scotland: The Later Middle Ages*, pp. 407–408.

60 Nicholson, *Scotland: The Later Middle Ages*, p. 408. Duncan's ascription was presumably on the basis of an editorial date of 1464/65 in *APS* xii, p. 31.

manuscript record.[61] All that matters for this discussion is that between the parliaments of 1461 and 1468 there is continuity demonstrated by the statute we now know to be from January 1464.

By 1464, over six years had passed since the previous detailed legislation on the Session, and King James III had succeeded to the throne in August 1460 as an eight-year-old minor. Mary of Gueldres, the guardian of the young king, had died in December 1463, and for the next eighteen months James Kennedy, bishop of St Andrews, was the "predominant figure in the royal government", whilst Archibald Whitelaw had begun in 1462 what was to be a thirty-year period of office as royal secretary.[62] It was at this stage in the reign, in early 1464, that the Sessions were re-appointed. Professor Nicholson explained this as a conscious effort by Bishop Kennedy to "wholeheartedly promote justice".[63] Precise dates were specified and the same locations as before (Edinburgh, Perth and Aberdeen). There was a concise statement of jurisdiction which encompassed that made in more detail in the 1458 legislation. The 1464 act gives the impression of having been drafted with its 1458 predecessor in mind and seems to do no more than continue the scheme devised then. An example is the statement in the conclusion of the principal chapter that the Lords shall have jurisdiction to sit "apone all actionis etc", without bothering to articulate the detailed rules, even the one excluding fee and heritage. The jurisdiction over spuilzie was more restricted, however, being now limited to "all spulzeis mayde sene the tyme of the cessing of the last Sessionis".

In 1468, Sessions of this type were again ordered to sit. The act was less compressed in form, but amounted to little that was new except for the naming of individual lords to sit. This was also the last legislative reference to "sessions" until the 1490s (by which time the expression applied to the conciliar model of Session, not the older auditorial one). The work which auditorial Sessions had performed up until the 1460s was increasingly to be dealt with by the King's Council instead. Dr Borthwick has remarked that, in contrast to the operation of Council during the minority of James II, "the general impression remains that the council was readily approachable for the obtaining of justice in the early 1460s, and that it was so used".[64] It is surely no coincidence

[61] Tanner, *The Late Medieval Scottish Parliament*, p. 179, note 60.
[62] Lynch, *Scotland*, p. 156.
[63] Nicholson, *Scotland: The Later Middle Ages*, pp. 407–408.
[64] Borthwick, "King, Council and Councillors", p. 287.

that, with the personal rule of James III underway from 1469, no more Sessions were ordained by Parliament. The administration of James III was notably static rather than peripatetic, with his Council more or less permanently based with him in Edinburgh.[65] Regular Sessions were likely to have become redundant if Council was a permanent fixture in one place, since such immobility constituted a form of regularity from the point of view of access. Even during the 1460s council meetings "often went on for periods of more than three months at a time", taken by Dr Macdougall to be "an indication of considerable pressure of business".[66] Indeed, Dr Borthwick has argued that "the decline of the Session was the result of greater activity by the council in judicial work in the 1460s".[67] The abandonment of the auditorial model of Session did not therefore reflect an abandonment of the underlying policy for a more accessible central administration of justice, but rather the abandonment of an expedient for judicial business which had become "unnecessary" in view of Council's judicial role and its accessibility.[68]

Conclusions on the auditorial Session, 1426–1468

It remains an impossible task to estimate the level of activity of the Sessions with certainty during the forty years or so of their existence in this form. The nature of the evidence, being almost exclusively in the form of isolated statutes, gives no clear impression of how the Session functioned in the long intervals between the parliaments and councils which produced these statutes. However, it seems reasonable to assume that we do at least possess most of the legislative references that were made to Sessions. Taken together, they suggest great continuity in retention of a particular conception of auditorial Sessions, as well as their increasing jurisdictional importance by the 1450s. They had not been set up *simply* to relieve other judicial bodies, such as Council, but to relieve them on an enhanced basis—by way of regular sittings in a certain place or places. The King's Council itinerated the country with the King, and until the personal rule of James III that involved great mobility. This must have impeded access to the Council, since its location and progress would be relatively uncertain. There would also

---

[65] See N.A.T. Macdougall, *James III: A Political Study* (Edinburgh, 1982), p. 120.
[66] Macdougall, *James III*, p. 304.
[67] Borthwick, "King, Council and Councillors", p. 286.
[68] Borthwick, "King, Council and Councillors", p. 287.

have been a disadvantage for the Council, in that wherever it did go there would be a constant stream of complainers ready to address to it their grievances, notwithstanding the limitations on its jurisdiction.[69] The Sessions would have provided litigants with a ready forum which gathered in a more predictable and regular way, and thereby must have relieved Council of at least some of its judicial work. Dr Borthwick has suggested that the 1456 and 1458 statutes were premised upon the idea of the Session as a regular and frequent event by comparison with the irregularity of Council's sittings. In a sense this was the policy behind the auditorial Sessions in general, and represents their real institutional innovation.[70]

In terms of the judges on the auditorial Sessions, it is not clear whether the authority or power to choose the lords who would sit on the Session would have been considered of special note. The only explicit references in the legislation are to either the King or the King and his Council having such a power,[71] whilst statutes which name members of the estates to sit never generally declare or otherwise indicate how the members were selected, leaving open the possibility that it was the King who had actually chosen the named lords beforehand. It seems inconceivable that the estates could have in effect forced councillors upon the King as Lords of Session. It could also be inferred from the requirement that the Sessions be drawn from members of the three estates that it was the estates themselves who chose the lords out of their own number, although this is not true of the 1426 statute. The role of the King and Council in filling gaps[72] or ordaining new Sessions[73] must have been the inevitable solution to manning the Session when the estates were not actually meeting in Parliament or General Council. For these reasons, it may be that the naming of members of the three estates in the legislation was a formality which does not reveal who was responsible for the selection, and that behind the formality it was the King who made the choice, as laid down in the original 1426 act. This would be consistent with his declared responsibility for filling

---

69 H.L. MacQueen, *Common Law and Feudal Society in Medieval Scotland* (Edinburgh, 1993), p. 220; MacQueen, "Pleadable Brieves and Jurisdiction in Heritage", pp. 254, 258.

70 Borthwick, "King, Council and Councillors", p. 287.

71 *APS* ii, p. 11, c. 19; p. 32, c. 1; p. 48, c. 5; p. 92, c. 7.

72 *APS* ii, p. 92, c. 7.

73 *APS* ii, p. 48, c. 5.

gaps and appointing members of subsequent Sessions, as previously mentioned. A requirement that the members had to be from the three estates and not simply of the Council, must have reflected the need for a wider pool of judges than provided by those regular in attendance at Council, especially since it would have been such regular members of Council who most needed relief from the pressure of judicial business. Another reason might have been that the Sessions could thereby have members from the representatives of all three estates, and, unlike Council, include a burgess element in a more representative way.

A final and important feature of the auditorial Sessions which would have made them attractive to litigants in addition to their regularity and frequency was the fact that no appeal was possible, thus giving final certainty in the resolution of any dispute upon which they decided. The 1426 act laid down that the Lords would "finally determyn" all causes which the King's Council could have heard. This is re-iterated in the 1458 legislation, which stated that "all uthir causis pertenande to the saidis lordis knawlege salbe wtirly decidyt and detirmyt be thame but [i.e. without] ony remeide of appellacione to the king or to the parliament".[74] There is no further mention of this condition, but the 1468 statute uses the phrase, "eftir the forme of the sessionis last haldin ande with siklik power", presumably carrying over the same restriction concerning appeal.

The auditorial Session was a way of placing central justice—whether of the sort previously available only from the parliamentary Auditors of Causes and Complaints or from the King's Council—on a more regular footing. Over the ten years following 1458, its jurisdiction was also expanded beyond the causes which it seems Council would normally have entertained, so as to include a wide range of civil actions, excluding always fee and heritage. Professor MacQueen noted that the reference to the exclusion of fee and heritage in the 1458 act is the first example of this formulation being used to define the limits of conciliar jurisdiction.[75] The theme of jurisdiction was indeed to be one of the most significant in the subsequent seventy-five years of ongoing development, and will be treated later in this book in greater depth, especially in relation to fee and heritage and the College of Justice in 1532.

---

[74] *RPS*, 1458/3/4; *APS* ii, pp. 47–48, c. 3.

[75] MacQueen, *Common Law and Feudal Society*, p. 235.

The judicial Council, 1468–1488

It is not possible to ascertain conclusively whether the auditorial Sessions continued beyond 1468. It seems that they fell into desuetude relatively quickly, though possibly continuing as far as 1472.[76] From this period onwards, it was Council which would be the main central forum for judicial determination of complaints apart from Parliament.[77] The Council can be seen functioning from the late 1460s as a general judicial tribunal, though it would be some twenty years before this aspect of its functions led to its sittings being referred to as "sessions". In addition to legislative evidence for these developments, the acts of the parliamentary Auditors of Causes and Complaints themselves become extant from 1466, whilst those of the Lords of Council are extant from 1478.

Procedural continuations and transfer of causes in 1466, 1467, and 1471

Professor Hannay noted references to the role of Council having widened by the late 1460s. Actions begun initially before the Auditors in Parliament were being carried over—"continued"—to the Council. For example, in 1466 a continuation was made of an action before the parliamentary Auditors to the King and his Council "quharc it happynnis his hienes to be". It was narrated that, with the consent of the parties, the Lords of Council "sall hafe the full power of parliament and of all uthir courtis".[78] Following Hannay, it might be inferred from this that "continuation from parliament to council was not yet regarded as a matter of course".[79] However, whether or not a "matter of course", it must be noted that even at this stage an express mandate was not always given to Council in such cases. Out of fifteen hearings by the Auditors on 17 October 1467, three were continued to the Lords of Council, without comment as to consent of the parties, two "to be decidit and endit" thereby.[80] What Hannay had in mind was a contrast with the later

[76] Chalmers, "The King's Council", p. 161.
[77] Chalmers, "The King's Council", pp. viii, 161.
[78] *The Acts of the Lords Auditors of Causes and Complaints*, ed. T. Thomson (Edinburgh, 1839), p. 6 [hereafter *ADA*]; Hannay, "Antecedents", p. 96; R.K. Hannay, "Introduction" to *Acts of the Lords of Council in Public Affairs*, ed. R.K. Hannay (Edinburgh, 1932), p. xxvii [hereafter *ADCP*, i.e. *Acta Dominorum Concilii (Public)*].
[79] Hannay, "Antecedents", p. 96.
[80] *ADA*, pp. 7–8.

situation whereby such continuation was to become so "familiar" that "the clerk would enter the date for the next hearing without specifying the court".[81] Continuations were often necessary when further action was needed by the parties or when time had run short in the immediate proceedings. Although Parliament sometimes ordained the Auditors to sit for longer terms, generally they were empowered by their commission to hear and decide causes for only as long as Parliament was itself in Session.[82] Besides which, once Parliament was coming to a close, it would be natural for members of the estates who had been elected as Lords Auditors to wish to depart. Hannay argued that the reciprocity between Auditors and Council from 1470 onwards meant that technical distinctions which existed up to that point thereafter lost "definiteness".[83] This was demonstrated by the way in which continuations from Parliament to Council were becoming a matter of course. Such technical distinctions had concerned the implications of specifying Parliament or Council in the summons, and the perceived need to formally confer the power of Parliament onto the Lords of Council, when continuing particular cases from Parliament to be heard by Council.

Evidence of such practices can be gleaned as early as the parliament of October 1467. It was ordained that "al summondis and causis that is left undecidit in this parliament salbe decidit before the lordis of counsaile the summondis standand as thai now do".[84] That this could be done without further comment implies that Council was considered to be exercising a jurisdiction equivalent to that of the Auditors in Parliament. Professor Duncan has stated precisely this in arguing that:

> in time of parliament, the council was in parliament, and its jurisdiction exercised by parliament through auditors. Sessions such as those of 1456–68 exercised conciliar jurisdiction by virtue of statute. It was always the council's jurisdiction which was transferred to other bodies and not *vice versa*.[85]

Of course, even this does not mean that Council and Parliament possessed identical jurisdiction—King and Council outwith Parliament seem

---

[81] Hannay, "Antecedents", p. 97.
[82] Chalmers, "The King's Council", p. 160.
[83] R.K. Hannay, "Early Records of Council and Session, 1466–1659" in *An Introductory Survey of the Sources and Literature of Scots Law*, Stair Society 1 (Edinburgh, 1936), pp. 16–24 at p. 20.
[84] *APS* ii, p. 88.
[85] Duncan, "The Central Courts before 1532", p. 333.

always to have had a more limited jurisdiction than the full parliament sitting as a fenced court. Similarly, however, Professor MacQueen has remarked in relation to the earlier fifteenth-century Council that:

> it would be unwise to suppose that the jurisdiction of the king and council was absolutely restricted to the complaints of the weak, and the church and to the control of royal officers. The council was the king's and, within the limits of the common law, he could use it as he wished.[86]

The implication seems to be that the Council did not need to be formally granted any particular jurisdiction, subject to the procedures of the common law, but could and did choose to widen the classes of action it was prepared to adjudicate upon by the 1460s so that in practice it was exercising an equivalent jurisdiction to the parliamentary Auditors. The 1467 ordinance is an example of a formal recognition of this fact on a particular occasion. It could be seen as serving a two-fold purpose. First, it directed those who had raised actions in Parliament, but which had yet to be heard, to proceed instead before Council. Secondly, it avoided the need to raise new summonses in the process of transferring the action.

Having considered this evidence of continuation from Parliament to Council in civil causes in 1466 and 1467, further evidence appears in 1471. The Auditors in Parliament in May 1471 continued all "undecidit actions" to the next Parliament (in August of that year) but allowed any party wishing to do so to take out in the meantime a new summons "til a schortar day" before Council and "dissolve" their action before the Auditors.[87] This contrasts with the earlier arrangements in 1467, when all undecided causes were simply continued to be decided by the Lords of Council.[88] After the Parliament of 1467 the next sitting of Auditors was not to come until two years later in November 1469. As we have seen, however, in 1464 and again in 1468 the auditorial Session also continued to function. This makes it hard to see the 1471 provision as a significant concession of some sort, as Hannay did. He noted that "the committee of auditors invariably continued cases to a day of parliament, if there was a commission to the lords 'havand power', and did not encourage application to the council".[89] But by

[86] MacQueen, "Pleadable Brieves and Jurisdiction in Heritage", p. 258.
[87] *ADA*, p. 14.
[88] *APS* ii, p. 88.
[89] Hannay, "Antecedents", p. 96.

1471, outwith time of parliament, Council was almost certainly the only operational central judicial body, since the statutory Session is likely to have fallen into desuetude by this point. The 1471 ordinance seems merely to recognise the central role in ordinary litigation which Council must have by this time possessed.

Dr. Chalmers has summarised the situation with the observation that:

> if the auditors had not managed to deal with all the summonses before them by the expiry of their jurisdiction, as they probably rarely or never did, the litigants had either to wait until the next parliament, or else approach chancery for a fresh summons before the lords of council, who generally commenced their diet as the lords auditors finished theirs. In practice, however, specific provision might be made for automatic conversion of unheard summonses before the auditors, into summonses before the lords of council.[90]

Of course, this inter-relation of the sittings of parliamentary Auditors and Lords of Council only becomes clear in detail from 1478 when the council register becomes extant. However, the general picture by the early 1470s is that with Council and Parliament both operating from Edinburgh (only one parliament of James III met outside Edinburgh—in Stirling in 1468),[91] Council was becoming a forum which could act as a simple alternative to Parliament in civil causes, whilst the old-style auditorial Sessions had completely ceased to function.

Judicial business in Council, 1470–1485

The situation just described represents an innovation not in terms of function or jurisdiction so much as in breadth of access. The Council, it may be inferred, was now prepared to hear a wide class of actions, tantamount to those traditionally heard by the Auditors of Causes and Complaints in Parliament. This development must have begun in the 1460s and seems to have been regular practice by the 1470s. However, so far there was no *institutional* innovation as such. The parliamentary Auditors and the Council retained distinct personnel during the reign of James III,[92] although a few men were common to both.[93] It is apparent,

[90] Chalmers, "The King's Council", p. 162.
[91] Macdougall, *James III*, p. 303.
[92] Chalmers, "The King's Council", p. 164.
[93] Chalmers, "The King's Council", p. 173.

however, that towards the end of a diet of the parliamentary Auditors their numbers would often fall, only for them to be "re-inforced" on an *ad hoc* basis by Lords of Council. By the late 1470s, we can see judicial sittings of the Lords of Council following on chronologically from those of the Lords Auditors. Moreover, Dr Chalmers has argued that whilst the judicial sittings of Council under James III were mainly composed of familiars of the King, there was nevertheless "sufficient differentiation of personnel to suggest that that the sederunts show a 'specialist committee' of the council rather than general sittings" and "by 1485, a diet of council was referred to as a 'session'."[94]

However, regular terms were not yet kept by Council in its judicial capacity. There was only regularity in so far as Council always now sat in Edinburgh, and litigants could expect it to hear civil causes after Parliament rose.[95] The practice came to be that the Lords of Council would sit as a distinct body to deal with the King's business at the same time as the Lords Auditors were sitting. Council would then simply take over unheard summonses from the Auditors.[96] Even this did not settle into a routine system. Dr Chalmers has argued in this respect that:

> [the] erratic pattern of holding parliaments in the late 1470s and 1480s, with repeated continuations and meetings in commission, precluded a more consistent policy of following a parliament with a council diet...the parliaments of James III did not provide a sufficiently firm and reliable basis for planning the diets.[97]

Nevertheless, during the personal rule of James III (until his death in 1488), Council normally exercised a general competence in civil affairs. This allowed it to despatch the judicial business which Parliament had not had time to consider, as well as presumably also attracting the business which the pre-1470 Sessions had previously transacted.

The acts of 1487 and 1488[98]

An act of the October parliament of 1487 signalled a radical departure from the way in which judicial work had come to be handled by

[94] Chalmers, "The King's Council", pp. 234, 249–250.

[95] cf. MacQueen, "Pleadable Brieves and Jurisdiction in Heritage", p. 272; Chalmers, "The King's Council", p. 231.

[96] Chalmers, "The King's Council", p. 231.

[97] Chalmers, "The King's Council", p. 232.

[98] *APS* ii, p. 177, c. 10 (1487); *APS* ii, p. 183, c. 17 (1488).

the central bodies. It was an attempt to end the role of Council as an equivalent body to the Auditors of Parliament by preventing all except certain privileged classes of litigant from raising a summons before Council *at all*. The contrast with the situation until that point is highlighted by the closing words of the statute that "al summondis that Is now Raisit or standis under continacioun dependand and undetermytt salbe decidit and endit before the lordis of consale".[99] Whether the new policy was seen as permanent is unclear, since it was stated that "this act and statut to endure quhil the next parliment", possibly implying that it was simply an expedient for the short term. Also unclear is the exact motive for this change. Was it simply to free the Council from the burden of its judicial business or rather to galvanise the ordinary courts?

The very next parliament, however, saw a dramatic reversal of this legislation, which in itself provides a clue as to the policy of the initial statute of 1487. The reversal is explicitly stated to be "Becaus the kingis hienes understandis that It wer deferring of Justice to mony partiis that couthe nocht gett law ministrat to thame before thair ordinaris". This gives a rare insight into the nature of the criticism of local justice which lay behind the development of central justice in the fifteenth century. In whatever way, the policy of the initial 1487 statute was considered to have been hindered by some unspecified inadequacy of the ordinary courts. This would suggest that it had been introduced to reduce the sphere of judicial competence of Council so as to relieve it of an unduly heavy burden of business. The 1488 statute demonstrates that by this time, however, Council had come to play an integral and essential role in the administration of justice which could no longer be fulfilled by the ordinary courts to the satisfaction of litigants. This realisation was no doubt the backdrop to the new methods of organising Council's judicial work which were to be adopted in the 1490s. In the meantime, the statute of 1488 provided that "it salbe lefull to all partiis in tyme tocum to Raise and persew summondis before oure soverane lord and his consale like as thai wer wont in tymes bigane nochtwithstanding the said statute".[100]

---

[99] *APS* ii, p. 177, c. 10.
[100] *APS* ii, p. 183, c. 17.

The conciliar Session, 1488–1504

The period after the accession of James IV in 1488 witnessed significant further institutional innovation in the conduct of judicial business by Council and Parliament. In particular, the two bodies constituted by parliamentary Auditors of Causes and Complaints and Lords of Council meeting in their judicial "sessions" seem to have become fused together. As a formality Auditors continued to be appointed in Parliament. However, they seem not to have sat as such after 1496 and it appears that no summonses to appear before them were issued after that year.[101] Dr Chalmers noted how under James III there had been a rigid division between parliamentary judges who sat as Auditors, and those Lords of Council who were council judges, with negligible overlap between them. Under James IV this changed, so that the same men who were elected as Auditors frequently also sat as judges in Council.[102] Therefore in the early years of the new reign, there was in effect a single body doing one type of work, whilst retaining technical distinctions of nomenclature and record.[103] This manner of duplication was retained until 1496, by which time there was little sense of any distinction left.[104]

The explanation of the fusion of personnel was noted by Hannay and more recently reiterated again by Dr Chalmers. This is that a group of men who had acted as judges in Parliament and sat on its auditorial committees under James III, but were not included in the King's Council, became reconciled with the new regime from 1488 onwards. Previously they had been out of favour with the King, but after the accession of James IV they were drawn into judicial work on the Council as well as the auditorial parliamentary committee, resulting in the *de facto* amalgamation of the two groups of judges.[105] It is worth noting that after 1496 there was in any event no sitting of Parliament for almost eight years. Whereas James III had held twenty-one parliaments in the twenty years of his adult rule, James IV held only three in the seventeen-year period after 1496.[106] By 1496, however, there had

---

[101] Duncan, "The Central Courts before 1532", p. 338.
[102] Chalmers, "The King's Council", p. 185.
[103] Chalmers, "The King's Council", p. 193.
[104] Chalmers, "The King's Council", p. 268.
[105] Hannay, "Antecedents", pp. 99, 101; Chalmers, "The King's Council", pp. 254–255.
[106] Lynch, *Scotland*, p. 158.

developed a single body of central judges whose work was to continue in Council through conciliar judicial Sessions, irrespective of the absence of full parliaments over the rest of the reign. In this way institutional structures can be seen to have been moulded by forces relating to politics and faction as much as administrative or governmental intent.

Already by the mid-1480s the "concerted, if irregular diets" of Council exercising its judicial competence had led to these diets being referred to as "sessions".[107] As we have seen, they were held immediately following upon sittings of the Auditors in Parliament. Between the diets of the judicial Council there would have been a general continuation of causes, except for privileged classes of litigant. The 1490s saw some disruption to Council sittings because of military operations and the itineration of King and Council, causing delay and the curtailing of diets.[108] Hannay noted examples of such disruption, commenting that:

> there were comparatively few lords available for much varied business. On 13th February 1490–1 the council had to turn to affairs of exchequer: it expected diplomatic debates in Lent: its next "session", or fixed term for civil causes, was to begin on 3rd March; the justice-ayres would have to be postponed. Parliament, called for April, had to be adjourned till May. A permanent order was scarcely attainable.[109]

In some sense, therefore, in the early 1490s it was at times a strain for Council to fulfil its role in judicial matters whilst carrying out its wider duties as the King's Council. It is no surprise therefore that this decade was to see administrative innovations in organising the despatch of this judicial business. Council was exercising in effect what had been the judicial functions of Parliament, but was now differentiating its own functions more systematically in their performance. These developments represented in Dr Chalmer's view a "modest upheaval in the council's organization" caused by the "need to adapt to the larger work-load which had formerly been shared by councillors and auditors".[110] Institutional change therefore arose in this context in a highly contingent manner from unrelated wider political developments.

---

[107] Chalmers, "The King's Council", p. 234.
[108] Chalmers, "The King's Council", p. 257.
[109] Hannay, "Antecedents", p. 102.
[110] Chalmers, "The King's Council", p. 283.

The pattern of development, 1488–1504

Professor Hannay saw the first fifteen or so years of James IV's reign as constituting the most significant period in the formation of the Court of Session. His view of the development of the Session and the foundation of the College of Justice will be discussed in greater detail in the next chapter. It is sufficient to note here that his overall interpretation can no longer be endorsed without significant qualification, even though his account of the developments in question remains indispensable. In short, he concluded that it was "probably correct to say that under James IV the Court of Session became a definite institution" and that by 1504 it "had definitely taken shape".[111] It is important to remember that Hannay expressed these points in framing the wider argument that the foundation of the College of Justice in 1532 was of much less importance in the history of the Session than commonly thought. Part of his argument was to demonstrate the greater claims which could be made for the significance of James IV's reign. Nevertheless, whilst Hannay's view of 1532 has come to seem controversial, his basic analysis of particular developments between 1488 and 1513 is highly persuasive.

We find from 1488 a plethora of ordinances governing the judicial activities of Council. The most significant consist of the following:

(i.) statute of 1490, nominating the "Secrett Consale"[112]
(ii.) election of specific Lords of Session in October 1490[113]
(iii.) statute of 1491, ordaining terms for the Session[114]
(iv.) election of specific Lords of Session in October 1495[115]
(v.) tabling ordinance of November 1495[116]
(vi.) tabling ordinance of June 1496[117]
(vii.) ordinance of June 1498 for a Session in Edinburgh[118]

[111] Hannay, *The College of Justice*, pp. 21–22.
[112] *APS* ii, p. 220, c. 11–12.
[113] *Acts of the Lords of Council in Civil Causes*, ed. T. Thomson (Edinburgh, 1839), p. 143 [hereafter *ADC* i].
[114] *APS* ii, p. 226, c. 16.
[115] *ADC* i, p. 386.
[116] *ADC* i, p. 423.
[117] *ADC* ii, p. 28.
[118] *ADC* ii, p. 210.

(viii.) ordinance of July 1498 for Sessions in Aberdeen, Perth and Edinburgh[119]
(ix.) ordinance of November 1500 for Session with geographical tabling[120]
(x.) ordinance of September 1503 with geographical tabling by divisions[121]
(xi.) statute of 1504 regulating "daily" Council[122]

Several trends can be detected during this period—the two of most note are the beginnings of a process of differentiation between Lords of Council and Lords of Session, and the development of more structured sittings and diets of the Session. In terms of the differentiation of Lords of Council and of Session, the individuals involved in this process were drawn from a wider pool of council judges than had existed before 1488. In part, of course, this was simply because of the merging of the personnel of parliamentary Auditors and Council members. The result of the process was that men might be made to sit on the Council with a view purely to their serving as Session judges.[123] Also apparent in relation to personnel is what Dr Chalmers perceived to amount to a rota system in the deployment of judges for the Session.[124] This was in evidence by 1496 though apparently lapsing again by 1501.[125] The implication of this trend is that there was some degree of professionalization emerging amongst the regular Session judges at the level of possessing specialised knowledge and skills. In other words expertise and experience in the law was becoming sufficiently relevant to Council business to lead to the nomination of lords who otherwise would not necessarily have served on Council at all. Part of that development must have been connected with the increasing proportion of churchmen who were active on the Council between 1478 and 1513, apart from a few years following 1488.[126] However, it also related to the growth of a core group of Session judges who, through cumulative

[119] *ADC* ii, p. 283.
[120] *ADC* ii, p. 417.
[121] Edinburgh, National Archives of Scotland, CS 5/14, fols. 186, 176; calendered in *ADCP*, p. lxi. (for comment see p. xxix).
[122] *APS* ii, p. 249, c. 2.
[123] Chalmers, "The King's Council", p. 261.
[124] Chalmers, "The King's Council", p. 260.
[125] Chalmers, "The King's Council", p. 274.
[126] Chalmers, "The King's Council", p. 287.

experience in dealing with large amounts of conciliar judicial business, had built up skill in deciding such matters.

Dr Chalmers drew a distinction between regular sittings of the Council for sustained concentration upon judicial business, and interim sittings between those longer diets. Following his analysis of the sederunts under James IV, he was able to state that "after 1488, a number of the regular lords of council occur as judges on the Edinburgh diets, but seldom or never as judges at the interim sittings; conversely, a few lords occur principally as judges outwith the sessions".[127] Regular Lords of Council were "supplemented by men who occur solely or principally as council judges, and who have little or no other involvement in the royal administration". In other words, these were "recognisable sessions judges".[128] Their appearance for the first time is a marked feature of James IV's reign. This development can be traced in the election of Lords of Session by the Council in October 1490, and by the King in October 1495.[129] This builds upon the insights of Hannay, who cited the 1490 nominations as evidence that "it had been decided that regular 'sessions' of council were inevitable; and we have a list of *domini sessionis communiter electi*".[130]

This differentiation of personnel occurred within a new structure of sittings of Council. Prolonged sittings of the Council in Edinburgh to deal with judicial business had become known as "sessions", inheriting the name previously used to describe the now defunct auditorial Session. The 1490s saw an increase in the number of interim sittings held outwith the main diets, however. These were held wherever the King and his court happened to be at the time.[131] Such interim sittings had been normal before the 1460s, when the auditorial Session had complemented the normal judicial work of Council. But at that time Council would have granted much more limited access to litigants. By the time that Council was apparently broadening this access in the 1460s, it was becoming the static, Edinburgh-based Council of the personal rule of James III. After the 1460s, it was also no longer complemented by auditorial Sessions outwith Edinburgh. The 1490s saw the gathering together and fusion of previous structures, in that prolonged sittings

[127] Chalmers, "The King's Council", p. 260.
[128] Chalmers, "The King's Council", p. 260.
[129] *ADC* i, pp. 143, 386.
[130] Hannay, "Antecedents", pp. 99–100.
[131] Chalmers, "The King's Council", p. 257.

in one place were combined with shorter interim sittings as the King itinerated the country, accompanied by his Council. Both types of sitting were, equally, ones of Council. It was the central sittings which were regarded as "sessions" and we first find terms stated for structuring the sittings of these judicial Sessions in a statute of 1491. In this statute, the phrase "lordis of Sessione" occurs in what Dr Chalmers has argued was by this time "a definite institutional sense".[132] Interim judicial sittings of Council outside Edinburgh were also supplemented in 1498 by Sessions to be held in Aberdeen and Perth as well as Edinburgh.[133] At a Council meeting in Edinburgh on 18 July 1498, it was declared that all summonses raised prior to 8 June had now been dealt with, but that all summonses raised since then would be referred to three regionally based sittings to fall between October and January and arranged chronologically between the three burghs. This revival of the idea of regional Sessions seems to have arisen directly from the failure of interim Council sittings to attend to and process complaints adequately, at the time when a justice ayre was also going around the country.[134] However, in turn the proposed Aberdeen and Perth Sessions were found to conflict with further justice ayres.[135]

In relation to the ordering of proceedings during the course of a Session, attempts were made from 1495 to structure the flow of business through a table of summonses. This meant that summonses would be ordered to call in waves on a day-by-day basis, instead of all at once at the commencement of a Session. We first see this strategy being propounded in November 1495, towards the end of a long Session in Edinburgh which had begun on 14 October.[136] The expense to litigants, and in particular the delays which followed from uncertainty about when a summons would be heard, were cited as the reason for the new system, the problem being diagnosed as the calling of all summonses on a single day. The new scheme involved existing but unheard summonses being continued to 8 February 1496, but all new summonses being divided up into groups, and set to call on particular days in the future. Eight summonses would be allocated to each day from 12 May

---

[132] *APS* ii, p. 226, c. 16; cf. Hannay, "Antecedents", pp. 99–100; Chalmers, "The King's Council", p. 267.

[133] *ADC* ii, pp. 283–284.

[134] *ADC* ii, p. 210.

[135] Hannay, *ADCP*, p. xxix.

[136] *ADC* i, p. 423.

1496 onwards. The intention was for the clerks to draw up a table which would show the King and Council how the summonses were set to call. Once such a "tabled" Session was underway, no further summonses for that particular diet would be issued. A similar method of calling and continuation is visible in Council proceedings some eight months later in June 1496. The summonses issued since the previous November which were to call in May appear not to have been heard because Council did not sit to deal with judicial business that month, and seems instead to have continued all summonses to June. The June ordinance is simply a general continuation to October, but it carefully stipulated that the new court day in October for a particular summons would fall to be determined by the original day of tabling in May.[137]

A different method of structuring the business of the Sessions was used for the first time in 1500. It was ordained that for the first two weeks of the forthcoming Session in Edinburgh, beginning on 3 November, only actions brought by litigants from south of the River Tay would be heard to begin with. Those from north of the Tay would have their actions continued to the fifteenth day of the Session in question.[138] This geographical method of structuring the table was adopted in more detailed form in September and December, 1503.[139] Summonses were to be tabled according to a division of the country into five groups of sheriffdoms, although the December ordinance laid down "a five-part division, using similar but more comprehensive shire groupings" for the March diet to follow.[140] There is a reference in the proceedings of the Parliament of March 1504 to one of these divisions being composed of the sheriffdoms of Fife, Lothian, Berwick and Renfrew.[141] This method of tabling continued to be used, and according to Dr Chalmers "the groupings of sheriffdoms usually have a geographical coherence within each group, but there is considerable variation from session to session in the composition of each set of shires".[142]

We find that by the time of the Parliament of March 1504 it seems to have been felt necessary to increase the opportunities for processing

[137] See the references given at the start of this section, especially see the June 1496 ordinance: *ADC* ii, p. 28.

[138] *ADC* ii, p. 417.

[139] *ADCP*, pp. xxix, lxi; Hannay, "Antecedents", p. 104; Chalmers, "The King's Council", p. 272.

[140] Chalmers, "The King's Council", p. 272.

[141] *APS* ii, p. 248.

[142] Chalmers, "The King's Council", p. 272.

the flow of judicial business in Council. Despite the developments noted above, there had been "greit confusioun of summondis at ilk sessioune".[143] It was enacted that for this reason a Council, chosen by the King, would sit continually in Edinburgh "or quhar the King makis residence or quhar it plesis him". It would hear causes "dayly as thai sall happin to occur, and sall have the samin power as the lordis of sessioun", the exact times of their sittings to be notified by proclamation.[144] Hannay seemed to view this as an innovation, commenting on how it had been "so ambitiously begun".[145] By contrast, Dr Chalmers has interpreted the act as simply giving "parliamentary sanction" to a pre-existing set of arrangements, namely interim sittings of the Council for judicial business.[146] He has pointed to references in the record to "sessioun dayly", which he equated with interim sittings, and "sessioun generale", which he equated with the sustained judicial diets of Council.[147] An example of the latter is the proclamation of 5 January 1503 referring to a "cessioun generale" to begin that month.[148] Such diets were held regularly, twice a year, from 1503 to 1513.[149] Since we have already noted the growth of interim sittings of the judicial Council in the 1490s, Chalmers' argument is compelling. It does seem probable that this statute is simply putting such hearings onto a formal footing, thereby integrating the system of interim hearings with that of the sustained Sessions.

One further development in Council's judicial business was that after 1498 it was the crown lands commissioners and the auditors of exchequer who would deal with judicial matters relating to their own particular responsibilities, such business having been heard previously in the main council chamber, privileged as the "king's own business".[150] Litigants with exchequer business began to be ordered to take out summonses before Council, returnable before the Exchequer.[151] This provides a glimpse of the process of differentiation of function within

[143] *APS* ii, p. 249.
[144] *APS* ii, p. 249.
[145] Hannay, "Antecedents", p. 106.
[146] Chalmers, "The King's Council", p. 279.
[147] Chalmers, "The King's Council", p. 279.
[148] *Acts of the Lords of Council Vol. III 1501–1503* ed. Alma B. Calderwood (Edinburgh, 1993), pp. 161–162.
[149] Chalmers, "The King's Council", p. 283.
[150] Chalmers, "The King's Council", p. 274.
[151] Chalmers, "The King's Council", p. 276.

the medieval council which had barely started in 1498 but was to assume much more prominence in the 1530s and 1540s following the foundation of the College of Justice.

Conclusions on 1488–1504

Dr Chalmers' analysis has clarified greatly the development of judicial business in Council and Session in the reign of James IV. In terms of its wider significance, he believed that "it is sensible to speak of the Council's judicial activities as constituting a 'court' by 1478 and probably earlier". In supporting Hannay's analysis, Dr Chalmers stated that "the Court of Session, in all but name, was in existence from the earlier part of James IV's reign".[152] In relation to institutional development, however, this claim is something of an overstatement, as well as lacking clarity in the concept of a court upon which it is premised. Hannay's own words were more qualified, stating that "it is probably correct to say that under James IV the Court of Session became a definite institution".[153] Hannay viewed as decisive the making of "adequate arrangements" for the hearing of civil causes by Council under James IV and the fixing of "stated periods appointed for the purpose", an example of which is found in the statute of 1491 which ordained Sessions.[154] However, in his more considered and detailed study, "On the Antecedents of the College of Justice", developments such as the 1491 statute are characterised by Hannay as marking merely *stages* in the evolution of the institution.[155] He noted that "though sessions of council had now been adopted as an expedient to deal with the administration of civil justice, there was still much indefiniteness and uncertainty".[156] Even the arrangements made by 1498 are described by Hannay as a "haphazard system", and the situation in 1503 raised for him questions of a "breakdown of civil justice".[157] Hannay went on to state that James IV "never succeeded in putting the administration of civil justice on a satisfactory footing". Dr Chalmers' view seems by comparison too categorical. Hannay simply meant to say that the Session became a

[152] Chalmers, "The King's Council", pp. 303, 316; cf. Hannay, *College of Justice*, p. 22.
[153] Hannay, *College of Justice*, p. 22.
[154] Hannay, *College of Justice*, p. 24; *APS* ii, p. 226, c. 16.
[155] Hannay, "Antecedents", p. 101.
[156] Hannay, "Antecedents", p. 101.
[157] Hannay, "Antecedents", p. 104.

definite *institution* under James IV, which is indisputable, but he would have stressed that this institution could hardly be equated with those of 1513, 1527, or 1532. The institution of the 1490s evolved to become those later institutions.

Furthermore, in terms of Dr Chalmers' view of a court, more must be required than sittings of a body of experienced men to decide civil causes if it is to be said that a central court has been established. It would be important to be able to point to a fixed and politically independent or at least autonomous body of judges, sitting self-consciously as such with reasonable frequency at regular and fixed times in a fixed place. Sheriff courts, for example, sat for three head courts a year, at Yule, Pasch and Michaelmas.[158] Apart from such institutional criteria, we should also expect a central court to have jurisdiction over "lower" courts. As late as 1513, however, Council and Session remained unable to hear certain actions which turned on questions of fee and heritage, in line with the later medieval common law rules on jurisdiction.[159] Of course it has to be admitted that there is nevertheless great continuity in the evolution of the Session under James IV and James V. Perusal of the council register in the early years of the sixteenth century reveals voluminous litigation, and heavy reliance upon Council as a central judicial body. However, by the end of James IV's reign the most that even Dr Chalmers claims is that "the Session in 1513 was poised awkwardly between being a function of the *curia regis* and becoming a professional judicature".[160] This is a much more accurate view, but is also inconsistent with the view that "the Court of Session, in all but name, was in existence from the earlier part of James IV's reign".[161]

The developments which have been discussed in relation to the period 1488–1504 were in no sense cumulative steps towards a "Court of Session". They were not intended as such, nor did they function as such. The differentiation of personnel which is traced in Dr Chalmers' work is only the beginning of a process which was certainly not exhausted by 1513. Dr Chalmers himself commented that:

---

[158] W.C. Dickinson, "Introduction" to *The Sheriff Court Book of Fife 1515–1522*, ed. W.C. Dickinson, Scottish History Society Third Series 12 (Edinburgh, 1928) p. xv.

[159] MacQueen, *Common Law And Feudal Society*, chap. 8.

[160] Chalmers, "The King's Council", p. 311.

[161] Chalmers, "The King's Council", pp. 303, 316; cf. Hannay, *College of Justice*, p. 22.

> the extent of differentiation between the lords' interim sittings and more general sittings of the secret council is a matter of uncertainty: many interim hearings have sederunts which suggest that the judicial business, and sometimes other administrative or miscellaneous matters, was being dealt with by the council-at-large.[162]

None of the developments which have been outlined led to the Session coming to be an established "court" in a meaningful institutional sense, though cumulatively they amounted to a massive step in this direction. The Session of the early 1500s was simply for the time being a relatively regular central forum in which to seek justice. To that extent it formed an important part of the evolution of the Session between 1426 and 1532. There were a number of different strands of institutional development in the evolution of the Session, but none concerned explicitly the issue at this point of "establishing" a court. The nearest to such a policy being articulated came with the foundation of the College of Justice in 1532, but even this was a reconstitution of the Session rather than the foundation of a new court. Continuous usage can serve to mask changes in underlying institutional character, and the fact that the "Session" had become an institution in the reign of James IV may be admitted without agreeing that this amounted to the formation of a central court distinct from the King's Council.

Besides the Session not yet being properly constituted as a central court, it must also be noted that many of the innovations of the 1490s had the character of temporary expedients, and that many were unsuccessful. The two which lasted were the sittings of "sessions general" twice a year, and the use of geographical divisions for tabling, although as we have seen these divisions were not themselves fixed in any permanent arrangement. Also, whilst there would have been an expectation by 1504 that "sessions general" be held, they still did not keep set terms as such. Instead they depended upon royal proclamations to determine their sittings, and remained liable to be disrupted by extranous events. For example, an ordinance of February 1509 prescribed "terms" for the forthcoming year. These were to be from April till August, and from October till the following March.[163] In mid-December 1509, however, the Lords abandoned the Session, announcing that the northern shires would now be dealt with at the time of justice ayres.[164] Though there

[162] Chalmers, "The King's Council", p. 303.
[163] *ADCP*, p. lxiv.
[164] Hannay, "Antecedents", p. 106.

was also at this time a core of regular council judges, as we have seen, they were merely the core of a wider, indeterminate pool of men who might serve as such.

Hannay charted the improvised and *ad hoc* nature of the innovations of the 1490s.[165] The flow of business into Council could not be dealt with adequately, even after the tabling ordinance of 1495. We have already seen how summonses which were to have called in May 1496 were continued first until June and then October. There followed attempts to combine interim sittings of the Council with the progress around the country of justice ayres—after all, important members of the Council would have had to be present at the ayres.[166] This scheme in turn broke down, since Council could not deal with all summonses before moving on to deal with the business of the ayre. The 1498 ordinance for a Session in Edinburgh was a direct response to this failure, and the link with the ayres was abandoned. Sessions were ordained later for Perth and Aberdeen, but this failed too, due to further clashes with justice ayres.[167] Hannay noted how:

> in September the parties who expected to be heard at Perth were postponed to January, and must come to Edinburgh: those of the north had to put up with a delay of four, and finally six months, and the hardship of travelling to the capital or where the King and Council happened to be.[168]

By November 1503, we witness the geographical division of shires, but the Session of that month was still "inadequate" in Hannay's view since the cases were not all heard by Christmas as planned.[169] This led to the statute of March 1504 concerning the daily Council, which constituted in Hannay's assessment an "expedient to remedy the congestion".[170] On the effect of the daily Council, Hannay remarked that "the numerous acts and proclamations for continuation, or adjournment, of session during the remainder of the reign prove that the ordinance for a Council to deal with civil matters 'dayly as thai sall happin to occur' had little effect in creating a court more constantly accessible", and that in any

[165] Hannay, "Antecedents", pp. 102–104.
[166] *ADCP*, p. xxix.
[167] *ADC* ii, p. 283.
[168] Hannay, "Antecedents", pp. 104–105.
[169] Hannay, "Antecedents", p. 104.
[170] Hannay, "Antecedents", p. 104.

case the statute "does not suggest a permanent institution so much as an energetic and temporary effort to dispose of arrears".[171]

The period 1488–1504 therefore saw a series of unsystematic expedients to deal with the flow of judicial business into Council, some of which survived or were retained to become institutional features of the conciliar form of Session. However, the Session of the 1530s had not yet taken shape, and in some respects the Sessions of James IV had as much in common with those of James I as of James V after 1532. The unifying thread is not by 1504 the development of a supreme central court, but merely the provision of organizational machinery designed to enable Council to meet the demands of litigants. This explains the evidence better than attempts to see the development of the Session as related to the notion of the Stewart kings engaging in a long struggle to "impose their authority on the whole country and build up their central institutions".[172] What does seem to be true, however, is that kings were forced to develop institutions capable of meeting the expectations of their subjects concerning that traditional and fundamental office of kingship, the dispensation of justice. Professor MacQueen correctly saw the institutional evolution as aiming "to relieve the increasing burden on council".[173] But conciliar justice also developed in the Sessions to enable the King to fulfil his natural and immemorial role within a changing society. Moreover, in this period we can be certain that the King was personally conscious of the task of dispensing justice because between 1503 and 1505 James IV was present at the Session in no fewer than eighty-four judicial meetings of Council over the course of sixty-seven days of hearings.[174]

Council and Session, 1504–1526

It appears that after 1504 no further institutional developments of significance occurred under James IV. Until 1513, Council and Session continued to function regularly, if not always smoothly. Professor Hannay viewed James IV as lacking full success in stabilising the operation of central justice, noting that "to the end of his reign the lords were

[171] *ADCP*, pp. xxx–xxxi.

[172] L.J. Macfarlane, *William Elphinstone and the Kingdom of Scotland 1431–1514* (Aberdeen, 1985), p. 93.

[173] MacQueen, "Pleadable Brieves and Jurisdiction in Heritage", p. 274.

[174] Macfarlane, *Elphinstone*, p. 423.

struggling ineffectually with persistent arrears", and that "the government, unable to provide for adequate 'sessions' in Edinburgh, oscillated between a centralised court and the itinerant system".[175] Hannay believed that the main developments after 1504 came only after the battle of Flodden in 1513. A Scottish army was famously defeated by the English and James IV killed, with consequences for Scottish government which have remained contentious. The fifteen years from 1513 to 1528 were ones of minority and extreme factionalism within the Scottish nobility, with successive rival regimes and resultant political instability until James V seized power for himself in 1528. The traditional view has been that such political instability must have had a damaging effect upon the operation of government and the administration of justice. On this view the operation of the Session was undermined compared to its success under James IV. Indeed, following from this, it could be said that the damage done after 1513 obscured the degree of that success, and therefore helped give an exaggerated impression of the innovation represented by subsequent reforms preceding the foundation of the College of Justice in 1532. The problem with this view is that its main premise is false. The Session carried on operating after 1513 with relative effectiveness, and it would be more accurate to emphasise the continuity between 1513 and 1532 than any discontinuity inflicted by Flodden and the political conditions of the minority.

Hannay's analysis of the period after 1513 was based upon the belief that the battle of Flodden had a disastrous effect on Scottish government generally, and the functioning of the Session in particular. He saw it as causing "the arrest...of the differentiating process and the marked shrinkage of the capacity to deal independently with two distinct classes of business" (i.e. justice and "public" affairs), adding that "the council was in fact so much taken up by public affairs that civil justice suffered".[176] These developments were reflected in the record, according to Hannay, where "minutes of business in general council, council, council in session, council in exchequer, council undefined, are mingled almost inextricably".[177] His conclusion was that "by 1517 the business of the session seems to have relapsed into the state which

[175] Hannay, "Antecedents", p. 108.
[176] Hannay, "Antecedents", p. 110.
[177] *ADCP*, p. xxxiii.

James IV had done much to remedy", i.e. certainly its pre-1504 state, if not its pre-1490 state.[178]

It is clear that the effect of Flodden, including the death of James IV and the succession of the infant James V, was profoundly disruptive in at least the short term. However, the view that there was a longer-term unfavourable effect on government has not been supported by modern research and has been directly challenged in a detailed study of the minority of James V by Dr Kenneth Emond.[179] The battle of Flodden took place on 9 September 1513. A proclamation of 12 July 1513 had previously continued the Session to 20 October, but in the event this was too soon after Flodden to be practicable.[180] In December, fewer than three months later, a Session was nevertheless ordained to begin on 8 January 1514 in Edinburgh "for ministracioun to be had of justice".[181] There was indeed a Session in January, though postponed by a few days "becaus the lordis have bene occupiit sen syne in greit materis concerning the gud of the realme sa that thai micht nocht vaik tharapon".[182] Nevertheless, this Session sat for at least a month, since on 25 February 1514 the chancellor "askit ane note that he protestit the lordis being present in the consell hous to remane in this town apon the ministracioun of justice and he suld remane with thaim".[183] As late as 7 April 1514 we find the first of a series of formal continuations of the Session.[184] The next formal sitting of the Session appears to be ordained by a proclamation of 30 May 1515, a few days after the arrival of the duke of Albany in Scotland as governor during the new king's minority.[185] At that point, on 5 June 1515, there was a "*sessio dominorum...per dominus electos ad consilium*".[186] Judicial activity may therefore have been slowed down by Flodden, but at least one annual Session was still being maintained.

---

[178] Hannay, *College of Justice*, p. 27.
[179] W.K. Emond, "The Minority of King James V" (University of St Andrews, unpublished Ph.D. thesis, 1988).
[180] *ADCP*, p. lxvii.
[181] *ADCP*, p. 7.
[182] *ADCP*, pp. 7, 9.
[183] *ADCP*, p. 11.
[184] *ADCP*, pp. 15–17.
[185] *ADCP*, pp. 31–31.
[186] *ADCP*, p. 34.

The Session in the regency of the duke of Albany from 1515

Hannay's account passes without comment over Albany's first period in Scotland as Regent (from May 1515 to June 1517), except for one remark that "there are indications, under Albany's government, that 'the lordis of sessioun' were resuming their former specialised functions; but the condition of things was so unsatisfactory as to emphasize the need for institutional progress".[187] However, in respect of other aspects of government, there is reason to see substantial continuity in the period after 1513. Dr Emond has pointed, for example, to continuity of personnel in government despite the great losses at Flodden. Although nine of the twenty Scottish earls were killed, only two left heirs who were too young to replace their fathers in Council, whilst of the twelve to fourteen Lords of Parliament who died, out of a total of thirty, only three left under-age heirs.[188] Moreover, the major offices of state were hardly affected in the aftermath, and Dr Emond's conclusion about the machinery of government was that it "did not grind to a halt".[189] We have noted that a Session did sit in January and February 1514, and Dr Emond drew attention to the large amount of judicial business in the year after Flodden relating to the heirs of those killed at the battle, and involving at least fifty-five separate cases.[190]

In terms of government, a council of regency was nominated in October 1513 to provide assistance to James IV's widowed Queen, Margaret Tudor, "for gude rewle to be kepit within the realme".[191] However, in August 1514 Margaret married Archibald Douglas, sixth earl of Angus. It was this as well as existing tensions between her and the other lords which resulted in her deposition as governor and tutrix of the King at a meeting of lords in Dunfermline in September 1514.[192] A request was also made to John Stewart, duke of Albany (1481–1536), a nephew of James III and heir presumptive to the throne, to come from France to Scotland (on his first ever visit to the country) to act as governor.[193] Therefore, it is probably true that for a year prior to the

[187] *ADCP*, p. xxxii.
[188] Emond, "The Minority of King James V", p. 6.
[189] Emond, "The Minority of King James V", p. 7.
[190] Emond, "The Minority of King James V", p. 9.
[191] *ADCP*, p. 6.
[192] *ADCP*, p. 28.
[193] See M.W. Stuart, *The Scot who was a Frenchman: being the life of John Stewart, duke of Albany, in Scotland, France, and Italy* (London, 1940).

arrival of the duke of Albany in May 1515, the judicial work of Council was disrupted by political events, and that there was no Session held. But it is significant that one of Albany's first acts was to hold a Session. Dr Emond regarded the Session which was held by Albany from 4 June to 1 August 1515 as the first signal of his success in restoring a measure of normality to government. Albany himself attended sixteen out of thirty-one recorded meetings which dealt with a large number of cases.[194] This evidence demonstrates that the political situation at large could affect very seriously the work of Council and Session, but also that Hannay's characterisation of the period as a whole was too sweeping. It was only in the twelve-month period before Albany arrived in Scotland that the Session appears not to have been able to function. Even so, it had sat in 1514 for a time at least. During Albany's first year in the country, the Session was then very active, and according to Dr Emond "there was a clear perception that land disputes, claims against theft and kidnapping and feuds could be redressed satisfactorily by the attention of the lords in session".[195]

By the autumn of 1516 Albany's government was firmly established, but the first sixteen months or so had witnessed some political instability and opposition to the Regent. However, the twenty months after Flodden, followed by the first sixteen months of Albany's regency, do not suggest that the system of Sessions was abandoned or much weakened, but rather that it was merely disrupted by political instability during particular periods. It is the period of twelve months following October 1516 which most shows Hannay's analysis to need fundamental revision, especially the period from January to June 1517. This period saw a huge number of cases brought before Council which amounted to more than 500 pages in the council register. The volumes of the register covering the twenty-two months from July 1516 to the start of May 1517 (Albany left Scotland in September 1517) amount to 862 pages. This compares with only 370 pages in the whole of the first twenty months after Flodden.[196] Moreover, the bulk of the business before Council from October 1516 to September 1517 concerned civil causes, not general council business in public affairs.[197] This evidence contradicts Hannay's argument, since it shows that Council's capacity

[194] Emond, "The Minority of King James V", p. 68.
[195] Emond, "The Minority of King James V", p. 60.
[196] Emond, "The Minority of King James V", p. 146.
[197] Emond, "The Minority of King James V", p. 146.

to process judicial business was in fact very striking in 1517. In this period civil justice in no way suffered because Council was distracted by "public affairs". Far from a "relapse", there seems to have been a revival of the business of the Session once Albany had arrived in Scotland, after a temporary disruption which was caused not by Council having to deal with other matters to the exclusion of civil causes, but rather by the wider political instability in the country. It is in this light that the proclamation of 20 June 1517 must be seen, coming twelve days after the departure of Albany from Scotland. It proclaimed a Session to run from 22 June to 30 October in line with a fourfold geographical division in the tabling of summonses.[198] This was not a measure to deal with the failure of Council to process civil business, but rather must have followed from the *success* of Council in its judicial business under Albany. The problem to which the tabling scheme was a response arose simply because the time available in Council was insufficient to hear the large number of cases. As Dr Emond remarked, "council was being too successfull in promoting its image as the place where justice could be obtained".[199]

The Session under the earl of Arran and the duke of Albany 1517–1521

That even the scheme of June 1517 did not enable Council to process an adequate proportion of judicial business is evident by 3 August of that year, when the first of a series of general continuations eventually pushed the next Session forward to February 1518, excepting a fairly wide class of privileged actions.[200] As Hannay noted, however, privileging classes of action became less a way of determining which cases Council would hear outwith terms of Session, and more a way of deciding which ones would be given priority within terms.[201] The Session did not really sit regularly for the best part of a year after August 1517, but again this can be seen to be because of a wider political instability which affected the whole of government, not because of the pressure of non-judicial business within Council. Dr Emond commented that it was only in the summer of 1518 that active government could be resumed in Edinburgh, in tandem—significantly—with a Session.[202] Emond has

[198] *ADCP*, p. 94.
[199] Emond, "The Minority of King James V", p. 172.
[200] *ADCP*, pp. 99, 106, 107, 108, 109, 112.
[201] *ADCP*, p. xxxii.
[202] Emond, "The Minority of King James V", p. 207.

argued that Albany restored stable government during his first regency, but that this success was based upon the effect of his personal presence as governor, representing royal authority. Amongst other things, this had "improved the image of the council as the place to obtain justice".[203] His departure in June 1517 led to politics and government becoming unstable again. The most notorious example of that was the assassination of Antoine D'Arces, Seigneur De La Bastie, agent and ally of Albany, royal lieutenant in the Merse (i.e. south east Scotland) and Lothian (central eastern Scotland south of the Forth), warden of the east marches and one of the seven vice-regents named by Albany at his departure. The killing occurred on 17 September 1517 and was carried out by David Hume of Wedderburn. It reflected a feud between Albany and the Hume family, exacerbated by the conflicting interests of Albany and the Humes in the Scottish Borders.[204] The government thereafter became very much pre-occupied with the state of the Borders as well as relations with England during this period.[205]

Council unanimously chose James Hamilton, earl of Arran, to succeed De La Bastie as governor of the Merse. For the next two years, until late 1519, Arran was the leading figure in the government. There followed another period of instability in 1520–1521, reminiscent of that of 1514–1515.[206] This instability followed from the recognition in Scotland by the autumn of 1519 that Albany would not be returning to Scotland so long as England and France were at peace (as they were at the time). This reflected pressure on the French king to respect Henry VIII of England's self-interested desire that Albany should not be permitted to return to Scotland as a hostile source of French influence. At this point Arran's on-going control of government seems to have become intolerable to other lords such as Angus. The Session had been fully active as recently as August 1517, but the discussion above indicates how six months of uncertainty and turbulence had followed, stimulated by the departure of Albany and the murder of his lieutenant, and the ensuing efforts of the government to stamp out the disruption caused by the culprits. A Session was finally ordained in Parliament for 22 February 1518, and sat on into March.[207] This Session was ordained

---

[203] Emond, "The Minority of King James V", p. 180.
[204] J.E.A. Dawson, *Scotland Re-formed 1488–1587* (Edinburgh, 2007), pp. 96–99.
[205] Emond, "The Minority of King James V", pp. 177–179.
[206] Emond, "The Minority of King James V", p. 178.
[207] *ADCP*, p. 116.

"becaus the executioun of justice civilie has bene lang deferrit to the kingis liegis sen my lord governouris departing for divers causis", and it seems likely that the occasion of Parliament was seized upon as facilitating the holding of a Session since the three estates were to "avis quhat lordis of every staite and to quhat noumer sall remane eftir the dissolutioun of the parliament for the ministratioun of justice".[208]

After six months without a Session one was felt to be necessary by February 1518, but because of the political situation, and associated military action by Arran in the Borders in March 1518, this Session did not really deal with the generality of summonses. However, as Dr Emond noted, the Session proper began again on 10 June and sat until 24 July, when it was continued until December.[209] Between July and November a wide class of actions was privileged so that they could be dealt with outwith Session, most notably "recent spuilzie".[210] In reviewing the period 1517–1518, Hannay commented that "the exigencies of state and unforeseen accidents constantly interrupted systematic procedure".[211] This is accurate in relation to a period extending from September 1517 to June 1518, but the preceding discussion suggests that *outwith* this narrower period the Session appears to have functioned regularly, albeit for comparatively short periods of a month at a time. Even within this narrower nine-month period, it sat for at least a month over February and March 1518. However, Hannay implied that his verdict related to the Session generally, even up to 1524. The evidence discussed here suggests that, on the contrary, whilst the political situation in the country could disrupt government during particular temporary periods, affecting the Session too, it did not prevent the Session from operating as normal when government itself was able to do so. This happened under Albany and again under Arran up to 1519. Dr Emond has even argued that "one aspect of Arran's government was therefore immensely successfull—it was seen to be capable of providing justice in civil causes and so the session was packed with cases which were finally heard".[212]

Unfortunately, the Council records from December 1519 to November 1522 are now lost, and so the operation of the Session over these

[208] *ADCP*, p. 112.
[209] Emond, "The Minority of King James V", pp. 208–209.
[210] *ADCP*, pp. 125–126, 132.
[211] Hannay, "Antecedents2, p. 111.
[212] Emond, "The Minority of King James V", p. 209.

three years cannot be traced. It must be conceded that it is likely that, between November 1519 and Albany's return in November 1521 for his second period of active regency, the Session could not have operated normally in what Dr Emond characterised as a "very disturbed period in Scottish government".[213] Nevertheless, Hannay's characterisation of the period up to 1519 clearly requires to be modified. He saw it as marking a definite set-back in a process of differentiation between Council and Session, which stemmed from the inability of the Session to function adequately in the prevailing conditions. Having considered the nature of politics in these years, though, there is an impression that whilst Hannay was right to stress the disruptions which occurred, he failed to recognise that there were periods when the Session did function, not just adequately, but very successfully, as under Albany in 1517. A more balanced synthesis would not view 1513 as marking any particular discontinuity in the administration of Sessions. From time to time there was disruption, but it affected the whole of government and not just the capability of Session. These periods of political instability and disruption do not appear to have caused any structural change, however, in the administration of justice by the King's Council and the Session. In terms of personnel, no development seems to have occurred either. Hannay observed that in 1524 "there is no sign of any body of men who are to be 'of council' with special regard to work on the Session".[214] The implication is that this represented his general view of the whole period 1513–24.[215]

The Session, 1521–1526

After four years abroad, Albany returned for his second residence in Scotland on 18 November 1521, and stayed for eleven months until 27 October 1522. His third and final visit was to last just over eight months from 20 September 1523 till 31 May 1524. As already mentioned, there are unfortunately no Council records extant for the first period of his return between 1521 and 1522. The register only becomes extant from shortly after his departure in 1522. In general terms, though, it seems probable that the Session resumed more regular meetings than would have been likely during 1520 and early 1521, in line with the galvanising

213 Emond, "The Minority of King James V", p. 277.
214 Hannay, "Antecedents", p. 112.
215 See also *ADCP*, p. xxxiii.

effect of Albany's arrival in 1515. Apart from a few dissident lords, Albany managed to achieve a wide range of support in this second, eleventh-month period, receiving cooperation from Queen Margaret and enjoying the support of the earls of Arran, Lennox, Huntly and Argyll.[216] The pattern of 1513–19 had been that the Session sat and heard a very large number of cases during periods of relative political stability, and it can be expected that the same pattern would have been present between November 1521 and October 1522.

It is telling that one of Albany's last instructions in 1522 was to order a Session to be held, expressed in a letter of 24 October.[217] The impression given by the tabling arrangements contained in the instruction is one of continuity, suggesting that at this time the Session was considered a normal and regular activity of the Lords of Council. The class of privileged summonses now contained so great a number of cases that three days a week out of six were set aside to hear them. The only obvious factor in this is the expansion of the definition of the category to include, for example, "recent spuilzie". In itself, the volume of privileged actions does not seem to imply any particular failing of the Session to function adequately. A Session *was* held from 6 November to 19 December 1522.[218] This dealt with a large number of cases, and the Lords in attendance were unusually strong in number, being between 14 and 16 on average.[219] The Session then resumed as planned on 15 January 1523 and sat until 17 February. Dr Emond noted that it was only the renewal of an active state of war with England which disrupted further hearings intended for May, leading to a general continuation until October.[220] After March 1524, the Session did not sit for a fifteen month period, until 12 June 1524, and in the meantime the duke of Albany left Scotland for the last time on 31 May 1524.[221]

It is quite clear that the Session was still considered a regular institution of government in the early 1520s, and that it did in fact sit in every year. Ten years earlier there would have been two "sessions general" a year following the pattern established in the second half of James IV's reign. In 1523 and 1524 there was only one, although in the second of

216 Emond, "The Minority of King James V", p. 299.
217 *ADCP*, p. 152.
218 *ADCP*, pp. 152, 158.
219 Emond, "The Minority of King James V", p. 328.
220 Emond, "The Minority of King James V", p. 328; *ADCP*, pp. 168, 173, 174, 175.
221 Emond, "The Minority of King James V", pp. 467, 294.

Albany's periods in Scotland in 1522 it is a possibility that there could have been two. It did not keep regular terms, of course, but this degree of regularity, and the expectation with which litigants would have been imbued that they would be able to bring cases before a Session, help to demonstrate that it had indeed maintained its institutional character in the period after 1513.

Just as he had done in 1515–1517, so too in his subsequent residences in Scotland did Albany bring stability and a measure of authority to government, which in turn stabilised the politics of the minority. This was so evident in 1524 that the Lords of Council refused to sanction Albany's departure from Scotland at the end of January. Dr Emond argued that "the main reason for the Lords' threatening Albany's governorship if he left without their license was the continued need for peace and good government within Scotland".[222] Emond assessed the early weeks of 1524 as being marked successes in the functioning of civil and criminal justice.[223] It seems likely that Albany saw to it that the Sessions functioned well.

Reviewing all three periods of Albany's presence in Scotland, two related points can be made. The first is the direct link which can be made between political stability and the effectiveness of central justice, and its very capacity to function. The second is the existence of a clear perception in Scotland of activity in the administration of conciliar justice as an index of good government. Under Albany, that perception seems to have been very strong, to judge from Dr Emond's research. The foremost evidence of this is the large volume of litigants which flowed into the Session when overseen by Albany. By 1524, in terms of its role in government, the general impression given by the operation of the Session is one of continuity over the previous twenty years. Whilst political turbulence could upset the work of the Session dramatically, as Hannay perceived, its nature as an institution did not change during this period.

Justice was a theme which continued to underlie the criteria of good government at this time, and Albany appears to have executed the traditional kingly office of dispensing justice very effectively on behalf of the monarch. The prevalence of this theme is highlighted by the way in which even English commentators remarked on the subsequent failure

[222] Emond, "The Minority of King James V", p. 384.
[223] Emond, "The Minority of King James V", p. 382.

of Queen Margaret's renewed regency (after Albany had left) to provide civil or criminal justice.[224] Judging by the difficulty which Council and Session clearly had in processing the volume of litigation pursued before it, even when working as smoothly as possible under Albany, Scottish society was becoming increasingly dependent on this central institution. Within ten years, the Session had further transformed itself, in ways to be discussed in subsequent chapters, in response to the pressure arising out of this dependence. By that stage, further differentiation of function between Council and Session had come about, but nothing in the period 1513–1524 appears to have reversed in any significant sense the position reached by the end of the reign of James IV.

After Albany's departure, a Parliament of August 1524 effectively restored Queen Margaret's regency. A new Council had not yet been provided for, but on 15 September 1524 specific lords were named to sit on Session and upon "all materis of consale concernyng our soverane lord".[225] It is suggestive that the "sessioune" was distinguished from "materis of consale concernyng our soverane lord", since this might tend to undermine Hannay's view that "there is no sign of any body of men who are to be 'of the council' with special regard to work on the 'session'."[226] The institutions of Council and Session were perceived to have distinctive if overlapping functions, even if we cannot at this time make out any particular Lords of Council whose only role was to sit on the Session. The appointment of lords who could sit on the Session in the September ordinance of 1524 was interpreted by Dr Emond as a sign of concern at the failure to hold a Session, following similar concern in the August parliament,[227] and there is a statute of the November 1524 Parliament apparently demanding the immediate holding of a Session, and expressing what seems to be a similar concern that the Lords of Session shall administer justice "evinly" to all parties. The concern is evident in the declaration that this shall be so, "nochtwithstanding ony requestes of oure soverane lord or quenis grace incontrare thirof".[228]

This failure to provide justice in 1524 was one of the symptoms of a wider failure which caused Margaret's government to fall by the spring

[224] Emond, "The Minority of King James V", p. 246.
[225] Emond, "The Minority of King James V", p. 419; *ADCP*, p. 210.
[226] Hannay, "Antecedents", p. 112.
[227] Hannay, "Antecedents", p. 426.
[228] *APS* ii, p. 286, c. 7.

of 1525, when a convention of the estates was called by the earls of Angus, Argyll, and Lennox, with archbishops Beaton and Dunbar, in defiance of Queen Margaret and the authority of the King under her charge. This led to a period of more conciliar government between February and November 1525, and an attempt at reconciliation between factions.[229] The new Council moved in mid-March 1525 to provide for justice through a Session, ordaining one for June 1525.[230] The Session then began on 12 June 1525,[231] the first for over a year. It ended up being one of the longest sittings for several years, such that "cases were heard with a frequency which suggests that the neglect of the Session must have been a matter of grave concern to those who had actions to be brought before the lords of council".[232] Adherence to the rules of tabling testifies to the Session operating in a regular and organized fashion when it sat. On 19 June 1525, for example, it was argued that a summons raised principally at the King's instance should not be heard "becaus this is nocht the kingis day in the sessioune", and because it "was nocht in the table" as required by act of Parliament.[233] This is a reference to the statute of the November parliament of 1524.[234] When the Session was continued in August 1525, it was to "have process according to the table".[235] This attention to procedure indicates an adherence to principles of organisation which serves to stress the continuity between the 1525 Session and those of the previous twenty or so years.

An ordinance of 12 February 1526 was regarded as significant by Hannay and Duncan, since it appeared to add specialist Lords of Session to the normal body of Lords of Council who would be sitting on the Session.[236] It stated that "the lordis has chosin thir persouns undir writin to be adjonit with the lordis of the secrete councale and ministeris of court to sitt apoun this nixt sessioune". They were to "cum and remane" and "sit continualie apoun the sessioune" with the Lords of Council.[237] It is not clear, however, whether it was specifically

229 Emond, "The Minority of King James V", pp. 453, 460.
230 *ADCP*, p. 215.
231 Emond, "The Minority of King James V", p. 467; *ADCP*, p. 226.
232 Emond, "The Minority of King James V", p. 467.
233 *ADCP*, p. 223.
234 *APS* ii, p. 286, c. 7.
235 *ADCP*, p. 226.
236 *ADCP*, p. 238.
237 *ADCP*, p. 238.

the additional Lords who were to sit continually or whether it was an injunction that all the Lords should be assiduous. Four experienced ecclesiastical judges were included in this extra number. The Lords of Session were not a discrete and fixed group, but this ordinance was perhaps intended to bring into the pool of possible Session judges a number of men who otherwise would not have been eligible for the Session since they were not Lords of Council. However, the phrase "of this nixt sessioune" also seems to imply that the measure was merely an expedient for a single Session.

Hannay implied that even having reinforced the Session with these men, its work was still unsatisfactory. He argued that "it is not to be supposed that this composite body, or even the greater part of it, sat regularly for civil causes. The court was sometimes very near debility. Important affairs brought out a larger attendance".[238] The evidence Hannay cited to illustrate this point was a letter from the King, to continue a case in December 1526, since "it is grete and wichty and requiris ane gret sete of our lordis".[239] Elsewhere, he explicitly linked this characterisation of debility to the belief that "attendance was irregular, the sederunt often very weak".[240] However, examination of the select listings of the sederunt numbers in *ADCP* for December 1526 reveals what seems like adequate levels of manning, with 22 Lords on 1 December, 14 on 3 December, 15 on 5 December, 17 on 17 December, and 13 on 20 December.[241] Only twice in this month—on 4 and 12 December—was the sederunt as noted in *ADCP* eleven or fewer. An equally plausible interpretation of this letter is that it reflected not at all upon normal manning levels, but represented a special concession of some sort to the pursuers by the King. For instance, it could have been that the pursuers wished to delay appearing before the Session until some particularly sympathetic Lords were there to hear the case. Also, the fact that a large sederunt is mentioned does not mean that the number of Lords on this occasion was viewed as being too low for Session business to be transacted satisfactorily. It could simply be that a larger than usual number was desired, for particular reasons associated with this case of which we are unaware. In itself, this letter does not constitute evidence of any particular "debility" in the Session.

---

[238] Hannay, "Antecedents", p. 113.
[239] Hannay, "Antecedents", p. 113.
[240] Hannay, *The College of Justice*, p. 30.
[241] *ADCP*, pp. 253–235.

We have noted how in the fifteenth century the categories of privileged actions were those which the King's Council would be prepared to hear outside time of Parliament or Session—its traditional judicial role—and how since 1513 the categories had come to be expanded and used as a means of regulating the selection of matters to be given priority within a Session. An indication of the pressure of business arising from the hearing of such matters even outwith the time of Session is given by the extension of the device of tabling to sittings of Council outwith terms of Session. Thus on 25 August 1526 the Lords of Council assigned Wednesdays and Fridays of each week to sittings on privileged actions. Presumably the intention was to free Council from the attention of litigants except on those days, since persons bringing such actions must "awayte apoun the said dayis".[242] That such a measure was necessary even after what seems to have been a long Session earlier in the year may imply that the organisation of the Session was neither failing nor inadequate at this time. Rather, it would suggest that the volume of litigation was greater, resulting in the intensifying of demands for a hearing before Council or Session. After apparent concern over the question of administration of justice through the Session in 1525, it seems to have sat frequently or at least for long periods of time in 1526 and 1527. It is at precisely this point that institutional innovations begin to be made with deeper implications for the conduct of the Session. These remaining developments prior to 1532 will be addressed in the next chapter along with the foundation of the College of Justice.

[242] *ADCP*, p. 252.

CHAPTER THREE

THE FOUNDATION OF THE COLLEGE OF JUSTICE

Introduction

The foundation of the College of Justice has generally been considered an unimportant event by modern historians. This view follows the seminal work of R.K. Hannay (1867–1940), Fraser professor of Scottish history and paleography at the University of Edinburgh from 1919 to 1940. In a series of studies published between 1918 and 1936, Hannay set out what remains the standard scholarly account of the history of the Court of Session. Hannay's interest was concentrated on the fifteenth and sixteenth centuries, and a recurring focus of his work was the significance of the foundation of the College of Justice in 1532. More exactly, he sought to question its significance and argued that claims for its importance were generally misconceived. The lasting quality of his work rests on its detailed grounding in the extant primary sources, and a range of scholarly vision encompassing church history, international relations and diplomacy, as well as political, legal, constitutional and administrative history. Hannay was also able to set his study of the College of Justice alongside his own wider studies of Parliament, General Council and Conventions of Estates, the history of seals, and the office of justice clerk. His expertise rested on a particular mastery of unpublished manuscript sources, especially the records of the King's Council and the Session. These qualities explain why historians have been slow to see any need to revise Hannay's work. It may also be that the dense style of presentation favoured by Hannay has not helped to encourage further research on the topics he explored. Although it is sometimes remarked that Hannay's prose style renders his work particularly difficult to digest, being unduly weighed down with examples and cautious qualifications, this is unfair. It would be more accurate to say that Hannay was simply not concerned to provide a general synthesis with boldly stated descriptive overviews. He favoured a discursive analysis, grounded in detailed discussion of documentary evidence. His work is therefore not an easy introduction to the subject, because it tends to presuppose a basic knowledge of the developments in question. Even the one monograph he published on the history of the College of Justice is in the form of a series of essays rather than a systematic descriptive account, being aptly entitled *The College of Justice: essays on the institution and development of the Court of Session*.

Nevertheless, though neither introductory nor elementary, Hannay's writings are readable and have a clear, analytical style which has dated well. In scholarly terms, the detailed citation of primary sources and very considered analysis gave Hannay's interpretation both rigour and an authority which did not invite serious challenge for over fifty years. So persuasive was Hannay's analysis, and his ability to ground it in the evidence, that most subsequent general historical accounts adopted it without criticism, including those by Gordon Donaldson, A.A.M. Duncan, Rosalind Mitchison, Bruce Webster, and Jenny Wormald. In one of the more recent accounts by Michael Lynch, Hannay's influence is still evident alongside awareness of other perspectives. Lynch does not explicitly refer to the debate over the College's significance, characterising the foundation of the College of Justice simply as "one of the pretexts of James V's early clerical taxation". However, he also views 1532 as the "fruition" of the longer-term developments.[1] Specialist studies have also generally found Hannay persuasive, despite an early dissenting approach by Hector McKechnie.[2] Hector MacQueen followed Hannay's basic analysis in accepting that no institutional innovation is apparent in 1532, though he argued that nonetheless it seemed to give "impetus" to the legal development of the Session.[3] The most notable exception in the historiography was W.C. Dickinson, Hannay's successor at Edinburgh University. He stated in 1961 that "the erection of the College of Justice was partly a financial expedient, partly an attempt to secure a more efficient administration of justice", but also noted his conclusion that the College equated to "a supreme central civil court".[4] But for his premature death in 1963, there is every reason to think that he would have gone on to produce "an authoritative statement on the origins and development of the judicial council in the fifteenth and

[1] M. Lynch, *Scotland: A New History* (London, 1991), pp. 107, 164.

[2] See the discussion of McKechnie below.

[3] H.L. MacQueen, *Common Law and Feudal Society in Medieval Scotland* (Edinburgh, 1993), p. 242.

[4] W.C. Dickinson, *Scotland from the earliest times to 1603* (Edinburgh, 1961), pp. 308, 307. Professor Duncan left these passages unaltered in his revision of Dickinson's book: W.C. Dickinson, *Scotland from the earliest times to 1603*, rev. and ed. A.A.M. Duncan (3rd ed., Oxford, 1977), pp. 305, 312 (n. 9).

sixteenth centuries" in tandem with editing the surviving manuscript records for publication.[5]

Only two other books to date have been published on aspects of the history of the Court of Session, and neither are concerned with the foundation of the College of Justice. They therefore do not seek to discuss or question the essence of Hannay's account.[6] Hannay's interpretation of the foundation of the College has eventually come to be challenged, however, first by Athol Murray and David Sellar, then in more depth by the present author and most recently by John Cairns. Nevertheless, the underlying research and general analysis of the development of the Court of Session which Hannay made continues to command acceptance and respect from all those who have studied the subject. The challenges relate more narrowly to the significance of the foundation itself, and have been based largely on a re-interpretation of the evidence Hannay himself presented rather than the discovery of new material. No source material of importance has come to light whose existence was not already known to Hannay. The main new evidence has come from a fresh scrutiny of the manuscript record of acts and decreets in relation to topics passed over by Hannay, especially the question of jurisdiction. Even in this regard, Hannay was familiar with the detail of the record but simply omitted to consider such questions. Whilst he acknowledged this in admitting that "the aspect of the evolution which relates to law and procedure is a matter for professional learning, prepared for laborious investigations which in present circumstances may hardly be undertaken by busy men", it seems that its possible relevance to the wider institutional history escaped his attention.[7] It is therefore the fresh perspective gained by attention to the functioning of the Session as a law court which more than anything has allowed revision of Hannay's view by recent scholars. In particular, this has increasingly led to the rejection of his interpretation of the foundation of the College of Justice.

---

[5] A.L. Murray, "Preface", in *Acts of the Lords of Council Vol. III 1501–1503*, ed. A.B. Calderwood (Edinburgh, 1993), p. v.

[6] N. Phillipson, *The Scottish Whigs and the Reform of the Court of Session 1785–1830*, Stair Society 37 (Edinburgh, 1990); Winifred Coutts, *The Business of the College of Justice in 1600*, Stair Society 50 (Edinburgh, 2003).

[7] R.K. Hannay, *The College of Justice* (Edinburgh, 1933), reprinted in *The College of Justice: Essays by R.K. Hannay*, ed. H.L. MacQueen, Stair Society Supplementary Series 1 (Edinburgh, 1990), pp. xiii–xiv.

Hannay was motivated by a strong desire to demonstrate how relatively insignificant the foundation of the College was in the development of the Court of Session. In his view, it was at other periods that the crucial stages in the evolution of mechanisms of central justice from the fourteenth to the sixteenth centuries occurred. He placed the emphasis much earlier, in the reigns of James III and James IV. Before we re-assess 1532 itself, therefore, it is necessary to examine Hannay's view and his grounds for holding it. Three preliminary points should be noted. First, it will be seen that his view was more nuanced than has generally been realised and that subsequent scholars relying on Hannay have tended to oversimplify his analysis. Secondly, Hannay's views were already fully developed when he first addressed the subject in 1918, but some change of emphasis is apparent over the years as his subsequent publications appeared.[8] Thirdly, since there is very little extant evidence relating to the step of establishing the College of Justice, and almost none on the policy behind it, Hannay's interpretation of this aspect of the history of the Court of Session was necessarily mostly based on conjecture flowing from the limited circumstantial evidence. He interpreted the foundation as insignificant but could not demonstrate it as such because of the nature of the evidence.

Hannay's general thesis was summarised in the opening sentence of *The College of Justice*, where he stated that "the Court of Session was the product of a long development, and was in action before the reign of James V, in whose time the growing institution happened to assume the unexpected form of a College of Justice". However, behind this lies a more detailed set of claims which relate specifically to the foundation of the College itself. First, Hannay was concerned to argue that the College was not "founded" or "instituted" in 1532, but emerged from a more complex set of steps lasting at least a decade.[9] Secondly, the foundation had significance not in any "creation" of a civil court but simply in securing financial endowment of an institution already in existence.[10] Thirdly, the creation of the College was simply the "incidental result of an astute diplomacy" directed towards finding a

[8] There is also commentary on the College of Justice in an even earlier work by Hannay, but since it was co-authored it is not strictly possible to attribute the views it expresses to Hannay personally. See J. Herkless and R.K. Hannay, *The Archbishops of St Andrews* vol. 3 (Edinburgh, 1910).

[9] R.K. Hannay, "On the Foundation of the College of Justice", *Scottish Historical Review* 15 (1918), 30–46 at p. 37.

[10] Hannay, "On the Foundation of the College of Justice", p. 43.

pretext for exploiting the wealth of the church, after James V failed in the early 1530s to find a wealthy bride.[11] It was "accidental".[12] Fourthly, the idea of a college of justice was itself "extemporised rather than a maturely considered plan", and its appearance in 1531 was "sudden" and therefore "remarkable".[13] Fifthly, the effect of the foundation was very limited, involving "much less breach of continuity with the old Lords of Council than is generally supposed".[14]

However, Hannay's view of the foundation of the College of Justice in its wider context was not totally dismissive. Even though seeing its main significance as relating to endowment, he still regarded this in itself as "an important stage in the development of a civil court".[15] He also recognised a connection between endowment and function, referring to "the Lords of Session, now endowed for a particular function" in the new college, and he appeared to accept that this entailed the Session "entering upon an independent career".[16] He could acknowledge that it "contributed to establish the separate identity of the civil court", and even referred to "the endowment of the Session in 1532 as a separate court".[17] The new statutes made to regulate the proceedings of the College in 1532 also marked, in Hannay's view, "a distinct advance in order",[18] though elsewhere he placed the emphasis rather on the continuity with what went before.[19] Above all, Hannay's account of those longer-term developments which he did regard as important—the development of the institution of the Session during the reigns of James III and James IV and thereafter, and the progressive "differentiation of function" in general in the King's Council in the fifteenth and sixteenth centuries—seems to envisage the foundation of the College of Justice as being the culmination of those developments, however

[11] *Acts of the Lords of Council in Public Affairs 1501–1554*, ed. R.K. Hannay (Edinburgh, 1932), p. xxxvi [hereafter *ADCP*]; R.K. Hannay, *The College of Justice*, p. 37.

[12] R.K. Hannay, "Early Records of Council and Session, 1466–1659", in *An Introductory Survey of the Sources and Literature of Scots Law*, Stair Society 1 (Edinburgh, 1936), pp. 16–24 at p. 17.

[13] *ADCP*, pp. xlii, xxxviii.

[14] Hannay, 'On the Foundation of the College of Justice', p. 43.

[15] Hannay, 'On the Foundation of the College of Justice', p. 43. Also R.K. Hannay, *The Early History of the Scottish Signet* (Edinburgh, 1936), p. 38.

[16] Hannay, *The College of Justice*, p. 38.

[17] R.K. Hannay, "On the Antecedents of the College of Justice", *The Book of the Old Edinburgh Club* 11 (1922), 87–123 at p. 108; Hannay, "Early Records of Council and Session, 1466–1659", p. 17.

[18] *ADCP*, p. xxxix.

[19] Hannay, *The College of Justice*, p. 38.

imperfectly realised. In terms of recognising a path of development, for example, Hannay concluded his most detailed examination of the antecedents of the College of Justice by stating that "the foundation and endowment of the College of Justice was the inevitable end of a long development".[20] In examining the earlier stages of that development, he recognised that the functioning of Council as a regular judicial tribunal tended to create impulses towards certain types of institutional change, noting for example that, in relation to the *ad hoc* interplay between Council and parliamentary Auditors evident by 1478, "the whole situation pointed to adequate and stated sessions of council as the next step in development".[21] In stressing that "the Court of Session was the result of an evolution", Hannay wished to draw attention to the origins of the court under James III, and argued that it is "probably correct to say that under James IV the Court of Session became a definite institution", and more specifically that by 1504 it "had definitely taken shape". He even talked of its "inception" being in the reign of James III or, with greater "justification", James IV.[22] Nevertheless, he also argued that, with James IV, "the administration of civil justice by the council under him never became satisfactory", and that he never came to "decisively abandon the itinerant system for one central and sedentary court".[23] Also, his claims for the reigns of James III and James IV can be seen to lack solid analytical foundations, since at no point did he state the criteria he was applying in recognising when the Session could be regarded as having become an institution, or, more specifically, a properly functioning court of law. Furthermore, in relation to the reign of James V, Hannay tended to regard *any* institutional instability as relating somewhat exclusively to a need for endowment to allow payment of judges, stating that under Albany, "the condition of things was so unsatisfactory as to emphasise the need for institutional progress".[24] "Expedients" which came in the 1520s "led rapidly in the direction of endowment", and by 1531 "the actual sederunts were often so unsatisfactory as to indicate that remuneration of professional men was becoming imperative".[25]

[20] Hannay, "On the Antecedents of the College of Justice', p. 122.
[21] Hannay, "On the Antecedents of the College of Justice", p. 97.
[22] Hannay, *The College of Justice*, pp. 22, 24.
[23] *ADCP*, p. xxxi; Hannay, *The College of Justice*, p. 20.
[24] *ADCP*, p. xxxiii.
[25] *ADCP*, pp. xxxiii, xxxiv–xxxv.

This general framework does in some ways point to the significance of 1532, despite Hannay's fundamental purpose of demonstrating the opposite. Even Hannay's belief that the College's foundation was primarily a matter of financial endowment was related by him to longer-term developments which "had reached a stage at which it was coming to be seen that the working of the court required assiduity and the engagement of professional skill", producing an "acknowledged need" which could only be addressed by endowment.[26] Although Hannay noted that "a fund to maintain the civil judges was made the pretext for imposing upon the Scottish prelates a perpetual subsidy", he had already acknowledged that such a fund was indeed needed for an entirely genuine purpose relating to endowment.[27] Hannay's treatment of "differentiation of function" in central governance, and recognition of a "differentiating process" whereby the functions of the late medieval King's Council were gradually separated out and associated with distinct institutions, also tended to point to 1532 being significant, even if only because, relative to what had gone before, "differentiation of function had advanced so far" by this point.[28] In this regard, Hannay seems to have accepted that the foundation of the College was significant in at least some of its effects too, commenting that "it was only by a very gradual process, after the endowment of the Court of Session and the erection of the College of Justice, that record of Session and of Privy Council was differentiated".[29]

That Hannay's analysis was nuanced at least to this degree would not be easily surmised from the orthodox, dismissive view of 1532 which most subsequent historians have derived from it. This was stated most pithily by Professor Duncan in his seminal article on the central courts before 1532, published in 1958, where he wrote that "it is clear that the creation of the College of Justice was no more than an excuse to mulct the Church".[30] The only difference he was prepared to recognise in the new institution was a greater degree of permanence: "the 'new' court was but the old session in more permanent form".[31] Generally

[26] Hannay, *The College of Justice*, p. ix.
[27] Hannay, *The College of Justice*, p. x.
[28] Hannay, "On the Antecedents of the College of Justice", pp. 109, 110, 123.
[29] *ADCP*, p. vii.
[30] A.A.M. Duncan, "The Central Courts before 1532" in *Introduction to Scottish Legal History*, ed. G.C.H. Paton, Stair Society 20 (Edinburgh, 1958), pp. 321–340 at p. 336.
[31] Duncan, "The Central Courts before 1532", p. 336.

this view has continued to dominate works on Scottish history. The only scholars to depart substantially from it were Hector McKechnie and W.C. Dickinson. McKechnie's view is notable since it was advanced in the context of a more detailed argument about the development of procedure and jurisdiction. He attributed the acquisition of jurisdiction over fee and heritage to the foundation of the College of Justice in 1532.[32] His views were overlooked or not taken up, however, and, as we have seen, Dickinson was never to write a detailed study of the Court of Session. The main refinement to the Hannay-Duncan interpretation only came in the 1980s when some of the scholars already mentioned departed from Duncan's view to argue that his account did not address significant aspects of the foundation of the College of Justice. Some argued that at least the consequences following the foundation were significant, especially in the apparent assumption of a full civil jurisdiction by the court.[33] David Sellar went as far as to interpret the legislation of 1532 as conferring a new jurisdiction of fundamental breadth and importance upon the Session in its new guise.[34] Sellar's analysis has inspired more detailed research from which it has been argued by the present author that the foundation of the College of Justice may have been jurisdictionally significant.[35] However, Duncan's view of the institutional significance of 1532, with his assertion that the foundation of the College was no more than an excuse to tax the church, does not seem to have been directly challenged until later still, first by the present author and separately in an important article by Professor Cairns.[36] Of course, this more recent work is massively

[32] H. McKechnie, *Judicial Process upon Brieves, 1219–1532*, 23rd David Murray Lecture, University of Glasgow (Glasgow, 1956), pp. 8, 25, 29.

[33] A.L. Murray, "Sinclair's Practicks", in *Law Making and Law Makers in British History*, ed. A. Harding (London, 1980), pp. 90–104; H.L. MacQueen, "Jurisdiction in heritage and the lords of council and session after 1532", in *Miscellany Two*, ed. W.D.H. Sellar, Stair Society 35 (Edinburgh, 1984), pp. 61–85; W.D.H. Sellar, "The Common Law of Scotland and the Common Law of England", in *The British Isles 1100–1500*, ed. R.R. Davies (Edinburgh, 1988), pp. 83–99 at p. 94.

[34] W.D.H. Sellar, "A Historical Perspective", in *The Scottish Legal Tradition*, ed. Scott C. Styles (Edinburgh, 1991), pp. 29–64 at p. 44.

[35] A.M. Godfrey, "The Assumption of Jurisdiction: Parliament, the King's Council and the College of Justice in Sixteenth-Century Scotland", *Journal of Legal History* 22 (2001), 21–36. See now chapters 5–7 below.

[36] A.M. Godfrey, "The Lords of Council and Session and the Foundation of the College of Justice: a Study in Jurisdiction" (unpublished Ph.D. thesis, University of Edinburgh, 1998), chap. 6, esp. pp. 281–296; J.W. Cairns, "Revisiting the Foundation of the College of Justice", in *Miscellany V*, ed. H.L. MacQueen, Stair Society 52 (Edinburgh, 2006), pp. 27–50.

indebted to Hannay, and does not seek to rehabilitate the views he succeeded in refuting. The kind of influential earlier tradition which Hannay reacted against is exemplified by Bishop Keith's *History of the Affairs of Church and State in Scotland*, published in 1734, in which Keith remarked that because James V:

> observed that his subjects were at a great loss for want of a settled Court of Justice, managed by Judges learned in the law, he first instituted in Scotland the Court of Session or College of Justice, consisting of fifteen Judges, to remain fixed in a certain place, as it subsists to this day.[37]

Keith's equasion of the foundation of the Court of Session with the College of Justice certainly became untenable in the light of Hannay's work. However, the work of those who have followed Hannay now requires revision.

The need for revision follows from recognising the inevitable limitation on Hannay's perspective. This derived from his not taking into account the legal implications of the judicial business of the Session when assessing institutional developments, especially in relation to jurisdiction and procedure. He only referred to the question of jurisdiction twice, and both times in relation to that of parliament.[38] However, his assessment of the institutional history is also vulnerable to criticism, since so much is based on indirect inference, as well as certain of his own assumptions. In addition he chose to emphasise particular aspects of the foundation unduly, notably in relation to finance, and administrative development, with consequences for the tone of his overall interpretation. Hannay's concentration on the question of endowment, for example, came to assume too great a prominence in how he regarded the institutional change effected by the College's foundation. Repeatedly, Hannay chose to interpret evidence of problems in the operation of central justice, or reforms to its operation, as primarily reflecting a deeper problem of lack of endowment. However, this seems to have led him to unduly minimise other forms of institutional problem of the sort which still existed by the 1520s, such as those which arose from not restricting the sederunt to Lords exclusively nominated for judicial business. Hannay preferred to explain almost everything in relation to

[37] R. Keith, *The History of the Affairs of Church and State from the beginning of the Reformation... to 1568*, ed. J.P. Lawson and C.J. Lyon, 3 vols, Spottiswoode Society (Edinburgh, 1844–50), vol. 1, p. 57.

[38] Hannay, *The College of Justice*, pp. 3–4.

progress towards endowment. His assessment is therefore coloured by these assumptions, and without them requires revision. It can be seen to be unbalanced in this particular respect once it is acknowledged that the 1520s and early 1530s witnessed a variety of reforms to the Session, none of which particularly suggest or articulate the issue of endowment as having been considered of pre-eminent importance. It was Hannay's own assumptions which led him to cast endowment as the core issue.

An example is his view that "it was the bull of Paul III [of 1535] which chiefly conferred such collegiate status as was enjoyed, recognising, as it did, the right of the president and the senators to collect the revenue...".[39] This allowed Hannay to fragment the significance of 1532 by presenting 1535 as in this respect the more significant year when compared with passage of the earlier parliamentary statute in 1532. He also assessed all the varied problems of the Session in the minority under Albany as together leading "rapidly in the direction of endowment".[40] Again, he perceived there to be a lack of attendance by judges which meant that by 1531 "remuneration of professional men was becoming imperative".[41] If the Session was to function more effectively it required "assiduity", "professional skill" and this in Hannay's view obviously required "financial recognition of judicial labours".[42] Hannay insistently saw the central problem in the development of the Session by the reign of James V as being that "some source of remuneration for the lords of Session had been for years obviously needful", but he never actually demonstrated that this was recognised as such by contemporaries.[43] Thus he tended to see endowment as the principal goal of incorporation as a college, and undervalue other institutional changes brought about at the same time. The concentration on the endowment and its implementation in turn allowed Hannay to stress the drawn-out nature of *that* development and to minimise the significance of any immediate changes achieved in 1532. These included, for example, changes brought about by the parliamentary statute of 17 May or the statutes of the court made following its inauguration on

[39] Hannay, "On the Foundation of the College of Justice", p. 43.
[40] *ADCP*, p. xxxiii.
[41] *ADCP*, p. xxxv.
[42] Hannay, *The College of Justice*, p. ix.
[43] Hannay, *The College of Justice*, p. 38.

27 May and which were ratified by King James the following month.[44] Hannay was thus able to characterise the establishment of the College in the 1530s as "partial and ill-defined".[45] When considering reforms prior to 1532, Hannay had recognised that "development towards specialism" was a matter independent of the question of endowment, for example in arguing that developments in 1527 had significance in those terms.[46] In his more searching account in the introduction to *Acts of the Lords of Council in Public Affairs*, he acknowledged the importance of ordinances in 1527 as "a fresh effort to provide for civil justice", without trying to connect this with any need for endowment.[47] In discussing developments from 1532, however, he subordinated such matters to the question of endowment.

Apart from the interpretive emphasis upon financial endowment, the other specific aspect of Hannay's approach which also calls for re-evaluation relates to his model of administrative development. As we have seen, this turned on a perceived process of "differentiation of function in the King's Council".[48] It is a useful and valid concept for analysing governmental change in the fifteenth and sixteenth centuries. However, it also runs the risk of being somewhat rigidly schematic, with discussion of one or other "branch of activity" of Council, assessments of "capacity to deal independently with two distinct classes of business" in Council, and the charting of a "process" together with those moments when this process suffered "arrest".[49] This schematic approach to analysing differentiation of function led Hannay to evaluate the significance of 1532 as it affected a "court which had been developing through the departmental activities of the royal council".[50] This led him to regard the foundation of a new college which attempted to separate the judicial function of Council from its wider institutional role as cutting across this organic development. In addition, Hannay perceived the very form of a college of justice to be structurally alien. It derived in his view from an Italian model, was thus "very foreign and outlandish" and therefore problematic.[51] Even this treatment of differentiation of function was

[44] To be discussed below.
[45] Hannay, *The College of Justice*, p. 73.
[46] Hannay, *The College of Justice*, p. 35.
[47] *ADCP*, p. xxxiv.
[48] *ADCP*, p. xxxii.
[49] Hannay, "On the Antecedents of the College of Justice", p. 110.
[50] Hannay, *The College of Justice*, p. xi.
[51] Hannay, *The College of Justice*, p. 49.

coloured by Hannay's view of the essence of the foundation of the College being the step towards endowment. He thought that from this perspective "the origin and circumstances of the endowment tended as much to stunt as to stimulate growth".[52]

The seminal and authoritative nature of Hannay's work means that it has been necessary to examine closely the nature of Hannay's interpretation, in order to make it clear why there is a need for a different approach. It has also been suggested already that his views were more nuanced than is often realised. In addition, the work he is best known for—his book on the College of Justice—happens to be the one in which he expressed his views most strongly, with something of a polemical edge. In this work he drew a particularly sharp distinction betweeen the development of the Session and the foundation of the College of Justice, referring to the "ill-considered suggestion for a 'college of judges in civil causes'" and to the "extraordinary supposition that the inception of the College of Justice was also the beginning of the Court of Session".[53] In addition, the account given in the *The College of Justice*, compared to the others he wrote, devoted more space to the diplomatic framework surrounding James V's quest for a royal bride than to those aspects of the College of Justice which reflected development of the Session itself. This naturally tended to result in an emphasis on the foundation of the College as an incidental by-product of these international negotiations. In such a presentation, the implications for the Session, as a court of law, of the foundation of the College were overshadowed. When Hannay's book is placed alongside his other studies, the nuances in his views and the thread of development in the history of the Session up to 1532 become more apparent. For all these reasons—namely the scope for offering new interpretations based on alternative inferences from the evidence, the removal of assumptions (about the role of endowment and the internal logic of administrative development in terms of differentiation of function), and the viewing of Hannay's work systematically as a whole—it is possible to accept almost everything in the substance of Hannay's account whilst arguing that his interpretation of the foundation of the College of Justice is unconvincing and ripe for review.

---

52 Hannay, "On the Foundation of the College of Justice", p. 44.
53 Hannay, *The College of Justice*, pp. 56, 38.

Institutional developments in the 1520s and early 1530s

The conclusion that the foundation of the College of Justice in 1532 was institutionally insignificant follows in large part from assessing its importance in isolation from the general path of development of the Session over the preceding years. Even when those developments are acknowledged, the foundation of the College is too often seen as an extraneous development, quite separate from those which had already unfolded in the 1520s and early 1530s. As we have seen, Hannay emphasised the connection the foundation had with Scottish diplomacy, international relations and royal marriage aspirations, the desire of the church for stable relations with the crown, and designs to raise crown revenue through taxation of the church. This was a question of emphasis, since Hannay also charted the pre-1532 development of the Session itself very carefully. Correspondingly, however, this emphasis heavily influenced his interpretation of 1532. At best he saw the foundation as of marginal immediate importance. If the College of Justice is placed primarily in the context of preceding developments in the Session, however, it becomes possible to recognise it as furthering coherent reforms which built upon and extended measures which had already been attempted or adumbrated in previous ordinances. There was something more than simple continuity. The vehicle for these reforms was nothing less then a new institutional framework, as realised by the incorporation of the College of Justice. That framework remained permanently thereafter. Even if it did not immediately result in wholesale operational changes in how the Session functioned, nevertheless the framework of the College conditioned the operation of the Session from 1532 onwards and gave it a corporate identity as a law court distinct from Council. But to place it in context, its connections with the developments of the 1520s and early 1530s require to be examined, and the reforming ordinances of 1526, 1527 and 1531 need to be surveyed. It will be seen that they were mainly designed to select particular Lords of Council to act as judges on the Session, and to exclude those Lords who did not receive this specific commission. There is a direct continuity of purpose with the College of Justice, since the main institutional change brought about by its foundation was restriction of the right of attendance to a smaller and more exclusive body of Lords of Session. Admission to their number had to be made by specific commission from the King, and in time might require the consent of the Lords themselves. Indeed, only with the College of Justice did the selection of a fixed number of Lords for the work of the Session become embodied in an institution which gave those Lords for the first time a distinct corporate identity.

The ordinances of 1526 and 1527

Professor Cairns has usefully characterised the second half of the 1520s as witnessing "a concerted attempt to deal with the problems of civil litigation".[54] By contrast, we can see the early 1520s as providing evidence of the importance of the Session in various pronouncements from the duke of Albany, the Council and Parliament, but not showing any attempt at reform. As we saw in the previous chapter, August 1524 marked something of a new beginning following the departure of the duke of Albany in May of that year. The regency of Queen Margaret was effectively resumed, with the support of the earl of Arran. The King was formally invested with personal authority in July, and attended Council in August, albeit this was for show and symbolic importance alone, given the King's youth.[55] Significantly, Gavin Dunbar, the King's preceptor, and now postulate of Glasgow (i.e. awaiting papal bulls of confirmation and subsequent consecration as archbishop of Glasgow) was already in attendance at the Council. Dunbar was to become president of the Session in 1527, chancellor of the kingdom in 1528, and later in his capacity as chancellor retained the right to preside as "principale" over the Session in its new form from 1532.[56] He seems in his person to provide the thread which links and gives pattern to the various changes to the Session from the mid-1520s onwards. At this stage in the summer of 1524 there is little sense of innovation in arrangements for the Session, but in September 1524 an ordinance made more clearly visible the arrangements for Council and Session, with the first resort in this period to the technique of naming those Lords eligible to sit. Sittings of Council and Session are implicitly distinguishable in the arrangements but a common list of names is given.[57] This is still probably not a reflection of any development in the Session, given that it occurred during the transition from Albany's rule to the short-lived revival of Margaret's control during these months. Dr Emond has characterised it more as a belated recognition of the need

[54] J.W. Cairns, "Revisiting the Foundation of the College of Justice", in *Miscellany V*, ed. H.L. MacQueen, Stair Society 52 (Edinburgh, 2006), pp. 27–50 at p. 30.
[55] G. Donaldson, *Scotland: James V–James VII* (Edinburgh, 1965), p. 38.
[56] See D. Easson, *Gavin Dunbar* (Edinburgh, 1947).
[57] *ADCP*, pp. 210–211.

to attend to the judicial business of Council, with the Session having initially been continued in early August until late October 1524.[58] An emphasis upon judicial business was evident in provisions of the Parliament of November 1524, which formalised many arrangements made under the new regime. The Session was to begin immediately, after lords and persons of "best knowlege and experience" had been chosen from the three estates to sit (the statute explicitly refers here to the three estates of Parliament).[59] In the same vein, little more than a year later an ordinance in February 1526 showed the Session being reinforced by Council with specialist named Lords, who, having been "adjonit with the lordis of the secrete counsale and ministeris of court", were urged to "sitt continuale apoun the sessioune".[60] By this time, the earl of Angus had seized control of the government and had custody of the young king. Although not unopposed, most Lords and most important royal officials accepted the Angus coup of November 1525, Archbishop Dunbar being one of those who continued to attend Council.[61] The importance of the conduct of judicial business in the Session was recognised, but still no structural reform is particularly evident. Noting that the additional Lords included ecclesiastical judges, heritable sheriffs and a lawyer, Cairns has commented upon the traditionalism of this expedient, pointing out that it marked "a return to an earlier practice of deliberate strengthening of the Council with trained and experienced lawyers".[62]

It is the ordinances from 1527 onwards which strongly suggest development, and provide the basis for Cairns' view that there was "a concerted attempt to deal with the problems of civil litigation". Detailed rules were made which reflect a move to regulate the Session more firmly. With an ordinance of 13 March 1527, there was the first important structural change to the institution of the Session since 1503, and one which served to enhance its identity as distinct from Council generally. The political context was that the period 1526–28 saw the dominance of the earl of Angus, following his retention of custody of the King's person in November 1525. In itself this does not seem to

[58] W.K. Emond, "The Minority of King James V" (University of St Andrews, unpublished Ph.D. thesis, 1988), p. 426.

[59] *APS* ii, p. 286, c. 6.

[60] *ADCP*, p. 238.

[61] Emond, "The Minority of King James V", p. 487.

[62] Cairns, "Revisiting the Foundation of the College of Justice", p. 31.

have informed any particular development of the Session as a matter of policy, though Archbishop Dunbar retained his influence, and Dr Emond has noted that under Angus the sederunts of Council (i.e. the daily list of those attending) do "reflect the basic reliance of the administration on lesser men who carried on government because the law was coming to be recognised as their profession".[63] The ordinance provided for an immediate Session, and named individually all those entitled to sit as judges. It was to be conducted "be the lordis and otheris personis of his [i.e. the King's] consell undirwritin".[64] The implication is that only those "undirwritin" were entitled to sit. Provision is made for a president, who was to be Archbishop Dunbar, with two alternatives named in case of absence. It is impossible to determine whether the nomination of a president has any institutional significance, since it could have simply been an expedient to fill the place of the chancellor, that office being vacant between the dismissal of Archbishop Beaton in July 1526 and the taking of the office by Angus himself in August 1527.[65] But clearly it could be suggestive of administrative differentiation of function that an office of president was created for the Session, and that this was subsequently retained and carried over into the College of Justice. It is also hard to know whether there could have been additional political and practical reasons for setting out the names of Lords in this way, rather than institutional ones. Such reasons could have stemmed from a need to provide a clear basis for the operation of the Session following the effect on attendance and business at Council of the changes of regime from Albany's in 1524 through Margaret's in 1525 to that of Angus in 1526, with associated factionalism and instability.

The thirty Lords eligible to sit under the March 1527 ordinance are listed, first the "spiritualite", second the "temporalite". The exclusive nature of the list is emphasised by the extension of membership in a separate clause to the absent James Beaton, archbishop of St Andrews, Gavin Dunbar, bishop of Aberdeen (and uncle of Archbishop Dunbar), and Colin, earl of Argyll "quhen tha returne agane", all along with "sum othiris that now ar absent be license of his grace".[66] In other words, had these three not been named, the implication is that they would not have been able to sit. If so, the idea of exclusively listing

[63] Emond, "The Minority of King James V", p. 549.
[64] *ADCP*, p. 256.
[65] Donaldson, *Scotland: James V–James VII*, p. 40.
[66] *ADCP*, p. 256.

Session judges, along with nominating a president, would seem to mark some further innovation, though again it is difficult to assess the extent to which this simply reflected contingent needs of the time. The actual sederunts of the Session in this period show that average attendance was smaller than the maximum would have permitted, often less than fifteen, except for the last months of 1527.[67] In the sederunts of this year Dr Emond has identified a core of what he describes as virtually professional administrators acting as judges. These included Adam Otterburn, the King's advocate, Nichol Crawford, the justice clerk, Archibald Douglas of Kilspindie, the treasurer, Sir William Scott of Balwearie and John Dingwall, provost of the collegiate church of Holy Trinity. Emond noted the continuity which was to follow through this group, apart from Douglas, becoming judges in the College of Justice at its foundation.[68] Dr Emond also argued that "the traditional rights of all Lords to come to the Council and act as judges had been eroded by successive attempts to define who were to be the judges on the Session".[69] Although to some extent this can already be seen in the September 1524 and February 1526 ordinances, it is harder to discern any serious erosion of this nature before the more significant ordinances from 1527 onwards.

The other important ordinance of 1527 is undated.[70] Hannay placed it in 1528 in his study "On the Antecedents of the College of Justice",[71] although in the nineteenth century Thomas Thomson had placed it in 1527. Hannay apparently reconsidered the matter, since he printed it in 1527 in *The Acts of the Lords of Council in Public Affairs*, published ten years after his earlier article. Following Hannay's final dating, it is here assumed to have been of December 1527. Nothing seems to turn on establishing the exact date, though it should be noted that Angus lost control of the King and of government in June 1528. The first article of this ordinance is highly significant, since it makes an explicit prohibition of any Lords, other than those named by the King, from sitting on the Session:

> in the first ye sall gar writ in a table with greit lettiris the namis of tham that we subscrivit to be on the cession, charging tham to await tharapon

[67] Emond, "The Minority of King James V", p. 549.
[68] Emond, "The Minority of King James V", p. 549.
[69] Emond, "The Minority of King James V", pp. 549, 569 (n. 155).
[70] *ADCP*, p. 272.
[71] Hannay, "On the Antecedents of the College of Justice", p. 115.

> and at all othiris lordis and othiris men knaw thaim selffe and ingeir tham nocht to the thing at tha ar nocht chosyne to, and affix this table on the conselhous dor to be seyn with eviry man at cummis tharto.[72]

This is a very stark statement of a completely novel principle, that even a Lord of the King's Council should be debarred from the council chamber when it was sitting as the Session, on the basis that Session was specifically a "thing at tha ar nocht chosyne to".

That explicit royal permission could formally be felt necessary before somebody could sit on the Session is hinted at by the fact that fifteen months later, in March 1529, James Colville of Ochiltree had to produce "ane writing subscrivit by the kingis hienes desirand the lordis to admitt the said James to be ane of the sessioune, chekkir, generale counsale, and all uthiris tymis as accordis". For whatever reason, this seems to have been felt necessary in order that he be admitted to the Session by the other Lords of Council and Session. We are told that the Lords admitted him because it was "thocht resonable" by them, implying some formal deliberation.[73] This example is difficult to generalise from, since Colville had shortly before stepped down from the office of comptroller, which had entitled him *ex officio* to sit on Council, and his subsequent special admission to a place on the Council reflected particular regard for him in the King's eyes and the desire to retain his services despite his demission from office. The King's letter concerning Colville stated that he had been given a lifetime gift of the office of director of chancery, and should be "ane of oure counsale and have place tharof in oure sessioune, chekkir, generale counsale and all uthir tymis as accordis". Colville's admission back into Council in this way may therefore not constitute a precedent for any general procedure. Nevertheless, the fact that matters were approached in this way in 1529 seems telling, especially the apparent recognition that, even following a decision on the matter by the King, it was still formally necessary for the Lords of Council themselves to "admit" a new member and recognise his status, in the light of the approach evident in the two ordinances of 1527. It was for the Lords to "adjunit" Colville to their number. However, this admission of Colville back into Council was also stated in terms which remind us that in 1529 the Session, Exchequer and Council were all still seen as a unity, as branches of the King's

[72] *ADCP*, p. 272.
[73] *ADCP*, pp. 306–307.

"great council", even though the 1527 ordinances seem to demonstrate some structural pulling away of the apparatus of the Session from the rest of the Council.[74]

Relative to 1513–1524, the years 1524–28 had seen the Session meeting in a more regular way. Although regimes still changed, the overall political instability of the minority was reduced. However, it also appears that the pressure of business was as high as ever. The ordinances of 1527 seem in part to represent attempts to re-articulate in some detail the proper form of proceeding in Session, and the ending of some particular abuses. Both were concerned with the "greit impediment to the lordis in proceding apon caus" due to the "inoportone solistation and crying" of people in the council chamber, as well as "lettres to stop justice" gained illicitly in the name of the King.[75] The second ordinance even recorded the King's instruction (no doubt drafted by Dunbar) to observe the stated "forme and ordour in mynistration of justice and reuling of the conselle hous".[76] As already discussed, it went on to dealt with how those who were to be on the Session (as opposed to Council more generally) were to have their names listed in a table, with a charge to them "to await tharapon", as well as detailed instructions as to who should be admitted to the chamber, and when they should receive "licence" to enter when the Session was meeting. Further rules were set out concerning the role of forespeakers, processing of simple bills of complaint, privileged matters concerning recent spuilzie or the reduction of letters, and safeguards for the Lords of the Session to deliberate in private. The two ordinances seem to represent an attempt to insulate the work of the Session from political pressures and interference, to streamline the protocols for its procedure and to try to ensure an adequate sederunt for it to proceed. Session was of course still seen directly as a function of Council, even if some of the expedients and practices adopted tended to separate it off in certain ways and entrench certain distinctions between different functions in terms of institutional identity. It seems possible, however, that at least a core of judges on the Session were developing something of a self-conscious

[74] I am greatly indebted to Dr Athol Murray for drawing my attention to the nuances behind the basic fact of Colville's admission, and generously sharing with me his own observations on the matter.

[75] See A.M. Godfrey, "Civil Procedure, Delay and the Court of Session in Sixteenth Century Scotland" in *The Law's Delay: Essays on Undue Delay in Civil Litigation*, ed. C.H. van Rhee (Antwerp, 2004), pp. 107–119 at pp. 116–117.

[76] *ADCP*, p. 272.

sense of identity by 1527. Hannay commented on this as a more general feature of the minority of James V, stating that since 1513:

> the Lords of Council, acting as representative of the prevailing political faction at a time when the authority of the crown was intermittent or feeble, developed a strong sense of their importance in administration... of which the admittance of Colville to the bench is an example.[77]

Whether this had any influence before 1532 in bringing about the jurisdictional change to be traced in later chapters is an interesting question. In any event, government during the minority was consistently through the Council, despite factionalism and instability having their effect, and the Session remained very directly a function of the Council.

By 1527, a formal change in the organisation of the Session had therefore occurred in terms of the structure of personnel, and the next five years saw further developments. The period 1513–1527 had seen as great a flow of judicial business to Council and Session as ever before. Innovations in organisation, just as before 1513, were designed to contain and process this business. It may be significant, too, that it was from 1527 onwards that decisive changes came about, because since the summer of 1526 the youthful James V had started to show a new independence of will.[78] An example is his asserting himself through the execution of a bond to the earl of Lennox, a leading opponent of Angus, at the end of June 1526.[79] By June or July 1528, James V was truly in control of government. Whether or not James displayed personal interest in the functioning of the Session, his personal rule brought to the heart of government men who did, above all Gavin Dunbar, who became James' chancellor in 1528. It is striking that within only four years of James V beginning his personal rule we see the foundation of the College of Justice.

The ordinance of February 1531

In 1531 there was for the first time since 1527 a major ordinance regulating the Session.[80] It specifically concerned the "ordouring of the sessioun and lordis that suld have voit tharin".[81] Although it constituted in part a fresh attempt to tackle some of the problems already addressed

---

[77] Hannay, "On the Antecedents of the College of Justice", p. 117.
[78] Emond, "The Minority of King James V", p. 486.
[79] Emond, "The Minority of King James V", p. 504.
[80] *ADCP*, p. 349.
[81] *ADCP*, p. 349.

in 1527, it also represented a more general and significant development in the recasting of the Session as a separable compartment of Council's business. Tellingly, it was "presentit" to Council by Archbishop Dunbar as chancellor, having had the ordinance subscribed by the King. It was concerned only with arrangements for the Session, not other Council business. Strikingly, the role of the chancellor is explicitly enhanced: he is clearly the leading figure in the Session, the one who is envisaged as sitting (and, implicitly, presiding) "daly", alongside those other lords in attendance. He has authority to license absences by other judges and to command their presence too. He is to give orders to the official acting as the macer (i.e. usher) in control of admission to the chamber. He is to decide who is allowed access to the chamber. He is responsible for enforcing all the regulations as to order, and any failure to do so is to be regarded as "negligence".

The arrangements for other Lords reveal a greater change still. Thirty-five Lords are named, not including the chancellor himself. However, "the prelatis and temporale lordis be bot present at thar plesour". The operation of the Session is to rely residually on the "remanent", who shall attend "daly with our chancelar and sworne to determe and decyde in all actiouns cuming befor thaim eftir thar connyng and knawledge". These included the royal office holders such as the justice clerk, secretary, treasurer and named men with professional experience of law and administration. Thus, the innovation of 1527 is repeated, in that there is a large pool of Session judges named, and "nane uthiris" are to have a vote or participate in Session business. However, a new provision is that, of this group of thirty-five, at least fourteen must sit with the chancellor in the holding of the Session, and may not depart without his permission. They must even "return again at his command or quhen he pleis to wryte for thame". The remainder of the provisions concern the more precise regulation of the manner of appearance by parties and advocates, and certain procedural matters. It would appear from the text of this ordinance that up until this time Lords of Council were coming to sit on the Session whether or not they had been nominated to do so after 1527, using their votes—and perhaps exhibiting partiality or bias—in the making of decisions, causing confusion, preventing justice being done and undermining the keeping of order in proceedings.[82] Since 1527, the keeping of order in the sederunt of the Session must have continued to be a problem,

---

[82] ADCP, p. 349.

it having been one of the purposes of the "table with greit letteris" of that year to overcome such difficulties.[83]

It is interesting, and arguably highly significant, that this ordinance of 1531 should have been made within a month of the arrival of Thomas Erskine, the royal secretary, in Rome on a diplomatic mission to the pope in tandem with the duke of Albany, and little more than six months before the papal bull concerning James V's supplication to the pope relating his desire to establish a college of justice in Scotland. It was of course only in this bull of September 1531 that we first hear of the project to establish a college of justice as such. Hannay did not seem to detect significance in the timing of the bull, even though it came only months after the earlier ordinance of 1531. This earlier ordinance had surely betrayed a failure to resolve long-standing difficulties in the work of the Session, and, as we have seen, had attempted to adapt more extensively than ever before the operation of the Session as a separate branch of Council activity in order to secure proper order in the transaction of judicial business. It is here that Hannay seems to have been unduly distracted by what he considered the mystery of how the proposal to incorporate a college of justice had come about. He seems to have assumed that the appearance of the idea of incorporation as a college of justice could not be explained except by pointing to the inspiration of some foreign model. For this reason, he considered that the proposal for a college of justice was likely to have been devised by Erskine during the course of the diplomatic mission in Italy, and then passed on to Albany, who remained behind in Italy to represent the interests of the Scottish crown. It does not seem to have occurred to Hannay that it could have represented an idea and an organisational concept for a reconstituted Session which had been thought out wholly in Scotland as the means by which the well-known problems in the running of the Session could be surmounted. The 1527 and 1531 ordinances alone imply that considerable thought was being given to the way the Session was functioning and how this could be improved. There is no direct evidence for the origin of the proposal for reconstituting the Session as a college of justice, but when seen in the context of the previous ordinances discussed it seems highly probable that it must have sprung from a considered domestic policy, as opposed

[83] *ADCP*, p. 272.

to being the improvised pretext of a crown servant preoccupied with papal diplomacy.

We have seen how a theme of these years was the nomination of particular judges for the Session, and the exclusion of members of Council generally unless so nominated. It is here that we can see a significant connection between the policy behind those ordinances and that behind the foundation of the College. In addition, there was a corresponding continuity in the selection of the same Lords of Council to be judges for the Session. However, this represents evidence for the *continuity* of an existing policy which was only finally realised in 1532, not evidence that 1532 somehow lacked significance because the choice of judges remained mostly unchanged. Fourteen of the fifteen judges nominated in 1532 had been named in 1531, and eleven of them back in 1527. This shows that the King and his closest advisers knew whom they desired to sit on the Session, but had to resort to formal devices both to ensure or legitimise their attendance and to bar other Lords from sitting. Since the Session was a judicial sitting of the King's Council itself, special rules would clearly be required if it was intended to exclude the generality of Lords who could sit on Council. Dr Andrea Thomas has commented upon "the number of names which can be located both within the royal court or household and within the Court of Session" in arguing that the nomination of a select bench for the College of Justice may in part have been "intended to extend the operation of the royal prerogative rather than solely to formalise the disinterested administration of impartial justice".[84] However, it is hard to see how the King's own interests were more readily advanced by litigation in the post-1532 Session, reconstituted as the College of Justice, instead of the pre-1532 Session. In addition, the overlap between the personnel of the royal court and household, the Session bench and the King's Council is itself not in any way surprising, given the relatively small and intimate nature of Scottish governance. As we have seen, the restriction of the Session bench through a policy of nomination dates back several years before 1532 in any event, and predates the start of James's personal rule in 1528. It is conceivable that the young James V would have approved of restricting noble influence over the judicial function of the King's Council by removing those functions

[84] A. Thomas, *Princelie Majestie: the Court of James V of Scotland, 1528–1542* (East Linton, 2005), p. 13.

to a specially nominated College of Justice over which he had more direct influence. However, the problem with such a thesis is finding any evidence to suggest this was a material consideration at the time. By comparison, there is reasonable evidence to suggest that nomination of select judges was part of a wider policy to reform the operation of the Session as a law court from the 1520s onwards.

The key theme of the ordinances since 1527 was to exclude Lords of Council who had not been nominated. The repeated naming of Lords has often been seen as a sign that the exclusionary nature of these rules was not being observed, and the terms of the 1531 ordinance themselves state as much. This is precisely the problem which we can see as having been successfully addressed, however, in the foundation of the College of Justice. The idea of conciliar work being undertaken by a fixed body of men separately constituted from the activity of the main Council would have been relatively novel, though the practice of the Parliament as well as the auditorial Session of the fifteenth century would have provided obvious institutional precedents. A sense of innovation compared to the normal practice of Council is suggested, however, by the need for repeated lists of nominees since 1527. Another reason may have been that the nominations tended to present themselves as governing only the particular Session which was forthcoming, rather than "the Session" in general. Short of the creation of a new institution to envelop it, the Session was not and could not be structurally separate from Council since it was by definition nothing more than a function of Council. The King's Council itself was not a fixed body of individuals and so it was problematic to make the Session comprise a fixed group of Lords. That is why, despite the growing exclusivity of the Session, the groups nominated to sit were usually well over thirty strong. Only some would sit at any one time.[85] In other words, the system used until 1532 was to have a large pool of Lords of Session, from which the Lords of particular sittings would have to be drawn. It was still not a fixed body of judges in 1531. Rather, the judges were drawn from an undifferentiated larger body which—without repeated ordinances such as were made from 1527—was equivalent to the full regular Council itself.

[85] See *ADCP*, p. 349 for the specific requirement in 1531 of fourteen Lords to sit with the Chancellor.

The other reason given for the February 1531 ordinance had been "to put all thingis in bettir form". It seems significant that the King and Council had this particular concern seven months in advance of the issuing of the papal bull which first mentioned the College of Justice. There is no explicit evidence to link the reform efforts of 1527–1531 with the conception of the scheme to establish a college of justice. However, as a matter of inference it seems highly probable that there must have been a link of this sort, rather than that Erskine or Albany invented the idea without previous consideration. After all, Sir Thomas Erskine, who had been royal secretary since October 1526, had himself been *ex officio* a Lord of Session since at least that point.[86] There were other royal servants and councillors sitting regularly too—Otterburn, the King's advocate; Crawford, the justice clerk; John Dingwall, the provost of Trinity College Church; Sir William Scott of Balwearie; Gavin Dunbar, the chancellor; and Alexander Mylne, abbot of Cambuskenneth. The ordinances since 1527 were being produced by some directing mind for James V to approve, and this must have been Dunbar, perhaps in consultation with others. It seems plausible to suggest that the impetus for these ordinances and the detail they contained may have derived from the work of these regular core-members of the Session. In this case, the idea for a college of justice is likely to have come from the same source. The mooting of some such scheme could have lent to James V a suitable pretext for an approach to Rome for money, but is hardly likely to have been simply concocted for no other reason than to justify such an approach. Hannay himself recognised this up to a point, in that he distinguished the plan to endow the Session (which he attributed to Archbishop Dunbar, and which related to longer-term development) from the scheme for a college of justice (which he attributed to Erskine and saw as an improvisation), but, even so, both seemed to him to form a single "pretext" for a papal subsidy.[87]

The diplomatic approach to the papacy

This reconsideration of the late 1520s and early 1530s suggests that once 1532 is seen in this context it assumes clear significance, especially when the coincidence in time is noted between measures being taken

---

[86] *ADCP*, p. 256.
[87] Hannay, *College of Justice*, p. 54.

in Scotland to reform the workings of the Session in February 1531 and the mission to Rome undertaken by Erskine, who had left Scotland in December 1530 with communications both for the pope and for Albany.[88] Albany too had already been instructed by James to travel from France to Italy on his behalf.[89] In 1530 James V's marriage diplomacy had become more active, and the King approved in the autumn a commission to Albany to represent his interests in relation to seeking the hand of Catherine de' Medici. Catherine was the orphaned daughter of Lorenzo II de' Medici, duke of Urbino and heir of the ruling family of Florence. Her mother was Madeleine de la Tour d'Auvergne, an orphaned Bourbon heiress whose sister happened also to be married to Albany. Albany therefore had a personal interest as Catherine's uncle. In addition, Cardinal Giulio de' Medici, who controlled Florence and became Pope Clement VII in 1523, was also *de facto* in as close a relation as an uncle, being the nephew of Catherine's great-grandfather, Lorenzo the Magnificent, and therefore a near cousin and in effect Catherine's guardian. Catherine had in fact grown up under the direct supervision of Clement in Florence in the early 1520s and moved to be with him in Rome in October 1530, returning to Florence in 1532.[90] Albany's mandate from James V to "convene with the ambassadouris of uthir princis to avise, treit, consent, concur and conclud sic thingis as sall be thocht expedient for the commoun wele of all Christianitie" had been exhibited to and approved by the Council in November 1530. A commission, instructions and other writings to be sent to Albany were also approved.[91] Albany had power to act as procurator for the King and to even contract the marriage *per verba de presenti*.[92] Apart from the need for Albany to consult with Clement and other members of the Medici family, there were complex questions relating to negotiation of the dowry and the provision and transfer of property as part of the dowry. But most interestingly, the marriage negotiations were not the only matter James wished to raise with the pope. This is apparent from further instructions to Erskine which are mentioned by James in a letter

[88] *Letters of James V, 1513–1542*, collected and calendered by R.K. Hannay, ed. Denys Hay (Edinburgh, 1954), p. 189.
[89] *Letters of James V*, p. 182.
[90] L. Frieda, *Catherine de Medici* (London, 2003), pp. 13–31; R.J. Knecht, *Catherine de Medici* (London, 1998), p. 12.
[91] *ADCP*, p. 342.
[92] *ADCP*, p. 343.

to the pope in November 1530.[93] Professor Cairns has suggested very plausibly that it was in these instructions to Erskine that the proposal for the College could have been relayed.[94]

The difficulty is that the royal letter in question does not reveal the content of the additional instructions. Hannay summarised James as stating to the pope that:

> though his business with the pope and the college of cardinals is in charge of Albany, James has matters of special secrecy in mind (*quedam secretiora mentis nostre*) which he will not commit to writing, and Albany may be preoccupied. He sends his secretary Erskine with instructions for Albany and to supply his place when it is permissible.[95]

It seems a reasonable inference that these matters of special secrecy certainly related, amongst other things, to proposals for a grant of taxation on the church by the pope, and this was Hannay's own view.[96] In a further letter to the college of cardinals, James stated (as calendered in Hannay's words) that he had "entrusted to Erskine certain business, partly concerning the royal affairs, partly for the honour and good estate of the church in Scotland".[97] We also know from a separate royal letter that one such matter was James' desire to see Dunbar given powers as papal legate *a latere*. However, given the continuity in royal personnel—Dunbar and Erskine especially—and the policies they were pursuing in relation to the Session, as well as the attempts of 1527 and the forthcoming attempt of February 1531 to reform the operation of the Session, it seems plausible to suggest that Erskine's instructions could also have contained the proposal for a college of justice. This would fit with the contents of the February 1531 ordinance, the basis for which must have been in the mind of Dunbar at some point over the preceding few months. This surmise would also remove the need Hannay felt to explain the proposal, when it came, as being an unpremeditated improvisation.

Against this view could be cited the failure of the pope's letter to the Scottish prelates of 9 July 1531, concerning taxation proposals, to

---

93 *Letters of James V*, p. 182; the full text in Latin is printed in A. Theiner, *Vetera Monumenta Hibernorum et Scotorum quae ex Vaticani, Neapolis ac Florentiae Tabulariis deprompsit et ordine chronologico disposuit* (Rome, 1864), p. 593.

94 Cairns, "Revisiting the Foundation of the College of Justice", p. 30.

95 *Letters of James V*, p. 182.

96 Hannay, *The College of Justice*, p. 47.

97 *Letters of James V*, p. 183.

refer to founding a college of justice but instead to the "protection and defence of the realm".[98] If the College of Justice was the main item of discussion in relation to the need for a papal grant of taxation, the failure to mention it at this point seems surprising. However, we simply do not know the full course of discussion in Rome in 1531, and only glimpses are afforded by the extant documents. We do know that once Erskine was in Rome he was aware by March 1531 that the proposed royal marriage to Catherine de' Medici could no longer be pursued, since Francis I of France had stepped in (through the offices of Albany) to secure Catherine as a bride for his second son Henry. Erskine then left Rome to return to Scotland, leaving Albany to represent Scottish interests.[99] Although Hannay suggested that Albany could have received fresh instructions by the summer of 1531, none has become extant.[100] The papal letter of 9 July makes it clear that a request for papal subsidy had explicitly been made by this time—and the "great tax" of 10,000 ducats a year would have been a very large subsidy indeed. The pope moved a week later to grant a lesser subvention *pro tempore* by unilaterally imposing a tithe on the church in Scotland for three years, referring to a variety of factors, not just defence of the realm, though again not mentioning the College.[101] It is only a further two months later that the College is the explicit basis for the subsequent papal bull of 13 September 1531.[102]

This chronology certainly does not preclude the possibility that the College of Justice proposal had been part of Erskine's instructions back in the autumn of 1530, nor that it had been put to the pope in the spring of 1531 once Erskine was in Rome. It was because of two particular assumptions that Hannay did not consider this possibility. First, he assumed that the failure of the College of Justice to be mentioned in July 1531 must have meant that it had not been canvassed at all by then. Though not an unreasonable assumption as such, this can only be a matter of inference, since we do not have evidence for all that transpired in Rome. Secondly, his assumption that the problems of the Session could all be related to a need for financial endowment meant that the significance of its sudden appearance as the basis for

[98] Hannay, *The College of Justice*, p. 52.
[99] Hannay, *The College of Justice*, p. 51.
[100] Hannay, *The College of Justice*, p. 51.
[101] Hannay, *The College of Justice*, p. 52.
[102] Cairns, "Revisiting the Foundation of the College of Justice", pp. 38–39.

the September bull was in his eyes also purely financial. The College proposal was therefore in Hannay's view a simple substitution of a new justification to give legitimacy to financial help which James V desperately needed in any event. In turn, Hannay assumed that the endowment issue would have only come into play once it was realised that new justifications were needed in the course of 1531 to buttress the King's proposal to the pope in relation to a subsidy. If, however, we dispense with these assumptions and instead view the problems of the Session in terms of its functions as a law court, and as more broadly institutional ones rather than narrowly financial ones, we can see how the idea of founding a college of justice could have been an item of business in its own right. Whilst such a foundation would naturally require endowment, endowment was far from being the only step required to realise the aims in question. Other institutional reforms would be needed too. On that assumption, all we may be seeing in the autumn of 1531 is the consolidation of different strands of existing and established policy and diplomacy into a single proposal to establish a college of justice, endow it, and have authorised a liberal grant of taxation on the church to sustain it. Even if King James, Sir Thomas Erskine and Archbishop Dunbar somehow introduced the College of Justice proposal by correspondence at a late stage in the summer of 1531 (as Hannay speculated—"there was just time for an interchange of letters"—though if so they do not survive),[103] this can still be interpreted as a marriage of two strands of policy which both, independently, had distinctive bases and were already in existence. Hannay may have been right to see as an extemporisation the linking of general taxation proposals with a plan to establish a college of justice, but his assumption that this implies that the idea of founding a college of justice was itself an extemporisation is unwarranted. Besides, even if the foundation of a college of justice were to have been progressed independently, endowment would still have been required. The nature of any extemporisation may have simply been that various proposals to exploit the wealth of the church were by the summer of 1531 collapsed together into one consolidated proposal in which the foundation of the College of Justice was elevated to providing the main purpose for the papal grant.

---

[103] Hannay, *The College of Justice*, p. 54.

The proposal to incorporate as a college

Further new arguments made by Professor Cairns in an important reassessment of the foundation of the College of Justice support the interpretation advanced so far. In particular, Cairns has concluded that the idea of establishing a college of justice "was certainly royal policy before 1531".[104] Amongst a wide range of new insights, two principal points presented by Cairns undermine Hannay's interpretation. First, Cairns has broken with the idea that the concept of endowing the Session in the form of a college of justice is puzzling and can only be explained by reference to foreign models. Hannay himself criticised an earlier tradition dating back to the seventeenth century, and associated with the seventeenth-century lawyer Sir George Mackenzie, which saw the parliament of Paris as the model for the court. Hannay effectively refuted this suggestion.[105] However, he then argued that there was a foreign model for the name, if not the institutional arrangements, which was to be found in the *Collegio dei Giudici* of Pavia. Erskine had been a student in Pavia and Hannay imagined that Erskine may have borrowed the idea of a college in order to make the Scottish proposal one which would be "intelligible to Italians, and would convey the requisite intention that the prelatical contribution was to be appropriated to this purpose".[106] Subsequently Professor Peter Stein followed this general approach, but suggested that, given Erskine's absence from Rome after April 1531 and the absence of any extant correspondence from Erskine on the matter, the duke of Albany himself was a more likely source for the proposal. Furthermore, since Pavia was but one of a number of Italian colleges of judges, Albany too could have been expected to have been familiar with the Italian model.[107] In fact, the more relevant point still which should now be added is that whatever Albany knew of Italian judicial institutions, he knew far more about the Scottish Session, since as governor during the minority of James V he had himself sat frequently on the Session and given strong support to progressing its judicial business during his three periods of residence in Scotland

[104] Cairns, "Revisiting the Foundation of the College of Justice", p. 37.

[105] Hannay, *The College of Justice*, pp. 22–24. See further comment in J.D. Ford, *Law and Opinion in Scotland during the Seventeenth Century* (Oxford, 2007), p. 313, especially n. 179.

[106] Hannay, *The College of Justice*, p. 54. See also pp. 49–50.

[107] P.G. Stein, "The College of Judges of Pavia", *Juridical Review* 64 (1952), 204–213 at p. 213; Hannay, *The College of Justice*, pp. 48–50.

between 1515 and 1524. In his involvement in plans relating to the Session in 1531, it was his own extensive experience of Council and Session which he would surely have drawn upon. And in other ways it is clear that even in the 1530s Albany remained actively involved in Scottish affairs even though outwith Scotland, for example in the conflict over jurisdictional rights and legatine powers between the two Scottish archbishops, Beaton of St Andrews and Dunbar of Glasgow.[108] Furthermore, Cairns has pointed out that "the idea of creating a *collegium* as an incorporated body to hold property for a specified institutional purpose was perfectly familiar in Scotland", citing the examples of collegiate churches and universities and noting that such bodies were also incorporated and confirmed by papal bull.[109] A letter of James V to Clement VII in March 1532, for example, could quite naturally refer to the Trinity Collegiate Church and Hospital in Edinburgh as simply "a college of some fame".[110] The only previous scholar to point out the significance of making the Session a college in this sense was W.C. Dickinson, who noted in this regard that "a 'college' is a society instituted for certain common purposes and possessing special rights and privileges".[111] Furthermore, Cairns has demonstrated that such terminology was normal at the European level in association with law courts, and does not need to be linked with particular national models in order to be made explicable. Thus there is no reason not to assume that the idea of creating a Scottish college of justice was a natural step which would have seemed quite obvious to James V and Archbishop Dunbar. It is therefore plausible to suggest that it could have been adumbrated in the years before 1532, especially if endowment was by this time seen as one of the particular needs of the Session (which would require a corporate legal structure in which the right to the endowment could vest).

The second important new point to be taken from Cairns' article relates to a close reading of the language used in the various documents relating to the Session and college of justice in these years, especially in the last of the earlier ordinances reforming the operation of the Session in 1531. Cairns demonstrates the presence of language which forms a unifying thread linking the attempts to reform the pre-1532

[108] Herkless and Hannay, *The Archbishops of St Andrews*, pp. 212–215.
[109] Cairns, "Revisiting the Foundation of the College of Justice", p. 29.
[110] *Letters of James V*, p. 217.
[111] Dickinson, *Scotland from the Earliest Times to 1603*, p. 307 (n. 3).

Session with the foundation of the College of Justice itself. This thread seems to imply the continuous involvement of Archbishop Dunbar. As Cairns puts it:

> close examination of the language used surrounding the project ... strongly suggests, as Hannay sometimes hints, that it was probably the result of a policy developed by Gavin Dunbar, who became chancellor in 1528, but who had started to influence royal thinking on justice the year before.[112]

Cairns draws attention to the close similarity between the February 1531 ordinance and provisions which appeared the following year in the statute of May 1532 concerning establishment of the College of Justice. However, he has also demonstrated a connection with the intervening papal bull of September 1531. The 1531 ordinance had referred to membership of the Session extending to the Lords spiritual and temporal and "persouns of cuning knawledge and undirstanding". The statute of 1532 which was to establish the College of Justice referred to the institution of "ane college of cunning and wise men". Cairns has pointed out that the bull of September 1531 refers to the pope having learned from Albany of James V's intention to establish a "*collegium proborum et literatorum virorum*", which Cairns translates simply as "a college of honourable and literate men". Cairns has also observed that, when phrases in the 1532 statute which resulted from (arguably) late amendments are put to one side, the original article before parliament can be acknowledged as "a very precise attempt to start work on the creation of a college of justice in line with the bull".[113] Finally, a further letter of James V proposing the allocation of the profits of royal seals to members of the College in 1532 referred to the "institution of ane college of litturate men of knawledge and experience".[114] Cairns concludes that "the bull, the act and the letter are all closely related in terminology and understanding".[115] As Cairns suggests, given Dunbar's likely authorship or responsibility for the 1531 ordinance and the 1532 letter, we can regard the four documents from 1531 and 1532 as all reflecting a single conception and scheme of development demonstrated

[112] Cairns, "Revisiting the Foundation of the College of Justice", p. 37.

[113] Cairns, "Revisiting the Foundation of the College of Justice", p. 34.

[114] The document is printed in Cairns, "Revisiting the Foundation of the College of Justice", p. 45, as published by Hannay in "On the Foundation of the College of Justice", p. 39.

[115] Cairns, "Revisiting the Foundation of the College of Justice", pp. 32–33.

by their reliance on related terminology. As we have previously noted, Dunbar had sat on the Session since 1524, was its first president in 1527, and assumed overall control of the Council from 1528 as chancellor. It is perfectly plausible to regard the 1531 ordinance as a preliminary step which presupposed the subsequent foundation of the College, but which further step would first require papal approval and arrangements for its endowment to be made. If so, this is a further reason why the "matters of special secrecy" entrusted to Erskine on his trip to Rome, and which James mentioned in his letter to the pope of 2nd November 1530, were likely to have included the plan to erect a college of justice and have it endowed through a papal subsidy.

The process of foundation

The events of 1532

Of the main claims made by Hannay which were outlined at the start of this chapter, two in particular remain to be discussed—that the College of Justice was not "instituted" in 1532 as such, and that the effect of founding the College was extremely limited. Both require an assessment of what happened in 1532, and what changes arose as a result. It has already been argued that the foundation of 1532 should be seen as a further step in the line of ordinances which regulated the work of the Session from the 1520s onwards, and not as a free-standing, singular or surprising development. It furthered a royal policy for development of the Session which was in evidence by 1527 at the latest. In relation to the form of the council register in 1527, Hannay had noted that "the record itself seems to indicate that resolute action began in this year".[116] The size of page expands in that year and the presentation and handwriting become neater and more exact. Just because the foundation of a college of justice could additionally function by 1531 as a pretext for a grant of clerical taxation far exceeding that which might be needed to endow such a college, it does not follow that it was intended to serve no other purpose.

1532 is usually taken to be the year of the foundation of the College of Justice because of the parliamentary statute of that year. The form which the foundation took involved the entrenchment of the

[116] Hannay, *The College of Justice*, p. 32.

pre-existing Session. As we have seen, this was a branch of the work of Council which possessed certain discrete institutional characteristics. As already argued, it is likely that a desire to entrench the Session in this way was responsible for prompting the scheme for a college of justice, and of course securing endowment would be an essential part of establishing the court on a lasting basis. Hannay himself acknowledged that the step to becoming a college entailed at least one formal change represented by the vesting of a "corporate right to levy the assigned ecclesiastical revenues".[117] The entrenchment of the Session would therefore have required financial subsidy from some extraneous source in any event. For this reason, it could lend itself to the procurement of a papal subsidy as part of the process of rendering the Session in collegiate form. As Cairns has persuasively argued, the choice of a collegiate form was a perfectly natural adjunct to such a reform of the Session. It should simply be seen as reflecting adoption of the normal vehicle of incorporation for such institutions—a standard institutional structure of the age.[118]

It is of course true that the process of establishing the College of Justice was in formal terms somewhat drawn out. At one level, it was not completed until 1541, though in fact most steps had been taken by 1536. Scrutiny of the significance and function of each stage in the process makes it clear, however, that it was the events of 1532 which were fundamental in institutional terms. Cairns has added further weight to this view by persuasively arguing that, quite apart from the need to recognise the significance of 1532, the suggestion of undue delay in the whole ten-year process is inaccurate and misleading. On the contrary, once the nature of the project is understood in a practical context, it seems neither unduly neglected nor left in a dysfunctional and ill-defined state following 1532. The duration of the proceedings can be explained by the practical complexity of arranging for two papal bulls, parliamentary legislation and a provincial council of the church, not to mention the working through of the financial measures to support the College. When measured against other foundations such as the establishment of the university of Aberdeen in 1495, as Cairns points out, the time taken over the College of Justice does not appear

---

[117] R.K. Hannay, "A Study in Reformation History", *Scottish Historical Review* 23 (1926), 18–33 at p. 24.

[118] Cairns, "Revisiting the Foundation of the College of Justice", p. 29.

unduly protracted. It can be seen that it was typical for the completion of such matters to require a substantial period of time.[119]

It could be added that the drawn out nature of the proceedings is in fact evidence of the opposite of inattention. This is because it can be taken to demonstrate the thoroughness with which King James and Archbishop Dunbar approached matters. First of all, this involved Erskine and Albany's mission to Rome in 1531 to secure papal approval for the College and formal agreement to the taxation of the church. Next it involved the securing of an act of parliament to establish the College back in Scotland.[120] Then there followed negotiations with the Scottish prelates which resulted in modifications to the initial papal grant of taxation (according to Hannay this took until September 1532)[121] and the need to send a further mission to Rome (the King was pressing his agent in Rome, John Lauder, in this regard in June 1533).[122] It is possible that some slight delay was caused by the death of Pope Clement VII on 25 September 1534, after which he was succeeded by Alessandro Farnese as Pope Paul III. It was then in March 1535 that the necessary papal bull was issued under the new pope, confirming the institution of the College.[123] This was possible once the necessary framework had been agreed institutionally and financially and the College established. This still had to be followed, once the bull reached Scotland, by the summoning of a provincial council of the Scottish church to give its approval in 1536.[124] The final step was the further act of parliament of 1541, but again Cairns has noted that this act was necessary simply to ratify the foundation and its endowment once the King had reached

---

[119] Cairns, "Revisiting the Foundation of the College of Justice", p. 35.

[120] *APS* ii, p. 335, c. 2; *ADCP*, pp. 373–377.

[121] Hannay, "A Study in Reformation History", p. 25.

[122] A. Teulet, *Relations Politiques de la France et de l'Espagne avec l'Ecosse au XVIe Siecle* vol. 1 (Paris, 1862), p. 93. The letter in question is undated, ascribed to 1535 by Teulet, but Hannay rejected this and finally placed it in June 1533 in *Letters of James V*, pp. 242–244, having initially implied a date around April 1534 in Herkless and Hannay, *The Archbishops of St Andrews*, p. 228.

[123] The process on the bull is printed in Keith, *The History of the Affairs of Church and State*, pp. 467–482 (the version cited by Hannay) and (with minor differences of transcription) in *The Acts of Sederunt of the Lords of Council and Session; From the Institution of the College of Justice, In May 1532, to January 1553* (Edinburgh, 1811), pp. 91–104. An extract from the latter is printed in Appendix 9 of Cairns, "Revisiting the Foundation of the College of Justice", pp. 48–49.

[124] *Statutes of the Scottish Church, 1225–1559. Being a translation of Concilia Scotiae Ecclesiae Scoticanae Statuta... with Introduction and notes by David Patrick*, Scottish History Society 54 (Edinburgh, 1907), pp. 238–242.

his age of majority—his "perfite" age of twenty-five years.[125] Not all of these steps related exclusively to the issues of financial endowment, for example the statutes of the court itself which the King ratified in June 1532.[126] When taken with the parliamentary statute of the preceding month and the inaugural sitting of 27 May, however, we can reasonably regard these statutes of the court as marking completion in 1532 of the institutional aspects of the foundation. Remaining formalities and the provision of the endowment caused the process of establishment to last until 1541, but upon closer examination this seems entirely understandable and suggestive of the seriousness with which the *ancillary* steps necessary for the foundation of a college on a permanent basis were pursued and completed.

Thus it is undeniable that 1532 does count as one of a series of significant dates in the foundation. Yet it is difficult to see any of the related measures as quite so significant as the parliamentary statute of that year. The other measures were all ancillary. Insofar as the statute lacked detail, it was provided instead in the statutes of the court which were approved shortly afterwards. As discussed already, it was the papal bull of 13 September 1531 which first mentioned the desire of James V to found a college of justice.[127] Subsequently, the bull of 1535 related that the pope had now been informed that the College—the *collegium justitie*—had duly been instituted by King James. Meanwhile, on 11 March 1532 the King had summoned a parliament specially to enact the statute for establishment of this college of justice. The proclamation made no mention of that particular purpose, using a more general form of words that the King "has divisit and ordanit ane parliament ... for certaine gret materis ... concerning the universale wele of this realm".[128] This, of course, was simply a standard form used in proclamations of parliament, and carried no particular import in this context. That Parliament was summoned especially with this intention in mind can be inferred from its subsequent proceedings, especially from the fact that only three general statutes were passed. One was simply an ordinance that previous statutes be more stringently executed. The other

[125] Cairns, "Revisiting the Foundation of the College of Justice", p. 37; *APS* ii, p. 371, c. 10.

[126] *ADCP*, pp. 373–377.

[127] Keith, *The History of the Affairs of Church and State*, pp. 464–466; *Acts of Sederunt*, pp. 85–87; appendix 1 of Cairns, "Revisiting the Foundation of the College of Justice", pp. 38–39.

[128] *ADCP*, p. 371.

was a traditionally expressed statute on the authority and freedom of the church which in one form or another was passed at the beginning of every parliament, though this one paid special tribute to Clement VII by name.

In the light of James' dealings with the papacy at this time, this profession of support for the church must have been considered diplomatically important, especially in the light of the pope's concern about the risk to Italy of an Ottoman campaign following those in Hungary in 1526 and 1529 (the latter penetrating as far as Vienna), and developments in the Mediterranean, not to mention the spread of heresy within Europe.[129] In May 1531 the Venetian ambassador to the French court was able to report to the Doge and Senate news from Istanbul which suggested an attack on Italy by the Sultan that very year, with rumours that it could even attempt to reach Rome itself.[130] The need for a show of support had seemingly been urged upon James by the papal nuncio Silvester Darius, who had travelled to Scotland in person to deliver papal letters on the matter which James considered in March 1532.[131] April 1532 was to see a third Ottoman land campaign in Europe, crossing the river Raab into Austria itself. Clement had severe concerns about the risk to Italy from the Mediterranean. It was only thirty years since Venice had been at war with the Ottomans. In 1532 Khair ad-Din Barbarossa, the leader of the Barbary corsairs and Ottoman governor of Algeria since 1518, became admiral of the Ottoman empire, a disturbing scenario for Clement as well as Charles V, given the corsairs' strength as a maritime power in the western Mediterranean. In 1534 Barbarossa did indeed carry out destructive raids on the Adriatic coast of Italy, prompting Charles V in 1535 to eject the corsairs from Tunis and La Goletta.[132] By 1538 hostilities in the Mediterranean were to have resumed between the Ottomans and the Holy League of Venice, Charles V and Clement's successor as pope, Paul III.[133] James wrote to the pope on 27 May 1532 referring to the concerns expressed to

[129] C.L. Stinger, "The Place of Clement VII and Clementine Rome in Renaissance History", in *The Pontificate of Clement VII: History, Politics, Culture*, ed. K. Gouwens and S.E. Reiss (Aldershot, 2005), pp. 172–174.

[130] K.M. Setton, *The Papacy and the Levant, 1204–1571*, 4 vols. (Philadelphia, 1976–84), vol. 3, p. 346.

[131] *Letters of James V*, p. 211.

[132] G.R. Elton, *Reformation Europe 1517–1559* (London, 1963), pp. 158–159.

[133] R. Bonney, *The European Dynastic States 1494–1660* (Oxford, 1991), pp. 137, 290–292.

him. This was the very same day that the Session first met following the act of parliament on the College of Justice ten days earlier. James stated that he had received from Darius papal letters discussing the "formidable preparations" of the Ottomans to invade Christendom, and requesting the King's aid "to defend Italy". At exactly this time Clement was seeking subsidies generally for this purpose, even requesting one from the college of cardinals.[134] It is possible that Clement's compliance in imposing taxation on the Scottish church was as much motivated by the desire to encourage James to provide a subsidy to him for defence against the Ottomans as to secure James' loyalty to Rome in religious affairs. In February 1533, Clement was to grant two tithes to Francis I, for example, in an attempt to encourage him to mount an expedition against the Ottomans.[135] James acknowledged the threat of the Ottoman fleet and related that, having consulted the magnates in parliament, he would send a representative to Rome to join in the provision of financial support.[136] It is also worth noting that the statute on the liberties of the church in 1532 was more elaborate than usual, and that a certified copy was ordered by the Lords of Council to be provided for Darius to give to the Pope.[137] Therefore, for external reasons this statute, though normally a formality, had special import.

Nevertheless, the only substantive legislation of the parliament of May 1532 was the statute concerning the institution of a college of cunning and wise men, which became commonly referred to as the College of Justice (as it was in the papal bull of 1535).[138] It is worth setting out the text of the statute of 1532 in full:

> Item, anent the secund artikle concerning the ordoure of justice, becaus our soverane is maist desyrous to have ane permanent ordour of justice for the universale wele of all his liegis and, tharefor, tendis to institute ane college of cunning and wise men, baith of spirituale and temporale estate, for the doing and administracioune of justice in all civile actiounes and, tharefor, thinkis to be chosin certane persounes maist convenient and qualifyit therfore, to the nowmere of xiiij persounes, half spirituale half temporall, with ane president; the quhilkis persounes sall be auctorizate in this present parliament to sitt and decyde apone all actiouns civile and nane utheris to have voit with thaim onto the tyme that the said college

[134] Setton, *The Papacy and the Levant*, p. 360.
[135] Setton, *The Papacy and the Levant*, p. 370.
[136] *Letters of James V*, p. 223.
[137] Hannay, *The College of Justice*, pp. 55–56; *ADCP*, p. 379, 17th June.
[138] *APS* ii, p. 335, c. 2.

> may be institute at mare lasare; and thir persounes to begyn and sitt in Edinburgh on the morne eftere Trinite Sonday quhill Lammes, and thereftire to have vacance quhill the xix day of Octobere nixt thereftir, and than to begin and sitt quhill Sanct Thomas evin effore Yule, and thereftir to begin apone the morne efter the Epiphany ["New Yer" deleted] ay and sitt quhill Palmsonday evin, and therefter to begyn on the morne efter *Dominica in Albis*[139] and sitt quhill Lammes; and thir persounes to be sworne to minster justice equaly to all persounes in sic causis as sall happin tocum before thaim, with sic utherir rewlis and statutis as sall pleise the kingis grace to mak and geif to thaim for ordouring of the samin. The thre estatis of this present parliament thinkis this artikule wele consavit and, tharefor, the kingis grace, with avise and consent of the saidis thre estatis, ordanis the samin to have effecte in all punctis and now ratifyis and confermes the samin and has chosin thir persounes underwrittin to the effecte forsaid, quhais processes, sentencis and decretis sall have the samin strenthe, force and effecte as the decretis of the lordis of sessioune had in all tymes bigane, ["that is to say" deleted] providing alwayis that my lord chancelare, being present in this toune or uther place, he sall have voit and be principale of the said counsell, and sic uther lordis as sall pleise the kingis grace to enjone to thaim of his gret counsell to have voit siclik to the nomer of thre or foure. That is to say, the Abbot of Cambuskynneth, president, Maister Robert Bothuile, Sir Jhone Dingwell, Maister Henry Quhite, Maister Robert Schanwell, vicare of Kirkcaldy, Maister William Gibsone, Maister Thomas Hay, Maister Arthoure Boyis, the Lard of Balwery, Schir Jhone Campbell, Maister Adam Ottirburne, James Colvile of Est Wemys, the justice clerk, Maister Francis Bothuil [and] Maister James Lausoune, and thir lordis to subscrive all deliverance and nane utheris eftire that thai begyn to sitt to minster justice.[140]

Hannay viewed this statute as hollow in content, commenting that "no scheme had been thought out" and "the ill-considered suggestion for "a college of judges in civil causes" was now found to involve serious practical difficulties in realisation", leading to "attempts to fix an extraneous type of institution to the "Lords of Council and Session" as they had evolved during the best part of a century".[141] This was something of an over-dramatisation by Hannay. As we have seen already, the College was not based conceptually on any such "extraneous" institution. Hannay was referring in particular to the inclusion of a right for the chancellor and up to three other Lords, nominated by the King, to sit. Hannay

[139] First Sunday after Easter: *A Source Book of Scottish History Volume Two 1424 to 1567*, ed. W.C. Dickinson, G. Donaldson and I.A. Milne (Edinburgh, 1953), p. 48.

[140] *The Records of the Parliaments of Scotland to 1707* [hereafter *RPS*], ed. K.M. Brown et al. (St. Andrews, 2007), 1532/5.

[141] Hannay, *College of Justice*, pp. 56–57.

argued on the basis of the phrasing of the parliamentary record, which plainly shows the deletion of certain words, that this represented a modification to the original legislative proposal.[142] This view has since been accepted by other scholars, Cairns characterising the additional text as an interpolation.[143] Hannay regarded this modification as otherwise inconsistent with the creation of a separate court, since it would conflict with both the role of the president of the College (who could be displaced by the chancellor) and the impartial status of the Session as a court (because it would be at risk of being weighted with additional nominees of the King). He saw the additional Lords as serving "to represent not only the interest of the King but an element in the Privy Council which could not with equanimity suffer civil justice to be left in the hands of persons qualified, it might be, to administer law, but feudally inconsiderable".[144] This was surmise on his part, since there is simply no evidence demonstrating why the original proposal for the College was modified in this way, if indeed it was. All we know is that modifications may have occurred during deliberations in parliament. Moreover, even if these provisions are regarded as contradicting the idea of making the Session structurally independent of Council, the fact is that they did not themselves modify that structural independence to any significant degree.

The effect of the supposed amendments was not to change the basic scheme for the College to include a president who would sit with fourteen other judges, but rather to supplement it. This could have worked to undermine the work of the Session if the general principle requiring special nomination to the College of Justice to sit as a Session judge was subverted by it. In practice, however, any potential undermining could only be to a minor degree, given the small and fixed number of additional Lords permitted, and the continuing close practical interrelationship of personnel on the Council and on the Session. More importantly, the principle of an exclusive membership requiring specific nomination was still formally preserved. In fact, the provision can be interpreted in the opposite way from Hannay. It strongly emphasised that the College of Justice was seen as structurally independent in a novel way, since otherwise there would have been no need to state an

[142] Hannay, *College of Justice*, p. 103.
[143] Cairns, "Revisiting the Foundation of the College of Justice", p. 34.
[144] Hannay, *College of Justice*, pp. 35–36.

explicit limit upon the numbers of additional Lords from the King's "grete counsell" which the King was entitled to nominate to sit in the Session after 1532. Hannay had considered that "the project conflicted with the traditional conception that 'Session' was a periodical function of the Council, enlarged rather than divided for the purpose".[145] He saw it as problematic for the College that the Session had hitherto been organically embedded in the overall structure of the King's Council, as "one department of the Council's activity, arranged and directed under the supervision of the chancellor, manned by royal officers, other privy councillors, and persons 'adjoined' for the special function".[146] Again, this point can be inverted to emphasise that the College of Justice could not have been regarded by contemporaries as insignificant but could only have been seen as a major innovation in these terms, notwithstanding the continuity which informed how the Session continued to function within the new structure.

Hannay was struck by the lack of detail in the parliamentary statute of 1532 and its stated reliance upon an intention to found a college, rather than an express and immediate act of foundation. However, in the context of establishing such an institution, this lack of detail seems far from unusual or unexpected. The royal supplication of 1495 for the foundation of the university of Aberdeen provides a useful comparison in the light of Leslie Macfarlane's assessment of it. He noted how it was in most respects expressed "in the simplest and most general terms". Furthermore, "all that one might suppose to constitute the most important details was omitted, and emphasis was given only to the need for such an establishment in Old Aberdeen". However, Macfarlane observed that "this... was the correct procedure. The details would take a long time to work out, and they would have to follow later, once the pope had given his initial *fiat*".[147] The parallel with the statute of 1532 is not exact, especially since many important details were in fact included in it, even at this stage. Furthermore, the statute of May 1532 was followed by a further detailed set of statutes made by the court itself and which James ratified in June 1532. Nevertheless, the example of Aberdeen cautions against the making of assumptions relating to the significance or otherwise of the level of detail in the 1532 statute.

---

[145] Hannay, *The College of Justice*, p. 35.

[146] Hannay, *The College of Justice*, p. 56.

[147] L.J. Macfarlane, *William Elphinstone and the Kingdom of Scotland 1431–1514* (Aberdeen, 1985), p. 293.

Hannay's negative view of the 1532 statute extended to his claim that it did not itself institute or found the College of Justice. It is true that there was from a formal point of view no single moment when the College was described at the time as being technically "instituted". In a sense the very method of foundation necessarily resulted in a process lacking one exclusively climactic moment. This was primarily because the process of foundation entailed a series of measures, including parliamentary statutes, papal bulls, resolutions of a church council, and the promulgation of statutes of procedure by the court itself. However, it was also because the "foundation" involved the reconstitution of an existing institution which was never itself dissolved but rather reshaped. However, to regard the College as having *never* in fact been instituted—as Hannay once did—is simply perverse in relation to the recorded proceedings of 1532 in Parliament and the Session.[148] First should be considered what may have been intended in 1532, and then what followed afterwards. It is true that the parliamentary statute of 1532 does seem to envisage a future moment when "the said college may be institute at mare lasare".[149] The 1532 act contains prefatory statements speaking by way of preamble of the King's intentions in instituting a college "of cunning and wise men" for the administration of civil justice. The specific clause of legislative enactment only seems to begin thereafter with the resolution that "the quhilkis persounes sall be auctorizate in this present parliament to sitt and decyde apone all actiouns civile and nane utheris to have voit with thaim onto the tyme that the said college may be institute at mare lasare".[150] Hannay seems to have come to view Pope Paul III's bull of March 1535 as responsible for finally "erecting" the College of Justice. However, the bull itself stated that (in Hannay's words) "recently King James informed his Holiness that he had, with advice of his estates in Parliament, actually instituted the College".[151] As a long-stop, the formal steps in creating

[148] See Hannay, "On the Foundation of the College of Justice", p. 37.

[149] *A.P.S.* ii, p. 336.

[150] *RPS*, 1532/5; *APS* ii, pp. 335–336, c. 2.

[151] Hannay, *The College of Justice*, p. 63. One section of the bull reads: "Cum autem, sicut prefatus Jacobus Rex nobis, qui dicto predecessore, sicut Domino placuit, sublato de medio, divina favente clementia, ad summum Apostolatus apicem assumpti fuimus, nuper exponi fecit ipse hujusmodi Collegium Justitie proborum et literatorum virorum, unius Presedentis, Prelati semper Ecclesiastici, ac quatuordecim aliarum personarum, quarum media pars in dignitate Ecclesiastica constituta semper existat, per eundem Jacobum et pro tempore existentem Scotorum Regem electorum et eligendorum, qui de dictis causis Regnicolarum predictorum, ut prefertur, cognoscant, illasque audiant,

the College had surely been fully completed with this bull of March 1535. However, the parties seem to have considered that the King had already instituted it some time before.

Given that the Parliament of May 1532 had been specially summoned with a view to establishing the College of Justice, it would in any event have left a period of two months or so to contemplate a scheme after the proclamation which led to the meeting of the Parliament. A further ten days followed from the passing of the statute on the College of Justice on 17 May until the next meeting of the Session on 27 May. The phrase "mare lasare" therefore does not imply that no scheme had been thought out (because one could have been thought out in the time available) but that it was considered obviously appropriate for the Lords of Session themselves rather than Parliament to make the detailed rules for the new college. Unlike the position forty or fifty years earlier, the Session had become a much more regular and coherent body, and one more capable of fulfilling such tasks as drafting a procedural code. The Lords could be delegated to do this by Parliament quite naturally. Besides, as we have seen, Archbishop Dunbar had fulfilled since 1527 a guiding role in the development of the Session, alongside a core of other regular council judges. Therefore, neither on the basis of its lack of detail nor its postponement of the moment of institution of the College can the parliamentary statute be regarded as unimportant on functional grounds. Its purpose can be seen as fundamentally political in enshrining in legislation the adoption of a formal statement of design, a framework to regulate the College of Justice, rather than as codifying a detailed technical scheme of operation. Sure enough, less than a fortnight after this parliament, we find that detailed rules were ordered to be made by the Lords of Session. The rules which followed carried detailed provision for the operation of the court.[152] The remaining aspects of institution not dealt with in May and June 1532 were concerned solely with the implementation of the financial endowment, and the formal confirmation of the arrangements by the pope and Parliament. Such confirmation is found as a formality in the papal bull erecting the College, necessary only because it was being funded by ecclesiastical monies. Ratification in the statute of 1541,

---

decidant, et fine debito terminent in ejus supremo Parliamento, de concilio et assensu trium statuum dicti Regni, sua regia auctoritate instituerit....". See Keith, *The History of the Affairs of Church and State*, p. 469; *Acts of Sederunt*, p. 92.

[152] *ADCP*, pp. 373–378.

as we have seen, was related to the King reaching his full age. These matters following 1532 were incidental to the functioning of the new college, whose establishment was otherwise complete in 1532.

The earlier moment of institution presupposed by the 1535 bull would naturally appear to refer to the statute of May 1532, were it not for the reference in that statute to the College being "institut at mare lasar". This might have referred to a *process* of further steps constituting institution as much as to a particular moment of inception. This might suggest a presupposition that 17 May marked the formal inception. Even if it was a future moment of inception which was being adumbrated in the statute, that still leaves one further intermediate step which can be plausibly regarded as the formal institution of the College. This was the meeting of the Session on 27 May, ten days after Parliament. The Session had last sat on 15 May, and so this was literally the first meeting since the enabling legislation had been passed. Attention to the precise details of what is recorded in the council register for that day justifies regarding this as the "institution"—or inauguration, as Cairns puts it—of the College. Cairns justifiably regards the parliamentary statute of 17 May as "moving towards creation of a College of justice", whilst the meeting of the Session on 27 May actually constituted its "inauguration". What remained in parliamentary terms was simply that "final confirmation of the College had to wait until the king's revocation" in 1541.[153] The meeting of the Session on 27 May was the materially important moment of institution, especially given the statement in the statute that institution was to follow at "mare lasare".

Numerous details on 27 May stand out as signifying an inauguration. As Hannay noted, "the record begins elaborately, and the first capital is decorated".[154] The King was present and, unusually, signed retrospectively every page of the register to show his approval of the statutes of the court subsequently set down there. These statutes were completed between 27 May and 10 June. The King's explicit instruction is recorded on 27 May that statutes should be drafted and they were ratified by a royal letter of 10 June which is copied into the register. The sederunt of 27 May lists the Lords present by describing the status of each individual in terms of the enabling legislation—Dunbar's membership by virtue of holding office as chancellor and Alexander

[153] Cairns, "Revisiting the Foundation of the College of Justice", pp. 34, 37.
[154] *ADCP*, p. 374. See fig. 1.

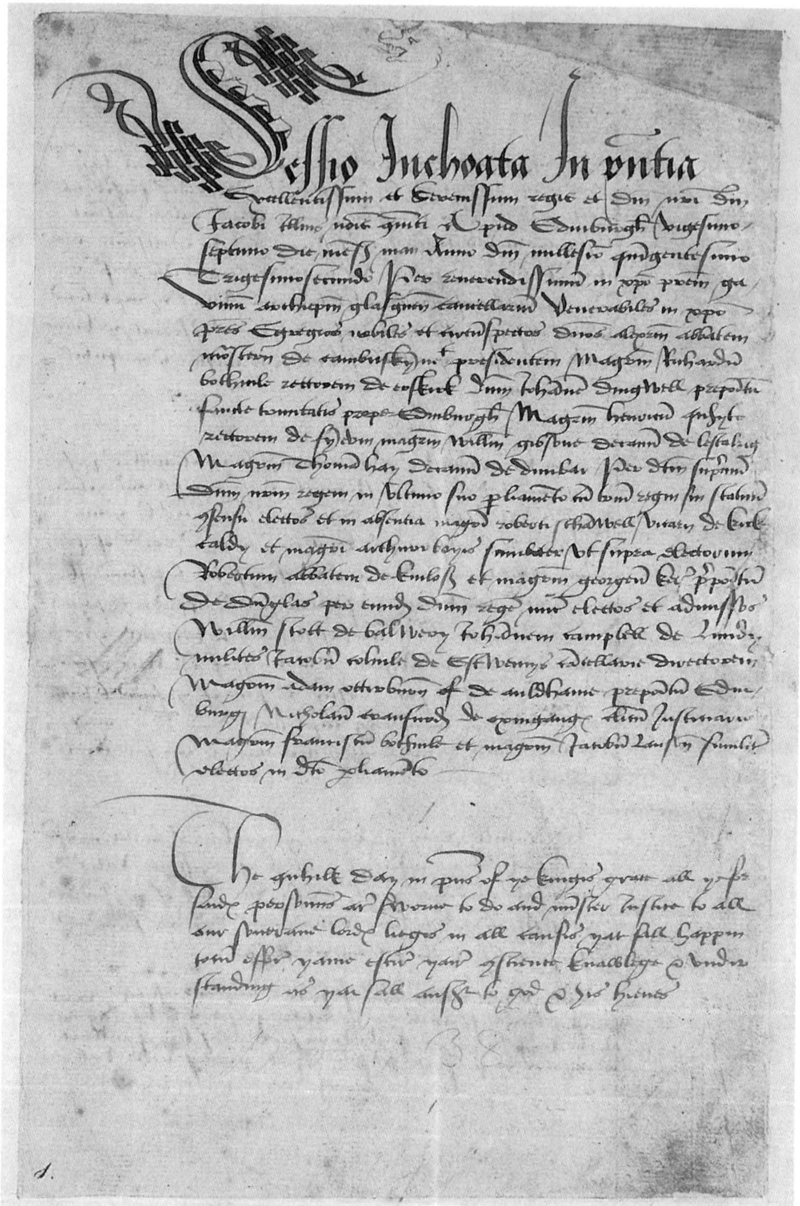
Sessio Inchoata In presentia

Fig. 1. Page from the Books of Council recording the sitting of the Session on 27 May 1532, following the Parliament which legislated for the College of Justice in the same month: NAS CS 6/1, fol. 1.

Mylne's as president are noted, the other Lords being described as "all chosen by the King in last Parliament with consent of the Estates" except two substitutes who are described as "now chosen by the King and admitted".[155] The declaration in the parliamentary act of 1532, that the "processes, sentences and decretis" of the Lords who had been chosen to be of the College "sall have the samin strength force and effect as the decretis of the lordes of sessioun had in all tymes bigane",[156] seems consistent with Parliament approving the scheme for the College but deeming it necessary to provide interim authority for the nominated judges until 27 May. This would avoid any doubt about their status and authority. At that point, following the "mare lasare" which Parliament had recognised as necessary, the institution of the new college could formally occur. In addition this provision stressed the continuity in the legal authority of the Lords of Session acting within the structure of the new college, and served to legitimate them by ensuring that despite any change that was recognised in the nature of the court, its sittings were still identified as the successors to judicial sittings of Council prior to May 1532.

That 27 May was a fresh beginning is also indicated by the first item of business being the swearing before the King by all the judges of an oath to do justice in all causes, the oath *de fideli administratione*.[157] As if to underline the extreme importance of this, it was also narrated that the King had:

> committit his power to my lord chancelar and abbot of Cambuskynneth, president, conjunctlie and severalie, to ressave the athis of thaim that ar absent, chosin and nemmit to be of this sessioun, and in thar absence the athis of ony uthir quhem his grace will nem tharto geif the saidis persouns cumis nocht.

This is clear evidence of a strong desire to undertake special formalities to mark the occasion. This can only be explained by the sitting being understood by those attending it as inaugurating something new. The register records that the King had:

> gevin command to the chancelar, president and lordis of the sessioun to avise, counselle and conclude upon sic rewlis, statutis and ordinancis as sall be thocht be thame expedient to be observit and kepit in thar man-

---

[155] *ADCP*, pp. 373–374.
[156] *APS.* ii, p. 336.
[157] Cairns, "Revisiting the Foundation of the College of Justice", p. 34.

> ner and ordour of proceding at all tymes and as thai devise conforme to resoun, equitie and justice.

These were then to be ratified by the King.[158] The King specifically commanded the Lords to spend the subsequent eight days devising these rules and statutes, but in the meantime to carry on as they thought best with judicial business. In the first of the statutes which followed, it was thought necessary to state that the Lords "sall begyne quhar thai left last in calling of the table". Instructions were also ordained for the physical arrangement of the layout of the court and for seating to be constructed, so that eighteen persons might sit "eselie". There then followed a very comprehensive attempt to set out the details of how practically the Session should proceed in its business, and a number of provisions of a constitutional nature setting out the duties of certain kinds of official. Whether the individual provisions were themselves innovative is of little importance compared to the innovation of setting them out in this manner, with an evident tone of a new departure necessitating this. Whilst not attempting any detailed reassessment of the College of Justice and, like Hannay, seeing these statutes as generally "not particularly innovative", Dr John Finlay has also argued that there was "considerable novelty" in the provisions relating to advocates and procurators, since they provided for "the creation of the office of general procurator of the council".[159]

In his subsequent letter of ratification of the statutes drafted by the Lords of Session, the King adopted a highly formal mode of expression, declaring of the statutes that "the quhilkis...we have subscrivit wyth our hand, heirfor of our awin free motive and propir will ratifiis and apprevis be thir presentis all and sindrie the saidis statutis".[160] This procedure and degree of formality is not evident in any of the earlier ordinances made up to this point by the Lords of Session or the King himself. The contrast with the ordinance of February 1531 is very noticeable, it having been simply a list of articles presented by the chancellor, and signed at the end by the King.[161] Moreover, the King bound himself not to ask the Lords of Session to do anything which would involve breaking these statutes "maide be thame at our

[158] *ADCP*, p. 374.

[159] J. Finlay, *Men of Law in Pre-Reformation Scotland* (East Linton, 2000), p. 53.

[160] *ADCP*, p. 378.

[161] *ADCP*, pp. 349–350.

command",[162] suggesting that the statutes were perceived as a kind of constitution for the court. The institution governed by these statutes was still "our daylie sessioun", but these observations suggest that all concerned viewed the foundation of the College as having brought about a formal change in the status of that "daylie sessioun", and that its nature was indeed different.

When he wrote on 10 June to confirm the statutes which the Lords of Session had made to regulate the court, the King made no reference to a particular moment of "institution" as such, therefore shedding no light upon the question when we may consider the College to have been instituted. He cited the 1532 parliamentary statute as though regarding this as the crucial step, but he did not express himself by using its language or terms such as "college".[163] He did talk of having "in our last parliament chosin ane certane number of personis spirituall and temporale to be upoun our daylie sessioun and to minister justice equallie".[164] However, the purpose of the letter of 10 June was primarily the ratification of the "statutes" made by the Lords, as well as the King offering some additional undertakings to the Lords in the carrying out of their role. These included punishing anyone found culpable of abusing the reputation of individual Lords, and it is made clear that the King would not tolerate anyone to "murmur" against those who "presentis our persoun and beris our auctorite in the doing of justice". In sum, the terms of the parliamentary statute taken with the ensuing proceedings of 27 May strongly suggest that the College was technically instituted on 27 May in the presence of the King, and perceived as having been so instituted. The detailed statutes of the court which the King commanded to be made at this inauguration were formally ratified on 10 June, but their text and the ratification were copied into the register as part of the record of proceedings on 27 May. The process of making these statutes and the terms of ratification by the King would therefore appear also to reflect this understanding of 27 May as the inauguration of the College. It would therefore seem to have completed the process of institution which the act of parliament had envisaged as happening at "mare lasare".[165] The papal bull of 1535

[162] *ADCP*, p. 378.
[163] *ADCP*, pp. 377–378.
[164] *ADCP*, p. 377.
[165] *Pace* Hannay, "On the Foundation of the College of Justice", p. 37: "But the College of Justice was not founded".

was even more of a formality, but did not add anything institutionally to what had been completed in 1532.

1532 as initiation of a supreme court

One of the reasons why Hannay placed so little weight on 1532, and saw the College of Justice as almost purely a financial vehicle to permit endowment, derived from the theoretical model he adopted in analysing the development of Council and Session. We have seen that this was stated in terms of the differentiation of function within the King's Council towards separate departments of activity. Hannay pointed to a "long development"[166] which saw "specialisation of function".[167] He came very close to implying that a supreme central court could only be recognised once the Lords of Session experienced "*complete* segregation from other activities of Council" (emphasis added).[168] There is no doubt that the concept of differentiation of function is a very useful analytical tool which can help to provide a theoretical expression of the course of development in the Council in the fifteenth and sixteenth centuries. However, the model seems to have misled Hannay into overlooking the true significance of 1532. He compared the College of Justice with his model, and, because it did not seem to conform, he concluded that this was not yet a supreme central court and that differentiation of function had not advanced far enough for this transition to have been made. This seems to give insufficient weight to the many strands of evidence already noted which imply that to contemporaries something new and significant happened in 1532.

Of course, it would be wrong to suggest that 1532 represented a uniquely momentous "turning-point", in the sense of a sudden discontinuity consequent upon the foundation of a new central institution. Refuting such a view was perhaps Hannay's main achievement. The foundation of the College of Justice is itself less significant than that it entailed the reconstitution of the Session, with decades of development already behind it. The College acted mostly to create a new corporate identity for the Session, distinct from Council. Even so, 1532 did witness institutional change, just as 1527 had done. There was therefore a definite development in 1532, and the question is how

[166] Hannay, "On the Antecedents of the College of Justice", p. 122.
[167] Hannay, "On the Antecedents of the College of Justice", p. 112.
[168] Hannay, "On the Antecedents of the College of Justice", p. 122.

significant was it? The institutional development involved does come to seem particularly significant when analysed along the lines already suggested above. When set beside the *jurisdiction* of the re-constituted body, this significance may come to seem even greater.[169] Investigating questions of jurisdiction to cast light upon the institutional importance of the foundation of the College of Justice has been a relatively recent development, and one pioneered by Dr Athol Murray. Dr Murray has been the first scholar since Hannay to *argue* for the point of view that the institutional development of 1532 was significant, though as we have seen that did seem also to be the view of some earlier scholars such as W.C. Dickinson. Murray set out the basis for his view in his study of Sinclair's "Practicks", a judicial notebook of a Session judge from the 1540s. Upon turning to consider the jurisdiction of the Session, Murray commented that "this was indeed a supreme court, and though historians have tended to play down the significance of the events of 1532, contemporaries saw them as marking a definite change in the nature of the court".[170] This comment was noted by Professor MacQueen, although more as an illustration of historiographical change.[171] It was also cited by David Sellar in support of the argument that there was a "jurisdictional shift" in 1532.[172] It should be noted that Dr Murray did not necessarily intend to give the evidence he cited this precise significance, since his comment was made in the context of a case of 1544, some twelve years after the foundation, and his observation can therefore be regarded as directed towards the views of "contemporaries" of the early 1540s. This means that on the basis of this item of evidence it can only be said that within twelve years of 1532 contemporaries saw the events of that year as marking a definite change in the nature of the court. Elsewhere, Dr Murray has stated his view that the effect of the changes in 1532 was "to make the Lords of Session a permanent, paid body of judges, with *what soon came to be a universal jurisdiction in all types of civil causes*" (emphasis added).[173]

---

169 The point about jurisdiction was strongly emphasised by Sellar in "The Common Law of Scotland and the Common Law of England", p. 94.

170 Murray, "Sinclair's Practicks", p. 98.

171 MacQueen, "Jurisdiction in heritage and the lords of council and session after 1532", p. 62.

172 Sellar, "The Common Law of Scotland and the Common Law of England", p. 94.

173 A.L. Murray, "Exchequer, Council and Session, 1513–1542", in *Stewart Style 1513–1542, Essays on the Court of James V*, ed. J. Hadley Williams (East Linton, 1996), pp. 108–109.

Even this point requires to be made cautiously, since the view expressed in the 1544 case was simply an argument submitted to the Lords, albeit one which they seem then to have approved. It had been argued that "the Lords of Council were also judges ordinary in all civil actions within the realm, by the first institution of the College of Justice".[174] However, the use of an argument to persuade a court to decide a particular way does not amount to evidence of any belief necessarily held by the pleaders who made the submission. The role of the pleader is to cite what argument and authority he can find in support of his submissions, since this is the nature of adversarial, forensic procedure. It is quite possible that the pleading was simply lifted out of the 1532 act to make an argument, rather than that it was a statement of a widely held opinion. That the jurisdictional proposition cited was not necessarily representative of a widely held opinion is quite possible, given that a series of different arguments was used in this case, with the Lords apparently commenting only on one in particular—that actions begun before them could not be "repledged" (i.e. tranferred) into any of the ordinary law courts, although it is not clear in the printed reports whether this was a pleading or a ground of decision.[175] It is not possible, then, to draw any definite inference from this case about the contemporary significance in 1532 itself of the foundation of the College. However, it draws attention to a second argument, that whether or not 1532 was seen at the time as being significant, nevertheless the consequences of 1532 were indeed significant, certainly by the early 1540s. An example would be the assertion of an exclusive jurisdiction over important matters such as fee and heritage, which at common law had been outwith the jurisdiction of Council and Session, but which the evidence surveyed later in this book suggests was by 1532 within it, although not yet exclusively so. This in turn raises the issue of whether those "consequences" were actually the products of 1532 or whether they resulted from a pre-existing path of development.

Institutional change with reference to the statutes of the court

It can be accepted that the foundation of the College of Justice was essentially a reconstitution of the Session, at the same time as arguing that it embodied particular institutional changes. As we have seen,

---

174 *Lord Bothwell v. Flemings* (1543), Mor. 7322.
175 Murray, "Sinclair's Practicks", p. 99.

Hannay did not stress any particular change, characterising the acts of sederunt of 1532 (i.e. the statutes made by the court itself) as marking "a distinct advance in order, but no breach of continuity with the past".[176] Such continuity is exactly what we would expect, and does not preclude significant changes having also occurred. Continuity followed on from the College being an adaptation of an older institution rather than the invention of a completely new one, but adaptation inevitably introduces new features. As we have seen, the content, form of composition and manner of promulgation of these statutes served to emphasise a change in the nature of the Session which was a product of the foundation of the College of Justice.

The act of parliament had explained that the College of Justice was to be instituted "becaus our soverane is maist desyrous to have ane permanent ordour of justice". This is in contrast to the transitory nature of the ordinances for the Session in the 1520s, when the various measures seemed very much designed for the forthcoming Session, rather than for the Session in perpetuity. An example would be the statement in the council register on 13 November 1531 that the "lordis of counsale in this present sessioune" ordained that the King's command for the last Session be observed "in every point".[177] A marked change seems to be evident when on 13 July 1534, the bishop of Ross was admitted to the Session, promising on oath to "observe and keip all statutis, actis and ordinancis maid be the kingis grace and lordis forsaid for ordouring of the said sessioun".[178] The implication is that after the institution of the College of Justice the Session was seen as a permanent institution in its own right, and that from 1532 its statutes and ordinances were considered to have an enduring quality requisite with the permanence now ascribed to the exercise of its functions in the form of a college.[179] Confirmation of this is found in the formal order from the King to the Lords of Session on 27 May 1532 to "avise, counsell and conclude upon sic rewlis, statutis and ordinancis as sall be thocht be thame expedient to be observit and kepit in thar manner and proceeding at all tymes". Once made they are to be "observit and

[176] *ADCP*, p. xxxix.

[177] *ADCP*, p. 366.

[178] *ADCP*, p. 426.

[179] To qualify the contrast I have made with the ordinances of the 1520s, it should be mentioned that when the King delegated his power to receive the oaths of lords named to sit, it was the oaths of those "nemmit of this session".

kepit by the saidis lordis of sessioun, advocatis and procuratouris of the samyne, and be all clerkis, scribes, maseris and uther ministeris of court *in all tymys cummyne*" (emphasis added).[180] That the institutional aspects of the process of foundation extended to this level of formality, detail and unlimited duration is compelling evidence that something of significance was happening to the nature of the Session in 1532.

There is a strong suggestion, too, that upon institution the Session acquired a greatly enhanced sense of corporate identity. Although the word "college" seems little used, nevertheless the nature of the Session from 1532 was that it was no longer simply an institution of conciliar government, merely a department of activity of the King's Council, but instead an autonomous corporate institution. As such it seems from its very instigation as a college to have acquired interests and privileges to protect and enforce, and this can again be traced in the King's letter of ratification of 10 June 1532.[181] James promised to "auctoris, manteyine and defend all the saidis lordis, thair personis, landis and gudis fra all wrang...be ony maner of persoun",[182] and to punish those who sought to harm them. As noted above, he would also punish those who falsely attacked or made unfavourable insinuations about the character and honesty of the Lords of Session, "becaus the saidis lordis...presentis our persoun and beris our auctorite in the doing of justice".[183] They should be "privilegit abone utheris" because of the office they exercised, and were to be exempt "fra all paying of tax, contribution and uther extraordinare chargis to be upliftit in ony tymes cuming". At "the saidis lordis consideratioun", those who offended or dishonoured the Lords could be imprisoned in Edinburgh Castle, or any other royal castle, whether "the falt be smal and injurious" or "grete". The letter is suggestive of a formal grant or charter, and its terms seem to signify a perception by the grantor, the King, that his Lords of Session were acquiring a new status by virtue of their office.

Why the King bound himself in this way with formal undertakings could be considered puzzling unless he saw the College of Justice as involving the reconfiguration of the Session so that in some way it was put on a new footing, and given a new form. Granting rights, privileges and protections to the Lords would seem to imply that they were now

[180] *ADCP*, p. 374.
[181] *ADCP*, p. 378.
[182] *ADCP*, p. 378.
[183] *ADCP*, p. 378.

to assume an identity distinct from that of the King's Council. This would have been a decision of principle. While a formal change in status occurred, however, it is important to note that this change could never have been followed by the kind of "complete segregation" of the Lords of Session from other activities of Council which Hannay looked for in assessing the progress of differentiation of function. To demand that such a test be satisfied before recognising the changes as of significance would be to impose an anachronistic standard in relation to the nature of sixteenth-century government. The government and administration of Scotland was conciliar in form, and for a king to rule was for him to do so as much through his councillors as personally at an executive level. The establishment of the Session as a college of justice would not lead to an expectation that it should now be wholly independent of King, Council and government generally, especially since the jurisdiction of the Session remained formally that of Council, albeit exercised from 1532 by members of the new college. The innovation represented by establishing the College of Justice was integrated into the evolutionary path being experienced by the Council generally in its development. Since government was by the King and his Council, a wholly distinct tribunal would have lacked a formal source of authority and an intelligible constitutional basis. The new college was neither a court with a traditional role in the procedures of the common law, nor one constituted directly by the King's Council. Indeed, it was institutionally independent and removed from the King and Council. Therefore, it was both natural and necessary that the Lords of Session remained formally as Lords of Council, and this connection is evident in the King's letter of ratification. Hannay also viewed complete segregation as impossible, but he ascribed this merely to "conservative feeling in the great ecclesiastical and temporal lords".[184] This was to see a political brake inhibiting development, when in fact from a constitutional perspective complete segregation would never have been feasible or desirable anyway.

We can see aspects of the foundation as reflecting the need to insulate the Session institutionally from the Council at large. The King's promise "nocht be ony privat writting, charge or command" to ask the Lords to do anything which would break their statutes or would go against justice is something which was necessary in part because the Lords of

[184] Hannay, "On the Antecedents of the College of Justice", p. 122.

Session were still Lords of Council.[185] The reconstituted Session was a central court, but remained within a curial framework (Hannay's term for the structure of conciliar government). Over the course of time it would naturally develop greater independence from this framework. It was in fact not until Charles I's reorganisation of the Privy Council in 1626 that judges were for the first time excluded from Council membership.[186] The logic of such a development could never have been worked through immediately in 1532, for reasons already mentioned. A very practical reason why the Session could not have experienced formal "segregation" was that it consisted of the same men whom the King continued to depend upon as Lords of Council. Scottish government was small-scale, intimate and carried out by a comparatively small core of councillors whose continued contribution would be necessary whether or not they were also Lords of Session in the reconstituted court. Together, these reasons also explain what Hannay viewed as the difficulty of adapting a foreign institution to fit the Lords of Council and Session and which led in his view to "curious anomalies"—by which, as we have seen, he probably meant the inclusion of the chancellor and other members of Council upon the bench.[187] Their inclusion, though, can be seen not so much as indicating a practical difficulty in realisation, but as evidence of the perception already described that even a central court dispensing the King's justice must be seen as operating within a curial framework.[188] On this view, the rights of the chancellor and additional lords nominated by the King were a necessary and residual institutional anchor connecting the College of Justice formally with the framework of the Council. Conceptually, this can be seen as the only way that contemporaries would have been able to think of the court, given its conciliar origin and function.

From the evidence discussed, it is possible to infer that change there was in 1532, and change which was perceived as such by King and Lords of Council alike. The statutes promulgated by them were a comprehensive code of "ordour", like rules of court, and introduced regulation of matters which had never been touched upon in previous

---

[185] *ADCP*, p. 378.

[186] Donaldson, *Scotland: James V to James VII*, pp. 290–291. See also M. Lee, Jnr., *The "Inevitable" Union and Other Essays on Early Modern Scotland* (East Linton, 2003), chap. 12 ("Charles I and the End of Conciliar Government in Scotland").

[187] Hannay, *The College of Justice*, p. 57.

[188] *Pace* Hannay, in *ADCP*, p. xlii.

ordinances of the Session, such as the conduct of advocates. The overriding impression is of an institution being demarcated as a court anew, so that those entitled to sit as judges—"to have voit tharin"[189]—should now exercise their jurisdiction within a discrete institution which was formally separated from Council though still conjoined through personnel. There is an analogy with the right of only specially nominated members of the United Kingdom Parliament's House of Lords to sit on its appellate judicial committees in modern times.[190] This impression confirms the remark of Dr Murray quoted earlier, about a definite change in the nature of the court, and the evidence discussed here suggests that perceptions of such a change by the 1540s might well have been rooted in similar perceptions from 1532 onwards.

Changes to the Session caused by the foundation of the College of Justice

Incorporation as an autonomous institution

Hannay observed that in 1524 "there is no sign of any body of men who are to be 'of Council' with special regard to work on the Session".[191] Duncan applied the same observation to the whole period 1513–1526.[192] Clearly in this period most Lords of Session were regular Lords of Council. However, as already discussed, it was in 1526, 1527 and 1531 that measures were adopted which began a process of restricting the right of attendance on the Session to a specified number of named Lords, and removed the right of Lords of Council to do so without specific commission. The 1532 parliamentary statute completed this process by making the Session institutionally autonomous through incorporation as the College of Justice. Incorporation under the terms of the act meant that the Lords of Session became a definite, exclusive, restricted and permanent body, which regulated admission to its own membership. The Lords of Session remained Lords of Council, and gave decree as Lords of Council, but from 1532 a Lord of Council

---

189 *ADCP*, p. 374.

190 Murray, "Sinclair's Practicks", p. 90. This comment applies to the operation of the House of Lords up to the inauguration of a new Supreme Court of the United Kingdom, which at the time of writing is projected to occur in October 2009.

191 Hannay, "On the Antecedents of the College of Justice", p. 112.

192 Duncan, "The Central Courts before 1532", p. 336.

was not *ex officio* a Lord of Session. The view of Professor MacQueen that "the erection of the College effected no change in the structure, personnel or record-keeping of the court" must therefore be significantly qualified.[193] In fact, a crucial change in the structure of the court was effected in 1532 from the point of view of the relationship between Council and Session.

The new structure was set down in the act. The King "thinkis to be chosin certane persounis maist convenient and qualifyit thairfore to the nowmer of xiiij persounis, half spirituale half temporall, with ane president". This was structurally a fundamental change from simply allowing any Lord of Council to sit upon cases in the Session. These Lords were to be authorised to sit on all civil actions "and nane utheris to have voit with thame onto the tyme that the said college may be institute at mare lasare".[194] The clear implication is that once the College was instituted it would only be those who had been admitted as members of the College who would have authority to exercise its jurisdiction. As we have already seen, the right of the chancellor to preside was retained, along with the right of "sic uther lordis as sall pleise the kingis grace to enjone to thaim of his gret counsell to have voit siclik to the nomer of thre or four". This clause plainly envisaged a separation between the two bodies of Council and Session, to the extent that it was necessary to have such a clause if any Lords of Council were ever to sit on the Session without being members of the College. Moreover, it is also possible that the purpose of this clause would have been in part a pragmatic one. It could have been designed to enable the sederunt of the Session to be more easily strengthened from time to time, for example in periods of vacation. It was not necessarily intended to secure some kind of constitutional right for the King to interfere by imposing Lords of Council onto the bench when he wished to exert some kind of special influence. It is true that this clause represents an exception to the general conception of an institutionally separate college of justice, but in its proper context it is as much a facet of the new structure of the court as the naming of fourteen Lords and a president to have exclusive control over Session matters. This is because the general right of the King to have any person serve as a Lord of Council is replaced in relation to the Session with a limited right to have his

---

[193] MacQueen, *Common Law and Feudal Society*, p. 242.
[194] *APS* ii, pp. 335–336, c. 2.

chancellor and only three or four Lords of Council adjoined to the Session *ex officiis*. Thus the King's freedom was considerably curtailed, and was merely preserved in limited form by statute as an exception to the general rule. The general rule was articulated again at the end of the act: only those named are to "subscrive all deliverancis and nane utheris eftir that thai begyn to sitt to minister justice".[195]

Reconciling such marginal qualifications to the autonomy of the College with an interpretation which emphasises the significance of 1532 is therefore possible. Such a view has also been advanced by Dr Athol Murray in his study of the relationship between James V's Exchequer, Council and Session. He drew attention to the fact that "under the 1532 act the Lords of Session became a restricted body, comprising only a president and fourteen ordinary senators of the College of Justice. This can be compared with the thirty-eight Lords chosen to sit in the Session as recently as December 1531. Henceforward new appointments could only be made as vacancies occurred, though the King did have power to nominate additional 'extraordinary lords'."[196] The Lords of Session therefore became "a permanent, paid body of judges".[197] The existence of this new structure was recognised in the council register itself, in a change in record-keeping which has not received significant attention before. If the sederunt listings of the Session are examined a change is immediately apparent after May 1532. Rather than listing individually the names of the Lords in attendance, it is very often recorded only that the Lords of Session sat, after which a list of those absent is given. This presupposes a fixed and recognised number of Lords constituting the court and thereby exercising collegiate authority as the Lords of Session. For example, on the first sitting of the Session after the foundation of the College the sederunt is given as "*sederunt domini sessionis except Decano de Dunbar*".[198] The authority exercised was that of the Council, but the right to exercise it was exclusively vested in the Lords of Session. This new practice of recording the sederunts was not invariably maintained, and is particularly, and perhaps significantly, in evidence in the first few months of the College's existence, but it was nevertheless new and would seem to reflect the new corpo-

[195] *APS* ii, pp. 335–336, c. 2.
[196] Murray, "Exchequer, Council and Session, 1513–1542", p. 110.
[197] Murray, "Exchequer, Council and Session, 1513–1542", pp. 108–109.
[198] Edinburgh, National Archives of Scotland [hereafter NAS], CS 6/1, fol. 9.

rate identity which had been assumed by the Lords of Session.[199] We have also already noted the impression of a new departure given by the unprecedentedly decorated and elaborate entry which records the institution of the College and the statutes of the court on that day.[200] Occasionally, further minor aspects of the record suggest to some degree a self-consciousness amongst Lords of Session as to the offices they held in the new college. For example, when taking instruments on a particular matter on 17 June 1532, the abbot of Cambuskenneth is designed as "precedent" in addition to his abbatial title.[201] Furthermore, that this new order and status in the Session was seen as enduring and as springing from the act of 1532 is confirmed by the way in which some new Lords of Session were appointed in November 1532. Three new Lords were named by the King, "to be ekit to the remanent of the lordis tharof chosin of befor, becaus thar is divers deid, sum seik and sum away of the saidis lordis of session, quharthrow thar is nocht sufficient nomer conforme to the act maid tharupon of befor".[202] The work of the Session from May 1532 was therefore regarded at the time as conducted within the framework of the new college. Tellingly, it was plainly seen as regulated constitutionally by the parliamentary statute of 1532, to which its operation should be "conforme". It is possible to find entries in the council register after May 1532 which formally distinguish the Lords of Council, the Lords of Session and the College of Justice itself.[203] This usage and the institutional categories relied upon provide a clear measure of differentiation of function which is consistent with viewing 1532 as marking an important change.

---

[199] Dr Murray also recognised this feature of the record and commented that it was "a change from pre-1532 practice, though decrees continued to be in the name of the 'lords of council'": Murray, "Exchequer, Council and Session, 1513–1542", p. 109.

[200] NAS CS 6/1, fol. 1. See fig. 1 on p. 138.

[201] NAS CS 6/1, fol. 25.

[202] *ADCP*, p. 389.

[203] 4th March 1533, *ADCP*, p. 398: "The thesaurer in presens of the lordis of counsale was contentit that na process sall pas apoun ony of the lordis of the sessioun for inbringing of the taxatioune put apoune thaim be vertu of the papis bullis, and realie dischargit thaim anent the thre teyndis except prelaciis, and presentlie commandit maistir Johnne Reid, provest of Symple, subcollectour of the said taxatioune, to ceis fra all proceding aganis thame or ony ane of thame for thar partis of the said taxtis, quharupoune maistir Williame Gibsoune, dene of Lestalrig, for him self and the remanent of the College askit instrumentis."

Jurisdiction

Jurisdiction is clearly a fundamental issue for any court, since it determines upon what matters the court may adjudicate in the first place. It is therefore of crucial importance to ask what jurisdiction was intended to be exercised by the College of Justice. The two most obvious possibilities are that it was either to be the same as that of the existing Session or expanded to a wider jurisdiction. The particular importance of this question lies in the older restriction under the common law upon the jurisdiction of the Session to determine heritable title. The question whether this restriction was still recognised by 1532 will be examined in chapters 6 and 7. There is also, however, a third, less clear-cut possibility alongside positing a still restricted or an expanded jurisdiction. This is that by 1532 the Session had already come to exercise a jurisdiction which was wider than its traditional one, extending to fee and heritage, but that it was only with the foundation of the College of Justice that this *de facto* state of affairs was first given formal recognition *de iure*. Whether or not the 1532 act was a *de iure* recognition of this sort, the evidence to be surveyed in later chapters on jurisdiction suggests that by 1532 there was indeed no remaining practical limitation on the Session's jurisdiction over fee and heritage. It will be argued that the deployment of alternative remedies bypassed the older restriction, and that by 1532 the jurisdiction of the Session over heritage could not be excluded if it was invoked in terms of the appropriate remedies.

In the early sixteenth century, Scotland possessed a complex pattern of local and national jurisdictions. There was no single omnicompetent court with jurisdiction over all matters dealt with in other courts. Obviously, Parliament and the King's Council occupied special positions in that they had jurisdiction in principle over the whole of Scotland and had virtually a full civil jurisdiction, the other secular courts consisting of primarily burgh, baron, sheriff, regality, and justiciar courts, as well as other extraordinary jurisdictions such as that of the admiral court. In addition there were the church courts—commissary and officials' courts, as well as the Roman Rota and the *ad hoc* courts of papal judges-delegate. That is one reason why the foundation of an institution which was or became a central omnicompetent court is of such interest, although even after 1532 various matters were to remain reserved to other jurisdictions and would not have been regarded as falling into the category of actions over which the College had jurisdiction as concerning civil matters. Until at least 1513, the Session was considered to have no general right or competence to determine issues of fee and heritage. This limitation grew up in the fifteenth century as the Session itself developed. It is therefore a significant omission in the analysis of both Hannay and Duncan that neither raised the question of the jurisdiction to be exercised by the College of Justice, let alone examined the evidence of the decisions of Session upon such matters at the time.

The word "jurisdiction" does not appear in the part of Professor Duncan's article which discusses the Council after 1489, and the College of Justice.[204] Hannay did remark of the 1532 act that "the continuity of the jurisdiction with that of the Session was expressly affirmed".[205] He was probably thinking here of the section of the act which gave decreets of the new college the same force and effect as those of the Lords of Council and Session, since in *The College of Justice* he drew attention to this clause as an example of "continuity", although without mentioning the question of jurisdiction.[206] However, this clause does not in any case have a bearing on jurisdiction as such, since a decreet is no more than an order of the court giving an executive force to its decision. The status of a decreet is an ancillary matter compared to the question of which issues may in the first place be decided, and so the concept of jurisdiction is wholly distinct. Provisions relating to the force of decreets would have been concerned with ensuring that the judgements of the court were observed, rather than determining upon which issues judgement could be given. Therefore, it seems that the work of both Hannay and Duncan rests upon the unexamined assumption that the jurisdiction of the College was the same as that of the Session. Whilst this might have proved to be a reasonable assumption, it would nevertheless be misleading if it were also assumed that this jurisdiction was the old restricted fifteenth century one and still did not extend to fee and heritage.

Sheriff Hector McKechnie was the first modern scholar to note the significance of the acquisition of jurisdiction over fee and heritage by the new college of justice. He did so in his seminal David Murray Lecture, entitled "Judicial Process upon Brieves, 1219–1532" and delivered in the University of Glasgow in 1956.[207] However, his insights on this point

[204] Duncan, "The Central Courts before 1532", pp. 334–336.
[205] Hannay, "On the Foundation of the College of Justice", p. 37.
[206] Hannay, *The College of Justice*, p. 39.
[207] McKechnie, *Judicial Process upon Brieves, 1219–1532*, pp. 8, 25, 29.

escaped the attention of the next generation of historians. It was only in 1980 that the question of jurisdiction was revived in the discussion presented by Dr Murray in his article on Sinclair's "Practicks",[208] and subsequently analysed with explicit reference to previous historiography by David Sellar in two articles published in 1988 and 1991.[209] However, the only detailed study of the jurisdiction of the Session after 1532 was published in 1984 by Professor MacQueen.[210] This investigated issues previously adumbrated in a slightly earlier article and subsequently developed by Professor MacQueen as part of a book-length study.[211] In his article on Sinclair's "Practicks", Dr Murray had already observed of the 1540s that the court could be seen to be claiming both concurrent jurisdiction over certain matters previously pertaining solely to other courts, and, in certain classes of action, exclusive jurisdiction over these matters as well.[212] Dr Murray was analysing only the cases reported in Sinclair's "Practicks", however, which record actions before the Session from 1540 onwards. Professor MacQueen surveyed a selection of evidence for the 1530s in addition to the 1540s and beyond, concluding that "the jurisdiction in heritage of the Lords of Council and Session seems therefore to have been developed over a period of years rather than in any one particular case". He also concluded that the parliamentary acts of 1532, 1541 and 1543:

> were not intended to be of particular significance, or to change the character of the court, at the time they were passed; but nonetheless as acts of the Scottish parliament they could be used to give legal authority to what clearly appears as an expansionist attitude of the court to its jurisdiction in the 1530s and 1540s.[213]

This was a plausible interpretation in itself, providing a coherent model of jurisdictional change. It supported Professor MacQueen's earlier view that "the institution of the College of Justice did not immediately affect

---

[208] Murray, "Sinclair's Practicks", p. 98.

[209] Sellar, "The Common Law of Scotland and the Common Law of England", p. 94; Sellar, "A Historical Perspective", p. 44.

[210] MacQueen, "Jurisdiction in heritage and the lords of council and session after 1532".

[211] H.L. MacQueen, "The Brieve of Right in Scots Law", *Journal of Legal History* 3 (1982), 52–70; MacQueen, *Common Law and Feudal Society*, especially chap. 8.

[212] Murray, "Sinclair's Practicks", p. 99.

[213] MacQueen, "Jurisdiction in heritage and the lords of council and session after 1532", pp. 82, 84–85.

the court's exclusively conciliar jurisdiction".[214] However, upon closer examination, the cases cited by Professor MacQueen do not provide unambiguous support for his interpretation. Indeed, they are open to a different interpretation which would not regard them as demonstrating any limitation on jurisdiction after 1532. I have set out the basis for favouring this interpretation elsewhere.[215] The effect of the act of 1532 has already been examined with reference to institutional development, and the conclusion drawn that the act effected significant changes. It will now be analysed from a jurisdictional point of view.

Jurisdiction and the parliamentary statute of 1532

Does the parliamentary statute of 1532 imply anything about a change in the jurisdiction of the Session? It is perhaps significant that the act of parliament made specific provision that "the quhilkis persounes sall be auctorizate in this present parliament to sitt and decyde apone all actiouns civile and nane utheris to have voit with thaim onto the tyme that the said college may be institute at mare lasare".[216] As already touched on, this clause did not confer authority on members of the College as such, but rather conferred interim authority for the time being on those who were to become members of the College when it was instituted. The emphasis seems to have been on maintaining continuity between the arrangements which were being put into effect immediately and those which would pertain once the College was properly established. Again, whatever the jurisdiction was, the clause seems to have been addressed to the question of who was entitled to exercise it during the interim period. There are in all three bodies at work in 1532: the Session; the interim Session, functioning on a provisional basis in anticipation of the College; and the Session functioning as the College from 27 May 1532. It may be significant that the interim Session required to have the jurisdiction of the College conferred upon it, and that it was not simply left to function as the old Session till further notice. The conferral of jurisdiction could have been simply to avoid confusion about whether the Session was being replaced and what the nature of the body now issuing decreets in the interim period was. It

---

[214] MacQueen, "Brieve of Right", p. 66.

[215] A.M. Godfrey, "Jurisdiction in heritage and the foundation of the College of Justice in 1532' in *Miscellany IV*, ed. H.L. MacQueen, Stair Society 49 (Edinburgh, 2002), pp. 9–36.

[216] *RPS*, 1532/5; *APS*, pp. 335–336.

certainly seems to have been seen as important to be precise about the nature of the body which was sitting, so as to be sure of its jurisdiction and who was entitled to exercise it. Despite the argument of this book that the College of Justice was inaugurated on 27 May 1532, it must be admitted that the parliamentary statute of 17 May was open-ended enough to confer authority until all formal aspects of the "institution" were completed, primary or ancillary.

One possible implication of the way in which the act distinguished the body which was to function up until the institution of the College from the College itself is that the jurisdiction of the College was understood differently from the pre-1532 Session. When the Session was ordered under the act "in the meyntym to deliver billis and call privilegit materis as thai sall think expedient",[217] while statutes of court were drafted following 27 May, this is not evidence that the old Session was merely functioning as it always had done and that the act had no effect upon it. We have already seen how it was felt necessary to expressly confer authority upon the nominated judges on an interim basis, until the College was instituted. The terms of the act do address directly the question of jurisdiction, although in a pithy and declaratory manner which does not allude to any particular matters of jurisdictional competence. Apart from the declaration that the purpose for which the College of cunning and wise men is to be instituted was "for the doing and administracioun of justice in all civile actions", it is also stated that its members were to minister justice "in sic causis as sall happin tocum befor thaim", and were authorised to "sitt and decyde apon all actiouns civile". Unfortunately, these phrases are not in the least conclusive as to whether "all civile actiouns" meant civil actions generally. If it did, this would have encompassed fee and heritage, and impliedly overturned the common law rule excluding such cases from the jurisdiction of Council and Session. Alternatively, it is also conceivable that such a phrase could have had a more restricted, technical meaning so as to indicate simply that class of civil actions which could have been brought before the Session as it normally functioned by 1532. This would have effected nothing which would have entitled the Lords of Session to hear matters outwith the commonly understood jurisdiction of that body. There could be a significance attached to the fact that the phrase "all civile actiouns" had never been used before in defining

[217] *ADCP*, p. 374.

which civil actions were within the jurisdiction of Council and Session. In the past, the classes of action so included were listed individually. However, unfortunately such argument can only be speculative.

David Sellar has argued for an immediate jurisdictional change occurring, which followed from these provisions of the act. This was the interpretation earlier put forward by McKechnie but never directly taken up by subsequent scholars.[218] Professor MacQueen, as we have noted, did not regard the act as conferring a wider jurisdiction. The act itself is certainly open to different interpretations, but neither Sellar nor MacQueen consider a third possibility: that those who enacted the 1532 legislation assumed that the Session *already* recognised no limitation on its civil jurisdiction. On this view the fee and heritage limitation had already been either discarded or had ceased to have an effect on the range of matters which could be adjudicated in the Session. It may be puzzling that after 1532 exceptions were still pleaded in the Session protesting that the Session did not have competence to determine questions of heritage, and that when this happened the jurisdiction clauses of the 1532 act do not appear to have been founded upon. In the present state of research, the first case which we know of where the act was expressly founded upon for the purposes of a jurisdictional argument is *Lord Bothwell v. Flemings* (1543),[219] when the act of 1532 was cited to meet a specific plea by the pursuer, who was arguing that the Lords were not competent judges in the matter. The absence of this type of submission until the 1540s is perhaps the most telling evidence against the act having been intended to effect a jurisdictional change, although it is only indirect evidence. To that extent David Sellar's analysis is undermined, whilst Hector MacQueen's argument that the act came to be seen as justifying a piecemeal expansion of the jurisdiction of the Session over a decade or more might be supported, although this view remains to be fully evaluated. What of a situation whereby the Lords already possessed jurisdiction in fee and heritage in 1532? If this was so, it could mean that by May 1532 it was the assumption of contemporaries that literally all civil matters could be decided upon by the new college, since the Session had already developed and established this jurisdiction. Or else, it could at least mean that a pattern of

[218] Sellar, "The Common Law of Scotland and the Common Law of England", pp. 94, 98 (n. 85).

[219] *Lord Bothwell v. Flemings* (1543), Mor. 7322.

deciding issues of heritage was sufficiently evident prior to 1532 that a jurisdiction in fee and heritage was already established in all but name. For direct evidence of how the act was understood and of the Lords' attitude to their jurisdiction we must look at individual cases when the Lords had to decide whether they were competent judges. Chapters 5, 6 and 7 will turn to assess in depth the jurisdiction of the Session before and after the foundation of the College of Justice in order to ascertain the extent to which the new college possessed or developed a full civil jurisdiction.

Conclusion

The conclusion of this chapter is that the foundation of the College of Justice was intended to and did cause a significant change in the organisation of central justice in Scotland. This change can be seen as possessing a new order of importance when compared with the developments from 1426 to 1526 analysed in the previous chapter. Professor Hannay's history of the Session and the foundation of the College remain of immense value as a series of works of comprehensive and outstanding scholarship. Nevertheless, his interpretation of the significance of 1532 has to be regarded as untenable in the light of the discussion presented in this chapter. This has embraced the institutional aspects of the foundation, but has also highlighted the relevance of assessing the jurisdiction of the Session as a court of law. This is necessary for understanding the effect of the legislation of 1532, as well as the nature of the Session before and after 1532. The institutional history alone—re-interpreted to suggest significant change in 1532—is consistent with and supportive of the suggestion that the act of 1532 might have been cast upon the assumption that the College of Justice would exercise a full civil jurisdiction. In that case the statute would not seem to have been a revolutionary legislative reform so much as a statutory recognition of the jurisdictional position which had already developed. Such an interpretation would have one particular merit in allowing the phrase "all actiouns civile" to be construed in a literal sense without supposing that the 1532 act necessarily purported to change or expand the jurisdiction of the Session. Nevertheless, as this chapter has also demonstrated, the wider terms of the act and the ancillary statutes of the court generally seem to speak to there having been a conscious and formal change in the institutional nature of the Session in 1532. It would therefore not be surprising if there had also been a formal *de iure* recognition in 1532 of the expanded jurisdiction which the Session had already come to exercise. On this basis, the institutional significance of the foundation of the College of Justice, together with this interpretation of its jurisdictional significance, would suggest that in 1532 the Session effectively became for the first time an autonomous central court, and one with unlimited jurisdiction across Scotland in civil matters. A separate institutional structure was created and it inherited a full civil jurisdiction from the King's Council. Evaluating in detail whether the evidence of jurisdictional change supports to this extent the evidence surveyed in this chapter of institutional change will be carried out in subsequent chapters, following examination of the ways in which the procedure and business of the Session in the period around 1532 provide indications of the nature of the court by this time, its relationship to other courts, and how this affected the pattern of jurisdiction across the kingdom.

CHAPTER FOUR

THE PROCEDURE OF THE SESSION

Introduction

Institutional change in 1532 created the College of Justice as a central court. However, we have noted how all historians since R.K. Hannay have emphasised that the vehicle of change was the pre-existing Session of the King's Council, with decades of development already behind it. One mature aspect of the Session which existed before 1532 was its procedural law. Indeed, this can be traced back to the fifteenth-century proceedings before parliamentary Auditors as well as the King's Council. This is therefore one feature of the history of the Session and the College of Justice in which there is a strong measure of continuity of the sort which Hannay emphasised more generally. Nevertheless, an analysis of the procedure of the Session is important in assessing how it operated as a court, and how this may have been affected in 1532. It is also important for a wider assessment of the foundation of the College of Justice, since ultimately the workings of procedure, remedies and jurisdiction within a legal system are closely related, and have consequences for substantive legal development. This is especially evident when considering the position of the Session in relation to the more established Scottish law courts. Finally, it also serves to place the Session in a European context of royal conciliar courts drawing upon the *ius commune* in framing a procedural law.

It is only comparatively recently that the history of Scottish civil procedure has begun to receive sustained scholarly attention, and this has so far concentrated upon the medieval period.[1] Civil procedure

[1] H.L. MacQueen, "Pleadable brieves, pleading, and the development of Scots law", *Law and History Review* 4 (1986), 403–422; H.L. MacQueen, *Common Law and Feudal Society in Medieval Scotland* (Edinburgh, 1993); J. Finlay, *Men of Law in Pre-Reformation Scotland* (East Linton, 2000), pp. 87–122; G. Dolezalek, "The Court of Session as a Ius Commune Court—Witnessed by 'Sinclair's Practicks', 1540–1549", in *Miscellany Four*, ed. H.L. MacQueen, Stair Society 49 (Edinburgh, 2002), pp. 51–84. Taking account of the Scottish position, see also J.M.J. Chorus, "Civilian Elements in European Civil Procedure", in *The Civilian Tradition and Scots Law*, ed. D.L. Carey Miller and R. Zimmermann (Berlin, 1997), pp. 295–305; R.C. van Caenegem, "History of European

during the sixteenth century is a crucial subject to investigate, however, because the period witnessed a fundamental transition in Scotland between contrasting medieval and early modern procedural models. Changes in the procedural framework were also fundamental in providing impulses towards development of substantive law, especially by facilitating the intensified influence of Roman and canon law. In this regard, Professor Baker has pointed persuasively to the role procedure could play in effecting legal change at a European level in this period. He has argued in relation to the German experience of a "reception" of Roman law, for example, that:

> [its] essence... was not, therefore, a replacement of medieval with classical law, but a wave of procedural and professional changes which brought about an increasingly scientific approach to decision-making, confining lay judges to questions of fact and turning more cases into questions of law for learned tribunals.[2]

The implications of this insight are worth considering for Scotland, since it clearly shared aspects of the German experience. The development of the Session also had a wider procedural influence over the legal system as a whole, since its Romano-canonical-influenced procedure became the basis for Scottish civil procedure generally within a few years of the foundation of the College of Justice. These changes were embedded a generation before the Scottish Reformation which unfolded after 1560. They therefore took root while the authority and practice of the church courts were still in place and subject to the wider authority of Roman canon law.

The central purpose of this chapter is to sketch some of the main features of the procedure of the Session at the time of its reconstitution in 1532. Providing a picture of Scottish procedural law in this period will also allow an underlying question of more general relevance to be addressed, namely what was the relationship in Scotland between Romano-canonical procedure as a supra-national source of procedural law and the development of a native and localised "style of court" or "practick"? What was the position by 1532? Addressing these questions will assist in elaborating the wider framework within which to evaluate

Civil Procedure", in *International Encyclopedia of Comparative Law*, 16, ed. M. Cappelletti (Tübingen, 1973), chap. 2.

[2] J.H. Baker, *The Oxford History of the Laws of England, Volume VI, 1483–1558* (Oxford, 2003), p. 10.

the content of Scottish procedural law. Such evaluation is problematic, since there exist no procedural commentaries or procedural ordinances providing codified statements of the Session's procedural rules, such as can be found for similar courts in other parts of Europe. In the Netherlands, for example, we find such ordinances being made for the Great Council of Malines in 1522 and 1559.[3] Without such sources, details of Scottish procedure therefore have to be gleaned as systematically as possible from combing through the surviving records of litigation on a case by case basis.

As already noted, a study of procedure at the time of the foundation of the College of Justice is also particularly relevant for exploring the shift in Scotland more generally from the established medieval procedural model to a fundamentally different early modern one. This is because the Session was the primary vehicle causing that wider procedural change to be instigated across the legal system. As we have already seen in earlier chapters, the period 1426–1532 was one of experiment and reform generally in the central administration of justice in Scotland.[4] From the point of view of the use of civil procedure, it witnessed a fundamental re-orientation of the legal system away from procedure by brieve (i.e. writ) and inquest and towards a Romano-canonical form of procedure. The reasons for this shift may themselves have been connected with the nature of the procedural law, since it seems likely that an important factor in the growing resort to central justice was dissatisfaction with the operation of local courts. Such dissatisfaction must have at least in part related to the forms of procedure and remedies available in those courts. Traditionally, of course, court actions had been structured around a series of jurisdictions rooted principally in the locality, united under the overall jurisdiction of Parliament. The procedure for most legal action until the fifteenth century required its initiation in these local courts. As we have seen, the fifteenth century seems to have witnessed a preference by litigants for central justice at first instance rather than merely as a residual final court of appeal, and in response Parliament gradually gave way to the smaller, more flexible King's Council as the primary central judicial forum. A possible implication of this is that central justice—and perhaps also its procedure—was

[3] C.H. van Rhee, *Litigation and Legislation: Civil Procedure at First Instance in the Great Council for the Netherlands in Malines (1522–1559)* (Brussels, 1997), p. 19.

[4] A.A.M. Duncan, "The Central Courts before 1532", in *An Introduction to Scottish Legal History*, ed. G.C.H. Paton, Stair Society 20 (Edinburgh, 1958), pp. 321–340.

regarded in this period as positively preferable and more effective than the traditional local forms available. This seems to be suggested by the way the period culminated in 1532 with the channelling of the judicial business of the King's Council—as transacted in the Session—into the College of Justice. This step must have powerfully enhanced the wider currency across the legal system of the Romano-canonical procedure which these conciliar bodies deployed, compared with the brieve system of the regular courts of the medieval common law.

Influences on sixteenth-century procedural law in the Session

The Romano-canonical nature of the civil procedure used in the Session is readily explained. As we have seen, the Session was from the 1490s until 1532 a normal form of sitting of the King's Council. The role of churchmen who were trained in canon law in the running of royal government, and therefore in taking leading roles on the medieval Council, must explain why in judicial matters the Council was inclined to adopt a form of Romano-canonical procedure to expedite the determination of legal complaints.[5] In an important sense, it was indeed the only generalised procedural law available, and the presence of churchmen provided the knowledge to apply it. Of course, Romano-canonical procedure was already a long-established element in Scottish legal culture, since it was applied routinely in the ecclesiastical courts of the medieval Scottish church. However, though the procedure of the Session possessed significant and recognisable Romano-canonical features, the *ius commune* of Roman and canon law texts and associated glosses, commentaries and other works of juristic exposition was not the only substantial influence upon it. The reasons for this are two-fold: first the medieval inheritance of Scots law, and secondly the legacy of the institutional antecedents of the Session, in particular the King's Council.

[5] For example, William Elphinstone (1431–1514), official of the diocese of Glasgow (1471–78). He was official of Lothian and Commissary General of the archdiocese of St Andrews (1478–83); member of parliamentary judicial committees and of the King's Council (from 1478); bishop of Aberdeen (1483–1514); chancellor (1488). See L.J. Macfarlane, *William Elphinstone and the Kingdom of Scotland* (Aberdeen, 1985), especially chapters 2 ("The Canon Lawyer at Work 1471–1488") and 3 ("Auditor of Causes 1478–1488").

In the first place, the fact that the Session evolved within an established legal system of some antiquity has a bearing. Native medieval procedural law existed and was a source and influence. As discussed in earlier chapters, a mature legal system had developed by the end of the thirteenth century, and was understood in terms of a distinctively Scottish common law.[6] The early formative influences in the twelfth and thirteenth centuries were Anglo-Norman, and the English common law was the source of much borrowing. As also noted in earlier chapters, Scottish brieves of dissasine, mortancestor and right were modelled on English writs, jurisdiction was granted to royal sheriffs and justiciars, proof depended upon juries through the summoning of an assize, and the principal source for the main medieval law book of Scotland was Glanvill's *Tractatus*, with its account of procedures in the English royal courts.[7] There was therefore a rich medieval procedural law already developed in Scotland by the time a central court matured in the sixteenth century. Despite some reliance upon *ius commune* sources, this was in origin not Romano-canonical as such, but rather reflected early English common law influences.[8]

In the second place, although the Session was only placed on a permanent institutional footing in 1532 with the foundation of the College of Justice, it nevertheless followed upon more than a century of institutional experimentation with the different forms of central tribunal examined earlier in this book, which themselves were initially supplements to the more established court of Parliament.[9] In terms of the fifteenth century experiments in central justice, the King's Council provides the thread of continuity in the development of the procedural model inherited by the College of Justice in 1532. From the 1460s, as discussed earlier, the King's Council had assumed an ever more important role. From

---

[6] W.D.H. Sellar, "The Common Law of Scotland and the Common Law of England", in *The British Isles 1100–1500*, ed. R.R. Davies (Edinburgh, 1988), pp. 82–99.

[7] T.M. Cooper, "Introduction", in *Regiam Majestatem and Quoniam Attachiamenta*, ed. T.M. Cooper, Stair Society 11 (Edinburgh, 1947), pp. 1–51 at pp. 32–40.

[8] On the influence of the *ius commune* see P.G. Stein, "The Source of the Romano-canonical Part of *Regiam Majestatem*", *Scottish Historical Review* 48 (1969), 107–123; P.G. Stein, "Roman Law in Scotland", *Ius Romanum Medii Aevi*, pars v, 13b, (Milan 1968), reprinted in P.G. Stein, *The Character and Influence of the Roman Civil Law* (London, 1988), pp. 269–317.

[9] R.K. Hannay, "On the Antecedents of the College of Justice", *The Book of the Old Edinburgh Club* 11 (1922), pp. 87–123, reprinted in R.K. Hannay, *The College of Justice and other essays*, ed. H.L. MacQueen, Stair Society Supplementary Series 1 (Edinburgh, 1990), pp. 179–215.

the 1490s onwards it was effectively the only central judicial tribunal, superseding the ordinary judicial functions of the medieval Parliament. By the 1490s it was becoming ever more routinised in its handling of judicial matters because of this institutional continuity. Therefore, the procedure of the Session itself was already well established *before* 1532 and must have been derived from the procedure adopted in its various fifteenth century antecedents. In turn, it seems reasonable to assume that this was informed to some extent by the procedure governing the determination of causes in the fourteenth and fifteenth century Scottish Parliament. This was a part of secular governance, though of course with a clerical estate which would have included trained canon lawyers in its number. When considering the procedure of the Session in the sixteenth century, therefore, the institutional changes represented by the foundation of the College of Justice sit alongside great continuity in procedural law, not only in one way but in several. The procedure of the Session did not require to be "adopted" in 1532 and it is impossible to imagine that any change to the basis of the existing procedural law of the Session was considered,[10] though examination of the statutes establishing the College of Justice in that year shows that they did provide for *regulation* of procedure. But it seems that the procedure already existed, and its adoption must be traced back to the fifteenth century King's Council.

In the light of these two considerations, a number of questions follow about how to characterise the procedure used in the Session by 1532. To what extent did the sixteenth-century Session operate a local variant of Romano-canonical procedure informed primarily by the *ius commune* (Roman and canon law, and the learned expositions and commentaries upon them), as opposed to an ever more distinctive native "practick" reflecting a more diverse range of influences and sources? Did the sixteenth century witness any important changes in this regard? What impact upon procedure was made by the foundation of the College of Justice in 1532? To some extent, answers to these questions will help locate the Scottish development of a central court within the broader European pattern of new central courts, which generally relied on Romano-canonical procedure mixed with some local features. Professor van Rhee has observed of one part of Europe, for example,

[10] As slightly implied in P.G. Stein, "The Procedural Models of the Sixteenth Century", *Juridical Review* (1982), 186–197 at p. 196.

that although French and Burgundian legal procedures were "highly indebted" to Romano-canonical influence, nevertheless "the procedures at the courts in the Netherlands had their distinctive features, which made the manner of litigation at each court more or less unique".[11] Even within the canon law there was diversity in formulating procedural law. Professor Helmholz has commented that "the procedural tradition of the *ius commune* left room for variation among the courts—the so-called *stylus curiae*".[12] Scotland is a particularly notable instance of embedding the procedural law of the *ius commune* within a distinctive native tradition, since its medieval legal system had developed such a mature procedural law already, drawing primarily upon Anglo-Norman sources rather than the *ius commune*. Professor MacQueen has observed that, despite the importance Romano-canonical procedure undoubtedly had as a source in Scotland throughout the medieval period, "there had developed a native system which was self-supporting and did not draw directly from canonical sources".[13] On this basis, he has drawn attention to the danger of characterising the court's procedure simplistically as "Romano-canonical", observing further that:

> the received view is that in matters of procedure the Lords of Council and Session adopted the Romano-canonical model. Evidence exists, however, of an elaborate system of pleading in the secular courts of the sheriff and justiciar when actions were commenced there by pleadable brieves. This system was founded ultimately on the Romano-canonical model and retained a close affinity to it, but it is probable that there was also borrowing from English law although, to some extent, the Scots evolved their own terminology and forms. Examination of this system suggests that the procedure used in the developing central courts at the end of the fifteenth century should be seen as less of a novelty and more as a continuation of an established, native tradition. The exact extent of this cannot be measured, nor can it be shown definitively that there was not also a continuing input of ideas and concepts from canon lawyers practising in Scotland.[14]

---

[11] Van Rhee, *Litigation and Legislation*, pp. 12–13.

[12] R.H. Helmholz, *The Oxford History of the Laws of England Volume I: The Canon Law and Ecclesiastical Jurisdiction from 597 to the 1640s* (Oxford, 2004), chap. 5 ("Civil Procedure and the Law of Proof"), pp. 311–353 at p. 313.

[13] H.L. MacQueen, "Pleadable brieves, pleading, and the development of Scots law", p. 422.

[14] MacQueen, "Pleadable brieves, pleading, and the development of Scots law", p. 405.

Pursuing such analysis further is problematic, given the limited nature of the procedural record in the later fifteenth century and the opening decades of the sixteenth century, as well the difficulty in this period of going beyond the mere identification of procedural influences to determining how the Session regarded and might have ranked the various sources of its procedure when deciding how its "practick" should be formulated. However, one theme of this chapter will be an evaluation of Professor MacQueen's view that "the procedure used in the developing central courts at the end of the fifteenth century should be seen as less of a novelty and more as a continuation of an established, native tradition".

In the present state of research, only preliminary rather than comprehensive answers can be attempted in trying to address these various questions.[15] At its widest, the argument to be advanced is that, notwithstanding the range of influences in the history of Scottish civil procedure before 1500, the procedure of the Session in the sixteenth century may fairly be characterised as Romano-canonical. The decisive factor leading to this was the development of the Session into a central court, re-orientating the legal system as a whole towards Romano-canonical procedure with the result that medieval procedure by writ and inquest was largely discarded.[16] The novelty of this does deserve emphasis, even whilst acknowledging the native medieval inheritance of Scottish civil procedure. By 1500, it seems likely that this inheritance had become secondary to direct Romano-canonical influence. The practical outcome of these developments in procedural models in Scotland can be seen in 1540 when Parliament legislated so that all other secular judges, above all sheriffs, the principal local judges, were ordained to adopt aspects of the procedure of the Session, and in particular a form of summary procedure.[17] Even in June 1532, the newly promulgated statutes for the College of Justice implied procedural misgivings about local justice, with one article stating that "fra thine furth that it be eikit in all deliverance direct to shereffis or uthir jugis ordinaries that thai admit to the partiis all thair lauchfull defensis and to minister justice equalie to baith the partiis as accordis", another indication of the way

---

[15] Though for another recent treatment see also Finlay, *Men of Law in Pre-Reformation Scotland*, pp. 87–122.

[16] Van Caenegem, "History of European Civil Procedure", p. 77.

[17] *The Acts of the Parliaments of Scotland*, ed. T. Thomson and C. Innes [hereafter *APS*], 12 vols (Edinburgh, 1814–1875), vol. 2, p. 358, c. 7.

in which the increase in litigation before the Session might have been in part a response to inadequacies in local justice.[18]

The foundation of the College of Justice

It has been suggested above that the development of the Session as a central court had a wider effect on civil procedure in Scotland. In view of this, the impact upon civil procedure of the foundation of the College of Justice in 1532 will now be examined. It is only after 1532 that any wider general effect becomes discernable, and certainly no fundamental reform of procedure was envisaged in the 1532 legislation. The parliamentary statute establishing the College was tersely expressed and did not attempt to set out or fix the procedure of the court. Since the College was a reconfiguration of a function of the existing King's Council into a new institutional structure, this is perhaps one area where great continuity was only to have been expected. If so, there would have been no pressing need to set out the content of a procedural law. A further consideration is that, as Professor van Rhee has remarked, "ordinances on procedure are invariably incomplete", not least because in systems resting on the Romano-canonical model it was considered superfluous to reproduce rules with which it could be assumed that practitioners and judges were perfectly familiar.[19] The act did not even purport to set out procedural rules. It simply referred to the ministering of justice by those judges who had been nominated, "with sic uthir rewlis and statutis as sall pleise the kingis grace to mak and geif to thaim for ordouring of the samin". Later, the act stated that the "processis, sentencis and decretis sall have the samin strength, force and effect *as the decretis of the lordis of sessioun had* in all tymes bigane" (emphasis added).[20] Greater detail is found in the subsequent short set of statutes produced by those Lords of Council and Session who were to sit on the new body. These statutes were the ones ratified by the King in Council in June 1532, a few weeks after the enactment of the parliamentary statute. They were to govern "the manner and

---

[18] *Acts of the Lords of Council in Public Affairs 1501–1554*, ed. R.K. Hannay [hereafter *ADCP*] (Edinburgh, 1932), p. 375.

[19] C.H. van Rhee, *Litigation and Legislation*, p. 16.

[20] *APS* ii, pp. 335–6, c. 2.

ordour of proceding at all tymes" and were to "conforme to resoun, equitie and justice".[21]

Much of the content of these statutes was administrative rather than strictly procedural in character, regulating the number required for a quorum, the order for hearing actions (i.e. "tabling"), other matters associated with tabling, calling and continuations, the roles of procurators, clerks and macers, and the fees they might charge. They did not amount to a comprehensive code. The two central procedural issues which are addressed were the taking of oral evidence from witnesses and the pleading of dilatory exceptions.[22] In addition there was guidance laid down for the Lords themselves about how they should deliberate and vote in reaching a decision. Both procedural items are characteristic of a Romano-canonical approach, in which a court would rely on written depositions of evidence, and in which certain types of defence to claims would be categorised in terms of the Romano-canonical taxonomy of "exceptions", originating in pre-Justinianic procedural law and elaborated further by medieval jurists.[23] Such depositions arose from separate ancillary hearings. Three Lords each week were deputed to sit separately to "examyne all witnes" for up to four hours every afternoon. We know from the records of their daily business that they would examine the witnesses in line with "interragoturs",[24] pre-prepared lists of questions handed in by the parties, and the resulting depositions would be then be "kepit in the register".[25] This business was quite separate from the plenary sittings of the Session as a whole, at which the submissions of the parties and their procurators were heard but not the oral testimony of witnesses. Following Romano-canonical procedure, the evidence taken was private until formally "published"

[21] *ADCP*, p. 374.

[22] An essential perspective is also provided in Finlay, *Men of Law in Pre-Reformation Scotland*, pp. 87–122.

[23] C.H. van Rhee, "The role of exceptions in Continental civil procedure", in *Adventures of the Law: Proceedings of the Sixteenth British Legal History Conference, Dublin, 2003*, ed. P. Brand, K. Costello and W.N. Osborough (Dublin, 2005), pp. 88–105.

[24] I.e. interrogatories (questions to be put to witnesses). In Romano-canonical procedure these were the questions put forward by the defender for examination of witnesses, whilst the factual questions for the pursuer were set out in "articles" which reflected the factual claims made in the "positions" which provided the detailed claims supporting the original "libel": Helmholz, *The Oxford History of the Laws of England Volume I*, pp. 322, 339.

[25] Edinburgh, National Archives of Scotland [hereafter NAS] CS 5/41, fols. 70, 131.

by the full court. It was laid down in the statutes that "all publicationis of witnes and uthir attestationis and examinatioun of proces be maid before the haill auditour", a reference to the whole court.[26] In relation to exceptions, a provision was made concerning:

> [the] proces and formalite to be kepit by advocatis in pleying befor the lordis, that ane delatour exceptioun being proponit and repellit be ane interlocutor of the lordis, that the advocatis, procuratoris or parteis tharselfis sall propone all the laiff of thair delatouris at anis.[27]

This last measure had a long pedigree in the *ius commune*, going back to the attempt made by Innocent III in the early thirteenth century to force litigants in the church courts to bring all their dilatory exceptions at once, thus reducing delay.[28] "Dilatory" exceptions were one of the three main categories of exception recognised in the *ius commune*, alongside "peremptory" exceptions and those which were difficult to classify and therefore "mixed".[29] Dilatory exceptions were particularly important to regulate, since under Romano-canonical procedure they could only be pleaded during the initial stages of the litigation up to *litis contestatio* or else they would be lost. Matters covered included fundamental issues such as objections to jurisdiction. It is telling that this specific aspect of procedure was singled out for treatment in the ancillary statutes of the College of Justice in 1532. Overall, however, the statutes clearly presuppose the continuation of existing rules of procedure in the Session, with nothing especially innovative beyond a degree of clarification. Nevertheless, it can be noted that they demonstrate significant reliance on Romano-canonical norms.

The structure of the Session as a collegiate court

Though not in itself a matter of procedure, another feature of the Session around 1532 which had important procedural implications

[26] *ADCP*, p. 376.

[27] *ADCP*, p. 377.

[28] L. Fowler-Magerl, *Ordines iudiciarii and Libelli de ordine iudiciorum (from the middle of the twelfth to the end of the fifteenth century)*, Typologie des sources du Moyen Age occidental, fasc.63 A-III.1 (Turnhout, 1994), p. 43. For some further comment on the issue of delay in procedure, see A.M. Godfrey, "Civil Procedure, Delay and the Court of Session in Sixteenth Century Scotland", in *The Law's Delay: Essays on Undue Delay in Civil Litigation*, ed. C.H. van Rhee (Antwerp, 2004), pp. 107–119.

[29] Helmholz, *The Oxford History of the Laws of England Volume I*, p. 323.

was its collegiate nature. This can be seen as reflecting a concept of a court very different from the medieval Scottish model of a court of suitors presided over by a feudal lord or royal officer such as a sheriff or justiciar. There was a bench of up to fifteen judges, and after 1532 a quorum was required of at least ten, as well as the chancellor or president, for giving decrees and other sentences. The association with the *ius commune* had a more direct aspect in institutional terms, since a prominent model for a collegial court was available in the fifteenth century *Sacra Rota Romana*, erected in 1418 into a collegiate court of 30 auditors, subsequently reduced to 12 in 1472.[30] The literal origins of the collegiate nature of the Scottish court are explained simply by its original structure being that of the King's Council. This was by definition an entity consisting of a number of individuals engaged in collective decision-making. Prior to 1532 the Session could be constituted with an even larger bench, but its collegiate nature was acknowledged more directly by its incorporation as a College of Justice in 1532. It sat as a whole court, with its daily composition or "sederunt" listed in its register of acts and decreets. We have already seen how evidence would be presented to such sittings in written depositions taken in hearings separate from the plenary sessions. This reflects one of the most typical procedural effects of adopting a collegiate model for a court as witnessed on the European continent. As Arthur Engelmann stated:

> for such collegial courts it was an obvious measure of economy to commit examinations of witnesses to one of its members deputed for the purpose, and this accordingly became a usual mode of proceeding, the court itself making its acquaintance with the testimony solely through the report of the examining judge.[31]

The decision-making of the Session remained collegiate in this way until the nineteenth century, when reforms to the structure of the court resulted in some modification which rendered it exceptional for the court to sit as a whole thereafter.[32]

---

[30] J.J. Robertson, "The Canon Law Vehicle of Civilian Influence with Particular Reference to Scotland", in *The Civilian Tradition and Scots Law*, ed. Carey Miller and Zimmermann, pp. 117–133 at p. 122.

[31] A. Engelmann et al., *A History of Continental Civil Procedure* (London, 1928), pp. 64–65.

[32] N. Phillipson, *The Scottish Whigs and the Reform of the Court of Session 1785–1830*, Stair Society 37 (Edinburgh, 1990).

In the previous chapter, the debate about the acquisition of the title of "College of Justice" was reviewed and it was noted that it is highly improbable that it was copied from any foreign model, as maintained by Stein and Hannay. Stein had pointed to the institution of municipal "colleges of judges" in the north of Italy from the thirteenth century onwards, and argued that the "proposal was explained to Pope Clement as a desire to establish a college of judges because it was thought that, if it were expressed in that form, Clement would understand substantially what [King] James intended".[33] As we have noted, Professor Cairns has persuasively countered this suggestion, commenting that "the idea of creating a *collegium* as an incorporated body to hold property for a specified institutional purpose was perfectly familiar in Scotland".[34] Moreover, as well as accepting Cairns' argument, it is even more important to note that the *structure* of the court along collegiate lines should be seen more simply as a native feature of the King's Council, and one which would surely have been most familiar of all to Pope Clement from the structure of the *Rota* itself.

What were the implications for procedure of the collegiate nature of the Session? From the statutes of 1532, as well as the practice of the court revealed in its records, it is clear that its collegiality was genuine, and that it determined or at least significantly informed the *modus operandi* of the court. We have already noted the implications for the taking of evidence. The Lords made their decisions collectively by carrying out a vote amongst themselves. The statutes made by the Lords related how submissions by parties were to be addressed to the whole bench. They stated that "the lordis beand sittin done and billis begune to be red, that silence be had amongis the lordis, and that na man commone nor speke of ony mater". After all of the arguments and disputations had been made, they further provided that the Lords should "haldand silence" while the chancellor or president asked for votes to be given "in the ordour be the actis and bukis of counsale...and that nane argone ane uthir in the gevin thairof".[35] The record demonstrates that parties were very alive to this aspect of the court's procedure. On 13 May 1529 it is recorded, for example, that the advocate Robert Leslie "allegit that the

---

[33] P.G. Stein, "The College of Judges of Pavia", *Juridical Review* 64 (1952), 204–213 at p. 212.

[34] J.W. Cairns, "Revisiting the Foundation of the College of Justice", in *Miscellany Five*, ed. H.L. MacQueen, Stair Society 52 (Edinburgh, 2006), pp. 27–50 at p. 29.

[35] *ADCP*, p. 376.

lordis yisterday vetit apoun the irrevalidatioun [*sic*] of the summondis and as he allegit gaif interlocutor that the libell was nocht relevant". Leslie protested that the summons should no longer have process.[36] Very occasionally, the controversial nature of a decision will be reflected in the record by the naming of those Lords who dissented from it. For example, on 28 April 1531 there was a summons called in the King's name against Sir David Young, chaplain, for "the contempcioune done be him contrar our said sovereine lord in breking of his act of parliament in the impetratioune of vicarage of Tibbermure" whilst Young was abroad in Rome. Young was found guilty despite a protest by the archbishop of St Andrews "for himself and all the remanent of the clergy" that nothing should prejudice the privileges of the church, and that they "apprevis nocht the act of parliament insofar as it may be any way contrar the privilege of halykirk".[37] However, unusually, it is comprehensively stated that "all the lordes spirituale and temporale except the abbot of Kinloss and dene of Dunbar declarit that Sir David Young had brokin the acte of parliament".[38]

Parties understood well the requirement in a collegiate court that only a bare majority of judges need be persuaded of the merits of their case. This could involve being attentive to the precise number of votes cast by the Lords in making their decisions. An action to reduce a decree could found upon any ambiguity in this aspect of the procedure. For example, on 9 December 1532 Andrew Seton of Parbroath brought an action for reduction of the decree against him which had been made in favour of William Scott, a burgess of Montrose. Five grounds of reduction were given in the summons, the second being that:

> the decreet assolzeis the said William fra the 4th reson of the said summonds simpliciter, howbeit ane grete part of the saidis lordis admittit the said reson and the remanent deliverit nocht simpliciter and determlie thirupon bot commonalie gif it wes the practik alanerlie quhairthrow the said Andro and hes procuratores protestit for nullite of the said decret.[39]

Although Seton was unsuccessful in getting the decree reduced, the illustration serves to reveal something of the openness of the deliberations of the Lords in deciding a case before them, and how the

---

[36] NAS CS 5/40, fol. 27v.
[37] NAS CS 5/42, fol. 169v.
[38] NAS CS 5/42, fol. 169v.
[39] NAS CS 6/2, fol. 25.

transparency afforded by this form of collegiate decision-making could be exploited by the parties.

In the ancillary statutes of 1532—those made by the Lords themselves following the legislation passed in Parliament—the collegiate nature of the court was accommodated by the formulation of rules governing how the judges should carry out their deliberations. Sitting in silence, seemingly the chancellor or president could require two Lords to "argone or dispute ony mater", during which no interruptions were to be made, and after which others could also be required to "argone the mater" again. Only then, "giff thai be any uthir of the lordis that hes ony oponyone or argument to mak, at thai ask leiff fra the chancellar or president, and than to argone as thai think expedient".[40] It would be interesting to know the extent to which this represented a renewed articulation of existing practice from before 1532, or whether the promulgation of new statutes prompted the formulation of some fresh and perhaps stricter rules of procedure, but this remains uncertain. Since the effect of 1532 was incorporation of the Session as a collegiate court institutionally distinct from the King's Council for the first time, this might suggest that the drafting of such rules would have been the occasion for incorporating some reforms of procedure or else some new measures to coordinate the functioning of the body in its reconstituted form. Against this is the fact that there would already have been, if anything, an even greater need for firm rules in the larger and more disparate pre-1532 bench. Generally, however, it was concluded above that the 1532 statutes of the court were likely to have constituted merely a written version of existing procedural norms and this view has been echoed in another recent study.[41]

Ius commune and procedure in the Session

The civil procedure of the Session involved a mixture of both oral and written proceeding. We have noted that in line with Romano-canonical norms there was no "trial" as such, in the sense of evidence being led from witnesses before a fact-finding jury and tested in a plenary sitting of the court in the presence of the judges collectively. Rather evidence was reduced to writing before being considered by the Lords.

[40] *ADCP*, p. 376.
[41] Finlay, *Men of Law in Pre-Reformation Scotland*, p. 53.

The evaluation of the evidence was in the hands of the judges who constituted the court, and was not put to any form of jury (though there could be some extraordinary forms of hybrid procedure which seem to have been exceptional, involving expert witnesses or assessors). The emphasis upon writing as an aid to the elaboration of argument can also be seen in occasional instructions from the Lords to a party to "geif in his allegeance and exception in writt that it may be mair cleirly understand to the said lords".[42] The hallmark of procedure before the King's Council, and therefore before the Session too, had been initiation of an action by summons under the King's signet following a bill of complaint, responsibility for which vested in the King's secretary. This reflected the general distinction between the calling of Parliament by precepts under the quarter seal out of chancery, and summons to Council.[43] The summons was a more flexible device than the brieve out of chancery, since brieves were in standard form, and essentially charged the relevant judicial figure with initiating the making of a determination of fact which would resolve the claim. A summons could narrate in as much detail as was wished the full terms of a claim, including material facts and allegations, as well as articulating a substantive legal ground justifying the remedy sought. It seems that the written documents upon which legal process was initiated in the Session were either the summons, bill of complaint or supplication, and that thereafter proceedings were oral except for the official record in the books of council, the interrogatours and depositions of evidence and the instruments which the parties might have drawn up recording particular matters of concern. No "articulated libel" in the late medieval sense of the English church courts (integrating "libel", "positions" and "articles") or equivalent "record" of written pleadings in the modern Scottish sense, focusing legal argument and relevant facts for proof in a single integrated document, was created or adjusted as the parties refined their case in successive hearings.[44] But though written pleading was relatively limited in scope, clearly there was a process of

[42] NAS CS 5/41, fol. 139 (7 December, 1530).

[43] R.K. Hannay, *The Early History of the Scottish Signet* (Edinburgh 1936), p. 25, reprinted in Hannay, *The College of Justice and other essays*, ed. H.L. MacQueen, p. 297.

[44] Helmholz, *The Oxford History of the Laws of England Volume I*, p. 322. The "record" has become a term of art in Scots law. More generally see W.A. Wilson, *Introductory Essays on Scots Law*, 2nd ed. (Edinburgh, 1984), pp. 63–70 ("Civil Procedure"); D.R. Parratt, *The Development and Use of Written Pleadings in Scots Civil Procedure*, Stair Society 48 (Edinburgh, 2006).

oral pleading based on the libel and any further written statements of pleading which happened to have been submitted.

So far as the court records reveal, pleading and procedure relied on terminology (and therefore concepts) informed by the *ius commune*.[45] Some have been touched upon already. Terms included that of the libel, litiscontestation (*litis contestatio*), the "intent" of a summons (*intentio*), the giving of "sentence" (*sententia*), "interlocutors" and "decree", the taking of evidence by commission and, as already noted, the use of written depositions of evidence and the categorisation of pleas as peremptory and dilatory exceptions. The record frequently reveals the pleading of exceptions classified explicitly on this basis. For example, in May 1529, in a case concerning the ward and marriage of Inverugie, John Hay, having claimed the assignation of these feudal casualties, protested through his "forspekar" that the Lords had "procedit to thar sentence in the haile mater nochtwithstanding that the said M. John had divers peremptour exceptiouns quhilk war nocht yit allegit nor shewin".[46] However, in this instance Adam Otterburn, the King's advocate, responded that, prior to the giving of sentence, the parties had been present before at all times and "suld nocht be admittit to sic exceptiounis now".[47]

Reference was also made to civilian and canonist sources such as the late thirteenth century and hugely influential *Speculum Iudiciale* of William Durantis, though the register of acts and decreets of the Council and Session does not tend to record such argumentation or reference.[48] However, judicial notes we find from the 1540s in the "Practicks" of John Sinclair add a helpful insight. In this regard, Professor Dolezalek has observed that, following examination of Sinclair's notes, "the methods by which the Scottish judges reached their decisions, and the law sources on which they based them, largely corresponded to those used in supreme courts on the European continent". He has also argued

---

[45] See J.A. Brundage, *Medieval Canon Law* (London, 1995), chap. 6 ("Canonical Courts and Procedure"), pp. 120–153. For a treatment of church court procedure in mid-sixteenth century Scotland see S. Ollivant, *The Court of the Official in Pre-Reformation Scotland Based on the Surviving Records of the Officials of St Andrews and Edinburgh*, Stair Society 34 (Edinburgh, 1982), chap. 6, pp. 95–118. See also R.H. Helmholz, *The Oxford History of the Laws of England Volume I*, chap. 5 ("Civil Procedure and the Law of Proof"), pp. 311–353; G.R. Evans, *Law and Theology in the Middle Ages* (London, 2002), pp. 91–104, 130–161.

[46] NAS CS 5/40, fol. 44r.

[47] NAS CS 5/40, fol. 44v.

[48] Finlay, *Men of Law in Pre-Reformation Scotland*, p. 89.

that "Sinclair's Practicks make it evident that the Court of Session in his time applied plain canon law whenever Scots domestic law did not expressly rule otherwise. The Scottish judges took it so much for granted that Scotland was governed by canon law as a subsidiary law that they did not even mention this as an issue".[49] This argument would benefit from being tested against further research in other sources, especially from the perspective of how conceptions of legal sources may have changed over time. The conceptualisation of canon law as a source in determining *secular* law in Scotland is something which until about 1600 can is difficult to infer, since the first notable attempt to discuss a hierarchy of sources of law in the Scottish courts came with the writing of Thomas Craig's *Jus Feudale* around 1599–1600, though David Chalmers of Ormond's little studied and unpublished "Dictionary of Scots Law" of 1566 may also cast some light.[50] Given the numbers of churchmen serving on the fifteenth and sixteenth century King's Council, however, the familiarity with *ius commune* sources is hardly surprising.[51] This was carried over in 1532. The institution of the new College of Justice in 1532 had stated that its fifteen judges would be those "persounis maist convenient and qualifyit thairfore" and this was to entail there being a president, with fourteen others, "half spirituale, half temporall". Since the president was in practice a churchman (and this was stated as a requirement by Pope Paul III in the bull of 1535), this meant that the pre-Reformation Session consisted of a majority of clerics, amongst them many trained canon lawyers and spiritual judges.[52] Reference is made in Sinclair's "Practicks" to over thirty glosses and commentaries, as well as the *Speculum Iudiciale*, *Practica Papiensis*, and Horborch's *Decisiones Novae*, implying that these sources were being habitually cited in

---

[49] Dolezalek, "The Court of Session as a Ius Commune Court", p. 52. See also J.W. Cairns, "*Ius Civile* in Scotland, ca. 1600", *Roman Legal Tradition* 2 (2004), 136–170 at pp. 141–147.

[50] On Craig's view see J.W. Cairns, "Historical Introduction", in *A History of Private Law in Scotland*, ed. K. Reid and R. Zimmermann (Oxford, 2000), p. 100. On Chalmers see J. Goodare, *The Government of Scotland 1560–1625* (Oxford, 2004), pp. 77–78. Generally, now see the extensive treatment in J.D. Ford, *Law and Opinion in Scotland during the Seventeenth Century* (Oxford, 2007).

[51] See also J.W. Cairns, "From *Claves Curiae* to Senators of the College of Justice. Changing Rituals and Symbols in Scottish Courts", in *Symbolische Kommunikation vor Gericht in der Frühen Neuzeit*, ed. R. Schulze (Berlin, 2006), pp. 251–268 at pp. 261–3.

[52] *APS* ii, pp. 335–336, c. 2. The bull stated 'unius Presidentis, Prelati semper Ecclesiastici': see R. Keith, *The History of the Affairs of Church and State from the beginning of the Reformation... to 1568*, ed. J.P. Lawson and C.J. Lyon, 3 vols, Spottiswoode Society (Edinburgh, 1844–50), vol. 1, p. 469.

the 1540s.[53] In terms of sixteenth century continental legal literature, Professor Dolezalek has commented that whilst reference was often made to "standard works which were 200 or even 300 years old...In contrast, very little use was made of contemporary legal literature". However, he has pointed out that this was in line with other courts of the time such as the Reichskammergericht and the *Sacra Rota Romana*.[54] Again, Scotland fits the continental pattern.

The "stile of court" as a source of procedural law

Returning to the issue raised at the beginning of the chapter about the extent to which procedure was Romano-canonical or native "practick", it is certainly a striking feature of the record that the Session did possess its own "style of court". This was its own normative set of rules of procedure, and clearly formed a *stylus curiae* in the *ius commune* procedural tradition. It therefore did not simply apply a diverse number of procedural rules drawn from disparate sources, but rather regarded these as cohering into a unified whole representing its own forensic practice. Given the long history of litigation before the King's Council, especially during the sustained development of the fifteenth century, this is hardly surprising. We find that the Lords of Session themselves often explicitly referred to the "stile of court" as their guiding principle. An example in 1529 involved an action of error which contested the process for confirming an heir in the succession to property. A secondary party to the action, who had already purchased land from the man who had been served heir, tried to call the heir in warrandice. This would have involved instituting process so that the heir as seller had to establish the disputed title or compensate with equivalent land. The Lords responded by ruling that "it is nocht the stile of court that any man may call a warand anent ane summond of error".[55] This would probably have been because in this case an action of error was not a direct challenge to a title. It was rather a challenge to the legal proceedings which had given rise to the title in confirming the status of the heir. In this case the Lords were therefore free to move swiftly to determine the allegations

[53] Dolezalek, "The Court of Session as a Ius Commune Court", p. 74.
[54] Dolezalek, "The Court of Session as a Ius Commune Court", p. 74.
[55] NAS CS 5/40, fol. 43.

of error alone, and they consequently reduced the retour of the inquest in accordance with the "style" of court.

Another form of expressing this kind of procedural norm was to refer to the "dailie use and practik" of the court. This was not just a loose reference to convention but to a body of rules seen as a source alongside the legislation of Parliament. On 31 March 1530, Alexander Ogilvy of Findlater's procurator alleged that Alexander should not have to answer a summons for reduction of a process of apprising and infeftment until the sheriff and inquest before whom the process had been led were also summoned. The argument was that "thai suld nocht be callit according to the actis of parliament of king James the third and to the dailie use and practik", though on this occasion these submissions were rejected by the Lords.[56] In March 1531 an allegation that a party had not been summoned with twenty-one days' notice was said not to be "conform to the practik and consuetude of the realm".[57] In January 1534 there was an allegation that the Lords had proceeded "wrangiously" and "contrar the stile practik and consuetude of court of sessioun".[58] The equation of the practick of the court with the "consuetude" of the realm, and reliance upon it in argument alongside statutes, implies that these matters were considered to be settled as firmly as if they had been matters of law. John Cairns has framed these issues more generally, arguing in relation to the 1540s that "we see Scots law as a largely unwritten customary system, cited imprecisely as 'practick' or 'custom', in contrast to *ius*, a term that nearly always refers to the *ius commune*".[59] But custom was in this sense a source *alongside* written law, however much the relations between the sources was open to juristic debate. There was imprecision up to a point, of course, since it was for the Lords to make a determination on any particular matter what the "consuetude" was, and sometimes the custom in question could not be clearly ascertained.[60] However, when it could be ascertained, the Lords sought to apply it.

---

[56] NAS CS 5/41, fol. 54v.

[57] NAS CS 5/42, fol. 133r.

[58] NAS CS 6/3, fol. 188.

[59] Cairns, "*Ius Civile* in Scotland, ca. 1600", p. 145.

[60] See an example of this in Cairns, "*Ius Civile* in Scotland, ca. 1600", pp. 145–146.

Other aspects of procedure in the Session

Decision-making

Until 1532 the Session was formally nothing more than a meeting of the King's Council (with some innovations in how membership was regulated from 1524 onwards). It therefore did not conform to the medieval Scottish idea of a "court", with its dependence upon the ritual of being "fenced" to certify that it had been duly constituted. The authority of such a fenced court had been considered to be vested in its suitors, and the calling of suits was part of the procedure of fencing, in which the bounds of the court would have originally been physically marked out as a ritual of constitution.[61] By definition the Council did not involve or require this form of constitution. This should not blind us to the fact that as an institution it nevertheless operated as a court. Its *authority* as a court was derived from its direct connection with the King, and this is why it had no suitors, juries or verdicts. Typically, it simply gave a decree binding the parties. The observation by Duncan that the medieval Council "made a 'decreet', it did not decide on a verdict. It was not a court, for it gave '*remedium*' but not '*iudicium*'..." seems to raise a narrowly formalistic distinction which, however pertinent it might have been to earlier centuries, lacks clear content when examining the late fifteenth and early sixteenth centuries.[62] By this time, decrees from the Council had a recognised general status in effecting a remedy which gave them just as much importance as the verdict of a jury following procedure by brieve. The differences between decrees and the retours of inquests simply reflected different forms of procedure. It is a question in its own right whether contemporaries classified the Session as a "court" or as some distinguishable form of royal tribunal, and, if so, what that distinction might have meant to them. In fact, interesting questions would arise from any evidence of a change in how the concepts in question were understood, were such evidence to come to light in relation to the Session. Professor Baker has reminded us of the need to remember that "our present image of a 'court' is the outcome of history, not the reflection of some

---

[61] P.J. Hamilton-Grierson, "Fencing the Court", 21 *Scottish Historical Review* (1924), pp. 54–62; W.C. Dickinson, "Introduction" to *The Sheriff Court Book of Fife 1515–1522*, ed. W.C. Dickinson, Scottish History Society Third Series 12 (Edinburgh, 1928), p. lxxxv; see also appendix A ("The Procedure of the Court"), p. 309.

[62] Duncan, "The Central Courts before 1532", p. 328.

constant truth which transcends history". Baker asks, "what is a court?", arguing that "when an institution has been labelled a 'court', it is easy to assume that this has somehow fixed its character, whereas in truth courts have not always shared the same characteristics".[63] In relation to the Session, we can in any event see that it behaved as a court. It made legally guided and enforceable decisions which bound the parties, explicitly drawing upon notions of reasonableness and justice in exercising a general jurisdiction.

In determining and applying the law, the Lords obviously exercised some discretion. In this regard, they often employed a test of reasonableness quite explicitly in deciding whether a submission to them should be accepted or not. An elementary example of this was when a party asked them to interpone (i.e. formally confer) their authority to a deed or agreement. In agreeing to such a request the Lords would typically declare that it was "thocht resonable". The reference to what was considered reasonable was neither purely formal nor rhetorical, as can be seen in cases where the Lords explicitly rejected a submission because it was *unreasonable*. An illustration of such a rejection came on 31 July 1532, when the Lords refused to implement a term in a lease because it was "nocht resonable". The abbot of Dryburgh had "set" (i.e. leased out) the teinds of the church and parish of Saltoun to William Crichton, "with conditione that he suld nocht suffer the teyndis of the parochin of Saltoun to be sett nor stakkit apoun the said kirklands under paine of tynsale of his tak".[64] The Lords decreed, however, that the abbot should allow the teinds to be "sett and stak...nochtwithstanding the allegeance maid be the said Maister Robert [i.e. Robert Galbraith, tutor to Lord Saltoun] in the contrar becaus the said lordes thinkes the said allegeance nocht resonable nor conforme to justice".[65]

Procedure: consent of party

Many procedures seem to have operated through the giving of the consent of the parties in the cause. There is often a formal note in the record that such consent has been given. Typical examples of this would be the procedure of "continuing" a cause (i.e. extending the hearing to

---

[63] J.H. Baker, "The Changing Concept of a Court", in J.H. Baker, *The Legal Profession and the Common Law. Historical Essays* (London, 1986), pp. 153–169 at p. 153.
[64] NAS CS 6/1, fol. 97.
[65] NAS CS 6/1, fol. 97.

a future date), or "advocating" it from another court (i.e. transferring it to the Session). However, occasionally a party would object and withhold their consent, although this did not necessarily entail a halt to proceedings. For instance, on 26 July 1530 James and Adam Wallace "dissassent to the continuation of the summonde aboune written", although they signalled that they would accept the "act" of Council in continuing the cause.[66] The action in question had already been continued, but had ended up being called during the sittings of the Exchequer. The Lords continued it again because the King had instructed them that "thai suld nocht proceid bot apoun chekkir materis".[67]

Pleading of exceptions

As Professor Helmholz states, "exceptions consisted of various means available to defendants of preventing further proceedings by objecting to one or another aspect of the plaintiff's case".[68] As we have noted earlier, dilatory exceptions required to be pleaded prior to liticontestation. This was the point at which the parties stated the matters in dispute and which required proof thereafter. The register usually gives little indication of the nature of the submissions on law which have been made prior to the Lords reaching their decision in an action, beyond relating a summary of the grounds of action founded upon in the summons. Allegations by the defender were usually recorded when, for example, they led to proof being taken. An example would be an allegation that an instrument had been forged. Occasionally, however, something of the legal debate was recorded, as when peremptory or dilatory exceptions were pleaded. A typical example was argument over what would today be referred to as a preliminary plea to the "relevancy" of the claim in law. This was one of the three main types of dilatory exceptions, along with those against the competency of the judge or court, or against the person or capacity of the claimant.[69] An instance of this occurred on 8 May 1529, when Robert Leslie, forespeaker for Lord Lovat, asked instruments that Adam Otterburn had produced a retour given for Lord Lovat concerning his being served heir to the lands of Lovat. Otterburn had "desirit to persew the retour of the dait anno 25 for

[66] NAS CS 5/41, fol. 94.
[67] NAS CS 5/41, fol. 94.
[68] Helmholz, *The Oxford History of the Laws of England Volume I*, p. 323.
[69] Helmholz, *The Oxford History of the Laws of England Volume I*, p. 324.

reduction thirof". There followed a classic statement of an argument to the relevancy, albeit with extreme concision: "the said Maister Robert allegit alwayis that he denyit not the secund punct but said the same was not relevant".[70] The facts might be true, in other words, but were not capable of supporting the legal claim being advanced. Two days later, Leslie appeared again to protest that "thai war remufit apoun the relevance of the summondis of error protestand that thai suld nocht proceid further anent the said sumondis quhill he war callit to use his defence".[71] In the event this action was referred to the discretion of the Lords for decision on the following day.[72] Relevancy was not simply a matter which might be raised by a defender. The Lords themselves can be found occasionally directing that a summons should be redrafted before being heard. For example, on 4 August 1529, in response to a summons raised by certain merchants from Danzig, the chancellor stated that the Lords were "redy" to hear the summons except that it was "nocht weile libellit", and the merchants' procurator should devise "ane relevant libell" instead.[73]

Another basis for pleading an exception, and which related to procedure, was that the defender had not been correctly served with the summons upon which the action proceeded. This meant that the formal "citation" of the defender had been incompetent. As Professor Helmholz has remarked, "a basic tenet of the *ius commune* remained that, without legitimate citation, further proceedings involving a person's rights or possessions were a nullity".[74] A submission that the summons had not been served was made by Lord Lindsay on 1 June 1529 in connection with an action against him for tinsel (forfeiture) of his office of sheriff of Fife. However, his allegation was contradicted by written proof of service: "the summondis is indorsit that the said lord was personally summond nochtwithstanding the exceptionnis proponit for the said lord that he had nocht gottin the copy of the said summondis".[75] The Lords' sentence interlocutor was also given despite Lord Lindsay's claim that he would thereby suffer prejudice. He had claimed that "he brocht not his defencis in that mater with him and desyrat ane term thirto". The

[70] NAS CS 5/40, fol. 20.
[71] NAS CS 5/40, fol. 21.
[72] NAS CS 5/40, fol. 22.
[73] NAS CS 5/40, fol. 82.
[74] Helmholz, *The Oxford History of the Laws of England Volume I*, p. 318.
[75] NAS CS 5/40, fol. 49.

"matter" to which he referred was his claim that he had been charged to enter the king's service.[76]

A further form of preliminary plea or exception was to claim personal exemption from the jurisdiction of the Lords, typically as a churchman. For example, on 20 August 1529 Henry Spittal, on behalf of Alexander Spittal, pleaded an exception that Alexander "was ane prest and suld nocht be haldin to answer befor the lordis". In this case, however, the Lords decided that he should answer, because he was summoned for intromitting with goods which pertained to the king as escheat by reason of bastardy. His status as a churchman did not of itself entitle him to exemption in such a case.[77]

Examination of witnesses

We have already noted that the taking of evidence was done separately by certain nominated Lords who were periodically delegated the task. Evidence was then produced before the whole court solely in written form. More detailed aspects of the procedures for examining witnesses can occasionally be established from the record relating to an individual case.[78] For example, on 6 April 1530 Robert Galbraith asked instruments that the Lords had assigned a certain number of individual Lords to examine the witnesses produced by John Brown in an action between him and Andrew Balony, and that he "protestit that thai suld be examinat apon the interragoturs to be gevin in".[79] Depositions of evidence from witnesses might be relevant to several different "punctes" of a summons, and could be "kepit in the register" so that the Lords could have further access them, prior to eventually giving sentence. James Douglas, earl of Morton, specifically requested the Lords to take this course during his defence of an action against him by the bishop of Galloway on 20 March 1531. In this case the depositions had already been opened and "publist". However, further allegations meant that the earl wished the Lords to maintain a record of the depositions so that they might be "avisit" by them again.[80]

[76] NAS CS 5/40, fol. 49.

[77] NAS CS 5/40, fol. 107v.

[78] For much additional and complementary information about taking of evidence see Finlay, *Men of Law in Pre-Reformation Scotland*, pp. 111–119.

[79] NAS CS 5/41, fol. 70.

[80] NAS CS 5/42, fol. 131.

In other situations, a party would compear before the Lords simply to ask "instruments" in order to record that evidence had been given. This involved the making of a notarised record of the proceedings. Although such instruments would typically relate to procedural decisions of the Lords or evidence from the parties, very occasionally the details of the evidence in question might also relate to the internal operation of the administration. These can provide a rare glimpse of such bureaucracy as there was, and its workings. For example, one case involved officials of the Chancery giving evidence in relation to deeds engrossed by them. On 11 May 1529 the laird of Wauchton asked instruments that Thomas Ballantyne, the "directour of the chancellarie", had been examined upon oath and had deponed that "he understandis that Isobell Hopper renuncit hir coniunct fee of the landis of blakbarony and as he rememberis the instrument of renunciatioune bure reservand to hir the liverent of the same for all the dais of hir lif eftir the deceis of Johne of Murray".[81]

The Lords could issue a special commission to have witnesses examined in geographically distant locations, with the resulting depositions sent back for their consideration. An example of this occurred on 22 March 1531. The Lords ordained letters to be directed in the form of a commission to the official and commissary of Moray to "summond ressave and call witnesses apon the intrometting with the teynd sharis" of the parsonage of Inverkeithing. The official was to "sumonde the party to compeir at certane dayis to hear the witnesses suorne and except agains thaime and to clois the said depositiounis of the witnesses under thair seile".[82] The depositions would then be sent to the Lords. Having been "avisit therewith", they would give their sentence.[83] When a party could not give evidence for justifiable reasons, the Lords could also order evidence to be taken under commission. For example, on 29 July 1529 a pursuer, Marion Mowat, was considered too "agit and feble throw infirmite" and it was accepted that she "may nocht travale" and so the Lords ordered letters in the form of a commission to be directed to the vicar general of Moray and his commissaries to "ressaif hir aith apon the premiss and as beis deponit befor him that he send the same agane closit undir his seile to the lordis of counsale".[84] These examples also

---

[81] NAS CS 5/40, fol. 22.
[82] NAS CS 5/42, fol. 134.
[83] NAS CS 5/42, fol. 134.
[84] NAS CS 5/40, fol. 67v.

show ways in which the secular and sacred jurisdictions interacted in a complex and intimate fashion which is not fully captured when they are portrayed as if they were wholly discrete jurisdictional systems.

Sometimes, the requirements of evidence-taking before the Lords went beyond the need to hear from witnesses and involved reliance on the findings of a judicial process in another court. One example shows the Session apparently issuing a commission to prompt such process in the church courts. In this case the Lords "continued" and thereby postponed the Session process so that a matter properly within the jurisdiction of the church courts could first be resolved there, after which the civil action was to carry on. This is suggestive of separate and parallel civil and ecclesiastical court processes being sometimes required in a given case. On 20 August 1529 William Wood of Bonnington, Arthur Panton and the King's advocate had brought an action against Alexander Dunbar for the moveable goods of the late Sir William Chancellor. The goods had fallen to the Crown as escheat upon William's death, since he "was borne bastard and deit bastard without lauchful airis of his bodie gottin and without lauchful dispositioune maid be him of his saidis gudis in his livetyme". The action, however, was continued for almost six months, and letters were ordained to "be direct in the form of commission at instance of said William and Arthur to persew and mak the said bastardry to be lauchfully and sufficientlie previt befor the spirituale juge competent and mak the same to be retourit agane to the saidis lordis", so that they could thereafter minister justice on "the punctis of the said principale summond".[85] Proof could not be made of this matter in the Council, even though the question of escheat was certainly within its jurisdiction. However, procedure was flexible enough to allow a retour to be made containing the findings of a church court in respect of matters pertaining to its jurisdiction. Such instances illustrate again an apparently easy interaction between process in the secular and spiritual courts.

The Session also had power to send out its own officials to take evidence in exceptional circumstances. For example, on 27 July 1532 the Lords ordained that:

> ane clerk of the court to pass over and exemine the auld failzeit personis allegit that best knawis this mater becaus thai ar waik personis and in danger that thai deceis in the meyntime and that thir deposicions be closit

[85] NAS CS 5/40, fol. 107v.

> quhill the said day [i.e. the continued hearing before the Session, set for 8 November] reservand to the party all lauchful defences in this matter and agains the said witnesses.[86]

The general power to have depositions taken elsewhere and then retoured to the Session in Edinburgh extended to evidence taken abroad. Scottish trade with the Low Countries was legally granted as a monopoly to a particular port known as the "staple". From 1508 this was Veere in the province of Zeeland. Scottish merchants could litigate before a "conservator" in the staple port.[87] But the Session might also rely in its own proceedings upon the prior conclusion of subsidiary proceedings in Veere. On 13 August 1532, for example, in respect of money that was alleged to be owing by John Moffat, "conservator of the privileges of the nation of the realme in Flanders", the Lords continued the action for six months and ordained Moffat to "have ane commission to the said lordis and jugis of the camfeir [i.e. Campvere/Veere] to ressave the witness to be producit be the saide Johne and writingis for preving thirof". They also ordered the pursuer, John Barclay, a burgess of Edinburgh, to compear personally or by procurator in Campvere "all the lauchfull dayis of the monethis of October, Novembre, Decembre and Januar" to see the witnesses sworn and writings produced, the results of which were then to be retoured to the Lords of Council.[88] Similarly, this form of procedure can be seen operating in reverse upon occasion. On 27 November 1533, for example, the Lords ordered depositions to be taken from a burgess of Edinburgh and an inhabitant of Leith, to be sent to the Lords of Mechelen (i.e. the Great Council of Malines, in the Netherlands). They had been presented with a supplication by John Forrester of Leith in which he explained how James Watson of Flanders had shipped "wyne and uther merchandice in the said Johns faderis schip and for fault of payment of the frauche [i.e. freight] thirof his fadir gart arest the said wyne".[89] Following this, Watson's factor, James Henderson, "allegit that he causit lows the said arest and found Francis Aikman burgess of Edinburgh and John Dalmahoy

---

[86] NAS CS 6/1, fol. 90v.

[87] A.D. Gibb, "International Private Law in Scotland in the Sixteenth and Seventeenth Centuries", *Juridical Review* 39 (1927), 369–407; D. Ditchburn, *Scotland and Europe: The Medieval Kingdom and its Contacts with Christendom, 1214–1560* (East Linton, 2001), pp. 12–13; M. Lynch, "Staple Ports" in *The Oxford Companion to Scottish History*, ed. M. Lynch (Oxford, 2001), pp. 590–591.

[88] NAS CS 6/1, fol. 101v.

[89] NAS CS 6/3, fol. 94.

in Leith sourteis...for the said frauch all that law will". Moreover, he claimed to have deposited certain monies with Francis and John to "relief" them of the surety, all of which they denied. The problem was that "for that caus the said James Watson now cumis and pleyis the said Johne befor the lordis of Machlyne". He also wanted to call Francis and John before them "be ane masour to declare the verite in the said matter".[90] Now that the matter was before the Session, and since Francis and John "beand sworn and diligentlie examinat declarit that James Henrisone lest na money with thaim", the Lords ordained a testimonial to be made to the Council of Malines "for declaration of the verite".[91]

That there were of course risks present in relation to the reliability of taking written depositions is brought out in a supplication of Gilbert Inglis which was heard on 20 June 1533. He explained that he was under summons before the Lords of Council (referring to appearing before those Lords of Council who constituted the Session of course) and that the pursuer had "divers witnesses examinat to preve the punctis of hir summondis". However, "the witness has said planelie that thai war nocht examat apon the punctis of the said summondis and the clerk writar of thir deposicionis wraite thame nocht as thai deponit". He now wished to summon the witnesses personally so that the "verite" of the depositions could be established. The Lords were obliged to order the witnesses to be summoned to appear in six days, to be "new examat".[92]

Pronunciation of decree

It is apparent from the record that, once the Lords gave their final decision in an action, there still had to be a formal pronunciation of the decree for it to have legal force. This requirement of public pronunciation of a sentence was discussed by Neilson and Paton in relation to their edition of the late fifteenth century council records, although more with reference to the history of other countries than directly to the Scottish evidence.[93] In the *ius commune* a sentence given in secret was invalid, hence the need for a definitive sentence such

[90] NAS CS 6/3, fol. 94.
[91] NAS CS 6/3, fol. 94.
[92] NAS CS 6/2, fol. 194.
[93] *Acts of the Lords of Council 1496–1501*, ed. G. Neilson and H.M. Paton [hereafter referred to as *ADC* ii] (Edinburgh, 1918), pp. xlix–lxiv.

as a decree to be publicly pronounced.[94] In the record between 1529 and 1534, reference to the procedure arose occasionally when a party requested that the pronunciation of a decree be suspended for a short period of time. For example, Robert Galbraith asked instruments on 27 January 1531 that the King's advocate consented to the suspension of the pronunciation of a decree given against the master and earl of Crawford in relation to the feudal casualty of non-entry. The reason for the twenty-day suspension was "gif instrument of seising war schawn of the land contenit in the sumonds" then the decree would "be drawn furth of the buke", and removed from the council register.[95]

In a case on 5 December 1532 involving the pronunciation of a decree, the Lords "delayt the same to divers termes". This was in order that both parties should "schaw baith thair ryte", apparently because the decree had been given "for null defens".[96] The case called again on 15 January 1533. The underlying dispute concerned the right attached to a vicarage to collect fruits and duties from certain parishioners. Alexander Hepburn, who had successfully prevented the decree being pronounced at the previous hearing, produced the letters issued to him in the matter. These would conflict with the decree were it to be pronounced in favour of Edward Cunningham. At this hearing, Hepburn's letters were examined and pronounced "iustlie procedit". The Lords then ruled that Cunningham's decree was "to stand and remaine unpronuncit and to be of nane availe na effect".[97] This was not the end of the matter, since the decree was simply to remain unpronounced until Hepburn's decree was properly reduced, something which would require a summons of reduction to be initiated. Cunningham protested strongly a few days later, alleging that he was "hurt be the lordis in the non pronunciation of the decrete" and asking for written instruments to be taken recording that he "apelit to the lordis of parliament".[98] Such an appeal would be of doubtful competence, as was discussed in chapter 1, and there seems to be no record of one being made. In another case on the same day, a complaint was made that a decree had been "written", suspending the validity of other letters, but that the "clerkes refusis to deliver...the copy of the said

[94] Helmholz, *The Oxford History of the Laws of England Volume I*, p. 343.
[95] NAS CS 5/42, fol. 12.
[96] NAS CS 6/2, fol. 24r.
[97] NAS CS 6/2, fol. 48.
[98] NAS CS 6/2, fol. 49.

act" due to a delay in the decree being pronounced.[99] Clearly, then, in some cases pronunciation was not merely a formality but was very much a live stage of procedure which provided parties with a further opportunity to raise objections and generally delay the conclusion of the action in question.

Excommunication and procedure in the Session

An important respect in which process before Council and Session could follow and depend upon process in the church courts was the civil procedure of putting to the horn, which meant being declared a rebel and in escheat of the Crown. It could follow process of "cursing", or excommunication, in the church courts. Excommunication was the ultimate sanction of the church courts but in Scotland had consequences in civil law by allowing civil remedies to follow. The canon law had early on come to the view that "where excommunication proved insufficient to secure obedience to its law, sterner measures that were otherwise unavailable to the spiritual courts, could be invoked".[100] Scotland, like England, was untypical in European terms, however, by putting secular jurisdiction "at the church's service".[101] A typical illustration is found in the supplication of the parishioners of the church of Crawford Lindsay on 23 August 1529, in which they complained that Sir Alexander Inglis had obtained royal letters "conform to the ordinaris letters" charging them to pay to him their teinds and fruits. They had complained to the official of Glasgow, but found themselves under cursing, and now wished to be assoilzied (i.e. absolved) from this and to see the judge ordinary's letters annulled and discharged, since they had paid their fruits. However, their approach to Council was necessary because Alexander meanwhile "intendis to put the saidis parishioners to the horn be our soveraine lordis letters of quhilkis ar past apoun the ordinaris letters now beand admittit". In consequence, the Lords intervened to suspend Alexander's letters, and relax the parishioners from the horn insofar as they had been declared rebels. In regulating such matters, the Session was the superior court to which aggrieved parties could turn for a remedy. Its role in this respect will

[99] NAS CS 6/2, fol. 49.
[100] Helmholz, *The Oxford History of the Laws of England Volume I*, p. 111.
[101] Helmholz, *The Oxford History of the Laws of England Volume I*, p. 111.

be further examined in the next chapter in considering its exercise of a supervisory jurisdiction.

Advocation

Advocation was a novel procedure which represents one of the most significant procedural developments of the early sixteenth century, carrying with it immense jurisdictional implications. It was the technical procedure which allowed the assertion of superior jurisdiction. By it a legal action could be transferred from a "lower" court to the Session by order of the Lords of Session. The regularisation of such a procedure itself indicates the extent to which the jurisdiction of the Council was becoming integrated by the early sixteenth century into the structure of jurisdiction provided for in the medieval common law. With the power of advocation, the Lords could insist that particular legal actions be brought before them. The significance of the use of such a power can hardly be exaggerated, especially when it is remembered that the Session, stemming from the King's Council as it did, was a new form of tribunal outside the medieval structure of courts, and hitherto had no established procedure for asserting jurisdiction over other courts. Such assertion would involve more than merely regulating and interfering with the legal process in another court. A substantive assertion of jurisdiction would involve reviewing the judgments of other courts, substituting a new determination, or else outright transfer of the legal action. Advocation involved such a wholescale transfer of the case to the Session from the "subordinate" court. Indeed, the existence of the procedure of advocation must have acted to define other jurisdictions as being subordinate in this sense. Until the 1530s, the more typical procedure had been to exclude the jurisdiction of a local court only on exceptional grounds and to grant a special commission to a sheriff *in hac parte* and in this sense derogate from the jurisdiction of the judge ordinary. However, advocation meant derogating from the judge ordinary in order to have the case determined directly by the Session.

Advocation was used regularly by the 1530s, but was still a novelty in that decade. It represents a procedural development whose profound institutional and jurisdictional implications are consistent with the overall argument of this book that the foundation of the College of Justice in 1532 was the decisive final step in the Session becoming a central civil court with an effectively supreme jurisdiction. It was seemingly not in evidence prior to 1500, and a preliminary examination of the council register between 1500 and 1530 reveals no mention of the procedure by name.[102] The point is hard to assess conclusively, since there may be instances of advocation in which the term is not deployed, though only two examples of this before 1530 have been noticed by the present writer in a search of the register. The first arose in 1508, when a party renounced and discharged a process before the sheriff of Ayr, though considering that it be "richt and just", in order that "the lordis mycht proceed in the said actioun".[103] The second arose in 1523 against the background of a feud, when at the instance of Andro Boswell, laird of Bargany, the Lords suspended letters directed to the sheriff of Ayr and his deputes. This was stated to be because of "inymite", and the Lords instead ordered the supplicant to compear before them and produce his right to occupy certain lands so that they might then decide the issue. The Lords accepted that Andro "may nocht surelie cum befor thame [i.e. the sheriff and deputies] to use his iust defencis".[104] Whatever further complexities might attach themselves to this example upon closer study, it does nevertheless resemble an advocation. Both of these examples, however, are more suggestive of an intervention to correct a default of justice arising from the partiality of the judge than an application of any more general procedure based on an assertion of an ordinary jurisdiction to transfer causes or review the decrees of lower courts.

Of course, the King's Council already possessed a long-standing jurisdiction of a supervisory nature over allegations of impropriety in courts and legal process, and this will be considered in the next chapter. The fifteenth-century Council could hear allegations of error in the giving of a verdict by an assize, for example, and this aspect of its role was enshrined in legislation.[105] However, the ideas which underlay that supervisory jurisdiction seem only to have crystallised in a more general way into a regularised procedural form by the 1530s. It was this development which provided procedural structures to allow the assertion of superior jurisdiction by the Session over other courts from this point onwards. Taking a sample of the five years between April 1529 and

[102] Of course, it is possible that a closer reading of the record may produce some examples, especially ones in which the term advocation was not used. It seems unlikely, however, that this would disturb the general analysis being presented.

[103] NAS CS 5/19, fol. 121v. (23 January, 1508).

[104] NAS CS 5/33, fol. 148r. (4 February, 1523).

[105] *APS* ii, p. 100, c. 9.

May 1534, there are no cases in the eighteen months between April 1529 and October 1530, but between October 1530 and May 1534 there are at least fourteen identifiable cases of advocation (of which eleven expressly involve advocation by name). After the first in October 1530,[106] there is one in July 1531,[107] none at all in 1532, and, remarkably, no fewer than nine between May and December 1533,[108] with three further cases in the first five months of 1534.[109] Since only this five year period from 1529 to 1534 has been closely surveyed, caution must be expressed in regarding this increase as being connected with the foundation of the College of Justice in 1532. However, it certainly raises the possibility that after the foundation of the College of Justice there was a greater desire and willingness by the Lords of Session to advocate actions before themselves.

In eleven of the fourteen cases found between 1530 and 1534 there is no doubt that a procedure was being used which was recognised by the parties and the Lords as advocation. This is because the word "advocation" is used.[110] In the other three this is a matter of inference.[111] Of these three, one is recognisably an advocation in all but name, displaying similar procedural steps to those in the explicit cases of advocation.[112] The other two stand out as involving a specific charge to the officers of the lower court to desist and cease their proceedings and refer or remit the action to the Lords of Council, the effect of which seems identical to an advocation.[113] The fourteen advocation cases related to a broad range of matters but involved rights in land in particular, though two concerned spuilzie (dispossession) and two concerned debt. The subject-matter of the actions otherwise included rights to the feudal casualty of non-entry (a matter which in any case seems to have been within the exclusive jurisdiction of the Lords when the King's interest was involved), the reduction of infeftments, cognition of the possession of

[106] NAS CS 5/41, fol. 120r.

[107] NAS CS 5/43, fol. 5v.

[108] NAS CS 6/2, fol. 158v.; CS 6/2, fol. 179v.; CS 6/2, fol. 182; CS 6/2, fol. 218; CS 6/3 fol. 58r.; CS 6/3, fol. 77; CS 6/3, fol. 80r.; CS 6/3, fol. 141v.; CS 6/3, fol. 142.

[109] CS 6/3, fol. 150v.; CS 6/4, fol. 2; CS 6/4, fol. 145v.

[110] NAS CS 5/43, fol. 5v.; CS 6/2, fol. 158v.; CS 6/2, fol. 182; CS 6/2, fol. 218; CS 6/3 fol. 58r.; CS 6/3, fol. 77; CS 6/3, fol. 80r.; CS 6/3, fol. 141v.; CS 6/3, fol. 150v; CS 6/4, fol. 2; CS 6/4, fol. 145v.

[111] NAS CS 5/41, fol. 120r.; CS 6/2, fol. 179v.; CS 6/3, fol. 141v.

[112] *Ogilvy v. Garden*, NAS CS 5/41, fol. 120r.

[113] *Lindsay v. Beton*, NAS CS 6/2, fol. 179v.; *Gray v. Achison and others*, NAS CS 6/3, fol. 141v.

lands, cognition of the existence of a tack (i.e. lease) over lands, cognition of whether lands pertained to their possessor in heritage, and the reduction of a tack on lands which were held in ward.

In eight of the cases in which explicit reference was made to advocation, the consent of the parties to the advocation is recorded. In five of the other six cases no consent is mentioned. Two involved a charge to the lower court to remit the matter, one of which apparently followed from a writing from the King charging the Lords to advocate the action to themselves.[114] It is striking that of three non-entry cases, in one it is recorded that the action is advocated with consent of the parties from the sheriff of Edinburgh,[115] whilst no consent is recorded in the other two. Presumably, as already noted, consent was not required to advocate such an action when the interests of the King were affected. This would follow when the issue related to non-entry to land by vassals who held of the Crown, in which case the matter ought originally to have been pursued before the Council.[116] Generally, though, it is not possible to demonstrate that the Lords would or could use their power of advocation against the will of one of the parties, even if it would seem likely that this might have been possible. The range of these advocations is nevertheless evident. It is notable that the actions in question were advocated from a variety of courts. Sometimes it was from a sheriff *in hac parte* acting under a special judicial commission. Other cases were advocated from the sheriffs of Edinburgh, Ayr, Peebles and Linlithgow, the regality court of St Andrews, a bailie court in Tranent, and the admiral court. In one case simultaneous proceedings before the barony court of Burleigh and the sheriff of Kinross were both advocated to the Lords.[117]

It should be mentioned that there were other actions which may well have been advocations in substance but which have not been included for discussion because an alternative characterisation is more appropriate, given the principal issue in the case. For example, on 8 May 1534, in relation to an action called before the commissary of Dunkeld, the Lords ordained "the mater to be callit and persewit befor thaim becaus

[114] *Barton and others v. earl of Bothwell and earl of Argyll*, NAS CS 6/3, fol. 58r.

[115] *Carnis v. Leis*, NAS CS 6/2, fol. 182.

[116] For helpful background see Craig Madden, "Royal Treatment of Feudal Casualties in Late Medieval Scotland", *Scottish Historical Review* 55 (1976), 172–194 at pp. 181–184 and R. Nicolson, "Feudal Developments in Late Medieval Scotland", *Juridical Review* (1973), 1–21.

[117] NAS CS 6/4, fol. 145v.

it concerns the non-entries of land quhilkis perteins to the kings grace and he his thesaurer and advocat hes interes in the mater".[118] This action had been treated as one concerning jurisdiction between courts, rather than the transfer of an action from one civil court to another. It is not clear whether it was regarded as an advocation or not.

Advocation seems to have involved a fairly standard procedure, which was often mentioned in the directions given by the Lords as to how the case was to proceed. If a matter was advocated from a court where proceedings had already commenced, then it would proceed before the Lords not by summons, but by a "simple bill of complaint", sometimes referred to as a simple supplication or bill. A simple bill of this sort required only fifteen days warning to proceed, but it would be provided that the action would otherwise proceed as though it was "a peremptour summons". The other kind of direction given for how an advocated action should proceed was that it should be "in the same maner as it suld or mycht have been procedit" before the judge from whom the action was being advocated.[119] Whether this even bypassed the need for a bill is unclear.

Appeal

The question of appeal was touched on earlier in this book in relation to attempts to appeal from the Session to Parliament. It was noted that there was never any such right of appeal, though sometimes parties alleged there to be one, and some exceptional examples exist of forms of interaction between the Session and Parliament. There was in fact no appeal beyond the Session in its fifteenth-century form or later, since Council operated independently of the ordinary legal processes of falsing the doom which had hitherto placed Parliament in a procedurally superior position to lower courts under the medieval common law. A party might try, however, to have the Session itself review one of its own decisions. The method was to raise a summons for "retreting" (i.e. reduction) of the decree. For example, on 30 July 1529 James Colville of Ochiltree supplicated the Lords for permission to raise a summons for reduction of a decree of recognition "sen the same was evill gevin and agains conscience", in response to which the Lords ordained that he

---

[118] NAS CS 6/4, fol. 129v.

[119] See e.g. *Dumduf v. Colquhoun*, NAS CS 6/3, fol. 77.

was to have a summons "as he pleis libell".[120] A summons for reduction of a decree of spuilzie raised by George Arnot of that Ilk laid out three grounds justifying the remedy, on which the Lords heard argument on 22 March 1530. First, the claim was made that George had never been lawfully summoned and that the decree had correspondingly been given for "null defence". Second, the decree was given "be depositionis of certaine suspect witnesses". Third, the pursuer had "na actione to persew", because the lands in question pertained to a third party in heritage, at the relevant date.[121] In this instance, however, the defender was assoilzied (i.e. absolved) and "quyte therefra in tyme tocum" from the summons "as it is now libillit".

An attempt on 30 March 1531 to have a decree reduced exhibits one of the few instances of the Lords of Council and Session finding themselves to be "na competent juges" to an action, although more in the sense of there being a bar and limitation on reducing the decree in question than that there was a jurisdictional bar stemming from another court being the appropriate forum. It was a question of procedural competence rather than jurisdiction. The objection came from the bishop, dean and chapter of Moray, and a chaplain to whose chaplaincy the land in issue had been mortified (i.e. bequeathed in perpetuity). An exception was pleaded that the Lords were not competent judges for "retraction" (i.e. reduction) of a decreet given previously by the Lords of Council in June 1496, because the decree had been "alterit" since then and the lands mortified to the Church. The Lords accepted that they could not reduce the decree "becaus it is aboune the space of xxx yeiris bigane sen the said decrete was gevin and als the same was alterit sen syne and the saidis lande mortifiit to the kirk".[122] It appears that in 1496 Alexander Innes of that Ilk had been decreed to pay 300 merks to the earl of Buchan, who had recovered the debt by apprising the land now in issue. Because this land had been mortified to the church, the decree itself could not now be reduced, even though Alexander protested that he "intendit nocht to desir na process of apprising nor mortificatioun to be reducit at this tyme".[123]

Occasionally, a party against whom decree had been given can be found protesting and alleging its nullity even before it had been

---

[120] NAS CS 5/40, fol. 79.
[121] NAS CS 5/41, fol. 30.
[122] NAS CS 5/42, fol. 154v.
[123] NAS CS 5/42, fol. 155.

pronounced. We find in such instances the adumbration of what might later become grounds for reduction in what would effectively constitute a kind of appeal. A case of this sort occurred on 31 March 1531, when Andrew Seton of Parbroath protested for "nullitie of the said decret" which had been given in favour of William Scott of Montrose. It was stated that this followed:

> in so far as it hapins to be gevin apon the thrid resone conteint in the sumonde rasit be the said Andro becaus thir wes na discussioun nor determinatioun maid be the lordes thirupoune and als becaus the lordis deliverit nocht determinantly geif it wer the practik.[124]

This example is particularly interesting since it involved such a specific allegation that the Lords had erred in the manner of reaching their decision. The Lords' discretion was expected to be exercised in accordance with commonly understood procedural norms as enshrined in their practick.

Though no appeal lay beyond the Session, and the Lords clearly saw the remedy for an unjust decree as a summons for its reduction, this did not stop an aggrieved party occasionally challenging a decision of the Lords by declaring that they would appeal to Parliament. On 18 January 1533, for example, Edward Cunningham complained that since the Lords refused to pronounce a decree given for him, he "appelit to the lordis of parliament" since he "knawand him hurt thirin".[125] Three days earlier the Lords had refused to pronounce the decree since another party also had a decree in the matter, which would have to be reduced before effect could be given to that of Cunningham.[126] However, the outcome of any "appeal" to Parliament in this case is not recorded, and there is no reference to such a complaint in the parliamentary register. The inference is either that no such judicial appeal was ever attempted, or that it was held to be not competent in the first place.

Whether or not such an appeal could be made to Parliament, there is no doubt that the Session could itself refer a matter to Parliament in the highly exceptional case of the law being considered impossibly ambiguous. There is an example of this in the parliamentary register on 10 June 1535, already referred to in chapter 1. James Kennedy of Blairquhan and Thomas McLellane of Gelston were in dispute over

---

[124] NAS CS 5/42, fol. 159v.
[125] NAS CS 6/2, fol. 49.
[126] NAS CS 6/2, fol. 48.

the mails and duties of the lands of Castlecrook and Killemanoth in Wigtownshire, and were conducting litigation before the Session. Thomas held the lands in heritage but James was his superior. Since Thomas had been at the horn for a year and a day (i.e. technically declared a rebel due to default in fulfilling his obligation), James laid claim to the mails and duties for the rest of Thomas' lifetime under the laws of the realm. However, the Lords of Session felt it necessary to refer "to the Lordis thre estatis of parliament for Interpretatioun of certane lawis of the realme schewin and producit befor the saidis lordis of Sessioun". This implies that the laws in question were written laws, most probably but not necessarily statutes. The question arose because "the saidis lawis war variante in thir selfis".[127] After hearing the parties, the parliamentary Lords of the Articles made their finding as to what "the use in tymes bigane hes bene" and enjoined that "the saidis lawis suld be sa interprete and usit in tymes cuming".[128]

This instance may be unique, and certainly is likely to be a rare example. It is, however, exceptionally suggestive, if perhaps a little puzzling too. It implies a degree of flux in institutional arrangements. The Session seems to have felt that, in the case of such ambiguity in what was probably parliamentary legislation, it was unable or unwilling to simply construc the law on the basis of its own authority as a court, either as the Session or indeed as the College of Justice. Instead it wished to be given a parliamentary restatement of the law to clarify any ambiguity or "variante". This does not seem to have been a "procedure" so much as an *ad hoc* request for clarification of the law. It may tell us something about the status of statute as opposed to the "practick" of the court, which the Session usually interpreted and applied for itself. In this example, however, it is striking that it was unwilling to resolve an ambiguity through an application of the enacted law in a way which went beyond the clear authority of Parliament. It may be impossible to make out definitively what the underlying norms were, even as to whether the Session could have been *obliged* to make such a reference, or simply preferred to do so. The example provides a rare glimpse of a new kind of institutional self-perception on the part of the Session, and a recognition that for either functional or normative constitutional reasons the Session should sometimes give way to Parliament in

[127] *APS* ii, pp. 349–350.
[128] *APS* ii, pp. 349–350.

ascertaining the law. It is a clear reminder that the structure of relations between institutions, and between their functions and roles, was itself subject to change and therefore doubt at this period of development. The 1530s and 1540s seem to have been a period of growing institutional self-consciousness in which these relations were worked out. The most obvious example of that is the shift towards declarations of exclusive jurisdiction by the Session, which will be considered in subsequent chapters.

Procedural abuse

Cases of abuse of procedure and court process could be brought for speedy resolution before the Lords. For example, on 30 July 1529 Alexander Snytoun, bailie to Lord St John of his temple land in the burgh of Perth, compeared in an action against John Bisset, a messenger, and William Ruthven of Ballindene. An action was already ongoing in the bailie court concerning the lawful warning of a tenant, presumably a warning to remove himself from the land in question, but William and his tutor "purchest privat letters under our said soveraine lordis subscriptioun and nocht signettit be sinister informacioun chargeand the said ballie to proceid", which he had done already. The upshot was that the bailie had been put to the horn wrongfully. The Lords therefore suspended the letters and the process of the horn.[129]

Another kind of abuse involved refraining from having a summons called while the defender was present, but suddenly going ahead after his departure. Obviously, the tabling of summonses as they were to call in court cannot have simply been a bureaucratic procedure. It must have also depended on the presence of the pursuer to initiate the calling once a summons was in fact tabled. For example, on 6 August 1529 Lord Somerville's procurator, Robert Galbraith, protested that Lord Somerville had "remanit continualie" for twelve days, "dailie desirand to have process" in respect of a summons by John Somerville, but "now the said lord was absent and the said Johne in his absence desirit to have his summondis callit". Galbraith protested that for "equite" he "desirit ane term to call the said lord sa that he mycht be present and iustice ministerit". John Somerville pointed out that Galbraith was already appearing as Lord Somerville's procurator, but Galbraith responded

[129] NAS CS 5/40, fol. 75.

that a procurator was "bot ane office of will and tharfor he wald nocht use the same at this tyme as ane procurator for the lord Somervale bot to excus him allanerlie".[130]

An abuse which was sometimes alleged was the obtaining of royal letters on false information. For example, on 19 January 1531 Andrew Baron alleged that he found himself under summons at the King's instance for forfeiture of land and goods for "certane crymis of lese majestie quhilk can nocht be be [*sic*] the law but geif that he had committit cryme in the kings person his realm...and thirfor that the lords suld nocht proceid".[131] Baron's explanation was that "the kingis grace is wrang informit in that behalf be private insolicitatioun of certane personis bot that thai avistly consider the same conforme to the commonis law". It appears that Baron was seeking to establish his rights to the estate of the late Sir William Brown, who had apparently been imputed with certain crimes. Incidentally, the case is also notable because the Lords ruled that Baron and his co-defenders should not have to answer to the summons "quhill thai compellit ane advocat or man to procurate for thame".[132] An instance of such compulsion is to be found only a few days later on 23 January 1531, when John Lethame, Thomas Marjoribanks and Henry Spittal protested that, since they had been "compellit be the lordis to procur" for John Tweedie of Drumelzier against Lord Fleming, Lord Fleming should consent in person that "thai mycht procure and use all thir diligence in the said mater without the displeasure of the said lord".[133]

Abuse of legal process could extend beyond the mere issuing of royal letters under some deception, and can be found in the simulation of valid proceedings through the holding of an inquest and the giving of a decree in contravention of an explicit prohibition from doing so. For example, on 26 January 1531 Paul Dishington and others called the bailies of the prior of Pittenweem before the Lords, together with the prior, for reduction of a decree given by them on 2 September 1530. This had reduced the tack and assedation of 80 acres of land in Fife granted by the prior to the late Thomas Dishington. The ground for reduction was argued to be:

[130] NAS CS 5/40, fol. 88v.

[131] NAS CS 5/41, fol. 158.

[132] NAS CS 5/41, fol. 160. See Finlay, *Men of Law in Pre-Reformation Scotland*, chap. 4 ("Compelling Counsel and the Procurators of the Court"), pp. 72–86.

[133] NAS CS 5/42, fol. 3v.

> becaus the said baillies procedit to the leding of the said process and gevin of the said pretendit decreet eftir and agains the inhibitioune maid to thaim in the said mater and efter that thai war dischargit of thir offices in that part for divers resonable caus.[134]

Moreover, the bailies had given decree in Paul Dishington's absence for "null defences" and had done so within the tolbooth of Edinburgh "quhar the pestilour was for the time".[135] The Lords correspondingly reduced the decree in the presence of all the principal defenders.

Access to copies of charters kept by the clerk register had to be regulated, and this was another area where abuse of legal process could occur. For example, on 4 May 1531 David Blair of Adamton gave in a supplication complaining that William Hamilton of Sanquhar Lindsay "laitly opteint ane deliverance" to the lord clerk register to deliver to him a copy of David's charter of the land of Adamton amongst other things, which was "express agains all equite and reson that ane party quhilk daly persewis ane utheris heretage and without titill of rycht suld have the copy of his partyis charteris to arm him with".[136] The Lords agreed and ordained the clerk register not to deliver any such copies "nochtwithstanding any deliverance or uther privat writinge purchest or to be purchest in the contrar".[137] This suggests that charters were seen as essentially private documents, despite their constituting the principal basis for asserting good title to land. As we shall see in later chapters, the move away from local procedure by writ and inquest to central regulation of title through process in the Session may have helped erode this perception, though without yet leading to a system of public registration of title.

Abuses often seem to have turned on the bypassing of proper public procedure through a private route. That such private resort was made seems typical of sixteenth-century political culture. However, this is another area where a tension existed between the legal culture promoted by the Session and the expectations informed by the wider political culture. Significantly, the Session of the 1530s seems to have had the authority to root out such abuse. There are sometimes references in the record to deliverances which have been "privatlie gottin", for example, although how they were procured and from whom is not

[134] NAS CS 5/42, fol. 10.
[135] NAS CS 5/42, fol. 10.
[136] NAS CS 5/42, fol. 178.
[137] NAS CS 5/42, fol. 178.

usually made clear. Such a deliverance could be overturned, however. On 23 July 1529 Agnes Lindsay, daughter and heir to Alan Lindsay, himself son and heir to Gilbert Lindsay of Glenmure, compeared to complain that a summons she had for reduction of an infeftment was a privileged one and could be called outwith the usual terms laid down by the Session. However, she alleged that the other parties had "privatlie gottin ane deliverance ordynand the said summondis nocht to be callit bot in the sessioun contrar the tenor of the said summondis". The Session intervened to order the parties to compear, notwithstanding this "deliverance".[138] The same problem is more amply illustrated in a case on 2 May 1531, which also shows reliance in procedural matters on the custom of the court. Margaret Allan and her spouse had obtained a decree against James Douglas of Parkhead for having intromitted with mails which were due to her. All manner of obstruction had been attempted to prevent her from enforcing her decree, including procrastination by the sheriff, and unsuccessful attempts by Douglas to solicit the intervention of the King on his side. We are told, however, that "his hienes havand sa greit consideration of hir lang truble and daly vixation be the space of ten yeris bipast with the mair wald do na thing to him therein bot would that justice equalie procedit".[139] Despite this, James had succeeded in obtaining decree from the Lords of Council suspending Margaret's decree, and she therefore complained that it is "nocht conforme to daily practik consuetude and use of court, that the execution of ane decreet dulie gevin suld be suspendit be ane private selistit bill the party nevir being callit".[140] The Lords appear to have agreed, since they went on to uphold this complaint, clearly based on the breach of basic procedural norms. Consequently they suspended the letters.

Sometimes the threat to legal process came externally, with a claim that the Lords were not entitled to proceed in a given matter. One type of interference came from the King.[141] After all, the Lords were exercising the jurisdiction of his royal Council. Occasionally, a party would attempt to persuade the Lords that they were barred from hearing an action because of an inhibition made by the King. However, the Lords would tend to resist such submissions, and were even

---

138 NAS CS 5/40, fol. 66.
139 NAS CS 5/42, fol. 174v.
140 NAS CS 5/42, fol. 174v.
141 Godfrey, "Civil Procedure, Delay and the Court of Session", p. 116.

occasionally beseeched by the King himself to be resistant to them. For example, in early February 1531 the chancellor registered a letter from the King which effectively ordered the Lords to ignore any royal letters for continuation of causes obtained from him by "inoportune solistatiouns".[142] In cases in which this arose, the letter therefore gave the Lords any additional authority which they required to reject such applications. For example, on 13 February, a week and a half after the registration of the King's letter, Robert Borthwick protested that despite presenting to the Lords a writing from the King under his signet "putting inhibition to thame to proceid apoun the letters purchest be Andro Murray against the said Robert quhill hes hienes war present himself", neverthless the Lords had proceeded, "sayand that thai war commandit be the kingis grace to minister justice equalie to all his lieges nochtwithstanding ony writis quhilk may stop justice".[143] It would be tempting to see this as an expression of the autonomy of the Session as a judicial body, though we should note that that it could also be seen as merely a direct implementation of the command of the King contained in the earlier charge to the Lords. It may also have simply reflected consciousness of their general commission to administer justice. The statement by the Lords of this general duty was certainly formulated in categorical terms, however, which may have resonated beyond the case with which they were immediately concerned.

Conclusion

By 1532 the Session had long possessed its own "stile practik and consuetude of court". It also took steps to regulate procedural abuse, and to develop its procedure so as to allow it to assert its jurisdiction over other courts. The question of jurisdictional authority over subordinate courts will be taken up again in the next chapter in relation to the supervisory jurisdiction of the Session. In relation to its own procedure, one of the conclusions of this chapter is that the practick of the court certainly displayed a Romano-canonical influence which suggests that its procedure was neither self-supporting nor grounded primarily in distinctive, native features. Given the strong element of institutional continuity in the development of the Session over the several decades before 1532,

---

142 *ADCP*, p. 348.

143 NAS CS 5/42, fol. 48v.

it seems unlikely that this was not already the case by the later fifteenth century, though further investigation would be necessary to confirm this or the degree of any change since then. Once adopted, Romano-canonical procedure was hard to displace. It possessed systematic and universal qualities. As Professor Helmholz has remarked, "the *ordo iuris* promoted a basic consistency in the settlement of disputes, gave rise to a common law of proof, and called into being a conception of due process of law that has been of real significance in the Western legal tradition". Romano-canonical procedural law "kept a fundamental identity across centuries".[144] In identifying Romano-canonical influence in the practick of the Session, a full and systematic analysis would require further research. As a preliminary step this chapter identified three indicators which were present: evidence in the procedural record of terminology which presupposes Romano-canonical conceptions (e.g. the libel), the application of Romano-canonical procedural mechanisms (e.g. the classification of defences as "exceptions" and proof through depositions of written evidence rather than the verdict of an assize), and citation of civilian and canonist literature in procedural argument before the court. The presence of these features seems to provide sufficient grounds for characterising the court as operating a local variant of Romano-canonical procedure. But there is a further question of a normative character which may affect this assessment. How was the whole body of procedural rules applied in the Session—its "practick"—understood as a source? Was the practick of the court seen as unique to that court, as a self-contained set of rules carrying only contingent marks of Romano-canonical influence? Or was it seen as that local court's adaptation of general norms represented by Romano-canonical procedure?

It is helpful at this point to acknowledge again that the concept of the "practick" of a court was informed by a wider European context. The valuable point has been made by Professor van Rhee that it was the European norm for secular courts using Romano-canonical procedure to formulate a particular "style" of court describing its procedure. None in fact simply applied unadulterated Romano-canonical procedure. As van Rhee states:

> When Romano-canonical procedural law was applied outside the ecclesiastical sphere the character of the literature on procedural law changed.

[144] Helmholz, *The Oxford History of the Laws of England Volume I*, p. 313.

> The totality of the learned procedure was not adopted, but the secular procedure was influenced to a greater or lesser extent by the Roman canon model. This fact explains the existence of a variety of "styles" of procedural law, that is to say, special forms of procedure specific to a given area or judicial body, which also imparted a local character to the literature on secular procedure.[145]

The various "styles" obviously shared much common ground. In relation to written accounts of procedures of particular courts, for example, van Rhee notes that usually the "styles of procedural law addressed by the various authors are at least related to the basic pattern of Roman law".[146] These comments perhaps help resolve the problem of how to characterise Scottish civil procedure. At an important level it may be that it is simply misconceived to regard native and Romano-canonical influences as though they were competing alternatives, since it would seem that all such courts in Europe formulated a style of court which blended native procedural tradition with the Romano-canonical model. The "style of court" in the Session could therefore have been understood as a locally determined source of procedural law, but in a way that sat very happily with the Romano-canonical colouring possessed by the procedural record. One would expect *both* native and Romano-canonical features to be present in the "practick" of any court of this nature. However, we have seen from the features traced above that by 1532 at least it was Romano-canonical influences which had become dominant in how the "practick" and "stile" of the Court of Session was being formulated. In its procedural law, as well as arguably in a more general sense, it was therefore "a *ius commune* court", in the words of Professor Dolezalek.[147] This overall analysis is supported by previous accounts of the court's procedure, which acknowledged both the Romano-canonical influence but also the evolutionary nature of the practick as formulated by the Lords of Session.[148] That such analysis is drawn not from juristic commentary but from examination of the record of acts and decreets of the Session adds to its weight as a reflection of practice. In the next chapter, the substantive business of the court will be treated following the same method in order to evaluate the nature and range of the jurisdiction of the Session more generally by 1532.

---

[145] C.H. van Rhee, "Civil Procedure: a European Ius Commune?", *European Review of Private Law* 4 (2000), 589–611 at p. 596.

[146] Van Rhee, "Civil Procedure: a European Ius Commune?", p. 596.

[147] Dolezalek, "The Court of Session as a Ius Commune Court", passim.

[148] Finlay, *Men of Law in Pre-Reformation Scotland*, p. 122.

CHAPTER FIVE

THE JURISDICTION OF THE SESSION

Introduction

The changes which caused the development of the Session resulted in the College of Justice inheriting and newly embodying a powerful institutional authority. The ordinary judicial role of the Council had been permanently ceded to the Session through statute in 1532. The Session continued to draw its authority from and function within the framework of conciliar governance, but was insulated from the *curia regis* after 1532 by the institution of the College of Justice. How the institutional authority of the Session was reflected in its jurisdiction by this time forms the subject of the rest of this book.

First, we should investigate the legal disputes which normally fell within that jurisdiction. What was the business of the court? Neilson and Paton stated in their introduction to *Acts of the Lords of Council 1496–1501* that:

> the jurisdiction of the Council is perhaps more significantly indicated by the few exclusions than it is either by direct grants by Parliament or by the actual cases heard... It will be enough to note particularly the absence of any commission whatever for cases of crime, the exclusion of cases belonging to ecclesiastical courts, and the reservation to the judge ordinary of questions touching heritable right.[1]

For the Council to be exercising this kind of general jurisdiction was a novel and relatively recent development, when compared with its role up to the first half of the fifteenth century. Nevertheless, some constraints still inhibited its authority.

Neilson and Paton were analysing the position at the end of the fifteenth century, but the only significant qualification needed in order to apply their remarks to the period around 1532 is in relation to fee and heritage, i.e. heritable title to landed property. The argument of this book is that fee and heritage appears to have been within the remit of

---

[1] *Acts of the Lords of Council 1496–1501*, ed. G. Neilson and H.M. Paton (Edinburgh, 1918) [hereafter *ADC* ii], p. xlv.

the Lords by the time of the foundation of the College of Justice. This claim entails rejection of existing interpretations of how the jurisdiction of the Session had developed by 1532 and will be discussed in the next two chapters. In this chapter the civil jurisdiction of the Session will be surveyed more generally, illustrating in detail the "practick" of the court and what disputes it adjudicated upon. Following the discussion of the procedure of advocation in the previous chapter, the emerging relationship of the Session with other courts by way of a supervisory jurisdiction will be examined in some depth. Three further areas within the jurisdiction of the Session were so significant that they will be treated in greater depth still in separate chapters to follow. First, questions of limitations upon the civil jurisdiction of the Lords will be treated in chapter 6 in a discussion of fee and heritage actions. Secondly, questions of the expansion of the Lords' jurisdiction to encompass fee and heritage through the novel exploitation of remedies will be discussed in chapter 7 in relation to the reduction of infeftments. Thirdly, the involvement of the Session in dispute settlement generally, but especially in alternative methods of dispute resolution such as arbitration, will be treated in chapters 8 and 9.

Academic discussion of the Session in the early sixteenth century has been mainly concerned with institutional organisation or limitations on jurisdiction. For this reason the judicial business of the court—the field of its general civil jurisdiction—has never received the kind of detailed scrutiny which will be offered in this chapter, though an invaluable earlier discussion is contained in Dr Athol Murray's analysis of the "practick" of the court in the 1540s in his discussion of Sinclair's "Practicks", supplemented by Professor Dolezalek's subsequent treatment.[2] Aspects of the case-load of the court for one year at the very end of the century have also been assessed by Dr Winifred Coutts.[3] Some treatment is offered indirectly in Dr Finlay's study of the early legal profession, but mostly in relation to procedure.[4] Though not concerned with the Session, Professor Dickinson's treatment of the business of the Sheriff

[2] A.L. Murray, "Sinclair's Practicks", in *Law Making and Law Makers in British History*, ed. A. Harding (London, 1980), pp. 90–104; G. Dolezalek, "The Court of Session as a Ius Commune Court—Witnessed by 'Sinclair's Practicks', 1540–1549", in *Miscellany Four*, ed. H.L. MacQueen, Stair Society 49 (Edinburgh, 2002), pp. 51–84.

[3] Winifred Coutts, *The Business of the College of Justice in 1600*, Stair Society 50 (Edinburgh, 2003).

[4] John Finlay, *Men of Law in Pre-Reformation Scotland* (East Linton, 2000).

Court also remains of great indirect value.[5] The reason for the general lack of attention is in part a practical one. The judicial business of the Session has tended to be ignored because such a survey is only possible by way of reference to the unindexed manuscript record, for the period after 1503. Only small selections of the record thereafter have ever been published. Hannay's edition of *Acts of the Lords of Council in Public Affairs 1501–1554* is in particular a highly selective volume. It is only a reliable guide to what he considered the administrative as opposed to the judicial business of the Council. It was, after all, described by him as "introductory" to the published series of volumes constituting the *Register of the Privy Council* which is extant from 1545.[6] Therefore the discussion in this chapter, based on examination of the manuscript record, will exclude the kind of public business which mainly forms the contents of Hannay's volume.

This chapter will be restricted to describing, illustrating and analysing the business which the Session transacted as a court of law. It will tend to severely undermine Hannay's judgment that "the decreets in civil causes, often valuable for family history, topography and social life, are apt to be disappointing to the student of law".[7] In fact, with an appropriate method of collation and comparison, the record proves surprisingly rich. The method adopted in selecting classes of action and particular illustrations for comment is to try and give an account of the main types of action which occurred with any frequency, and to describe variations in the circumstances which underlay the raising of such actions. Attention will be given largely to the actions brought and remedies craved rather than the underlying legal rules upon which a claim depended, although occasionally some treatment of the legal rules can also be given. The result will be that a comprehensive picture of the judicial business of the Session should emerge, at least as

[5] *The Sheriff Court Book of Fife 1515–1522, Transcribed and Edited, with an Introduction, Notes, and Appendices by William Croft Dickinson M.A., Ph.D.*, ed. W.C. Dickinson, Scottish History Society Third Series 12 (Edinburgh, 1928), pp. 325–343 ("Appendix B: The Work of the Court").

[6] *Acts of the Lords of Council in Public Affairs 1501–1554*, [hereafter *ADCP*] ed. R.K. Hannay (Edinburgh, 1932), p. v; B. Webster, *Scotland from the Eleventh Century to 1603*, The Sources of History: Studies in the Use of Historical Evidence (London, 1975), p. 210. On the beginnings of a separate Privy Council see J. Goodare, *The Government of Scotland 1560–1625* (Oxford, 2004), pp. 128–131, and the extremely valuable overview in *Guide to the National Archives of Scotland*, Stair Society Supplementary Series 3 (Edinburgh, 1996), pp. 19–22.

[7] *ADCP*, p. viii.

it was carried out in the years around 1532. It should be noted that in many cases a particular example could be used to illustrate a number of different aspects of the Session's business, but will have been cited only with reference to one of those aspects. More generally, the body of material to be discussed in this chapter has been subdivided and treated in sections under particular headings, and these sections have themselves been classified loosely into groups, but these subdivisions and groupings have been adopted for ease of presentation rather than to reflect any underlying jurisdictional principles. The groups of actions have been classified firstly in relation to what can be characterised as the supervisory aspect of the Session's jurisdiction; secondly, actions relating to property; and thirdly, other substantive actions.

Some published commentary already exists on the judicial business of the Session. Ian Shearer (Lord Avonside) edited for the Stair Society an edition of decisions of the Session arising in 1532–1533, but the volume is of limited value for present purposes since it is extremely selective and frequently resorts to summary and calendar. Shearer's introduction is concise and contains barely any illustration of the record or detailed description of legal actions before the Session.[8] J.A. Clyde (Lord President Clyde) produced an introduction to the Stair Society volume covering 1501–1503 which contains a more detailed analysis of the business of the court, but is discursive rather than descriptive or illustrative in character.[9] Neilson and Paton's introduction to their volume of Council business for 1496–1501 contains discussion of particular matters such as the constitution of procurators,[10] warrandice claims,[11] pronunciation of sentence,[12] arbitration,[13] protestations,[14] oaths,[15] lawburrows,[16] and

---

[8] *Acta Dominorum Concilii et Sessionis 1532–1533*, ed. I.H. Shearer, Stair Society 14 (Edinburgh, 1956), pp. xiii–xxiv ("Introduction").

[9] *Acta Dominorum Concilii 1501–1503*, ed. J.A. Clyde, Stair Society 8 (Edinburgh, 1943), pp. xiii–lx, especially pp. xxxiv–lx. The circumstances which resulted in Lord Clyde writing this introduction are described for the first time in T.H. Drysdale, "The Stair Society: the Early Years", in *Miscellany Five*, ed. H.L. MacQueen, Stair Society 52 (Edinburgh, 2006), pp. 243–260 at pp. 253–55. The Council of the Stair Society noted at a meeting in 1943 that there were a large number of errors in the transcription of the record itself, though this was by a hand other than that of Lord Clyde.

[10] *ADC* ii, p. xlvii.

[11] *ADC* ii, p. xliii.

[12] *ADC* ii, pp. xlix–lxiv.

[13] *ADC* ii, pp. liv–lv.

[14] *ADC* ii, p. lxiii.

[15] *ADC* ii, pp. lxiv–lxix.

[16] *ADC* ii, p. lxx.

spuilzie,[17] but is more a commentary arising out of a concern with particular points than a general description. Particular points are also discussed by Dr Athol Murray in his "Introduction" to *Acts of the Lords of Council, Vol. III, 1501–1503*, but more with reference to the function and form of the record, a subject of very great importance in its own right but not to be treated here.[18] In this chapter no attempt will be made to describe systematically every facet of a particular type of action, though the record has itself been comprehensively examined for the five year period 1529–1534. Rather, the choice of topics being presented has been determined by the material contained in the record. A representative account will be attempted in relation to the actions which happened to arise in the period surveyed, and an assessment of the nature of the Lords' jurisdiction made, relying as closely as possible upon descriptive detail from the record itself.

Supervisory jurisdiction

The use of the term "supervisory jurisdiction" is not predicated upon the existence of a distinct jurisdiction exercised by the Session over and above its usual one, but is used simply to characterise that part of its normal jurisdiction which had a supervisory character. This related to due process, legality and the rule of law, and resulted in a jurisdiction to quash other legal proceedings and redirect them, rather than to overturn the substantive decisions of other courts on the merits of the legal case.

Supervision by the Session of other courts

At a European level, the development of central courts can be seen as tending towards the promotion of central authority and jurisdictional unity or integration within a legal system. Part of the jurisdiction of Council and Session was supervisory in nature and related to the conduct of legal process in other courts. In the Scottish context, this was the particular mode through which centralisation of judicial authority had the greatest effect, buttressed by the procedure of advocation.

---

[17] *ADC* ii, p. lxxi.

[18] *Acts of the Lords of Council, Vol. III, 1501–1503*, ed. A.B. Calderwood (Edinburgh, 1993), pp. xxv–xxviii.

A typical example might concern a case in which a litigant alleged intimidation by another party or his or her supporters. The Session could transfer the action to be heard elsewhere geographically. This could be in Edinburgh or another part of the country. If transferred to Edinburgh, it could be arranged for the action to be heard in the town's governmental building, the Tolbooth, and the safety of all parties guaranteed to a reasonable degree. The Edinburgh Tolbooth was where the King's Council and the Session usually tended to meet prior to 1560.[19] An example of such a complaint was that of Gilbert Wauchop of Niddry Marshall. He complained on 23 August 1529 about John Edmonston of that Ilk in respect of a dispute between them about certain "landis debatable". Gilbert had been charged by the sheriff principal of Edinburgh and his depute to compear on the debatable ground itself to hear final sentence be given. However, "at the first court day he durst nocht compeir to except agains the personnis that was apoun the inquest nor to use his iust defencis for feir of his lif becaus his said party gaderit agains him... for slauchter and distructioun". Moreover, he had only had notice served on him the previous day. Gilbert was personally present at the Session and John represented by a procurator, and with their consent the Lords continued the court from "this instant day" and ordained the sheriff depute, officers of court and officers that were upon the inquest to compear in the Tolbooth of Edinburgh. Gilbert was then to have the right to plead all his lawful exceptions concerning the sheriff, the members of the court and those who served upon the inquest. In due course the sheriff and inquest were to proceed and "pass apoun the ground of the landis pleyable, but nane of the partiis nor nane utheris in thir namis" were to compear upon the ground when sentence was given. In this way, the Lords were able to intervene to regulate the procedure of a sheriff court in order to overcome the hazard of intimidation.[20]

The Lords could also decide on disputes over jurisdiction between two sheriffdoms. For example, on 31 August 1529 the sheriff of Renfrew, Lord Sempill, appeared in an action against the sheriff of Linlithgow, John Hamilton. The allegation was that Hamilton had wrongly called the free tenants of certain lands to give suit of court in the sheriff court

[19] H.L. MacQueen, "Two Visitors in the Session, 1629 and 1636", in *Miscellany Four*, ed. H.L. MacQueen, Stair Society 49 (Edinburgh, 2002), pp. 155–168 at p. 155.

[20] Edinburgh, National Archives of Scotland [hereafter NAS], CS 5/40, fol. 109.

of Linlithgow, and as a result of their non-compearance had "unlawis thame and hes poyndit and takin thir gudis". However, the lands in question "ar anext to the sherifdom of Renfrew and ar haldin of our soveraine lord as Stewart of Scotland, and the tennentis of the saidis landis suld gef sute and service thirfor in the sheriff court of Renfrew and hes bene in use of the same past memor of man". The Lords charged Hamilton to stop his proceedings and to restore the goods poinded (i.e. seized as security for debt). Without the exercise of this supervisory jurisdiction by the Lords it is easy to imagine how deadlock could have ensued and such a matter remain unresolved between two jurisdictions.[21]

Commissions could be granted out of Chancery to constitute judges in a particular action, often as sheriffs *in hac parte*, i.e. in that "part" or "cause". However, the Lords could intervene to protect the interests of the judge ordinary who would otherwise have possessed jurisdiction to hear the action. On 16 October 1529 they suspended a commission constituting bailies *in hac parte* in the burgh of Lanark, which was to have led to the serving of a brieve of succession in the Tolbooth of Edinburgh, albeit in relation to land situated in Lanark. The bailies of Lanark had complained that the lands to which the heir was to be served were indeed "within the said burgh of Lanark quhilk commission is purchest without ony resonable caus in hurt of the previlege and fredome of the said burgh".[22] The Lords implicitly asserted their right to be the judges of what "resonable caus" might be, and suspended the commission in favour of the bailies, protecting the rights of the burgh but also thereby the jurisdiction of the judge ordinary.

Another aspect of this supervisory jurisdiction, however, involved exempting an individual from the jurisdiction of a local court. For example, on 17 March 1530 a summons of exemption of this kind was considered by the Lords. It was raised by William Murray of Tullibardine, and was against the sheriff of Perth, Lord Ruthven. The exemption was claimed not only for William, but also "his kyn, tenentes and servandes", and the exemption was to be "fra the said sheriff and hes depute office and juresdictioun in all tym tocum".[23] The summons was continued in this case, but an exemption granted on an interim

[21] NAS CS 5/40, fol. 113.
[22] NAS CS 5/40, fol. 126v.
[23] NAS CS 5/41, fol. 16.

basis. The reason for the exemption is not given, but typically might have related to the existence of a state of feud or other kind of personal enmity. On other occasions a dispute over suit of court might involve an alleged suitor turning to the Session to resolve the disputed claim. For example, on 14 November 1530 William Cardney appeared under a supplication to complain that Lord Methven "callis him and his tenents to his barony courte" for lands in the barony of Methven, but which William held directly of the Crown. Lord Methven insisted on "sute and service" and "unlawis poynde and take his gude therefor wrangusly".[24] The matter would have to go on to be the subject of proof and was accordingly continued, but the principle of the Session regulating jurisdictional disputes of this sort is clear.

Clashes between remedies sought from different jurisdictions could also find their resolution before the Session. For example, on 15 November 1530 Alexander Montgomery complained that whilst a lawful poinding had been executed, those men who had been poinded had taken out letters to the sheriff of Renfrew charging him to "tak cognition geif the said Alexander spuilzie the gudis". The complaint was that Alexander resided in the bailiary of Cunningham and that the sheriff of Renfrew therefore had "na jurisdiction apone him".[25] Montgomery also alleged that in the sheriff court of Renfrew he had formally made protest and taken instruments that he "declynit the juge" and "nocht entirit a pley effor him admittand him juge to him in the mater aboune written". Now it had transpired that the sheriff and his clerk would not deliver to him the "autentik copy of the said protestation and actis".[26] The Lords were able to set the matter down for proof and order the delivery of the documents.

The procedure of "repledging" allowed a feudal superior to transfer to his own court an action which properly pertained to his jurisdiction but which had been raised initially in another forum.[27] At common law this seems to have been the acknowledged means of asserting jurisdictional rights.[28] It is therefore telling to find an equivalent procedure in the Session, where under its supervisory jurisdiction it could

[24] NAS CS 5/41, fol. 123v.

[25] NAS CS 5/41, fol. 125.

[26] NAS CS 5/41, fol. 125.

[27] See Professor Dickinson's account in *The Sheriff Court Book of Fife 1515–1522*, ed. Dickinson, pp. 344–346.

[28] *Regality of Dunfermline Court Book 1531–1538*, ed. J.M. Webster and A.A.M. Duncan (Dunfermline, 1953), pp. 3–4.

bar proceedings in one court so that they might properly be raised in another and thereby effect a replegiation. Repledging would normally have involved a direct transfer between the courts of the two competing jurisdictions without reference to a third higher court of superior jurisdiction. An example of such an action in the Session can be found on 15 March 1533, when James Douglas, earl of Morton, appeared against John Bannatyne, the holder of a liferent in Roberton within the earl's regality of Dalkeith and in the sheriffdom of Lanark. Bannatyne had called some tenants of the land before the sheriff of Lanark for the taking of cognition and "the said sheriff has set Tusday nixt tocum and sua tendis to draw the tenentis of the saidis land fra the said erle and his iuresdiction howbeit he is thir juge ordinar be resonis of his said regalite and thai suld be callit befor him", otherwise "the same may hurt the said erle gretly in his office and privilege of regalite".[29] The Lords accepted that such proceedings were "preiudiciale" and suspended Bannatyne's letters. Whether it was because it was simply more effective to do so, more expeditious or more authoritative, the case illustrates an apparent preference for bringing an action before the Session to resolve a matter traditionally dealt with directly between two courts at common law. The jurisdiction of the Session to suspend or reduce legal processes, deeds or instruments gave it the means to carry out this supervisory role, though it could also make positive directions for how further process should be carried out and in which court this should be done.

Such resort to the Session might be the only recourse if an attempt to repledge failed. For example, on 28 May 1533 the provost and bailies of Montrose gave in a supplication against Robert Wood as admiral depute, complaining that James Roland, an inhabitant of Flanders, had called William Scott, also a burgess of Montrose, before the admiral's court in pursuit of a sum of money due under an "obligation". However, the provost and bailies alleged that the admiral and his depute were "na jugis competent…for dett" in these circumstances, "but thai alanerlie". Nevertheless, despite their request, and an accompanying offer of "caution" (i.e. security), the admiral would not admit their claims for repledging, and his depute was charged to send the "autentik copy of the clame" for the Lords to assess. The result in this case

[29] NAS CS 6/2, fol. 120v.

was that the admiral and his depute were charged to desist from any proceeding in the matter.[30]

However, on another occasion the Lords refused to intervene when the abbot of Holyrood complained that a man who lived within his regality was being sued for spuilzie before the sheriff of Edinburgh and his deputies, who "ar na competent jugis to the said Adam". The abbot alleged himself to be "hurt... gretulie in his privilege of his said regalite", since he and his bailies were "jugis ordinar in the said matter".[31] However, the Lords simply provided that "it salbe lefull to him to replege Adam Dais to his courtis siclik as the saidis letters had nocht been grantit".[32] Repledging was therefore competent but the Lords were not prepared to stop proceedings before the sheriff of Edinburgh themselves. The implication is that it was up to the abbot to repledge, and only then would the Lords intervene, if the sheriff, for example, were to refuse to cooperate. We also see the Lords sometimes refusing to order a replegiation which had already failed because it was not raised at the appropriate procedural stage. This was simply a question of due process. In a case in March 1534 the Lords refused to order that an action be repledged from the sheriff of Ayr to the stewart of Kyle "becaus the said mater was enterit in pley befor the said sheriff of Air and his deputis and litiscontestation maid thirin".[33] As we saw in the previous chapter, an exception against the jurisdiction of a court had to be entered at the appropriate preliminary stage of proceedings before *litis contestatio*, and replegiation was treated in the same way.[34]

Those such as sheriffs who exercised local jurisdictions can also be seen recognising the jurisdiction of the Lords to supervise their authority. For example, Hugh Campbell of Loudon, sheriff of Ayr, protested on 28 January 1531 that, since the Lords had previously ordained him to make John Crawford of Drongane and Adam Wallace of the Newton his deputies in all actions pertaining to the laird of Blairquhan, he should not as sheriff be held responsible, should the deputies "procedit nocht justice". The reason for his inability to take responsibility was that the deputies were "to sit and hald thir courte at the kirk of Allbay besyd the brig of Abine quhar he mycht nocht cum with his folke to

[30] NAS CS 6/2, fol. 179v.
[31] NAS CS 6/3, fol. 127.
[32] NAS CS 6/3, fol. 127.
[33] NAS CS 6/4, fol. 100v.
[34] *The Sheriff Court Book of Fife 1515–1522*, ed. Dickinson, pp. 344–345.

se that justice war done".[35] Exception had already been taken to Hugh Campbell sitting upon the action due to the existence of a feud, and as sheriff he now sought to safeguard his position by entering a protest in the books of council. In this case James Kennedy of Blairquhan had sought a full exemption from the jurisdiction of the sheriff, but the Lords had settled for the case being heard by appointed deputies, albeit in Deeside.[36]

Of course, a party who took objection to the jurisdiction of a court before which he was being sued would not necessarily succeed in having his complaint upheld by the Lords, if only on preliminary procedural grounds, as discussed already in relation to replegiation. The Lords would repel such complaints if the complainer had already appeared as a party to the proceedings in the relevant court, for example. Again, the test was whether litiscontestation had occurred. For example, on 31 March 1531 the Lords ruled against William Scott, burgess of Montrose, in his attempt to have an action declared incompetent, which had been brought against him by Gilbert Strachan before the conservator of Aberdeen. Having had the process produced before them, the Lords "ordanis the mater to be procedit upon and have process before the said conservator becaus the said Gilbert Strachauchin producit ane testimoniale under the seile of the conservator of Abydene quhare the said William Scott be hes procurator maid litiscontestation in the said matter".[37] Seemingly, it had already "procedit to divers actes and to the continuation in the mater befor the said conservator".[38]

The jurisdiction of the Session extended to examining the substance and form of the decrees of other courts. Indeed, some of the most typical actions before the Session, such as that on a summons of error, were premised upon such a remit being competent. However, even outwith such standard actions the Lords were able to invalidate decrees and rolments of court if they were inadequate on the face of the record. For example, on 5 December 1533 the Lords reduced three court rolments of the earl of Eglinton as bailie of the regality of the abbey of Kilwinning. These had been delivered by an inquest on 2 October 1527. The reason for the reduction was that "the said rolmentis hes nowther form nor figur of sentence or decrete nor conteins ony caus

[35] NAS CS 5/42, fol. 17v.
[36] NAS CS 5/42, fol. 18v.
[37] NAS CS 5/42, fol. 156.
[38] NAS CS 5/42, fol. 156.

relevant quharefor the said Janet [Fairlie] suld have bene decernit to have forfaltit hir said maling".[39] The bailie court did have the jurisdiction to make such a decision, but the Lords were able to insist that due process of law be followed in its exercise. Moreover, the Lords also went on to offer Janet a remedy when she appeared before them on 12 December 1533. She complained that the abbot of Kilwinning wanted to "remove hir fra hir said maling wrangusly howbeit sche be rentalit thirof... quhilk rentale the said abbot will nocht now deliver to hir entendand be sic menis and wais to put hir to utir heirschip quhilk is ane agit wedow".[40] The Lords ordered the abbot to compear on 18 January to "geif his aith quhidder he hes this rentale or not or geif he had it and geif he knawis geif this Jonet wes in the said rentale or nocht in tymes bipast", and they warned him that the matter would otherwise be referred to Janet's oath.

Regulation of legal process

A further aspect of the supervisory jurisdiction of Council and Session was to regulate legal process in other courts if called upon to do so. An example of this would be when a party had used an incompetent form of court process. On 16 February 1531, for instance, Lady Bothwell complained that tenants of land which she held in liferent in Lanarkshire had claimed that they "knawis nocht perfitlie the marchis thirof" and had taken out letters to the sheriff of Lanarkshire to take cognition on the question of the correct boundaries of the property. However, she pointed out that "the knawing of and schawing of marchis suld be brevis of perambulatioun and nocht be sic letters quharthrow the same is wrangwislie and unordourlie procedit".[41] The Lords accepted this and suspended the letters, going on to direct two men as "justicis depute to pas aponis the ground of the said lande for perambulatioun thirof in dew forme". It is particularly interesting to see procedure by brieve and inquest being strictly enforced by the Lords in a question of determination of boundary disputes at a time when the use of the parallel procedures by pleadable brieve for determining ultimate "right" seem to have fallen into desuetude, as will be discussed in subsequent chapters.

[39] NAS CS 6/3, fol. 114.
[40] NAS CS 6/3, fol. 125v.
[41] NAS CS 5/42, fol. 60.

On 20 December 1533 a similar case arose of an incorrect mode of court process being used. James Livingstone had purchased letters to the sheriff of Lanark to take cognition upon the "ground right" of "thirl multures" attaching to the mill of Robert Dalziel of that Ilk. Multures involved the right to levy an exaction for the use of a mill to grind grain, and were considered a right of property. Robert complained that the sheriff was not a competent judge "thirto be cognition bot be ane brieff of ryt or utheris wais requirit thirto of the law".[42] Thirl multures were classifiable as relating to heritable right, and were thus matters of fee and heritage. Under medieval Scots law the brieve of right would have been the appropriate remedy when the ultimate right was in issue. The Lords went on to reduce James' letters as "unordourlie procedit" but the only reason given for this was "becaus thai ar direct to tak cognition upon the ground ryt of the said thirle multur".[43] It is not made clear whether the competent form of action would have been to raise an action in the Session or to proceed under a different process before the sheriff, perhaps even by a brieve of right. Given that multures were matters of fee and heritage, and given the apparent desuetude of the brieve of right by this time, it may be that the Lords viewed a decision on "ground right" as being more appropriately brought before them. Frustratingly, this example does not make the answer clear. It simply records that such a simple form of cognition was incompetent for determining such proprietary interests.

Suspension of letters

Under a system of administration of justice where writs of various kinds could be issued to a complainer as a purely administrative act without judicial warrant and simply upon payment of a fee, the Lords of Council came to occupy a fundamental role in policing the use of such writs or "letters". Strict Romano-canonical procedure would have required the commencement of an action to take place before a judge who would safeguard due process, but the European experience generally was that on pragmatic grounds this was not always observed.[44] This could lead to a lack of certainty about the regularity with which

[42] NAS CS 6/3, fol. 142.
[43] NAS CS 6/3, fol. 142.
[44] R.H. Helmholz, *The Oxford History of the Laws of England Volume I: The Canon Law and Ecclesiastical Jurisdiction from 597 to the 1640s* (Oxford, 2004), chap. 5 ("Civil Procedure and the Law of Proof"), pp. 311–353 at p. 318.

writs might have been issued. Similar problems arose in relation to other types of writ or legal orders by "letters". Typically, the party who found himself charged by royal writ to act in a certain way to which he objected would come before Council to complain, and require those who had taken out the letters to answer to his complaint. He would hope that it could be shown that they were not entitled to their writ, perhaps by proving that the underlying state of affairs, which the terms of the writ presupposed, did not exist. The remedy to be sought from the Lords was suspension of the writ, and this would be granted automatically if the other party failed to compear. For example, on 6 April 1529, Alexander Hay, parson of Turriff and tutor at law to William Hay, sixth earl of Errol, appeared before Council under letters raised against Elizabeth Hay, countess of Errol and William's mother, and Ninian, Lord Ross, her spouse. Elizabeth had purchased "letters in three forms" requiring Alexander to pay to her and Ninian £40 per annum for years gone past and £80 for future years in order to recompense them for their "keping" of the earl and to pay for his "sustentatioun". Such letters represented the ecclesiastical courts' sanction for failing to meet an obligation. Alexander, however, considered the letters to have been purchased by "sinister and wrang informatioun". In the event, neither Elizabeth nor Ninian compeared to produce their letters for examination whether they were "ordourlie procedit and of justice or not", and Alexander thereby gained the remedy he sought: suspension of Elizabeth's and Ninian's letters, though only as an interim measure "ay quhill thai be producit".[45]

Letters of suspension could of course themselves be suspended upon a relevant complaint. For example, on 10 April 1529 John Campbell of Lundy appeared before the Lords under supplication in order to explain how Robert Leslie had been "warnit be ane masour" to produce letters he had "impetrat" on behalf of Richard, Lord Innermeith. Leslie's letters had suspended earlier letters purchased by Campbell putting Lord Innermeith to the horn. Campbell protested that, since Leslie would not produce these letters for examination, his own letters should have effect after all. The Lords "admittit" this protest.[46] Part of the reason for seeking suspension of such letters could be that a party with an interest to defend had not been called to appear when the

[45] NAS CS 5/40, fol. 8.
[46] NAS CS 5/40, fol. 9.

letters were granted. This ground underlay the complaint of George Pettullo on 16 April 1529, in respect of the fruits of a chaplaincy to which he had been "lauchfully providit", and in relation to which he had had "the ordinar letters with our soveraine lordes letters conform thirto be deliverance of the lordis of counsale to mak him be answerit of the frutis thirof". The defender, David Crammond, had also taken out royal letters to execute "diligence" and enforce his right to the fruits of the chaplaincy extending back over the course of two years. Pettullo alleged that Crammond had been issued with these letters "be sinister and wrang information and without cognition in the caus". The implication of the phrase "without cognition in the caus" would seem to be that the letters issued to David Crammond had not been issued by deliverance of the Lords of Council or by virtue of court process based upon judicially supervised findings of fact, and therefore without any judicial determination of the issue in question. The alleged flaw in this procedure had been that Pettullo had never been "callit thirto for his enteres". The Lords of Council were called upon to examine David's letters to determine whether they were "ordourly procedit", but since he failed to compear the letters were suspended until they were produced before the Lords.[47]

This practice of challenging the legality or competence of writs and letters could easily lead to abuse of process where unfounded allegations were made so as to protract or confuse a dispute. The large number of actions throughout the council register relating to suspension of letters may imply that this kind of abuse was fairly common, as parties manipulated legal process tactically so as to inconvenience their opponents and delay a formal resolution of the issue. For example, on 6 April 1529 Roland Donaldson's letters interdicting Sir Alexander Scott from alienating property so as to defraud his creditors were suspended at Alexander's instance. Roland did not compear to contest the action. However, the matter appeared in a different light on 16 April when Roland did compear and had his letters of interdict declared "ordourly procedit". Roland explained that Alexander had indeed called him "be ane masour" before the Lords but went on to allege that "als lang as he was present the said Sir Alexander wald nocht cum and persew the same and in said Rollandis absence the said Sir Alexander has for null defence gettin ane act suspendand the said letters ayand quhill

47 NAS CS 5/40, fol. 10.

producit".[48] On this occasion Alexander was the one who did not compear and Roland saw the suspension lifted.

Normally, if a pursuer refused to appear to hear his summons called, the defender was entitled to have the action dismissed so that the pursuer would have to start again with the serving of a new summons. For example, on 8 May 1529 Lord Livingstone protested that he had been summoned at the instance of the King and his advocate, Adam Otterburn, for reduction of an instrument of sasine. Otterburn "wald nocht compeir to persew the said summondis" and therefore "he suld nocht [be] compellit to answer in the said mater quhill he war summond of new and his expens refoundit". The Lords declared that he should not be compelled to answer in the matter until "warnit be new letters thirto apoun 20 dais warning".[49] This step was with the consent of Otterburn, and the reasons why he did not pursue the summons are not stated. Suspension was, of course, in essence an interim remedy, but the Lords could also proceed to declare letters simply void and therefore reduce them. For example, on 29 March 1530 a procurator asked instruments to record the fact that letters of removing directed to the sheriff of Fife in respect of property, possession of which was disputed, were reduced because "the sheriff excedat the bounds of hes office in execution thereof".[50] It should be remarked, incidentally, that reduction on such grounds would seem consistent with both the Lords' general jurisdiction over reduction and their jurisdiction over royal officers and courts, this also being supervisory in character.

When legal actions were pursued in more than one court, but in connection with the same dispute, the Session played an important supervisory role as well. The remedy of suspension could be used to avoid multiplicity of actions and prevent an action proceeding in more than one court. One type of example was where an action in the sheriff court led to a further action in the Session on a related but subsidiary matter, but in circumstances in which, meanwhile, one of the parties attempted to progress the action in the sheriff court prior to the Session having reached its decision on the matter upon which the sheriff court action was depending. For example, on 28 April 1529 a dispute came before the Lords which had arisen over two conflicting leases

[48] NAS CS 5/40, fol. 10v.
[49] NAS CS 5/40, fol. 20.
[50] NAS CS 5/41, fol. 47v.

in the barony of Marnoch in Ayrshire. Patrick Hamilton of Boreland claimed the "assedation" of these lands, held of Alexander Hepburn of Richardton. He alleged that his lease was to run for another five years. However, John McAdam also claimed to hold the lands under an assedation from Alexander, and had called Patrick before the sheriff of Ayr, accusing him of spuilzie and putting him "furth of said maling". McAdam had "optenit ane rolment of court agains" Patrick. However, Patrick had then obtained a decree of the Lords of Council which decerned the rolment of "nane avale". Following this, both assedations had been produced before the Lords of Council in the presence of the alleged grantor, Alexander, to whose oath was referred the question "quhilk of thaim was just and of verite". Alexander was granted a continuation so that he could be "avisit" on the matter. However, in the meantime, John McAdam had taken out new letters to the sheriff of Ayr to take further cognition and proof in this matter, despite the fact that Alexander had not yet declared the "verite" of the assedations. McAdam did not compear and the Lords suspended his newly obtained letters until they were produced for examination.[51]

"Impreving" of instruments

An action commonly raised before the Session was that of impreving (i.e. proving invalid) instruments or deeds. An example of such a deed would be a reversion, whereby land was held under a condition that the other party had the right to take it back upon payment of an agreed sum. For example, on 30 April 1529 Thomas Duddingston of Southhouse called Janet Duddingston, daughter of the late Alexander Duddingston, before the Session. Janet claimed to have an instrument "berand in effect that umquhile [i.e. deceased] Williame Duddingstoun the gudschir to Thomas gaif to umquhile Alexander heretablie the landis of Westlogy undir reversioun contenand sum of 300 merks". However, Thomas alleged this instrument to be "fals and fenzeit in the self" and wished it to be "sene and considerate" by the Lords and to "heir and see" it be "civile imprevit". In this case the action was continued so that Thomas might summon both the witnesses named in the instrument and also "the kepar of the Notaris protocol buke to produce the same".[52] This occurred on 14 May 1529, when the instrument was

[51] NAS CS 5/40, fol. 14v.
[52] NAS CS 5/40, fol. 15.

"impreved" by witnesses giving evidence that the handwriting of the notary by whom the instrument had allegedly been made was different from that in the instrument. The witnesses named in the instrument and "divers notaris and autentik notaris quhilkis knew the said umquhile M. Nicholl and his writingis" were of this view because of their "inspectioune of divers autentik instruments under said M. Nicholes signe and subscriptioune ferr deferent baith in writting and proportioun fra the signe manuale of the fenzeit instrument".[53] A separate ground of reduction of an instrument might be that it had not been issued in proper accordance with the "ordour of the chancellarie", if it was a writ issued out of chancery, such as a precept of sasine. An example of a reduction action of this sort occurred on 24 February 1531, when the countess of Cassillis alleged that a precept had been "counterfetit by the ordoure of the chancellarie but [i.e. without] ony retour brief or uther warand passand of befor".[54]

Interponing authority

The Lords could be called upon to interpone their authority to a private declaration or renunciation of rights. Common instances were cases involving reversionary interests in land. For example, on 14 May 1529 Robert Galbraith appeared as procurator for Patrick Brown, a burgess of Ayr, and on his behalf proceeded to "renunce, overgeif and discharge all ryt and titill of ryt propirtie and possession that he has had or may have in and to the landis of borrowfeild of air... and renounces it, be ryt of ane reversion". The Lords interponed their authority to this renunciation.[55] Another type of case would arise when a minor sought to grant a charter, but desired the authority of the Lords to be interponed so as to guarantee its status and validity. On 6 August 1529 Gavin Douglas, canon of Aberdeen, together with Thomas Annan, both acting as procurators, compeared and produced two charters made by the earl Marischal "with auctorite of his freyndis and curatoris and desirit the lordis of counsale to interpone thir auctorite thirto". This was "thocht resonable" by the Lords in deciding to do so.[56]

[53] NAS CS 5/40, fol. 35v.
[54] NAS CS 5/42, fol. 54.
[55] NAS CS 5/40, fol. 34.
[56] NAS CS 5/40, fol. 87.

Constitution into an office

Throughout the council register there are notes of compearances by individuals to appoint or "constitute" men to the office of procurator in order that they might be represented in court. In noting the rule stated in the medieval *Regiam Majestatem* and still accepted in the later sixteenth-century *Practicks* of Sir James Balfour, Dr John Finlay has explained how "a litigant who wanted a man of law to act on his behalf before a judge had to appear personally in court and formally constitute one or more procurators to act for him".[57] However, this manner of constitution was only one particular instance of a wider phenomenon of coming before the Lords to be constituted into a variety of offices, particularly ones which entailed representation of the interests of another party who for one reason or another was unable or incompetent to safeguard those interests personally. For example, on 7 May 1529 Allan Hamilton of Bardowny compeared to constitute as his curators *ad lites et negotia* Nichol Crawford, the justice clerk, and William Stirling of Glorat.[58] Conversely, individuals would sometimes appear before the Lords to formalise discharge of an office. For example, on 22 May 1529 James Foulis protested that he had been chosen as an arbiter by John Somerville, but that "the said John wald nocht compeir to geif him informatioun". He therefore wished to be "exonerat of his aith and his conscience anent the said mater".[59]

Other offices carried with them associated property rights, such as to receive the fruits of certain lands. When conflicting claims to such offices arose, they could be brought for resolution before the Lords. For example, again on 22 May 1529, Walter Kennedy, parish clerk of the Inch, appeared in an action against Henry Arnot who "clamand the said paroche clerkship to pertene to him", and "trublit the said M. Walter and the parochinaris of the said kirk thrifor befor ane reverend fader in God Henry bischop of Galloway & his commissaris".[60] Walter's complaint was that he and the parishioners had appealed to the archbishop of Glasgow, but Henry had already taken out letters entitling him to collect the fruits. In this case the Lords did not proceed to decide directly upon the right to the office, but instead suspended

[57] Finlay, *Men of Law in Pre-Reformation Scotland*, p. 21.
[58] NAS CS 5/40, fol. 18v.
[59] NAS CS 5/40, fol. 24v.
[60] NAS CS 5/40, fol. 24v.

Henry's letters in the interim. This incidentally provides yet more evidence of the way in which there was commonly a smooth interaction between legal process in the church courts and the Council, with the Session intervening here in a process before the commissary courts of the archbishop of Glasgow.

Another kind of office or status which parties would take upon themselves with formal notice to the court was that of cautioner (i.e. standing as surety by way of security for performance of an obligation). Thus, for example, on 22 May 1529 Alexander Ogilvy of Finlater compeared and "oblist him to releif and keip scathless" Lord Lovat in relation to payment of 300 merks, in part payment of an overall sum of 750 merks which Lord Lovat owed to Margaret Tudor, the Queen Dowager.[61] Parties would also compear to "become lawborowis" (give surety for themselves as a pledge against their causing harm to a specified person).[62] As well as being constituted a procurator, there were other offices of the court such as a sheriff *in hac parte* (i.e. "in that part", i.e. cause) to which the holders would be sworn in before Council. For example, on 14 July 1529, whilst the Exchequer was still sitting, James Johnston and John Produven, macers of the court, compeared to swear that "thai suld lelely and trewly minister in the office of sheriffship within the tolbuth of Edinburgh anent the cognition taking apoun the commissioun rasit...tuching the land of Pollinfeith...and half landis of Sandelandis".[63]

Tinsel of office

Part of the traditional jurisdiction of the King's Council was to exercise a disciplinary jurisdiction over royal officers, and this is illustrated in an action in the King's name against Lord Lindsay, the sheriff of Fife, on 1 June 1529. The basis of the action was legislation which established that a sheriff should forfeit his office for culpable or partial proceeding in the administration of justice.[64] In this case Lord Lindsay was held to have "parcially and wilfully procedit in the sheriff court

---

[61] NAS CS 5/40, fol. 44.

[62] NAS CS 5/40, fol. 93v.

[63] NAS CS 5/40, fol. 57.

[64] Statutes on this matter were passed from 1450 onwards, e.g. *The Acts of the Parliaments of Scotland*, ed. T. Thomson and C. Innes [hereafter *APS*], 12 vols (Edinburgh, 1814–1875), vol. 2, p. 35, c. 5. See the discussion and reference to subsequent legislation in *The Sheriff Court Book of Fife 1515–1522*, ed. Dickinson, p. xxxiii.

of Fiff" in respect of a contested claim to lands. The dispute arose from a process before the sheriff of Fife initated by a brieve of inquest which saw Robert Orok entered to certain lands. Orok subsequently seems to have been the innocent party. Another party, David Boswell, brought a wrongful occupation action against Orok, and appears to have violently dispossessed him from the property. A decree of the Lords of Council had held that Boswell had spuilzied the lands from Orok, along with taking Orok's charter, tailzie, letter of tack (i.e. lease) and an associated assignation, and that Boswell ought to restore Orok. Boswell nevertheless did not do so but instead proceeded against Orok again. This was before the sheriff and involved "tuching the cognition taking" in relation to the assertion by Boswell of a right of lease of his own. This cognition contravened letters which had also been issued charging the sheriff and his deputies not to proceed against Orok in this regard until he had been restored to his lands.[65] Prior possession was to be protected. On this basis the sheriff forfeited his office and within two weeks letters had been served on him demanding that he hand over to a macer his seal and signet of office, his court book and related writings and rolments. We know this because on 15 June 1529 Lord Lindsay compeared personally to complain at this course of action.[66]

Forfeiture

It was Council which was used as the judicial instrument by which the penalties for crimes such as treason were put into effect. For example, after the earl of Angus had been convicted of treason and lese-majesty in Parliament in September 1528, his property was confiscated as an escheat to the Crown through forfeiture. The effect of this upon particular properties can also be seen in legal process before Council. For example, on 22 March 1529 Adam Otterburn (as King's advocate) appeared in an action against the free tenants of Kirriemuir in order to seek a declarator from the Lords of Council that the lands and lordship of the regality of Kirriemuir now pertained to the King in property, having previously been the heritable property of Archibald Douglas, sixth earl of Angus. The crucial point of this for the holders of the "tenandrys" as residual possessors was that the property was now to

[65] NAS CS 5/40, fol. 49r.
[66] NAS CS 5/40, fol. 55.

be "brukit and disponit be his hienes at his pleasour in tym cuming according to the said process and dome of forfaltour".[67]

Deforcement of messengers

The Council's jurisdiction extended to overseeing the enforcement of its decrees, and a common action was a summons in the name of the King's advocate against men who had "deforced" (i.e. resisted violently or otherwise) a royal messenger in the course of his duties, most often in the execution of diligence to enforce a decree for debt. Such an action occurred on 15 April 1529, for example, with a summons against John Oliphant and Alexander Smith, chaplain, in relation to a deforcement on 16 February, some two months earlier. A messenger, Robert Chapman, had travelled to the lands and barony of Kelly with royal letters issued "be deliverance" of the Lords of Council, in order to poind (i.e. attach as security) some movable goods for payment of 40 merks annual rent owed to the master and bedesmen of the Hospital of Our Lady and St Paul's Work in Edinburgh, a late fifteenth-century charitable foundation. The allegation was that the defenders had "violentlie stoppit and tuke the said gudis fra the said officiar and deforsit him in the execution of his office". They were now to answer to the King and his advocate for the "contemptioune done to his hienes and to be punist".[68] The defenders in this case failed to compear and it was decreed that they had done "wrang" and were now to be punished. In a separate case on 5 May 1529, relating to the deforcement of William Duncan, three horses had been poinded by William. As he was delivering them to market for apprising, the defenders came upon him, took back the horses and thereby deforced him in the execution of his office. The record in this case describes William's symbolic and procedural response, which was that he "brak his wand and tuk witness".[69]

---

[67] NAS CS 5/40, fol. 7r.
[68] NAS CS 5/40, fol. 9v.
[69] NAS CS 5/40, fol. 16v.

Actions relating to property

Protection of property rights

An extremely large proportion of litigation concerned disputes over land. The remedies were often both proprietary and delictual, being drawn in part from the law of obligations concerning "wrang" as well as from the law of property. The Lords of Council would give remedies against dispossession from property, including property held on a heritable title. This was mainly through actions of spuilzie, wrongous occupation and ejection. However, the Lords did not merely safeguard possession but would also adjudicate over conflicting claims of title, and correspondingly protect the possession of someone who could show rightful title. Typically this might involve protecting the possession of the rightful owner. However, title might also arise from temporary and non-heritable interests such as a lease, a life-rent or a widow's right of terce. Heritable title was of course the ultimate right in land but conflicting heritable claims had been beyond the jurisdiction of the King's Council. The difficult questions relating to jurisdiction over such matters of ultimate but contested right and associated jurisdictional change will be treated in the following two chapters. Heritable title was perhaps the one area where the development of the jurisdiction of Council was significantly inhibited by the structure of medieval jurisdiction as determined by the common law. Nevertheless, this inhibition did little to prevent the Session handling the large volume of litigation which had developed by the early sixteenth century in which a wide range of remedies relating to property disputes were dispensed.

Rights to land and conflicts and disputes arising from them in a feudal order could take many forms. For example, on 12 April 1529 Andrew Murray of Blackbarony compeared against Adam Dundas and complained that Adam had obtained a "pretendit" gift from the King of Andrew's feuferme lands and heritage of Ballincrieff, having alleged that they had been his mother's lands as her conjunct fee and had come into the King's hands as escheat. Andrew alleged that this was "sinistre informatioun and nocht of verite for his modir has na coniunctfeftment thirof bot hir terce allanerlie". Adam was to produce his gift and the letters he had obtained as a consequence of it. Both parties were present in court, and the Lords gave decree that Adam should "decist and ceis" from intromitting with the lands in question, which were "to be brokit and joisit be Andro as he sall think expedient eftir the forme and tenour of his charter of few and instrument of seising thirupoune".[70] In essence the Lords had upheld the rights of the heritable proprietor, but the complex nature of the dispute reflected the interrelationship between different forms of interest in land, exaction of feudal rights by a superior, and exploitation of those rights through the King making a gift of them to a third party. Andrew's mother had merely a widow's life interest of "terce", and the exaction of the escheat had been invalid. The basis for the Lords' decision was simply examination of the written deeds. This took the form of the charter, and evidence of Andrew's feudal investiture through the taking of sasine.

Land disputes could therefore compell the Session into making a sophisticated evaluation of conflicting claims to title, often arising ultimately from disputes involving the exaction of feudal rights by the superior. In a system in which documentary evidence of title was simply the responsibility of the claimant to be able to produce, legal transactions could easily run their course on the basis of contestable claims. The only way to resolve the resulting disputes was through litigation. The Session came into its own as a forum in which such disputes could be resolved. To take another example, on 22 May 1529 we find the Lords assessing claims to mails, ferms, profits and duties under escheat against a newly infeft proprietor of the land in question. Following the forfeiture of Archibald Douglas of Kilspindie, Patrick Hepburn of Wauchton had received from the King the assignation of an escheat of land in the sheriffdom of Peebles which had belonged to Elizabeth Hoppar, the spouse of Douglas. Hepburn had already "apprehendit" sheep and other goods from the land, and the Lords held that these were correctly his escheat goods because they were in Archibald and Elizabeth's possession when Archibald was forfeited. However, the Lords refused to award the mails of the land to Patrick since they "has sene ane autentik instrument of saising bering in effect that the said Andro Murray is saisit in the samyn". Andrew Murray's instrument of sasine was to be considered valid unless it was reduced "or ellis ane sufficient reservacioun of the said Isabellis coniunctfeftment of the saidis landis be schawn and producit".[71]

We see again from this example how the Lords would look to the underlying right in land claimed by the possessor, and would if neces-

[70] NAS CS 5/40, fol. 9r.
[71] NAS CS 5/40, fol. 26.

sary adjudicate upon competing instances of such rights. The language of the record brings this out clearly in a decision of the King which was registered on 3 June 1529. A party was to "produce and schaw the day befor his grace ane gretar richt...for the broiking and joising of the landis", but failed in this and had "schew na ryt nor comperit". Decree was therefore awarded against him.[72] Given the need to prove the nature of the title under which the land was held, a party would sometimes come before Council simply in the hope of getting an order to another party to hand over evidence such as a charter which it was alleged he or she was withholding. Alexander Shaw of Sauchy sought this remedy against William Lumsden of Ardre in Fife in June 1529, alleging that William retained Alexander's charter. On this occasion, Shaw was granted a continuation to prove his allegations, though William continued to deny them.[73] Litigation and formal adjudication in court were therefore crucial aspects of promoting security and clarity of title in the sixteenth century. The contentiousness inherent in the complex structure of landed tenure required the possibility of authoritative judicial intervention. The Session provided an essential form of adjudicative oversight of the written basis for land title which was especially important in a feudal tenurial order. By the seventeenth century this was to have become the foundation of a more settled system of title, through the direct regulation by the Session of notaries and their protocol books by the second half of the sixteenth century, the formalisation of a register of deeds from 1554, and the requirement from 1617 of registration of writs relating to land transactions.[74] But in the early sixteenth century, securing tenurial rights required greater judicial intervention and the development of the Session fulfilled this role.

Error

A common action raised in the King's name was that of a summons of error, whereby the retour of an inquest which had purported to serve an heir to lands was reduced. Error was an important framework within which the remedy of reduction was commonly applied. This

[72] NAS CS 5/40, fol. 51v.
[73] NAS CS 5/40, fol. 55.
[74] Webster, *Scotland from the Eleventh Century to 1603*, pp. 209–210, 213–214; J.W. Cairns, "Historical introduction", in *A History of Private Law in Scotland*, 2 vols, ed. K. Reid and R. Zimmermann (Oxford, 2000), vol. 1, pp. 14–184 at pp. 88–89, 132.

type of jurisdiction was essentially supervisory in character. Its development was seen by Hannay as "initiating a movement which slowly but surely diminished the calls made upon Parliament as a court of appeal, and which in proportion opened the approaches by direct complaint to the privy council".[75] This is a very important claim but one which has not tended to be pursued by subsequent scholars. The expansion of conciliar error jurisdiction and associated remedies could be seen to mark the decisive *terminus a quo* in the fifteenth century for the development by the Session of a general and unlimited jurisdiction in the sixteenth century. If so, this may have provided a specific impetus for development by the 1520s and 1530s of the scope of the remedy of reduction, whose importance in establishing a heritage jurisdiction will be assessed in chapter 7.

Research on the history of the action of error has advanced very little beyond the incidental treatment encountered in the work of Hannay, and the concise but highly suggestive analysis of Hector McKechnie in his David Murray Lecture of 1956.[76] McKechnie succeeded in adding significantly to the observations of Hannay on how the summons of error may have reflected deeper jurisdictional change. The action could involve summoning the sheriff, members of the inquest as well as the alleged heir who had initiated the process. It had been regulated by statute since the fifteenth century. An act of 1471 had been directed against "manswearing" (perjuring) by members of inquests and assizes to the harm of the lieges, and "specialy by the inquestis in thar heretage".[77] It was from that time open to someone with a complaint of this nature to summon under this statute the whole assize before the Council and lead evidence of the misconduct of its members. If the allegations were proven, then the tainted legal process could be nullified, and the assize punished. Significantly, though, this procedure was not to apply to the pleadable brieves (dissasine, right etc.), which of course provided the main fifteenth-century proprietary remedies. In 1487 a statute was passed which in part re-asserted Council's residual jurisdiction to hear complaints against royal officers such as sheriffs for

[75] R.K. Hannay, *The College of Justice* (Edinburgh, 1933), reprinted in *The College of Justice: Essays by R.K. Hannay*, ed. H.L. MacQueen, Stair Society Supplementary Series 1 (Edinburgh, 1990), p. 10.

[76] Though also briefly treated in relation to fee and heritage jurisdiction in MacQueen, *Common Law and Feudal Society*, p. 224.

[77] *APS* ii, p. 100, c. 9. (6 May, 1471).

"wranguis and inordinat proceding", with provision for summoning them before Council with their rolments of court in order to reduce and annul any court process tainted by their wrongful conduct.[78] Error seems to have experienced development as a cause of action in the later fifteenth century, and also exemplifies the expansion of the jurisdiction of the King's Council. In this regard, Hector McKechnie argued that, during James IV's reign, "while brieves remained in active operation, they were increasingly duplicated by other royal writs under the Privy Seal or signet". He pointed to error as a significant example of the way in which the newer procedure by summons before Council tended to absorb the substance of the older forms of action by brieve, and noted the existence of "the brieve of summons of error" as an example of this shift.[79] His broader argument was the brilliantly insightful one that "it was not so much that the summons superseded the brieve as that the brieve passed into the summons".[80] Consequently, in our survey of the business of the Session in the 1530s, it is no surprise to find the summons of error as a particularly significant form of action before the court.

A typical example of a summons of error in the later period around 1532 came on 21 May 1529 in relation to a brieve of inquest (i.e. service of an heir) raised by Robert Bruce. In this case the error lay in wrongly retouring the nature of the tenure under which the land was held as "blanchferme", even though there were "na evidentis thirupon shown to inquest".[81] This error action was the first in a series of six heard that day. In another case, the complaint was "inordinat proceding" because of failure to produce an instrument of sasine of the deceased man, and an undervaluing of the lands in question.[82] On the following day, the complaint was against John Ross, son of Walter Ross, "pretendit" sheriff depute of Elgin and Forres, for "inordinat and parciale process" through proceeding on the serving of the brieve of inquest whilst "havand na power nor commission thirto bot as ane privat persoun havand na iurisdictioune".[83] Also from a more technical point of view, the inquest had been held in time of Parliament without

[78] *APS* ii, p. 177, c. 10.

[79] H. McKechnie, *Judicial Process upon Brieves, 1219–1532*, 23rd David Murray Lecture, University of Glasgow (Glasgow, 1956), pp. 22–23.

[80] McKechnie, *Judicial Process upon Brieves*, p. 28.

[81] NAS CS 5/40, fol. 40.

[82] *King v. Alexander Bailze et al.*, NAS CS 5/40, fol. 40v.

[83] NAS CS 5/40, fol. 43v.

a dispensation. In the decree the retour was reduced explicitly for the latter reason.

There was a variety of further technical bases which could ground an action of error. In one instance it was alleged that the brieve had been put to an inquest despite "nocht beand lauchfullie proclamit and the membris of court nocht sufficientlie suorne thirto".[84] A subsidiary factor in this case was also that there had been an inhibition put on the sheriff from proceeding with the inquest. This was at the instance of the "donatour" of the ward and lands in question, who was away in France in the King's service.[85] Another potential cause of error was that an inquest had been mistaken in assessing who was the nearest lawful heir. For example, on 23 July 1529 the retour serving Margaret Hope as heir to John Hogg of Foulsland was reduced because the inquest had wrongly found Margaret heir, "howbeit William Hogg is brother jarman and nerest and lauchful air".[86] Equally, objection might be taken to the persons on the inquest as "suspect",[87] or to the way they gave their retour. This might be because "thai answerit not noyther affirmative nor negative to the punctis of the said breif", for example.[88] Decrees of error were, of course, themselves subject to reduction. On 4 April 1530 the Lords reduced such a decree after hearing submissions that "the said sumondes was never tabulit by the tolbuth dure", that it had not been raised or pursued within three years, and that the inquest had not been wrong in ascertaining who had died last seised in the land.[89] The decree of error being reduced, the Lords ordained the original retour to stand.

A summons of error did not lie only against an inquest of succession, serving an heir to lands. Other actions such as a process of apprising for debt could also be the subject of a summons of error. For example, on 23 March 1531 Oliver Maxton, a macer and sheriff *in hac parte*, was pursued under a summons of error in relation to his apprising of the lands and goods of David Boswell of Glassmount. In this case the process of apprising was challenged on the basis that "thai procedit in the halding of the saide lande for sum of 400 mk as

[84] *King v. William Hamilton*, NAS CS 5/40, fol. 47.
[85] NAS CS 5/40, fol. 47.
[86] NAS CS 5/40, fol. 67.
[87] NAS CS 5/40, fol. 77.
[88] NAS CS 5/40, fol. 77.
[89] NAS CS 5/41, fol. 64v.

perteining to David Boswell in heritage" when this was untrue, and it pertained in heritage to William Larbert. The challenge failed, however, and the record baldly states in simple terms that the Lords assoilzied the defenders.[90]

Redemption of lands

The redemption of lands under a reversion was often considered a transaction of such importance that it ought to be carried out or registered in the presence of the Lords of Council, particularly in cases where there had been dispute over some aspect of the redemption. A typical example is the compearance on 15 July 1529 of Alexander Inglis of Tarvit and William Inglis, vicar of Cupar, his curator, to renounce "all clame of ryt that thai have or micht have in and to the landis of Wemyss Tervale". This land had been redeemed by David Wemyss of that Ilk, and Alexander now "deliverit in presence of said lordis" his "evidentis" relating to the land and "made faith that thai had na ma evidentis of the same and that thai had done exact deligence to seik and gett all evidentis perteining thirto". A decree had been given against Alexander and his curator on this account, and the Lords now discharged the process of the horn which had been led against them.[91]

Transactions involving reversions could easily lead to disputes. The buyer of land to be held under a reversion might refuse to deliver the deed of reversion, thus depriving the seller of the legal document necessary to redeem the land in the future. On 20 March 1531, for example, John Ormiston complained to the Lords that Alexander Cockburn and his spouse had not yet delivered to him a reversion of land which "he sauld and analyit thame... heretablie be charter and seising... and thai band and oblist thaime to have deliverit to him ane reversion in dew form for redemption of the saide lande".[92] Although Ormiston alleged this to be "incontrar the band and oblissing" and a breach of their agreement, the Lords assoilzied the defenders without explanation, according to the record. In another similar case on 31 March 1531, John Lindsay of Colinton complained that, having charged Janet Telfer, relict of John Graham, burgess of Edinburgh, to deliver a reversion to him or enter into ward, failing which she should be put to the horn,

[90] NAS CS 5/42, fol. 139.
[91] NAS CS 5/40, fol. 60v.
[92] NAS CS 5/42, fol. 131v.

she had entered into ward in the castle of Blackness "to eschew the process of the horn and to caus the said Johne tyne [i.e. forfeit] the privelege of the redemptioun of hes auld heritage". The record went on to state that "sche fraudfully enterit in ward...and thir to remain all hir dayis sche beand ane agit woman and able hastelie to de".[93]

Tinsel of property

Adjudicating upon title was the main way in which the Lords possessed jurisdiction over rights in land. This could ultimately involve reducing an infeftment which they declared to be invalid, the implications of which for jurisdiction over heritage will be discussed in chapter 7. But the Lords also had jurisdiction to declare someone forfeited of their lands through failure to perform their obligations to a feudal superior or landlord. For example, on 23 July 1529, the earl of Crawford was found to have forfeited his tack (lease) of lands in the sheriffdom of Fife because he had "nocht maid payment of the mailis fermes and dewiteis thirof eftir the form of the rentale". The land was now to "turn again to the kingis grace to be disponit be his hienes as he sall think maist expedient".[94] Having failed to appear, the earl of Crawford turned up the following day protesting.[95] A similar action failed on 30 March 1530. It was in relation to a summons to hear James Grant of Freuchy declared to have "tynt and forfaltit hes heritage of the saide landes because he and hes fadir had failzeit to pay to our soveraine lord the said few be the space of 17 years". The King sought payment of the "few mailis" as well, which was granted. However, Grant did not forfeit his property because he was able to produce "ane writing under the privy seile ratifiand and apprevand the charter of few maid to the said umquhile Johne the Grant of the said landes". James Grant apparently claimed that he had paid these mails to the earl of Moray over this period, and an action on this account was reserved to him.[96] Although the King failed to seize the land in question, the action was successful in gathering revenue and can be seen as an illustration of the many royal actions which were motivated by the desire to increase revenue to the Crown which in turn helped sustain royal patronage.

---

[93] NAS CS 5/42, fol. 156.
[94] NAS CS 5/40, fol. 68v.
[95] NAS CS 5/40, fol. 69.
[96] NAS CS 5/41, fol. 50.

Concerted efforts to raise summonses of error and to collect feudal casualties or to apprise lands in lieu of payment of such dues are all evidence of this, and related to the wider "systematic fiscal exploitation of feudal casualties" by the Crown which had been in evidence since the reign of James III.[97]

By the same token, a superior could forfeit his superiority for failing in his obligations towards his vassals. For example, on 7 November 1530 John Charteris forfeited his superiority over lands in Perthshire for his lifetime, because he had been charged by his vassal Janet Gray, Lady Wemyss, to enter to his superiority, and had failed to do so. Lady Wemyss and her spouse were to be entered into their lands and to hold of their over-superior for her lifetime.[98] The disadvantage suffered by a vassal whose superior did not enter the superiority is clear from a similar action five days later, brought by Thomas Colquhoun. The allegation was that the superior "lyis out in defraud of the said Thomas and will nocht entir to his superiorite thereof causand the said Thomas thairthrow to want his mails and deweteis".[99]

Generally, the Session seems to have been seen as a particularly appropriate forum for airing and resolving disputes arising from relations between vassal and superior in respect of the tenurial bond. In a sense that had always been the role of royal as opposed to feudal justice, and the Session simply offered royal justice in a new form. For example, on 24 January 1531 the earl of Rothes compeared to protest that he had called Robert Lumsden to compear before him in his own court ten days earlier, in the chapel of Glendook, in order that he might receive new infeftment of certain lands after the form of his "auld infeftment", but that Robert had refused. Now the earl came to the Session and "as of befor in the presens of the saidis lordis requirit him personalie thirto and offerit him ready to infeft the said Robert", protesting that the land should meanwhile be regarded as in non-entry so that this feudal casualty should accrue to him in the meantime.[100]

[97] C. Madden, "Royal treatment of feudal casualties in late medieval Scotland", *Scottish Historical Review* 50 (1976), 172–194 at p. 192; see also R. Nicolson, "Feudal Developments in Late Medieval Scotland", *Juridical Review* NS 18 (1973), 1–21.

[98] NAS CS 5/41, fol. 118.

[99] NAS CS 5/41, fol. 122v.

[100] NAS CS 5/42, fol. 4v.

Infeftment and entry to lands

Where a superior refused to invest a vassal in lands, the vassal had a remedy in an action before Council. For example, on 31 May 1531 Duncan McKellar, as heir to the late Thomas McKellar of Barskeet, sued Lord Herries in relation to his lands of Barskeet in the barony of Norton, lands which had been recognosced (i.e. taken into the superior's hands). They had apparently been granted to John Murehead of Bulleis, but this infeftment had been "laitlie retretit" (i.e. reduced) by the Lords of Council. Now Lord Herries was "enterit to the said haile barony with power to infeft their first tennent to thir tennandris of the same".[101] However, Lord Herries refused to enter Duncan to his land despite being charged to do so within fifteen days. The Lords continued the cause so that Lord Herries could make "liquid" the composition for the lands (i.e. fix a value of the feudal casualty for gaining entry to the lands) "with certificatione to him and he do nocht the said lordes will decerne and ordains him to entir the said Duncane to the propirtie of the said land, he findaind cautione to do that suld bedone be the law".[102]

R.M. Maxtone-Graham charted the history of the action of showing the holding, and pointed out that by the second half of the sixteenth century such actions were being raised in the Session.[103] Such actions had originally been raised by a lord in his own court as part of his "disciplinary" jurisdiction. They required a tenant to answer for his lands by bringing his charter to show in the lord's court and demonstrate thereby his written title. They seem to represent a survival of the lord's disciplinary jurisdiction free from the procedures of the common law, since no brieve was required.[104] Litigation arising from such actions could take place before the Session, as illustrated by the case of Janet Dickson and her spouse, William Tait, on 22 April 1534.[105] Janet had complained that she held land in chief of James Gladstains, which she had been entered into by James's father, but now James "hes maid him to lede ane pretendit process agains hir and hir said spous for schawing of thir halding". Unfortunately, they could not produce an

[101] NAS CS 5/42, fol. 184v.
[102] NAS CS 5/42, fol. 184v.
[103] R.M. Maxtone Graham, "Showing the Holding", *Juridical Review* NS 2 (1957) 251–269 at p. 267.
[104] MacQueen, *Common Law and Feudal Society*, pp. 120–121.
[105] NAS CS 6/4, fol. 106v.

instrument of sasine at the relevant time, although "thai offerit to preve be the ballie that gave the sesing and uther witnesses that was present thirat that sche gart the same and wes sesit thirin". This James and his bailies would not allow as evidence and "dome of propirte" was given. Janet appealed, but James and his bailies refused to give her a copy of the process. The Lords therefore ordered that a copy be delivered to Janet by 12 May or else the process itself might be declared null. This illustration shows the extent to which the Session exercised by this time a central, supervisory and effectively supreme jurisdiction over other Scottish courts, since a lord who refused to observe due process of law could find legal process in his own court simply declared void. From a wider European perspective, the Session provides in this sense a vivid Scottish example of the effect of centralisation upon jurisdiction and the dominant role which the newer generation of central courts could play in enhancing the unity of the legal system within a state.

Warrandice

Parties whose title to land was challenged or thrown into doubt would be entitled to have resort to an action of warrandice, or if the challenge took the form of legal action against them, could call their warrantor to defend the action. An action on 26 March 1530 shows clearly such a claim in warrandice being upheld by the Lords. John Lockhart of the Bar appeared against Matthew Stewart, earl of Lennox, and his tutor. John wished Matthew to be "decernit be decrete of the lordis of counsal to warand acquiet and defend" certain lands in Ayrshire, "to be brukit be him peceablie in tyme tocum eftir the forme of the charter of vendition and alienation thereof maid" by the late John, earl of Lennox. The point of the warrandice claim, however, is revealed in the decree, which states that the earl should defend John in his possession of the land, but if necessary should alternatively provide "als mekle als gud landis of als greite availe als weile liand and als weile haldin as the said landis".[106]

Spuilzie

One of the most common actions before the Session was spuilzie (i.e. spoliation, dispossession) of goods or livestock. The action of spuilzie

[106] NAS CS 5/41, fol. 38r.

seems to have had its origin in canon law and to have developed as a ground of action in summonses before Council in the fifteenth century, though as a remedy it shares some features with the brieve of novel dissasine. Neilson and Paton long ago remarked for the period around 1500 that "no form of action was so much in use as that of Spuilzie", and noted its regulation in legislation passed in 1438, 1449, 1457 and 1503, as well as commenting upon its origin in the canon law.[107] These canonist origins relate to the *actio spolii*, which was a medieval development of a form of action which protected against dispossession and was first formulated as the *condictio ex canone redintegranda* by Sicardus of Cremona in his *Summa* of 1180. As Gabriel Le Bras demonstrated, the *condictio* itself was a development of a defence already recognised in canon law in the ninth century on the basis of the canonistic principle *spoliatus ante omnia restituendus*.[108] Typically, canonists considered the matter in relation to cases of bishops being dispossessed because of crimes they were alleged to have committed.[109] Before facing prosecution canon law insisted on the bishop's right to be restored to possession of his see. Gratian's *Decretum* of 1140 gave an account of spoliation and stated the *canon redintegranda*—the rule of restitution, applied by Gratian more generally to one who had been dispossessed.[110] Subsequent to the formulation of Sicardus, the action then seems to have been taken up and provided for in a canon of Innocent III made in 1215.[111]

Little seems to have been published on the *actio* since the late nineteenth-century account by Francesco Ruffini, though it has been discussed in analysis of its possible influence on the development of English writs. In this context, Donald Sutherland argued that it was certainly "a very close canonist equivalent of the assize of novel dissei-

---

[107] *ADC* ii, p. lxxi; *Habakkuk Bisset's Rolment of Courtis*, vol. 3, ed. P.J. Hamilton-Grierson, Scottish Text Society New Series 18 (Edinburgh, 1926), p. 121. See also the treatment in MacQueen, *Common Law and Feudal Society*, pp. 224–8.

[108] G. Le Bras, "Canon Law", in *The Legacy of the Middle Ages*, ed. C.G. Crump and E.F. Jacob (Oxford, 1926), pp. 321–361 at pp. 350–51. Though concise, this is a short and authoritative account of the history of the *actio*.

[109] H.J. Berman, *Law and Revolution: the Formation of the Western Legal Tradition* (Harvard, 1983), p. 240.

[110] Berman, *Law and Revolution*, pp. 240–241.

[111] A. Engelmann et al., *A History of Continental Civil Procedure* (London, 1928), p. 581.

sin".[112] More generally, Harold Berman has summarised its importance in stating that:

> the actio spolii was available for any kind of spoliation (including spoliation by fraud); it could be used to recover possession of incorporeal rights as well as of moveable and immoveable things; it was available against third persons, including persons not in possession of things claimed; and the plaintiff was not required to show title to the land or goods or rights which he claimed. Finally, the action was available even to one who was himself wrongly in possession.[113]

Whilst it was a remedy from the canon law, it appears to have provided the remedial concept for the secular, civil action of spuilzie in the Scottish royal courts. As Professor Cairns puts it, the canon law action "crossed over into Scots law to provide a category in which to deal with wrongs".[114]

The idea that this was wrongful conduct which should be redressed was, however, already present in the Scottish common law. The canon law simply provided the model for Council replicating a form of possessory remedy for itself which was already provided for in the common law, principally by the brieve of novel dissasine. In that sense, we witness here the grafting of a new remedial form onto an existing type of liability, and not the extension of the substantive common law. This development fits the pattern described by McKechnie and already noted above as "the passing of the brieve into the summons".[115] Significantly, it was precisely this step—of replicating a form of remedy already provided for in the common law—which Council was traditionally unable to accomplish in relation to the determination of fee and heritage. There its jurisdiction was still limited, at least in the fifteenth century, by the medieval common law. Here too, the ultimate acquisition of jurisdiction by Council was to arise indirectly through the development of its own form of remedy (reduction), but in relation to the established structure of legal rights in land as defined by the common law.

---

[112] F. Ruffini, *L'actio spolii: studio storico-giuridico* (Turin, 1889); D.W. Sutherland, *The Assize of Novel Disseisin* (Oxford, 1973), pp. 20–21, with ensuing discussion of the contribution of the civilians as well. But see the review of the debate in J. Martinez-Torrón, *Anglo-American Law and Canon Law: Canonical Roots of the Common Law Tradition* (Berlin, 1998), pp. 175–177.

[113] Berman, *Law and Revolution*, p. 241.

[114] Cairns, 'Historical Introduction', p. 73.

[115] McKechnicc, *Judicial Process Upon Brieves*, p. 22.

The narration of the ground of action typically followed a common form, as in the summons of George Dalzell against Hew Crawford, called on 17 April 1529. It was for "wrangous, maisterful and violent spulze... awaytaking and withhalding... recently on 15 March of aitis".[116] If the case was proved, the defender was decreed to have done "wrang" and the remedy was restitution of the goods. In this particular case it was ordained that the defender "sall restor and deliver" the oats. Commenting on the late fifteenth and early sixteenth century council proceedings in relation to spuilzie, Dr Neilson observed that "in a very considerable proportion of the cases the spoliation was rather a technical wrong than an act of mere violence".[117] Professor Dickinson argued to the contrary that actions such as spuilzie should not be seen uniformly as relating to merely technical breaches of procedure, such as when property was seized under a flawed warrant, frequent though such instances might have been. Rather they must often have encompassed a real degree of violence as well in the course of the dispossession.[118] The evidence considered here supports Dickinson's emphasis, together with evidence to be considered later relating to ejection and wrongous occupation.

As was generally the case, of course, a spuilzie action did not necessarily reach final decree, and could be abandoned if the defender simply returned the goods in question. On 7 May 1529, for example, Sir James Wychtand discharged a summons of recent spuilzie which he had raised against James Wedderburn, because "the gudis contenit in the said summondis" had been delivered again to him.[119] Disputes could arise over whether or not such goods had been restored, and it was obviously a defence to a spuilzie action that they had been. For example, on 23 March 1531 the Lords made a ruling on an exception put forward by Ninian Chirnside of East Nesbit "to preve that he restorit and deliverit 8 kyn and hors of the 52 kyn and 4 hors aboune written". The Lords assoilzied Ninian in respect of these seven "kyn" and a horse "because the said Ninian hes maid payment thereof".[120]

It is worth pointing out that spuilzie was not simply an action associated with the Session, as might be expected given its canon law back-

[116] NAS CS 5/40, fol. 11r.
[117] *ADC* ii, p. lxxi.
[118] *Sheriff Court Book of Fife 1515–1522*, ed. Dickinson, p. 326.
[119] NAS CS 5/40, fol. 18v.
[120] NAS CS 5/42, fol. 144.

ground and the special composition of the Session with its experienced canon lawyers. Although it has never been studied in depth, spuilzie is usually regarded as an action developed before the King's Council in the fifteenth century, where a canon law influence would be readily explicable. In fact, as Neilson and Paton noted, legislation was passed as early as 1438. Under this legislation, jurisdiction lay with the sheriff in the first instance, and under that of 1450 jurisdiction was recognised separately in both the sheriff and the Council.[121] Certainly by the 1520s, and probably therefore considerably earlier, the action of spuilzie was generally competent in the sheriff court.[122] On 28 April 1529, John Spens of Marisoune called John Chalmers and Steven Duddingstone before Council. He explained that he had "optenit ane decret of spulze befor the sheriff of Fiff and his deputis" against John and Steven, but that this had been "retretit", the retreting taking place "for the sheriffis unordourlie proceding alanerlie".[123] On 10 March a messenger had served royal letters upon John Spens allegedly in relation to this decree "quhilk as he traist is nocht of verite". Spens wanted the messenger to show him the letters so that he might "ken the effect thirof", but he refused, and now the defenders had also failed to compear to allow the letters to be examined.[124] This provides an incidental example of the Session exercising its supervisory jurisdiction in relation to matters which had already been the subject of a preliminary legal action in the sheriff court.

The record of litigation before the Session shows that it could be open to argument—at least in the eyes of litigants—to question exactly how the elements of a spuilzie action should be defined. For example, on 14 May 1529 there were submissions in which a distinction was drawn between spuilzie and "wrang". James Foulis, forspekar for the laird of Burleigh, protested that if process were led against the laird "bot apoun spulze that thai suld nocht proceid apon the wrang and gif thai did for nullitie of the process, becaus be the privilege of the summondis thai may nocht proceide but be way of spulze".[125] The pursuer,

---

[121] *APS* ii, p. 32, c. 2 (1438), p. 34, c. 8 (1450); p. 36, c. 7 (1450). See Hannay, *The College of Justice*, pp. 8–9; *Sheriff Court Book of Fife 1515–1522*, ed. Dickinson, p. 326; *ADC* ii, p. lxxi.

[122] *Sheriff Court Book of Fife 1515–1522*, ed. Dickinson, pp. 325–327, where the fifteenth-century history is also reviewed.

[123] NAS CS 5/40, fol. 14v.

[124] Ibid.

[125] NAS CS 5/40, fol. 33v.

Thomas Scott, referred to "his summondis of spulze and wrang",[126] but the laird of Burleigh "allegit the summondis was libillit for spulze and nocht for wrang".[127] However, the Lords had already given their sentence interlocutor that they could proceed because the summons was for "wrangwis spoliatioune".[128] The explanation for these submissions may be that the wording of the summons did not explicitly allege "wrang" but only spuilzie, and had therefore been drafted inadequately for the action intended. However, it is hard to see how the Lords could determine spuilzie without determining "wrang", since spuilzie was by definition wrongful and subsumed within a larger category of the law of "wrang".

The submissions in this example may simply reflect a rather misconceived and disingenuous attempt to stall proceedings, relying on tenuous objections. Alternatively, they may reflect accurately the extremely technical nature of pleading, and the importance of strict matters of form. Even more so, however, they might also reflect the uncertain course of juridification of rights in a system with no authoritative legal treatises or enactments capable of providing definitive analysis of such novel or evolving forms of liability. Legal pleading could expose and exploit conceptual doubt or confusion about how to classify and explain the underlying substantive basis of a remedy in the course of contesting the application of that remedy to the case in hand. In 1529 Scotland was still several decades away from the first sustained attempts to develop a legal literature which attempted systematic analysis of the law.[129] However, by the 1530s the development of the Session was helping to crystalise the common understanding of the "practick" of Scotland, as well as specific points of doubt which its decisions could act to resolve.

Certainly by the 1520s, one element in a spuilzie action could be the allegation of having been spuilzied of the possession of property, as distinct from wrongous occupation or ejection. This suggests spuilzie of an abstract right or state of control in itself and clarified that it was rights flowing from possession and not ultimate right to title which was in issue. If this is more than simply a question of how legal claims were

---

[126] NAS CS 5/40, fol. 34.

[127] NAS CS 5/40, fol. 34v.

[128] NAS CS 5/40, fol. 33v.

[129] On that subsequent course of development see J.D. Ford, *Law and Opinion in Scotland during the Seventeenth Century* (Oxford, 2007).

being expressed, it could represent the conceptual step towards a decoupling of a truly possessory remedy from proprietary ones involving the protection of title. Understanding possession in this way could have led to conceptual advantages in the development of the law. For example, it could have helped clarify if necessary that a possessor need not be personally in occupation or have control of spuilzied property, but need only have vicarious or "civil" possession.[130] It could also aid conceptualisation of the spuilzie of an incorporeal right such as jurisdiction, to be discussed further below. If there was in fact development here, it would seem to have involved abstraction of the nature of the dispossession, which might have acted to broaden the scope of spuilzie. This would be entirely consistent with the canon law remedy, as well as the tradition of novel dissasine, based as it originally was upon the English writ of novel disseisin.[131] Practically speaking, it may also have simply put the effect of spuilzie onto a similar footing to the brieve of novel dissasine. However, this way of regarding the protection of possession does not seem to have been a feature of spuilzie actions in the records up to 1500 and it would be interesting for a more systematic study to be made in order to test this point as well as to chart the development of possessory remedies more generally. Such apparent development in the characterisation of spuilzie may also simply reflect in a fragmentary manner the underlying functional shift by which it finally superseded the older form of action by brieve of novel dissasine.

Since novel dissasine is thought to have begun to fall out of use in the second half of the fifteenth century, it seems very likely that the development of spuilzie was directly influenced by the understanding of the Session judges of the prevalent canon law concept. An example of the mature action came on 14 May 1529, when James Crichton of Cranston Riddale appeared in order to pursue his summons against Katherine Rutherford, Lady of Traquair, for the "wrangwis and maisterful recent spulzie of him of his iust possessioun of his steding and land of Schotingleyis" and "putting and halding of livestock apon the same recently in May 1527".[132] The Lords went on to decree that Katherine

[130] This is just a hypothetical example rather than a claim that this consequence did in fact follow in sixteenth-century legal development. For civil possession in property law, see K.G.C. Reid, *The Law of Property in Scotland* (Edinburgh, 1996), pp. 105–106.

[131] Martinez-Torrón, *Anglo-American Law and Canon Law*, p. 177; Berman, *Law and Revolution*, p. 455.

[132] NAS CS 5/40, fol. 37r.

had done wrong. Sometimes, of course, a spuilzie action might be brought only for it to transpire that the seizure of goods in question had in fact been lawful. For example, it may have been carried out in the execution of diligence (i.e. enforcement of a decree for debt). An illustration of such an action came on 1 February 1531 when John Nesbit of Newton renounced his summons of spuilzie against William Hay because he "grantit that the gudes takin fra him be the kinge officiar war lauchfullie apprisit to the said William and utheris eftir the form and tenor of the said Johnes bond maid to him".[133]

In terms of the scope of a spuilzie action, we have seen that an abstract state of control such as possession could be spuilzied. Another similar example is the spuilzie of jurisdiction. An action was heard on 6 February 1531 in which the provost and bailies of Edinburgh and Alexander Little, a burgess of Edinburgh, sued George Forester, an inhabitant of Leith, for recent spuilzie on 14 June 1530. He was alleged to have spuilzied goods from the shore of Leith and thereby also to have committed "wrangwis spulze of said provost, baillies, counsel of thir possession and jurisdiction of arresting halding of courte and attachement making apoun thir said shore be hes pretendit coulorit aresting thirupon as bailze of Leith", contrary to their "auld infeftment" constituted by a charter from the laird of Restalrig to the town of Edinburgh. The Lords upheld the claim in full.[134] This example is not unique. On 31 March 1531, Andrew Murray of Blackbarony complained against Robert Borthwick "for the wrangwis using and excerting of the said Androis office of bailzerie perteining to him in few ferme and heretage of the tone and lande of ballincreif... and wrangwis haldin of bailzie courte thereon without tak or licence of the said Andro".[135] This was alleged to be despite the King's inhibition against doing so, and thus Andrew had suffered the "wrangwis spoliatioun of him of hes possession of the said office" and the Lords duly declared Robert to have done "wrang". Here we see jurisdiction treated simply as a property right, possession of which could be spuilzied, and therefore fall to be restored according to Andrew's infeftment. At what stage spuilzie came to be understood with this breadth is unclear, but it would seem illustrative of what must

[133] NAS CS 5/42, fol. 30.
[134] NAS CS 5/42, fol. 35.
[135] NAS CS 5/42, fol. 159v.

have been a gradual crystallization of the scope of application of this newer form of remedy before the Session.

Ejection and wrongous occupation

An action often associated with spuilzie—and perhaps hard to differentiate from it, being also very common and often brought concurrently within the same summons—was that of ejection, which arose when someone was dispossessed of his or her land. It may be that the difference from spuilzie related to whether the subject of the dispossession was land or goods, though further research would help to clarify this. Professor Dickinson noted that legislation of 1458 recognised spuilzie as being in relation to either moveables or lands, but argued that it soon became "confined" to movable goods.[136] The established view is that spuilzie was associated with dispossession of moveable goods and that ejection and wrongous occupation related to dispossession of land, but even after 1458 this may contain an element of oversimplification, given the application of spuilzie to a wide range of types of possession, including possession of jurisdiction.[137] It is worth reiterating incidentally that in the canon law the *actio spolii* itself did not apply only to moveables.

A typical example of ejection occurred on 5 May 1529 in the action of James Johnston, burgess of Edinburgh, against Nichol Moffat and John Johnston for "wrangous violent and maisterful intromitting, occupatioune, ejectiounne and outputting" of two tenants of James, from the land of Blacklaw which he possessed in heritage in the stewartry of Annandale. The "outputting" occurred in 1522, and the action encompassed the wrongous withholding of the profits of the land over a seven-year period. The Lords decreed that Nichol and John had done wrong and should desist and cease from occupying the lands, and that James should enjoy possession of them on the basis of his infeftment. These were, incidentally, the standard terms in which accounts of such actions in the record were narrated.[138] Sometimes an action was concerned solely with recovering the profits of land which had been wrongously occupied, in which case the ground of action would be

[136] *Sheriff Court Book of Fife*, ed. Dickinson, p. 325.
[137] *ADC* ii, lxxi. The most detailed analysis is MacQueen, *Common Law and Feudal Society*, pp. 222–228.
[138] NAS CS 5/40, fol. 17v.

the intromitting with and withholding of profits. James Johnson had an action of this sort on 5 May 1529, which was for payment of "the malis and proffitis that he mycht haif had of ane third part of his landis of Nether Blaklawis", which lands had been withheld from him "without tak or licence" for ten years.[139]

Clearly, in an action for ejection the nature of the possession claimed might come under challenge from an opponent. For example, on 16 July 1529 Sir John Campbell of Lundy and his wife, Dame Elizabeth Gray, who held the lands of Pettormo in conjunct-fee, appeared against James Gray. James had been under summons of spuilzie and ejection a month earlier at the instance of Elizabeth and her children. However, James alleged that "sche had na uther possessioun bot came to his place in freindle manere as sche was wonit to do and remanit twa nytis thirin and departit at hir awin pleasour and quhen sche ged furth of the gett his servand stekit the gett and held hir furth".[140] James claimed to hold the land under a tack (i.e. lease) of the previous proprietor, Lord Lyle.[141]

Ejection and wrongous occupation were civil actions, but occasionally the Lords entertained actions which were in substance similar but libelled in terms redolent of the form of a criminal action, as might have been indicted in the justice ayres. Professor Dickinson noted that spuilzie had a criminal connotation, given the close similarity between its cause of action and the crime of theft, and we can extend this point to ejection too.[142] For example, on 29 March 1530, we find an action alleging "wrang" in the "violent and maisterful laying waist of the 40 s. land of auld extent... throw manissing [i.e. menacing] and baisting [i.e. beating] of tennentes and servandes and putting of thaime and thir servandis furth of the said maling", which was held under assedation (i.e. lease). Moreover, the defender had wrongly "suffirit him hes tennentes and servandes to have occupiit the same".[143] In the decree given by the Lords, the rule of law is asserted and the necessity of legal process underlined by the declaration that the pursuer is to enjoy

[139] NAS CS 5/40, fol. 17.
[140] NAS CS 5/40, fol. 61v.
[141] NAS CS 5/40, fol. 62v.
[142] *Sheriff Court Book of Fife*, ed. Dickinson, p. 326.
[143] NAS CS 5/41, fol. 47.

the lands during the term of his lease "and further quhill that he be lauchfullie callit and ordourlie [put] therefra".[144]

The essence of an action for wrongous occupation seems to have been that the possession was wrongful, violent and without title of right. The question of proving violence for a claim to lie was examined above in relation to spuilzie. Though it might seem plausible to imagine that claims of violence were regarded as merely necessary for the sake of legal form without necessarily implying that there was any actual violence, this must be set against some evidence that the Lords could require proof of violence for the action to lie. For example, on 5 December 1533, Katherine Watson lost an action she had brought against Beatrice Semple for the profits Katherine should have received had not Beatrice "maisterfullie and on force... occupiit lauborit and manurit" her lands of Akinbar. The Lords assoilzied Beatrice because the pursuers "have nocht previt the violence conteint in the said sumondis as it is libillit".[145]

Other aspects of the concept of possession

Possessory remedies in general have now been considered. However, on occasion the nature of the possession seems to have been founded upon in the course of making a further personal claim, which gave rise to a fuller statement of legal argument than normal. One particular case from January 1531 illustrates a party using the concept of possession in good faith to justify a claim we might regard as based on grounds akin to unjustified enrichment and the remedy of recompense following possession of a property to which title was disputed. The procurator for Janet Rowat, the defender, gave in a "protestation" in connection with a dispute over title to a house. The pursuer claimed to have been seised of the property prior to the defender. However, the point of the protest was to argue that even if the court were to accept the pursuer's claim, nevertheless, since the defenders had incurred expense in maintaining the property, they should be paid for their expense before being required to give up possession. They "puttand ane meikle ruff apoun the same", and incurred expenses of 300 merks which they wanted "refundit and payit". The justification offered was that "we war in actuale possession be chartir and seising" and were therefore "bone

[144] NAS CS 5/41, fol. 47.
[145] NAS CS 6/3, fol. 114.

fidei possessiares", and it was argued that at the very least no decree of reduction of the sasine should be given before the expenses were refunded.[146] The Lords assigned a day for both sides to produce "sic lawis and resonis quhy the protestatioun aboune written suld be admittit and have effect". The case is a rare illustration of the record containing a relatively clear statement of the legal arguments which underlay a dispute. It is not clear whether the legal issues would have been easily resolved or would have involved the Lords in developing their practick in new ways. The matter was left open for debate.

Reduction of leases

The remedy of reduction has a special relevance to the development of the Lords' jurisdiction over title and disputes over heritable infeftments and this will be examined separately in chapter 7. However, this was only one aspect of their general jurisdiction to reduce legal instruments. It took another form through their jurisdiction to declare a lease void and thereby reduce it. For example, on 28 March 1530 William Stewart, the provost of Lincluden, appeared in an action against multiple defenders, including James Douglas of Drumlanrig, Lady Borthwick and William McClellan, tutor of Bombie. The defenders were:

> to heir and see the pretendit takis maid to thaime and ilkane of thame of the lands undirwrittin…pertaining to the college and provost of Lincluden be ane reverend fader in God David Bishop of Galloway and be Henry now Bishop of Galloway to be decernt be the decrete of the lordis of counsale to have bene fra the begynning and to be now and in all tymis cuming of nane availe.[147]

This the Lords did, because they accepted that the bishops "had nene rycht in and to the said provostry", as had already apparently been decided by the pope and the auditors of the Roman Rota. The right of the provost to set, use and dispone the lands was upheld, although actions of warrandice were reserved to the tack holders against the bishop.[148]

[146] NAS CS 5/42, fol. 3.
[147] NAS CS 5/41, fol. 40.
[148] NAS CS 5/41, fol. 40.

Other substantive actions and grounds of action

Feudal casualties

Casualties such as non-entry, ward and marriage were frequently the subject of litigation, not least because they were assignable and carried with them rights over property with potentially great financial value. That casualties could be assigned gave them an obvious commercial utility. This is apparent in an action before the Lords of Council raised by Nichol Cairncross, who compeared on 22 May 1529 to explain how he had "maid finance" of the sum of 1,400 merks to William Hamilton, who had "passand in France", in return for which "the said Williame maid him assignay to the ward and marriage of Houstoune". He was now concerned that his position should not be prejudiced by anything which could alter relations between William and the Laird of Houston. His appearance in court was simply to note his interest and thereby secure his position to pursue an action as he saw fit.[149]

Casualties such as ward were pursued not only in connection with profits arising from land. Physical possession of the heirs who were in ward was pursued as well, in order to have control in relation to any marriage which might be arranged. For example, on 28 July 1529, Sir James Sandilands of Calder appeared in order to claim the "keping" of the daughters of the late Margaret Ramsay, since they would hold lands of him by service of ward and relief. Their father, Edward Sinclair, was refusing to give them up. The Lords ordered him to deliver the heirs specifically so that James "may dispone apoun thir marriage".[150] The heirs to lands which were held in ward could themselves look to the Council to protect their interests. For example, on 31 March 1531, Lord Crichton of Sanquhar complained that "his lande and heritage hes bene of lang tyme bigane in ward and hes na blanchferme lande to susteine him and the wardoure of the said landes and heritage will geif him na part thirof to his sustentacioun".[151] This was an action

[149] NAS CS 5/40, fol. 24. There is incidentally a remote possibility of confusion in whether the scribe wrongly identified this party as Nichol Cairncross instead of Nichol Crawford. The entry states: "Comperit Nichol Carncors and exponit how he had maid finance to William ~~Craufurd~~ [*sic*] Hamiltoune passand in France of the sum of 1400 Mk or thirby for the quhilk the said Williame maid him assignay to the ward and marriage of Houstoune."

[150] NAS CS 5/40, fol. 71.

[151] NAS CS 5/42, fol. 161.

known as one "to modify thirby ane competent leving thirof" to the "sustenatioun" of the heir. On this occasion Lord Crichton produced retours of the cognition of the value and extent of his heritage made in 1530 by the sheriffs of Dumfries and Perth. The Lords went on to set a "resonable leving" of £20 per annum up to the age of ten, to be followed by 40 merks per annum up to the age of sixteen, and 100 merks per annum between the ages of sixteen and twenty-one, "quharthrow he ma be honestlie susteint in his less age according to equities", the total rental from his lands being 967 merks per annum.

Actions of non-entry were very important, since as a result of lands having fallen into non-entry through the failure of the heirs to receive investiture, apprising could follow in order to satisfy the debt constituted by the casualties incurred. The whole property could be judicially disponed to the King or whoever was the feudal superior, or else to a chosen assignee. For example, on 30 March 1530, the King and David Bonar, the "donator" to whom the casualty in question had been given by the King, pursued the earl of Buchan and others for the non-entries of land in Forfarshire, the defenders being the "herituris" of the land. The King sought declarator of non-entry over a fifty-year period, and "the ground of the said lande to be apprisit for the same" in respect of mails and duties. In this case the defenders were assoilzied after the production of a gift of the non-entries in question by King James IV to James Beaton, who was archbishop of St Andrews by the time of this litigation.[152]

Interdiction from alienation of property

(1) *Interdict by creditor*

The modern Scots procedure of "inhibition" to prevent property being alienated in the face of outstanding claims of debt is found in the early sixteenth century in the form of an interdict against alienating property. Commonly this form of letters was taken out by a creditor. It was not necessary to come before Council to obtain the grant of such letters, but it was Council which exercised a supervisory jurisdiction over such matters through its authority to suspend royal writs. On 6 April 1529, for example, Alexander Scott, parson of Middleby, supplicated Council to suspend letters of this kind taken out by a burgess of Edinburgh,

[152] NAS CS 5/41, fol. 51.

Roland Donaldson, who alleged himself to be Alexander's creditor. The basis of the interdict from Roland's point of view was that Alexander was "awand to him grete soumes of money and is not responsale [i.e. capable of providing security to pay the debt] thirfor in movable gudis", but Alexander alleged that Roland was also Alexander's debtor, and owed more than £100 to him. The effects of Roland's action had been severe. Alexander found himself charged by "opin proclamacioun" at the mercat cross of Edinburgh not to sell or "analie" any of his lands or heritage "in fraud" of Roland, and there was a general charge to the lieges (i.e. the general public) not to buy or take in wadset (i.e. security) any of Alexander's lands, and "gif ony deis in the contrare the same salbe of nane avale" and therefore null.[153] Roland failed to compear, and Alexander received his remedy of suspension of the letters "ay and quhill thai be producit". They were in fact produced ten days later and at that point declared to be "ordourly procedit".[154]

(2) *Interdict in relation to a marriage settlement*

Such an interdict could similarly be employed in relation to a marriage settlement, to guarantee to one of the contracting families that the other family would not diminish by alienation the likely inheritance to be expected from its property. For example, on 17 April 1529 Andrew Reidpath of Grenlaw appeared before Council by way of supplication to state his desire that "of his fre motive" he be interdicted by the Lords' authority "fra all selling, wedsetting and alienatioune" of his lands, annual rents and heritage. This was in connection with the "fulfilling of ane contract of marriage betwix him and Steven Brounefeild of Grenlawdene anent the contracting of matrimone betwix his son and the said Stevins dochter and for conservatioune of his hous and heritage and in favouris of his airis".[155]

(3) *Interdict of minors*

For his own protection a minor might supplicate the Lords to interdict him from alienating property. On 11 May 1529 Walter Borthwick explained to the Lords that he was "ane child of 18 or 19 yeiris of age" and intended to travel to France to "leire the use of merchandice".

[153] NAS CS 5/40, fol. 8.
[154] NAS CS 5/40, fol. 10.
[155] NAS CS 5/40, fol. 12.

Because "thir has bene divers young men maid contractis and has bene seducit to sell thir landis and heretage in tyms bigane, thai beand in ferr partis fra thair frenndis and dreide to be siclik seducit to inconementis", he wanted the Lords to grant such an interdict against him.[156]

(4) *Loosing of interdict*

A party under interdict from alienating property would require to compear again before the Lords themselves if it was desired to alienate any of the property so interdicted. The Lords seem to have had a discretion in making such a decision, since their consent is usually expressed in the form that they "thocht resonable" the request, and if the interdict had been made at the instance of a third party then his consent might be required as well. For example, on 24 January 1531 Lord Lyle compeared to supplicate for the loosing of such an interdict. The circumstances were that before the interdict had been made, "part of the saide lande quhilk is verray proffitable wes wadsett" (i.e. alienated in security for debt with a conditional right of redemption) and now Lord Lyle wished to redeem it. However, in order to do this he needed to alienate some other land in Renfrewshire which was less profitable than the wadsetted land. The Lords "lowsis the interdict" for this specific request, and it is clearly stated that the grounds upon which they deemed the loosing reasonable were that "the same is for his [i.e. Lord Lyle's] utilite and mair profett".[157] Further proceedings two days later illustrate the procedure by which the transaction would be allowed. The Lords "interponit and interponis thir auctorite with decret irritant thereupon" and ordained royal letters to be sent to the sheriffs of "the shyris quhar any of his saide lande lyis". Also, there would be publication of the revised interdict at the market cross of the head burghs of these shires. This particular set of proceedings was not just personal to Lord Lyle but bound all the king's "lieges".[158]

Caution, surety and lawburrows

Agreements for caution (i.e. surety for debt or guarantee of another obligation) could be registered before the Lords. As we have seen, cautioners could be constituted as such through a formal appearance

156 NAS CS 5/40, fol. 22.
157 NAS CS 5/42, fol. 5.
158 NAS CS 5/42, fol. 10.

before the Session. The Lords also dealt with complaints that such agreements had been broken. The particular type of security known as "lawburrows" involved pledging not to cause harm to a person. It was a significant private method of securing the peace during the period of a dispute. Neilson and Paton commented that such agreements can be found entered in the parliamentary register in the fourteenth century, and were already at that time a matter of "common form".[159] They also pointed to a body of fifteenth-century legislation concerned with "law borowis" or "borowis of pece".[160] Unsurprisingly the first of these statutes had been passed under James I, relating what should follow "gif ony of the kingis liegis haf ony doute of his life, outhir be dede or manauce or violent presumpsioun, ande he ask souerte of thaim that he doutis".[161] Neilson and Paton took the view that in the long run "the decline of the process of lawburrows in the seventeenth and eighteenth centuries was to be the gradual register of victory for the King's peace".[162] This obviously must have had a connection with the decline of the bloodfeud in Scotland in the early seventeenth century.[163] Professor Dickinson, however, noted signs of earlier decline, stating that "in the Fife records of the latter half of the [sixteenth] century the action had become comparatively rare".[164] But in the 1530s, the institution of lawburrows was still a routine matter and one which was brought to the Session. On 6 April 1531, for example, Robert Adamson, a burgess of Edinburgh, and his spouse appeared in order to pursue an action against John Sinclair on the basis that he had "found suretie and lawbarowis" that Robert and his wife should be unharmed. They complained that this undertaking had been broken since they had been "invaidit and struke". They wanted new lawburrows to be

---

[159] *ADC* ii, pp. lxx–lxxi.

[160] In 1429 (*APS* ii, p. 19, c. 20); 1432 (*APS* ii, p. 21, c. 9); 1439 (*APS* ii, p. 32, c. 2); 1449 (*APS* ii, p. 35, c. 2); 1457 (*APS* ii, p. 51, c. 29); 1466 (*APS* ii, p. 85, c. 6); 1491 (*APS* ii, p. 225, c. 8).

[161] *APS* ii, p. 19, c. 20 (6 March 1430). For a critical apparatus important to understanding the manuscript traditions behind this statute and different readings see: *The Records of the Parliaments of Scotland to 1707*, ed. K.M. Brown et al. (St. Andrews, 2007), 1430/24.

[162] *ADC* ii, p. lxxi.

[163] J.M. Wormald, *Court, Kirk, and Community: Scotland 1470–1625* (London, 1981), p. 164. See generally J.M. Wormald, "Bloodfeud, Kindred and Government in Early Modern Scotland", *Past and Present* (1980), 54–97 and K.M. Brown, *Bloodfeud in Scotland 1573–1625: Violence Justice and Politics in an Early Modern Society* (Edinburgh, 1986)

[164] *The Sheriff Court Book of Fife*, ed. Dickinson, p. 330.

found, but the Lords continued the action for proof of the breaking of the pledge.[165]

Modification of assythment

The Lords had a jurisdiction to "modify" or set the exact terms of an assythment. Assythment was the term for compensation, but also had a formal role in discharging legal liability for wrongfully caused harm. Compensation of this sort was treated more as a criminal than a civil matter in the sixteenth century, though in fact the boundary between the two forms of liability and jurisdiction was not yet fully developed. Assythment was nevertheless a necessary step before a remission from criminal prosecution could be granted. An action of modification in court seems to have been necessary if a party did not voluntarily offer assythment.[166] As early as 1425 there had been statutory provision for a jury to assess the level of assythment in particular instances.[167] Professor Robert Black has described with reference to a slightly later period how "the *quantum* of compensation might be remitted from the Justiciary Court to the Court of Exchequer. In time, the whole action of assythment came to be competent also in the Court of Session".[168] Evidently, as early as the reign of James V it would seem that the "whole action" was already competent in the Session, albeit following upon proceedings in justice ayres. For example, on 28 July 1531 Gelis Guthrie, relict of David Garden of Braktullo, and others sued James Rynde of Cass as pledge and surety for Lord Ogilvy, who had been indicted in the last justice ayre of Dundee for art and part of the slaughter of David Garden, and had been granted a respite for this act. Gelis wanted "ane competent assithment to be modifyit" by the Lords, who therefore gave decree for "assithment to be maid...in maner form and effect as eftir followis modifyit be the saide lordis avisesly".[169] Obligations were laid down for prayers to be said, a pilgrimage to be undertaken, the public asking of forgiveness to be made, the payment of compensation and

[165] NAS CS 5/41, fol. 69v.

[166] For some discussion see Brown, *Bloodfeud in Scotland 1573–1625*, pp. 52–57.

[167] *APS* ii p. 8 c. 25. See also A. Harding, "Rights, Wrongs and Remedies in Late Medieval English and Scots Law", in *Miscellany Four*, ed. MacQueen, pp. 1–8 at p. 7.

[168] R. Black, "A historical survey of delictual liability in Scotland for personal injuries and death", Part 1, *The Comparative and International Law Journal of Southern Africa* 8 (1975), pp. 46–70 at p. 59.

[169] NAS CS 5/43, fol. 21v.

the issue of "letters of slains" (certifying receipt and acceptance of the assythment by the victim and kin).[170]

This involvement of the Lords in the fixing of compensation in relation to a private settlement shows an uncontroversial and standard involvement in the world of private justice which echoes their role in the conduct of arbitrations which will be examined in chapters 8 and 9. It is striking that by the 1530s (if not since 1425) regulation of such a core part of private dispute resolution and the "justice of the feud" was capable of being entrusted to the courts by at least some disputing parties.[171] The business of the Session demonstrates this feature more than half a century before James VI's celebrated legislation on feuds, which was to encourage arbitration and settlement instead of violent retaliation. The impetus in Scotland towards submission to legal adjudication and a more peaceful culture of settlement arose long before James VI, and is clearly evident at the time of the foundation of the College of Justice in 1532. This will be discussed further in chapters 8 and 9.

Payment of mails

A familiar process in the Session was a summons for payment of mails, duties and profits of lands (i.e. the rents) from a defender who had been receiving payment without right. For example, on 24 March 1530, William Hamilton of Macknairston appeared against Adam Wallace of the Newton and William Wallace, tutor of Craigie, in such an action. Adam had been "accusit" in the last justice ayre of Ayr of the "reif and oppressions", spuilzie and "violent occupation" and "labouring" of the lands in question. William's title derived from an assignation and disposition from John, Lord Lindsay, as heir and executor to the late Patrick, Lord Lindsay. The Lords duly decreed that Adam was to pay four years' worth of mails and profits. With that action resolved, the parties went on to submit the underlying question of disputed ground right to arbiters.[172]

When parties laid claim to the mails of land to which they both alleged themselves to have title, an action might be raised by the tenants

---

170 For letters of slains and a brilliant wider treatment see Wormald, "Bloodfeud, Kindred and Government in Early Modern Scotland', p. 62.

171 For the measures taken from 1598 onwards see Brown, *Bloodfeud in Scotland*, chap. 9.

172 NAS CS 5/41, fol. 37.

of the land to prevent their being exposed to "double poynding". On 26 March 1530, for example, the "pur tennentes" of Balquhidder had their action called against the earl of Rothes and Lady Glamis. The earl claimed to have from the King the gift of the ward of the lands since the death of Lord Glamis, whilst Lady Glamis claimed part of the lands by reason of her widow's right of terce. The point of the action was that the defenders were "to produce and schew before the saidis lordis sic rycht as ilkane of thame will use for the double poynding". Calling them to appear before the Session would force them to do so. In this case, the earl claimed that the late Lord Glamis had already granted out these lands to a third party in liferent, so that they should fall to be included in the ward lands, and he was ordered to prove this at a hearing a few days later. However, the tenants received an interim remedy as well, since the Lords "als ordanis the gudes now poyndit pertening to the said pur tennantes be relizit and deliverit to thame agane to remaine with thame ayand quhill it be decidit to quham thai suld pay thir mailis and deweties".[173]

Enforcement of bond

A straightforward action before the Session was the enforcing of a contract or bond between two parties. For example, on 18 June 1532 Patrick Strageth sued Lord Drummond and his tutor, seeking a charge from the Lords that Drummond should resign into the King's hands his lands in the stewartries of Menteith and Strathern and sheriffdom of Perth, so that they could be given to Patrick as heir to his brother, in excambion (i.e. exchange) for the land of Strageth, or else to infeft Patrick in the land directly as his successor, to be held of the King under a confirmation. The ground of the action was that the late Lord Drummond "bound and oblist him and hes airis to the said umquhile Johne Strogeith [i.e. the brother of Patrick] and airis to do the same".[174] The Lords issued letters in the form requested after examining the "letters obligaturis" and bond.

---

[173] NAS CS 5/41, fol. 38.
[174] NAS CS 6/1, fol. 26.

Assignation

It is only occasionally that the recorded decision of the Lords contains sufficient reasoning to illuminate underlying legal rules. A case of 22 May 1529 turned on the law of assignation, for example, even though the nature of the rights in question—the casualties of ward and marriage—was feudal. A dispute had arisen over the right to these casualties in respect of the heirs of Inverugie, the King having made consecutive gifts of the same to the earl of Errol and, after his death, the earl Marischal. The countess of Bothwell, Lord Maxwell, the earl Marischal, the earl of Errol and John Hay, provost of Guthrie, had all been summoned by the King to "produce and schaw quhat ryt our soveraine lord or thai has". The late earl of Errol, it transpired, had made "divers pretendit assignations" of the casualties gifted to him, but these were "fenzeit" [i.e. false in some way] and "of nane avale because thai war maid *inter vivos* and thir followit na possessioune of the said assignatiounis but the said umquhile William earl of Erole remanit in possessioune of the said ward and mariage... quhill his deceis". It is not clear whether "possessioune of the said assignatiounis" meant narrowly the delivery of the deed of assignation, or more broadly the collection of the dues which pertained to the assignee as a result of the assignation. However, the assignations in this case were ineffective and the casualties "returnit again to our soveraine lord" to dispone again as he pleased.[175] Possession in this context may well have had to include physical possession of the lands and not just delivery of a deed. This is suggested by another entry in the same case where a procurator protested that there *had* been possession "be holding of courtis".[176]

Sale of goods

Disputes over the ownership of goods or livestock in connection with sale can be found before the Lords, even for disputes over a single horse. It says something for the availability of central royal justice that the owner of a horse should consider it necessary or feasible to to supplicate the Lords of Council for a remedy in such a matter. On 2 June 1529, for example, John Chalmer gave in a supplication against John Barns alleging that he had loaned his horse to James Bassenden,

---

175 NAS CS 5/40, fol. 26v.
176 NAS CS 5/40, fol. 28v.

a burgess of Edinburgh, to travel from Dunbar to Edinburgh, but that "be the gait he and the said hors war takin be Gawyn Hume" and others, servants to Archibald Douglas, formerly earl of Angus. Now Bassenden had found the horse again, and wished delivery of it. Barns alleged that he "coft" (i.e. acquired, perhaps by barter) the horse from William Charteris, servant to Lord Bothwell, whom he now called in warrandice. The matter was meanwhile continued.[177]

Executry

Distribution and control of property after its owner's death could lead to difficulty and dispute. Occasionally, problems relating to executries were brought before the Lords by a supplication. An example, which also offers an incidental insight into the practicalities of confirmation and executry procedure, occurred on 14 May 1529 when Christine Anderson, the relict of Alexander Adamson, a burgess of Edinburgh, complained that after Alexander's recent death his friends had entered his house and "intromittit and tuk up all hir gudis and keyis of hir kistis... and has lokkit the same in ane grete kist sa that sche may nocht gett hir clething, schetis, blancaitis and uther necessaris as uther wifis has and suld have of resoun".[178] The Lords ordered Christine to remain with the house and goods "quhill the testament be confermit and equalie distributioune of the gudis be maid, sche fundand sufficient cautioune that the saidis gudis salbe furth cumand to Alexander's executors".[179] The executors had acted with unnecessary stringency.

Ecclesiastical affairs

Occasionally, disputes which seem to have had no implications in civil (i.e. secular) law were brought by churchmen before the Lords of Session. For example, on 31 January 1531, the archbishop of St Andrews, James Beaton, supplicated Council to forbid the abbot of Glenluce from carrying out a visitation of Cistercian abbeys in Scotland. The abbot had received in 1530 a commission from the mother house of Citeaux to undertake this visitation, but the archbishop alleged that it was he who had the right to carry out visitations of nunneries within

177 NAS CS 5/40, fol. 50.
178 NAS CS 5/40, fol. 37.
179 NAS CS 5/40, fol. 37.

the diocese of St Andrews. The Lords agreed with this, at least until such time as Glenluce should compear and prove the terms of his right. The basis for the decision was that the Lords accepted that "it is notourly knawin to all the said lordes" that this was an "auld privilege" of the archbishop of St Andrews.[180] This litigation before the Session echoed a much wider political dispute over such visitations between King James V and the abbey of Citeaux. Dr Mark Dilworth noted that "the Cistercian visitations of the 1530s resemble a stubbornly waged campaign" which created tensions with the Scottish crown. In the same month that Beaton supplicated the Council, James was writing to the abbot of Citeaux requesting a specially designated abbot to act as visitor. Dr Dilworth argued that James had found the abbot of Glenluce "too zealous".[181]

Litigation over property rights affecting revenues such as from teinds (i.e. tithes) seems also to have been within the civil jurisdiction of the Session, though normally a matter within spiritual jurisdiction. Teinds were an ecclesiastical exaction representing a tenth of a parish's grain crop.[182] However, in sixteenth century Scotland the right to teinds was not usually vested in parish clergy. As Dr Sanderson has noted, "since the majority of parishes and their teinds were by the sixteenth century annexed to monasteries, cathedrals and other churches, the teinds were collected on behalf of these institutions and their clergy". In addition, teinds had become commodified. Dr Sanderson has observed in this respect that "they were often set in tack for an annual tack-duty".[183] All of this enhanced the scope for dispute and litigation. However, the extent of civil litigation appears to have related primarily to a form of supervisory jurisdiction by the Session. Beyond this it was limited to what would now be called execution of diligence, i.e. the judicial attachment of goods with which to discharge the debts in question. Jurisdiction to decide upon the right to teind sheaves seems to have belonged to the church courts, even to the extent of reducing an assedation (i.e. lease) of teinds. This is made clear in a decision on 7 June 1531, following letters of the archbishop of St Andrews against Sir

[180] NAS CS 5/42, fol. 24v.

[181] M. Dilworth, *Scottish Monasteries in the Late Middle Ages* (Edinburgh, 1995), p. 37; *Letters of James V, 1513–1542*, collected and calendered by R.K. Hannay, ed. Denys Hay (Edinburgh, 1954), p. 187.

[182] M.H.B. Sanderson, *Scottish Rural Society in the Sixteenth Century* (Edinburgh, 1982), p. 33.

[183] Sanderson, *Scottish Rural Society in the Sixteenth Century*, p. 33.

William Hamilton, executor of Robert Forman, dean of Glasgow. William alleged that the executry estate included an assedation of certain teind sheaves, and had taken out letters as a matter of civil process charging the archbishop and Hew Spens, as judge delegate, to cease proceeding against William for reduction of this assedation. However, the Lords suspended these letters relating to civil process, stating that "thai ar past without cognition in the caus... and als becaus the said mater concernis teyndis quhilk suld haif process... befor the spirituale juge and nocht in temporale court".[184] In other words, in principle the Lords did not consider that they had jurisdiction.

However, further proceedings in the same case on 28 July 1531 reveal that even once process was initiated in the church courts, the Session still had a residual role through its supervisory jurisdiction. These further proceedings showed that the ecclesiastical judge delegate in question had been charged by the Lords of Council to send to them "the autentik copy of the libell" in question, so that they could consider "gif the same be intentit be vertu of the bull callit bulla paulina". The Lords seem to have been intervening in order to assert a right to quash proceedings which were intended to give effect to church law when this was in conflict with secular law. If the basis for seeking reduction of the assedation had indeed been the *Bulla Paulina* then the Lords would apparently have intervened to stop further process, even in the church courts. Having considered the libel, however, they found it too "generale" and stated that they "can nocht cleirelie undirstand be quhat law the said Juge intendis to proceid in the said mater". Correspondingly, the Lords ordained the ecclesiastical judge not to proceed on this libel, and instructed the pursuer to "found ane new libell and to specify clerelie therein apoun quhat law and caus it beis foundat" so that the Lords might consider whether or not the action was proceeding "super bulla paulina".[185]

The *Bulla Paulina* had been issued by Pope Paul II in 1468 for restraint of alienation.[186] Under the bull, the leasing out of the right to teinds might be prohibited as constituting an unlawful alienation of church property. It would seem that, beyond the question of respecting the proper jurisdiction of the church courts, the Lords could nevertheless

[184] NAS CS 5/42, fol. 185v.

[185] NAS CS 5/43, fol. 23v.; *ADCP*, p. 360.

[186] See Neilson and Paton's brief discussion in *ADC* ii, p. lvii. The canon law source is Extrav. Comm. 3.4.1.

regulate the granting of remedies by the church courts on the grounds of the type of legal claim being raised, even when the subject matter itself was a matter ordinarily within spiritual jurisdiction.[187] In some ways this intervention by the Lords in spiritual matters perhaps reflected a deeper concern for consistency in decisions which affected the binding force of obligations, such as those created under an assedation, and which were subject to the jurisdiction of both secular and spiritual courts. In such matters, the church courts were required to interpret secular legal institutions such as an assedation according to secular legal principles. It is hard to imagine any civil court other than the Session being capable of regulating the exercise of ecclesiatical jurisdiction in this way. This therefore represents another way in which a central court could affect the structure of jurisdiction across a legal system as a whole.

Parties might also complain to the Lords that a civil action was being wrongly pursued in the church courts. On 20 July 1531, for example, Lord Lindsay complained that land he had redeemed ten years earlier was subject to a claim of terce from a widow, who had subsequently assigned her terce rights to a chaplain, John Balfour, who in turn "callis and trublis the said lord" before the official of St Andrews. Lord Lindsay alleged that the action was "civile and prophane concerning the said Johne Lord Lindesay's heretage and the said officiale na competent juge thirto".[188] Thus he demanded that the official send to the Lords of Council "the autentik copy of the libell gevin in before him" to see whether it was civil in nature. The Lords upheld the complaint and barred the official from further proceeding. If, however, such a case was not "prophane", then the Lords might do the opposite and remit the action to the church courts, as they did on 27 January 1534, in a case involving Hugh Farny and Thomas Meldrum. The former had complained that the commissar general of the official of St Andrews was not a competent judge to their dispute.[189] It had been unsuccessfully argued that "the said commissar suld nocht intromettit thirwith considering the same is ellis in effeir jugit and decernit first before the said sheriff and secundlie befor the saidis lordis of counsal".

Presentation to ecclesiastical chaplaincies was essentially the conferral of a property right, but would normally have been within spiritual

[187] *ADCP*, p. lvii.
[188] NAS CS 5/43, fol. 13.
[189] NAS CS 6/3, fol. 181.

jurisdiction. However, in such cases the Lords also seem to have been able to entertain related legal actions in which they acted in a supervisory role. For example, on 3 June 1532 Andrew Kirkcaldy sued Sir Walter Ninian because Ninian had been collated to a chaplaincy by the archbishop of St Andrews in his capacity as "ordinary" of the diocese. However, Kirkcaldy claimed the same chaplaincy, given that he had been presented to it himself by William Williamson, "undoutit patronne of the rude alter within the parish kirk of kirkaldy", but for which the archbishop had refused to "gif him collation".[190] Kirkcaldy had lodged an appeal against this decision in the ecclesiastical courts, but now Ninian was trying to take possession of the chaplaincy. Kirkcaldy complained that this was incompetent since he had appealed in due time, and his appeal should prevent further legal process in the interim. The Lords granted a two-week continuation and ordained Kirkcaldy to produce "the foundation of the said alterage" so that the rights in it might be proved. This might imply that the Lords were willing to decide the dispute themselves, or at least that they wished to satisfy themselves that Andrew's claim had some merit before they intervened further.

Custom

Occasionally, there is reference to custom in the decisions of the Lords, but not necessarily in the context of the "practick" of the court. Rather, we can also find it in relation to what appears to be local custom which, if proved, would be recognised by the Lords as providing the rules by which a legal question should be determined. For example, on 5 July 1533 the Lords heard the summons of Beatrice Semple, a widow. She was ordained to summon witnesses "to preif that the auld rite use and consuetude is that women eftir thir husbandis deceis haifand any feld landis or akeris within the fredome of the burgh of Dunbertane broikit josis and occupys thir tercis of the saidis landis and swa has bene usit observit and kepit thir 40 yeiris bipast or thirby be consuetude of the said ton".[191] The point was that "na burrowland in this realm gevis ony tercis thirof" as was explicitly argued in further proceedings on 31 July.[192] The "use rite and consuetude" of Dumbarton would therefore be

[190] NAS CS 6/1, fol. 10.
[191] NAS CS 6/2, fol. 225v.
[192] NAS CS 6/3, fol. 48r.

an exception to the general rule at common law, if it could be proved that this was indeed the use. In fact, although Beatrice therefore had an arguable case, she failed to prove it and so the Lords assoilzied the other parties "for all that thai have yet sene".[193]

Effectiveness of legal remedies

Despite the pervasive influence of legal process throughout the ordering and governance of Scottish society, the provision of legal remedies can sometimes be seen to have had limited effect. Complaints reflecting this type of failing were made directly to the Council and even the King upon occasion, at least through the offices of the Lords of Council. On 10 May 1529, for example, John Multrare of Seafield compeared and "exponit how the lard of Raith had oftymis invaidit him and his son for thir lifis and distructione of thame and had inlikwis rest and spulzeit his cornys apoun the quhilk he had optenit decretis". Despite the obtaining of such decrees, Raith had "sett apoun him in Kirkaldy...and upon forthocht felony slew twa honest gentilmen for the quhilk the said lard of Raith was now present in the castell beand summond to undirlie the law for the said crimes". Multrare came now "besekand the lordis that thai wald solist the kingis grace to caus him have iustice sen he is sa evill done to".[194] The rule of law could not always be relied on, but this did not deter Multrare from returning to the Session with his complaint.

Conclusion

The purpose of this chapter was less to enter into any particular historiographical debate than to draw a picture demonstrating the variety of judicial business transacted by the Session. Such a picture is revealing in its own right but also provides the necessary context for the discussion elsewhere in this book of particular aspects of that business. In particular, the development of remedies is strongly illuminated by the history of error jurisdiction and of spuilzie, whilst the development of jurisdiction is illuminated by an understanding of the supervisory role of the Session. The most striking feature of the survey attempted in this chapter is the sheer range of the jurisdiction which

[193] NAS CS 6/3, fol. 48r.
[194] NAS CS 5/40, fol. 21.

the Lords exercised, combined with an apparently unlimited authority to intervene in and overrule all other civil courts, nullify their decrees, order new process to be undertaken, and transfer actions to be heard by themselves. In its exercise of the remedies of suspension, reduction and advocation in particular, the Session commanded a supreme position amongst civil courts in Scotland, and used its procedural powers of intervention to interfere with any civil legal process upon cause shown, effectively supervising the administration of justice in Scotland as well as entertaining the broadest possible range of complaints at first instance.[195] Dr Athol Murray's observation for the 1540s, that "this was indeed a supreme court", can in these respects be justifiably applied to the late 1520s and 1530s as well.[196] Moreover, we have seen that the supervisory jurisdiction of the Session clearly extended into the sphere of ecclesiastical jurisdiction as well. In so far as jurisdictional restraints upon the Lords had remained in the early sixteenth century, they related essentially to fee and heritage, which will be discussed in the two chapters to follow. It will be argued that such restraints were no longer being applied by the 1520s if not earlier. The broader context of litigation conducted before the Session provides some circumstantial support for this particular conclusion, since we have seen the notable extent to which many actions relating to rights in property were being heard by the Session. Any jurisdictional limitation on the competence of the Session to decide questions of fee and heritage would have stood out as exceptional and anomolous, both in relation to its general jurisdiction over property and its superior jurisdiction over other courts, and would surely have received explicit enunciation in the record if it were any longer recognised.

Professor Peter Stein has observed, in relation to the evolution of national courts manned by professional judges by the early sixteenth century, that "the judges and advocates who appeared before these national courts realised that each court had its own practice, which, as in England, constituted a forensic custom or *usus fori*".[197] Scotland fits this pattern too. As we saw in the previous chapter, the *usus fori* of the Session included in a narrower sense the procedure of the court.

---

[195] Professor MacQueen also discusses advocation in *Common Law and Feudal Society*, p. 240, and suggests reasons why it was attractive to litigants.

[196] Murray, "Sinclair's Practicks", p. 98.

[197] P. Stein, "Common Law and Civil Law in historical perspective", *Zeitschrift fur Europäisches Privatrecht* 5 (1997), p. 390.

However, by the 1530s the Session had evolved so that it had a much wider "practick" of which its judges and advocates were well aware, and which was recorded by members of the bench informally from 1540 onwards, if not earlier.[198] We have seen that the jurisdiction of the Session appears to have been very fully extended by the 1520s, and we will see in subsequent chapters that there were developments in the 1530s which had the effect of consolidating this. If there was any change that was likely to have promoted judicial and institutional self-consciousness in the Session in the 1530s, it was most likely to have been the foundation of the College of Justice. In previous chapters it has already been argued that this development did bring into effect significant changes in the nature of the court. Although in its "practick" the Session seems already to have been operating as a supreme central court by 1532, its reconstitution as the College of Justice, in addition to instigating particular institutional changes, seems to have stimulated its recognition by contemporaries as exercising that role too. The best illustration of the process of recognition is the example cited by Dr Murray from 1544. This involved the submission in a legal argument before the Session that "the lordis of counsall were also judge ordinaris to all civill actioun within the realme be the first institutioun of the college of justice maid be the king and the thre estattis in parliament".[199] In the next two chapters, the disappearance of the one remaining jurisdictional limitation upon the Session which it inherited from the medieval Council will be examined in order to complete this picture of the court's judicial role in the period around 1532.

---

198 Murray, "Sinclair's Practicks", p. 91.
199 Murray, "Sinclair's Practicks", p. 91.

CHAPTER SIX

JURISDICTION OVER FEE AND HERITAGE

Introduction

The previous chapters have traced the institutional history of the Session, reassessed the significance of the foundation of the College of Justice, and presented an analysis of the "practick" of the court which demonstrated the breadth of litigation taking place before the Session and the superior nature of its jurisdiction by 1532. It could be said that until recently the preoccupation of historians with assessing the institutional significance of the College of Justice has distracted them from examining the underlying work of the court in sufficient depth to appreciate the very great scope of its judicial role by 1532. In chapter 5 both the range of legal actions and the centrality of the role of the Session in the legal system was emphasised. The Session was already functioning in effect as a central court, except for its lack of institutional autonomy. Nevertheless, the argument has been advanced in this book that the provision of institutional autonomy through the foundation of the College of Justice was of fundamental importance. The received account deriving from the seminal work of R.K. Hannay is no longer tenable. 1532 can truly be seen to represent the establishment of a central civil court through the reconstitution of the Session on a separate basis from the residual Council. Although the Session was still closely connected with the Council in practical terms, it now embodied a distinct and autonomous institutional structure for central judicial business.

We have noted how an earlier set of arrangements presaging features of the sixteenth-century Session had first been introduced in 1426, but had evolved significantly during the fifteenth century. Moreover, the evolution was desultory and involved the adoption, adaptation but also abandonment of different forms of central tribunal, constituted in different ways and exercising jurisdiction of varying scope. In the background, the parent bodies of Parliament and Council continued to provide the institutional basis for such tribunals and their jurisdiction. Whilst it is true that by the 1490s the Session had acquired a more settled form, even this more settled institution was subject to further development and was still operationally an aspect of Council's business. Significant reforms came in the later 1520s and early 1530s before the decisive step of incorporation and reconstitution as the College of Justice was taken in 1532. During this lengthy period the Session also developed for itself rules of practice, procedure and law, as examined in the previous two chapters. Even after a large degree of institutional stability had emerged, this "practick" of the court seems to have been constantly evolving as new cases tested the precise meaning and extent of the competence of the Session.

Why was this competence only made clear gradually and incrementally? Medieval Scotland possessed a diffuse range of jurisdictions, and one achievement of the medieval common law had been to provide a degree of order, hierarchy and coherence within this jurisdictional complexity. However, it did not provide any central source of authority of the kind embodied in the Session by 1532, with an omnicompetent and superordinate governing role. The King in Council and Parliament had exercised something of this type of role, but constrained and defined by the procedures of the common law. These procedures acted to limit the exercise of such a role in important respects, not least in relation to the pleadable brieves. In contrast to this, the Session was by 1532 not only a new central tribunal but a new form of tribunal, given the immense scope of its authority, unconstrained in practice by the procedural models of the medieval common law. It exercised the residual authority of the King's Council, within as well as concurrently alongside the course of the common law. That authority could only be given definition and expression incrementally, however, by the development of the "practick" of the court.

No code or juristic treatise existed to explain the extent of the judicial authority of the Session in the early sixteenth century. Even the bald legislative statement in 1532 of the competence of the College of Justice to decide all civil actions is exceptional in this respect, but as we have seen its meaning is far from clear and it is problematic to interpret. In this context, the acts and decreets issued by the Lords of Session between the 1490s and the 1530s therefore tell us as much about the development of the meaning of the authority of the Session as lists of formal ordinances and parliamentary statutes, though as sources they too present severe difficulties of interpretation. This type of development in the "practick" of the Session is in evidence up until 1532 and beyond, though the argument of this book is that the most significant developments towards full competence as a central court occurred prior to 1532. The College of Justice of 1532 was therefore not merely the Session "in a more permanent form", as Duncan regarded it. It was quite simply the Session fixed in permanent form within the legal order as a whole. After all, the statute of 1532 had itself narrated how King James was "maist desyrous to have ane permanent ordour of justice".[1] The College of Justice embodied this permanent order. It can readily be admitted that there begins in 1532 not the history of the Session, but of the College of Justice. What requires a renewed emphasis, however, is that the beginning of the College of Justice did mark a new beginning in the history of the Session.

One fundamental aspect of the analysis remains to be considered, however, and forms a crucial element in this re-evaluation of 1532. This is the question of the extent of the jurisdiction of the Session by 1532. Was the new College still exercising, like the medieval Council, a residual and essentially supplementary jurisdiction, however wide it had become in practical terms? Or was it now possessed of a full civil jurisdiction which extended over the whole range of the common law? Only the latter would signify the existence of a fully empowered central civil court. In the previous chapter, we saw how diverse and extensive the jurisdiction of the Session had become by 1532. Already by 1500, it would seem, no significant limitation on its jurisdiction remained except one. However, that limitation was in formal terms highly significant since it barred the Council from deciding questions of land ownership. More technically, as we have seen, this meant title to heritable property, "fee and heritage" in terms of Scottish feudal land law.[2]

Fee and heritage was, of course, a legal concept of great antiquity in Scots law with a provenance extending back to the twelfth century in charters recording grants of land.[3] It only seems to have acquired a jurisdictionally framed definition by the fifteenth century, however, at the time the jurisdictional bar on the central tribunals became elaborated. However, this constraint did subsequently come to be thrown

---

[1] *The Acts of the Parliaments of Scotland*, ed. T. Thomson and C. Innes [hereafter *APS*], 12 vols (Edinburgh, 1814–1875), vol. 2, p. 335, c. 2.

[2] There were naturally conceptual difficulties, recognized by medieval jurists, in reconciling the structure of feudal interests in land with the clear civilian distinction between ownership and possession: H.L. MacQueen, *Common Law and Feudal Society in Medieval Scotland* (Edinburgh, 1993), p. 157.

[3] H.L. MacQueen, "Tears of a Legal Historian: Scottish Feudalism and the *Ius Commune*", *Juridical Review* (2003), 1–28 at p. 11.

off. We know that by the middle of the sixteenth century the Session quite explicitly regarded its jurisdiction as unrestricted from this point of view. It had even asserted an *exclusive* jurisdiction over matters of fee and heritage. However, we do not know how, when or why this important development occurred.

The rules on jurisdiction were important because they profoundly affected the remedies available to parties in relation to enforcing or protecting their substantive rights. In the civilian tradition, the right of ownership is a fundamental institution of the law of property, but its elaboration within any particular system of property law depends upon other related concepts. In particular, its vindication and protection require a separate concept of title.[4] Title concerns "the types of rule which legal systems adopt in order to decide who is to own a thing and, if two or more persons have claims to a thing, how priority between them is to be settled".[5] The medieval common law had developed sophisticated rules on title to land and remedies with which it could be protected.[6] These remedies took the form of brieves, which as we have seen initiated procedure by inquest (i.e. a form of "civil" jury) in certain prescribed and locally constituted courts. The medieval King's Council, like the late medieval English Court of Chancery, developed its role outside the existing structure of remedies provided by the common law. The way in which those common law remedies had developed meant that the Council could not intervene in such matters. It possessed neither jurisdiction nor appropriate procedures. This was despite the fact that by the fifteenth century it was increasingly concerned with land litigation when possession was in issue, adjudicating upon civil and specifically proprietary wrongs such as spuilzie, wrongful occupation and ejection. Nevertheless, though this jurisdiction over civil wrongs made great inroads into property disputes, the determination of title was still excluded from its jurisdiction.

This is somewhat reminiscent of the formal exclusion of legal title to land from the jurisdiction of the English Court of Chancery, itself in origin an offshoot of the English King's Council. In England, title was properly the preserve of the common law court of Common Pleas, despite a situation in which, by the early sixteenth century, "the

---

[4] K.G.C. Reid, *The Law of Property in Scotland* (Edinburgh, 1996), para. 3, pp. 8–9.

[5] A.M. Honoré, "Ownership", in *Oxford Essays in Jurisprudence*, ed. A.G. Guest (Oxford, 1961), p. 107.

[6] H.L. MacQueen, *Common Law and Feudal Society* (Edinburgh, 1993), chap. 4–7.

majority of cases in chancery concerned landed property", owing in part to the development of the trust as an interest in land.[7] There was also a wider shift in England at this time in "the law and practice of real actions" whereby "the vast majority of actions involving title to land...were now personal actions: forcible entry, replevin, and—first and foremost—trespass".[8] However, whilst this allowed the development of the jurisdiction of the common law courts by means of trespassory actions, it still left the formal restriction upon Chancery in tact.

Significantly, it was the jurisdiction not of Chancery but of the common law court of King's Bench over civil wrongs, and trespass in particular, which developed to encompass title to land with the action of ejectment, though not until the 1550s.[9] In Scotland, we also find the same movement towards personal, possessory actions, posing remedial and jurisdictional difficulties when their resolution depended upon disputes over title. However, the institutional structure of law courts in the Scottish kingdom allowed an integrated jurisdictional solution to eventually emerge through the development of the Session. There was no serious risk of any rigid degree of institutional separation building up in Scotland between the older courts allocated jurisdiction over land by the medieval common law and the newer conciliar tribunals which were denied it, as did happen in England. This was precisely because there was no existing Scottish central court capable of rivalling the new jurisdiction of the Session, given the fifteenth-century withdrawal of Parliament from this role. As Professor Harding observed, "in Scotland, the Court of Session came to fill the place of both a Chancery and a King's Bench".[10] In England the difference lay in the existence of vastly more strongly developed common law central courts, since "by 1450, the three central courts of common law had been in existence for over two centuries".[11] Nevertheless, in Scotland, were the exclusion of title from the jurisdiction of the Session to have persisted, this would have

[7] J.H. Baker, "The superior courts in England, 1450–1800", in *Oberste Gerichtsbarkeit und Zentrale Gewahlt im Europa der Frühen Neuzeit*, ed. B. Diestelkamp (Cologne, 1996), pp. 73–111 at p. 95.

[8] J.H. Baker, *The Oxford History of the Laws of England, Volume VI, 1483–1558* (Oxford, 2003), pp. 719–720.

[9] Baker, "The superior courts in England, 1450–1800", p. 80; Baker, *The Oxford History of the Laws of England*, p. 724.

[10] A. Harding, "The Medieval Brieves of Protection and the Development of the Common Law", *Juridical Review* (1966), 115–149 at p. 148.

[11] Baker, "The superior courts in England, 1450–1800", p. 78.

distorted the development of civil remedies and the law of property, even if not generating separate jurisdictions akin to equity and common law. This would have dramatically inhibited the development of a supreme central civil court in the early modern period in Scotland. Jurisdiction would have been fragmented within an incoherent and asymmetrical institutional structure.

The development of the jurisdictional restriction on the central judicial bodies in Scotland has been convincingly analysed by Hector MacQueen against the background of land litigation between the thirteenth and fifteenth centuries and the development of property-related remedies.[12] The restriction crystallized in the fifteenth century, and—crucially—survived beyond what Alan Harding has characterised as "the break-out of the common law...from a pre-occupation with tenure to the whole field of civil injuries".[13] The "break-out" stemmed from the development of the jurisdiction of the central tribunals, beginning with Parliament and its auditorial committee for first instance complaints in the fourteenth century, but above all with Council and the Session in the fifteenth century. The process turned on the development of judicial process by bill of complaint and summons instead of brieve, and of course it was this form of process which was used before all the various central tribunals, including the Session, Council and the parliamentary Auditors of Causes and Complaints. Indeed, the jurisdictional restriction was in a sense a necessary organisational rule which had the effect of providing procedural integration and coherence between the very different remedies of the earlier medieval common law and those which arose later from the developing central jurisdictions. The limits of the jurisdiction of Council and the various forms of "Session" required definition, but significantly the restriction also applied to the first instance jurisdiction of Parliament, whose Auditors of Causes and Complaints can also be found declining jurisdiction in the later fifteenth century over cases which "aw nocht to Resort nor be determyt befor thaim because it is fee and heritage".[14]

---

[12] MacQueen, *Common Law and Feudal Society*, chap. 8.

[13] A. Harding, "Rights, Wrongs and Remedies in Late Medieval English and Scots Law", in *Miscellany Four*, ed. H.L. MacQueen, Stair Society 49 (Edinburgh, 2002), pp. 1–8 at p. 3.

[14] *Acts of the Lords Auditors of Causes and Complaints*, ed. T. Thomson (Edinburgh, 1839) [hereafter *ADA*], p. 10.

Evidence for the existence of the jurisdictional bar comes in the form of challenges to jurisdiction made procedurally by the pleading of an "exception", whether in Council, Session or before the parliamentary auditorial committee.[15] The Scottish "exception declinatour" matched the canonist category of declinatory exceptions (a form of dilatory exception) as being "against the competence of the judge or the jurisdiction of the court".[16] The jurisdictional bar was not provided for as such in any statute, but was a rule of the common law. It was for the defender to an action, when this related to title, to raise by such an exception a preliminary defence contesting jurisdiction. If the exception was upheld then the action could proceed no further before the Lords and would invariably be referred by way of a remit "to the judge ordinary". This was whoever was the relevant judge in terms of the established procedures of the common law. It would be a justiciar, sheriff or bailie of a burgh, before whom procedure would have to be re-commenced by the relevant brieve. Since the proprietary remedies of the medieval common law had been established and structurally grounded in a system with no central court other than Parliament, they were not capable of simple adaptation to accommodate the grafting on of a new central tribunal such as the Session. Parliament's own role as a central court had been severely circumscribed by procedure as well as its own nature as an irregular assembly. For fee and heritage actions, however, the procedures and remedies of the common law meant that it was only Parliament which could take jurisdiction after process before the judge ordinary.

The fifteenth century Session—in both auditorial and conciliar forms—possessed its own distinctive forms of remedy, operated with procedure by signet summons on a bill of complaint. In principle it originally possessed only a residual jurisdiction outside the procedures of the common law, though institutional development by the end of the century must have made this increasingly irrelevant. Fee and heritage cases had to be progressed under the old procedures initiated by brieves, however, and that excluded the newer central judicial tribunals. Again, this also applied to Parliament, which generally had no first instance jurisdiction in relation to the proprietary remedies in question.

---

[15] H.L. MacQueen, "Pleadable brieves, pleading, and the development of Scots law", *Law and History Review* 4 (1986), 403–422 at p. 410.

[16] MacQueen, "Pleadable brieves, pleading, and the development of Scots law", p. 411.

Parliament's role and formal jurisdiction had only developed after the common law remedies were already in place in the thirteenth century. In relation to such matters, it could only normally extend to the falsing of dooms. Besides all of this, the central tribunals were handicapped since they also possessed no inherent regular procedure for fact-finding in the localities, such as developed in England. There we find a system of assizes and jurisdiction "nisi prius", whereby central court judges went around the country on circuit.[17] In Scotland, the appointment of sheriffs *in hac parte* under special commission from the Lords of Council to hold an inquest and retour the verdict may well have provided the potential by the sixteenth century for a similar mechanism. This would have allowed the Session to overcome some of the problems of taking evidence by way of proving a claim, but this aspect of its proceedings has been little studied, and its significance remains to be investigated in future research. In any event, it seems likely that such appointments remained exceptional and did not become a routine substitute for the exercise of local jurisdiction.

Examination of the pleading of jurisdictional exceptions on the ground of fee and heritage is the most obvious method of assessing the application over time of the jurisdictional restriction on the newer central tribunals, including the Session as it developed in the late fifteenth and early sixteenth centuries. In the absence of sources which describe the jurisdictional norms directly, we can at least examine evidence of attempts to have the norms applied. Of course, from an evidentiary point of view this exercise will often merely reveal the arguments which litigants or their counsel thought worth submitting, rather than providing direct evidence of the jurisdiction of the Session. However, the jurisdiction can be inferred on those occasions when the decision of the Lords in relation to an exception is recorded. Even then it is often only stated in the record that the exception is repelled, or that the Lords are competent judges, but with no explicit assertion or articulation of the basis of jurisdiction over fee and heritage. Nevertheless, the pleading of such exceptions is the nearest we have to direct evidence of the application of the jurisdictional restriction.

Although the jurisdictional bar has been long known about by historians and jurists, and often commented upon, its precise workings have remained unstudied. Indeed, it has never before been systematically

---

[17] Baker, "The superior courts in England, 1450–1800", p. 84.

examined.[18] Generally it has been regarded as enshrining a broad policy that the central courts should not interfere in questions of heritable title. An incidental assumption underlying this view is that any remedy directly or indirectly affecting such questions of title was beyond the competence of Council, regardless of the underlying cause of action. On this view, when applying the fee and heritage rule, no distinction was drawn at a technical level between the different types of action which were in some way concerned with title. By an examination of the pleading of exceptions, however, we will discover that the rule itself was far more nuanced than this would suggest. In particular, it will be argued that the jurisdictional bar was more technical and far narrower in scope than has previously been realised. This insight will allow us to probe beneath the surface of the procedures and chart the relationship between the jurisdictional bar and the general nature of disputes concerning heritage to which it was applied. This will reveal patterns relating to when jurisdiction was and was not contested, and how jurisdiction over heritage was understood. All of this has significant implications for our picture of possible jurisdictional change up to 1532.

Exceptions on the ground of fee and heritage did continue to be pleaded throughout the period 1466–1532 (and indeed after 1532), but we will discover that their incidence and success fluctuated dramatically. Whether there was any pattern to this, and what any such pattern might suggest about jurisdictional change, therefore become important questions. In particular, can we discern, buried in the litigation of this period, what John Baker has termed in a different context "a subtext of jurisdictional readjustment"?[19] If so, did it take the form of express encroachment by the Session into questions previously beyond its competence and reserved to other jurisdictions, or was it accomplished by indirect means such as the development of alternative remedies outwith the scope of the previous rules? Above all, can we tell what the jurisdiction of the Session was by May 1532 so as to ask how this might have informed understanding of the parliamentary statute of that month which established the College of Justice? Claims for the institutional importance of 1532 would be weakened if the new court

[18] The first such examination, which this chapter draws upon, was A.M. Godfrey, "Jurisdiction over Rights in Land in Later Medieval Scotland", *Juridical Review* (2000), 242–263.

[19] Baker, *The Oxford History of the Laws of England*, p. 15.

was still one with a restricted jurisdiction, as has been argued by Professor MacQueen. On the other hand, if the statute was intended to change the common law so as to confer a new and unrestricted civil jurisdiction on the Session, as argued by David Sellar, then the significance of 1532 would be very much greater than the institutional case alone would suggest. To assess these views requires first an analysis of what type of action constituted a fee and heritage action, and then an evaluation of the nature of challenges to the jurisdiction of the Lords before 1532 on the ground of fee and heritage.

The evidence of jurisdictional challenges

It was the work of David Sellar and Hector MacQueen which illuminated for the first time the deeper significance of jurisdiction as an aspect of the foundation of the College of Justice and the evolution of the Session. Hector McKechnie had much earlier argued in his David Murray Lecture of 1956 that the foundation of the College reconstituted the court so as to confer "for the first time a full jurisdiction in matters of fee and heritage", but the potential significance of this claim simply failed to be realised by subsequent historians.[20] Besides, McKechnie seems to have assumed that the statute of 1532 did confer such a jurisdiction, without showing any awareness that evidence of jurisdictional challenges after 1532 undermine such a categorical assertion and mean that additional supporting arguments are required before such an assumption can be endorsed. Sellar and MacQueen dramatically advanced the debate by recognising the importance of the question, and the need for a more complex analysis. Like McKechnie before them, however, they assumed for the sake of argument a highly static model of the nature of the jurisdictional bar and how it was applied in the period before 1532.

The MacQueen and Sellar view would hold that an action before the Session might be seen to affect the heritage of one of the parties and fall foul of the jurisdictional bar if it involved an adjudication of some sort upon heritable title. The bar is thus seen as wide in scope, encompassing any action the result of which could have been interference in a question of heritable title. In such a case, that party would be entitled

[20] H. McKechnie, *Judicial Process upon Brieves, 1219–1532*, 23rd David Murray Lecture, University of Glasgow (Glasgow, 1956), p. 8; see also pp. 25, 29.

to raise a declinatory exception at the outset of proceedings, denying that the Lords were competent judges. If the allegation was accepted, the Session would then refuse to progress the action and would "remit" it to the judge ordinary. By treating the period 1466–1532 as a whole (records only becoming extant from 1466), this view tacitly assumed that the frequency with which such remits were made because of fee and heritage would have been reasonably constant, or at least that the limitation was continuing to be consistently applied. It was also explicitly assumed that remits were common. David Sellar noted that "time and again in the fifteenth century the Council and the Lords Auditors of Causes and Complaints had declined jurisdiction because it concerned fee and heritage". Professor MacQueen stated that "anyone reading the printed records of the *Acta Dominorum Concilii* or of the *Acta Dominorum Auditorum* will quickly become familiar with the remit to the judge ordinary of matters concerning fee and heritage by these bodies". The view has been shared by others too. Dr Alan Borthwick, in referring to fee and heritage exceptions, stated that "such a plea would become a commonplace in causes heard by the lords of council".[21]

Adopting this static model created a focus upon the identification of a particular moment at which the medieval jurisdictional bar was dropped. It could be assumed on one view that ongoing evidence of the pleading of fee and heritage exceptions could only mean that the bar had not yet been abandoned and that it therefore remained valid. On this view it did not seem relevant to explore systematically the operation of the fee and heritage exception over time. There would have seemed little apparent value in considering the evidence of particular remits and exceptions, or questions relating to the form in which this type of judicial business before Auditors and Session was recorded, and whether this itself was changing over time. Also left out of account was the extent to which the record made it clear which procedural steps had been followed and upon which precise grounds decisions to remit had been taken. In particular, no separation was made between the question whether a procedural order—of remitting to the judge ordinary—had been given and the prior question of what claims had

[21] W.D.H. Sellar, "A Historical Perspective", in *The Scottish Legal Tradition*, ed. S. Styles (Edinburgh, 1991), pp. 29–64 at p. 44; A.R. Borthwick, "The King, Council and Councillors in Scotland, c. 1430–1460" (University of Edinburgh, unpublished Ph.D. thesis, 1989), p. 351; H.L. MacQueen, "The Brieve of Right in Scots Law", *Journal of Legal History* 3 (1982), 52–70 at p. 64.

first been put forward to justify the making of the procedural order, and how frequently such claims were accepted. Remits were noted but not necessarily the nature of the underlying exception pleaded, nor whether it related to fee and heritage in the first place, nor whether there were also fee and heritage exceptions which were unsuccessful.

We can only know that parties contested jurisdiction to the extent that jurisdictional exceptions were recorded. When a remit was made, it was often stated in the record that this was because of fee and heritage, thereby demonstrating that there had indeed been an exception on that ground pleaded first. Sometimes, however, it is not clear why a remit was made, and in such cases it might not be because of the medieval jurisdictional bar over fee and heritage actions but for another reason such as a claim of spiritual jurisdiction. In such a case the judge ordinary would be the spiritual judge ordinary. Furthermore, if the recording of the pleading of exceptions is examined in its own right, whether or not remits were then ordered, it becomes possible to consider not only how often jurisdiction was declined but also how frequently it was asserted, from the evidence of exceptions *repelled* by the Lords. The static model does not take account of the frequency with which jurisdiction was challenged, nor with what rate of success. It also does not explain the precise bounds of the jurisdictional bar, and why some types of action which might *seem* to affect a title—summonses of error against an assize, in particular—were permissible before the Session.

Analysing these questions is problematic in a number of evidentiary ways. The record is procedural and concise in character. As Professor Gordon has noted, the typical content of the register of the Council is made up of decrees, protestations, continuations and engrossments of deeds (such as alienations of property), contracts and submissions to arbitration.[22] Dr Athol Murray has also discussed its contents, as well as the history of its binding and arrangement, and provided an analysis of the likely state of the record in the sixteenth and seventeenth centuries. This has uncovered further difficulties in analysing the development of the Session in terms of the recording of its business.[23] 1466 represents the first year for which continuous records of the Auditors of Causes and Complaints are extant (their business is recorded up until

[22] W.M. Gordon, "The Acts of the Scottish Lords of Council: Records and Reports", in *Law Reporting in Britain*, ed. C. Stebbings (London, 1995), p. 59.

[23] A.L. Murray, "Introduction", in *Acts of the Lords of Council Volume III 1501–1503*, ed. A.B. Calderwood (Edinburgh, 1993), pp. viii–xxxvi.

1496—no formal proceedings occurred after 1494 as recorded in the parliamentary register and 1496 as recorded in the council register[24]). All extant proceedings before the Auditors are available in a modern edition. Council records become extant from 1478 and are published in three volumes up to 1503. These are supplemented by an unpublished transcription in the National Archives of Scotland for those of 1503–1506, prepared for a further, subsequently abandoned volume of the acts of the Lords of Council. Records beyond 1506 are generally available only in unpublished manuscript form. Even the extant manuscript record does not represent a complete account of recorded business by any means, since lacunae are known to exist where various volumes are missing, or individual folios have been lost or misplaced.[25] Nevertheless, for most of the relevant period most of the record does survive and provides a sufficient sample to attempt some analysis of fee and heritage questions in relation to jurisdiction.

One particular problem in trying to provide a more detailed account of jurisdictional challenges before 1532 is that little is said in the record about the formal grounds of decision or even about the nature of the procedural steps preceding and following a decision. Still less in the way of legal reasoning is ever set down in the record of acts and decreets. Answering questions about jurisdiction therefore has to rely heavily upon making a series of inferences rather than trying to find authoritative statements of rules, even in cases of explicitly recognised jurisdictional significance. The record itself does not contain any systematic account of jurisdiction—in ordinances or rulings—or even of what was required in order to show that a case concerned fee and heritage and should be remitted to the judge ordinary. To some extent this is hardly surprising

---

[24] *Acts of the Lords of Council 1496–1501*, ed. G. Neilson and H.M. Paton (Edinburgh, 1918) [hereafter *ADC* ii], pp. xxvi–xxvii; see *Guide to the National Archives of Scotland*, Stair Society Supplementary Series 3 (Edinburgh, 1996), p. 104 and the important analysis of the record in A.L. Murray, "Introduction", in *Acts of the Lords of Council Volume III, 1501–1503*, ed. A.B. Calderwood (Edinburgh, 1993), p. xx.

[25] Note there are no council records for 1481, 1482, 1486 and 1487, whilst in 1483 there are eight months" worth of council records missing, in 1484 some gaps, and in 1485 only one month"s worth of records survives. A recent summary of the state of the records, including the existence of a now lost council register from before 1478, volumes thereafter which are now lost, and missing or misplaced folios is contained in Gordon, "The Acts of the Scottish Lords of Council: Records and Reports", 57–59. Account has also been taken of the observations contained in A.A.M. Duncan and M.P. McDiarmid, "Some Wrongly Dated Entries in the Acts of the Lords of Council", *Scottish Historical Review* 33 (1954), 86–88.

given the extremely complex remedial and jurisdictional developments which had eventually given rise to the fee and heritage rule.[26] Very few decisions reveal their grounds even as clearly as that concerning Sir John Auchinleck in January 1493, which stated that:

> the lordis of Consale decrettis deliveris and declaris that albeit the said Sir Johne Auchinlek allegit the said landis to pertene to him in fee and heretage yit nevertheless our soverane lord his parliament or consale micht be jugis thirto as it wes persewit because our soverane lord clamit for the tyme bot the ward of the said landis.[27]

In this example, we see Auchinleck's exception being held irrelevant because the action did not concern a heritable right in the land, but merely the transitory royal claim to the feudal casualty of ward, exigible until the vassal's age of majority.

In this chapter the treatment of issues relating to fee and heritage questions in the fifteenth and early sixteenth century records of Council and parliamentary Auditors will proceed by collation and analysis of decisions concerning challenges to jurisdiction. This will provide a general picture of how the fee and heritage restriction was being applied prior to 1532 as well as a point of reference and comparison for discussion of the significance of 1532 itself. The analysis will have two aspects. First, it will clarify what elements were required in order to characterise a case as concerning fee and heritage. Secondly, it will offer a view of the pattern of jurisdictional challenges relating to such fee and heritage actions between 1466 and 1532, against which the significance of the foundation of the College of Justice can be assessed.

In relation to the first aspect of the analysis, a definition of fee and heritage in jurisdictional terms will be arrived at which can explain why particular cases were remitted to the judge ordinary, and others not. This definition will identify the scope of the jurisdictional bar, and whether it was as wide as suggested by the static model. From this, it will be possible to evaluate the extent to which the fee and heritage bar was an absolute and comprehensive one, as assumed by the static model. The crucial question is whether there were types of case before the Session which did at some level affect rights relating to heritable title, but which were not precluded by the jurisdictional bar. Having arrived at a

[26] Traced authoritatively in MacQueen, *Common Law and Feudal Society*, chap. 8.

[27] *Acts of the Lords of Council in Civil Causes*, ed. T. Thomson (Edinburgh, 1839), p. 263 [hereafter *ADC* i].

definition of the jurisdictional bar, it can then be applied to the period around 1532 to test whether the jurisdictional rules had changed at all, in substance or application. A further question to address is whether any jurisdictional change occurring by then had proceeded through explicit jurisdictional encroachment by the Session into previously forbidden areas, or indirectly through the development of alternative remedies which could meet the needs of litigants. In relation to the second aspect of the analysis, the period 1466–1532 will be treated at two levels. The main analysis will rely heavily upon the evidence available from the published records of decreets between 1466 and 1503, supplemented by unpublished transcripts in the National Archives for 1503–1506 (though of course this is also available in original manuscript form too). This will help construct a model and provide a detailed picture over four decades of how the jurisdictional bar operated during its classic age in the later fifteenth century. The remaining period from 1506 to 1532, for which the record can only be examined in its manuscript form, will then be taken into account to chart any changes affecting this picture or notable developments which occurred before 1532.[28]

Criteria for remitting to the judge ordinary

In the remit cases, why was the decision made that they should be determined before the judge ordinary? What *type* of action had to be remitted? There are definite limits upon our capacity to answer these questions using the evidence of the council and parliamentary registers, given the usually terse nature of the record. Nevertheless, some inferences can be drawn from the later fifteenth-century evidence in which the application of the jurisdictional bar is apparent. The reason for remitting a case which concerns us is jurisdictional competence, where the matter being brought before the Council was said to be one which pertained to the jurisdiction of another court, *and* which was outwith the jurisdiction of Council (and therefore Session) or Auditors. At its simplest level, in such cases the register would record the fact that a case was called, together with the procedural order made by the court as a result—perhaps a continuation to a subsequent date or a final decreet,

[28] The manuscript records for the sample period 1529 to 1534 have been minutely examined, but due to the sheer quantity of the record those from 1506 to 1529 have been read in their entirety but examined in a more cursory fashion.

or else a direction that the matter must now be adjudicated in a different forum, thus ending proceedings before Council or Auditors. Very occasionally all that is recorded is the calling of a case and that it was then remitted to the judge ordinary, without any reason being given. The judge ordinary was simply the generic term for the relevant judge with jurisdiction under the common law.[29] More often, however, there will be a few explanatory words relating, for example, that the decision has been made "because the matter concerns fee and heretage".

The disposal in such cases, however, does not usually record any finding that the Lords of Council are not competent judges. A party might allege that "the lordis was na Jugis to thaim"[30] or that the action "suld nocht remain befor the lordis",[31] because "it concernit...fee and heretage".[32] It would then typically be recorded that the Lords had decided that "the question of the richt dependis apon heretage"[33] or "the mater dependis apon the question of the hale heretage betwix the said partiis",[34] and that therefore "thai may nocht of law be Jugis thirto",[35] because both parties claimed in heritage the land relating to the dispute and had shown their "lauchful enteres thair apone".[36] Such a decision might deprive either party of their heritage for ever,[37] in which situation the case should be remitted to the judge ordinary "eftir the forme of law".[38]

Most cases with an explanatory clause of this sort explicitly stated that in some way it was the existence of a fee and heritage issue which had led the Lords to remit them to the judge ordinary, although various different forms of words were used to express this. Most suggestive, perhaps, are cases in which it was stated that the case "tuichis" or "depends" upon fee and heretage.[39] Clearly, these formulations do not reveal much in detail about the reasoning which led the case to be remitted. What is important, however, is the implication that the

[29] See MacQueen, *Common Law and Feudal Society in Medieval Scotland*, pp. 217–218.
[30] *ADA*, p. 21.
[31] *ADA*, p. *123.
[32] *ADC* i, p. 405.
[33] *ADC* i, p. 22.
[34] *ADC* i, p. 25.
[35] *ADC* i, p. 57.
[36] *ADC* ii, p. 258.
[37] *ADC* ii, p. 434.
[38] *ADA*, p. 8.
[39] For some other forms of words noted see Godfrey, "Jurisdiction over Rights in Land in Later Medieval Scotland", p. 255.

action could not be decided without a determination of some incidental question of fee and heritage. This is also seen more explicitly in some of the wrongful occupation cases where the remit was made because both parties were said to claim that the lands pertained to them in heritage, or that the litigation might have excluded one of them perpetually from their heritage. In such cases any dispute over possession would ultimately give way to one governed by determining title—the right of ownership—if it could be made out. Whilst certain types of action did typically seem to raise a jurisdictional question of this sort, in sum the form of words used in these cases implies that there was no particular set of actions or types of case which were *prima facie* excluded from Council's jurisdiction. Rather, any action raised before Council or Auditors could on the facts be considered to turn upon a matter of fee and heritage, and as such have to be remitted to the judge ordinary.[40]

Nature of a remit

What can be inferred from the discussion so far about the nature of the jurisdictional limitations upon Auditors and Council in respect of heritage? First, it does not seem to have been a question of an action being raised in Council or Parliament which was in itself incompetent. It was not as simple as having as nominate list of excluded actions. Rather, as has already been suggested, the problem was that any action could raise or depend upon an incidental issue of fee and heritage, meaning that an otherwise valid summons could not be determined in either Council or Parliament. Presumably such a "complaint" to either body could not be adjudicated upon without a prior determination of the heritage claim. In such cases, the claim would clearly depend upon legal process before the judge ordinary, as yet either uninitiated or unresolved. Such complaints therefore turned out to raise additional incidental issues for Council and Auditors which were beyond their competence, because they depended upon settling a question of fee and heritage.

[40] A few cases are harder to fit into this model: see A.M. Godfrey, "The Lords of Council and Session and the Foundation of the College of Justice: a Study in Jurisdiction" (University of Edinburgh, unpublished Ph.D. thesis, 1998), pp. 35–41.

The second inference we can draw about the nature of the jurisdictional limitation is that the remit would follow from the fact that two competing titles to fee and heritage were in issue. This would seem to be the crucial technical aspect of the jurisdictional bar which is not captured in the "static" model relied on by Borthwick, MacQueen and Sellar to represent the fee and heritage rule. This model regarded *any* action affecting a heritable title as subject to the bar. However, examination of decisions by Council or Auditors suggests that those affecting the title of one party alone were not beyond the jurisdiction of the central judicial bodies. This can be demonstrated through examination of cases involving reduction by Council or Auditors of charters, infeftments and instruments of sasine, and retours following from the determination of brieves of succession and of right. This occurred in the exercise of the error jurisdiction discussed in the previous chapter. Though in effect "reduction of an infeftment would destroy a title to land", in the words of Professor MacQueen, this did not necessarily mean that such an action could be characterised as a fee and heritage case.[41] It is therefore questionable whether the Lords could ever have been barred from hearing an action on jurisdictional grounds merely because the action affected a title to land and a person's claim to be seised of that land in fee and heritage. It was *competing* claims which were at the heart of the jurisdictional bar.[42]

Cases before Council or Auditors which "touched" heritage

A definition of the fee and heritage restriction based on the idea of decisions which would "touch" heritage in this sense would therefore be too wide. In 1471, for example, the process of a brieve of right, with doom, sasine, possession and "all uther thingis folowing uppon the said breif", is stated as having been reduced by "the lordis of parliament" (i.e. the Auditors of Causes and Complaints).[43] The ground

41 Quoted from H.L. MacQueen, "Jurisdiction in Heritage and the Lords of Council and Session after 1532", in *Miscellany Two*, ed. W.D.H. Sellar, Stair Society 35 (Edinburgh, 1984), p. 82. The argument advanced in this chapter thus casts doubt on Professor MacQueen"s earlier view that "doubts as to the lords' jurisdiction to reduce infeftments must have arisen because such actions touched heritage".

42 In his discussion of the late fifteenth century Professor MacQueen has also noted the idea of competing claims as being relevant to the operation of the fee and heritage restriction upon Council: MacQueen, *Common Law and Feudal Society*, pp. 222, 224.

43 *ADA*, p. 16 (Robert Spens v. James and Robert Nory).

of reduction was that the process was "unlachfully and unorderly procedit because the last court quhen the assise past and the dome was gevin was withein feryale tyme on gude Wednisday in passione woulk". This action certainly invalidated a title to land and therefore touched heritage, but was nevertheless competent in Parliament. Why would this not have been considered a fee and heritage action? The distinction must reflect the fact that in reducing this process no final determination of right was made and thus no one was being excluded perpetually from their heritage, and no order was being made that someone else be now infeft in the property. The common law remedy of a brieve of right remained available, and the issue in the reduction could be characterised as essentially procedural, in that there was a flaw in the method of determining title but not necessarily in the substantive determination of right. Yet from the point of view of the litigant whose title had been previously upheld by the assize, he had now lost sasine of the lands, even if this was only until he was able to rectify matters through initiation of further legal process.

In another example, from 1478, we find a hearing fixed by the Auditors to allow the defender, John Stewart, to "fals and inpung...civily" an instrument of sasine because "the notare of the said sesing callit Robert Marschiale put in the uthir landis in the said instrument of sesing without his consent or sesing gevin of thaim".[44] Of course, this reveals a limited amount, since it is not stated that the sasine was of the heritable fee of the lands, as opposed, for example, to a fixed-term interest such as a lease. If it related to the heritable fee, though, it would demonstrate another reduction on procedural grounds, with reference to a flaw in the transfer of the land. Again there is no assessment of competing titles, although if John failed to "impreve" the instrument, the residual dispute might then have been one which could only be approached as relating to two competing heritable titles.

The classic case of an action which could be brought before Council or Auditors and which "touched" on heritage but was not characterised as a fee and heritage case was the summons of error. When examining this in the previous chapter, we noted the jurisdictional potential of summonses of error, as remarked upon by Hannay.[45] If error was

---

[44] *ADA*, p. 84.

[45] R.K. Hannay, *The College of Justice* (Edinburgh, 1933), reprinted in *The College of Justice: Essays by R.K. Hannay*, ed. H.L. MacQueen, Stair Society Supplementary Series 1 (Edinburgh, 1990), p. 10.

proved successfully, this entailed the reduction of any infeftment given, and all that followed upon the retour recording the inquest's verdict. Of course, the declaration of a retour and infeftment as null was in itself a step which "touched" heritage, although we have already seen that this kind of reduction might be distinguished as concerning specifically a flaw in the legal process which brought that particular infeftment into being. So, determination of a summons of error did not necessarily entail assessment of a fee and heritage issue.

On 14 October 1478, for example, there was a hearing before the Lords of Council of the action of Alexander Hething against John Ellis, bailie of Dundee, for "wranwiss and unordeourly proceding in the serving of a breif of Inquest of our sovuarane lordis chapel... apon certane landis and tenementis in Dundee".[46] The specific allegations were that:

> the balye proclamit nocht the said breif lauchfully in Dundee on 15 days and because he warnit nocht the partii to be at thir defence and because he continuit the serving of the breif fra a day to ane uther but consent of partii and als because he put the mar part and noumer of the persons that past apon the inquest of burges of Edinburgh and les noumer of the burgh of Dundee.

John did not compear, and the Lords decreed that he had wrongously and in unorderly manner proceeded in the service. They decerned the retour, sasine and all that followed upon them to be of no force. The brieve had been raised by Alexander Strachan, who was not present at the Council hearing. If he had been present, could he have successfully pleaded a fee and heritage exception?

Professor MacQueen considered that actions of error against inquests were "probably the commonest types of case" where a fee and heritage exception was pleaded.[47] There are at least ten such cases in the first forty years of the record to 1506 in which an action of error was remitted to the judge ordinary. However, there were many more summonses of error in this period which were not so remitted. What distinguished the summonses of error which were remitted from those which were not? Was it that procedural error could be heard by Council or Auditors, but that error which turned on an assessment of the substance of competing heritable claims could not? Presumably a case such as *Hething v. Ellis*

---

[46] *ADC* i, pp. 10–11.

[47] MacQueen, *Common Law and Feudal Society*, p. 224.

could be regarded as one in which a decision could be made without such an assessment, because the error was clearly procedural. What, then, might have been involved in assessing the *substance* of the verdict of an inquest? Those cases which were remitted to the judge ordinary might have been those in which it was alleged that the assize had come to the wrong verdict on the evidence, perhaps, as expressed in one case, through "errour and wrangwis determinacioun in the serving of the said bref eftir the hering of the resons and allegacons of bath the partiis".[48] A specific example of this might have been when error was alleged in the finding of the inquest that the deceased proprietor had not in fact died "last vest and sesit of fee of the land".[49] Another would be the converse case, as in one example where it was found that the deceased had "deit last vestit and sesit as of fee of the saidis landis... howbeit the said landis wer gevin and grantit be the said Humphrey's predecessoris to umquhile John Banory and his airis male, the quhilkis failzeand to return to the successoris of the first giffare".[50]

That explanation is undermined, however, by the fact that there are also cases of this sort which were not remitted and which were decided by Council. An example is the action of John Blair in 1498 against the inquest impleaded by himself, where he successfully alleged "wrangus delivering and retouring that the sade umquhile David, grantschir to the said John, deit nocht vestit and saisit as of fee of the saidis landis of Wester Bawluny... the said umquile David being vestit and saisit as of fee in the said landis heretably be charter and saising".[51] The Lords found that David had been vested and seised of the lands "eftir the forme and tenor of his charter... schawin and producit before the Lordis". This would seem more than a procedural error, and more a case of the Lords finding the retour wrong in substance after considering the evidence of a charter. However, it should be noted that there was no rival claim to consider in coming to this decision. This may therefore explain why this was not characterised as a fee and heritage case. The structure of an error action did not field rival claims against each other but considered a title on its own terms. A similar kind of case which involved substantive error, but not competing claims of fee and heritage, was when an assize was alleged to have falsely retoured

48 *ADC* i, p. 6.
49 *ADC* i, p. 25 (case of Margaret Knichtson).
50 *ADC* i, pp. 222–223.
51 *ADC* ii, p. 169.

that the land was held on a particular kind of tenure, for example blanche-ferme instead of ward and relief.[52] Another common ground of error was that a retour contained an incorrect assessment of the value of lands.[53] These three main examples illustrate the reduction of retours due to fault in the process leading to the retour, and reduction of an instrument of sasine because of inaccuracy in its terms. They were apparently not considered to be fee and heritage cases in terms of the jurisdictional bar, but turned on some fault in process or transfer. They did not involve competing claims to heritage which were being backed up by independent, conflicting evidence as to title. No final judgement was made as to who should have the heritage.

A common thread in tracing the competence of Council and Session to adjudicate upon heritage disputes in this way is the remedy of reduction. This is significant, since, whilst the jurisdictional bar prevented Council from directly providing a remedy in such cases which was already provided for by the common law, it did not prevent Council offering supplementary remedies. We noted in the previous chapter how jurisdiction over error might have played a significant role in the fifteenth-century Council in developing its competence to grant reduction as a remedy. General actions raised to reduce an infeftment seem to have been uncommon in the fifteenth century, but there are some instances. For example, in 1492 there is one which shows Council again deciding a matter which touched on heritage but was not a fee and heritage case. This is the action of James Ramsay, burgess of Cupar, against Henry Wardlaw, "for to bring with him the pretendit infeftment maid to him be Johne Hunter of a parte of a land and tenement... to here the sammyn decernit and declarit to be of nain avale nor effect", on the grounds that it was made after the land and tenement had been apprised to James and because it was done to defraud Henry's creditor.[54] The Lords went on to reduce the infeftment because it was "done in fraude of the creditor".[55]

There are also examples of Council apparently deciding whether a particular piece of land pertained to one or another person's infeftment. Thus in 1498 the tutors of Robert White raised an action against Sir

---

52 See e.g. *ADC* ii, p. 92.

53 See e.g. *ADC* ii, pp. 133, 377, 393, 407, 406.

54 *ADC* i, p. 238.

55 For similar reduction cases with an infeftment made in defraud of an heir, see *ADC* ii, pp. 391, 455.

Laurence Mercer for wrongous uptaking of a yearly sum from a tenant in Easter Balladur for a part of the lands which were occupied by the tenant.[56] Lawrence admitted the uptaking but denied that the lands in question were part of the lands of Easter Balladur. The pursuers were assigned a day to prove that they were. Again, there is doubt whether the pursuer had the fee and heritage of the land in issue, but there is no mention of a competing claim as such, just an allegation that this land is not part of the land of Easter Balladur. The parties were back before Council a month later for proof of Robert White's title.[57] It seems that the proof failed to resolve the matter since the Lords ordered an inquest to be held by the sheriff to "inquere gif the landis quhilk the sade Janet occupyis ar ane part of the saidis landis... and quhilk of the saidis partiis has bene in state and possessione thareof and be qhat space and tyme". The verdict was to be retoured to Council. In fact, no record of this retour or further council proceedings is extant. This would seem to be a case where the original complaint did depend upon an incidental issue of fee and heritage. The reason an inquest was ordered, though, was apparently not because Council was not a competent forum for proof, since it had already ordered a proof by Robert White's tutors, but rather because the evidence produced before Council had not been capable of supporting the contention that the disputed land was part of Robert White's infeftment. It was this which necessitated the taking of "cognition"—i.e. judicially supervised fact-finding—by an inquest. What would seem to mark this out as not constituting a fee and heritage case is the absence of a competing claim. This is because, whoever else this land might have pertained to, they were not a party to this action. If Sir Laurence Mercer had been able to show some kind of *prima facie* heritable claim of his own, then that would perhaps have allowed him to plead the fee and heritage exception.

Other examples of Council reducing an infeftment include further cases where correct procedures had not been followed. On 11 July 1498 an action was heard relating to the case of Margaret White against the aldermen and bailies of Ayr and the inquest which served and retoured Marion and Elizabeth White to a tenement.[58] The cause of action was that the service had not been retoured to Chancery and instead

[56] *ADC* ii, pp. 167–168.
[57] *ADC* ii, p. 197.
[58] *ADC* ii, p. 65.

infeftment had been given directly at the hands of the bailies. Council then declared the sasine to be a nullity. This is another case where it was the intrinsic validity of a title which was in question. Council could therefore determine it, as opposed to cases where two independent and competing claims presented themselves. Finally, another type of reduction of infeftment case could follow from a decision of Council to reduce one of its own decreets when that decreet had contained an order that someone be infeft in lands.[59]

The judicial competence of Parliament in fee and heritage

Such was the extent of the limited jurisdiction affecting heritage which Council already had in the later fifteenth century. But why is it assumed that *Parliament* was bound in the same way as Council and Session? The evidence for treating both as being similarly bound derives from the evidence of remits made by Council and parliamentary Auditors of Causes and Complaints. If remits because of fee and heritage were being made by both Council and Parliament (through its Auditors) then it is a logical assumption that the test for remitting an action was the same for either body, and that therefore the jurisdictional bar was the same for both. Indeed, the discussion in this chapter has proceeded so far on the basis that the jurisdictional limitations upon Council in respect of fee and heritage in the later fifteenth century applied also to Parliament as a court of law.

Evidence in support of this view would seem to be found in the eleven remits to the judge ordinary by the Lords Auditors of Causes and Complaints.[60] There is no apparent difference in form or substance between these remits and those made by Council because of heritage. As it happens, in none of these cases did the Auditors expressly declare themselves not to be competent judges in such actions. The most they say is that it "aw nocht to resort nor be determyt befor thaim becaus it is fee and heretage", and that is said in only one case.[61] Normally, the decreet just states that it is because it concerns fee and heritage that

[59] *ADC* ii, p. 331.

[60] See appendix 1, based on Godfrey, "Jurisdiction over Rights in Land in Later Medieval Scotland", pp. 260–261, though two of the 13 *ADA* remit cases listed there are here reclassified as being unrelated to fee and heritage: Graham v Graham (*ADA*, p. 8) and Ouchterlony v Hair (*ADA*, p. 93).

[61] *ADA*, p. 10 (abbot and convent of Lindores v. Philip Mowbray).

the cause is remitted to the judge ordinary. However, when set against identical prescriptions which emanated from Council (alongside at least some incidental declarations that the Lords of Council were not competent judges in such matters) there would seem little reason not to assume that Parliament was subject to the same jurisdictional limitations as Council in this respect, and that these matters were remitted because Parliament was not a competent forum for their determination. Another way of stating this would be that Parliament—and its Auditors of Causes and Complaints—had no first instance jurisdiction over fee and heritage, because the procedures of the common law confined determination of fee and heritage to procedure by brieve and inquest. That would still leave a residual jurisdiction for Parliament, through its other auditorial committee on falsed dooms. However, this simply flowed from those same procedures of the common law which provided for procedure by brieve and inquest in the first place. It was consistent with the fee and heritage limitation. This residual role would only be triggered in the question of falsing. It will be considered below.

This view of Parliament as being without fee and heritage jurisdiction is broadly shared by Professor MacQueen, subject to some qualifications. It particularly requires discussion, however, because it has been cogently questioned by Dr Alan Borthwick in an extremely suggestive study of one fifteenth-century case. Both views will therefore be evaluated. Taking Professor MacQueen's analysis first, he does not argue that Parliament *could not* decide matters of fee and heritage, but rather in a more nuanced way that "the auditors had no jurisdiction in such cases because parliament generally did not exercise jurisdiction in them either".[62] He also adds the qualification that "this is not to say that parliament had no jurisdiction in fee and heritage cases. It would be more accurate to say that parliament was generally not concerned to deal with cases where there was a remedy in the general common law". This way of putting the argument might appear somewhat inconclusive. However, it attempts to recognise that as the supreme legislative and judicial body in the kingdom, Parliament cannot lightly be characterised as being without jurisdiction in any given legal matter.

This latter concern relates to Professor MacQueen's general thesis about the development of the jurisdictional bar on the central judicial bodies. He has argued that "in the course of the fifteenth century the

[62] MacQueen, *Common Law and Feudal Society*, p. 219.

idea that parliament and council could not act where there was a common-law remedy was gradually superseded",[63] but not necessarily in "cases relating to land and in particular in relation to disputes about ownership".[64] This was because of "the continuing force of the common-law rule that, when a pursuer sought to recover lands from the possession of another, he had to proceed by way of a pleadable brieve".[65] However, rather than marking out all questions relating to the wider tenurial category of "freehold", Professor MacQueen has suggested that a distinction between possessory and proprietary jurisdiction may explain why it was exclusively fee and heritage upon which Council and Parliament could not decide an action.[66] Freehold could involve rights to possess which were not based on full ownership. Fee and heritage was not merely a possessory right, but the ultimate right of heritable title. Thus it was fee and heritage which could have been seen as the *proprietary* interest excluded from Council's jurisdiction by the earlier procedural rules, whilst leaving possessory questions as competent to be raised without pleadable brieve. The result was that the only actions now remaining outwith the jurisdiction of Council and Parliament were fee and heritage ones, to which they were not competent judges and for which the parties continued to have to resort to the common-law remedies available.

Dr Borthwick's challenge to this view came in an article on the mid-fifteenth century dispute between the burghs of Montrose and Dundee. The dispute concerned their trading privileges, in particular the right to indict forestallers at chamberlain ayres.[67] He examined the history of the dispute before the chamberlain ayre itself, the court of the four burghs, Parliament, and the King and Council. Following examination of the pleadings of Montrose, Dr Borthwick characterised the case as one of fee and heritage. He argued that "both burghs seem to have accepted that parliament had jurisdiction in their case", Montrose protesting at one point that "we refer us to the parliament quhar debatis off

[63] MacQueen, *Common Law and Feudal Society*, p. 235.
[64] MacQueen, *Common Law and Feudal Society*, p. 236.
[65] MacQueen, *Common Law and Feudal Society*, p. 237.
[66] MacQueen, *Common Law and Feudal Society*, p. 237.
[67] A.R. Borthwick, "*Montrose* v. *Dundee* and the Jurisdiction of Parliament and Council over Fee and Heritage in the Mid-Fifteenth Century" in *The Scots and Parliament*, ed. Clyve Jones (Edinburgh, 1996), pp. 33–53.

bondis of burowis off fee and heritage aucht off law to be determyt".[68] Dr Borthwick underlined the various distinctions between the King's Council and Parliament. In particular, he emphasised the Council's traditional more limited concern with actions which the King wished it to hear. In addition, he noted Parliament's status as a fenced court in which dooms could be pronounced, which might have implied that, as a supreme court of law in the immemorial sense, its jurisdiction was unlikely to be limited.[69] As a second line of argument in support of this contention, Dr Borthwick pointed out that "parliament as a whole might be faced with fee and heritage matters on appeal. It was quite possible that the doom awarding ownership of property after the execution of a pleadable brieve could be falsed all the way to parliament".[70]

To take the second point first, it is not clear that in the falsing of a doom concerning fee and heritage parliament would thereby engage in the determination of a fee and heritage matter. It would only be doing so if it quashed the previous doom and then adjudicated upon the pronouncement of a new one itself, but that does not seem to have been within the remit of a court which falsed a doom. Professor MacQueen would appear to accept the same view as Dr Borthwick in this regard, arguing that falsing the doom "was significantly different from the action of error applying to retourable brieves in that the appellate court's verdict was substituted for that given below and did not merely quash it",[71] citing an article by Sir Philip Hamilton Grierson in support of this statement.[72] This body of work has already been considered more generally in chapter 1. Hamilton Grierson merely states that "the judgement of that court [i.e. the court of review] was limited to a pronouncement that the judgement of the court below was either 'wele gevin and evil againsaid' or 'evil gevin and wele againsaid', and to the imposition of a fine on the judges whose judgement had been 'evil gevin'."[73] No reference is made to the court going on to determine its

[68] Borthwick, "*Montrose* v. *Dundee* and the Jurisdiction of Parliament and Council", p. 48.

[69] Borthwick, "*Montrose* v. *Dundee* and the Jurisdiction of Parliament and Council", p. 49.

[70] Borthwick, "*Montrose* v. *Dundee* and the Jurisdiction of Parliament and Council", p. 51.

[71] MacQueen, "Pleadable brieves, pleading, and the development of Scots law", p. 408.

[72] P.J. Hamilton-Grierson, "Falsing the Doom", *Scottish Historical Review* 24 (1926), 1–18.

[73] Hamilton-Grierson, "Falsing the Doom", pp. 1–2.

own doom on the original question in relation to which the first doom had now been falsed.

Whilst a doom could perhaps be shown to be incorrect in the light of some further evidence, it could hardly be substituted except by a determination from a new inquest. Parliament did not itself constitute inquests. Even if some types of case were capable in theory of being resolved on their merits in Parliament following the falsing of a doom, this cannot have extended to *all* questions of fee and heritage. Procedure by brieve and inquest must usually have required to be reinstituted. Thus on this argument, falsing the doom *does* in fact appear to bear a close analogy to determination of a summons of error, leaving the parties to reinstitute proceedings at common law. In that case, falsing of a doom relating to fee and heritage would not place Parliament in the position of deciding upon such matters directly.

A further element is that it should not be assumed that legal understanding of such matters did not change over time to reflect developments in jurisdiction and procedure. If there were earlier cases in which Parliament substituted a verdict for a falsed doom this would not be conclusive about the general position. The attitude in the fourteenth century to what falsing the doom involved may have been different to that of a century later. By then the operation of the Session and the fee and heritage rule had been integrated into the legal system. In the late fifteenth century, we find the Auditors of Causes and Complaints refusing to hear fee and heritage actions. It would seem inconsistent if the position was that they were unable to make substantive determinations of fee and heritage, but that their sister auditorial committee could do so upon falsing a doom. Until further study of procedure on falsing of dooms suggests otherwise, the most compelling view remains that Parliament and Council were equally bound and that falsing the doom did not involve jurisdiction over fee and heritage.

With respect to Dr Borthwick's first point, it is important to note that the evidence he has adduced in respect of jurisdiction relates to the pleadings of the parties, and not to any determination by Council or Parliament as to their actual jurisdiction. Pleadings could be made for no other reason than to win that party some advantage in the case, and the making of a submission does not necessarily imply that it was an accurate statement of the law. Several further possible doubts about Dr Borthwick's argument should be mentioned as well. First, what sorts of right counted as fee and heritage? It should not be too readily accepted that the right in question—that of a burgh to indict forestallers at the chamberlain ayre—really was a matter of fee and heritage. It was a corporate privilege more redolent of questions of jurisdiction and public order than landed property right. The only fee and heritage cases we know about which are not directly concerned with holding the heritable fee of land are cases involving ground annuals, thirl multures, or fishing rights, and even multures were no more than a way in which income could be raised from a service relating to particular mills on particular pieces of land. The traditional types of fee and heritage cases do at least bear a concrete and directly revenue-bearing relation to land, even when they do not relate to the heritable fee itself, but to other heritable interests. They seem to be matters of property rather than a jurisdictional privilege such as the right to indict forestallers. Secondly, even if the matter was properly speaking one of fee and heritage, the motives of one or both parties in wishing to have the matter decided by Parliament may simply have been that they considered Parliament to be *tactically* the most favourable forum for a decision affecting their rights. Indeed, Dr Borthwick has indicated that Montrose may have had reason to prefer the determination of Parliament to Council at this time. A further complication in this case, unfortunately, is that we do not know whether Dundee also accepted the matter as being one of fee and heritage.

A third and final point to consider in relation to Dr Borthwick's argument is that a corporate dispute between burghs raised particularly complex issues which might have tested the orthodox understanding of jurisdictional concepts. It would not have been the typical type of case in which the fee and heritage bar had been developed. Such disputes were in a sense beyond the normal procedures of the common law. It is hard to see which court would have been the "judge ordinary" in the action other than the court of the four burghs, which the King had interdicted from proceeding in this case. Possibly, though, it could be argued that Parliament itself was the judge ordinary. However, in relation to fee and heritage cases, the judge ordinary is one to whom a pleadable brieve could have been addressed, and that would have excluded both the court of the four burghs and Parliament at first instance. Neither could constitute an inquest. Moreover, it is hard to see which pleadable brieve would have applied in a dispute of this kind. In other words, the circumstances of this case mean that it is unusually complex and is hard to fit into any procedural and jurisdictional model provided for in the common law.

It seems reasonable to conclude that the case is too far removed from the mainstream fee and heritage cases to allow a reliable generalisation to be made concerning the general jurisdictional competence of Parliament over fee and heritage. Perhaps there was a jurisdictional loophole in the medieval common law in this regard which only Parliament could fill. But this would be exceptional. In due course such cases would certainly come before the Session in the sixteenth century. In any event, although Dr Borthwick's analysis might support the suggestion that there was no formal rule restricting Parliament's role in fee and heritage, his conclusion is in fact the more limited one that "the rule restricting their role was not strictly applied".[74] However, the discussion above would suggest that the *Montrose v. Dundee* case does not necessarily support even this view, and that Professor MacQueen's view remains preferable. Besides which, it could be argued that in unusual or anomalous circumstances Parliament's hearing of a fee and heritage dispute would not necessarily be seen to interfere with the normal jurisdictional rules. Overall it seems that Parliament was restricted by the common law from deciding fee and heritage except to the extent that it adjudicated upon the falsing of dooms, but that these generally involved no more than the quashing of dooms already given by lower courts.

Frequency of Remits to Judge Ordinary and Declinatory Exceptions 1466–1513

We have examined what kind of action was affected by the fee and heritage jurisdictional bar, and how the rule seems to have governed the jurisdiction of all central tribunals, including Parliament. But how frequently was jurisdiction over heritage contested in the later fifteenth century? The record does not often reveal explicitly whether an exception was pleaded. Thus it commonly does not contain a procedural record of an objection to the jurisdiction of the tribunal. Instead it is merely the procedural order which must have been the result of such a plea that is recorded, stating that the case is to be remitted to the "judge ordinary". It is a fairly straightforward matter of inference from this that an exception was pleaded, though less easy to say that it was

[74] Borthwick, "*Montrose* v. *Dundee* and the Jurisdiction of Parliament and Council", p. 51.

because of fee and heritage that the case was remitted. Nevertheless, as we have seen, the connection with fee and heritage is in many cases explicitly acknowledged in making the remit. The greater problem is in establishing how frequently jurisdiction was *unsuccessfully* contested, by reference to exceptions which were *not* followed by a remit. What we cannot know is whether there were ever unsuccessfully pleaded exceptions which were just not recorded and how any convention about recording them may have changed over time.

The one type of procedure which it seems reasonable to assume was always recorded was the remit to the judge ordinary. This was effectively a disposal of the action. These can be picked out and examined over the whole period, excluding those instances where it is apparent that it is the spiritual judge ordinary to whom the case is remitted—confusingly, the term "judge ordinary" had both a secular and a church court usage, and the record uses the term indistinguishably. Over the half-century or so from 1466 to 1513 there are sixty-three known remits to the secular judge ordinary which related or probably related to heritage.[75] This would suggest an average of under two cases a year, out of many hundreds. Therefore, the suggestion of Borthwick, MacQueen and Sellar that remits were commonplace seems to go too far. Indeed, the relative infrequency of remits to the judge ordinary might even suggest that the kind of remedies which litigants sought very rarely related to or were dependent upon deciding an issue of fee and heritage. If so, that might suggest that the fee and heritage restriction may not in practice have even been a very significant one for Council in the conduct of its business, although legally and jurisdictionally significant.

Given that the restriction itself has been shown to arise from a succession of technical developments in medieval Scots law rather than from the implementation of any policy designed to restrict the competence of the central tribunals, care should be taken not to make exaggerated claims for the significance of the existence or erosion of the fee and heritage bar by 1532. After all, it would be surprising if land titles in early sixteenth century Scotland were *generally* contestable, given centuries of reliance upon written charters and infeftments, and

[75] Two remit cases previously categorised as related to fee and heritage in A.M. Godfrey, "Jurisdiction over Rights in Land in Later Medieval Scotland", *Juridical Review* (2000), 243–263 are here re-classified and regarded as being remitted for other reasons: Graham v Graham, *ADA*, p. 8; Ouchterlownie v Hair, *ADA* p. 93. They are therefore excluded from the list in appendix 1.

the protection offered by the medieval common law. This might be so notwithstanding the contentiousness generated by the exploitation of feudal land rights discussed in the previous chapter. It is also not to say that there was not still significant scope for title disputes, or that deeper changes in how the scope of a title was regarded, how it should be asserted, and how it should be protected, might have been underway in a manner which affected wider change in the legal order. It is also worth observing that as long as the jurisdictional bar was being seen as still applicable, this would surely have discouraged many litigants from the apparent futility of bringing fee and heritage issues before the Session in the first place. If everyone—or at least lawyers advising clients—understood that such cases were properly to be brought by another procedure in other courts, then we would not expect to find many fee and heritage cases before the Session.

Equally, it might not have always been immediately apparent that an action did concern fee and heritage. Some actions would only have raised a fee and heritage issue after they were initiated if the defender sought to advance a defence which focused the issues in terms of heritable title. In such cases what might have been a normal and commonplace legal action, otherwise competent, might have come to be a "fee and heritage" case once the defender entered an appearance and sought to defend the action. Regardless of the practical importance of the jurisdictional bar, however, it is nevertheless a pertinent historical question to ask how, and indeed why, the application of the rule may have changed over time. The wider importance of this relates to tracing the incidence of contested jurisdiction as institutional evolution towards a central court continued. The institutional development of a central court is of course also likely to have been a contributing factor in how a full jurisdiction eventually became established.

Remits to the judge ordinary did not always flow from contested jurisdiction or from fee and heritage. They could sometimes be on other grounds. Indeed, when fee and heritage is not specifically mentioned, it can be doubtful whether remits involved questions of title as such. For example, in 1467 the first remit recorded in the extant auditorial record was "anent the abstractioune of the water of Northesk fra the ald gang", which does not seem to raise legal questions which turn on disputed title directly but rather on the wrongful act constituted by changing the course of a river. The brieve which the auditors must have had in mind in making a remit would therefore not be of right but *de aqueductu*.[76] There was also another remit in 1479 which is silent on its precise jurisdictional basis but is probably unrelated to fee and heritage. First it stemmed from a claim in warrandice and involved the "impreving" of an instrument purporting to grant a "sett"—i.e. a lease, not the heritable fee. The warrantor was resisting the warrandice claim by alleging that the instrument of lease itself was forged. Secondly, it would appear that, though not explicitly stated, the judge ordinary here was the spiritual judge ordinary, in the light of slightly later proceedings by the same litigants before Council in which it was stated that a sentence was awaited on the validity of the instrument from the official of Glasgow.[77]

General trend in remitting to judge ordinary 1466–1513

Between October 1467 and December 1513 there are 143 recorded cases in which parties disputed the jurisdiction of the central judicial bodies because of fee and heritage: 63 remits to the judge ordinary, and 80 examples of the unsuccessful pleading of a fee and heritage exception, or else a protest to the effect that the Lords were not competent judges. We have already noted that this means that remits were not especially frequent. In addition, the distribution in the half century to 1513 was not even. It appears that fewer and fewer cases were remitted to the judge ordinary over time, whilst, as discussed further below, more and more exceptions were being recorded in relation to the jurisdiction of the Lords of Council over fee and heritage. The implication might be that during the reign of James IV Council and Auditors became less inclined to remit a case to the judge ordinary, or else that cases which once would not have been brought before the central tribunals were now being brought more often in Council and Session. This might seem to be especially the case by about 1500. By this time sittings of the Session had quite recently become the regular unified vehicle for central justice, in practical terms superseding the parliamentary Auditors after 1496.

[76] For this brieve and discussion of this example see MacQueen, *Common Law and Feudal Society*, pp. 158–161, 235–236.

[77] *ADC* i, p. 59.

One explanation could be that traces of this unwillingness to remit have been left behind in the record in the form of the recording of protests and exceptions to the jurisdiction of Council made by dissatisfied parties but plainly repelled. Alternatively, the degree of institutional development represented by the aggrandisement of the jurisdiction and business of the Session in the 1490s might have prompted more challenges to its jurisdiction. This seems improbable, however, given that for many years prior to the 1490s there had been jurisdictional integration between causes dealt with consecutively or concurrently by parliamentary Auditors and by Council, and both were subject to the jurisdictional bar concerning heritage. A further explanation might be that more actions were being raised before the Session in ways which disguised or circumvented the articulation of the underlying legal dispute as one which ultimately depended upon conflicting titles. Though such a case might have been accepted as technically competent by the Lords, this could have prompted defenders to raise the jurisdictional issue in the vain hope of forcing the action to be progressed in the traditional way in a local forum.

Although some kind of change must have been occurring, this rather broad analysis is too crude in itself to permit a firm conclusion. This is because the figures of contested jurisdiction alone tell us a limited amount unless they are broken down to reflect how many fell in particular years. Even then, of course, caution is still required in their interpretation because the relative quantity of judicial business in any given year as compared to other years varied. For example, there were as many as nine remits in 1478 and in 1480, three in 1490, and none in 1492.[78] Overall, it is very difficult to find a simple pattern. For example, the evidence shows that the only three years with more than two or three cases were 1471 (before the Auditors), 1478, and 1480 (these last two before the Council), with four, nine, and nine cases respectively. Thereafter there are between one and three cases in any year, or else none. And whereas Council business is recorded for thirty-four and thirty-two days respectively during 1478 and 1480, if we look at the period 1501–1506 there is a potentially significant contrast. For a start, there are a mere six remit cases over the six-year period, which is below average. However, Council was often also conducting business on more

[78] See appendix 1; for some further comment see Godfrey, "Jurisdiction over Rights in Land in Later Medieval Scotland", pp. 252–254.

than double the number of days that it did in 1478 or 1480, and thereby presumably deciding upon many more cases by comparison.[79] This again supports the view that after 1500, if not for some time before, remits to the judge ordinary had become less frequent in proportion to the amount of judicial business conducted by Council.

General trends in pleading of fee and heritage exceptions 1466–1513[80]

It is striking that up until 1500 there are only six recorded instances of *unsuccessful* exceptions and protests made against the jurisdiction of Council and which did not lead to a remit to the judge ordinary, whereas over the course of the thirteen succeeding years there were more than seventy. This is a much more clear-cut case of a definite trend than that of remits to the judge ordinary. There is plainly a substantial increase in the number of such protests and exceptions by litigants, or at least the recording of such protests and exceptions, which denied that Council was a competent judge to them in matters of fee and heritage. None was known before 1492. Approximately 95 per cent of cases in which jurisdiction was *recorded* as contested on grounds of fee and heritage before 1500 were successfully remitted. After 1500, the position changes. There were as many as seven unsuccessful protests or exceptions in 1501 alone, three in 1502, nine in 1503, thirteen in 1505, two in 1506, and then thirteen in 1507. How can this incidence be explained? Of course, even such striking figures are difficult to interpret. How do we know, for example, that they do reflect an increase in the pleading of such exceptions and protests as opposed to the recording of them by the clerks of court? After all, record-keeping habits do not necessarily remain rigid or static over time. However, even supposing that it is not certain that the increased number of recorded protests reflected anything more than a change in record-keeping practice, the question would remain why the record style had changed with such dramatic consequences in disclosing unsuccessful instances of contested jurisdiction. Why would it have come to be considered important to note such protests when in the past there had been no need to do so? Had the

[79] See appendix 2.
[80] See appendix 1.

whole question of jurisdiction been relatively settled and uncontroversial before 1500, but become heavily contested thereafter?

At the very least, therefore, this evidence would seem to be indicative of the jurisdiction of Council over fee and heritage having somehow become a matter of controversy or dispute around about 1500. Subject to the various caveats already expressed, the record of protests and exceptions would seem to support the view that some kind of jurisdictional change was underway around 1500, with fewer cases remitted to the judge ordinary, and many more litigants protesting about the jurisdiction of Council, although to little effect. This interpretation may seem to have even more potential significance given that the 1490s had been such an important decade in the evolution of the Session. It is not possible to do more than speculate on how to interpret these features. The recording of jurisdictional protests and exceptions may well be an indicator that from the 1490s Council and its judicial Session were providing an ever more accessible forum in which royal justice could be dispensed, so that parties were more likely than ever to find themselves summoned before it. The protests and exceptions may reflect this, as well as that a wider range of cases may have been coming before Council. This could have increasingly provoked protests by defenders, if only as a tactical ploy to hold back the judicial resolution of a dispute over that most valuable source of wealth, status and power—their heritable property. The pleading of protests and exceptions of this sort may have had less to do with asserting or establishing jurisdictional norms, than with using any available means to hinder litigation, the efficient resolution of which would be a source of inconvenience or patrimonial loss if decree was granted against the defender. Preventing litigation from running its course might also have been advantageous in strengthening the bargaining position of a party who wished to achieve settlement on favourable terms.

Remits and fee and heritage exceptions 1513–1532

We have examined the operation of the fee and heritage exception in its "classical" period up to the early sixteenth century. After 1500 jurisdiction seems to have become more contested, whilst remits were being made less frequently. But in order to assess the jurisdictional position by 1532, it is necessary to examine how this situation developed over the first three decades of the century. On 1 March 1507 the Lords were still able to declare that a summons relating to contested multures concerned the heritage and ground right of the parties, to which they were not competent judges. The case was therefore referred to the judge ordinary.[81] Nearly a year later, on 18 February 1508, we find another remit to the judge ordinary because a summons "concernit the ground rycht of the mater".[82] The practice of remitting to the judge ordinary because of fee and heritage was therefore still a live one in 1508, continuing the pattern of the previous few decades whereby in almost every year there had been at least one such remit. Given the continuity of these final years of James IV's reign, it would perhaps be surprising if the Session had changed its practices significantly in the period up to 1513. At least seven further remits were indeed made between January 1509 and March 1513.[83] A remit to the judge ordinary was still considered a valid recourse in May 1513, though the decision in the case in question was deferred to allow further hearings for the production of evidence of the conflicting titles.[84]

When we look at the subsequent period between 1513 and 1532 as a whole there is a very striking contrast indeed. It appears that there were no further remits to the judge ordinary at all because of fee and heritage, suggesting that this practice had ended after 1513. Furthermore, compared to what may have been a highpoint in the first three months alone of 1507, when there were twelve protests or exceptions against the competence of the Lords because of fee and heritage, we find a noticeable change after 1513. Although exceptions continued to be pleaded up to 1513 and afterwards for many years, their number declined dramatically. Between 1513 and 1532 only twelve exceptions were pleaded in total on grounds of fee and heritage, most arising from 1527 onwards. Their distribution suggests that the practice of contesting the heritage jurisdiction of the Lords fell away almost completely between 1513 and the later 1520s. The instances between 1513 and May 1532 occurred respectively in 1517, 1525, 1527 and 1528, twice

---

[81] CS 5/18(2), fol. 237v.

[82] CS 5/19, fol. 183v.

[83] CS 5/20, fol. 69r. (29 Jan., 1509); CS 5/20, fol. 70r. (29 Jan., 1509) [these first two are separate actions arising out of the same dispute]; CS 5/20, fol. 173v. (27 April, 1509); CS 5/20, fol. 185v. (5 May, 1509); CS 5/23, fol. 68r. (24 July, 1511); CS 5/24, fol. 93v. (16 Dec., 1512); CS 5/24, fol. 151v. (1 March, 1513).

[84] CS 5/25, fols. 85v–86v.

in 1529, twice in 1530 and four times in 1531.[85] A previous study has shown that the pleading of such exceptions also continued after the foundation of the College of Justice in May 1532, with single instances in 1532, 1533 and 1534, but again always unsuccessfully, with no remits to the judge ordinary as a result.[86]

The implications of this are difficult to make out. However, the most important would seem to be that after 1513 the Lords of Council never again accepted that a case should be remitted to the judge ordinary because of fee and heritage.[87] This clearly has a major bearing on the debate over the jurisdiction of the Session in 1532. The fee and heritage restriction on the jurisdiction of the Session was the concomitant of protecting the privative jurisdiction of the judge ordinary and the integrity of process by brieve and inquest. The protection was given effect procedurally by the pleading of an exception and a subsequent remitting of the action to the relevant judge ordinary. If by 1532 there had been no such remit for almost twenty years, though occasional exceptions were pleaded, it suggests that the jurisdiction of the Lords of Council had come to be no longer limited in substance. Subsequent evidence shows that by 1560 at the latest the Session possessed not only jurisdiction in heritage, but a wholly exclusive jurisdiction in such matters.[88] We therefore know that the jurisdictional limitation was formally superseded at some point in this period. Previously the debate conducted by Sellar and MacQueen tended to focus on events after 1532, by way of assessing the effect of the foundation of the College

[85] CS 5/29, fol. 91r. (16 March, 1517); CS 5/35, fol. 69v. (3 July, 1525); CS 5/37, fol. 228r. (30 August, 1527); CS 5/39, fol. 72r. (4 February, 1529); CS 5/40, fol. 74r. (28 July, 1529); CS 5/40, fol. 81v. (4 August, 1529); CS 5/41, fol. 4 (12 March, 1530); CS 5/41, fol. 22v. (19 March, 1530); CS 5/42, fol. 40 (9 February, 1531); CS 5/42, fol. 46 (11 February, 1531); CS 5/42, fol. 119r. (15 March, 1531); CS 5/43, fol. 92v. (23 November, 1531).

[86] A.M. Godfrey, "Jurisdiction in Heritage and the Foundation of the College of Justice in 1532", in *Miscellany Four*, ed. MacQueen, pp. 9–36 at p. 18.

[87] Of course the record after May 1534 remains to be examined and could in theory contain such a remit. If the analysis presented in this chapter is correct, however, this is not in the least bit likely. I also acknowledge that an even slower and more painstaking search of the council register from 1513 to 1529 *might* uncover remits I have so far missed, but again this seems to me to be unlikely.

[88] A.M. Godfrey, "The assumption of jurisdiction: Parliament, the King's Council and the College of Justice in Sixteenth-Century Scotland", *Journal of Legal History* 22 (2001), 21–36 at p. 24; Godfrey, "Jurisdiction in Heritage and the Foundation of the College of Justice in 1532", p. 13. The primary source is "Discours particulier D'Escosse, 1559/60", ed. P.G.B. McNeill, in *Miscellany Two*, ed. W.D.H. Sellar, Stair Society 35 (Edinburgh, 1984), pp. 82–131 especially at pp. 109, 113.

of Justice upon the "static model" of jurisdictional limitation which it was assumed had existed until that time. The evidence just discussed would suggest, however, that the "jurisdictional shift" was likely to have occurred before 1532, though no earlier than 1513. It seems plausible to suggest that a lengthy transitional period may have occurred during which the practice of the Session changed in how it approached heritage disputes, but that contemporaries struggled to assimilate this.

The explicit recognition of a jurisdiction in heritage by the Lords may have been difficult to rationalise until the College of Justice had become established and had articulated its "practick" during its first decade or so of existence. This particularly involved asserting its superiority to other courts, for example through advocation, and defining aspects of its jurisdiction as exclusive. It would therefore not be surprising to discover that there may have been a time-lag between a heritage jurisdiction being exercised by the Lords and it being expressly acknowledged as such. To make these observations naturally raises many other questions which must be pursued in the attempt to give an adequate account of the nature of jurisdictional change in this period. In particular, the fact that jurisdiction in heritage continued to be contested after 1532 needs to be explained. At a deeper level, we must also return to the question whether the jurisdictional limit had been formally discarded, or had simply been superseded by the development of different remedies. And how were heritage disputes now being resolved? Finally, how can the account of change prior to 1532 presented here be reconciled with the detailed analysis given by Professor MacQueen? In his discussion of the development of a heritage jurisdiction by the Lords, he argued that the 1530s and early 1540s constituted the crucial period in which jurisdiction over heritage was gained.[89] All of these matters will be pursued in more depth in the next chapter.

Changing perceptions of Council as a forum to decide heritage

The fee and heritage jurisdictional bar was a legal rule which stated that such cases *could not* be decided by the central tribunals. In turn, the legitimacy, appropriateness or relevance of the jurisdictional bar must itself have rested on deeper normative assumptions about the

[89] As well as the next chapter, for more detailed discussion see Godfrey, "Jurisdiction in Heritage and the Foundation of the College of Justice in 1532".

importance of observing the manner prescribed in the common law for resolving certain kinds of important disputes. But there must have come a point when the continued survival of the bar began to seem incongruous, if not anomalous, given the extent to which the remedies and jurisdiction of the Session had developed by the early years of the sixteenth century. It is therefore pertinent to ask whether there is evidence which suggests that there was a change in perception favouring the adjudication of the Session over heritage in general, if not yet generally over fee and heritage disputes as such.

We have seen that the jurisdiction of the central judicial tribunals was excluded from only certain types of heritage case, which arose when two competing titles were in opposition. A range of other heritage-related matters could be addressed, in particular when the remedy of reduction was sought from the Session. By 1500, we have seen that there was a falling away of remits, but an intensification of challenges to jurisdiction. However, there is also some evidence that, despite the medieval jurisdictional bar, parties did sometimes desire their heritage disputes to be decided by Council and Session, even though regular procedure would not normally permit this. This possible evidence of changing perceptions is apparent in the hearing of actions by the Session, with the consent of parties, on the "ground right" of the parties in dispute. This seems to have gradually become a more significant practice by 1532. It could and did sometimes encompass fee and heritage disputes. Its importance was that in giving their consent to the extraordinary submission of such questions to the determination of the Lords and the waiving of declinatory exceptions (thus perhaps implying that the action would otherwise have been outside the Lords' jurisdiction) the parties circumvented the jurisdictional limitations upon Council which would otherwise have led in the past to a remit to the judge ordinary. Such submissions would seem to reflect a changing perception of the Session and its role in dispute resolution, as a result of which litigants were coming to prefer the central forum of the Session for deciding upon their heritage. The beginnings of such a trend in the early years of the sixteenth century would fit in with the evidence already considered of declining numbers of remits to the judge ordinary and increasing numbers of declinatory exceptions, which also implied that some change was underway.

It is towards the end of 1504 that we find what may be the first extant case of a submission of a determination of "ground right" to the Lords of Council. This was in relation to a summons of error raised by Thomas Wemyss against the sheriff of Fife and the assize which had served William Forbes his brieve of inquest. The action was part of a long-running dispute which has been charted by Professor MacQueen.[90] It is not clear how the error proceedings turned out, even whether they were pursued at all, but we find that the procurators are said to have obliged themselves of their own free will to cause William Forbes and Thomas Wemyss to compear before the Lords and "produce charters and evidentis as they will use for the verray ground right of the matter" and to admit the Lords as judges in the said matter "without exception determinat [*sic*], dilatour or peremptour to be raised against said judges, and shall abide at the lords' deliverance without appeal or reclamation thereafter".[91] The implication is that, without such an admission of the Lords as judges, the cause would have been vulnerable to a jurisdictional challenge. This is the earliest extant case of this type noticed by the present writer. The terms of the submission are very close to an arbitration agreement, though there would seem to be no previous case in which, as here, the submission was made generally to Council as a corporate institution, instead of to individually named judges. Such a procedure was a departure from the normal course whereby the summons of error would have been determined, and the parties would have had to raise new brieves of inquest if the retour had been reduced. In this case we find the Lords reducing the retour but also going on to decide the ground right too, an outcome which was also to become more common by 1532.

There are other examples which show that submission of "ground right" to Council's determination was in some sense a procedure which was in issue around 1504. On 22 January 1505, we find William Hamilton, forespeaker for John Weir, asking instruments that he preferred to put the ground right of the matter of Folkirtone before the King and Lords of Council, to be decided by them.[92] Procedural debate followed on 30 January, during which John Ferny, forespeaker for John Menzies and Catherine Folkart, the pursuers, asked instruments that William Hamilton, the forespekar of Robert Hamilton and John Weir, had "pretermittit [i.e. passed over] the exception declinatour again the

[90] MacQueen, "Jurisdiction in Heritage and the Lords of Council and Session after 1532", p. 77.

[91] Edinburgh, National Archives of Scotland [hereafter NAS], CS 5/16, fol. 76v., 13th February 1504/5. See NAS transcript p. 200.

[92] NAS CS 5/16, fol. 24v. See NAS transcript p. 58.

lordis as jugis". This was said to be "becaus he except of before or he proponit the exception declinatour again the summondis, falsand to the said Johne his justice defens again the said exceptione declinatour".[93] It is hard to be sure exactly what significance this had, due to the absence of further contextual information, but then on 1 February we find an agreement that the summons raised by Catherine and John against Robert Hamilton and John Weir was to be continued to a later date, at which time the defenders consented to compear without exception declinatour and to admit the Lords as judges in the said matter. We are then told that these proceedings were not to prejudice other actions which there may yet be. Catherine or John were also reserved the option of raising a new summons against Robert or John. The latter agreed to answer to any new summons, admitting likewise the Lords as judges. Further statements were made in this case that the admission of the Lords as judges was not to prejudice other parties from pursuing brieves of right or processes thereupon afterwards and that the admission was made with consent of party. This may imply that there was a novelty in these proceedings and that they were out of the ordinary course of litigation. If so, that presumably differentiated this situation from one in which the Lords ordered a case to be brought for decision before themselves in formal proceedings in a manner consistent with the common law.

The provisions of the agreed course of action in this case are revealing because they show that apart from agreeing that the Lords may hear an action, it was felt necessary to show how this related to ordinary common law procedures and the jurisdictional rights of the judge ordinary. The upshot seems to have been that whilst the parties in question were to receive a decreet resolving their dispute, this was not to prevent other parties with some interest from resorting to conventional proceedings before the judge ordinary. Together, these instances show an apparently novel development in the type of dispute brought for decision before Council, a development which followed from the desire of the parties to have their dispute resolved in this way. Admittedly, these examples are small in number, and only reveal a small and incomplete amount of information about the disputes in question. Also, they occur during the period when the fee and heritage jurisdictional bar continued to

[93] NAS CS 5/16, fol. 46v. See NAS transcript p. 118.

be observed, remits to the judge ordinary continued to be made and exceptions because of heritage continued to be pleaded. However, they nonetheless illustrate something new in the type of dispute which can be found coming to Council, and anticipate features of the judicial activity of Council and Session at the time of the foundation of the College of Justice in 1532. These will be examined in the next chapter.

Conclusion on 1466–1532

The main purpose of this chapter has been to examine the workings of the fee and heritage restrictions on the jurisdiction of Council and Auditors, so as to produce a more detailed account of the elements which led an action to be characterised as one which should be remitted to the judge ordinary because of fee and heritage, and to ascertain any pattern in the making of jurisdictional challenges and consequential remits over the period 1466–1532. We have observed that there does seem to be some kind of pattern and that it suggests an increase in contested jurisdiction around 1500 and a decline in cases being remitted. It has also been argued that only certain kinds of heritage-related actions were barred by the fee and heritage rule. The elements of actions which were remitted seem to have been that the action depended upon a decision on an *incidental* matter of fee and heritage, that this matter involved more than one competing claim to a disputed title, backed up by showing lawful interest in the title, and that the decision would involve a final determination of right. Under this definition it remains possible to explain how Council was able to hear other actions which have a fee and heritage element. Such adjudication was on the basis that Council and Session could examine the intrinsic validity of title and reduce such titles when some cause of invalidity was shown such as fault in transfer or incidental legal process. Thus we can characterise the role of Council in fee and heritage matters as indirect and one of review. It was something like a supervisory jurisdiction, essentially looking at the legality of the way things had been done in constituting a particular title, rather than at matters of substance of the sort which might have arisen in resolving competing claims, and which would require further process in order to make new findings of fact of the sort traditionally instigated by the pleadable brieves.

There is still a question, though, whether the jurisdictional position governing fee and heritage was itself coherent once the King's Council had developed its judicial role by 1500. Did the apportionment of jurisdiction over heritage represent a stable way of integrating the different systems of remedies offered in the different forms of court or tribunal in late medieval Scotland? Afterall, the underlying function of the fee and heritage rule was to provide jurisdictional integration and preserve the integrity of different structures of remedy and procedure. It would seem likely that in many genuine fee and heritage cases the underlying issue causing the competing claims might be some previous invalid transfer or legal process. If that were so, there would seem to be the anomalous position that Council could generally determine such legal issues but not if they arose in the context of a fee and heritage action pitting competing titles against each other.

On the other hand there are many other reasons why a claim to fee and heritage might have been contested, for example because of dispute over whether a reversionary agreement had been fulfilled, or whether heirs had taken entry in previous generations, or whether the land had been recognosced and so on. However, in themselves these particular questions would also seem to be ones which Council could hear. In other words, again we see that the fee and heritage restriction did not relate to decisions which were restricted to the judge ordinary because of their substance, but rather because of the consequences of making such a decision in the context of the particular dispute which had come before Council. This was that at the instance of their adversary a party would be put out of what they claimed as their heritage. The restriction therefore seems to flow more from procedural rather than substantive legal considerations, relating as much to the law of remedies as to jurisdiction *per se*. Traditionally, the appropriate remedy for disputed heritable title could only be dispensed locally by pleadable brieve and inquest.

The argument may now be put that this understanding of the basis of the restriction holds the key to how the Session came to exercise a heritage jurisdiction after 1500. In 1513 any formal assertion of jurisdiction over heritage by the Lords was still more than 25 years ahead, but remitting to the judge ordinary because of heritage had ceased. The primary jurisdictional readjustment would therefore not seem to have happened through direct encroachment into the field traditionally given over to procedure by brieve and inquest before the local judge ordinary. It seems clear therefore that there was indeed "a subtext of jurisdictional readjustment" taking place in precisely these decades.[94] Since there does not seem to be an explicit arrogation to itself by the Session of jurisdiction over fee and heritage, the most likely way it acquired jurisdiction was therefore through the development of alternative remedies by which heritage disputes could be resolved—a development to be examined in depth in the next chapter.

The elaboration of a new heritage jurisdiction by the Session and its development into an exclusive one did not therefore begin in 1532 but simply began to be more explicit after 1532. This explanation of jurisdictional change suggests that the period before 1532 witnessed the crucial developments. That in turn opens up the possibility that the legislation of 1532 may not have been intended to effect a jurisdictional change, but rather was cast upon the assumption that the Session already possessed jurisdiction over fee and heritage. Whether or not any contemporary advocate or Lord of Session would have regarded the jurisdictional bar on fee and heritage as abrogated is hard to say, especially since it had certainly not been formally rescinded. Nevertheless, the development of new remedies through which any dispute over contested title could instead be handled may have achieved the same result, meaning that the statute of 1532 should be read literally as conferring jurisdiction in all civil matters on the judges of the College of Justice. Contemporaries may have understood the jurisdiction of the Session in 1532 to be a full civil one, without acknowledging explicitly the implications of that for the traditional rule barring the Lords from fee and heritage. To test this argument further requires examination of the main form of remedy which had always allowed Council to interfere with questions of title, as is certainly evident in the later fifteenth century. This was the remedy of reduction. Can the development of this remedy explain the desuetude of the fee and heritage limitation of the jurisdiction of the Session?

[94] Baker, *The Oxford History of the Laws of England*, p. 15.

CHAPTER SEVEN

THE JURISDICTION OF THE SESSION OVER FEE AND HERITAGE

Introduction

Having examined the nature of the jurisdictional bar on fee and heritage, its incidence, and the pattern of remits to the judge ordinary before 1532, we can now turn to assess the period around 1532 itself. A particular concern is the bearing which the foundation of the College of Justice had on jurisdictional change. It is the 1530s and the 1540s which previous study of jurisdiction over fee and heritage has concentrated upon. This has been for two reasons. Firstly, the decade or so after 1532 is quite obviously of interest because of the proximity of the date of the foundation of the College of Justice. Secondly, we find the citation in later sixteenth-century sources such as Balfour's *Practicks* of a small quantity of decisions from this time which address jurisdictional issues. These subsequently reported decisions have presented clues to historians about the effect of the legislation of 1532 on heritage jurisdiction. They have been thought by some to bear signs of a process of jurisdictional expansion by the Session. This process has been argued by Professor MacQueen to have led to a jurisdiction in heritage being established in consequence of the foundation of the College of Justice. The conclusions of the previous chapter provide a basis for reconsidering this view. This is important for establishing the significance of 1532 in the creation of a fully empowered central court. What form did jurisdictional "expansion" take, and did it occur before or after 1532? The central question in this regard is whether the College of Justice possessed jurisdiction over heritage at its inception, or came to acquire it for the first time at some point after 1532.

Whether or not a process of jurisdictional expansion occurred in the 1530s and 1540s, there certainly was an important change over the longer term. This amounted to a "jurisdictional shift", as David Sellar has put it.[1] The shift is clear from the fact that by some decades later

[1] W.D.H. Sellar, "The Common Law of Scotland and the Common Law of England", in *The British Isles 1100–1500*, ed. R.R. Davies (Edinburgh, 1988), pp. 83–99 at p. 94.

the heritage jurisdiction of the Session had become very categorically established. A contemporary account of 1560 portrayed the Lords of Session as "the last and supreme judges in this kingdom in civil matters", with "full cognizance in all civil causes".[2] It is hard not to see a reflection in that description of the terms of the legislation of 1532, covering "justice in all civile actiounis". The legislation had empowered judges of the new College to "decyde apone all actiouns civile". Significantly, the 1560 account emphasised the subordinate nature of local jurisdiction. It contrasted the position of the Session with the position of the sheriff. The latter was barred from heritage, *despite* being admitted in this account to be "judge ordinary in the county" ("iuge ordinaire du pays"). He had "jurisdiction and cognizance in all civil causes in the first instance, except matters concerning lands and heritages, as for claims for the same in which the said sheriff has no jurisdiction".[3] Evidently the fifteenth-century jurisdictional rules, and the procedure of remitting to the judge ordinary in heritage cases, had been abandoned. More strikingly still, the rules had been reversed so that *only* the Lords of Session could pronounce on questions of heritage by 1560. In contrast, as the previous chapter demonstrated, such questions were still being routinely remitted to the judge ordinary up until 1513.

We therefore see completely opposite jurisdictional positions in 1513 and 1560 in respect of heritage. This represented a revolution in relations between centre and locality. The principle of the medieval legal system which gave priority to local judicial process had been replaced by one which insisted on the pre-eminence of central justice. Though this was a longer term transition stretching back a hundred years to origins in the early fifteenth century, the substitution only finally materialised between 1513 and 1560. Between these two dates we also find lasting and significant institutional change which culminated in the foundation of the College of Justice. What connection might there have been between jurisdictional and institutional change, and how has this been previously explained? The relationship between the two types of change must have been in evidence across Europe more generally in the fifteenth and sixteenth centuries, given the new generation of central courts which were developing. The newly assertive courts had to find

[2] "Discours Particulier d'Escosse 1559/60", ed. P.G.B. McNeill in *Miscellany Two*, ed. W.D.H. Sellar, Stair Society 35 (Edinburgh, 1984), pp. 86–131 at p. 113.

[3] "Discours Particulier d'Escosse 1559/60", ed. McNeill, p. 109. The quotation is in Dr McNeill's translation.

an accomodation with the existing networks of jurisdiction. The Scottish example is a particularly relevant one because of the well-attested existence of the formal jurisdictional bar on the medieval Council. There was thus a distinct category of jurisdiction associated with local and never central justice in the medieval period. Lifting this bar so as to allow the Session to function fully as a central court meant rewriting the medieval common law rules. The exact process by which this development occurred has always seemed opaque. The only detailed analysis of the question in relation to the College of Justice is that of Professor MacQueen. We have already seen in previous chapters that along with Alan Borthwick and David Sellar, Professor MacQueen regarded the jurisdiction of the Session as still limited in 1532. He saw the period before this as essentially a static one in which the jurisdictional bar over fee and heritage cases continued to be applied with consistency. For this reason, the fifteen years or so following 1532 were the focus of MacQueen's account.

Professor MacQueen pointed to a number of sources cited in later juristic works which shed light on jurisdictional debate in the 1530s and 1540s. Using such evidence and searching for a *terminus ante quem* for the establishment of jurisdiction in heritage, Professor MacQueen noted that "later sixteenth-century writers cited cases of the 1540s as authorities for the proposition that the lords of session enjoyed what had become an exclusive jurisdiction in heritage".[4] These cases were *Wemyss v. Forbes* (1543) and *Caldwell v. Mason* (1545), cited by the later sixteenth-century jurists Sir John Skene and Sir James Balfour respectively.[5] Professor MacQueen examined these decisions against the background of several cases from the 1530s and argued that "both *Wemyss* and *Caldwell* seem...to be links in a chain of decisions by which the court established its 'practick' and, in a piecemeal, step-by-step way, the meaning of its jurisdiction in heritage", given that "the general jurisdiction in heritage...seems to have been accepted by the end of the 1530s".[6] The two cases were therefore taken to represent the application of an emerging general principle to particular situations brought before the

[4] H.L. MacQueen, *Common Law and Feudal Society in Medieval Scotland* (Edinburgh, 1993), p. 239.

[5] Discussed in H.L. MacQueen, "Jurisdiction in Heritage and the Lords of Council and Session after 1532", pp. 61–85, with transcriptions of the Council record of the cases, and the texts of Skene's and Balfour's accounts of them.

[6] MacQueen, *Common Law and Feudal Society in Medieval Scotland*, p. 241.

court. This reflected the new jurisdictional competence which the court had been coming to regard itself as possessing, and which was on this view cumulatively established by the late 1530s. Suggesting this model of jurisdictional change is buttressed by the view that the Lords did not have fee and heritage jurisdiction in 1532. Such a view is still implicit in Professor MacQueen's analysis, following his argument that in 1532 "it was still *arguable* that the Lords had no jurisdiction in such cases" (emphasis added).[7] It should be noted that the evidence certainly shows that this was sometimes argued. How *arguable* the point was is itself open to debate, however. Nevertheless, on this view the jurisdiction of the Lords over heritage was gradually and incrementally articulated and thereby "established" as cases involving heritage happened to arise.

On its own terms, Professor MacQueen's analysis is a highly plausible account of how the heritage jurisdiction of the Session might have been acquired. The suggestion of a process of establishing the practick of the court in piecemeal fashion after 1532 might also seem to fit well with the argument touched on at the beginning of the previous chapter. This suggested that there was a general process of establishing the meaning of the *authority* of the Session before and after 1532 through articulating its jurisdiction in the circumstances of particular cases. Its authority had to be given definition within the legal order, since it had moved from a supplementary role to exercising a superior central jurisdiction. The argument of this book, however, has been that such an articulation was not necessary in order to establish or *constitute* the Lords' jurisdiction after 1532 but merely to expressly *assimilate* the jurisdictional change which had already occurred up to 1532. Assimilation simply required the renewed assertion of jurisdiction by the Lords in the circumstances of those cases in which it was challenged or doubted. The unbounded nature of its authority was thus clarified. But the jurisdiction had already been assumed. There is no reason to imagine that such assimilation was not underway already before 1532. Indeed, this would be consistent with the argument of this book that the Session had already developed its substantive heritage jurisdiction before 1532. We have noted how the pleading of exceptions against the jurisdiction of the Session in fee and heritage seems to have revived in

[7] MacQueen, *Common Law and Feudal Society in Medieval Scotland*, p. 241. See also MacQueen, "Jurisdiction in Heritage and the Lords of Council and Session after 1532", p. 62 and H.L. MacQueen, "The Brieve of Right in Scots Law", *Journal of Legal History* 3 (1982), p. 66.

the late 1520s. Perhaps this was a sign of friction caused by a reaction to the extent of jurisdiction which the Session appeared to be exercising by this time. However, the main course of assimilation in articulating jurisdictional competence in the face of jurisdictional challenges seems to follow the foundation of the College of Justice.

These claims are supported by scrutiny of practice relating to heritage cases made possible by systematic examination of the manuscript record, and a rejection of the static model of how the jurisdictional bar operated. As we will see, the heritage jurisdiction of the Session had been developed through a wider use of the remedy of reduction. On this approach, Professor MacQueen's specific argument about how heritage jurisdiction developed becomes less convincing. The evidence cited by Professor MacQueen has been re-examined elsewhere, and it has been argued that, whatever else it suggests, it neither shows the Lords declining jurisdiction over heritage after 1532, nor explicitly expanding the technical extent of their heritage jurisdiction.[8] The principal basis for this view was that the evidence in question related largely to actions for the reduction of infeftments. The Lords possessed an established jurisdiction to reduce infeftments which is evident in the late fifteenth-century records. We have noted this in examining cases arising from summonses of error. Deciding such matters was therefore not innovatory in 1532 or thereafter, given the conclusions of the previous chapter. The exercise of such a jurisdiction could therefore not in itself be equated with the exercise of the previously forbidden form of jurisdiction over fee and heritage. And yet it permitted the Lords to decide questions of heritage as long as they were approached in terms of the established remedy of reduction.

Thus the evidence from the 1530s and early 1540s had little significance in terms of jurisdictional *expansion*. However, there was a novel feature which followed from and supplemented assimilation of the heritage jurisdiction established before 1532. This was the assertion of *exclusive* jurisdiction over certain actions, such as claims to the feudal casualty of non-entry, long leases and, most importantly for understanding heritage jurisdiction, the reduction of infeftments. None of this evidence, however, provides a commentary directly upon

[8] A.M. Godfrey, "Jurisdiction in Heritage and the Foundation of the College of Justice in 1532", in *Miscellany Four*, ed. H.L. MacQueen, Stair Society 49 (Edinburgh, 2002), pp. 9–36.

the old jurisdictional restriction over fee and heritage. Its status by the 1530s is opaque. It was seemingly no longer observed by 1532 and must have been hard to rationalise in terms of the remedies through which heritage disputes before the Session were being approached. It therefore seems to have simply withered into desuetude. In that respect, the cases considered by Professor MacQueen were not concerned with establishing jurisdiction by way of making technical inroads into the old fee and heritage restriction. This restriction had already ceased to be applied long before 1532. These cases of the 1530s and 1540s are best seen as traces of a fresh development which saw the Session coming to be regarded as the most appropriate forum to decide *all* legal issues relating to heritage. This would have been utterly foreign to the medieval legal system. It represented a fundamental change of emphasis, even though some forms of local judicial process would still have remained necessary after 1532 for determining certain questions of fact in relation to heritage. The novel step after 1532 was heritage-related cases being defined by the Lords as exclusively within their jurisdiction. Reduction of an infeftment and thereby a heritable title would be the pre-eminent example.

The argument is therefore that not only did the Session possess jurisdiction over heritage by 1532, but that it also began to stop heritage disputes being resolved in any other forum from 1532 onwards. Part of this development involved decisions upon such actions which affected heritage coming to be regarded *by litigants* as particularly appropriate to the Session. The overall argument of this book is therefore that heritage was beginning to be accorded special importance by the Session in the 1530s, though there was no direct expansion of the scope of jurisdiction of the Lords following 1532. Direct expansion was not necessary because, in effect, a heritage jurisdiction was already being exercised by the Lords before 1532. The 1530s and 1540s simply witnessed increasing assimilation of this position, intensified by the institutional authority gained by reconstitution of the Session as the College of Justice. The jurisdictional bar over fee and heritage had developed in the fifteenth century to provide procedural and jurisdictional integrity between the older jurisdictions of the common law and the supplementary role of the central tribunals. By 1532 the Session had long since ceased to exercise a merely supplementary role. It was at the centre of the common law. Whilst the pleadable brieves appear to have fallen into disuse, the Session had come to decide upon heritage through the remedy of reduction. By 1532 the jurisdictional bar had not been applied for a generation and it is hard to see how it could have still been considered intelligible. It is certainly hard to see how it could have been regarded as *applicable* to the jurisdiction of the Lords over reduction of infeftments.

The means by which the new heritage jurisdiction of the Session was accomplished seems to have been twofold. The first was the ever greater use of the remedy of reduction. The second was the structuring of heritage disputes directly around questioning the validity of a particular title. Both involved the manner in which litigants chose to characterise their disputes. In effect, the conceptual legal framework for understanding the nature of a dispute over title seems to have been recast into a remedial form which made it competent to be brought before the Lords. That still left open the technical issue of whether the jurisdiction of the Lords over fee and heritage was still considered to be restricted in the old way. But in a sense the functional basis for requiring such a jurisdictional bar had dissolved as a result of the Session moving towards becoming a central court instead of a supplementary tribunal. Not only the jurisdictional bar, but also the very framework within which it made sense, had been superseded.

This may explain why the Lords never seem to have directly declared themselves to have acquired a general jurisdiction in heritage. The old jurisdictional bar did not need to be abrogated in this way. It had simply been overtaken by the more general application of remedies which the Session had always been able to dispense. When the Lords repelled jurisdictional challenges after 1532 they were as much defending their traditional jurisdiction as asserting a new one. They preferred to articulate their competence in relation to particular forms of action, as and when challenges arose, rather than in relation to the general categories of abstract rights which underlay such actions. I have argued elsewhere that neither of the cases from 1543 and 1545 discussed by Professor MacQueen (*Wemyss v. Forbes* and *Caldwell v. Mason*) reveal an assertion of direct jurisdiction over heritage.[9] However, another case from 1540 does at least seem to pre-suppose such jurisdiction to exist, and already to be exclusive to the Session. This was the case of *Cameron of Lochiel v. Maclean* in 1540 which was noted by John Sinclair, Lord

[9] Godfrey, "Jurisdiction in Heritage and the Foundation of the College of Justice in 1532".

of Session, in his "Practicks".[10] There Sinclair stated that "according to the custom of Scotland he [the sheriff] can only cognosce concerning possession, and the cognition of lordship and property [*cognitio dominii et proprietatis*] belongs to the lords of council [*ad dominos consilii pertinet*]".[11] Further confirmation of the shape of these developments would require a search of the manuscript register from the second half of the 1530s onwards, but this awaits further research. Nevertheless the outlines seem clear.

The purpose of this chapter is to consider in more depth the immediate period to either side of the foundation of the College of Justice in 1532. There will be discussion of evidence from a five year period between 1529 and 1534. This will examine exceptions pleaded to the jurisdiction of the Lords because of fee and heritage,[12] and the implications of the absence of any remits to the judge ordinary. This will allow in turn an assessment of any signs that the attitude of the Lords to their jurisdiction had changed by comparison with the period before 1513. In the previous chapter we saw that 1513 seemed to mark the point beyond which the practice of remitting to the judge ordinary because of fee and heritage ceased, though it is not clear why this was so.

Analysis will also be made of actions raised for the reduction of an infeftment in order to assess the role of such actions in resolving heritage disputes, again by comparison with the earlier period. A particular aim will be to test the hypothesis that by the 1530s a party who sought redress in a dispute concerning heritage was likely to attack his opponent's alleged title directly through having his or her infeftment reduced by the Lords of Session. This would contrast with the nature of later fifteenth-century litigation when court actions and the structure of remedies more frequently produced disputes turning on *competing* titles which then had to be referred to the judge ordinary. It seems likely on this hypothesis that a party would have been able to circumvent the old jurisdictional restriction on fee and heritage through arguing for the reduction of an infeftment as a means to clarify contested title. It

[10] I am greatly indebted to Dr Athol Murray, who first drew my attention to this case.

[11] Edinburgh University Library, Laing MS III 388a, c. 16 (Ewan Alenson (Cameron of Locheil) v. John Maclean of Coll), discussed in Godfrey, "Jurisdiction in Heritage and the Foundation of the College of Justice in 1532", pp. 32–33; a provisional text of Sinclair's Practicks prepared by Dr Athol Murray is available at http://www.stairsociety.org/sinclair.pdf.

[12] See appendix 3.

is worth noting at this point that it would still have been unlikely that every dispute relating to heritable title could have been resolved in such a simple manner through actions to reduce infeftments. This may be one reason why, by the 1530s, we can find some complex disputes over land being brought before the Lords by extraordinary consent-based procedures or submitted to them as arbiters. The procedure of advocation was examined in chapter 5, whilst the role of the Lords as arbiters and related matters will be examined in the final two chapters of the book.

Remits to the Judge Ordinary and Declinatory Exceptions around 1532

As we have seen, perhaps the most striking feature of the record of Council decisions between 1513 and 1532 is that not a single action was remitted to the judge ordinary because of fee and heritage. The evidence surveyed in this chapter will concentrate upon the period immediately around 1532. It will be shown that the absence of such remits persisted after 1532, none being apparent in the two years for which the record has been comprehensively examined between May 1532 and May 1534. As we have seen in the last chapter, this was despite a mild revival in the late 1520s of the practice of pleading exceptions to jurisdiction because of fee and heritage. By comparison, up to 1513 there were only very occasional years in which no cases were remitted because of fee and heritage. Between 1500 and 1513 there were just two years in which no remit was made at all.[13] The longest continuous period between 1490 and 1513 without a remit was from November 1495 to April 1498, amounting to roughly two and a half years.[14] By 1532 the equivalent period had lasted for some nineteen years.

Thus, insofar as we can judge from the state of the records, they demonstrate that until the first decade or so of the sixteenth century it was not out of the ordinary for Council hearings to proceed for one or two years without any cases being remitted to the judge ordinary. However, the period of more than twenty years after 1513 in which

---

[13] I.e. 1504 and 1510.

[14] *Acts of the Lords of Council in Civil Causes*, ed. T. Thomson (Edinburgh, 1839), p. 429 [hereafter *ADC* i]; *Acts of the Lords of Council in Civil Causes 1496–1501*, ed. G. Neilson and H.M. Paton (Edinburgh, 1918), p. 175 [hereafter *ADC* ii].

not one case was remitted in this fashion was completely without precedent. It can be clearly recognised that after 1513 the Lords, as a matter of fact, no longer remitted cases on these grounds. It is more difficult to ascertain why this was so. More difficult still is to ascertain at what point remitting on those grounds ceased to be considered competent. One possible inference is that by 1532 the Lords had ceased to recognise any jurisdictional obligation to remit cases of this sort to the judge ordinary. Other evidence of the generally assertive attitude they displayed to the nature of their jurisdiction at this time might support this claim. If by 1540 express recognition had arrived or was not far off that the Lords could decide upon heritage *generally*, then it seems inherently unlikely that they could have been persuaded to remit such a case for lack of jurisdiction in the 1530s, when no similar case had occurred during the preceding twenty years or more. It would make sense to regard the remitting procedure for fee and heritage cases as therefore having fallen into desuetude before 1532. Litigants occasionally still attempted to invoke the procedure in order to argue that the Lords were not competent judges, but what is striking is that by 1532 such arguments were never successful. Indeed it seems that beyond 1513 they were never successful. Against this background, as already suggested, the very rationale of the jurisdictional bar over fee and heritage could hardly have seemed intelligible by 1532. The structure of remedies provided in the legal order had already mutated sufficiently to obscure its former basis.

This development amounted to a notable reversal of the situation which existed up until the early 1490s, when all such exceptions which we know about were successful, though of course there is no way of knowing whether unsuccessful exceptions pleaded before that time were simply not recorded. The first recorded pleading of an unsuccessful exception before Council came in 1493.[15] Simply taking the first forty years for which records survive as representative of the fifteenth-century position, we saw in the previous chapter that in the period up to 1506 about half of the cases of contested fee and heritage jurisdiction were remitted to the judge ordinary.[16] Over the first five or six years of the

[15] *ADC* i, p. 263.

[16] The record has been published to 1503, and the transcriptions in the National Archives of Scotland continue until March 1506/07. The problems of assessing the period 1466–1506 are therefore slightly less overwhelming than for the period thereafter, for which the record must be consulted in its original manuscript form.

1500s the proportion remitted had fallen and was less than 20 per cent. So a highly significant change is evident in the period between 1513 and 1534 (and beyond, we may assume), during which no case was remitted at all. As these figures also make clear, the pleading of such exceptions in the first place was far less common by 1532, especially when compared with the early years of the sixteenth century. Including those which resulted in a remit to the judge ordinary, in each year from 1500 to 1505 there were anything up to fifteen exceptions pleaded to fee and heritage actions. By comparison, in each calendar year between May 1529 and May 1534 there were usually one or two and at most four exceptions of this sort.

There is also a qualitative difference to be discerned between the most common types of case which were remitted in the late fifteenth century and those which parties attempted to have remitted around 1532. The actions from the earlier period up to 1506 most often related to wrongous occupation or spuilzie (i.e. dispossession), with fourteen or fifteen examples of each over the forty-year period. The other actions which constituted a sizeable proportion of the remit cases were for error and payment of annualrent, with nine or ten examples of each.[17] However, there were also other types of action which were occasionally remitted. These concerned wrongfully withholding charters, payment of thirl multures, casting of peat in a moss (i.e. the digging up of peat from a peat bog), and on one occasion the reduction of the resignation of the heritable fee of lands. By contrast, in ten out of the eleven exceptions pleaded in the 1529–1534 sample and for which the cause of action is clear, all related to an action for the reduction of an infeftment, and not to the traditional categories of action which featured in the later fifteenth century. The eleventh case is not explicitly revealed as a reduction of infeftment case, but concerned a "biggin" (i.e. building) in a borough which was in point of "tynsell" (i.e. forfeiture). This sounds like an action for apprising (i.e. attachment or judicially sanctioned seizure of property in realisation of a debt), but conceivably could have involved the reduction of an infeftment as well.[18]

The sample around 1532 shows a continuation of the pre-1532 pattern of rejecting fee and heritage exceptions, which still continued to arise in small numbers. This was despite the slight revival in the late

---

[17] See appendix 1 for a list of all the cases of contested jurisdiction up to 1513.

[18] *Adam Hoppar v. Janet Turing & William Adamson*, CS 5/40, fol. 74v.

1520s of attempts to get the Lords to decline jurisdiction on grounds of heritage. We may conclude that the old jurisdictional restriction upon the Lords could not yet have been considered formally abandoned. Neither was the legislation of 1532 regarded as abolishing it. Otherwise it would presumably have been futile for parties to plead a fee and heritage exception at all. On the other hand, this does not mean there was an intelligible basis for declining jurisdiction in the cases in question. The pleading of the fee and heritage restriction only made sense in the context of competing claims to title, as well as the availability of local judicial process by pleadable brieve before an inquest. The remedy of reduction was technically outwith its scope. If it was realised amongst procurators that there had been no remit because of fee and heritage since 1513, then arguing for jurisdiction to be declined must also have seemed close to being futile. All we can be certain about is that exceptions were pleaded, were rejected, and that no remits for fee and heritage were made. Though this seems to have been the position since 1513, other developments had in the meantime also intervened. The Session itself had developed as an institution compared to 1513, especially through the foundation of the College of Justice. The Session was by 1532 as busy as ever, and possessed as strong an institutional identity as ever before, to the extent that it was declaring or assuming itself to be the *only* competent forum to hear certain kinds of action. It was in November 1532, for example, that the Lords considered their jurisdiction over nineteen-year tacks (leases), stating that such actions *required* to be pursued before them and that this had been the "consuetude" in "tymes bipast".[19] With a field of jurisdiction over heritage developed since 1513 through actions to reduce infeftments, and jurisdiction over "all civile actiounis" under the legislation of 1532, the post-1532 period was able to witness consolidation and assimilation of the established jurisdictional competence of the Session.

It should be noted that the development or assertion of exclusive jurisdiction was mainly in relation to actions concerning land. The 1530s show such claims made by the Session over rights arising from the feudal casualty of non-entry as well as long leases, and the 1540s show assertion of exclusive jurisdiction over the reduction of infeft-

[19] Edinburgh, National Archives of Scotland [hereafter NAS], CS 6/2, fol. 5v.; see Godfrey, "Jurisdiction in Heritage and the Foundation of the College of Justice in 1532", p. 34.

ments. In making these claims the Lords were not staking out new areas of jurisdiction but were removing the right of other courts to hear certain actions, primarily when interests in land were at stake. This is nevertheless noteworthy, since it shows the Lords of Session taking an initiative in defining their jurisdiction in a way which cannot simply be regarded as responding to the needs of litigants. In fact, it seems a sign of self-consciousness on the part of the court that it started placing constraints upon the jurisdiction of other courts in relation to general categories of action. It seems extremely unlikely that in the face of this development the old restriction on fee and heritage could have carried on being recognised by the Lords. Developing an exclusive jurisdiction over subsidiary and dependent interests in land hardly seems compatible with a prohibition from determining the ultimate interests on which they depended, i.e. heritable title. Of course, we know that in fact the prohibition was not maintained, and the real question is how the transition occurred whereby the restriction was first rendered irrelevant and then finally abandoned. The fact that virtually all of the fee and heritage exceptions pleaded between 1529 and 1534 arose in the context of reduction of infeftment actions is significant in this context. It would seem to support the suggestion made above that such actions had become an important means and perhaps the primary means of settling disputes over heritage. The nature of the reduction cases in which exceptions against jurisdiction were pleaded must therefore be examined.

In most of the eleven cases of fee and heritage exceptions being pleaded in our 1529–1534 sample, the allegation was simply that the Lords were not competent judges in the action, although in one it was specifically that "thai suld be na jugis in ground rycht".[20] That the idea (if not the practice) of remitting to the judge ordinary still had some currency with pleaders is specifically brought out in one case, in which the Lords "decernis that thai ar competent jugis to the said mater as it comes befor thaime nochtwithstanding that it is allegit that the samyn concernis the heritage and suld be decydit befor the juge ordinar".[21] Even this merely provides evidence of a plea being put forward, and does not disclose the attitude of the Lords towards whether there could

[20] NAS CS 5/42, fol. 119r. (15 March 1531).
[21] NAS CS 5/41, fol. 4. (12th March 1530).

still have been cases which, under other circumstances, ought to have been remitted.

In more than half the 1529–1534 sample, some kind of reason was offered why the Lords were not competent judges. In August 1529, for example, John Crichton of Strathurd's forespeaker alleged that the Lords were not competent judges to a summons "raisit at the instance of the kingis grace for the nonentres of the landis of Tulibody", to which the Lords responded that they were competent judges, "nochtwithstanding the allegeance maid...that the said mater concerns the fee and heretage of the saidis landis".[22] The action here was characterised as one concerning non-entries, and establishing a right to this casualty was undoubtedly the ultimate goal of the action. The means by which this was to be achieved was through the reduction of an infeftment. The threat that this constituted to John Crichton's heritage must have been why he sought to contest jurisdiction. We can see, however, that it was not a fee and heritage action in the technical sense, because there were no competing titles. The action merely "touched" heritage. However, John Crichton stood to lose his title, which depended upon that of Ninian Seton of Tullibody. Ninian's infeftment would be invalidated by the reduction of the resignation and infeftment of his ancestor, Alexander Seton. Since the *de facto* result of the King's action would be the loss of Crichton's title, it is readily apparent why he tried to argue tactically that it was a fee and heritage action. This would have allowed him to defeat the claim before the Session without the validity of his title ever being examined. However, as an action for the reduction of an infeftment it was unambiguously within the jurisdiction of the Lords.

In most other cases the reason given for the pleading of the exception was simply that the action "concernit fee and heritage".[23] However, in two cases the allegation was specifically made that it was because it was a reduction of infeftment action that the Lords might not hear it. In February 1531, for example, the plea was made against a summons by Finlay Spittal's procurator that the Lords were not competent judges "because the same was for reducing of ane infeftment".[24] In November 1532 the procurator of one of the tutors of Melchior Cullen, defending an action raised by Margaret Inglis, alleged that the Lords were

[22] NAS CS 5/40, fol. 81v.
[23] NAS CS 5/42, fol. 40.
[24] NAS CS 5/42, fol. 46v.

not competent judges "becaus the said action concernit the retreting of ane infeftment and sua the rycht of hes heretage".[25] Thus in at least one case the argument was explicitly mounted that a reduction of infeftment case was a fee and heritage action because it concerned the "rycht" of the defender's heritage. Of course, the point of a reduction of infeftment action was not that the pursuer had a greater "rycht" to the lands to which the infeftment related, but that the defender's "rycht" was in itself a nullity and could not provide the basis for a claim to the lands. Consistent with the argument of this book, the Lords rejected the exceptions in these cases.

It is telling, perhaps, that the terms used by the Lords in asserting their right to hear this last case were narrowly reflective of the particular grounds as pleaded by the pursuer to justify the reduction. There was no general statement that by their "practick" all such cases were customarily heard before them. In the *Spittal* case, for example, the Lords declared that "thai war competent juges in the said mater becaus the said infeftment was gevin be circumventioun".[26] In the *Inglis v. Cullen* case the Lords decerned that "thai mycht proceid apon the sumondis...becaus the mater wes intendit agains the said Melchiores fadir and dependand be summondes the tym of hes decess".[27] It is hard to know how to interpret such abbreviated explanations, especially since the record was made up by a clerk and not a Lord of Session. In the *Spittal* case, for example, circumvention was clearly going to be the main ground for reduction, but does the way in which the record expressed the decision imply that jurisdiction in such an action was potentially open to question? Could it be that only some types of reduction of infeftment actions, pleaded on particular grounds such as circumvention, necessarily fell within the Lords' jurisdiction? Or was the mention of circumvention simply a means of incorporating into the ruling on jurisdiction a statement of the reason why there was a *prima facie* case for reduction? It is difficult to answer these questions, given the terse nature of the procedural record. The mode of expression in recording such decisions is not free of ambiguity in the 1530s. There is a tendency towards a highly casuistic approach in which reasoning is expressed narrowly in terms of particulars arising from the case rather

[25] NAS CS 5/43, fol. 92v.
[26] NAS CS 5/42, fol. 46v.
[27] NAS CS 5/42, fol. 93.

than deductively in terms of wider categories of abstract rights. Nevertheless, the range of reduction cases decided by the Session makes it hard to imagine any coherent basis for declining jurisdiction in some types of reduction action but not in others. Moreover, the fact is that in our sample period there is not a single case of it being declined.

In what terms did the Lords assert their jurisdiction in the nine other cases? In *Adam Hopper v. Janet Turing and William Adamson* we do not even have a record of a sentence interlocutor by the Lords.[28] In *The King v. John Crichton & Ninian Seton* a simple assertion of jurisdictional competence was not elaborated upon.[29] In *Janet Rowit v. Alison Ruche* we find the apparently more limited statement that they are competent judges to the said matter "as it comes befor thaime".[30] In *Alexander Innes v. Alexander Ogilvy* the Lords stated that "thai ar competent juges anent the sumondis aboune writtin as it is libellit and causis contenit thirintill libellit apounis falsat".[31] In *Alexander Innes v. Lord Oliphant* there was an allegation that the Lords were not competent judges but this does not seem to have been treated as an exception since no sentence interlocutor was recorded. In the case of *Helen Rutherford v. Mark Kerr* the Lords seem to make another qualified assertion by decerning themselves competent judges "becaus the said Mark bound himself be his obligatioun [to Helen]...geif he failzeit therein the bonde to turn to the said Helene".[32] In *Wigtown v. Whithorn* nothing was said beyond stating that the Lords were competent judges notwithstanding the exception.[33] The same was true of *Thomas Duddingston v. Steven Duddingston*.[34] Finally, in *The King and Prebendaries of Crieff v. William Drummond* the allegation was made that the Lords were not competent judges, but the action was continued, so it would seem that procedurally the exception had not yet been formally pleaded. The action had not yet been called again by 5 May, to which date it had been continued.

In these cases we do not meet with blanket assertions of jurisdiction. As noted above, when explanatory reasoning is given or hinted at, it tends to rely upon particular features of the action rather than identifying the action as within a general class of actions which the

[28] NAS CS 5/40, fol. 74r.
[29] NAS CS 5/40, fol. 81v.
[30] NAS CS 5/41, fol. 4.
[31] NAS CS 5/42, fol. 40.
[32] NAS CS 5/42, fol. 119r.
[33] NAS CS 6/2, fol. 19r.
[34] NAS CS 6/2, fol. 219.

Lords will hear, such as "reduction of infeftments". Significantly, this was not the case by the time of *Caldwell v. Mason* in 1545, when we find more explicitly deductive and categorical reasoning of the sort already noted in relation to jurisdiction over nineteen-year leases in 1532. In *Caldwell* the Lords asserted that "thai ar in use to tak the decisioun of all actiounis of retretting of infeftmentis, evidentis or seisingis to thame selfis".[35] On the other hand, in relation to the early 1530s, the stress on the particular circumstances of contested cases to explain jurisdiction does not equate to implicitly acknowledging limitations in competence. In several cases no reasoning at all was given and the record merely reveals that the Lords considered themselves competent judges to those cases in the most general terms. The assertions of jurisdiction by the Lords throughout the 1530s and 1540s were therefore likely to have been premised upon a common view of unlimited jurisdiction which pre-dated 1532. The difference between 1532 and 1545 lies in how assertions of jurisdictional competence were expressed in relation to the controversial field of heritage. There seems to have been a tendency towards an increasingly categorical mode of expression by the Session in declaring its jurisdictional competence after 1532. It seems likely that this was just part of the more general process we have identified of the Session establishing the meaning of its authority through articulating its jurisdiction in particular cases, especially after 1532. But this was simply about giving expression to jurisdiction which the Lords both possessed and exercised already.

We should also remember that there is no way of knowing to what extent the record can be relied upon to reveal with any precision what the Lords thought or said in court when reaching their decisions, or even whether they took a direct interest in formulating the way their decisions were expressed in the register. It is therefore all but impossible to evaluate the subjective attitude of the Lords to their jurisdiction over heritage in 1532 and to the old limitations upon it, by comparison with the attitude of the Lords of Council and Session in the later fifteenth century. We can only proceed by cautious inference from the formal record of their decisions. It is possible that in formal terms they might still have recognised that their jurisdiction was theoretically limited. The old jurisdictional bar had never been specifically abrogated and

[35] MacQueen, "Jurisdiction in Heritage and the Lords of Council and Session after 1532", p. 81.

the pleading of fee and heritage exceptions still continued. However, the fact that no cases were remitted to the judge ordinary and that the exceptions almost all related to the reduction of infeftments seems to bear out the suggestion that the circumstances which triggered the proper application of the jurisdictional bar were considered no longer to arise in practice. A kind of surface-level jurisdictional impasse had been reached, whereby the jurisdictional restriction remained technically in place but had no further application, since as a matter of practice there seemed no longer to be circumstances in which the restriction would be held to apply. The remedy of reduction had unlocked the jurisdiction of the Session over heritage. This formed the "subtext of jurisdictional readjustment" (in Baker's apt phrase) which renders explicable the otherwise apparently contradictory pleas, arguments and rulings of the 1530s.[36] A new structuring of remedies was in place in the legal order but the implications of this for jurisdiction took time to be given expression.

The structure of jurisdiction had changed by 1532 in relation to the remedies offered by the Session. If the correct remedy was sought in a heritage dispute then its jurisdiction could not be excluded even though title was in issue. This was perfectly consistent with the original basis of the fee and heritage rule, which was that Council's jurisdiction was limited out of respect for the established procedures and remedies of the common law. By 1532 Council had developed alternative remedies but these were alternatives and not direct substitutes for those which the common law had provided. The impasse was symbolised by the paradox that virtually all attempts to make the Lords decline jurisdiction over heritage from 1529 to 1534 were in cases which happened to relate to reduction of infeftments—a category of action traditionally taken before Council, and which within a further decade was held to pertain exclusively to the Lords' jurisdiction. It must be significant that this was also the period in which, as we have noted, a judicial "activism" was apparent in the development of a number of exclusive jurisdictions by the Lords of Session. Nevertheless, by 1529–34 the exercise of the Session's jurisdiction over reduction of infeftments seems to have experienced development in its own right when compared with

[36] J.H. Baker, *The Oxford History of the Laws of England, Volume VI, 1483–1558* (Oxford, 2003), p. 15.

the early years of the sixteenth century, and this development will now be assessed.

Actions for the reduction of infeftments

The late fifteenth-century record does not suggest that reduction of infeftments was an especially important class of action in proceedings before Council at that time. It was certainly not a common one in its own right. Council's main business in reducing infeftments occurred in the course of deciding upon summonses of error. In error cases, a disgruntled third party challenged the procedure which had conferred title to land onto an heir. The retour of an inquest serving the heir to the property would be declared invalid so that the ensuing infeftment of the putative heir would also be rendered invalid. In terms of remedies, the retour and all subsequent steps in the conveyance and infeftment would fall to be reduced. In the remainder of this chapter the scope of the remedy of reduction by 1532 will be surveyed. Decisions involving the reduction of an infeftment by the Session between 1529 and 1534 will be examined, in order to assess whether such actions had become more common and what underlying characteristics they shared. The significance of these cases will be assessed, particularly in relation to the traditional jurisdictional restriction over fee and heritage actions. The grounds upon which reduction actions proceeded will be described in order to analyse the width of application of such grounds, and a comparison made with the later fifteenth-century evidence. Finally, the extent to which such actions could be used as a means to resolve disputes over heritage without contravening the traditional jurisdictional restrictions will be assessed.

It has already been noted that actions for the reduction of infeftments *per se* were relatively uncommon in the later fifteenth century. By comparison, a sizeable number of such actions was raised in the period covered by our sample. Between May 1529 and May 1534 there were thirty-six reduction of infeftment actions in total.[37] The distribution of such actions over the five years was relatively even, with typically as many as seven a year. Actions for error are not included in these figures, but only those non-error actions where the principal determination

[37] These are individually described and analysed below.

sought was the reduction of an infeftment. In error actions the focus was on the deliberations of the inquest and the procedures surrounding these, and it was the decision of the inquest rather than a flaw in the transfer of the land or the intrinsic validity of the title which was being attacked. Error actions thus resulted in reduction, but only on these specific grounds to do with a failure of legal process. Moreover, error formed a distinct category of action which was as prevalent in the fifteenth century as the sixteenth, and so it seems potentially misleading to include such actions in a survey seeking to establish the degree of change which may have occurred during this period as a whole. The significant development in this regard was the increasing emergence of reduction as a remedial category of action in its own right. This opened the way to define invalidity in a title as a separate cause of action, and this in turn provided the substantive framework for the heritage jurisdiction of the Session.

Although reduction of infeftment actions from 1529 to 1534 were not very numerous in comparison with the probable numbers of some other actions such as spuilzie or wrongous occupation, it would be wrong to infer from this that it was an unimportant type of action. The number of disputes which related to heritable title was never large when compared with disputes which could be resolved through a possessory action. Only some land disputes turned on deeper issues of contested title. This was to some extent evident in the previous chapter, in that the number of cases remitted to the judge ordinary in any given year up to 1513 was relatively small, although this is obviously in part because actions to resolve heritage disputes directly should not have been raised before Council in the first place at that time. Accepting, though, that the number of reduction of infeftment actions could be expected to be quite low, what becomes significant about the years 1529–1534 is that in relative terms there would seem to have been an increase in the frequency and regularity of such cases, compared to the later fifteenth century. If the Session sat for about one hundred days a year between 1529 and 1534, we can see that there were enough reduction of infeftment actions for one to be called every third week or so on average. In the early years of the century such actions are not easily traceable at all, let alone in any quantity. By 1529 they formed a small but regular part of Council's judicial business. It was a remedy which was by that time regularly sought from the Lords and, as discussed above, within a decade they were declaring that it was a remedy which only they could dispense. The nature of such cases from 1529 to 1534 will now be examined, and the particular grounds of reduction pleaded before the Session will be described. The greater importance of such actions by 1529–1534 seems likely to have been because they provided a competent procedure and remedy through which heritage disputes could be resolved by the Session without breaching directly the old jurisdictional limitations. How the evidence of reduction actions supports this view will also be assessed.

Grounds of reduction

Cases from the later fifteenth century have already been cited to illustrate grounds which were pleaded for the reduction of infeftments in that period (whether in error proceedings or not). They included procedural faults in the serving of brieves and the making of retours; infeftment of a third party to defraud a creditor; mistaken inclusion of extraneous lands in an instrument of sasine by a notary; incorrect findings by inquests about who had died last vested and seised of the fee of lands or about the correct valuation of or tenure under which lands were held. Given the greater number of such cases between 1529 and 1534 it is perhaps to be expected that a wider range of such grounds would be in evidence, and this is the case. The presence of a wide range of grounds, as well as greater numbers of such cases, also implies that reduction of an infeftment was not a narrowly applied action or one which could only be used in limited situations. Instead it had become by the 1530s a broadly framed remedy which could be used across a whole spectrum of disputes over title in order to resolve contested claims. Of the thirty-six cases there are nine in which no grounds were stated in the record, but from the remaining twenty-seven it is possible to chart at least fourteen distinguishable grounds of action used in requesting this remedy. They provide a taxonomy of invalidity as a cause of action in relation to title to property. The individual grounds fall roughly into one of four general categories, each exemplifying a common basis.

The two main categories relate to situations where a person was infeft in lands invalidly, either because his claim to receive infeftment was without right, or because the granter of the title had been himself without right to make infeftment. A third category relates to the fraudulent infeftment of a third party with intent to frustrate a future rightful claim to the lands in question. There is also a fourth category in which the infeftment was said to be invalidated by the failure of the new holder to perform a previously specified obligation in return. Together these grounds of action, when put alongside the customary grounds used in error actions, seem to have encompassed the full range of situations in which an infeftment might have been invalid or somehow vitiated. Therefore, the variety of grounds evident between 1529 and 1534 shows that the theoretical competence to reduce infeftments which Council had always possessed was now being very widely applied by the Session to a much greater extent than in the later fifteenth century.

Before considering the individual grounds of action exemplified in these cases, the nature of the nine cases in which no grounds are recorded will be discussed. In *The King v. Alexander, Lord Livingstone* in May 1529, nothing was revealed about the nature of the action at all beyond the fact that it was for the reduction of an instrument of sasine.[38] In *Thomas Duddingston v. Steven Duddingston* in July 1533 all that was revealed was that it was for reduction of an infeftment of 1524.[39] Of the other cases, two concerned non-entry, in which the pursuer's claim for the casualty of non-entry for certain lands was met with the production by the defender of an instrument purporting to prove that sasine of the lands had been taken.[40] This meant that the conveyance of the land had been completed through feudal investiture in the property, and presumably that the feudal casualties had been paid. Two other actions were simply for the reduction of charters or resignations and the subsequent infeftments.[41] Another two further cases related specifically to infeftments in annualrents.[42] Finally, there was the case of *George, Earl of Rothes v. Robert Lumsden* in July 1533 in which the earl apparently wished to reduce the infeftment of his vassal Robert Lumsden. However, the Lords declared that the summons was "generale" and that "ane speciale decrete couth not be gevin thirupon".[43] The earl's procurator then intimated that the earl would require Robert to come in person the following morning to exhibit to him, as his overlord, his

[38] NAS CS 5/40, fol. 20.

[39] NAS CS 6/2, fol. 219.

[40] *James Kennedy v. John Mure* (10 Feb., 1531), NAS CS 5/42, fol. 45r. *The King v. Janet and Marion Cathcart* (21 June, 1532), NAS CS 6/1, fol. 36v.

[41] *The King and Sir John Paterson and James Gordon, prebendaries of Crieff and canons of the Chapel Royal at Stirling v. William Drummond* (13 March, 1534), NAS CS 6/4, fol. 65v. *John Fiff v. George Heukers* (18 March, 1534), NAS CS 6/4, fol. 93v.

[42] *Robert Berton and Thomas Erskin, Secretary v. Sir John Carmano and George Bishop of Dunkeld* (19 July, 1533), NAS CS 6/3, fol. 31v. *John Gledstanis v. Andro Douglas* (7 May, 1534), NAS CS 6/4, fol. 126v.

[43] NAS CS 6/3, fol. 18v.

"auld" infeftment and receive from him a new infeftment "conforme to his auld infeftment", protesting otherwise for the non-entry of the lands. Unfortunately, the grounds for reduction were never stated and Robert failed to compear the next day.[44] The remaining cases, however, all reveal something of the specific grounds of reduction and will now be assessed.

Particular grounds for reduction

Invalidity due to infeftment without right in the granter

There are seven distinguishable types of ground in this category. The first ground to be discussed is exemplified in three cases where the granter of a heritable fee was in fact merely the holder of the frank-tenement (i.e. freehold) or the conjunct fee in the land (i.e. the fee was jointly held between husband and wife). The first arose in August 1529, and was an action raised on behalf of the King against John Crichton of Strathurd and Ninian Seton of Tullibody. It was directed towards establishing the King's claims to the casualty of non-entry for these lands. The claim would have been established if a resignation, charter and infeftment dating from the reign of James II (1437–1460) could be reduced as invalid. Alexander Gordon, earl of Huntly, had resigned the lands of Tullibody into the hands of King James II, in order that Ninian's ancestor, Alexander Seton, could receive infeftment.[45] However, it was successfully argued that at the time of the resignation the earl "was allanerlie coniunctfiar with hir [i.e. his spouse] of the same and sua at that time mycht nocht resigne the heretable fee of the saidis land", since the earl's spouse, Dame Gelis Hay, was the "heretar" of the lands. The earl did not have title to dispone. The resignation and infeftment were accordingly reduced. This meant that the lands had been in non-entry for fifty years since the death of Alexander, earl of Huntly. Over four years later, in December 1533, we find the earl of Huntly raising an action to reduce this decree of the Lords, arguing that, in relation to the reduction, the cause "wes nocht of verite becaus the said umqhile Alexander erle of Huntlie the tyme of the resignation of the saidis landis wes heretar thirof and heretablie infeft in the same",

[44] NAS CS 6/3, fol. 27.
[45] NAS CS 5/40, fol. 84v.

entailing that the resignation in favour of Alexander Seton was "gud and lauchfull in the self".[46] However, this action failed. Perhaps somewhat inconsistently, though, the earl had meanwhile lodged in court a charter made by Gelis Hay in 1438 to Alexander Seton of the lands of Tullibody, confirmed by James II and in 1505 by James IV. Two weeks later the earl compeared to receive a transumpt (i.e. certified copy) of the charter.[47] Perhaps he was preparing the way for another action to reduce the decree of non-entry by showing that there existed another infeftment of Alexander Seton which remained valid.

The possibility of the decree of non-entry being reduced was of concern to John Crichton of Strathurd, since in 1529 the King had proceeded to infeft him in the lands of Tullibody which Ninian Seton had lost.[48] However, at the same time, Ninian Seton was attempting to reduce the process of apprising which had led to John Crichton's infeftment.[49] The basis of Ninian's action was in part his own claim to have had a gift of the non-entries back in 1527. The process of apprising was reduced at Ninian's instance, although the reason was said to be for the "wrongus iniust and inordinat proceding" of the sheriff, and the Lords specifically held back from expressing a view about the claims to non-entries, stating that "this decrete mak nowther strenth nor prejudice to any of the saidis partiis rytis be reson of the said pretendit gift of the non-entries".[50] That these actions were also of great concern to the tenants of the lands in dispute is shown by an action raised by some of John Crichton's tenants in January 1530, against both John Crichton and Ninian Seton. They complained that they were "double poindit" and that Ninian had spuilzied them for mails and duties which they owed to John for the land. John and Ninian were to bring with them to court "baith their rychte quhy thai poynd the saide pure tenantes for double mailes".[51]

None of these examples was a fee and heritage action, although we saw previously that John Crichton had unsuccessfully alleged that the King's action for non-entries was such an action and as such beyond the jurisdiction of Council. However, in none of them were two competing

[46] NAS CS 6/3, fol. 105v. (2 Dec., 1533).
[47] NAS CS 6/3, fols. 93v, 122v.
[48] NAS CS 6/3, fol. 93v.
[49] NAS CS 6/3, fol. 111v. (4 Dec., 1533); NAS CS 6/3, fol. 118 (10 Dec., 1533); NAS CS 6/3, fol. 123r. (11 Dec., 1533).
[50] NAS CS 6/3, fol. 124v.
[51] NAS CS 5/40, fol. 153r.

claims pitted against each other. Nevertheless, the complexity of the various claims, and the ways in which these claims were pursued or attacked over the course of many years through different actions and stages of litigation must have generated scope for the parties to dispute their conflicting titles directly. This makes it easy to envisage how the facts of such disputes could have given rise to competing heritable claims, which could have been made good in the course of actions of wrongous occupation or spuilzie of mails. However, this was not the form in which the dispute was approached before the Session. Deploying instead a reduction of infeftment action allowed the claim of invalidity to be focused clearly into a relevant cause of action for rendering a particular title void. In considering the claim for reduction in this case, we find the Lords being prepared to look behind a heritable title to the transactions which brought it into being, and to declare it null on the basis of an invalidity in its transfer over ninety years earlier. This must have been decisive in helping resolve a long-running dispute. Earlier litigation had not done so. At least one earlier wave of litigation in the dispute can be traced as far back as 1505.[52]

Another action exemplifying this ground arose in November 1531 when Margaret and Marion Inglis, daughters and heirs of Margaret Drummond, Lady Colquhoun, together sued Melchior Cullen. The action was for reduction of an infeftment of lands made to Melchior's father, Jasper, by Lord Erskine, the superior, after an "assignation" into his hands by Margaret Drummond.[53] The ground of reduction was that:

> befor the making of the said pretendit infeftment...the said umquhile [i.e. deceased] Margaret Drummond than being heretar of the said lands resigned the same in the handes of umquhile Thomas lord Erskine superior thirof quhilk...gaif heretable stait of all and hail the forsaide landis...to the said umquhile Margaret and to Jhone Inglis than hir spous in coniunctfee and their airis...quharthrow the heretable fee was transferrit fra the said Margaret in the said Jhone Inglis and she alanerly secludid fra all maner of resignation or alienation thirof and...denudid of the heretable fee of the Bass...and the conjunct fee remanent with hir alanerallie.

[52] NAS CS 5/18(1), fols. 90v, 91v, 92r, 121r, 132r; cf. NAS transcript, pp. 178, 181–182, 232, 254.

[53] NAS CS 5/43, fols. 85–86.

Margaret's right to alienate the lands had become qualified through the fee being shared and held as a "conjunct fee" with her husband. The upshot was that "she mycht mak na ryt of the heretable fee to any other person".

The third action exemplifying this ground occurred in November 1532 when William, master of Glencairn, sued Janet Langmuir and her sisters for reduction of an infeftment, charter and precept of sasine given to them by William's father, Cuthbert, earl of Glencairn, to which infeftment William was also alleged to have been a party.[54] The principal ground of reduction was that Cuthbert:

> had na power thirto nor mycht not give the same nor infeft na personis heretablie thirintill he beand at youth as he was in verite distitut of the heretable fee... and alanerlie wes but franktenementar [i.e. holder of the freehold] and William master of Glencairn in heretable fee.

William denied that he had ever consented to this transaction or made the infeftment personally.[55] Again, it is possible to see how a fee and heritage action could have arisen out of these circumstances, since Janet Langmuir and her sisters had a *prima facie* valid heritable infeftment, and so it seems did William, master of Glencairn. In this case, although we do not know the arguments, William failed to prove his case and the Langmuir sisters were assoilzied (i.e. absolved). But we can see how the structure of the action for reduction had focused the dispute around the issue of invalidity in a title.

The next ground of reduction to consider relates to a situation where the granter wrongly claimed the right to transfer land which was not part of his own infeftment. The main example of this is found in the action raised by Archibald Spittal against Finlay Spittal in February 1531, for reduction of an infeftment, charter and sasine made by the King to Thomas Spittal, Finlay's father, and the subsequent sasine now taken by Finlay. The reason put forward for the reduction was that:

> long befor the said pretendit infeftment maid to the said umquhile Thomas the said Archibald was heretably infeft in fifty shilling land in Cessintuly quarof the said 10 merkland is ane part and pendikle... the said Thomas by sinister information circumnevand the kinges grace, nocht makand mention of the same, optenit ane preteindit infeftment and als

[54] NAS CS 6/2, fol. 14r.
[55] NAS CS 6/2, fol. 96. (20 Feb., 1533).

> the pretendit seising now takin thereof be the said Finlaw his son and ar be the common law null in the self.[56]

In other words, Archibald claimed to have already been infeft in the land in question, when Thomas received fresh infeftment in the same land from the King. In order to prove whether the ten-shilling land was part of the fifty merklands, the Lords commissioned the stewart of Menteith to take "cognition", which would have involved local process with a jury. The ascertained facts were held to favour Archibald. On 29 April 1531 the infeftment was reduced, since all the land pertained to Archibald, "as wes clearlie previt befor the saidis lordis be ane rolment of court producit be the said archibald gevin be the stewart of menteith".[57] This case clearly shows the Lords deciding upon heritable title, after first commissioning a local finding of fact presided over by a local judicial figure. This seems akin to the mechanism of a commission to a sheriff *in hac parte*, except that the commission is here subordinated to central judicial process. This fusion of forms of central and local judicial process within the exercise of jurisdiction by the Lords of Session is highly significant, in that it suggests that all practical and procedural obstacles to their developing a full heritage jurisdiction had been potentially overcome even before 1532.

Again, it is apparent that the facts of this case could easily have given rise to a fee and heritage action with two competing titles. A few decades earlier, this would have been open to being remitted to the judge ordinary. Both parties could lay claim to the ten-shilling lands, and it was not apparent from the face of Archibald's charter whether or not they pertained to his property. In fact, a year after the original action of reduction arose in court, we find in February 1532 a new action raised by Archibald against Finlay in relation to precisely the same lands, this time for wrongous occupation. In the record of the new action the previous proceedings leading to the reduction of Finlay's infeftment were narrated. The new allegation was then made that "nochtheless the said Finlay and Janet his modir wrangously and by way of deid intromettis and occupyis the said land & will nocht decist thirfra without thai be compellit".[58] Finlay and Janet did not compear but were ordered to desist and cease from occupation of the lands. These

[56] NAS CS 5/42, fol. 48r.
[57] NAS CS 5/42, fol. 172v.
[58] NAS CS 5/43, fol. 160v.

proceedings therefore provide an exact illustration of how the fee and heritage restriction might have been circumvented through the use of a reduction of infeftment action. Archibald's first act was to establish an undisputed title for himself through reducing Finlay's infeftment, and his second was to remove Finlay through a wrongous occupation action to which Finlay would have no defence since his previous title to the land had been reduced.

The other example of this ground is provided by litigation between the earl of Glencairn as franktenementer of the lands of Cluny (i.e. holding the freehold), the master of Glencairn as fiar (i.e. holding the heritable fee), and Margaret Campbell against William Hamilton. Margaret was relict [i.e. widow] of the late William Cunningham, previously holding the lands in conjunctfee with him. The earl and others had a summons against William Hamilton "tuching the land of clune",[59] whilst William Hamilton had a summons against them for reduction of their infeftment of the lands of Cluny, previously made by King James IV in 1498 to the master of Glencairn. The summons for reduction was called again on 5 March 1533, but the defenders pleaded an exception that the lands of Cluny were a pertinent of the lordship of Kilmaurs, in which the earl and master and their predecessors were infeft.[60] We are told that William Hamilton's claim arose from a process of apprising for the non-entries of the lands of Cluny, the gift of which non-entries he had presumably received from the King. It is presumably this same process of apprising which, in November 1532, we also find the earl and others trying to reduce. Unfortunately, we do not know for certain the ground of reduction pleaded by William in relation to the infeftment of 1498, but it seems apparent that the issue was in part whether the lands of Cluny were part of the lordship of Kilmaurs, and this was an issue which the Lords would be determining in order to decide whether to reduce the infeftment. Both sides can be seen attacking the title of the other in separate actions. Success would presumably have allowed them to establish title from which to establish a right to lawful possession of the lands. If necessary this could have been accomplished through an action of wrongful occupation, as happened in the Spittal case.

[59] NAS CS 5/43, fol. 147r. (8 Feb., 1531/32).
[60] NAS CS 6/2, fol. 108.

The next ground to be considered in this first category relates to the situation where the granter of an infeftment held the title on the basis of an invalid process of apprising. In other words, the land had been judicially seized for debt, but invalidly. Such circumstances underlay an action in 1531 between Alexander Innes and Alexander Ogilvy, William Stewart and Adam Otterburn (as King's advocate). Alexander Innes' action related to an infeftment, charter and gift, with precept and sasine, made by King James IV to James Stewart of lands which were in his hands "be virtue of ane pretendit apprising maid to him of the same be reason of nonentres".[61] The ground for reduction was that James IV "had na rycht" to the mails for which the lands were apprised for debt at that time. We are informed that "divers sufficient acquittance of payment" were produced to demonstrate this. This meant that the allegation that the lands were in non-entry:

> was nevir of verite and swa the fundimant of the said infeftment quharupon it procedit was fals and fenzeit in the self qhuarfor our said soverane lord had na rycht to the said landes and fisching and mycht nocht dispone the same.[62]

In fact the reduction action was abandoned because the parties submitted the dispute to the Lords as arbiters, who allowed Alexander Ogilvy to retain the lands in return for paying compensation of 600 merks.[63] However, the case is another telling illustration of how a complex dispute over title might arise and how the remedy to which the complainer might resort in order to resolve such a dispute was the reduction of his antagonist's infeftment.

The next two grounds in this category both relate to crown property. First, there is the reduction of infeftments which were made by the King in his minority without the advice and consent of Parliament, and which therefore fell under the general revocation of such grants. Thus in February 1533 the King and his comptroller sued Robert Hunter on this ground, as well as because the land had been:

> in all tymes bigane fre forest and fens for the kingis grace & his predecessors wyld bestis & nevir was sett in assedation of befor and now ar sett

[61] NAS CS 5/43, fol. 134r. (19 Dec., 1531).
[62] NAS CS 5/43, fol. 173. (27 Feb., 1532).
[63] NAS CS 5/43, fol. 173.

> in assedation for 5mk of few allanerlie howbeit thai ar worth 30 marks yeirlie.[64]

A related ground of action in *The King v. James Crichton of Frendraught* in 1530 was that a charter and infeftment of feu of crown lands should be reduced, and James decerned to have "tynt" (i.e. forfeited) his fee and heritage, because the charter had been made in diminution of the King's "rental".[65] Also, in February 1533 the King's advocate pursued the earl of Morton for reduction of a charter of feuferme made by the King because it had been made in his minority and to the diminution of his "rentale".[66] These two grounds of action are perhaps slightly distinguishable from the others, in that they related to King's actions of the sort which it must always have been the business of the King's officers to pursue on his behalf before Council. By 1529, however, such actions represented but one part of the Lords' generally applied jurisdiction to reduce infeftments. What may have been a remedy once applied above all for the benefit of the King had by this period therefore achieved a general utility.

The final two grounds in this category are more narrowly technical in nature. The first instance is where infeftment was made after a resignation into the hands of someone who was not in fact the superior of the lands but who then purported to make a re-grant as though in the position of a superior. In March 1533 John Scrimgeour, "heretable possessour" of the lands of Nether Myres, sued Alexander Scrimgeour, his son and apparent heir, for reduction of an infeftment and instrument of sasine of the lands of Nether Myres made into the hands of the bailie of Auchtermuchty in 1520.[67] John was ordered to produce his "auld infeftment" along with the terms of erection of Auchtermuchty as a free burgh. On 23 June 1533 the sasine of Alexander was reduced because the resignation had been made into the hands of the bailie, "he havand na power to ressave the said resignation, but the same suld have bene resignit in our soveraine lordes handes befor the geving of any new infeftment thirof". The reason was that "the sadis landis ar not haldin of our soveraine lord be reson of fre borrewage nor yit lyis

---

[64] NAS CS 6/2 fol. 99v.
[65] NAS CS 5/40, fol. 157v.
[66] NAS CS 6/2, fol. 101r.
[67] NAS CS 6/2, fol. 136.

within the freedom of the said burgh but ar haldin of our soveraine lord by uther service".[68]

Secondly, there is the ground of reduction arising from a variation between a transumpt of an instrument of sasine (i.e. an official copy of the deed constituting the infeftment) and the legal record of it contained in the notary's protocol book from which the transumpt was taken. Such a ground supported James Douglas of Parkhead's action against Margaret Allan and her spouse John Stanehop in 1531. James Douglas was pursuing an action for non-entries, but Margaret produced a transumpt of the record of an instrument of sasine which must have purported to show that entry had been taken of the lands.[69] However, in January 1532 James proved the transumpt false "because the same is variant fra the prothogoll producit befor the saidis lordis of year 1492 and in transsumpt the year 1488".[70] Having "impreved" this instrument, James Douglas was then awarded possession of the lands by virtue of his gift of non-entries when the question of the ground right came up on 4 June 1532. We are informed that he had received this gift from the earl of Angus in 1518.[71]

Both of these actions show how legal documents which were intrinsically invalid could come into existence and be used to support a claim to heritable title. Both demonstrate how the jurisdiction of the Session to reduce infeftments could be deployed to provide a remedy whereby such claims could be declared invalid and the infeftment void. Suppose, for example, that John and Alexander Scrimgeour had fallen into dispute with one another over the lands of Nether Myres. Both would have been able to produce heritable titles to the land—Alexander his infeftment at the hands of the bailie of Auchtermuchty, and John his "auld" infeftment. Would not an action of wrongous occupation between them have had to be referred to the judge ordinary under the traditional jurisdictional rules which we see being applied in the late fifteenth century? By raising a reduction of infeftment action, litigants were able to attack the titles of their opponents separately, before moving on to attack their possession of the property. The evidence being considered in this chapter would seem to suggest that this pattern of litigation had become common by 1529–34, and formed the new

[68] NAS CS 6/2, fol. 200.
[69] NAS CS 5/43, fol. 121r.
[70] NAS CS 5/43, fol. 140.
[71] NAS CS 6/1, fol. 12v.

paradigm for litigation over heritable title. Litigants were adopting a more sophisticated approach to the remedies they sought in order that the whole course of a dispute about heritage could be transacted before the Session. The judicial remedies and authority of central justice were preferred. No doubt this was on the advice of the professional men of law who undertook most procuratorial work in the Session by this time.[72] Certainly, title was now being attacked directly through reduction of infeftments more often than heritage actions in the past had ever been remitted to the judge ordinary.

Invalidity due to infeftment without right in grantee

The second category of grounds for reduction relates to cases where a person gained entry to lands without duly established "right". There are five specific grounds exemplified in the nine cases which fall into this category from our sample covering 1529–1534. The first is represented by the case of *Agnes Lindsay v. The King* for reduction of an infeftment made by King James IV to John Lindsay, the second son of Gilbert Lindsay of Glenmure. Agnes was the daughter of Alan Lindsay, Gilbert's son and heir, and she wished to reduce John's infeftment because it was "in defraude, hurt and disherising of the said Agnes". She also wished the Lords to give decree that she should be infeft by the King in the same land as the lawful heir.[73] Unfortunately, we discover no more in the record about how these circumstances had arisen.

A second ground of reduction is illustrated by three cases which concerned infeftments given without "coursable" brieves or "cognition in the cause", in other words without the requisite formality of judicial process before an inquest. In November 1529, Sir Alexander Elphinstone, brother and heir "of tailzie" to the late Andrew Elphinstone of Selms, sued Marion Elphinstone, daughter and heir of line to the late Andrew. An instrument of sasine of Marion's was to be reduced "because the same wes privatlie gevin to hir as air of lyne thirof without brevis coursable and cognition in the cause".[74] The second example is *Alison Ruche v. Janet Rowit and William Wallace* in February 1531. The wider context is difficult to infer from the record, but the

[72] See generally J. Finlay, *Men of Law in Pre-Reformation Scotland* (East Linton, 2000).
[73] NAS CS 5/40, fol. 82v. (4th August, 1529).
[74] NAS CS 5/40, fol. 135.

ground of action in this case was that an instrument of sasine should be reduced:

> becaus the said pretendit seising...wes gevin without cognition in the caus nocht expremand ony manner of rycht throw the quhilk the same wes gevin to him nowther as ayre therof to the said umquhile Laurence hes fadir nor to any uthir person, nor zit be resignation of any person, and by the stile and ordour of geving of seisingis within borrowis observit & keipit in siclik causis past memor of man.[75]

The infeftment had not been duly constituted and so reduction should be made. The third example of this sort of case is the action raised in December 1531 by Gelis Berclay against Thomas Alison and the archbishop of Glasgow. Gelis wished an infeftment which had been given to Marion Gibson, Thomas' mother, to be reduced. Thomas was his mother's heir. The reason for reduction was "becaus the said pretendit seising wes gevin privatly be ane precept [i.e. of the archbishop]...without brevis cursable". The sasine was also given "eftir that the said Gelis had optenit ane decret of wilfull error apon the persons thirof of before had retourit the said umquhile Marion nerrest and lauchful air to said umquhile Margaret of the saidis landis". Therefore the infeftment was "without cognition in the caus" since "the pley beand dependand betwix thaim quha suld succeid".[76] In turn, Gelis alleged David Berclay, to whom she was the heir, to have received infeftment in the lands, and produced an instrument of sasine of 1505 to show this. On 4 June 1532 the Lords accepted the validity of this infeftment and reduced that of Marion Gibson. Marion's procurator had offered to prove Gelis' instrument false, but had obviously failed to do so. Perhaps not technically, but at least functionally, the Lords were therefore essentially deciding a question of fee and heritage of the sort previously beyond their jurisdiction. They reduced one instrument of sasine and upheld the right of Gelis to succeed as heir to the lands in question on the basis of a separate instrument of sasine whose validity the Lords accepted.

The third ground in this category is exemplified by the case of *Nichol Crawfurd v. Andrew Hay* in February 1534. Nichol successfully sought reduction of Andrew's infeftment. The reason was that, ostensibly, Andrew had been infeft by the superior of the lands after the form of

---

[75] NAS CS 5/42, fol. 31v.
[76] NAS CS 5/43, fol. 125v.

charter and "auld infeftment" which had pertained to his predecessors. But this made him:

> heretor heretablie succedand to his predecessors heritage...howbeit the said Andro is be the law ane person unhabill to succeid to the heritage of ony of his predecessouris and specialie to his said fader becaus he is ane bastard gottin and born in bastardy...betwix Sir Thomas and Marion Forestar his concubyn eftir his promotion to the ordour of prestheid.[77]

Andrew was barred by his illegitimacy. Nichol, the justice clerk at this time, is described as holding the land of Howburn "tenend and tenendrys, in heritage". Andrew had been infeft in an acre of land of the lands of Howburn, implying that Nichol had now acquired this land. Presuming that this was the case, it is easy to see how a fee and heritage action might then have arisen in the past, and how the reduction of infeftment action permanently averted such a prospect.

The fourth ground for reduction within this category is when disruption to the feudal order caused by a forfeiture provided an opportunity for title to be dishonestly taken to the forfeited property. The particular situation in question was when the tenure being claimed was falsely alleged to have existed prior to the forfeiture of the superior of the lands. An opportunity for dispute could arise because sasine had to be given again by the new superior through the re-entry of the rightful heir. Dispute as to which party really had held the land prior to the forfeiture could break out. The first example of this is William Kerr's summons against Patrick Murray in January 1531, for "impreving" and reduction of an instrument of sasine. William's son, Adam, held certain lands of the earl of Angus in heritage. After the forfeiture of the earl in 1528, Adam had been re-entered to his lands, reserving a liferent to his father, William. Adam took sasine on 12 September 1528, one week after the doom of forfeiture against the earl had been given in Parliament.[78] However, Patrick's father, James, had alleged that the lands pertained to him in heritage before the forfeiture, and on that basis he had allegedly already obtained a gift of the lands from the King following the forfeiture. Nevertheless, there was allegedly "ane fenzeit and fals instrument of sesing gevin be Sir Jhone Michechill notar thirupon of the dait the 8 September with ane antedait befor

[77] NAS CS 6/3, fol. 215; NAS CS 6/4, fol. 59.

[78] *The Acts of the Parliament of Scotland*, ed. T. Thomson and C. Innes, 12 vols., (Edinburgh, 1814–75), vol. 2, p. 326.

the sesing takin be the said William and his son".[79] However, "all the cuntre knawis that he [William] and his said son gat seising thereof 24 days befor the pretendit seising takin be the said umquhile James".[80] Patrick was ordered to produce the instrument, but on 10 February 1531 the Lords simply declared it "fra the begyning and to be now and in all tymis tocum of nane availe force nor effect but fals and fenzeit in the self". In fact, another instrument of sasine of James Murray had been produced by the notary John Mitchell, but it was dated 6 October 1528. The notary went on to declare that no other instrument had been made by him for these lands prior to that date.[81]

This dispute seems very close to a fee and heritage action, since there were two competing titles in the form of instruments of sasine taken in relation to the same land. There were two competing infeftments. The primary issue concerned the question which of them had been given first. However, one possible way of distinguishing this situation from a fee and heritage action proper would be that in this example only one of the parties, William, appeared to possess sasine himself. Patrick Murray was said to be son and heir to the late James Murray, but it was the instrument of the sasine which James allegedly took of the land which was reduced, and we are never told whether Patrick had tried to take sasine on the basis of James' title. Obviously, if Patrick had taken sasine, then the ground for reducing his title would still have been the invalidity of his father's title, and so the substance of the action would have been identical to the action which did ensue. Nevertheless, this action again illustrates how a litigant could approach what was essentially a dispute about conflicting claims to heritage through trying to have the infeftment of his opponent reduced.

Another case illustrates the same type of ground in slightly different circumstances. In February 1531 Duncan McKelly, son and heir of Thomas McKelly, sued John Muirhead and Adam Otterburn (as King's advocate) for the "pretendit infeftment" made to John Muirhead's father by James IV. This was to "be annullit be decrete of the lordis".[82] The reason was that the land had allegedly pertained to the late Thomas McKelly, before the recognition of the barony of Merton into the hands of James IV and its subsequent forfeiture. Thomas had held the

[79] NAS CS 5/42, fol. 23r.
[80] NAS CS 5/42, fol. 23r.
[81] NAS CS 5/42, fol. 44r.
[82] NAS CS 5/42, fol. 76r.

land in "property", having been heritably infeft by charter and sasine. As such the land should now pertain to Duncan, given that all vassals and subvassals were meant to have been newly infeft in their property and tenandry after the forfeiture. This would have involved "ilkane in thir part payand thir part of the composition lik as the said Duncan offirit".[83] However, after the lands had been recognosced and doom of property given, John Muirhead:

> be sinister information allegiand the same land befor the forfaltour perteint to him in propirtie [and] optenit new infeftment to him of the same the said Duncaine beand of less age and in keping of the said Johne as he that had hes ward.[84]

Duncan was under John's control because of his age and John had exploited this to his advantage. The Lords reduced the infeftment and thus we see them invalidating sasine on the basis that there was no rightful claim to heritable title underlying it.

The fifth and final ground in this category is the reduction of an infeftment because it encroached on the boundaries and freedoms of a burgh which had not consented to the encroachment. This is exemplified in the case which arose between the burghs of Wigtown and Whithorn in 1532. Wigtown sought reduction of the charter and infeftment made to Whithorn by King James IV. The reason was that:

> the toun of Wigtoun wes maid and creat be umquhile king James the second and utheris our soverane lordis predecessoris kingis of Scotland ane fre burgh with all privileges and freedoms of fre burghs within all the boundis of Quhithorn and Galloway…and the inhabitantes of the said burgh hes bene in possession of the said fredome past memor of man quhair thirthrow our said umquhile soveraine lord mycht not tak fra the inhabitaris of the said burgh thair fredom without thair avis and consent and gif the same to the town of quhithorn.

This consent we are told they never gave and never will give.[85] Although Whithorn was assoilzied and the action failed, it is interesting to find the same action raised again over a year later in March 1534.[86] To adjudicate on this reduction action seems particularly close to deciding fee and heritage, since the reason for reducing the defender's title would

[83] NAS CS 5/42, fol. 76r.
[84] NAS CS 5/42, fol. 76r.
[85] NAS CS 6/2, fol. 94.
[86] NAS CS 6/4, fol. 71.

have been that it conflicted directly with that of the pursuer. Therefore a comparison of the two conflicting titles would have to be made by the Lords. Indeed, at the outset of the proceedings on 2 December 1532 an exception had been pleaded that the Lords "ar na competent juges in the said mater", though this was rejected.[87] Perhaps it can then be said that this case illustrates particularly well how a dispute which was in substance one over fee and heritage could nevertheless be adjudicated upon by the Lords through their jurisdiction to reduce infeftments. We may also note that any previous difficulty apparent in the fifteenth century in defining the appropriate forum to resolve such a dispute between two burghs, such as in the case involving Montrose and Dundee, had now given way to an acceptance of the authority of the Session.[88]

Invalidity due to fraudulent infeftment

The third category of ground for reduction of an infeftment concerns the fraudulent infeftment of a third party in order to defeat a future rightful claim to the land in question. There are five cases of this type which concern an infeftment made in order to defraud a creditor, and one in order to defraud a spouse in advance of divorce proceedings. In one example Alexander Innes sued Lord Oliphant in March 1530 for the reduction of his infeftment in various lands, including reduction of his charter, sasine and confirmation. This was because the property had been alienated by Andrew Oliphant to Lord Oliphant, "his tendir kinsman in secund and third degrees of consangunite", in defraud of Alexander as Andrew's creditor. A crucial point seems to have been that this occurred "lang eftir that the said umquhile Andro as air and successor to umquhile Constance Sutherland hes modir was under sumondis befor the lordis of counsale" at Alexander's instance. Alexander had been assignee to the feudal casualty of marriage which had been due upon Constance's marriage. This represented a debt for which he had been pursuing Andrew up until his death. In other words, prior to the alienation, a valid claim had already been made against the property, although not attached to any security in the modern sense, and the alienation had left Andrew a debtor with no means. As

[87] NAS CS 6/2, fol. 19.

[88] See chapter 6 above for discussion of this case and the analysis of it presented by Dr Borthwick.

the record states, he was "not responsale nor distrenzeable" in other lands or goods for the considerable sum of 5,000 merks.[89] Alexander was therefore attacking the fraudulent infeftment which had taken the land in question out of Andrew's patrimony.

In another case in 1530, Sir Alexander Scott had resigned lands to his son, William, after decree had already been given by the official of Lothian for a debt of £100 owed to Roland Donaldson. Moreover, there had been "opin proclamatioun apoun our soveraine lords letters lang befor the said alienatioun that the said Alexander suld nocht analyt nor put away hes land nor gudes in fraud nor prejudice of said Roland Donaldson".[90] The use of a proclamation constituted public notice that dealings with Sir Alexander might be vitiated by his failure to satisfy the existing decree for debt against him. Thus the infeftment was "in fraude of the creditour" and was reduced, and the land apprised. Actions of this sort were effectively forms of the procedure of diligence, whereby creditors enforced their decrees by means of reducing fraudulent alienations, before judicially attaching the property to realise their debts in the same action. Apprising also followed reduction in *Marjory Mowat v. Walter Kynnard*.[91]

In another case the fraudulent infeftment appears to have been made to evade third party claims in warrandice against the granter. Here the allegation was that the newly infeft proprietor was in bad faith. Property had been transferred to Gilbert Inglis by his brother John. It was alleged that Gilbert "knawand perfitly" that his brother was liable in warrandice to Margaret Allan, and knew that at the time of the fraudulent alienation John was not "responsale" in other lands. There is also a hint that Gilbert had pretended to be purchasing the lands at a market value but without making any payment to John.[92] This alienation had occurred in 1512.[93] In another case of this sort, the Session was asked to intervene in a dispute between William Kynard, burgess of Dieppe, and Robert Brown, burgess of Edinburgh, and to reduce all infeftments made by Robert's wife in defraud of William, their creditor.[94]

---

89 NAS CS 5/41, fol. 22v.
90 NAS CS 5/41, fol. 53r.
91 NAS CS 5/42, fol. 178v. (4 May 1531).
92 NAS CS 6/2, fol. 166.
93 NAS CS 6/2, fol. 118v.
94 NAS CS 6/2, fol. 218.

The final example of this ground of reduction relates not to a creditor but to a spouse who was about to be "divorced".[95] Robert Lauder was summoned in March 1534 by his sometime wife Janet Logan, to have an infeftment reduced which he had made to his son. This was because it had been made "eftir that he had movit pley of divorce agains Jonet", knowing that if divorce was granted "he wald be condampnit be the same sentence to refound all the sums that he ressavit with her".[96] Moreover, after the divorce he then purported to infeft Janet (fraudulently) in the same lands in which he had already infeft his son. As a result of this, it would seem that two infeftments existed for the same land, something which would inevitably cause a dispute over the fee and heritage of the land. Again, a reduction of infeftment action would solve the fee and heritage dispute by leaving only one valid title, although in this particular case the defender was assoilzied because the "punctis" of the summons were not proved as libelled.

Invalidity due to failure to perform obligation under condition of the grant

Only one example of this ground occurs between 1529 and 1534. It concerns a situation where an infeftment was vitiated by the failure to perform an obligation which had been undertaken in return for the infeftment. In March 1531 Helen Rutherford appeared in relation to her summons against Mark Kerr, in which he was summoned for:

> reducing of an infeftment maid be hir to said Mark of certane landis gevin to him to defend hir in hir heritage. Nochttheless he did na diligence therein bot suffirit Thomas Ruderfuird to occupy her land & castell of Edzarstonne & deit in possession thereof.[97]

Therefore he had not acted "conforme to the obligatioune" made to Helen in this respect. This case shows a further aspect of the Lords' jurisdiction to reduce infeftments, although the facts are not immediately as suggestive of a fee and heritage case as those of some of the other examples already considered. However, a fee and heritage dispute could have arisen from Helen producing her "auld infeftment"

---

[95] For the limited notion of divorce in Scotland prior to the Reformation—either as full annullment or mere separation through divorce *a mensa et thoro* see R.D. Ireland, "Husband and Wife" in *Introduction to Scottish Legal History*, ed. G.C.H. Paton (Edinburgh, 1958), p. 90.

[96] NAS CS 6/4 fol. 78v.

[97] NAS CS 5/42, fol. 124v.

and setting it against that of Mark, which she might then have alleged to be invalid.

Conclusion

The regular number of reduction of infeftment actions by 1529–1534 and the considerable variety of grounds pleaded in them suggest that such actions were a particularly significant aspect of the Lords' jurisdiction. Although such actions were not technically fee and heritage ones in the old sense, they nevertheless touched heritage and involved the Session interfering directly in matters of title. In the examination of these actions it has been shown how a number of common forms of heritage dispute, which could have led to a remit to the judge ordinary and the declining of jurisdiction in the past, here seem to have been approached competently using other grounds of action. Such disputes could be adjudicated upon by the Lords when the remedy requested was the reduction of an infeftment. The apparent growth in the number of such cases at the same time as the Lords appear to have ceased to remit cases to the judge ordinary because of fee and heritage, together with the fact that the fee and heritage exceptions which were pleaded were made in reduction of infeftment actions, is significant. It implies that litigants and their legal advisers had realised that if heritage disputes were approached on these grounds then the old jurisdictional restriction on Council could be effectively circumvented.

Therefore, through a comprehensive jurisdiction to reduce infeftments the Lords were able to resolve many typical disputes about heritage, but without any formal repudiation of the old jurisdictional restriction. This hypothesis seems to render explicable how the Session could have developed a comprehensive heritage jurisdiction without such a repudiation. Crudely put, the sixteenth-century Council developed an important jurisdiction over heritage by means of its jurisdiction to reduce infeftments, and this rendered obsolete the restriction which prevented the fifteenth-century Council from hearing actions which depended upon fee and heritage. As already noted, a shift in the structuring of remedies within the legal order could be said to have transformed the underlying jurisdictional norms. This development seems to have happened as a result of litigants approaching disputes on different legal grounds, motivated by a desire for a remedy which was available before the Session, and possibly a wider preference for its adjudication in general. It could therefore be only a matter of time before the formal recognition occurred that the Session was no longer barred from deciding fee and heritage as such. The failure to remit because of fee and heritage after 1513 opened the way for this, and the institutional impetus of 1532 must have been decisive in its realisation. This recognition materialised through the incremental voicing in particular cases of the jurisdictional implications of deciding heritage cases through the reduction of infeftments. This is what has been characterised in this chapter as an assimilation after 1532 of the jurisdictional change already completed before 1532.

It seems probable that the Lords of Session realised that their newly developed jurisdiction over heritage conflicted to some extent with the basis of the medieval jurisdictional model embodied in the common law. This would account for their hesitancy in asserting jurisdiction by way of a declaration of general competence over fee and heritage, and their preference for articulating their jurisdiction on a case by case basis in relation to remedial categories of action. The confidence to define their jurisdiction more categorically only seems to be in place by 1540. Since the legislation of 1532 did not express any limitation upon the jurisdiction of the College of Justice, it might have been expected that it would have been founded upon from 1532 onwards to give authority for the Lords' jurisdiction over heritage. However, since the statute of 1532 did not purport to change the jurisdiction of the Lords, that might have seemed something of a circular argument to contemporaries, at least at first.[98] The enhanced involvement of the Session in heritage jurisdiction by 1532 might have been difficult to render explicable in the light of the jurisdictional bar on the medieval Council. Nevertheless, it was properly an emanation of its traditional pre-1532 competence to reduce infeftments. This jurisdiction to reduce infeftments had allowed the Lords to shape a new form of heritage jurisdiction after 1513 based around invalidity of title. By the 1530s the meaning of their authority to do so was being more expressly articulated and acknowledged. These developments clearly have great significance for re-assessing the significance of the College of Justice in 1532. From a jurisdictional

[98] But of course, in time arguments were constructed which sought to found upon the institution of the College of Justice (and therefore implicitly upon the statute of 1532) as authority for assertions of jurisdiction and cases from the 1540s demonstrate this: see Murray, "Sinclair's Practicks", p. 98.

perspective, the foundation of the College allowed the full jurisdiction developed by the Lords before 1532 to be embodied in a reconstituted institution which could function for the first time as a form of supreme central court. However, apart from the development of the jurisdiction of the Session, there were other ways in which its wider authority was also in evidence by the 1530s. These involved developments outside the ordinary procedures of litigation, particularly the use of extraordinary procedures to submit disputes to the Session, either as a law court or as a group of arbiters, as well as the advocation of actions from other courts. The remaining two chapters will address these matters.

CHAPTER EIGHT

LITIGATION, ARBITRATION AND DISPUTE RESOLUTION BEFORE THE SESSION

Introduction

The development of the jurisdiction of the Session enhanced the scope of litigation which it could entertain. As we saw in the previous chapter, this did not necessarily mean the extension of jurisdiction to encompass or directly take over existing and well-defined claims previously reserved to other courts, such as those which involved the pleadable brieves. It rested upon a dynamism in the development by the Session of its own remedies to address new types of claim which litigants wished to make. The development of the remedy of reduction by 1532 is the pre-eminent example. However, by this time the records of Council and Session also contain references to a wide range of alternative methods and procedures for resolving disputes in a way not evident in the fifteenth century. They illustrate the relation of these methods to formal litigation and emphasise the role which the Session could play in dispute resolution outside the formal course of litigation. This evidence is also important for illuminating the significant authority and status which the Session enjoyed in Scottish society by 1532.

The complexity or intractability of a legal dispute could lead parties to look beyond formal litigation in their efforts to achieve a resolution. On 16 November 1531, for example, the Lords of Session sat in their ordinary judicial role to determine the "pley debatable" between the second earl of Menteith, Alexander Graham, and Thomas, Walter and Patrick Graham. The latter were assignees of the late countess of Menteith, grandmother of the earl. The dispute concerned a valuable claim to the lands of Ross. However, the outcome of the hearing was not a court decree. Rather, the Lords gave their determination "as juges arbitors for stansching of all pleis quarell and debate amangis the said partiis".[1] The matter had already been litigated locally in 1530

[1] Edinburgh, National Archives of Scotland [NAS] CS 5/43, fol. 79; the general dispute is passingly referred to in J.S. Cameron, *James V: the Personal Rule 1528–1542*, (East Linton, 1998), p. 138.

before the sheriff principal of Perth, but the decree resulting from that process had been reduced. This was because of the culpability of the sheriff in "wrangeous and parciale proceding". He had previously been discharged from hearing the action because he was alleged to be a "parciale and suspect juge" to the earl.[2] Apart from these earlier judicial proceedings, the parties had referred the matter to a set of "jugis arbitratours" between July and November 1531, but by November it was recorded that there was "na thing done therein".[3] The dispute had also entailed undesirable legal consequences for the earl during the course of the litigation. Part of his estates had been appropriated by the Grahams in 1530 as a judicial security for their ongoing claim against the lands of Ross.[4]

The Graham dispute illustrates tellingly the wider process of dispute resolution in early sixteenth-century Scotland. Three features stand out. We see the invocation by parties of the jurisdiction of more than one court at both a local and national level. This included the highest civil tribunal in Scotland—the Session. A second feature is the appointment of private arbiters, described specifically as "arbitratours". The third feature is that the final resolution of the matter was transacted in the Session by means of a deliverance of the Lords of Session themselves, acting as arbiters. These features underline several aspects of the nature of dispute resolution in sixteenth-century Scotland. They make plain that it often cannot be exclusively categorized as either based on state "public" justice, or informal "private" justice. The Graham case contained a mixture which encompassed both types of approach. The working out of the dispute over the lands of Ross cannot be seen as principally dependent upon the justice of the courts or the private justice of arbiters, mediators and simple compromises. It relied on both. Nevertheless, it seems significant that the "fynale end" of the dispute was determined in the Session by the supreme civil judges of Scotland. Their authority was instrumental in bringing the parties to a resolution. However, this was only after they had assumed the capacity of private arbiters. The conclusion is that their institutional role and status were important enough to make them the appropriate body to resolve the

[2] NAS CS 5/43, fol. 12 (20 July, 1531).

[3] As narrated in proceedings on 15 November 1531: NAS CS 5/43, fol. 75.

[4] Cameron, *James V*, p. 138; *Registrum Magni Sigilli Regum Scotorum* 3, ed. J.B. Paul and J.M. Thomson (Edinburgh 1883), no. 960.

dispute, within or without the framework of litigation. This was accomplished in this case through the procedure of arbitration.

Another type of complication in dispute resolution was the way in which different forms of jurisdiction might confront one another without formal mechanisms to resolve any conflict between them. In this regard, ecclesiastical jurisdiction could add immeasurably to the complexity of disputes, both legally, politically and through the introduction of an international dimension. In a dispute in March 1534 over the lordship of Stow in the Scottish Borders, the matter was now said to be pending in the "court of Rome... to the gret consummyng and spending of the substance and money of this realme".[5] Indeed, at a previous calling before the Session two weeks earlier, it had been stated that one reason for seeking concord in the dispute was "for eschewing of truble and exhorbitant expensis".[6] The dispute was between Lord Borthwick and the archbishop of St Andrews, together with the archbishop's tenant, David Hoppringle. The King had commanded the "convencionnis of the said partiis... that be gud mediation the saidis partiis mycht be drawn to concord", and the Hoppringles were granted a period of time to "be avisit with frendis".[7] Lord Borthwick accepted that the matter should be submitted "in amicablewis" to be decided before the Lords of Council, though the Hoppringles claimed that they were not free to take such a step since their interest was as mere tacksmen (i.e. lease holders) of the archbishop of St Andrews.[8] The extraordinary outcome to this dispute was that it was eventually placed in the hands of the King personally—as "arbitrator" in Professor Hannay's view[9]—by Pope Paul III in February 1538. A royal letter was transcribed into the council register and records the King stating that "we have tane the samin on us be our haly fader the papis brief direct to us tharupon to remane in our handis to be amicably aggreit for wele of thaim baith", though it should be noted that the wording might imply mediation rather

[5] NAS CS 6/4, fol. 70r. (13 March, 1533/34). This dispute is also discussed in R.K. Hannay, "Some Questions Regarding Scotland and the Canon Law", *Juridical Review* (1937), 25–34, especially from p. 30.

[6] NAS CS 6/4, fol. 16v. (23 February, 1533/34).

[7] NAS CS 6/4, fol. 16v.

[8] NAS CS 6/4, fol. 70r. A selection of references to this dispute appears in *Acts of the Lords of Council in Public Affairs 1501–1554*, ed. R.K. Hannay [hereafter *ADCP*] (Edinburgh, 1932), pp. 211, 220–221, 415, 421, 465–466.

[9] Hannay, "Some Questions Regarding Scotland and the Canon Law", p. 31.

than an imposed resolution.[10] Secular and ecclesiastical jurisdiction at national and international level had been invoked, as well as private arbitration. The arbitration was through the offices of the Lords of Session, but also embraced the King and the papacy. Again it is notable how arbitration, though a distinctive alternative procedure, could be readily integrated with ongoing legal process before a variety of courts in relation to diverse aspects of a dispute.

The interaction between the courts and arbitration has a special relevance to sixteenth century Scotland due to the development of a central court. As we have seen, this development resulted in the establishment and incorporation of the judicial Session of the King's Council as the College of Justice in 1532. We have also seen how this development involved a restructuring of jurisdiction through the novel application of remedies. The sixteenth century is thus a period when the public administration of justice was becoming strengthened through the evolution of new forms of central authority. This evolution is a feature of the development of institutions of central government across Europe in the late medieval and early modern period. According to the European pattern, "justice was originally handled by the king in his council, although later parts of the council split off to become the highest law courts".[11] In the fifteenth and sixteenth centuries there are numerous courts which reflect something of this, such as the College of Justice in Scotland, the King's Council in Denmark, the Great Council of Malines in the Netherlands, the English Court of Chancery and to some extent the imperial Reichshofrat and the Reichskammergericht in the Holy Roman Empire. The broader question which will be touched on in the next chapter is what effect the enhancement of "public justice" had upon existing practices of private dispute resolution?[12] To what extent was "private justice" in Europe displaced or over-shadowed by the "public justice" of the newer and more powerful judicial bodies,

[10] *ADCP*, p. 466; Hannay, "Some Questions Regarding Scotland and the Canon Law", p. 31.

[11] P.M. Ribalta, "The Impact of Central Institutions", in *Power Elites and State Building*, ed. W. Reinhard (Oxford, 1996), p. 23; see also R.C. van Caenegem, *An Historical Introduction to Private Law* (Cambridge, 1992), pp. 100–101; B. Guenée, *States and Rulers in Later Medieval Europe* (Oxford, 1985), p. 125.

[12] The underlying theme of J.M. Wormald, "Bloodfeud, Kindred and Government in Early Modern Scotland", *Past and Present* 87 (1980), 54–97. Considered also in J.W. Cairns, "Academic Feud, Bloodfeud, and William Welwood: Legal Education in St Andrews, 1560–1611", *Edinburgh Law Review* 2 (1998), 158–179, 255–287.

whose authority was after all drawn typically from the executive authority of royal government itself? In this chapter there will be an attempt to evaluate the reasons for deploying private methods such as arbitration in the first place, in order to understand the interaction between "public" and "private" forms of justice. A related and even broader enquiry is to examine the intelligibility for sixteenth-century Scottish society of the very distinction between concepts of public and private order and justice. Historians have tended to rely on such concepts somewhat uncritically.[13]

The main concern of this chapter will be to adduce evidence of why arbitration procedure was attractive to disputants and had utility even within the context of disputes already being conducted through litigation. It will be demonstrated that resort to litigation often went hand in hand with resort to arbitration but that the incidence of the latter did not necessarily imply weakness in the administration of justice. Rather, in the wider context of dispute resolution, arbitration and litigation were simply alternatives. In this wider context, litigation was not necessarily an autonomous activity, but one which often presupposed the simultaneous pursuit of other strategies to resolve a dispute. It was also not necessarily the most important of the various approaches to disputes. Dr Gerald Harriss has even commented of fifteenth century England that "it is clear that men embarked on litigation less to settle a dispute than because it offered an honourable method of affirming and protecting their rights".[14] Other means apart from litigation might be used to achieve a final settlement. In the next chapter it will be demonstrated that the Session had itself developed a significant role in dispute resolution outside litigation, as well as in deciding upon conventional legal actions. This suggests that contemporaries acknowledged the Session to possess a strong degree of institutional authority beyond the coercive power to issue decrees. Its wider role will be analysed and placed in the context of the debates over the respective spheres of private and public justice. The present chapter will be concerned more narrowly with identifying the nature and advantages of arbitration as one method commonly used in Scotland when disputes were resolved outwith judicial structures.

[13] S. Reynolds, "The Historiography of the Medieval State", in *Companion to Historiography*, ed. M. Bentley (London, 1997), pp. 117–138 at p. 125.

[14] Gerald Harriss, *Shaping the Nation: England 1360–1461*, The New Oxford History of England (Oxford, 2005), p. 197.

What does the use of arbitration reveal about the modes of ordinary litigation? What made it attractive to disputants? Were there different forms of arbitration? Is there anything distinctive about the operation of arbitration in Scotland? These questions are important in a Scottish context, but also resonate at the European level, where forms of arbitration were part of the Romano-canonical legal tradition, and played a part alongside litigation in the resolution of disputes generally. The Scottish evidence to be surveyed here relates to the same sample period of 1529–34 which was discussed in the last chapter in relation to reduction of infeftments. It will be similarly drawn from the records of Council and Session. The history of arbitration in Scotland and its role in dispute resolution has received surprisingly little attention, especially compared to the considerable body of work which has now been carried out in relation to late medieval England, in particular the series of studies by Edward Powell.[15] Dr Powell has argued that the use of arbitration cannot be taken to reflect a lack of confidence in the court system in fifteenth-century England, for it was often deployed hand in hand with litigation, rather than as a substitute.[16] Arbitration was simply one form of dispute resolution but one which did possess a range of distinctive features which could help achieve settlement, or at least an outcome both parties would agree in advance to accept.[17] Powell has

---

[15] See generally Harriss, *Shaping the Nation*, pp. 197–202 ("Dispute and Disorder in Gentry Society") but in particular Edward Powell, *Kingship, Law, and Society: Criminal Justice in the Reign of Henry V* (Oxford, 1989), pp. 91–107; Edward Powell, "Arbitration and the Law in England in the Later Middle Ages", *Transactions of the Royal Historical Society* 33 (1983), pp. 49–67; Edward Powell, "Settlement of Disputes by Arbitration in Fifteenth-Century England", *Law and History Review* (1984), pp. 21–43. See also Ian Rowney, "Arbitration in Gentry Disputes of the Later Middle Ages", *History* (1982), pp. 367–376; J.B. Post, "Courts, Councils and Arbitrators in the Ladbroke Manor Dispute, 1382–1400" in *Medieval Legal Records Edited in Memory of C.A.F. Meekings*, ed. R.F. Hunnisett and J.B. Post (London, 1978), pp. 289–339; C. Rawcliffe, "That Kindliness Should be Cherished More, and Discord Driven Out: the Settlement of Commercial Disputes by Arbitration in Later Medieval England", in *Enterprise and Individuals in Fifteenth-Century England*, ed. J. Kermode (Stroud, 1991), pp. 99–117; B. Hanawalt, "The Power of Word and Symbol: Conflict Resolution in Late Medieval London", in B. Hanawalt, *"Of Good and Ill Repute": Gender and Social Control in Medieval England* (Oxford, 1998), pp. 35–52. In relation to a much earlier period, see also another contribution to the debate on the nature of dispute resolution in medieval society which argues persuasively for "the importance of the normative" even in dispute resolution outside court procedures: John Hudson, "Court Cases and Legal Arguments in England c. 1066–1166", *Transactions of the Royal Historical Society*, 6th series vol. 10 (2000), pp. 91–115.

[16] Powell, "Arbitration and the Law in England in the Later Middle Ages", p. 57.

[17] See P.C. Ferguson, *Medieval Papal Representatives in Scotland: Legates, Nuncios, and Judges-Delegate, 1125–1286*, Stair Society 45 (Edinburgh, 1997), p. 183, for a similar

also highlighted the important role of the English Chancery in "fostering arbitration", whereas the role in arbitration of the Session has not been examined in any depth hitherto.[18] This chapter will provide an account of the position in Scotland in the years around 1532.

Arbitration in Scotland

As already demonstrated in the earlier chapter on civil procedure, Scotland was a typical late medieval European kingdom with a legal culture informed by the *ius commune*. Predictably, therefore, an important formalised method of resolving disputes outwith judicial structures was arbitration, governed at an early stage by juridical concepts and models already developed in canon law. The particular appropriateness of arbitration as a method must be understood as conditioned by the social context within which disputes occurred, especially when this social context was that of a kin-group. The social structure of Scottish society generally, but especially the Highlands and Borders, rendered the arbitration model particularly appropriate.[19] As David Sellar has noted, "society in the Highlands and Islands of Scotland remained kin-based until well into the eighteenth century".[20] The kinship networks of the Borders have also been emphasised by Dr Maureen Meikle.[21] In this context formalised juridical procedures could be of less value. When activity such as slaughter caused disputes, it was often "the advice and assistance of the kin" which was likely to be of greatest importance.[22] This was due in part to the form of legal liability to compensate which was owed in Scotland through "assythment", discussed earlier in chapter 5. This was the term for compensation for injury. However, the liability

analysis of how a preference for arbitration over litigation before judges-delegate in thirteenth century ecclesiastical disputes in Scotland was not due to "the inefficiency or failure of the judge-delegate process".

[18] Powell, "Arbitration and the Law in England in the Later Middle Ages", p. 65.

[19] See A. Cathcart, *Kinship and Clientage: Highland Clanship 1451–1609* (Leiden, 2006), especially the discussion at pp. 97–98, 126–128; J.E.A. Dawson, *The Politics of Religion in the Age of Mary, Queen of Scots: The Earl of Argyll and the Struggle for Britain and Ireland* (Cambridge, 2002), pp. 67–68; A.I. Macinnes, *Clanship, Commerce and the House of Stuart, 1603–1788* (East Linton, 1996), pp. 6–8.

[20] W.D.H. Sellar, "Assistance in Conflict Resolution in Scotland", *Transactions of the Jean Bodin Society* 64 (1997), pp. 267–275 at p. 268.

[21] M.M. Meikle, *A British Frontier? Lairds and Gentlemen in the Eastern Borders, 1540–1603* (East Linton, 2004), chap. 1 *passim* and pp. 230–232.

[22] Sellar, "Assistance in Conflict Resolution in Scotland", p. 269.

extended to the wider kinship group. Remissions for crimes could not be obtained from the King without certification that assythment had been given.[23] Indeed, this provides a point of departure for the whole subject of the Scottish bloodfeud, to be touched on again in the next chapter.[24]

In this context, scholars such as David Sellar and Jenny Wormald have emphasised the long history enjoyed by arbitration in Scotland since the thirteenth and fourteenth centuries.[25] Arbitration could follow from private attempts to negotiate a settlement as much as from court proceedings. Consequently, resort to arbitration can often be clearly traced in the records of a dispute. Especially in kin-based societies, however, it may be that negotiation, mediation and arbitration were not always clearly distinguishable processes or stages in the resolution of such disputes. A recent short but valuable treatment of arbitration in Scotland by David Sellar represents one of the few attempts to begin writing its history within a broader framework, building upon the earlier work of Lord Cooper.[26] Tracing its history is relevant to an understanding of the interaction of the courts with private and informal methods of dispute resolution. Arbitration seems to imitate the formality of court procedure, taking account of legal rules, and yet operate primarily within the private sphere, forming a bridge between what we have been referring to as public and private justice. This point

[23] See generally H.L. MacQueen and W.D.H. Sellar, "Negligence", in *A History of Private Law in Scotland*, ed. K. Reid and R. Zimmermann (Oxford, 2000), chap. 17, pp. 520–521, also published as "History of Negligence in Scots Law" in *Negligence: the Comparative Legal History of the Law of Torts*, ed. E.J.H. Schrage, 22 Comparative Studies in Continental and Anglo-American Legal History (Berlin, 2001), pp. 276–277; Wormald, "Bloodfeud, Kindred and Government in Early Modern Scotland"; A. Harding, "Rights, Wrongs and Remedies in Late Medieval English and Scots Law", in *Miscellany Four*, ed. H.L. MacQueen, Stair Society 49 (Edinburgh, 2002), pp. 1–8 especially at pp. 5–8; R. Black, "A Historical Survey of Delictual Liability in Scotland for Personal Injuries and Death", Part 1, *Comparative and International Law Journal of South Africa* (1975), pp. 46–70.

[24] K.M. Brown, *Bloodfeud in Scotland 1573–1625* (Edinburgh, 1986), p. 1; Wormald, "Bloodfeud, Kindred and Government in Early Modern Scotland", p. 57.

[25] Sellar, "Assistance in Conflict Resolution in Scotland", pp. 267–268, 270–271; Wormald, "Bloodfeud, Kindred and Government in Early Modern Scotland", pp. 86–87.

[26] Sellar, "Assistance in Conflict Resolution in Scotland", pp. 267–275; T.M. Cooper, "Introduction" to *Select Scottish Cases of the Thirteenth Century*, ed. T.M. Cooper (Edinburgh, 1944), especially pp. xlix–l. Other valuable overviews include R.L.C. Hunter, *The Law of Arbitration in Scotland* (2nd ed., 2002), chap. 2 ("The History of Dispute Settlement Law in Scotland"); W.J. Gilmour, "The Development of Arbitration in Scotland", *Arbitration* 41 (1974), pp. 199–202.

has been stressed by Jenny Wormald in her work on the bloodfeud in Scotland when noting how "the procedure used in the private settlement could very well mirror that of the courts, for arbitration was common in both".[27]

We should note that investigation of the Scottish position involves understanding how the *law* of arbitration operated. In England, by contrast, arbitrations seem to have been largely social rather than legal facts, although inevitably there could be interaction with the procedures of the common law and more particularly the Chancery. Violent feuds in England could on occasion occur and be sufficiently disruptive to attract the attention of the King and be brought to an end by "an arbitration award embodied in an act of Parliament".[28] The medieval English common law, however, does not appear to have regulated the conduct of arbitrations as a matter of law.[29] Dr Powell has commented of the late Middle Ages that "the common-law courts did not make direct provision for the enforcement of arbitration", though John Baker has noted that "there could still be litigation as to whether the arbitrators had made a valid award or whether the parties had performed it".[30]

In Scotland, by contrast, over time the medieval common law does appear to have extended to the regulation of arbitration procedure, and to have adopted a variety of legal rules to this end. By the fourteenth

---

[27] J.M. Wormald, "The Sandlaw Dispute", in *The Settlement of Disputes in Early Medieval Europe*, ed. W. Davies and P. Fouracre (Cambridge 1986), p. 203.

[28] J.H. Baker, *The Oxford History of the Laws of England, Volume VI, 1483–1558* (Oxford, 2003), p. 723.

[29] Holdsworth attributes the creation of a law of arbitration in medieval England entirely to the English common law courts: W. Holdsworth, *A History of English Law*, 14 (London 1964), pp. 187–188. Dr Powell states for the fifteenth century that "arbitration procedure followed a well-defined pattern. While not implying direct judicial supervision of the practice, this undoubtedly reflects the influence of legal development, and the active participation of lawyers in many arbitrations": Powell, *Kingship, Law and Society*, p. 104. Dr Powell traces the extension of the forms of "ecclesiastical arbitration" to lay disputes in the thirteenth and fourteenth centuries, with a notable increase in the evidence for this after 1350. By the fifteenth century the court of Chancery was developing a supervisory role. However, he does not suggest that the canon law rules were themselves received into the common law, rather that there was "widespread imitation of the precise, legalistic formulae of canon-law arbitration, suitably adapted for the requirements of the common law", though the common law courts did not yet supervise arbitration or enforce arbitral awards: Powell, "Arbitration and the Law in England in the Later Middle Ages", pp. 54–55, 62–64. For a general overview of the role of arbitration in medieval English society see M.H. Keen, *English Society in the Later Middle Ages* (Harmondsworth, 1990), pp. 209–212.

[30] E. Powell, "Arbitration and the Law in England in the Later Middle Ages", p. 63; Baker, *The Oxford History of the Laws of England, Volume VI, 1483–1558*, p. 334.

century, such rules were incorporated for the first time into the secular legal treatise known as *Regiam Majestatem*, the most important surviving medieval Scottish law book. The rules in question were not native inventions, however, but clearly derive from thirteenth-century canon law, which was in turn reflected in Scottish thirteenth-century practice. In particular they adopt the language and reflect the distinctions of the canon law between the offices of arbiter, arbitrator and amicable compositor. In order to explain the status of the Scottish rules, this chapter will set in context the influence of the Romano-canonical *ius commune* on arbitration in Scots legal practice between the thirteenth and sixteenth centuries. The process of reception or borrowing of the thirteenth-century canon law rules has already been demonstrated in a seminal article by Peter Stein, but it is also necessary to place this development in a broader context of the development of arbitration in the *ius commune* and how such borrowings may have been understood in Scots law.[31]

Terminology in Scotland

Whilst suggestive, the mere adoption of medieval canon law rules in a treatise like *Regiam Majestatem* tells us little directly about the practice of arbitration, the practical significance of its terminology or how this developed between the thirteenth and sixteenth centuries. The starting point is therefore to adduce some other evidence of practice in Scotland and especially whether the practice of arbitration did rest upon usage of the canonist terms arbiter, arbitrator and amicable compositor. The terms were certainly not restricted to appearances in treatises, being frequently referred to in records of arbitrations, compromises and court proceedings, and to this extent the canon law model of arbitration

[31] I acknowledge that, though convenient, the label "Scots law" is somewhat anachronistic in relation to the period, since it did not yet have a clear technical meaning or presuppose a single fixed hierarchy of legal sources. I am using it in this context to stand for the medieval statute and common law of Scotland. It was for the Scottish "institutional writers" of the 17th century to formulate a broader view of "Scots law" which incorporated a role for other sources such as the *ius commune*. See J.W. Cairns, "The Civil Law Tradition in Scottish Legal Thought" in *The Civilian Tradition and Scots Law*, ed. D.L. Carey Miller and R. Zimmermann (Berlin 1997), pp. 190–223 at p. 199; J.W. Cairns, "*Ius Civile* in Scotland, ca. 1600", *Roman Legal Tradition* 2 (2004), pp. 136–170; J.W. Cairns, "Attitudes to Codification and the Scottish Science of Legislation, 1600–1830", *Tulane European & Civil Law Forum* 22 (2007), pp. 1–78.

clearly became firmly embedded in Scottish legal culture. Whether or not the terms were used with any distinct technical definition in mind poses a difficult question, but they were certainly used.

In Lord Cooper's *Select Scottish Cases of the Thirteenth Century*, for example, not just arbitration but amicable composition is featured, though Cooper's presentation of translated summaries of the records does not distinguish between "arbiters" and "arbitrators"—he uses the term arbiter, but it is unclear whether he has adopted it as a generic term or whether it is a literal translation of the term found in the records.[32] However, if we move forward to the sixteenth century, the first century in which Scottish court records survive in copious amounts, we find the Lords of Council in 1531 sitting judicially but then determining *as arbiters* the "pley debatable" noted above between the second earl of Menteith, Alexander Graham, and Thomas, Walter and Patrick Graham.[33] As we saw, the record stated that decree was given "as juges arbitors for stansching of all pleis quarell and debate amangis the said partiis".[34] On another occasion a matter was submitted "in amicablewis" to be decided before the Lords of Council, seemingly a phrase indicative of amicable composition.[35]

Did any of these terms carry a technical significance? Was any technical difference understood to arise between an arbiter and an arbitrator? In the sixteenth century, when a dispute was submitted for private rather than judicial determination to the Lords of Council, the capacity in which they were to act is variously narrated as "judges arbiters and amicable compositors", "judges arbitrators and amicable compositors", "judges arbiters" or just as "amicable compositors". Were the different terms adopted intentionally? What lay behind these distinctions and especially the appointment of the Lords in more than one capacity? To establish the meaning of these terms in the context of Scottish legal practice may prove elusive, but in order to frame such a discussion it is first necessary to consider their meaning in canon law, and the nature of the borrowing from canon law which sees them appear in *Regiam* by the fourteenth century.

---

[32] *Select Scottish Cases of the Thirteenth Century*, ed. Cooper, p. 49.

[33] The latter were assignees of the late countess of Menteith, grandmother of the earl.

[34] NAS CS 5/43, fol. 79; the general dispute is passingly referred to in J.S. Cameron, *James V: the Personal Rule 1528–1542* (East Linton, 1998), p. 138.

[35] NAS CS 6/4, fol. 70r.

Terminology in the ius commune

Arbitration procedure and terminology derived historically from Roman law.[36] In the Roman *legis actio* and formulary systems there was little distinction made between *iudex* (judge) and *arbiter* since both acted in a private capacity following reference from the magistrate. Professor Buckland observed that "there was no fundamental distinction; an *arbiter* was a *iudex*".[37] Whereas initially the arbiter "was probably an expert who decided questions involving the exercise of discretion", the *iudex* "in later law certainly exercised the functions of *arbiter* also".[38] The *iudex* of classical law was of course, like the arbiter, a layman. Justinian's *Digest* contains many extracts of detailed opinions on the operation of arbitration.[39] However, the later currency of arbitration stemmed from its development in late antiquity, in particular through the role of the bishop in the early church as "a mediator and reconciler of disputes between members of his congregation".[40] By the fourth century bishops could be seen as exercising the role of an arbiter more generally,[41] James Brundage commenting that "the judicial functions of bishops in the early stage of this development mainly involved arbitration".[42]

Norms regarding procedure in episcopal courts therefore embraced the practice of arbitration from the earliest times, drawing at first upon rules developed by the Roman jurists.[43] From these antecedents, and following the twelfth-century revival of Roman law, it is therefore of no surprise that by the thirteenth century there were many sources in the canonist literature which treated procedure by arbitration, and which the Scottish texts in *Regiam Majestatem* resemble. Such texts include Goffredus de Trano's *Summa in Titulos Decretalium* and it is this which has been proved to be the most likely source for the account in the Scottish *Regiam*, as established by Peter Stein's pioneering research.[44] By

[36] For an overview of the development of the *compromissum* and the role of the *arbiter* in Roman law and the *ius commune* see R. Zimmermann, *The Law of Obligations* (Oxford, 1996), pp. 526–530. For a more general but informative account, see P.G. Stein, "Arbitration under Roman Law", *Arbitration* 41 (1974), pp. 203–206.

[37] W.W. Buckland, *A Textbook of Roman Law*, 3rd ed. (Cambridge, 1963), p. 636.

[38] Buckland, *A Textbook of Roman Law*, p. 617.

[39] *D*.4.8.

[40] J.D. Harries, *Law and Empire in Late Antiquity* (Cambridge, 1999), p. 192.

[41] Harries, *Law and Empire in Late Antiquity*, pp. 201, 210–211.

[42] J.A. Brundage, *Medieval Canon Law* (London, 1995), p. 12.

[43] Brundage, *Medieval Canon Law*, p. 12.

[44] Comparisons considered in P.G. Stein, "The source of the Romano-canonical part of Regiam Majestatem", *Scottish Historical Review* (1969), p. 109.

way of further explanation, it is sometimes argued that the thirteenth century seems in more general terms to have witnessed increasing resort to arbitration across the whole of Europe. This is evidenced by the fact that Gratian's *Decretum* of 1140 made only passing reference to arbitration, whereas the *Liber Extra* of 1234 placed a number of decretals under the title *De Arbitris.*[45] Decisions arising from references in Scottish arbitrations account for some of the decretals included in the *Liber Extra.*[46]

It is clear, however, that whatever the significance of the arbiter in Roman law, the concept was heavily developed through its association with ecclesiastical courts and the jurisdiction of the bishop from late antiquity. Scholars of the medieval distinctions between arbiter, arbitrator and amicable compositor have indeed traced a complex development. Here the work of Karl-Heinz Ziegler and Linda Fowler-Magerl is fundamental. Apart from the well known distinction between the *arbiter* deciding according to law, and the *arbitrator* and *amicabilis compositor* deciding according to justice,[47] three further questions are significant for present purposes in the developments they have discussed. First, did proceedings result in a sentence or were the parties left to come to an accord? Second, was there a formal procedure or not? Third, was the result subject to review?

The mature proposition was that an *arbiter* decided according to law and by formal procedure. By the thirteenth century this is contrasted in the canonist literature with the appointment of an *arbitrator* who could decide according to justice and without formal procedure. The distinction is present in the late thirteenth-century *Speculum Iudiciale* of Durantis.[48] The term "arbitrator" as opposed to "arbiter" seems to have been unknown in Justinianic Roman law.[49] Early canonical jurists exploited and defined the term in the late twelfth and early thirteenth centuries so as to adapt the Roman institution of *arbiter* to the practice of arbitration as it had developed, in particular to surmount the bar to

---

[45] K.-H. Ziegler, "Arbiter, Arbitrator und amicabilis compositor" (1967) 84 *Zeitschrift der Savigny-Stiftung für Rechtsgeschichte (Rom. Abt.)*, 239–276 at p. 378. I am very grateful to Philip Simpson, Advocate, for providing me with his own English translation of this article.

[46] Sellar, "Assistance in Conflict Resolution in Scotland", p. 270; *Select Scottish Cases of the Thirteenth Century*, ed. Cooper, p. 15.

[47] Ziegler, "Arbiter, Arbitrator und amicabilis compositor", p. 376.

[48] Ziegler, "Arbiter, arbitrator und amicabilis compositor", p. 376.

[49] Ziegler, "Arbiter, arbitrator und amicabilis compositor", p. 379, n. 29.

a *iudex* acting as *arbiter* which was prescribed by Roman law,[50] as stated by Ulpian in D.4.8.9.2 (13 *ad edictum*). After appointment as a *iudex* in a particular case, it would have been *ultra vires* for the *iudex* then to act as an *arbiter* in the same dispute.

In any event, "arbitrator" became the distinctive office which was superimposed, in Linda Fowler-Magerl's words, onto "the already existent concept of an amicable agreement".[51] As Durantis put it, "*Arbitrator vero est amicabilis compositor*".[52] At first the arbitrator was understood, as in amicable composition, as not delivering a sentence but facilitating a settlement between the parties, though by the mid-thirteenth century arbitrators can be found acting in this respect like arbiters in deciding disputes themselves.[53] By this time, therefore, there seems to be a two-way distinction between arbiters (and sometimes arbitrators) on the one hand, and arbitrators and amicable compositors on the other, the latter acting merely in amicable composition without giving a sentence.[54] In terms of outcomes, however, the distinction between an arbiter and an arbitrator seems to have become blurred relatively early.

The main difference established by Linda Fowler-Magerl between arbiters and arbitrators was one of formality in procedure.[55] An arbiter used a formal procedure in imitation of a court of law. The arbitrator proceeded informally. At first there was also a difference in whether a party could appeal the decisions of arbiters and arbitrators, but during the thirteenth century the distinction was elided as the *arbitrium* of the arbiter came to be regarded by jurists as just as reviewable as the *arbitratus* of the arbitrator.[56] It was a feature of thirteenth century practice, however, that despite the development of these juridical concepts, parties tended to refer disputes to arbitration under a multi-jurisdictional

---

[50] Ziegler, "Arbiter, arbitrator und amicabilis compositor", pp. 378–379.

[51] L. Fowler, "Forms of Arbitration", in *Proceedings of the Fourth International Congress of Medieval Canon Law*, ed. S. Kuttner (1972), pp. 133–147 at p. 136.

[52] Zimmermann, *Law of Obligations*, p. 529.

[53] Fowler, "Forms of Arbitration", p. 143.

[54] In modern French arbitration it seems that arbitrators can be required by the parties to decide according to equity rather than the strict application of legal rules through being asked to act as "amicable compositeurs". A decision in these circumstances which applies legal rules rather than equity can be set aside due to a failure to respect the "mission" of the parties: *Halbout and Matenec H.D. v Hanin*, Cour de Cassation, Chambre civile 2, 2001–02–15, 98–21324, Bull. Civ. 2001 II Nœ 26 p. 19. I am very grateful to James Hope for this point and reference.

[55] Fowler, "Forms of Arbitration", pp. 143–144.

[56] Fowler, "Forms of Arbitration", p. 142.

commission to act as arbiter, arbitrator and amicable compositor, suggesting that the distinctions under discussion were those which jurists recognised as important but which it was not necessarily found relevant to emphasise in practice. It has been suggested by Linda Fowler-Magerl that "the litigants apparently did not care on the whole *how* the matter would be handled; they allowed the arbiter to decide this, and they defined the juridical relationship only when they wanted to question the outcome".[57] Fowler-Magerl regarded this as advantageous for parties in providing for their convenience by promoting flexibility. In other words, when a submission was made the parties would not necessarily be sure or indeed care whether the resolution was achieved in the form of an *arbitrium* or a mere composition, and by deploying the widest form of commission they permitted the most appropriate form of disposal to be used in the light of the course of the arbitration.

Though perhaps generally true of the thirteenth century, in at least one Scottish example this argument is open to question, however. The argument could be made that, having agreed to submit to the jurisdiction of an arbiter, the parties might sometimes have expected to come away with a decision rather than still be able to insist on a negotiated settlement. This stricter model seems to be reflected in the Scottish case of *Inchcolm Abbey v. William de Hercht*, dating from 1240.[58] It turned on a boundary dispute, which was referred to arbiters who found that, after taking evidence, they were unable to reach a determination. They advised the parties to submit to amicable composition, which they did. The original arbiters (who presumably then facilitated the settlement) subsequently oversaw the marking out of the boundaries as agreed. The original commission was not apparently multi-jurisdictional, suggesting that at first the parties *might have* cared about having the matter determined through an arbitration and were not initially prepared just to settle. It was only in the light of the inconclusive arbitration proceedings that the parties considered and opted for amicable composition, on the suggestion of the arbiters themselves.

In the end, therefore, these particular parties did seem to have regard for the capacity in which the arbiters were determining their dispute, though the case also suggests that it may often have been the achievement

---

[57] Fowler, "Forms of Arbitration", pp. 143–144.

[58] *Select Scottish Cases of the Thirteenth Century*, ed. Cooper, p. 49; *Charters of the Abbey of Inchcolm*, ed. D.E. Easson and A. Macdonald, Scottish History Society Third Series 32 (Edinburgh, 1938), p. 19.

of a resolution which was the supreme aim of such proceedings, with the choice of procedure being a secondary matter influenced by the circumstances most likely to achieve this aim. Other Scottish evidence lends some support to Linda Fowler-Magerl's analysis. Paul Ferguson has discussed the thirteenth century case of *Simon de Noisiaco, Rector of Dysart v. Dunfermline Abbey*,[59] in which the parties submitted to arbiters so that "they should have cognisance of the aforesaid cause, without appeal, just as the judges-delegate themselves, or that they should amicably and legitimately make a compromise between the parties".[60] Perhaps the reason for multi-jurisdictional commissions was that disputes referred to arbitration may by definition have often been incapable of a clear-cut legal resolution, if only due to lack of appropriate evidence. When such an impediment to a determination of the dispute by an arbiter was anticipated, it may have been convenient, though not necessary, to authorise arbiters in advance to resort to mediation.

Reception in Scotland

How were these concepts and institutions of the *ius commune* received into Scots law? As indicated already, arbitration occupies a notable part of the fourteenth century *Regiam Majestatem*, the main medieval law book of Scotland.[61] It was largely a manual to procedure in the King's Courts modelled on the late twelfth-century English treatise attributed to Glanvill, the *Tractatus de Legibus et Consuetudinibus Regni Anglie*. It also represents the first significant native source to give a treatment of arbitration and is thought to have been written sometime not long after 1318.[62] The "preface" of *Regiam* is almost identical to the prologue of Glanvill, except for one addition: the attribution of

[59] *Registrum de Dunfermelyn*, ed. C. Innes, Bannatyne Club 74 (Edinburgh, 1842), pp. 66–68 (no. 111).

[60] P.C. Ferguson, *Medieval Papal Representatives in Scotland: Legates, Nuncios, and Judges-Delegate, 1125–1286*, Stair Society 45 (Edinburgh, 1997), p. 182.

[61] See generally P.G. Stein, "Roman Law in Medieval Scotland", in P.G. Stein, *The Character and Influence of the Roman Civil Law* (London, 1988), pp. 269–317 at pp. 280–288; A. Harding, "Regiam Majestatem Amongst Medieval Law Books", (1984) *Juridical Review*, 97–111; H.L. MacQueen, "Regiam Majestatem, Scots Law and National Identity", *Scottish Historical Review* (1995), 1–25; Sellar, "Assistance in Conflict Resolution in Scotland", pp. 270–271.

[62] A.A.M. Duncan, "*Regiam Majestatem*: a Reconsideration", *Juridical Review* 6 (1961), pp. 199–217.

the work to a command of David I of Scotland (1124–53), with the advice and consent of the whole realm.[63] This is obviously mythical since almost none of the sources of *Regiam* yet existed in his reign, let alone a legal system of the sort described in the treatise. However, by adopting this quasi-legislative formula, the intention of the author seems to have been to present the work as officially sanctioned as describing legal rules observed in the courts, legitimated by immemorial tradition dating back to good King David.

The section on arbitration is one of the main canonist parts of a treatise which is otherwise based largely on *Glanvill.* About two thirds of the work is more or less copied from Glanvill, with some editing and revision at various points. Peter Stein first identified the additional canonist source as the thirteenth-century *Summa in Titulos Decretalium* of Goffredus de Trano.[64] The passages from Goffredus are edited and modified as they appear in *Regiam*, presumably in order to reflect local Scottish practice and conditions. If so, this clearly implies that arbitration was not just a practice but an established procedure which was within the purview of the common law in Scotland in the early fourteenth century.[65] Evidence of arbitration hearings adduced by Lord Cooper demonstrates its practice in the thirteenth century. Writing of that period he remarked that "even in these early days there was evidently a marked demand for methods more flexible and equitable than those of the ordinary judicial tribunal, clerical or lay, and we find in a decrescendo of formality the *judex*, the *arbiter*, the *arbitrator*, and the *amicabilis compositor*".[66] However, during the thirteenth century arbitration seems to have been regulated only as a matter of canon law, and was associated particularly with resolving disputes which otherwise might have been argued before ecclesiastical rather than secular common law judges. No systematic study has been made of arbitrations in this specific period, but of the nine examples cited by Lord Cooper in his *Select Scottish Cases of the Thirteenth Century*, four were initially disputes subject to litigation,

[63] T.M. Cooper, "Introduction", in *Regiam Majestatem and Quoniam Attachiamenta*, ed. T.M. Cooper, Stair Society 11 (Edinburgh, 1947), pp. 1–51 at pp. 57–58; cf. *Tractatus de legibus et consuetudinibus regnie Anglie*, ed. G.D. Hall (Oxford, 1993), p. 3 ("Prologue").

[64] Stein, "The source of the Romano-canonical part of Regiam Majestatem", p. 109.

[65] Stein, "The source of the Romano-canonical part of Regiam Majestatem", pp. 110–111 for a discussion of significant changes introduced by the redactor.

[66] *Select Scottish Cases of the Thirteenth Century*, ed. Cooper, p. xlix.

and in every case this was before judges delegate or papal legates rather than secular courts administering the common law.[67]

To what extent arbitration was yet regulated in the secular courts in the fourteenth century is another difficult question. Given the ecclesiastical origins of arbitration, it seems far more likely that disputes over the conduct of an arbitration following a *compromissum* would be determined in the church courts, since the rules governing such matters were part of canon law. How and why the rules on arbitration were considered relevant to an account of the common law is therefore an interesting question. Their place in *Regiam* followed upon the other principal borrowing from Goffredus, which was a series of chapters concerning pacts. There is a certain logic to the place of treatment in *Regiam* since the section on pacts followed one on procedure which ended with a title on concord by the parties. This was based on Glanvill VIII.1 concerning "concords made in the king's court". Here Glanvill stated that "it often happens that cases begun in the lord king's court are ended by amicable composition and final concord subject to the consent and license of the lord king or his justices". *Regiam* repeated this whilst omitting the need for the consent of the King or his justices and adding the explanation that the concord may have arisen as a result of the agreement of the parties *or by arbitration*. Here *Regiam* added the words "*ex pacto conventu seu per arbitrium*". This gave a logical basis to the insertion thereafter of the canonist passages dealing with pacts and arbitration. Moreover, this ordering was one which was customary to any medieval canonist. In Book II of Justinian's *Codex* the title *De Pactis* was followed by another, *De Transactionibus*, dealing with submissions to arbitration. This arrangement tended thereafter to be followed in the various collections of *Decretales*.[68]

The author of *Regiam*, widely argued by scholars to be a canonist himself, might simply have been adopting a standard systematic structure in his account by discussing pacts and arbitration at this point, perhaps drawing as much upon canon law practice as describing accurately what we would regard as the common law, as applied in the secular courts. The compiler may have been concerned with recording the relevant legal norms, and not with distinctions between the nature

---

[67] *Select Scottish Cases of the Thirteenth Century*, ed. Cooper, pp. 3, 13, 17, 34. Whether this may simply reflect the nature of the sources both extant and examined by Lord Cooper is a difficult question.

[68] I am very grateful to Gero Dolezalek for this point.

of the sources of those norms. Quite apart from this doubt, however, since *Regiam* came to be regarded as an authoritative account of the common law, the rules on arbitration seem in any event to have been received into it, regardless of whether this pre-dated their inclusion in *Regiam* itself.

Effect of reception

Through Goffredus the canon law of arbitration was therefore received with modifications into the Scottish common law as described in *Regiam Majestatem*. The matters dealt with included how many arbiters should be appointed; who could act as an arbiter; what questions could be referred to arbitration; the effect of an award by an arbiter; and how arbitrations should be ended procedurally. A detailed comparison of Goffredus' *Summa* and its Scottish redaction has been made by Peter Stein, in what remains the fundamental study of the canon law influence on *Regiam*.[69] A number of points can be drawn from Professor Stein's analysis in relation to arbitration. The bar on the *iudex*, or in the Scottish context the *ballivus ordinarius* or judge ordinary, acting as an *arbiter* was carried over from Goffredus, as well as the allowance that a *ballivus* could nevertheless act as an *arbitrator* in order to resolve a dispute through amicable composition.[70] On such matters the Scottish position was fully in line with canonist thought as it stood in the mid-thirteenth century. The *arbitrator* was not yet recognised as possessing power to decide a dispute. On some other matters, the Scottish redactor formulated rules differently from Goffredus. Whereas Goffredus merely observed, for example, that the enforcement of an award could be assisted by the threat of a penalty, in *Regiam* the validity of the award was itself conditional upon there being a penalty prescribed for non-observance.[71] *Regiam* required an arbiter to be of good repute whereas Goffredus stated that the character of the arbiter had no bearing on the validity of an award.

[69] Stein, "The source of the Romano-canonical part of Regiam Majestatem", pp. 107–123.

[70] *Regiam Majestatem* 2.4, in *Regiam Majestatem*, ed. Cooper, pp. 106–107; Stein, "The source of the Romano-canonical part of Regiam Majestatem", pp. 110–111, 116–117.

[71] Stein, "The source of the Romano-canonical part of Regiam Majestatem", pp. 110–111, 116–117.

One difference which is at first slightly puzzling is that although Goffredus stated that matrimonial causes could not be compromised or settled, but required adjudication by *maiores iudices, Regiam* appears to depart from this. It stated that causes relating to matrimony, personal freedom and crimes could not be decided by arbiters, but compromise *was* apparently allowed through arbitrators and amicable compositors.[72] Clearly, though, questions such as the validity of a marriage could not under any circumstances have been the subject of out-of-court compromises, and so the allowance in *Regiam* must have concerned the incidental and especially financial consequences of a marriage or the *de facto* separation of a married couple.[73] For example, a reference to an arbitration from 1509 is recorded in a protocol book from the archdiocese of Glasgow concerning a dispute over a husband's "non-adherence to his spouse and for not treating her with matrimonial affections" ("*pro non adhesione sue sponse et pro non tractatione matrimoniali affectione eiusdem*").[74] A decree and sentence arbitral had been pronounced against the husband, George Lisle, concerning these matters, and financial penalties imposed.

As already mentioned, the practice of arbitration was clearly in evidence in Scotland in the thirteenth century, and has been discussed in an ecclesiastical context by Paul Ferguson in his analysis of the jurisdiction of papal judges-delegate,[75] as well as by Lord Cooper.[76] Though it is unknown whether *Regiam* was composed with official sanction,[77] it certainly came to be regarded as a formal source of Scots law by the fifteenth century, though still at this time wrongly attributed to David I.[78] The continuing importance of arbitration as a common

[72] Stein, "The source of the Romano-canonical part of Regiam Majestatem", p. 110; *Regiam* 2.6 begins "Potest utique compromitti in causis pecuniariis, temporalibus et spiritualibus. Sed in matrimoniali, in liberali et causa criminali de jure non compromittitur in arbitros sed in arbitratores et amicabiles compositores": see *Regiam Majestatem*, ed. Cooper, p. 108.

[73] I am very grateful to Gero Dolezalek for this point.

[74] Described in Gilmour, "The Development of Arbitration in Scotland", pp. 199–200; see *Liber Protocollorum M. Cuthberti Simonis*, ed. J. Bain and C. Rogers, Grampian Club (1875) vol. 8:1, no. 362, p. 435 (English translation), vol. 8:2, pp. 280–281 (Latin).

[75] Ferguson, *Medieval Papal Representatives in Scotland*, pp. 182–184.

[76] *Select Scottish Cases of the Thirteenth Century*, ed. Cooper, p. xlix.

[77] The most recent assessment by Professor Hector MacQueen "supports suggestions that *Regiam* had 'official' rather than 'private' origins; that is, the author was closely connected to and was perhaps commissioned by the king's court": MacQueen, "Regiam Majestatem, Scots Law and National Identity", p. 6.

[78] Cooper, "Introduction" to *Regiam Majestatem*, ed. Cooper, p. 2.

method of resolving disputes in the fifteenth century is suggested by the intervention of Parliament in 1427 to legislate on certain aspects of arbitration procedure, imposing a requirement in any submission to arbitration that there be an uneven number of arbiters, reinforcing a rule present in *Regiam*.[79] Parliament laid down a procedure for choosing an "oversman" where a submission provided only for an even number of arbiters. In relation to clerics, the local bishop should choose one; for laymen, the choice fell to the local sheriff; for burgesses, it was the local provost and burgh council. It is interesting that the provisions of this statute suggest that arbitration in the early fifteenth century in Scotland could quite naturally be subject to the supervision of regular judicial officers, as well as to legislation emanating from Parliament. This supports the view that the appearance of the rules in *Regiam* on arbitration signal their reception into the common law of Scotland. Furthermore, it supports the argument that the courts which administered the common law of Scotland were not seen as occupying a separate plane from other methods of dispute resolution, and correspondingly do not seem to have been perceived as remote from the use of such methods.

Canonist writings such as the *Speculum Iudiciale* supplemented *Regiam* and statutory sources, though not necessarily so clearly as a source of the Scottish common law as such. That styles of submission to arbitration taken from the *Speculum* were in routine use, though, is certainly evident in the later fifteenth century in litigation before the King's Council.[80] Unsurprisingly, given the absence of any juristic treatise on Scots law between the fourteenth and early seventeenth centuries, the statements concerning arbitration made by Sir James Balfour in his *Practicks* (completed in the early 1580s) do not represent any particular advance on those contained in *Regiam Majestatem*, which in fact constitute his main source.[81] They suggest, however, both that arbitration

[79] *The Acts of the Parliament of Scotland*, 12 vols, ed. T. Thomson and C. Innes, (Edinburgh, 1882–1914) vol. 2, p. 14, c. 6. I am very grateful to John Cairns for this reference.

[80] George Neilson, "Introduction" to *Acta Dominorum Concilii: Acts of the Lords of Council in Civil Causes, vol. II, A.D. 1496–1501* [hereafter *ADC* ii], ed. G. Neilson and H. Paton (Edinburgh, 1918), pp. liv–lv; W.M. Gordon, "The Acts of the Scottish Lords of Council in the Late Fifteenth and Early Sixteenth Centuries: Records and Reports" in *Law Reporting in Britain*, Proceedings of the Eleventh British Legal History Conference, ed. C. Stebbings (London 1995), pp. 55–71 at p. 59, n. 15; J.W. Cairns, "Historical Introduction", p. 72.

[81] *The Practicks of Sir James Balfour of Pittendreich*, vol. 2, ed. P.G.B. McNeill, Stair Society vol. 22, (Edinburgh, 1963), pp. 411–417 ("Anent Arbitrie").

remained a commonly used procedure, and that its supervision formed a regular part of the business of the Session, a suggestion to be further examined in the remainder of this chapter as well as the following chapter. Balfour may have simply plundered Regiam for a set of rules to plausibly fill in the relevant section of his *Practicks* whether or not those rules bore an exact relation to the actual conduct of arbitrations in sixteenth century Scotland. However, this seems improbable. With an eye to practice and procedure, he does state that in the tabling of actions matters concerning decrees arbitral were "commoun privilegit actiounis".[82] The late sixteenth century Court of Session therefore maintained a case-load deriving in part from arbitration. Whether this role owed much directly to the presence of canonist rules on arbitration in Scots law as recognised in *Regiam* or whether it merely reflects the acquisition by the Session of the kind of institutional role which the English Chancery had possessed in relation to arbitrations since the fifteenth century is another question. The canonist terminology itself certainly remained part of Scots law, styles of appointment such as "judge-arbitrator and amicable compositor" being found at the end of the eighteenth century and beyond.[83]

Arbitration and the Lords of Council and Session as arbiters

By the sixteenth century, there were various ways in which parties tended to involve the courts in the conduct of their arbitrations, for example through registering and sometimes requesting the interpretation of agreements to arbitrate. These will be discussed in the next chapter. The remaining discussion in this chapter will focus upon why parties might prefer arbitration to litigation in the first place and what its distinctive features were. In terms of the application in Scotland of the juridical norms of arbitration, questions may arise such as whether recognition was given to the technical distinctions between the offices of arbiter, arbitrator and amicable compositor which have been discussed in relation to medieval canon law.

[82] *The Practicks of Sir James Balfour*, ed. McNeill, p. 272. I am very grateful to John Cairns for this reference.

[83] Gilmour, "The Development of Arbitration in Scotland", p. 202.

The manuscript record of the Lords of Council and Session over the five year period around about the year 1532 provides the primary evidence for the discussion (i.e. 1529–1534). If "arbitration" is taken to be the generic term encompassing the work of arbiters, arbitrators and amicable compositors (assuming for the time being that meaningful distinctions between the three were recognised), then between April 1529 and May 1534 there are thirty-two cases in the council register which involved the submission of a dispute to the Lords in one or other of these capacities. It should be noted incidentally that the business of the Session continued to be recorded after 1532 in the main council register and a separate privy council register is only extant from 1545.[84] Apart from the thirty-two arbitration cases, there are a further thirteen general references of a decision to the deliverance of the Lords with no explicit mention of the capacity in which they are to act, other than as Lords of Council. Two further cases involve a similar reference to the King personally. It should be noted that Lords of Session were always technically Lords of Council as well, both before and after 1532.

These cases usefully illustrate two points in particular about the terms of commission of judges in arbitration proceedings. First, it is possible that recognised distinctions between the offices of arbiter, arbitrator and amicable compositor may be implied by the separate use of these terms in the clauses narrating the appointment, although this would not seem consistent with earlier medieval usage. Of the thirty-two arbitration references to the Lords of Council, in nine they were to sit as judges arbiters and amicable compositors; in nine as judges arbitrators and amicable compositors; in ten merely as amicable compositors; in two merely as judges arbiters; and in two as judges and amicable compositors with no reference to arbitrators or arbiters. Secondly, although these distinctions may have been recognised, it is clear that most commonly two offices were combined, as in arbiters and amicable compositors, to the extent that appointment as arbiter or arbitrator almost invariably carried with it appointment as amicable compositor. Whether there was any difference in practice in the conduct of proceedings under these various offices is, however, very difficult to say. For example, if amicable

[84] See observations on the creation of a separate privy council register in *Guide to the National Archives of Scotland*, Stair Society Supplementary Series 3 (Edinburgh, 1996), p. 20; Bruce Webster, *Scotland from the Eleventh Century to 1603*, The Sources of History: Studies in the Use of Historical Evidence (London, 1975), p. 210.

composition was merely mediation without power of determination, it is hard to explain cases where the Lords did give decree as amicable compositors, an example of which will be cited later. Overall, the variety of uses may imply that nothing turned upon the distinctions between terms such as arbiter and arbitrator. Such a conclusion would seem consistent with the earlier medieval practice already described by which appointment was often to all three offices so as to allow maximum flexibility in determining the dispute.

Distinctiveness of arbitration procedure

What made arbitration procedure distinctive and why might parties prefer it to litigation? It is a feature of the record that litigation before the Session was quite often abandoned for arbitration, by an agreement known as a "compromit" (*compromissum* or compromise), that is to say a submission of the dispute to the Lords as arbiters. The reverse situation in which an initial arbitration was superseded by litigation seems to have been rarer. One of the main advantages of arbitration was that it was intended to avoid the protracted duration and procedural complexities of litigation. Typically, a very short timescale was established, lasting no more than several weeks, within which the arbiters had to give their decision. When matters were submitted to the Lords as arbiters, commonly during ongoing litigation before the Session, they would often give decree immediately at that very hearing.

By the 1520s, submission of disputes to the Lords as arbiters was not simply a matter of appointing a chosen number to sit in a private capacity. A new feature was their appointment collectively—as a whole court—to be arbiters. This is significant, since it represents the submission of a dispute to a court, and the judges collectively of that court, but with the procedure of the court displaced through a preference for that of arbitration. This brings out pointedly the fact that parties themselves must have been well aware of the distinction between and respective advantages of litigation and arbitration. This is especially striking in situations in which the matter was already under summons before the Lords of Council.[85] The practice of appointing the Lords

[85] Ironically, in the eighteenth century the Court of Session was criticised for using a procedure so flexible that it was likened to being "not so much a court of law as a court of arbitration": N. Phillipson, *The Scottish Whigs and the Reform of the Court of Session 1785–1830*, Stair Society 37 (Edinburgh, 1990), p. 59.

collectively as arbiters (as opposed to appointing a series of named individuals) seems to have been virtually unknown in the period up to 1500, though George Neilson pointed out an instance of the fifteenth-century parliamentary judges, the Lords Auditors of Causes and Complaints, being named in the early 1470s as oversmen "all as ane" in the event of a disagreement between arbiters.[86] However, it is certainly a feature of the record by the end of the 1520s. It is an open question how the practice may have developed between 1500 and the 1520s.

What was distinctive about the collective appointment of the Lords as arbiters was that the matter was in effect being submitted to whoever happened to be in attendance at the Session of that day. In such cases, the credibility of the Session as a sufficiently balanced and independent tribunal must have justified to parties the sacrifice of the right to select the arbiters personally. As noted above, following such a submission, the Lords would very often move immediately to deliver their decree arbitral. This kind of involvement in disputes enhances the extent to which the records of the Lords of Council can be exploited in relation to the sixteenth century for incidental information relating to arbitration and provides a substantial basis for this and the next chapter. Importantly for the main theme of this book, it also seems to demonstrate regard for the institution of the Session in the years around 1532, above and beyond mere regard for the authority and expertise of individual Lords. This seems to mirror increasing recognition of the *judicial* authority which the Session possessed during the course of the early sixteenth century, and which lies behind the development of its jurisdiction in heritage after 1513. This general growth in the authority of the Session was underway before the foundation of the College of Justice, but the foundation of the College can only have reinforced it.

An example of the collective appointment of Session judges is that of Hew, Lord Somerville, and John Somerville of Cambusnethane binding themselves on 1 April 1531 to "keep the decreet and sentence of lordis of counsale namyt be the kinges grace upon the Sessioun as jugis arbitrators and amicable compositors".[87] The dispute seems to have arisen from the slaughter of a certain John Maitland by John Somerville, but the terms of the Lords' appointment embraced "all

[86] George Neilson, "Introduction" to *ADC* ii, p. liv; *The Acts of the Lords Auditors of Causes and Complaints*, ed. T. Thomson (Edinburgh, 1839), p. 22.
[87] NAS CS 5/42, fol. 165.

clames of heretage" and "all otheris slauchteris" as well.[88] Clearly the approach to the Lords as arbitrators was against the background of a feud, since Lord Somerville appeared not merely personally, but on behalf of "his near kyn and servants, allyas and part takaris". There was also an existing summons of spuilzie (i.e. dispossession) against John Somerville as well.[89] This kind of use of the Lords of Session may imply a shifting perception of them by the later 1520s if not earlier. They may have been seen in this context less as a politicised body of undifferentiated royal councillors and instead as possessed of a more fixed, institutional and corporate identity. As such they would have been perceived to have the capacity to rise above the separate interests concerned in a feud in order to exercise a truly adjudicative role. The comparative frequency of such collective appointment may also imply that whatever the composition of the Council or Session in terms of particular judges, it was generally considered to offer sufficiently impartial adjudication in this sense. The terms of the resolution represented by the decreet arbitral arising from this particular arbitration broke down by July 1531. However, the parties continued to seek redress from the Lords of Council, thus underlining the central role of the Lords in the handling of the dispute as well as the role of arbitration within the context of court proceedings.[90]

The stress was as much upon avoiding interminable legal process as simply upon reaching a speedy resolution of the dispute. There was more than one disadvantage to prolonged litigation, not least expense. A common explanation given in the record for why the parties were submitting to arbitration was "staunching of plea", i.e. a desire to terminate conclusively further legal proceedings. An example of this is the dispute between James Douglas of Parkhead and Margaret Allan over the lands of Sandilands. The dispute had already involved an action before the local judge, the sheriff of Lanark. It featured in the council register in 1531, and again in 1532, when Margaret raised a related action of warrandice against Gilbert Inglis.[91] At the end of July 1533,

[88] NAS CS 5/42, fol. 165.

[89] NAS CS 5/42, fol. 165v.

[90] NAS CS 5/43, fol. 18v. There is no reference to the arbitration in this subsequent record of proceedings but simply to the fulfilling of a decreet given by the Lords of Council between the parties which John Somerville claimed to have fulfilled in all points, the language of which might imply that it was a decreet arbitral to which he referred.

[91] NAS CS 6/2, fol. 114.

after eleven previous hearings before the Lords since December 1531,[92] this second action was submitted to the Lords as arbitrators and amicable compositors "to decern and determine in the said action amicablie and to geif thir finale sentence and decret betwix the saidis partiis as thai think maist expedient for staunching of pley in tymes cuming". The Lords went on to "desertis the said sumondis for evir" before giving a complex disposal of the dispute.[93] Although this involved a financial settlement, curiously it was made dependent upon the result of a fresh legal process which the Lords ordained Margaret Allan to raise by summons "with all diligence", which summons would be "privilegis" when called in court. Therefore, although the decree arbitral did not conclude matters, perhaps the aim of "staunching of pley" can be regarded as accomplished by the setting of a precise framework by the Lords within which the dispute should be finally resolved in this case.[94]

Similarly in December 1532, though arbitration is not mentioned as such, George Leslie, earl of Rothes, and David Garden of the Newton consented that "for staunching of lang process" the Lords should be "jugis" to decide whether certain lands were redeemable under a contract of reversion.[95] Sometimes the Lords even used the phrase themselves when giving their decree as arbiters. In the dispute between Alexander Graham, earl of Menteith and Thomas Graham in 1531, it was stated that the Lords gave their decree "as juges arbitors for stansching of all pleis quarell and debate amangis the said partiis".[96] In the dispute already described in 1534 between Lord Borthwick and the archbishop of St Andrews, the stress upon speedy resolution arose because of the "gret consummyng and spending of the substance and money of this realme",[97] amounting to "exhorbitant expensis".[98] Unusually, when these parties had first come before the Lords at the command of the King, they had been assigned a period of time following which they were to "schaw and declare thir myndis to the lordis of counsale gif thai war inclynit to pas to concord and submit thaim to the saidis

[92] NAS CS 5/43, fols. 121r., 140; CS 6/1, fols. 12v, 15v; CS 6/2, fols. 77v, 114, 118v, 119v, 166, 187v, 194v, 195v, 218. CS 6/3, fols. 24, 58v.

[93] NAS CS 6/3, fol. 58v.

[94] NAS CS 6/3, fol. 58v.

[95] NAS CS 6/2, fol. 33r.

[96] NAS CS 5/43, fol. 79.

[97] NAS CS 6/4, fol. 70r. See Hannay, "Some Questions Regarding Scotland and the Canon Law", pp. 25–34.

[98] NAS CS 6/4, fol. 16v.

lordis in the caus debatable".[99] This demonstrates the Lords exercising a regulatory role at the instance of the King in seeking to encourage settlement of a dispute, not merely acting as judges or arbiters on the initiative of the parties.

Occasionally, it is explicitly stated that the submission to the Lords came after long and therefore presumably inconclusive argument. For example, on 23 March 1530 a summons of the King and George Leslie, earl of Rothes, against John Kinnaird of that Ilk was called. It related to the right to the feudal casualty of avail of marriage. It was stated that "eftir lang argumente and disputatioune and productionis of documentis bath the saidis partiis referrit the said matter to be decidit be the lordis as amicable compositouris", after which the Lords gave immediate decree.[100] This outcome also implies that the Lords had power to determine the dispute in this capacity, contrary to the general understanding of the amicable compositor as a mediator, as outlined earlier. Another example is the submission of the dispute between James Bannatyne and other tenants and James Livingstone and Robert Dalziel in February 1534. The tenants were complaining of being forced to pay their thirl multures twice over, concurrently to each laird, and both men were charged to produce their "right".[101] The record states that:

> thare rytis, resonis and allegationis with the productionis of divers charteris, infeftmentis and evidentis, togidder with ane decrete arbitral... eftir lang argumentis and disputatiounis, baith the saidis partiis referrit the said action for thir rytis to the lordis of counsale to be decydid be thaim in amicable wiss as jugis arbitouris and amicable compositors.[102]

The implication is that arguments had failed to resolve the matters in dispute, or perhaps had revealed the need to prove certain points which the parties had realised would prolong their dispute significantly.

The purpose of arbitration

These were some of the principal obstacles which could be overcome by submission to arbitration. But in what ways did arbitration have a

[99] NAS CS 6/4, fol. 70r.
[100] NAS CS 5/41, fol. 32v (23 March 1530).
[101] Thirl multures conferred the right to payment to the proprietor or tenant of a mill of a duty in kind on corn ground there.
[102] NAS CS 6/4, fol. 6v (14 February, 1534).

distinctive purpose compared to litigation? What criteria did arbiters use in making their decision? Often the parties explained that it was for "amity" that they were resorting to arbitration. This supports the orthodox thesis that private methods of dispute resolution aimed at settlement through compromise, though it is perhaps questionable whether such language amounted to more than superficial rhetoric in some cases. For example, at the end of February 1532 Alexander Innes and Alexander Ogilvy submitted a land dispute to the Lords of Council as arbitrators and amicable compositors "for the mair sicker tendir life and amite to be had amangis thame in tymis cuming".[103] This was the ninth hearing in this dispute in two years. It embraced at least two successive litigations and two arbitrations, and came before the Lords thirteen times in all between 31 March 1530 and 22 November 1533.[104] In the decree arbitral which the Lords immediately delivered, Ogilvy was ordered to pay Innes 600 merks in settlement, but the role of "amite" was again hinted at when it was stated in the decree that the payment was to be made "for his gude will rycht and clame".[105] These sentiments did not prevent the parties returning to court to persevere in their dispute, however.

Amity was therefore an elusive goal. An arbitration submission to the Session involved asking the Lords to determine how best to achieve it. In a dispute between Isabel and Janet Inglis and their spouses and Alexander Shaw of Sauchy and the inquest which had served him to the lands of Ardmure in 1533, for example, the matter was referred to the Lords as amicable compositors. This was so that the Lords would "decid thirupoune in amicable wys as thai think maist profitable for the weile of baith the partiis".[106] But amity also depended upon acceptance and implementation by both sides. In the case of Lord Lindsay of the Byres and Andrew Kinninmonth in July 1532, after the submission of the parties to arbitration concerning a dowry payment, the Lords of Council gave sentence and "willand the weile of baith the saidis partiis, kindness and friendship to stand among thaim thir kyn and friendes".[107] As in the Ogilvy-Innes dispute, the decree arbitral does not in this case

[103] NAS CS 5/43, fol. 173 (27 February, 1531/32).
[104] NAS CS 5/41, fol. 54v; CS 5/42, fol. 40, 58, 61; CS 5/43, fol. 133v, 146v, 148, 167, 171, 173; CS 6/2, fol. 64v, 193; CS 6/3 fol. 44v, 146.
[105] NAS CS 5/43, fol. 173.
[106] NAS CS 6/3, fol. 8.
[107] NAS CS 6/1, fol. 59v.

appear to have closed the matter, if for no other reason than that the implementation of the decree could and did become a fresh cause of dispute, undermining the amicable objectives of the arbitration. As early as the end of August 1532, one of the parties returned to the Lords and disputed the execution of the decree. Both sides had to be ordained to appear to "hear and see it be pronuncit and ordourit how the said decrete... sal be put to execution".[108] It was only on 18 January 1533 that this joint appearance eventually happened, however.[109] The Lords then seem to have effectively revised the terms of their decree arbitral rather than simply interpreting it for the parties. Even this was not enough to persuade the parties to implement the decree since they returned again in May and October 1533 complaining of non-fulfilment.[110]

The rhetoric of amity could extend to the condition of both the parties and the kingdom as a whole. In a dispute over a coal mine between the abbot of Newbattle and James Ramsay of Cockpen in 1532 the Lords gave their decree as arbiters and amicable compositors after "beand ripelie avisit havand ee [i.e. eye] to the weile of the saidis partiis and common weile of the realme for the myning of colys to sustene the kingis lieges".[111] The sort of language used in these cases suggests strongly that at least in a formal sense the grounds upon which arbitration proceeded were distinguishable from those relevant to legal action, and even suggest the promotion of "love" rather than "law". This distinction has been emphasized by Michael Clanchy in his discussion of the basis for dispute resolution in the medieval period.[112] Clanchy has addressed the broad principles underlying dispute settlement in writing that "law (standing for learning and the application of rules) and love (standing for common sense and bonds of affection) can be seen as contrasting styles in the settlement of disputes in the Middle Ages".[113] This contrast will be discussed further in the next chapter in relation to private and public justice. It is sufficient to note here that arbitration in early sixteenth-century Scotland carried with it a distinctive rhetoric which resonates with Clanchy's model.

---

[108] NAS CS 6/1, fol. 108v.

[109] NAS CS 6/2, fol. 50 (18 January, 1532/33).

[110] NAS CS 6/2, fol. 162v; CS 6/3, fol. 69v.

[111] NAS CS 6/1, fol. 105v.

[112] M.T. Clanchy, "Law and Love in the Middle Ages", in *Disputes and Settlements*, ed. J. Bossy (Cambridge, 1983), pp. 47–67 at p. 52.

[113] Clanchy, "Law and Love in the Middle Ages", p. 52.

Another distinguishing feature of arbitration was that it could encompass not just a particular dispute, but all outstanding matters of dispute between two parties. An example is that of Alexander Dunbar of Cumnock and Huchon Rose of Kilravock, who compromitted before the Session on 30 August 1529.[114] In the compromit, the scope of their dispute was expressed at three levels: first, "anent the nonentres of the land and barony of Sanquhar"; secondly, "all utheris rytis that ay of thame can ask, has had or may haif to the saidis landis"; and thirdly, "all utheris materis debatable betwix thaim".[115] Sometimes parties adopted an extremely expansive approach and simply submitted to arbitration "all materis, questions, cravinges and pleyis that any of thame has againis utheris any maner of way and be quhatsumevir caus". This occurred under a compromit between Lord Hay of Yester and George Hay on 31 March 1530, who submitted themselves to Gavin Dunbar, bishop of Aberdeen, George, coadjutor of Aberdeen, and James Hay, bishop of Ross.[116] In this instance no particular matter of dispute was specifically identified as being within "all materis".

Broadly speaking then, arbitration was evidently intended to enable a determination to be reached swiftly and to take into account the best interests of both parties, even if in practice this was difficult to achieve. Moreover, as already noted, a reference to arbitration could encompass all outstanding matters of dispute between the parties, and thus realistically hope to establish lasting "concord" if the decree arbitral was implemented. However, arbitration also differed in the nature of the remedy granted. It could go beyond simply providing a remedy to make good a particular wrong suffered, and could require further acts of contrition or reconciliation by the parties. This is where the rhetoric of "amity" seems to have had more substance to it through requiring a party to demonstrate outwardly feelings of contrition, perhaps through a ritual performance of some kind. Barbara Hanawalt has demonstrated for fifteenth-century London how "not only the participants in a reconciliation needed outward ceremony to bind their agreement, but the symbolic exchanges reinforced the urban values of harmony", and we might suppose that this observation could apply equally well to other types of community or society in this period.[117]

[114] NAS CS 5/40, fol. 111v.
[115] NAS CS 5/40, fol. 111v.
[116] NAS CS 5/41, fol. 52.
[117] Hanawalt, "The Power of Word and Symbol: Conflict Resolution in Late Medieval London", p. 38.

Ritual observances were certainly prescribed in Scotland as part of settlements imposed by arbitration before the Lords. In a decree arbitral given by the Lords as arbiters and amicable compositors between Lord Fleming and John Tweedie of Drumelzier in March 1531 for example, the Lords decreed that Tweedie "sall infeft ane chaplane perpetualie to sing within the kirk of Biggar to pray for the soule of umquhile Johne Lord Flemyng havand the sum of £10 yearlie of annuell to spend and ane foundation to be maid thereof of the said Johne Twedy's heritage and lande".[118] Tweedie and Fleming were also to join hands in the presence of the King and the Lords of Council.[119] Again, the role of the King in encouraging the pursuit of an arbitrated settlement before the Council is apparent. Lord Fleming had earlier stated that "he mycht get the kinges mynde to submit him to the lordes as amicable compositours. And woll he knawis his grace of gude mynd thereintill tharfor he wald at the kinge's grace plesour submit him and presently submit him to the lordis of counsel in that behalf".[120] Tweedy stated in response that he would submit as well, "at the request of the lordis of counsell", and would do so "in all charge his heritage and lif being except".[121] The intention of both parties to effect concord as soon as the arbitration was underway is displayed in the manner in which both acted to "assure" each other and their kindreds (i.e. guarantee their safety) until the feast of Beltane, Lord Fleming specifically doing so by "the ostensioun of his hand".[122] The parties then "band oblist and compromittit thame be their gret aithis" to abyde by the result of the arbitration.[123] Arbitration procedure allowed the parties to stake their personal honour and reputation on mutual acceptance of the outcome. It also allowed the giving of a formal oath to be secured with further ritual gestures which promoted the sense of being bound by personal honour and not merely legal formality.

Another obvious advantage of arbitration was that the parties could choose the arbiters individually. Often, the arbiters would consist of a mixture of kinsmen and influential patrons of both parties, or on other

---

[118] NAS CS 5/42, fol. 93 (4 March 1531).

[119] These are merely instances in a severe feud that had been active since the murder of John, Lord Fleming in 1524: see J. Finlay, *Men of Law in Pre-Reformation Scotland*, East Linton 2000, pp. 77–78.

[120] NAS CS 5/42, fol. 23v.

[121] NAS CS 5/42, fol. 23v.

[122] NAS CS 5/42, fol. 24.

[123] NAS CS 5/42, fol. 25r.

occasions experienced men of law or Lords of Session who may have had little personal connection with either party. Or, as we have seen, parties seem to have come to regard the King's Council, usually in its specifically judicial guise as the Session, as itself a suitable arbiter. In these cases they seem to have been willing to forego further involvement in the selection of individual arbiters by nominating the Lords collectively. Upon occasion all the possibilities would be combined, as when in 1530 the prior and convent of the Dominican friars of Perth and John Ross of Craigie consented to submit their dispute to the Lords of Session, with the archbishop of St Andrews, the bishop of Aberdeen and the Laird of Balwerie, Sir William Scott, "being present with the saidis lordis of sessioun for that tyme".[124]

The same example also illustrates how, when parties bound themselves to arbitration, they submitted to certain conditions which were evidently intended to fulfil the objectives of speed and finality. The two principal conditions of a technical nature in this category were that there should be no dilatory exceptions pleaded and that there should be no appeal from the deliverance of the arbiters. The Dominicans and John Ross bound themselves to "stand at thir sentence howevir thai deliver therein bot ony dilatour exceptionis or appellationis".[125] Similarly, in 1529 John Johnston of that Ilk and William Hamilton of Maristoune bound themselves "in the maist straite forme of compromitt without reclamatioun or revocatioun", with the Lords of Council to give decree as amicable compositors on a summons of error.[126] As we saw in an earlier chapter, dilatory exceptions were pleas which advanced "objections to the form in which an action was brought, rather than to its substance" and concerned some procedural or jurisdictional flaw in the case.[127] They could hamper the progress of litigation considerably. As for appeals, the whole point of arbitration was to bring a dispute to

---

[124] NAS CS 5/41, fol. 126v. The need to nominate Sir William Scott of Balweary is puzzling since he sat as a Lord of Session at this time anyway, being named in the ordinances of 12 February 1526, 13 March 1527, and 14 February, 1531: *ADCP*, pp. 238, 256, 349. However, prior to the foundation of the College of Justice and its first meeting on 27 May 1532 it is not possible to speak of a fixed body of nominated Lords of Session who were exclusively assigned the judicial business of the King's Council, which other Lords of Council could not have attended to *ex officiis*.

[125] NAS CS 5/42, fol. 126v.

[126] NAS CS 5/40, fol. 22v.

[127] H.L. MacQueen, *Common Law and Feudal Society in Medieval Scotland* (Edinburgh, 1993), pp. 77, 258; Finlay, *Men of Law in Pre-Reformation Scotland*, p. 106; Brundage, *Medieval Canon Law*, p. 130.

an end conclusively, not with a narrowly based legal decision but with a settlement capable of commanding the assent of all the parties and which they had agreed in advance to accept. After all, the defender in a court action was not required to consent to the adjudication of the court if it possessed jurisdiction. A remedy could be granted against him whether or not he entered the proceedings. However, arbiters were by definition appointed by both parties, and a concomitant of that was the acceptance of their decision irrevocably. There were certainly occasions when parties would come back before Council in relation to a decree arbitral, but this was normally to question whether it was being fulfilled correctly and not to have it overturned.

However, apart from agreeing to forego formal appeal against the decision of the arbiters and dilatory exceptions, parties also commonly bound themselves to promise to observe whatever sentence was pronounced. The Dominicans and John Ross did so and in 1532 the prior of Pittenweem, Eufame Ramsay and Paul Dishington submitted to the amicable composition of the Lords and "oblist thaim to abyde at thir sentence howevir thai deist thirin".[128] In February 1534 James Bannatyne, his fellow tenants, James Livingstone and Robert Dalziel submitted to the arbitration of the Lords and "hes suorne to abyde at thir deliverance".[129] This condition tended to be mirrored in the giving of the decree arbitral when the Lords would use words such as "decern and deliver and for finale sentence pronuncit".[130] On other occasions such as the dispute over a gable wall in 1531 between Christine Gray, James Abernethy and Gilbert Logan, the finality of the decision is brought out in the terms of the decree where the Lords "putte perpetuale silence to the said Cristaine and James, thair airis and assignais of all clame tuiching the said gabill and steppis of the said stair in tyme tocum".[131] Again, practice and theory may have diverged, since in both these last two examples a previous decree arbitral had already been delivered, though not by the Lords of Council and Session. This suggests incidentally that the authority of the arbiters had to be great enough in the circumstances of the dispute to secure observance of the decree arbitral delivered by them. In the Gray-Abernethy-Logan case, an additionally authoritative element in the arbitration was that

---

[128] NAS CS 6/2, fol. 10r.
[129] NAS CS 6/4, fol. 6v (14 February, 1534).
[130] NAS CS 6/1, fol. 59v (*Lord Lindsay v. Andrew Kinninmonth*, 9 July, 1532).
[131] NAS CS 5/42, fol. 160.

the Lords gave their deliverance "with the avise of the principalis maseris and wrytes of Edinburgh", the reliance upon expert opinion presumably enhancing the finality of the decree arbitral.[132] In another arbitration already mentioned which followed on from an action by summons, the Lords gave their decree arbitral and signalled the finality of the resolution by pronouncing that they "desertis the said summondis for evir".[133]

Beyond the pattern which has just been outlined, there were further occasional variations which can be found in particular submissions to arbitration. For example, sometimes specific powers were conferred on the arbiters. Hew, Lord Somerville, and John Somerville of Cambusnethane appointed the Lords of Council as arbitrators and amicable compositors in April 1531, specifically "with power to the saidis lordis to prorogat the said terme of deliverance to sic uther dais as thai sall ples and think maist expedient provyding always that thai pronunce thair decret herin befor the rysing of this your sessionis".[134] The parties consented in advance to the Lords exercising a discretion over precisely when they would be in a position to give their decree arbitral.

Sometimes a matter under summons could be referred to the Lords as judges arbiters but only apparently for their advice and counsel, with a view to the parties then reaching "concord" amongst themselves. Such a procedure appears close to the idea of mediation and amicable composition, though these terms may not in fact be used by the parties. Thus on 17 March 1531 Alexander Innes and Alexander Dunbar (dean of Moray) and the chapter of Moray:

> referrit to the saidis lordis as jugis arbitours to avis with the ground rycht and poyntis of the summondis and to give thir counsale thirupoune to the dene and chapter of Murray how thai think suld be done in the said matter...and end the action be way of concord.[135]

The Lords accepted this commission and deputed twelve of their number to act as "neutrale and discrete men to consider the said summonde and merite of the caus and thereftir geve thir consale thirupoune", stating that if their counsel is not accepted then the summons will simply

[132] NAS CS 5/42, fol. 160.
[133] NAS CS 6/3, fol. 58v.
[134] NAS CS 5/42, fol. 165 (17 March 1531).
[135] NAS CS 5/42, fol. 123.

be continued till the third day of the next Session.[136] The practice of taking the "counsel" of the Lords is also displayed in some cases of litigation without an arbitration element. For example, in November 1531 Patrick Hepburn, earl of Bothwell, won an action against Andrew Kerr of Gradane, apparently for wrongous occupation of the lands of Sandestains, for which Andrew had claimed an assedation (i.e. lease).[137] However, Andrew went on to ask instruments that, despite having obtained his decree, the earl was "contentit" to "use the counsale of the lordis anent the matter".[138]

Finally, it should not be assumed that arbitration was always preferable to other courses of action open to the parties. Parties might have their own reasons for resisting such a recourse. For example, on 11 July 1532 Gavin Carmichael compeared in relation to disputed lands in Uddingston in the Lordship of Douglas, and it is noted in the register that "the lordis desirit the said Gavin to submit the mater betwix him and Jane Carmichael to the lordis of counsal as juges arbitouris and amicable compositors betwix them...and thai suld dress the matter according to justice and saif the kinges honour". However, the record bluntly informs us that "the quhilk the said Gavin refusit to do".[139] Arbitration's distinctiveness and flexibility might be unattractive to a party determined to fully vindicate his rights or to stall resolution of the dispute for tactical reasons.

Jurisdiction and arbitration

Did the role of arbitration also operate to allow courts to determine disputes they could otherwise not entertain? Arbitration could potentially have been a means of allowing a court to determine a dispute unconstrained by the normal formalities of procedure or jurisdiction. In Scotland, the question arises whether such a side-stepping of conventional limitations through the Session acting in arbitration could have played a part in the jurisdictional change witnessed in the period around 1532. It might have provided a means of circumventing the jurisdictional bar on the King's Council in order to allow it to hear a

[136] NAS CS 5/42, fol. 123.
[137] NAS CS 5/43, fol. 94r.
[138] NAS CS 5/43, fol. 94v.
[139] NAS CS 6/1, fol. 60v.

matter which would otherwise have been open to jurisdictional challenge. In the fifteenth and early sixteenth centuries, as we have seen in earlier chapters, such jurisdictional challenges could arise in the context of disputes over title to land. However, there is little evidence in the council register to suggest that arbitration was adopted to overcome this limitation. After all, if a defender was in a position to object to the competency of the action successfully on jurisdictional grounds, he was hardly likely to consent to the Lords determining the issue instead as arbiters. Of course, an arbitrated solution by the Lords *could* sometimes have been acceptable in circumstances in which their legal determination of a particular dispute was not. For example, arbitrated outcomes could encompass a broader range of disputes, or find a more balanced way of making redress to both sides. However, if a defender consented to arbitration for those reasons this would signify an intention to reach a resolution. The dispute would be resolved, but through arbitration procedure rather than legal action. Enough has been said in this chapter to show why parties might have cause to hold this preference. Jurisdictional issues *as such* therefore do not seem likely to have prompted submissions to arbitration.

However, one example shows how resort to arbitration might sometimes have been made when the preferred alternative of litigation was precluded for some reason, but parties wished to pursue the matter before the Lords in some capacity. The instance in question is the action already mentioned between Isabel and Janet Inglis and their spouses and Alexander Shaw of Sauchy concerning the lands of Ardmure in June and July 1533. Isabel and Janet were pursuing a summons of error against Alexander and the inquest which had served him as heir to the lands of Ardmure, but on 20 June 1533 the parties and their procurators consented to a continuation of a week so that they could "compromit" (i.e. compromise) the question of the error of the inquest and the general "ground right" of the land. They agreed to submit the matter to the Lords of Council as arbiters and amicable compositors.[140] However, when they compeared again on 27 June the pursuers' procurator, Robert Leslie, asked the Lords instead to carry on and proceed upon the summons of error, but added that he was content to "cast in" the ground right as well. There is no indication that the Lords acted as arbiters at this point. Alexander Shaw confirmed that he too was

[140] NAS CS 6/2, fol. 195.

happy that the ground right should be decided "be the lordis as jugis".[141] However, at this stage Shaw stated that "gif thai found ony deficulte or doute thirin, the lordis to deceid thirupon as jugis arbitouris and amicable compositours". It is not entirely clear what this anticipated difficulty could have been. However, it does not appear to relate to jurisdiction because Shaw stated by way of explanation that this offer was made notwithstanding an "inhibition" produced by him, and so the difficulty appears to stem from the terms of that "inhibition".

The "inhibition" was contained in a letter from the King which discharged his royal interest in the summons of error and discharged the Lords of Council from proceeding upon it "in all poyntis concerning us and for our part rasit at our instance...insafar as concerns our interest".[142] Robert Leslie argued that despite this inhibition the Lords "suld and mycht proceid" at the instance of the party, but the Lords rejected this for the reason that "the kingis inhibition standand".[143] The following day, however, with the consent of both parties the Lords assigned 5 July for calling of the summons of error and for proceeding to determine the "ground right". In what way this was consistent with the Lords' decision of the previous day is not clear. However, they ruled that "the summondis of erroure be first decidit and thireftir the ground ryt decidit incontinent but [i.e.without] langar delay becaus the partiis forsaid had referrit the said matter to the saidis lordis as said is". They added that "the said summondis and ground ryt be all decidit at a tyme and pronuncit togidder".[144] On 9 July, however, the parties referred "the mater dependand betwix thame tuching the landis of Auchmure to the lordis of counsale as amicable compositors, of the quhilk the ground ryt thirof was referrit to the lordis as in the actis maid thirupon of befor".[145] This appears to have finally put the entire matter of error and ground right into the Lords' hands as amicable compositors. That was not, however, what was to transpire, at least on the face of the record. On 12 July 1533 the Lords gave decree of error and reduced the retour of the sheriff and inquest, but after apparently having heard the action as a normal summons. However, the Lords did go on to decide the question of the ground right (in any case beyond the scope

[141] NAS CS 6/3, fol. 210.
[142] NAS CS 6/3, fol. 210v.
[143] NAS CS 6/3, fol. 210v.
[144] NAS CS 6/2, fol. 212.
[145] NAS CS 6/3, fol. 8.

of a summons of error) as amicable compositors, and decreed that it pertained to Shaw of Sauchy in fee and heritage for ever.[146]

From the evidence in the record, it is not possible to judge conclusively why the resolution of this dispute took this form. Given the jurisdictional change we have charted in this period in relation to fee and heritage, it might seem possible that problems over jurisdiction could have been behind this complex set of proceedings. However, it also seems clear that the doubt or difficulty which was foreseen was the inhibition (from hearing the original action of error) which emanated from the King. Prior to mentioning this difficulty, the parties had already indicated that they were content to "cast in" the ground right, and this is eventually precisely what they did. It would appear that, despite the Lords' decision that the King's letter precluded them from hearing the summons of error, they did exactly that in the end. The hearing did proceed as originally envisaged, and the Lords were then able to decide the ground right too. In terms of illuminating the purposes of arbitration, this example does suggest that arbitration could play a tactical role in the course of litigation, where there was a reason why a summons could not proceed, or where a matter germane to the dispute needed to be decided but fell outwith the scope of the summons. Arbitration does not appear to have played a role in developing the jurisdiction over heritage, however. There was indeed no jurisdictional need for it to play such a role. As argued in the previous chapter, the Session could simply approach such matters under its conventional jurisdiction to reduce infeftments.

Other references to the Lords of Council and the King

Apart from the thirty-two instances of submission to arbitration by the Lords of Council over the five years surveyed between April 1529 and May 1534, there are a further fifteen general references of matters to the determination of King or Council, with thirteen to the Lords and two specifically to the King.[147] In these examples there is no explicit reference to arbitration as the basis upon which the submissions were

[146] NAS CS 6/3, fols. 15, 16.

[147] The two cases referred to the King are *Earl Bothwell v. Laird of Cessford* (1529), NAS CS 5/40, fol. 23; *The King v. Earl of Crawford* (1531), NAS CS 5/43, fol. 122r.

made. They therefore illustrate a further related method of dispute resolution which bears a great resemblance to submission to arbitration but which stopped short of it. It merely placed matters in the discretion of the court, whilst sometimes appealing to some of the same criteria which we have noted as underlying a preference for arbitration itself. For example, on 11 May 1529 Lord Lovat, having been called in connection with a summons of error, referred all related actions depending between himself and Lord Methven to the Lords of Council. On 8 and 10 May his forespeaker had been protesting against the relevancy of the error summons.[148] However, at the next hearing on 11 May Lord Lovat's forespeaker suddenly declared to the Lords that "quhat thai pleis to deliver thirin owther be way of composition or uther wayis he suld stand contentit thirwith".[149] Such a concession must have been tantamount to abandoning any defence of the action.

Matters could be submitted for decision by the Lords through the ordinary procedure of supplication, which involved them exercising their normal competence rather than a specifically conferred office such as arbiter. For example, on 6 July 1531 William Cockburn of Newhall supplicated the Lords in connection with a dispute over the fulfilling of an agreement involving a reversionary right to land. The Lords had previously given a decree that George Hay keep the lands until they were redeemed by payment of 550 merks before Whitsunday. William now alleged that he had fulfilled these conditions and that George had acknowledged this but refused to vacate them for a further year, until the following Whitsun. The record states that "for stancheing of pley baith the partiis ar contentit that the said matter be decidit befor the lordis of counsale that it may be kenit quhilk of thame [has] ryt tharto".[150] George was present and granted that he had no right or interest to the lands, whereupon the Lords decerned the lands lawfully redeemed at the previous Whitsunday, discharged George from any intromitting in the meantime and issued "letters" to this effect.

An example of a less formal reference came in November 1532, in connection with a dispute between David Beaton, abbot of Arbroath, and his uncle and predecessor as abbot, James Beaton, archbishop of St Andrews. The dispute concerned the fruits of the abbey of Arbroath.

---

148 NAS CS 5/40, fols. 20r, 21r.
149 NAS CS 5/40, fol. 22r.
150 NAS CS 5/42, fol. 193v.

Both men were being sued by the tenants of the abbey since they were both concurrently charging the tenants to make payment of the mails, teinds and fruits of the lands and churches of the abbey.[151] The dispute had been a long-running one, more or less since David had become abbot in 1524.[152] At this stage in the dispute (which was not finally resolved till the matter was decided in Rome in 1535) we find that David:

> referrit him in the mater debatable betwix the archbishop of St Andrews and him to the lordis of counsale or any thre of thame as thai thocht expedient or quhat thai counsalit him to do conform to justice, he suld fulfill the same.[153]

It is hard to assess exactly what lay behind such an offer, but it shows a willingness to take direction from the Lords of Council as to how to resolve the dispute in question in the most expedient fashion, as opposed to seeking their determination of the issue on strictly legal grounds.

The reference of such matters to the Lords seems to have amounted to an established procedure which could allow the direct resolution of more complex disputes. Disputes over title could easily fall into this category. For example, on 23 November 1532 Andrew Kinninmonth of Craghall and William Lindsay of Preston "referrit thame" to the Lords of Council "anent the ryte that ilkane of thame allege to have to ane quarter of the land of Ceras now occupiit be the said William".[154] This reference of the "variance and debaite" between the parties came up again on 18 January 1533,[155] and proceeded to a proof as with any normal action by summons.[156] The matter was finally disposed of after various continuations[157] on 21 May 1533.[158] The record narrated the proceedings in the "action and caus persewit be Andro Kynynmonth of Craghall v. William Lindesay of Preston", and set out the facts and the libel. Then, after recording that both parties "referrit thaim to the lordis of consell anent the ryte that ilkane of thaim allegis to have to the saidis landis", the details of the proof were related. It is stated that

---

151 NAS CS 6/2, fol. 8.
152 M.H.B. Sanderson, *Cardinal of Scotland: David Beaton, c. 1494–1546* (Edinburgh, 1986), pp. 21–22.
153 NAS CS 6/2, fol. 9r.
154 NAS CS 6/2, fol. 11v.
155 NAS CS 6/2, fol. 49 (18 January 1533).
156 NAS CS 6/2, fol. 49v.
157 NAS CS 6/2, fols. 75, 119, 152.
158 NAS CS 6/2, fol. 165v.

William founded on a "rolment" of the sheriff court of Fife which Andrew had failed to "impreve" and thereby prove invalid.[159] The court roll showed that the seller from whom William had purchased the land had been lawfully entered to it in 1518. Therefore the Lords assoilzied William.

This example shows a "reference" to the Lords as a fully integrated part of normal procedure. In fact the proceedings really turned upon this attempt by Kinninmonth to "impreve" and reduce the court roll in question, something which was a perfectly conventional matter to bring before the Lords. A similar situation occurred between the earl of Rothes and David Garden of the Newton in December 1532 in respect of a reversion of land which the earl claimed entitled him to redeem the lands of Innerleithen. For "staunching of lang process" the parties consented that the Lords of Council "be jugis and to decyde quhidder the said landis ar redeemable be virtue of the said reversion".[160] This also shows again a desire in litigants for speedy and flexible procedure which could be adapted to the nature of the dispute in hand. More generally, these examples presage the continuing development in the 1530s and 1540s of the Session and College of Justice as a supreme form of civil court. As such, it not only articulated and defined its jurisdiction as though it was both superior and unlimited, but also was clearly regarded by many parties as a tribunal to which they were only too willing to refer their disputes, as a court of law or as a body which could arbitrate.

Conclusion

This survey of dispute resolution in the 1520s and 1530s before the Lords of Council and Session demonstrates that although arbitration was not the only procedural alternative to litigation, it occupied a central role in meeting the needs of parties when the nature of their disputes meant that they could not readily be resolved in an appropriate manner through court action or other means. A variety of advantages could accrue from appointing arbiters to resolve a dispute, mainly deriving from the flexibility such agreements allowed to reflect the voluntary wishes of the parties about how a resolution should be reached, and

[159] NAS CS 6/2, fol. 165v.
[160] NAS CS 6/3, fol. 33r.

the prospect of a speedy and conclusive end to the dispute. Relying on the impression and flavour of the evidence more than anything else, perhaps the most important advantage was the way in which the scope of an arbitration could be defined by the parties and was not constrained by categories of legal claim and associated remedies. It could thereby embrace a potentially wide range of matters in dispute between parties personally but also between their adherents. This last aspect was particularly important when the wider interests of a kin-group were at stake, or the processes of feud had involved that wider kin-group in the conduct of the dispute.

Arbitration therefore allowed the use of an agreed procedure free of the constraints of pleading and discrete grounds of action in law. Perhaps just as important was the speed with which the arbitration could be decided—typically ranging between the immediate issuing of the decree arbitral and its subsequent pronouncement within a few weeks. Finally, it might be supposed that the freedom to agree a choice of arbiters was particularly important, though here the increasing frequency with which the Lords of Council were themselves appointed as arbiters does perhaps signal a change in the sixteenth century. The advantages of choosing several private arbiters to reflect the balance of interests of the parties and to promote the acceptance of the decree arbitral were arguably diminishing in the face of the increasing authority of the Lords of Council as exercised in the Session by the 1530s. Arbitration procedure clearly retained its attractiveness, but concern with exercising choice in the selection of the arbiters appears to have been capable of satisfaction upon occasion by submission to the judges of the Session as much as it would have been by submission to a determined number of individuals. In other words, a preference for arbitration by the 1530s does not necessarily imply distrust (if it ever did) of the persons who administered ordinary judicial process in relation to the Session as a central judicial tribunal. This might represent an important strand in explaining the ongoing development of an enhanced role for the courts in dispute resolution in sixteenth-century Scotland and the subsequent decline of the feud by the early seventeenth century.[161] Overall, when evaluating the advantages of arbitration in this period it is not clear that its use was necessarily more effective than litigation, though it seems likely that

[161] See generally Wormald, "Bloodfeud, Kindred and Government in Early Modern Scotland"; Brown, *Bloodfeud in Scotland 1573–1625*.

it often could be. It seems at least to have allowed the resolution of a dispute to be approached in what the parties themselves considered to be the most appropriate way in the particular circumstances.

A further point confirmed by the evidence surveyed is that in the sixteenth century the offices of arbiter, arbitrator and amicable compositor were recognised and employed in Scots law, the specific rules being a thirteenth or fourteenth-century borrowing from the canon law. By way of qualification to this, it seems that the individual offices may have been used interchangeably, and without particular technical significance beyond denoting a submission to arbitration generically. Broadly speaking this may reflect a slightly corrupted tradition deriving from medieval practice in appointing arbiters under multi-jurisdictional commissions as arbiters, arbitrators and amicable compositors.

As in fifteenth-century England, arbitration was not primarily a way of overcoming perceived deficiencies in the legal system, but was often closely associated with the use of the courts through litigation, as will be further discussed in the next chapter. The Scottish council records suggest that arbitration was often used in conjunction with litigation, and that a strong degree of interdependence existed between the two procedures in resolving disputes. It seems likely that this pattern would have been replicated in other European countries, as it was in England. The enhanced opportunity for litigation in the late medieval period through newer central courts would thereby have been smoothly accomodated within existing forms of dispute resolution. In sixteenth-century Scotland, moreover, the way in which the frequency and vitality of resort to arbitration is displayed so fully in the council records also implies a great enhancement in the authority and role of the Session by the 1530s when compared with the early years of the century. There was a structure of methods of dispute resolution in Scotland by 1532 whose overall character was increasingly defined by the opportunity to seek central adjudication from an authoritative civil tribunal possessing a new degree of permanence and status. This was the Session, whose authority was sealed by its reconstituted in 1532 as the College of Justice.

The role of privately negotiated settlements and arbitrated resolutions was not and could not be entirely displaced by a central court. This still leaves the question why alternative forms of resolution featured so noticeably in the record of the Session in the 1520s and 1530s, particularly in the form of references to arbitration. Many instances exist of parties to arbitrations and mediations appearing before the Session to register their compromises and arbitration agreements, or else to seek the authority of the court in interpreting or enforcing such matters. These will be discussed in the next chapter. Rather than displacement of the alternatives to litigation, there seems to have been integration between the worlds of judge and private arbiter, demonstrated above all by the increasing frequency with which the Lords of Council and Session were themselves corporately appointed as arbiters and invited to assume that role in the settlement of a dispute. "Public" and "private" are of course classificatory labels which may not do justice to the historically contingent sense of a developing public order and its association with the provision of justice by the central institutions of the state, as witnessed in the sixteenth century. However, if the labels have to be used, it can be stated that the public justice of the courts and the private justice of arbiters, mediators and simple compromises were far less in opposition to each other than such labelling might imply.

CHAPTER NINE

THE ROLE OF THE SESSION IN DISPUTE RESOLUTION

Introduction

Recent scholarship has tended to supplement a traditional concern with the development of law courts with an attempt to place the pursuit of legal action within the wider context of dispute resolution. This often involves emphasising other, less formal methods of achieving a conclusion to a dispute, and elaborating upon themes of compromise, settlement, the role of the feud, and the use of procedures such as mediation and arbitration as alternatives to litigation.[1] This reflects a recognition that the maintenance of order and social stability in many medieval and early modern polities did not rest exclusively upon legal sanctions associated with the formal administration of justice, important though legal rules and courts of justice were. Justice could be achieved in other ways too, and the resolution of disputes through legal process had not yet achieved its subsequent degree of pre-eminence.

This approach has been evident in the context of Scottish history. However, it has a special relevance to the sixteenth century in Scotland. As we have seen in earlier chapters, this period witnessed extraordinary change in the system of law courts which was inherited from the

[1] In the Scottish context, see J. Wormald, "Bloodfeud, Kindred and Government in Early Modern Scotland", *Past and Present* 87 (1980), 54–97; J. Wormald, *Lords and Men in Scotland: Bonds of Manrent, 1442–1603* (Edinburgh, 1985); J. Wormald, "An early modern postscript: the Sandlaw dispute, 1546", in *The Settlement of Disputes in Early Modern Europe*, ed. W. Davies and P. Fouracre (Cambridge, 1986), pp. 191–268; K.M. Brown, *Bloodfeud in Scotland 1573–1625: Violence, Justice and Politics in an Early Modern Society* (Edinburgh, 1986). Other examples include R.R. Davies, "The Survival of the Bloodfeud in Medieval Wales", *History* (1969), pp. 338–357; H. Zmora, *State and nobility in early modern Germany* (Cambridge, 1997); H. Kaminsky, "The Noble Feud in the Later Middle Ages", 177 *Past and Present* (2002), pp. 55–83; S. Carroll, "The Peace in the Feud in Sixteenth- and Seventeenth-Century France", 178 *Past and Present* (2003), pp. 74–115; S. Carroll, *Blood and Violence in Early Modern France* (Oxford, 2006). A pioneering earlier work was O. Brunner, *Land und Herrschaft: Grundfragen der territorialen Verfassungsgeschichte Österreichs im Mittelalter*, 4th ed. (Vienna, 1965), also available in English as O. Brunner, *Land and Lordship: Structures of Governance in Medieval Austria*, trans. with introduction by H. Kaminsky and J. Van Horn Melton (Philadelphia, 1992).

mature medieval legal order of the fifteenth century. These changes in the administration of justice in the sixteenth century were themselves an important aspect of the wider development of the machinery of governance typically associated with the development of the early modern state. Assessing the implications of those changes for dispute resolution raises again the question posed in the previous chapter, namely what effect did the enhancement of "public" justice have upon existing practices of "private" dispute resolution? Furthermore, how does any effect of this sort provide a measure of deeper social or ideological change?

The previous chapter examined the history and nature of arbitration in order to provide a basis for analysing the role of the Session in dispute resolution generally, placing formal litigation alongside arbitration as a commonly used alternative method. There is a temptation to overlook this wider context, and the place of alternative methods of dispute resolution within it, since medieval Scotland was a land of common law, and the fundamental condition for the evolution of a common law in Scotland, as in England, had been the development of the jurisdiction of royal courts. Courts and legal forms of redress therefore form a natural focus of study, assisted by their tendency towards reliable record-keeping. Nevertheless, careful attention to methods of dispute resolution in the wider sense has been evident in relation to recent work on sixteenth-century Scotland, where particular insights have been gained from the fact that bloodfeud and the evidence for it is considered to have survived late by European standards.[2] Famously in 1599 James VI had criticised the Scottish nobility in his *Basilikon Doron* for their readiness to "tak up a plaine feid" and to "bang it out bravely, hee and all his kinne".[3] The extent of this royal concern was evident towards the end of the sixteenth century, and in 1598 the well-known "Act anent removeing and extinguisching of deidlie feids" was passed.[4] Notably, the main feature of the legislation was an attempt to force feuding parties to submit their disputes for resolution, but through private arbitration, rather than involving the full state legal apparatus in

[2] Brown, *Bloodfeud in Scotland 1573–1625*, p. 1; Wormald, "Bloodfeud, Kindred and Government in Early Modern Scotland", p. 57. Scotland was not unique however: Carroll, "The Peace in the Feud in Sixteenth- and Seventeenth-Century France", pp. 78, 81.

[3] King James VI, *Basilikon Doron*, in *The Political Works of James I*, ed. C.H. McIlwain (London, 1918), p. 24.

[4] *The Acts of the Parliament of Scotland* [hereafter *APS*], ed. T. Thomson and C. Innes, 12 vols., (Edinburgh, 1814–75), vol. 4, pp. 158–159.

order to impose a judicial determination.[5] Particularly from the 1580s, the Privy Council and the King personally were actively involved in achieving settlement of feuds and the suppression of the disorder consequent upon them.[6]

Using a broader approach to dispute resolution, highly plausible accounts of the operation of the bloodfeud have now been given in relation to Scottish evidence in the sixteenth and seventeenth centuries. The pioneering account by Dr Jenny Wormald was followed by Professor Keith Brown's book-length study, and more recently Professor John Cairns has published a detailed study of a bloodfeud in the burgh of St Andrews in the last decade or so of the sixteenth century.[7] A wider study of Highland clanship by Dr Alison Cathcart has also added much to our understanding of the workings of the Scottish feud.[8] A common feature in the work of Brown, Wormald and Cairns has been charting the decline of the bloodfeud as well as its role and function. All three historians recognise that (in the words of Cairns) "the disappearance of the bloodfeud in Scotland…left the legal profession and the law as the main means of resolving disputes".[9] Stemming above all from the foundation of the College of Justice as a central court in 1532, Cairns notes how by 1590 "there had developed in Edinburgh an organised legal profession, largely trained in the Roman and canon laws, practising before a professionalised central civil court that had adopted an essentially romano-canonical procedure".[10] The historiography therefore agrees upon a clear picture emerging of a "feuding society" giving way to a recognisably more modern one which depended upon specialist lawyers and judges to achieve the rectification of wrongs and offer technical forms of legal redress. The sixteenth century appears to be the crucial transitional period.

It is equally important, however, to recognise that the law, the lawyers and the courts had always been at least part of the framework within which disputes were conducted in medieval Scotland. If sixteenth-century Scotland was indeed a "feuding society", then perhaps it was

[5] Brown, *Bloodfeud in Scotland*, p. 242.

[6] Brown, *Bloodfeud in Scotland*, pp. 56–57, 216–218, 239–246.

[7] Brown, *Bloodfeud in Scotland*; Wormald, "Bloodfeud, Kindred and Government"; J.W. Cairns, "Academic Feud, Bloodfeud, and William Welwood: Legal Education in St Andrews, 1560–1611", *Edinburgh Law Review* 2 (1998), pp. 158–179, 255–287.

[8] A. Cathcart, *Kinship and Clientage: Highland Clanship 1451–1609* (Leiden, 2006).

[9] Cairns, "Academic Feud, Bloodfeud, and William Welwood", p. 167; Brown, *Bloodfeud in Scotland*, p. 260; Wormald, "Bloodfeud, Kindred and Government", p. 91.

[10] Cairns, "Academic Feud, Bloodfeud, and William Welwood", p. 160.

at least as much a *litigating* society. Indeed, there is some danger of distortion which must be guarded against whenever the label "feuding society" is used. This is because it runs the risk of elevating a single characteristic of society (however significant) into an unduly reductionist statement of its general character, representing the feuding nature of society as the primary and dominating feature which governed all others. Characteristics which may seem more familiar to modern eyes might also have been at least as typical in how disputes were approached, but can end up being unduly minimised in importance through the emphasis upon the "feuding" nature of society.

Most obviously in this regard, there can be a tendency to minimise the prominence of the law in dispute resolution. However, the role of law was just as much a part of the structure of Scottish society as the feud, owing to the existence of a Scottish common law since the thirteenth century, the dominance of feudal tenure, coextensive with national boundaries and royal jurisdiction, the structuring of lordship through grants of jurisdiction, and the exercise of ecclesiastical jurisdiction in the application of canon law. In the Anglo-Norman era, medieval land-holding had been rooted in the disciplinary jurisdiction of the courts of feudal lords.[11] From this ensued the presence of royal court-holding across the whole of Scotland as royal intervention created the remedies and procedures of the common law. This allowed the possibility of resolving a dispute by reference to law, even if ultimately this might not always have been the most effective means of doing so. Apart from its development of forms of criminal liability, the common law in this way elaborated a substantial range of civil remedies and rules which governed private disputes. Land law was always the most developed, but gradually in the later medieval period the notion of a civil wrong developed in complexity as well.[12]

Beyond litigation, law and its procedural norms also conditioned the wider framework in which feud operated. We saw in the previous chapter that, so far as practices of private dispute resolution went, the

[11] H.L. MacQueen, *Common Law and Feudal Society in Medieval Scotland* (Edinburgh, 1993), chap. 2.

[12] A. Harding, "Rights, Wrongs and Remedies in Late Medieval English and Scots Law", in *Miscellany IV*, ed. H.L. MacQueen, Stair Society 49 (Edinburgh, 2002), pp. 1–8; R. Black, "A Historical Survey of Delictual Liability in Scotland for Personal Injuries and Death", Part 1, *Comparative and International Law Journal of South Africa* (1975), pp. 46–70; H.L. MacQueen and W.D.H. Sellar, "Negligence", in *A History of Private Law in Scotland*, ed. K. Reid and R. Zimmermann (Oxford, 2000), chap. 17.

law of arbitration had been received into Scots law at an early date. Therefore, by deploying arbitration, even private resolutions of disputes often looked to a formal legalistic process governed by agreed rules of procedure.[13] Indeed, the practice of arbitration had always had a bearing on the settlement of feuds, Professor Brown acknowledging that "the framework on which a more effective means of ending feuds was built already existed in private arbitration".[14] Questions therefore arise about how to explain the relationship between the various means of resolving disputes in Scottish society prior to the disappearance of the bloodfeud, and the subsequent establishment of modes of formal legal redress as the dominant approach in achieving such resolution. In particular, how can the roles of litigation, arbitration and mediation, respectively, be assessed? To what extent did they accommodate other methods such as feud, or have any bearing upon the resolution of feuds during this period?

The later fifteenth and sixteenth centuries afford historians a new point of departure in seeking fresh insights into these questions. This is because patterns of dispute resolution were in flux, with new courts, procedures and remedies both enlarging the opportunities available to parties in resolving their disputes and providing a new record source in the acts and decreets of the Lords of Council which reveals much about the relationship between the various means of doing so. As we have already seen, the incidence of litigation in Parliament and the King's Council had risen in the fifteenth century. Pressure of judicial business had led to the development within the structure of the King's Council of a new central judicial tribunal in the form of the Session.[15] As previous chapters have sought to demonstrate, the administration of justice in Scotland was increasingly carried on by the Session or was subject to its review, above all after its reconstitution as the College of Justice in 1532. In this chapter the records of this court from around 1532 will be examined in order to illuminate the broader picture of dispute settlement in the early sixteenth century. This will allow an

---

[13] P.G. Stein, "Roman Law in Scotland", *Ius Romanum Medii Aevi*, pars v, 13b (Milan, 1968), p. 17.

[14] Brown, *Bloodfeud in Scotland*, p. 239.

[15] See chapters 1 and 2; see also R.K. Hannay, *The College of Justice* (Edinburgh, 1933), reprinted in *The College of Justice: Essays by R. K. Hannay*, ed. H.L. MacQueen, Stair Society Supplementary Series 1 (Edinburgh, 1990); A.A.M. Duncan, "The Central Courts before 1532" in *Introduction to Scottish Legal History*, ed. G.C.H. Paton, Stair Society 20 (Edinburgh, 1958), pp. 321–340.

assessment to be made of the relationship between formal methods of dispute resolution in the courts and the informal methods already touched upon in the last chapter and which were apparently of such importance in a "feuding society".

Two particular questions to be addressed are how legal remedies related to the other means available, and how a court such as the Session could be involved in achieving extra-judicial settlements between parties in dispute. Formal legal remedies were obviously only one means by which a dispute could be resolved, and the exclusive pursuit of a court judgement was not necessarily the most effective means of doing so. However, debates about the respective roles of "private" and "public" justice in Scottish society suggest a complex interaction rather than a sharp divergence between their respective spheres, and this illuminates in turn the ways in which the jurisdiction, procedure and remedies of courts such as the Session were relevant to dispute resolution, whether in relation to private or public justice.

Dispute settlement, private and public justice

In order to inform such study of dispute resolution, particular views of public order have been developed by historians, as well as the distinction between public and private justice. As discussed in the previous chapter, Michael Clanchy has addressed the broad principles underlying dispute settlement in arguing that "law (standing for learning and the application of rules) and love (standing for common sense and bonds of affection) can be seen as contrasting styles in the settlement of disputes in the Middle Ages".[16] It is the workings of the law which have generally preoccupied historians, but in recent years the role of "love" in Clanchy's sense of "a bond of affection, established by public undertakings before witnesses and upheld by social pressure"[17] has begun to be examined in more depth. By this means historians have realised the extent to which peace and order in medieval and early modern societies depended not just upon "public" or publicly administered justice delivered by kings and their courts, but also upon "private" justice commonly negotiated through the agency of lordship, kindred, private arbiters or a combination of all three.

[16] M.T. Clanchy, "Law and Love in the Middle Ages", in *Disputes and Settlements*, ed. J. Bossy (Cambridge, 1983), p. 52.

[17] Clanchy, "Law and Love in the Middle Ages", p. 47.

What distinguished these different approaches to achieving a resolution from each other has not always been clearly analysed. Most accounts have concentrated on pointing out differences in the mechanisms involved and have simply emphasised the distinctive role of compromise and settlement in private justice. From this perspective, the main difference between private and public modes of justice does indeed seem to have been the nature of the resolution achieved. The purpose of a court judgement was to provide a legally correct answer in a dispute and to grant the appropriate remedy to vindicate the rights of one party against another. By contrast, a private settlement was essentially founded upon a measure of compromise so as to minimise the extent to which either party was left with an outstanding sense of grievance. As we noted in the last chapter, a private settlement could more easily extend towards inclusion of a range of interested parties, especially the wider kin, and a range of technically unrelated disputes. Furthermore, the sanctions for breach of private settlements and court judgements differed. In principle they were informal, social and potentially violent in the former case, and formal, coercive and legally defined in the latter. Defying a court decree could lead to being excluded from the King's "peace". However, following informal resolution of a dispute, an unwillingness to defy the authority of powerful lords at the head of kin groups implicated in a dispute might be a more powerful guarantee that a settlement would be honoured than such formal legal sanctions.

The studies already referred to by Jenny Wormald remain the most telling and influential studies of private justice in fifteenth and sixteenth-century Scotland. In her seminal article, "Bloodfeud, Kindred and Government in Early Modern Scotland", Dr Wormald investigated the demarcation between the respective spheres of public and private justice and attacked the notion that "public and private order, represented by government and kindred respectively, conflict because they are essentially incompatible".[18] With particular reference to surviving bonds of manrent, maintenance and friendship she demonstrated "[the] survival of the private settlement as a customary and practical method of dealing with crime or civil dispute".[19] Given that in Scotland people

[18] Wormald, "Bloodfeud, Kindred and Government in Early Modern Scotland", p. 55.

[19] Wormald, "Bloodfeud, Kindred and Government in Early Modern Scotland", p. 72.

"sought justice close to home" and that the emphasis was therefore on the "local settlement", this survival of the private settlement should, she argued, be mainly attributed to its effectiveness in resolving disputes.[20] In practice it could often be more "effective" than a court decree.

Of course we should be careful not to construct an overly simplistic model in terms of which consensually arranged private settlement is viewed simply as the alternative to choosing to fight out disputed claims in the courts in pursuit of ultimate legal vindication. Arbitration, mediation, negotiation, compromise and consensual settlement were and always had been processes carried out against a background fabric of legal rights and available legal remedies. The strength of legal rights and remedies must always have been a factor in the degree of compromise or satisfaction which parties looked for or were prepared to make in private settlement. However, even in a society premised on the rule of law, with law courts and a system of legal remedies to redress harm and enforce rights, the private settlement nevertheless retained its distinctive value for a variety of reasons. Not the least of these was that contestable or disputed legal rights could never be relied upon with complete security. No disputed legal claim could be regarded as certain and incontrovertible until adjudicated upon, but adjudication itself always carried risk. The outcome of adjudication could never be guaranteed. This was as true in the sixteenth century as it is now. For this reason, as well as the differences in approach embodied in private methods of dispute resolution, the private settlement would survive. The end of the sixteenth century was to witness the decline of the feud and changes in the methods of achieving private settlement, but not the end of the private settlement itself.

Three main themes from Dr Wormald's work are relevant to this chapter, and are developed by her in a further study concerned with a sixteenth-century dispute relating to the lands of Sandlaw in the north-east of Scotland.[21] First, we have the theme that "private settlement was still... a prevalent and effective force in Scottish justice", and was not in conflict with public justice.[22] The Sandlaw dispute itself illustrated this point, since it was ultimately resolved without invoking public authority, although court actions had been undertaken during

[20] Wormald, "The Sandlaw Dispute", p. 203.
[21] Wormald, "The Sandlaw Dispute", p. 203.
[22] Wormald, "The Sandlaw Dispute", p. 203.

the dispute.[23] Moreover, it could be added that the specific evidence relating to bloodfeud in Scottish society in the sixteenth century would support the same conclusion, since liability to make settlement and the right to receive it vested in a kinship group, and a feud could only be resolved through the giving of assythment by way of compensation, in exchange for letters of slains. These were both practically and technically extra-judicial, private procedures, but ones which remained common throughout the sixteenth century.[24] Secondly, Dr Wormald argued that it is misleading to draw too sharp a contrast between court actions and private settlements on the basis of formality and authority.[25] Dr Wormald's view is that:

> in terms of its procedures, the dividing line between public and private authority was as blurred as that between criminal and civil justice. The procedure used in the private settlement could very well mirror that of the courts, for arbitration was common in both, and had been at least since the thirteenth century.[26]

Thirdly, Dr Wormald argued that the sixteenth century was "the last great age of the private settlement in Scotland", although noting that it is difficult to explain exactly how this came about.[27] Dr Wormald suggested that men came to prefer "the greater elaboration and professionalism of the world of the lawyers and the courts" in resolving their disputes.[28]

These themes contribute to building up a highly persuasive account of dispute resolution in sixteenth-century Scotland. Dr Wormald's analysis naturally prompts further questions, however, about the role of law courts in disputes, and in the present context about the role of the Session and the significance of its reconstitution as a College of Justice in 1532. The main purpose of this chapter is to draw on these themes and to examine private justice *in the context of* the administration of public justice. It should be possible to assess to some degree the extent to which the records of the Session bear out Dr Wormald's thesis that public and private justice did not conflict with each other in this period. In addition, an assessment will be made of the degree of relation

---

[23] Wormald, "The Sandlaw Dispute", p. 202.
[24] See Brown, *Bloodfeud in Scotland*, pp. 52–55.
[25] Wormald, "The Sandlaw Dispute", p. 192.
[26] Wormald, "The Sandlaw Dispute", p. 203.
[27] Wormald, "The Sandlaw Dispute", p. 205.
[28] Wormald, "The Sandlaw Dispute", p. 205.

and interaction between public and private justice, as demonstrated in proceedings before the Session. In particular, the active involvement of the Session in the procedures and administration of private justice outwith the normal course of litigation will be examined. In turn this should illuminate Dr Wormald's suggestion that "the demarcation between state or government on the one side and kindred or bloodfeud on the other may be too rigid".[29] It will be demonstrated that in sixteenth-century Scotland legal action before the courts was an important means of resolving disputes which was often used alongside other means before a final settlement was reached. This fits with the conclusion of the previous chapter that the sixteenth century witnessed not opposition but increasing integration between the worlds of judge and private arbiter. The degree of integration between public and private justice will be demonstrated in this chapter through examining the way that Lords of Council and Session, as well as administering the common law, were also frequently approached using the modes of private justice, particularly when parties wished to submit to arbitration.

The role of Council and Session in arbitration

The most notable involvement of the Session with private justice came in relation to the conduct of arbitrations. Evidence of the conduct of private arbitrations is disclosed in various ways in its proceedings.[30] The evidence to be examined will be drawn from the years immediately before and after the foundation of the College of Justice in 1532. Through the registration before the Session of agreements, termed "compromits" (clearly deriving from the romano canonical usage of *compromissum* as an agreement to submit to arbitration) or "appunctments", and submissions to arbitration, it was given the role of formalising such agreements and the subsequent stages of procedure which followed upon them, even though it was not being asked to resolve the underlying dispute itself. The Lords of Council and Session were thus perceived to constitute the appropriate body before which parties could appear

[29] Wormald, "Bloodfeud, Kindred and Government", p. 56.

[30] Apart from what follows, see now J. Finlay, *Men of Law in Pre-Reformation Scotland*, Scottish Historical Review Monograph no. 9 (East Linton, 2000), especially pp. 166–167.

to formalise both a decision to "compromit" and the subsequent steps in what was essentially a private matter under arbitration. Although the practice of registering such agreements can be seen in the earliest extant council records from the 1470s, it would appear that the Lords did not at that time directly assume a role so as to actively "interpone" (i.e. formally confer) their authority to such agreements, as became the later practice.[31]

An example of parties binding themselves before the Session to observe a compromit, already mentioned in the previous chapter, is that of Alexander Dunbar of Cumnock and Huchon Rose of Kilravock on 30 August 1529.[32] In this case the arbiters were Alexander Dunbar, subchantor of Moray; James Dunbar of Tarbert; Thomas Urquhart, sheriff of Cromarty; and Robert Innes of Innermarkie. James Stewart, earl of Moray, was oversman. Although a private settlement, the parties must have felt the need to seal it by involving the King's Council as the highest civil authority in the land below the King personally. The dispute was over the right to the feudal casualty of non-entry for the lands and barony of Sanquhar in the sheriffdom of Elgin and Forres. We should be careful, of course, not to assume that registration before Council meant that the substance of the compromit was necessarily carried out or that the arbitration process automatically led to a resolution of the dispute. For example, we find that in this case, over six months later and without explanation of what has passed in the meantime, the same dispute had to be brought before the Lords again on 21 March 1530.[33] This time the parties bound themselves "to abyde by a decreet" of Gavin Dunbar, the chancellor, and archbishop of Glasgow, and Gavin Dunbar, bishop of Aberdeen (and uncle of the archbishop).

A more complicated example can be seen on 1 April 1530, when William Scott, burgess of Montrose, made an appearance before the Lords to make a complaint directed against Andrew Seton, laird of Parbroath. Seton had summoned William for reduction of a decreet obtained by William against him.[34] The following day, however, the parties appeared again, and compromitted themselves to abide by the

[31] Athol L. Murray, "Introduction" in *Acts of the Lords of Council, Vol. III, 1501–1503*, ed. A.B. Calderwood (Edinburgh, 1993), p. xxvi.

[32] Edinburgh, National Archives of Scotland [hereafter NAS], CS 5/40, fol. 111v.

[33] NAS CS 5/41, fol. 26r.

[34] NAS CS 5/41, fol. 56v.

sentence of five arbiters, all Lords of Session.[35] However, it was necessary for Andrew Seton's procurator, Robert Leslie, to come before the Lords again four days later to obtain a formal charge to the arbiters to proceed in the manner envisaged in the compromit. It seems that new letters had meanwhile been obtained from the King which contained a clause discharging the arbiters from proceeding, but that some form of misrepresentation had been behind this which had now been uncovered. The King wrote personally to the chancellor and the Lords on 6 April, the letter seemingly being produced to the Lords on Seton's behalf by Leslie as his procurator. The King explained that he had neither been aware of the inclusion of a discharge in the earlier letters nor that the commission was to amicable compositors, and stated that the judges named in the compromit should now proceed to give their decree arbitral after all.[36] All these steps were taken through the Session—the King did not charge the arbiters directly to proceed, but directed the Lords to issue this charge to them.

When parties themselves agreed to discharge arbiters whom they had commissioned, such a step might also be formalised before the Session. On 12 August 1529, for example, the arbiters chosen between Robert Forman, dean of Glasgow, the prior of Pittenweem and others, and the laird of Ardross, were discharged "fra all proceding or labouring apoun the said compromitt" in the presence of the parties and the Lords of Council. All of the arbiters were themselves Lords of Council and Session: Alexander Mylne, abbot of Cambuskenneth; George Learmonth, prior of Pluscarden; Adam Otterburn, King's advocate; Nichol Crawfurd, justice clerk; James Lawson and Francis Bothwell.[37]

A reason why parties conducted the formalities of private settlement before the Session in this way is suggested by the registration on 15 March 1530 of an "appunctment" between Janet Rowat, the relict of an Edinburgh burgess, and Alison Ruche. Registration of such a deed in the books of council gave it the force of a decree. This would mean that the private agreement could then be more effectively enforced through legal process. The parties bound themselves to "stand and undourly the sentence and decrete arbitrale of honourable personis", these being Adam Otterburn, James Simson (official of Lothian), John

[35] NAS CS 5/41, fol. 59.
[36] NAS CS 5/41, fol. 70; *Acts of the Lords of Council in Public Affairs*, ed. R.K. Hannay (Edinburgh, 1932), p. 326.
[37] NAS CS 5/40, fol. 94r.

Bothwell and James Lawson. They had been appointed as "jugis arbitral and amicable compositours".[38] It would be interesting to know the subsequent history of this arbitration and its result, but what is equally interesting is simply to note the apparent desirability of securing a formal legal status for the settlement, along with the agreement to accept the "sentence" of the chosen arbiters. This tends to confirm Jenny Wormald's observation in a more general context that "Scottish society by the sixteenth century had an extraordinary degree of confidence, both in public authority and in private arbitrators".[39] This is brought out even more clearly in relation to another registered agreement in a hearing on 4 March 1531. It concerned David Blair of Adamton and William Hamilton of Sanquhar. Their dispute was over title to land, and on 4 March the matter was submitted by them to arbitration. The nature of the regard which parties must have had for registration in the books of council is shown by the provision that the decree given by the chosen amicable compositors was to be put in the "buke of counsell" and to have the strength of a decree "as it had bene gevin be the hale lordis of the session".[40] Decrees of the Session are being held up here as providing a special benchmark of authority.

Another reason for registration, more directly concerned with enforcement, is suggested by a compromit submitted in February 1532 by William Hamilton of Sanquhar Lindsay. He was in dispute with James Wallace of Carnell and Adam Wallace of Newton, in relation to a claim to the common land of Sanquhar Lindsay in Ayrshire. Letters to command, charge, compel and distrain the parties were issued as a result of registration, and the compromit itself was "insert" in the books of council "for the mair securite of the fulfilling of the promiss".[41] Once registered with the consent of both parties there could be no dispute about the terms of the agreement, or any need to verify what one or other party thought were its terms, beyond reference to the council register. This in turn meant that the parties had the security of knowing that their future conduct could be tested against an objective and unimpeachable public document. Without this precaution a party who objected to a decree arbitral could attempt to renounce it, as did the earl of Crawford on 7 July 1531. He referred to a "pretendit decret

[38] NAS CS 5/41, fol. 9.
[39] Wormald, "The Sandlaw Dispute", p. 203.
[40] NAS CS 5/42, fol. 94.
[41] NAS CS 5/43, fol. 153.

arbitrale" given between him and his son Alexander, but claimed he "knew nevir na compromit nor decreit nor wald consent to the same and thirfor renuncit the said decretit arbitral".[42]

In the giving in of an appunctment on 19 February 1532 by Dame Isabell Campbell, countess of Cassillis, and Alexander Kennedy of Bargany, the idea that compulsion of the parties could follow from registration in the books of council is explicitly referred to. The appunctment was given in "and baith [the parties] to be compellit to fulfill thair part of the same".[43] The sanctions for not fulfilling a court decree were more severe than the civil remedies available for breach of an agreement, since they could amount to being declared rebel and put to the horn and thereby excluded from the King's "peace". This was explicitly recognised in some appunctments. For example, on 27 February 1532, Hew, Lord Lovat, and George Richardson, son and executor of the late Robert Richardson, a burgess of Edinburgh, asked that their appunctment be inserted into the books of council to have the strength of an act and decree, with letters to command and charge the parties to fulfil its terms, under pain of being declared rebel and put to the horn. Their dispute centred on payment of £43 for silk cloth and other merchandise, and the appunctment laid down a form of structured repayment by installments. It is hard to know the practical effect of being put to the horn in a case like this, but nevertheless it was technically a severe sanction.

Compulsion was not only available to the original party, since another advantage of registration of the decree arbitral itself was that it could then be transferred like a normal court decree to the successors in title of the original parties in dispute, to whom the rights under the decree would thereby be assigned. On 25 June 1532, for example, a decree arbitral which had been "insert" in the books of council on 12 April 1527 was transferred to Gilbert Kennedy, third earl of Cassillis, and Helen Crawford. Helen was the widow and "relict" of Thomas Corry of Kelwood. Thomas had been awarded £300 against the second earl of Cassillis, who had been assassinated in 1527.[44] Again, an approach to the Session was seen as necessary in implementing a private settlement.

---

[42] NAS CS 5/42, fol. 195r.
[43] NAS CS 5/43, fol. 162.
[44] NAS CS 6/1, fol. 40r.

Arbitration and litigation before the Session

By the years around 1532, the Session was therefore not only a central court but a forum in which settlement or other forms of dispute resolution could be formalised, including the arrangement of arbitration. We have noted a variety of ways in which the Session offered additional security and assistance to parties in underwriting their privately initiated processes of settlement. Whether there was any tension between its identity as a law court and as a facilitator of settlement is difficult to say, but it seems unlikely in the light of the evidence discussed above. Moreover, the Session derived its authority ultimately from its direct connection with the King's Council, with which it was in practical terms synonymous until 1532 and whose jurisdiction it continued to exercise after 1532. The Council's role as a regular law court was relatively recent, going back forty or fifty years, and a residual authority deriving from it being part of the *curia regis* still infused the Session, even after the formal separation of 1532. Afterall, Lords of Council ceased to be Lords of Session *ex officiis* in 1532 but Lords of Session were by definition still Lords of Council. In this way, the Lords of Session continued to give their decrees in their capacity as Lords of Council after 1532.

Given that through its wider involvement in dispute resolution the Session bridged the separation between the worlds of public and private justice, it is hardly surprising to discover that in the course of a single dispute it might have played more than one role on consecutive occasions. Sometimes parties approached the Session for the first time with a compromit already agreed. But it was also common for a dispute to have already come before the Session under formal legal process initiated by summons, prior to a submission to arbitration being made, and the litigation thereby abandoned. For example, on 19 June 1533 Sir John Stirling of Keir and James Kinross bound themselves to arbitration in relation to matters contained in a decree of recognition "as in ane summond for retreting of the said decrete of recognition" raised by Kinross.[45] Similarly, the appunctment already mentioned between Janet Rowat and Alison Ruche followed the raising of a summons by Alison Ruche and her husband John Mair.

[45] NAS CS 6/3, fol. 24v. The procedure of recognition is discussed in J. Finlay, "James Henryson and the Origins of the King's Advocate in Scotland", *Scottish Historical Review* (2000), 17–38 at pp. 28–30.

Arbitration might sometimes be chosen only after protracted legal process. For example, on 10 November 1531 the Lords received a supplication from Sir David Bruce of Clackmannan against his spouse Janet Blackadder. Janet had apparently obtained a sentence or judgement against him before the official of St Andrews, under which he had been required to make payment to her and infeft her in certain lands. David appealed, but Janet sought to enforce the judgment through letters of apprising against his lands and goods. She alleged that due process had been complied with since he had been under "cursing" for forty days. She took out letters to poind and distrain him as well. At the hearing on 10 November, the parties agreed to the arbitration of the chancellor, the comptroller, and the prior of Pittenweem. In the meantime the action was continued to the 4 December, and "all letters, process and proceeding" were to cease.[46] Public justice was to be suspended while private justice was allowed to operate.

In these ways public justice tended to play a role even in disputes which were primarily approached in terms of private justice. Moreover, if the social pressures to honour private agreements failed, then by the early sixteenth century public justice tended to fill the vacuum. In a supplication of Alexander, prior of Pluscarden, for example, we find reference to a dispute resolved by an appunctment, but followed by litigation over the fulfilling of that appunctment. William Wood of Bonnington and Arthur Panton, the other parties, had alleged that the prior would not fulfill the contract and appunctment he had entered into, and obtained letters charging him to fulfill his obligations. The prior raised a summons on them to produce these letters. However, the "term peremptour" having arrived in July 1532, Panton produced a compromit providing for arbitration. The parties were reverting to the modes of private justice. At this point we are told that the Council superseded ("supersedes") the legal action until the third day of the next Session.[47] It was not terminated, however, but merely superseded. In another case, on 30 April 1534 John Dickson of Ormiston tried to get William Dickson to fulfil a decree arbitral and hand over his charters to some disputed land. It was mentioned that "eftir lang pley movit betwix thaim anent the landis of Ormiston... thai compromittit the same".[48]

[46] NAS CS 5/43, fol. 68v.
[47] NAS CS 6/1, fol. 93.
[48] NAS CS 6/4, fol. 115v.

Again, this shows settlement through arbitration arising only after a long period of litigation. In such cases it is difficult to tell whether there had been frustration at the failure of legal process to achieve a resolution, whether legal process had simply taken time to serve the purpose of exerting pressure on the other party to compromise, or whether it had simply been intended to prevaricate and postpone any resolution for as long as possible through the use of cout action.

Of course, private justice was itself not necessarily effective, even once settlement was reached. Agreements did not necessarily hold, and could also end up being reopened and superseded by further agreements, as was apparently the case with Alexander Dunbar and Huchon Rose in the instance already cited. In proceedings involving another case on 29 January 1532, William Cockburn, as brother of the late John Cockburn of Newhall, handed in an agreement to be registered before Council concerning the redemption of lands under a reversion, and which was explicitly said to supersede a previous agreement.[49] In other cases, the inability of private justice to achieve a resolution led to the public justice of the courts being invoked. In this way, agreements to use private modes of justice could be superseded by formal litigation when the private methods proved ineffective or had simply come to be abandoned. For example, on 17 June 1533 James Charteris came before Council by way of supplication. His complaint was that he had previously had Alexander Kirkpatrick of Kirkmichael under summons before the Lords of Council for the profits arising from peaceable occupation of lands which Alexander had denied to James.[50] However, that summons had been continued to 26 January 1530, after it had called in court on 12 December.[51] As was quite typical, James Charteris had raised his civil action after Kirkpatrick had first been criminally indicted in the justice ayre of Dumfries, with Lord Maxwell having stood as his pledge and surety. The case therefore illustrates incidentally the relations between criminal and civil process. When compearing in June 1533, Charteris explained that the previous summons before the Session had simply not been pursued, and that he and Kirkpatrick had "compromitted" and submitted their dispute to arbiters. However, the arbitration had apparently never happened, since it was stated that the compromit was

[49] NAS CS 5/43, fol. 141.
[50] NAS CS 6/2, fol. 188v.
[51] NAS CS 5/41, fol. 145v.

"fundin by the lordis of nane availe and expirit in the self". Charteris was now appearing in court to reinstate his summons so that he could call witnesses on the basis that the Lords might "proceid and do justice in the said mater".[52] The Lords then authorised letters to be issued summoning Alexander to compear on 8 July "to answer in the said matter eftir the form of the last act of continuation", which had been over two years earlier.[53] Kirkpatrick had not compeared at this hearing, but was personally present at the next one on 12 July, and the matter now proceeded as a normal action under summons.[54]

In terms of the interaction between private and public justice, clearly opting for one approach could have consequences in wholly excluding the other. Sometimes a party raised an action before the Session by summons when the dispute appeared to have been fully resolved already by some form of arbitration or mediation. For example, on 23 July 1533, John Hepburn, the parson of Hawick, summoned Walter Scott of Branxholm for spuilzie of the teinds and profits of his benefice, parsonage and vicarage of the kirk of Hawick in 1530, and the occupation of his kirklands.[55] However, Scott compeared personally and alleged that he and Hepburn had "compromittit thaim... anent frutis", and that the friar to whom they had submitted the dispute had accepted the commission and already given his sentence. In any event, Scott submitted, the matters contained in Hepburn's summons were already the subject of an action in the commissary court of Glasgow, from which Scott had appealed to Rome. Hepburn's summons was put to one side and Scott ordered to prove his allegations. The next hearing was not until 10 November 1533, at which point Walter Scott abandoned his exception, and chose instead to refer the whole matter to proof by the oath of Hepburn.[56] On the same day a supplication was heard from Scott, in which he complained that he had now been put to the horn by Hepburn, again alleging that he was thereby wronged because of the existence of an "appunctment" between them which had been ratified by Hepburn. Hepburn denied this and the matter was continued for him to "liquidate" (i.e. ascertain) the sum sued for. On 21 November 1533 the Lords gave decree against Walter Scott. If

[52] NAS CS 6/2, fol. 188v.
[53] NAS CS 6/2, fol. 188v.
[54] NAS CS 6/3, fol. 15.
[55] NAS CS 6/3, fol. 38.
[56] NAS CS 6/3, fol. 73.

there had been a compromit, Walter certainly failed to produce it. The case does illustrate, however, the variety and interaction of remedies, formal and informal, which parties in dispute could deploy. In addition, it seems clear that they may sometimes have been deployed in bad faith simply in order to be obstructive for tactical reasons. Indeed, the bad faith of litigants seems likely to have been a far greater problem in the administration of justice in the Session than bad faith, partiality or corruption in the judges.

An agreed choice by parties to make private settlement should in principle have acted to bar any formal proceedings which sought thereafter to invoke public justice. In another case in 1529, for example, it was alleged that a dispute under summons had already been resolved formally by a decree arbitral. Elizabeth Hamilton and her spouse James Dundas had raised a summons against Elizabeth's son James Stewart of Craigiehall.[57] At the calling of Elizabeth's summons, James had pleaded an exception and shown that there was a decree arbitral given between him and his mother already, which decree was now to be produced in evidence. On 15 May, the following day, James Stewart stated that since the raising of the summons against him, he had compromitted with his mother, and that a decree arbitral had been given absolving him from the allegation of spuilzie, and thus decree should not be pronounced against him. Not only does this example show how different methods of resolving disputes interacted, but also how a resolution achieved by one method did not necessarily mean that a dissatisfied party would not attempt to overturn it by another. Nevertheless, a decree arbitral should have barred further litigation.

Attempts to re-open a dispute could occur many years after its apparent resolution. At the end of 1530, for example, we find decree being given against Neil Montgomery, son of the earl of Eglinton, in favour of Marion Ross, relict and executor of Edward Cunningham of Auchinhervy. The legal action had re-opened a matter Montgomery claimed had been settled by a decree arbitral seven years earlier.[58] Decree was given on 5 February 1531 and Montgomery found liable for payment of 800 merks for what had apparently been a violent raid on the home of Cunningham. Montgomery had been indicted for the offence in the justice ayre of Ayr on 17 January 1529. However, two days after the

[57] NAS CS 5/40, fol. 33v.
[58] NAS CS 5/42, fol. 78.

giving of decree, Montgomery's brother, Robert Montgomery, bishop of Argyll, appeared on Neil Montgomery's behalf to allege that the complaint upon which Marion's action had been founded had already been considered and addressed in a decree arbitral between the earl of Eglinton and Lord Kilmaurs.[59] On 28 February, Neil Montgomery compeared himself by way of a supplication, explaining that the damage for which the action had been brought had already been "assythed" (i.e. settled through payment of compensation) and made the subject of a compromit between the earls of Glencairn and Eglinton and their kin (it is unclear whether this might be the same settlement as the one in the compromit mentioned by the bishop of Argyll). Neil went on to say that a decree arbitral had been given on 13 March 1523 in Edinburgh, and produced an acquittance from the late Edward Cunningham acknowledging that he had been fully assythed by the earl of Glencairn on Neil's behalf.

Here we have, incidentally, a classic vignette of the settlement of a feud, with the compromise and compensation being agreed by the respective lords, and the kin-group being party to it.[60] The pronunciation of the decree against Neil was suspended, but the action continued since Marion's husband compeared on her behalf and alleged that the acquittance in question was false.[61] The ramifications of settling a dispute between two powerful figures could be notable, and a decree arbitral could encompass relations between such figures and a wide variety of their friends and servants, making it at least in this respect an ideal mechanism for the termination of a feud. However, the complexity of such comprehensive settlements could create new problems of enforcement and render them hard to interpret if fresh sources of dispute arose between supporters of the principal parties. On 9 March 1534, for example, John Somerville of Cambusnethane complained to the Session that Patrick Mure of Arniston had raised an action of lawburrows against him when this contravened a decree arbitral already given involving Sir James Hamilton, of whom he was "man and servand".[62] There could be a tension between the rights of the individual to redress according to the standards of public justice, and the sanctity of a wider settlement made within the context of private justice. Modes

[59] NAS CS 5/42, fol. 65v.
[60] See J. Wormald, *Court, Kirk, and Community* (London, 1981), pp. 36–37.
[61] NAS CS 5/42, fol. 78.
[62] NAS CS 6/4, fol. 46.

of private justice could not necessarily provide clear solutions in such circumstances, but the Session as an institution of public justice seems to have been increasingly accorded a regulatory role in order to resolve such problems of interpretation.

The effectiveness of private justice clearly drew to some extent upon the ultimate sanction available of turning instead to public justice. Sometimes formal legal action was merely suspended to make way for negotiation and the possibility of a private settlement, but on the explicit understanding that if such a settlement was not reached within a certain period of time then legal process would be resumed. This is illustrated at one point in the protracted dispute of many years duration between Lord Fleming and John Tweedie of Drumelzier, and touched on in the previous chapter.[63] On 26 January 1531 John Tweedie appeared in order to ask instruments (i.e. a notarised extract of a sentence) following the Lords of Council having continued his summons against Lord Fleming "in hope of concord" until the coming Tuesday. He wished a formal record of his submission that if no agreement was reached between them by that point then without further delay the Lords should proceed on the summons and "minister" justice.[64] By 31 January both parties were in fact prepared to submit their dispute to the Lords of Council as amicable compositors, apparently after the personal intervention of the King.[65] Similarly on 30 July 1532, Alexander, prior of Pluscarden, appeared in order to answer an accusation that he had refused to fulfil a contract and appunctment between himself and William Wood of Bonnington and Arthur Panton concerning intromission with escheat goods, and to see Panton prove the allegations against him or grant him an absolvitor. However, at this point Panton produced a compromit which bound the parties to accept the verdict of certain arbiters. As we saw earlier, the Lords of Council superseded the action until the third day of the next Session, so that in the interim the arbiters could give their sentence.

Given the complexity of patterns of dispute resolution, institutions of public justice were in an advantageous position to provide essential regulation of the rights of the parties when this was desired. As we have been seeing, in a variety of ways the Session was well able to perform

[63] The feud involved the murder of John, Lord Fleming in 1524. See Finlay, *Men of Law in Pre-Reformation Scotland*, pp. 77–78.

[64] NAS CS 5/42, fol. 8.

[65] NAS CS 5/42, fol. 24.

this role by the early part of the sixteenth century. A situation could arise, for example, in which it would appear that a court decree had by consent of the parties been superseded by an arbitrated settlement, but following which one side went back to try to enforce the court decree. Clearly this was an abuse of process. Arbitration rendered the previous court decree irrelevant in this context. The enforcement of a prior court decree was subject to any subsequent agreements made between the parties. When one or more of the parties behaved inconsistently in this regard, clarifying the relations between them inevitably required additional court process. This scenario is apparent on 21 March 1534 when John Steel of Kilmaurs and John Boyd compeared. Boyd had called Steel before the sheriff of Ayr and been awarded the sum of five merks, but thereafter both parties referred the matter to arbiters who proceeded to give decree arbitral. However, Boyd obtained letters charging the sheriff to put the court decree to execution and to ensure that Steel made payment, but omitting any reference to the decree arbitral. Steel then found himself poinded for the sum in question. Upon his protest, the Lords decided that he should be allowed to prove that the reference to arbiters had been made, and ordained him to summon the arbiters and the witness and notary mentioned in the decree. The notary was ordained to produce his protocol book. The dispute over whether there had been an arbitrated settlement was going to have to be laboriously proven.[66]

The courts could therefore have a surprisingly direct involvement in assisting private processes of dispute resolution. Sometimes it is even apparent that the Lords of Council had themselves chosen arbiters to hear a dispute between parties. Of course this did not necessarily guarantee that the arbitration would resolve matters, but it suggests that public justice could again step in to supplement the actings of parties who were attempting a private resolution. On 23 October 1531, for example, a supplication was heard from Adam Wright and Edward Thomson against William Buchan. The complaint was that Buchan had not fulfilled the terms of a decree arbitral, and it was narrated that the arbiters—the bishop of Ross and the provost of Edinburgh—were "juges arbitratours chosen be the lordis of counsal betwix the said personnis".[67] The Lords had at first assisted in promoting the option

[66] NAS CS 6/4, fol. 100v.
[67] NAS CS 5/43, fol. 59.

of arbitration, but were now being required to assist in policing the enforcement of its outcome.

Private resolutions might still require to be enforced, and public justice could again be invoked in situations in which other informal sanctions appeared to have been ineffective. There are many examples of parties to arbitrations coming before the Session seeking orders to compel the other party to fulfil a decree arbitral. This type of situation seems to exemplify perfectly the interaction of public and private modes of dispute resolution. It involved a settlement which had been achieved through private arbitration being seamlessly channelled into a form of official enforcement procedure. For example, on 31 July 1529 James Kennedy compeared as procurator for Gilbert Kennedy of Kirkmichael and produced letters which had been served on Gilbert charging him to fulfil a decree arbitral or else to compear and show a reasonable cause why he should not do so. In this case, the procurator protested successfully that Gilbert should not have to answer in this matter until he was served with a new summons on twenty-one days notice by Janet Dunbar and her spouse Gilbert Boyd.[68] The results of the arbitration were now absorbed into the technical formalism of court procedure.

A more extended dispute over the fulfilling of a decree arbitral is described in an action between Archibald Fairlie, fiar of the land of Braid, and Robert Bruce, burgess of Edinburgh, in February 1532. Archibald appeared before Council by supplication to complain that a decree arbitral had been given between him and Robert which Robert "postponis and deferres to fulfill". This was despite the fact that "eftir he was requirit thirto he promittit to fulfill the samyn", as could be seen from an instrument produced by Archibald. Robert had already been charged to compear "to heir him decernt to fulfill the said decrete arbitrale for his part or ellis to shaw ane resonable caus quhy he suld nocht do the sammyn". He was now simply charged again to fulfil the decree, since he had failed to compear.[69] Both parties then compeared on 2 May 1532, with Robert alleging that he had fulfilled the decree in all points.[70] The Lords were now being called upon to determine whether the decree arbitral had been fulfilled or not. Robert alleged that Archibald had "by sinister and wrang information" procured

[68] NAS CS 5/40, fol. 79.
[69] NAS CS 5/43, fol. 166.
[70] NAS CS 5/43, fol. 185v.

letters of cursing against him, and was putting him to the horn "bot [i.e. without] lauchful caus". The Lords continued the action for two days for Robert to prove that he had fulfilled the decree. The parties compeared again as instructed, and after seeing a reversion and letter of assignation "uncancellat" of six acres of the land of Braid, and various other documents produced by Robert, the Lords suspended Archibald's letters and declared Robert to have fulfilled the decree arbitral.[71]

This example serves to reinforce the point that just because parties sought a resolution of their dispute through arbitration did not mean that formal legal process was of no further interest or practical use. In fact, royal letters and charges were often obtained to help enforce the fulfilling of a private settlement. Public and private justice were therefore in this way often closely interrelated. This is amply illustrated by the dispute between John Inglis of Kilmany and William Lindsay of Preston. John came before the Council on 7 May 1532 to complain that the Lords had granted letters to William which charged John to fulfil a decree arbitral between them. John, however, had appealed to the Lords of Council against this decree and summoned William to compear and produce the letters which he had been granted. The Lords were now told that "the said Johne standand in hope of concord divers dais the said William hes this secund day of May instant opteint ane decret as the said Johne is informit to put the said letters to execution and intends thirby to put the said Johne to the horne".[72] These letters were now reduced as "unordourlie procedit". Four days later both parties compeared again, and John protested that he had been charged to fulfil the decree arbitral but was ready to explain why he should not have to do so.[73] The next appearance of the parties was on 5 June, when the Lords were moved to declare explicitly the nature of their authority over the arbitration. They stated in a sentence interlocutor that:

> thai ar competent juges to understand quhether letters suld be gevin apoun ane decret arbitrale... becaus the compromitt quharupoune the decret is gevin is actit in the bukes of counsale havand the strength of ane decret of the lordis to the quhilk thai ar competent jugis.[74]

John Inglis had tried to claim otherwise in an appeal by way of "instrument of reclamationne". The Lords' response is extremely telling, since

---

[71] NAS CS 5/43, fol. 188v.
[72] NAS CS 5/43, fol. 191.
[73] NAS CS 5/43, fol. 195.
[74] NAS CS 6/1, fol. 16r.

it shows them choosing to assert their authority in technical terms of jurisdiction. Even in the world of private settlement the language and concepts of the law could envelop the outcome, at least at the point at which the terms of the resolution in question had to be performed or enforced. The Lords went on to find that John had failed to fulfil the decree arbitral, which awarded to William the "rycht" of the teind sheaves and fruits of the parsonage and vicarage of St Michael's kirk of Tarvit. Letters to command and charge John to fulfil the decree arbitral were consequently issued. William was also able to procure royal letters to make himself be "answerit" of the teinds and fruits.

However, the matter came up again on 18 June, with William claiming that John had "maid him to interpone ane further reclamation fra the said decrete arbitrale out of dew time" and that in consequence he had summoned William before the official of St Andrews for reduction of the decree arbitral.[75] William submitted that the official was not a competent judge in this instance, and had been charged to send a copy of the "appellacion and reclamacion" to the Lords on 4 July. The Lords declared themselves again to be the competent judges and ordained letters to be directed to the official of St Andrews requiring him to cease further process in the matter. John was told in no uncertain terms that any grievance which he had in this matter was to be brought before the Lords of Council. The case illustrates how even though the substantive resolution of a dispute might be removed from court and entrusted to arbiters, nevertheless parties still looked to use—and might find it necessary to use—the full panoply of the law in enforcing the eventual decision of the arbiters, or equally to obstruct its implementation.

Again, this case demonstrates how private and public justice were not distinct spheres apart from one another. Interaction of this kind with the spiritual courts was also not unusual. An appeal to the court of the official could sometimes be considered desirable even when arbitration had been used. For example, on 27 March 1533, Margaret Dalgleish complained against her son Hercules Guthrie that he had not fulfilled a decree arbitral between them, despite being charged either to do so, or to compear before the Lords. On this occasion, though, Hercules was assoilzied, because he had reclaimed against the decree arbitral to the official of St Andrews, as a testimonial under the seal of the official

[75] NAS CS 6/1, fol. 28v.

confirmed.[76] This appeal would probably have been in relation to a "compromit" which the parties had chosen not to register in the books of council. The basis of the appeal is unclear and it could suggest that the rule against appeal from an arbitral award was not always adhered to. It is more likely, however, that the appeal would not have been on the merits but rather would have concerned a flaw in process.

Clearly, a further difficulty could arise in respect of a decree arbitral apart from merely enforcing it. This would be the question of interpreting how it was to be fulfilled, if this was on the face of it ambiguous or if the circumstances which the arbiters had taken into account had changed. The authority of the arbiters would depend on the terms of their commissions, and these would contain a strict time limit. Normally, once they had delivered their decree they would cease to have any formal involvement in the dispute or in the enforcement of the decree. This was another reason why parties who had opted for private arbitration would still look to the machinery of legal process and the law courts to enforce, interpret or modify decrees arbitral.

An example of this latter situation arose on 15 July 1531, when John Tweedie of Drumelzier came before the Lords of Council, who had acted collectively as arbiters in this instance. Tweedie and Lord Fleming were personally present to see the decree arbitral interpreted in respect of certain points they had raised, and for the Lords to make a declarator to this end. One of the main points was that under the decree John Tweedie was to have ensured the removal of all the persons who were at the slaughter of John, Lord Fleming (the cause of the Fleming-Tweedie feud) from Scotland and England, but Tweedie had been unable to fulfil this because some of these persons had now become "men" of Malcolm, Lord Fleming. The Lords assoilzied Tweedie from failing to comply with this point of the decree, thus formalising the position and thereby allowing Tweedie to say that he had fulfilled the decree in all points. Both parties wished for such a formal declaration and it was the Lords of Council who were best placed to give it. Lord Fleming stated that "gif the lordis findis ony poyntis unfulfillit he sall fulfill the same", so that "na process suld be led apoun him in tyme tocum".[77] It was also important for each side to accept that the other had fulfilled all points of the settlement and to this end Lord Fleming

[76] NAS CS 6/2, fol. 140.
[77] NAS CS 5/43, fol. 8v.

also asked instruments to record the fact that Tweedie "grantit that the said lord tuk him be the hand befor the kingis grace and chancellar and for that part had fulfillit the said decret in that punct".[78] The rituals of peace had not merely to be enacted as agreed, but recorded as having been accomplished.

Interpreting agreements to arbitrate was another function which an institution of public justice such as the Session was particularly well placed to perform, and which the modes of private justice found it difficult to provide for. Such interpretation could involve supplying terms and conditions which the parties had failed to decide upon or express, but which were necessary to enable the relevant procedures to work. It was not always the case, for example, that a compromit contained exhaustive conditions as to how an arbitration was to proceed. On occasion parties might first register a compromit and then look to the Lords to determine further procedure. On 10 May 1531 Alexander Scrimgeour and his wife compromitted with Oliver Maxton and his spouse, for example, in relation to actions of spuilzie and reduction of court process in which they had been involved. They registered their "compromit", which named eleven arbiters but stated that any five of the eleven could hear the cause.[79] However, the record then states that the Lords of Council assigned to the arbiters a particular day to "accept and tak the said compromit and mater in and apoun thaim", and also ordained the parties to compeir before the arbiters in Edinburgh on the same day to "persew thair actionis sa that iustice may be ministrat".[80] This example is particularly illuminating since it demonstrates the language and formality of litigation being unproblematically carried over into the realm of arbitration. Private and public justice were again so interconnected here that they could almost be regarded as drawing upon a common procedural discourse.

The interaction between different courses of resolving dispute, and the important role which the Session could play in such interaction, even in private arbitrations, is shown vividly in a dispute between the prior of Pittenweem, William Dishington, fiar of Ardross, and Thomas Scott of Petgormo in 1533. The parties had "compromitted" and referred their dispute to arbitrators, but the prior came before the Session on

[78] NAS CS 5/43, fol. 8r.
[79] NAS CS 5/42, fol. 180v.
[80] NAS CS 5/42, fol. 181.

10 March 1534 to explain that although the matter had been so referred, nevertheless "the saidis arbitratoris thinkis the mater difficult to thaim". The result had been that in a new compromit of 21 January 1533 the parties had referred the matter to the Lords of Council instead and assoilzied the arbitrators from the previous compromit.[81] Clearly, whatever the difficulty, there was perceived to be either greater authority, objectivity or expertise in the Lords of Council than in the original arbitrators. A further element in the resolution of this dispute was the personal involvement of the King, who had written to the chancellor, president of the Session and Lords of Session on 27 February from Cupar, where he was at the time. The letter is copied into the council register, and in it the King asks the Lords to "accept the samin apon you" and to "end the samin to the eis of all partiis that thai may leif in frendschip, doand na wrang to owther of thaim". He stated that "we pray you to do as ye will do us singular emplesour, becaus all the saidis partiis hes requestit us to this effect".[82] There also seems to have been some element of delay on one side or other, since the prior declared himself "redy to obey and fulfill the compromit", but had also made a point of stating that "it stud nocht in him the nonfulfilling of the said compromit nor writing [of the King] forsaid bot in the said William Dischington alanerly".[83] So in sum we see here the involvement of chosen arbitrators, as well as the Lords of Council, and also the separate petitioning of the King personally, with the final outcome being that the Lords of Council are to sit as arbitrators in the dispute. The fact that accepting the office of arbitrator was a voluntary matter probably explains why the King merely asked the Lords to accept the commission rather than commanding them to do justice as he might have done if the action was proceeding by royal summons. Nevertheless, the outcome of the dispute was a product of the convergence of public and private justice and authority.

Public justice was not just able to better facilitate the operation of private justice. It was also able to supervise it when the parties required this. This simply reflected the way in which the Session's superior jurisdiction naturally transcended the operation of private authority. On the

[81] NAS CS 6/4, fol. 53r.

[82] The letter is printed in *Acts of the Lords of Council in Public Affairs 1501–1554*, ed. R.K. Hannay (Edinburgh, 1932), pp. 419–420; NAS CS 6/4, fol. 53v.

[83] NAS CS 6/4, fol. 53r.

question of exercising authority to quash the decision of arbiters in a particular matter, for example, it seems that the Session did exercise in this regard something which amounted to a form of supervisory jurisdiction similar to that exercised over the operation of other law courts. It would reduce a decree arbitral in cases when evidence upon which the arbiters based their decision proved to be false, for example. The invocation of such a jurisdiction may in effect be what contemporaries regarded as an appeal in relation to an arbitration. For example, on 28 May 1533 Huchon Dunning appeared before the Session to pursue a summons against John Scott, alleging that John was troubling him in the enjoyment of lands he held with others under lease after the two of them had compromitted in an earlier dispute over the lands. The land had apparently been alienated to John by a certain George Gorthy after the assedation to Huchon had already been made.[84] The arbiters had decreed that since the assedation preceded the alienation and had four years to run then Huchon should continue to possess the lands, although he should also pay mails and duties (i.e. rent) to John Scott. However, Scott alleged that:

> the said pretendit decret arbitrale wes of na effect nor valour and the lordis aucht nocht to compell him to fulfill the same becaus it wes gevin eftir the form and tenor of ane pretendit letter of assedation... quhilk was fals and fenzeit in the self, maid with ane antedait efter that he [i.e. George Gorthy] had analyt the said lands to said Jhone.[85]

The Lords then assigned John a court day to prove his allegation, and made it clear to the parties that "meyntime... na innovation be maid thirin quhill it be understand and decydit be the saidis lordis quhilk of the saidis partyis hes ryt to the saidis takkis".[86] The action was continued to 20 June but it was 25 June before it came up again. At this hearing, the Lords reduced the decree arbitral because they accepted that the assedation was false.[87] Notably, Huchon had refused to produce the letter of tack which he was relying upon as evidence of the lease, advancing the weak excuse that he would not produce it since John Scott's procurator "impugnit the same".[88] This case shows that

---

[84] NAS CS 6/2, fol. 180r.
[85] NAS CS 6/2, fol. 180v.
[86] NAS CS 6/2, fol. 180v.
[87] NAS CS 6/2, fol. 206.
[88] NAS CS 6/2, fol. 203.

jurisdiction was not to be excluded by submission to arbitration if it could be proved that there was a flaw in those arbitration proceedings. In this case false evidence had been relied upon.

In another case on 31 March 1531, a decree arbitral was challenged because it had allegedly been given "outwith the day expunt in the compromitt".[89] Christine Gray and her son James Abernethy were pursuing an action against the arbiters in a decision over the ownership of a gable wall between two properties in the Canongate, adjacent to Edinburgh. The decision of the arbiters was overturned, but somewhat unexpectedly the Lords did not explicitly reduce the decree in the manner craved by the pursuer, but simply gave decree anew as judges and amicable compositors with the advice of the principal masons and wrights of Edinburgh, aiming at "the mair eisiamente of baith the partiis".[90] It is not immediately clear whether acting in this capacity was under the guise of arbitration or litigation, and whether it was technically a decree of the Lords of Council or a decree arbitral which was pronounced. There is no mention of the matter being submitted to the Lords as arbiters. However, it does show a dissatisfied party to an arbitration coming before Council to have a decree arbitral reduced or superseded by virtue of a technical flaw. Moreover, it symbolises clearly not just the compatibility between and frequent convergence of public and private modes of dispute resolution, but also the ambiguity of form sometimes arising from their close relationship in practice.

Simple submissions and mediation

The examples cited so far have related almost exclusively to disputes which parties had submitted to the decision of arbiters through a "compromit". In a sense, it is easiest to discuss those procedures for which records were made, and evidence survives, and arbitration satisfies those conditions more than any procedure outside formal litigation. However, arbitration was but one method, albeit a common and important one. It is striking that other *ad hoc* arrangements were also used and often committed to writing. This tendency to cast such arrangements into written, legalistic forms suggests a cultural impetus towards the rendering of dispute resolution mechanisms generally into more juridical form.

[89] NAS CS 5/42, fol. 160.
[90] NAS CS 5/42, fol. 160.

After all, the rights which were the subject of dispute would have often themselves been in written form. It is perhaps too easy to overlook the extent to which legal culture in this sense permeated norms of conduct in sixteenth-century Scotland, even in situations in which parties might tend to eschew litigation and the courts. That there should have been such permeation should not surprise us, given the centuries-long experience of royal jurisdiction, feudal courts and common law, together with the church courts and canon law in a society where title to land was based on the written charter. Of course, the source being considered here is the register of the Council, which would naturally show a bias in favour of such evidence. How representative it is of approaches to dispute resolution more generally would require further investigation, but the variety to be found in the council register alone may suggest that this evidence is typical.

Further examples in the council register illustrate the reference of disputes to the discretion of an individual, as well as the resolution of a dispute through individuals acting as mediators rather than arbiters. For example, on 18 March 1531 Mark Kerr of Dolphinton and Helen Rutherford of that Ilk bound themselves before Council to "keep the sentence and interlocutor of Walter, abbot of Glenluce tuching the perambulation of the merches betwix landis".[91] A specific procedure was set down whereby the abbot was to visit the site of the ground in question with the abbot of Melrose as well as certain "gentilmen of the cuntre", and with reference to charter evidence assess the correct marches of the land. In another example, the defender in an action simply referred it to the discretion of the pursuer. In this case, Alexander Mylne, abbot of Cambuskenneth, and various tenants of the abbey were pursuing various persons for the spuilzie of goods. When their summons was called on 28 February 1532, however, the defenders, represented by Henry Spittal, referred the matters in the summons "to the said venerable faderis consuence and will". After this the abbot rather than the Lords of Council assigned the 16 March for the parties to appear in Stirling "to heir and see him declair his will".[92] The spuilzie had occurred over six months earlier, at the end of the preceding July, and the implication of the case might be that it was the involvement of the abbot in the pursuit of the action which led the defenders to abandon

[91] NAS CS 5/42, fol. 127.
[92] NAS CS 5/43, fol. 174.

it in order to submit to his judgement. After all, Mylne was one of the leading judges on the Session—in line to become the first president of the College of Justice within months—and therefore a man of significant influence at the royal court.[93]

A further variation of the reference to an individual or party is illustrated by a dispute which came before Council on 12 November 1530. This was between William Murray of Tullibardine and Agnes Gorthy, relict of Thomas Murray of Troon.[94] William had called Agnes before his own bailies for her to be declared to have lost or forfeited her right to a tack (i.e. lease) of the land of Troon and which was his heritage. However, it is narrated that "the said Agnes be her pur meins has optenit letters dischargeing the said William and his bailies of all preceding in the said matter quharthrow he ma nocht use his fredome and privilege of courte", for which reason he had summoned Agnes before Council. However, in an apparent reversal for William the Lords decerned Agnes' letters to be "ordourly procedit". However, William then asked instruments to record the fact that he was prepared to subscribe to an agreement which would set up what seems to have been an unusual hybrid form of resolution, mixing elements of arbitration and mediation. The proposal would have seen Agnes "resarvit the mater debatable betwix hir and William Murray of Tulibardin to the said William and his weil avisit counsale, the quhilke William in presens of the said lordis promittit till use the counsale of my lorde of Dunkelde, lord Ruthven, and Justice Clerk in said matter and to do na thing by uthir avise".[95] It is not apparent whether this course was then adopted by Agnes, but its formulation is suggestive of alternative, informal methods by which disputes might upon occasion be resolved.

Other examples suggest the use of simple mediation. For instance, the lairds of Wauchton and Niddry compeared before Council on 15 November 1531. The laird of Niddry had raised a summons, but both parties now "war contentit to use the consale of the provest of Edinburgh, the Iustice Clerk, the provost of the College [i.e. Trinity Collegiate Church], Maister Frances Bothwile, Maister James Lawson…

[93] A. Thomas, *Princelie Majestie: the Court of James V of Scotland, 1528–1542* (Edinburgh, 2005), pp. 13, 117; J. MacQueen, "Alexander Mylne, Bishop George Brown, and the Chapter of Dunkeld", in *Humanism and Reform: The Church in Europe, England and Scotland, 1400–1643*, ed. J. Kirk (Oxford, 1991), pp. 349–360.

[94] NAS CS 4/41, fol. 123.

[95] NAS CS 5/41, fol. 123v.

in all materis debatable amange thaim anent the tak of West Trako".[96] Here, though, the intention seems to have been to use this counsel by way of mediation in order to bring the parties themselves to a compromise. This is suggested by a condition which stated that if the parties had not reached an appunctment by Saturday or Sunday following, then the laird of Niddry was to have process on his summons. The case is a simple but telling illustration of the dynamics of dispute resolution, in that litigation was used to force an opponent to answer to a complaint and was then suspended whilst negotiations could be held to establish a satisfactory settlement with the help of mediators giving their counsel, but with a time limit and the threat of a resumption of formal legal process. What looks even more like mediation is the set of arrangements agreed on 4 February 1531 between David Douglas of Pittendreich and John Kinnaird of that Ilk. Legal process was suspended so that the parties could compear in Aberdeen before the bishop of Aberdeen "to the effect that my lord of Abydene may aggre the said partiis in all materis".[97]

On 9 December 1532, a case arose in which mediation was mentioned explicitly. William Lindsay of Preston raised a complaint against Thomas Trail, John Inglis of Kilmany and Sir William Inglis, apparently to block legal action in the church courts in respect of matters already agreed upon and entered into the books of the official. John Cantuly, the archdeacon of St Andrews, apparently acting as factor to Donald Ard, the parson of Tarvit, had granted Lindsay an assedation of lands relating to St Michael's church, Tarvit. The parson was now in Rome but through the agency of John Inglis was pursuing Lindsay in court over the fruits of the parsonage. However, this seems to have been in breach of a previous agreement following earlier litigation over the land. It is narrated that, previously, "eftir lang pley thai war compromittit" and William Lindsay had obtained a decree arbitral to which the Lords of Council had then interponed their authority. We are told that "eftir all this be mediation of frendes with baith the sadis partiis consentis thai war finale aggreit lik as ane act made in the officiles buke purportes".[98] It is not made clear in precisely what manner the "mediation of frendes" was instrumental, but clearly it had a definite

[96] NAS CS 5/43, fol. 74v.
[97] NAS CS 5/42, fol. 30.
[98] NAS CS 6/2, fol. 26.

role. The present dispute simply arose from the fact that the parson of St Michael's had summoned William Lindsay to Rome to answer for the fruits of the parsonage or pay 500 ducats unless he made payment of the fruits. The precise nature of the dispute is not clear from the record, but the Lords now proceeded to ordain the mandate for commencing proceedings which had been given by the parson to be produced in court by Sir William Inglis. Mediation had played its role without ultimate success, and had been unable to contain the contentiousness present in the dispute.

Another example of litigation being suspended "in hope of concord", with mediation envisaged as the means of reaching concord, is Gilbert Wauchop's action against the minister of Peebles, which came before Council on 7 May 1534. With the consent of the parties, the Lords of Council continued the action until the following week "so that thai may in the meyntime tak freindes and aggre thame betwix and the said day".[99] It is worth mentioning that the phrase "in hope of concord" was a standard one used in any context where it was hoped that the parties to a dispute might reach a private settlement, without the sanction of a court judgement, in this sense relying upon "love" rather than "law" in the terms used by Dr Clanchy in his analysis of medieval disputes. It seems that the objective of "concord" is what underpinned all the private methods of dispute resolution, and it may be significant that it was never used to denote the objective of litigation. This might confirm that the contrast between private methods of resolving dispute, based on compromise and settlement, and public methods of vindicating rights through court decrees was to some extent explicitly recognised in the sixteenth century. In one case the objective of an arbitration was said to be "that ane finell and gude concord may be had betwix the said partiis".[100] In May 1529, Huchon Rose of Kilravock complained that the laird of Cumnock had raised a summons against him concerning a matter "quhilk he [Rose] desyre to be ordourit amangis fryndis and nocht be the rigour of law". Rose explained that there "has bene greit kyndness betwix the lardis of Cumnok, him and his forbearis".[101]

Sometimes the Lords of Council simply continued an action for apparently the sole reason of allowing a period of time to elapse during

[99] NAS CS 6/4, fol. 125v.
[100] NAS CS 5/43, fol. 97v.
[101] NAS CS 5/40, fol. 43.

which efforts could be made "in hope of concord", as in the continuation of Patrick Murray of Fallowhill's summons against Walter Scott of Branxholm on 17 February 1532.[102] Sometimes the parties themselves consented to the continuation of their various actions "under hop of concord", as in the brieves of inquest taken out for lands in the earldom of Crawford by David, earl of Crawford, and Elizabeth Lindesay in July 1532.[103] Again we find the phrase in February 1534, when George Robson's procurator protested that any submissions made by him at this stage were "intendit be na way to pley nor answer" to the summons raised against George by Agnes, countess of Bothwell, but "was bot to persuad the party to concord".[104]

Occasionally, it is not entirely clear in what capacity a dispute was referred to the determination of named individuals. In March 1531, George, Lord St John, and John Robson bound themselves to "abyde at the ordinance and deliverance" of the archdeacon of St Andrews, William Gibson, dean of Restalrig, and James Lawson, burgess of Edinburgh. They were simply designated as "jugis" and directed to "give furth thir sentence and mak ane fynale end therein".[105] Again, in December 1531, Andrew Fernie of that Ilk and Elizabeth Lundy "submittit thaim in all actions and materis betwix thaim" to the comptroller, the bishop of Galloway, and John Lethame, "quhilk sall decyde thirin betwix and this day 8 dais", without there being any explicit indication of the capacity in which they were to act or the procedure to be used.[106] There are various possible explanations, including the failure of the record to reveal adequately the terms of such a submission, or that such submissions would always have been implicitly understood as relating to arbitration. It could also have been akin to referring a decision to the discretion of an individual. Consideration of the various possibilities reminds us how flexible arbitration itself was, since we have already seen in the previous chapter how medieval juristic debate about the nature of arbitration had taken account of all these different bases for the procedure. If Scotland was a litigating society, it was also most certainly an arbitrating one too, and more generally one in which lordship and hierarchical social relations were seen as providing

[102] NAS CS 5/43, fol. 157v.
[103] NAS CS 6/1, fol. 61.
[104] NAS CS 6/3, fol. 202v.
[105] NAS CS 5/42, fol. 135.
[106] NAS CS 5/43, fol. 122v.

the framework for resolving disputes in a wide range of informal ways. All of this adds a wealth of support to Dr Wormald's stress on "the underlying principle that disputes should be settled and not prolonged, in the most effective way possible".[107] This did not necessarily reflect anything special about a "justice of the feud" in this "feuding society", however, but rather a deeper and even more general principle about the nature of disputes in medieval and early modern Scotland. Litigation, arbitration, mediation and feud were all means of bringing about settlement of a dispute or at least a resolution in some form. A formal end to a dispute would often be achieved through a combination of some or all of these, whether by court decree, decree arbitral or agreed compromise. By the early sixteenth century, public and private justice typically functioned together in the achievement of such an outcome. Indeed, whether private justice could proceed by this time without the involvement of public justice in many cases, especially where landed right was concerned, must surely be doubted. Once a central court had emerged with the authority which seems to have been possessed by the Session by 1532, private justice must inevitably have come to function with at least a residual dependence upon the role of public justice.

Conclusion

Dr Wormald's observation that "private settlement was still . . . a prevalent and effective force in Scottish justice" in the sixteenth century has received strong confirmation and support from the evidence surveyed in this chapter. Of course, if "settlement" were taken to include settlement of court actions (with the consequent abandonment of litigation without the award of decree), then the statement would still be just as true of dispute settlement in modern Scotland, and would have a universal validity of sorts. Therefore the idea of "private settlement" must be taken to signify something more in this historiographical context. It was observed at the beginning of this chapter that the distinctive feature for sixteenth-century Scotland related to the reliance upon "private" authority, particularly through lordship and kinship structures. This created pressure and meaningful sanctions for upholding settlements. In addition, private settlement thereby became more capable

[107] Wormald, "The Sandlaw dispute", p. 191.

of incorporating a wide range of interests, contested matters and various disputants, particularly the wider kindred when this was relevant. Because of the development of the Session in the fifteenth and sixteenth centuries, the fate of this sort of private settlement has to be examined against the development of central justice. Of course, those agreements of which we have evidence in the council record cannot represent the total number which were made to resolve disputes. However, for the sixteenth century it is clear that parties often sought to enhance the stability of their private settlements through the involvement of Council and Session. The private settlement therefore belonged not to some compartmentalised sphere beyond the purview of the courts. The parties themselves often chose to bring their settlements into the world of the courts to enhance their stability.

When we talk here of the courts, though, we particularly mean the King's Council, and in its judicial guise, the Session. At this period it seems unlikely that local courts could have possessed the same authority. As a central civil court the Session was to play a uniquely formative and unifying role in the legal system of Renaissance Scotland, and its routine involvement in solidifying even private settlements in the sixteenth century is testimony to the idea that the development of central justice was not in opposition to more traditional forms of dispute resolution, and could even be seen as itself a response to the demands of people in dispute and litigants in particular. As such, we should never have expected a conflict between this new form of "public" justice and the traditional forms of "private" justice. Dispensing justice was after all a matter of resolving disputes.

The idea that public modes might be in conflict with private modes arises much more from the very particular sphere of criminal justice, and the gradual shift towards criminal liability being a matter deserving of prosecution and punishment by the state, as opposed to a matter for the injured party to prosecute in court or be compensated for. Even in the early seventeenth century, prosecution of crime was still largely a private matter.[108] It was only when the state came to develop its own interest in prosecution, without regard to the interests of the particular injured party, that the possibility of a conflict could become more real. Once the state came to reject the idea of discharging criminal liability

---

[108] M.B. Wasser, "Violence and the Central Criminal Courts in Scotland 1603–1638" (University of Columbia, unpublished Ph.D. thesis, 1995), pp. 12, 15.

and escaping punishment in return for compensating the victim, and once a sense of public order had developed to a high enough degree that the threat of feud was absent, then a shift might have been likely to occur which would create opposition between the public and private spheres of dispute resolution when criminal liability was involved.

Following such a change, the older system of compensation for harm which was criminal—assythment—would be undermined and ultimately destroyed by such developments. Compensation for harm would become a purely civil matter. A public interest in imposing justice would become structured by the criminal law alone. So in that very particular sphere, a debate might present itself about possible conflicts between private and public justice. But hitherto scholars have tended to treat criminal and civil justice together in terms of an undifferentiated concept of public justice. Just because the concepts of crime and civil obligation were evolving in the sixteenth century did not mean that no distinction was made between them in the *administration* of justice. If criminal justice is distinguished, the picture we have of the transitional sixteenth century is far more coherent, and we realise that a strong degree of integration and harmony between modes of private and public justice existed, and was only to have been expected. Moreover, the operation of private justice to some extent depended upon institutions of public justice.

Dr Wormald's work has demonstrated the compatibility between public and private justice in large part, and the evidence of this chapter intensifies the strength of some of her conclusions. But it also advances beyond them to suggest that the level of integration was much greater than previously thought. In addition, the degree of integration between public and private justice is also evident much earlier than is usually supposed. Integration of this sort is as much an early sixteenth century phenomenon as a later sixteenth or seventeenth century one. The role of the King's Council was largely responsible for this, the growing authority of the Session being symbolised by and embodied in the foundation of the College of Justice in 1532. Not only was there no conflict, but private and public justice seem to have been closely interrelated. The evidence of bringing "compromits" before Council for registration, discharge, interpretation and enforcement shows how effectively the mechanisms of public justice could be applied to fulfilling private settlements. Moreover, the insights into arbitration in fifteenth-century England to be found in the work of Dr Powell hold true for sixteenth-century Scotland. The Scottish Council records suggest that arbitration was often used in conjunction with litigation, and that a strong degree of interdependence existed between them in resolving disputes. The collusive legal actions found in England are paralleled in the registration of decrees arbitral in the books of council in Scotland. We also find the Session fulfilling a very similar role to the Court of Chancery in fifteenth-century England, in being used to lend authority and formality to arbitration procedure, agreements and awards, and to resolve disputes about arbitration, as well as to foster arbitration in relation to those disputes brought before it, by helping arrange it or even by sitting as arbiters. The integrated nature of private and public justice is apparent in the telling detail of the Lords of Council on occasion requesting a litigant to submit to arbitration. Overall, Powell's statements that "legal action was often pursued, not as an end in itself, but as a practical preliminary or accompaniment to arbitration", and that "the resources of the law were... harnessed to provide support and protection for arbitration", seem to hold also for Scotland.[109] All of this is evident by 1532.

Parties in dispute seem to have recognised the distinctive options open to them in litigation, arbitration, mediation and negotiation. However, what is so striking is that outwith the course of litigation there was evidently still a desire to take advantage of the formality, authority and sanctions which followed upon legal process in the courts. In this sense, Dr Wormald is also right to regard as false a distinction which contrasts "cases which came before the courts with private settlements, seeing in the first a formality and an authoritative quality which was lacking in the second."[110] However, a qualification must be made to this view in relation to a change in the sixteenth century. It is clear that whilst parties may have reached their settlements privately, they also felt the necessity—at least by the sixteenth century—of turning to the courts in order to lend an additional degree of formality and authority to them. They must have wanted the most effective form of settlement, it is true, but by the early sixteenth century this often did mean involving state institutions and legal processes even for the privately agreed settlement of a dispute. Thus there is reason to qualify Dr Wormald's statement

[109] Powell, "Arbitration in the Late Middle Ages", p. 62; in a recent study embracing legal disputes in early sixteenth century Scotland, Dr John Finlay also notes that "there can be little doubt that formal legal proceedings were sometimes raised by a party in order to encourage his adversary to negotiate": Finlay, *Men of Law in Pre-Reformation Scotland*, p. 122.

[110] Wormald, "The Sandlaw Dispute", p. 192.

that "in mid-sixteenth-century Scotland persuading parties to end their dispute was still more likely to be achieved by the pressure brought to bear by the social *mores* of the locality than by outside intervention from above, by state or central court".[111] We should also remember that involving the Session in local disputes was not exactly "outside intervention from above", since it could only happen at the instigation of one of the parties in the "locality". What is more important is to understand how centralisation of judicial authority manifested itself within the locality, reinforcing existing norms and structures of legal right rather than introducing new ones from "above".[112]

In fact, the evidence surveyed in this chapter suggests that it is most profitable to reject a stark contrast between different systems of dispute resolution, state and government versus kindred and bloodfeud, public versus private justice. These are highly abstracted concepts which tend to become organised into rigidly exclusive and discrete categories. In practice, there was also no absolute ranking of the effectiveness of different methods of resolving disputes, but simply a spectrum of methods open to parties in dispute, some or all of which might be and often were pursued contemporaneously. If anything, the most notable feature of dispute resolution by this time was that whichever method was used, legal process and the courts seem to have invariably become involved, even if not to generate the final outcome.

In turn, this suggests yet again that it would be mistaken to overemphasise the character of Scottish society in the sixteenth century as a "feuding society" if that was to imply that courts and legal process were somehow relegated to a secondary role. The feud existed alongside the law and not above it. Feuds usually related to landed interests, and these could not be dissociated from the structures of legal rights which were governed by the common law. By the end of the sixteenth century the feud was coming to seem an increasingly ineffective way of safeguarding such legal rights. The view of Keith Brown that "neither the law nor the judges who enforced it were ever thought of as objective and somehow above the world of the feud" and that "judges and assizes were themselves too much of a product of a feuding society in which obligations to friends and kinsmen, and extensive corruption, made it

[111] Wormald, "The Sandlaw Dispute", p. 192.

[112] See the insightful wider analysis of the operation of central and local power in the locality in J. Goodare, *The Government of Scotland 1560–1625* (Oxford, 2004), pp. 114–117.

impossible for the law to be seen as the repository of anything other than a partisan kind of justice" does not sit easily with the evidence and conclusions of this chapter.[113] If he were right, it would become almost impossible to explain meaningfully the development of the Session between the 1490s and the 1540s, let alone beyond that date. The sixteenth century was a period of transition in which these perceptions, if they ever existed, ceased to be reflected in the resolution of disputes in Scottish society. If, as Dr Wormald suggests, the sixteenth century was the last great age of the private settlement (in her very specific sense), then one reason for this was already apparent by the early decades of the century. Even at that point it seems to have been attractive to parties to use the courts in achieving private settlements of one sort or another. The operation of the Session by 1532 demonstrates a gradual process in which the state and its "public justice" was coming to be central to the resolution of disputes at all levels of society, integrating with rather than supplanting "private justice".

[113] Brown, *Bloodfeud in Scotland*, p. 44.

CONCLUSION

With the foundation of the College of Justice in 1532, a Scottish central civil court with supreme jurisdiction was fashioned out of the Session. By this step it ceased to be merely a sitting of the King's Council and instead acquired its own distinct identity. Until very recently, historians have generally failed to grasp the significance of this development. The argument of this book is that it should be interpreted as one of fundamental importance, though naturally its implications took time to be worked through. Indeed, some were still being worked through almost a century later in the course of Charles I's reforms to the Session and the Privy Council in 1626.[1] This should not obscure their importance from the very inception of the College of Justice, however. At the same time, it must be recognised that the foundation of the College did leave the existing institution of the Session essentially intact, and in most dimensions of its work there was great continuity. However, from 1532 it existed in a reconstituted and permanent form within the formal structure of a new institution. By this time, developments in the procedural law and remedies of the Session had also come to liberate it from the medieval constraints on the jurisdiction of the King's Council. Furthermore, they had provided the Session with the procedural means to assert its authority over other courts and to supervise more generally the exercise of jurisdiction and legal authority in Scotland.

The Session as a *ius commune* court

The foundation of the College therefore acted as both the capstone of the late medieval evolution of the Session and as the foundation for a fundamental new beginning in the administration of justice in early modern Scotland. Of course, there continued to be further development, not least through the Scottish Reformation leading after 1560 to the absorbtion of ecclesiastical jurisdiction into the sphere of the

[1] See M. Lee, Jnr., *The "Inevitable" Union and Other Essays on Early Modern Scotland* (East Linton, 2003), chap. 12 ("Charles I and the End of Conciliar Government in Scotland").

secular courts.[2] It is significant, however, that the College of Justice was founded a quarter of a century before such developments occurred and that the Session had by that time already assumed its role as a fully empowered central court. The Session therefore reached this stage of its development whilst operating unquestionably as a *ius commune* court, one in which the common learning of the medieval Roman and canon lawyers was drawn upon by advocates and judges alike. With more than half of the collegiate bench required to be of clerical background, the judges of the College of Justice were steeped in *ius commune* learning in a way which must have helped solidify such learning as perhaps the single most important influence on legal culture and the development of Scots private law in the sixteenth and seventeenth centuries.

Of course, even without the foundation of the College, the Session would have had the same basic character as a *ius commune* court. Its development *before* 1532 was decisive in this regard. However, the institutional tradition and structure of the College may have made this character more secure in advance of the Reformation, given the effect that this had upon the authority of canon law and ecclesiastical jurisdiction. This is especially apparent in the wider context of considering how the Romano-canonical procedural law of the Session appeared to become the dominant form of process in the legal system as a whole following the foundation of the College of Justice.

All of this is important when placed in a European context. The sixteenth century witnessed a wider cultural and intellectual transformation across Europe in the nature of the *ius commune*, something which becomes evident from the middle of the century onwards. Though historians of private law have sometimes mistakenly assumed that the *ius commune* can simply be regarded as forming a common legal culture for Europe from the Middle Ages to the French Revolution, it has become clear that this view takes insufficient account of the political and religious fragmentation of European legal culture from the sixteenth century onwards. The more homogenous medieval world of *ius commune* became complicated so as to produce a new level of differentiation tending towards what Douglas Osler has called "*ius diversum*". In other words, the operation of the *ius commune* (and the printing, reprinting

---

[2] See D.B. Smith, "The Spiritual Jurisdiction 1560–64", *Records of the Scottish Church History Society* 25 (1995), 1–18; J.W. Cairns, "Historical introduction", *A History of Private Law in Scotland*, ed. K. Reid and R. Zimmermann (Oxford, 2000), vol. 1, pp. 14–184 at pp. 83–84.

and circulation of books) became subject to political and religious constraints resulting from the Reformation and the political division of Europe upon confessional lines. Dr Osler has argued that this caused "the disintegration of the legal unity of the Medieval world, itself largely based on the canon law of the universal church".[3] But the College of Justice was an institutional anchor for the enduring legacy of the *ius commune* in Scotland from the early to mid-sixteenth century onwards, before this disintegration came to affect Scotland in any substantial way. This can only have enhanced the extent to which the *ius commune* tradition continued to underpin the legal culture of the College over the succeeding two centuries, even as European legal culture continued to experience further fragmentation and movement towards a "process of formation of national law".[4]

General claims

The interpretation advanced in this book has largely arisen from bringing a new perspective to bear on the history of the Session which encompasses its operation as a court of law. Such a perspective informed the reconsideration of 1532 in earlier chapters, setting it against the longer-term institutional developments in which the medieval Parliament ceded its judicial role to the King's Council and ultimately to the Session. This served to clarify and emphasise the institutional importance of the foundation of the College in terms of the constitution of a central court. With closer attention to the institutional characteristics of a central court and to the legal question of jurisdiction, the old argument that the foundation was no more than an excuse to exploit the wealth of the church can be seen to become untenable. The foundation of the College was an integral part of the development of the Session and completed the fundamental stage of its development as a central court. The process of foundation which culminated in the

[3] D.J. Osler, "The Fantasy Men", *Rechtsgeschichte* 10 (2007), 169–192 at p. 184. See also D.J. Osler, "A Survey of the Roman-Dutch Law", in *Iuris Historia: Liber Amicorum Gero Dolezalek*, ed. V. Colli and E. Conte (Berkeley, 2008), pp. 405–422; D.J. Osler, "The Myth of European Legal History", *Rechtshistorisches Journal* 16 (1997), 393–410.

[4] K. Luig, "The Institutes of National Law in the Seventeenth and Eighteenth Centuries", *Juridical Review* (1972), 193–226 at p. 193. This is a translation of a revised version of K. Luig, "Institutionenlehrbücher des nationalen Rechts im 17. und 18. Jahrhundert", *Ius Commune* 3 (1970), 64–97.

inauguration of the new College suggests an acknowledgement and appreciation of this change amongst contemporaries at the time. The importance thus ascribed to 1532 is also consistent with a comparative perspective in which the development of central courts in the fifteenth and sixteenth centuries forms a common European pattern. This pattern is especially visible when, as in Scotland, it was the judicial role of a royal council which provided the vehicle for such development. Most importantly, analysing the operation of the Session as a court of law reveals for the first time the breadth of its litigation, the impressive scope of its authority and the supreme and unlimited nature of its civil jurisdiction by 1532.

These conclusions constitute a new interpretation which reverses the orthodox view of 1532, dating back seventy-five years to the work of R.K. Hannay. They have implications for understanding developments in the administration of justice in Renaissance Scotland, as well as the nature of legal and jurisdictional change more generally in Renaissance Europe. These implications can be drawn out in relation to four main themes, all of which have been freshly illuminated by the understanding presented in this book of the Session as a court of law. These consist of the way in which the evolution of the Session reflected the growing importance of central authority in late medieval Scotland; the way in which changes in the relationship between state and society came to be apparent in terms of public and private forms of justice and the settlement of disputes; the changing role of law, legal rights and legal norms within society; and the nature of legal change more generally in Scotland as a late medieval European society, in terms of its effect upon the relations between judicial institutions, legal remedies, the development of private law and patterns of jurisdiction.

Central authority

The changing role of central authority constitutes perhaps the most important theme touched on by the history of the Session. Scotland was not the only European state in which a new form of judicial tribunal came to exercise jurisdiction more widely by the sixteenth century alongside established law courts, necessitating jurisdictional and procedural development so as to maintain the integrity of the legal order. As we have seen, such development in Scotland can be taken to illustrate aspects of what Sir John Baker has characterised as "a subtext of jurisdictional readjustment, not only between central and local but also between lay and spiritual courts", when discussing in an English context the changing role of King's Bench as a central court.[5] The example of the Session may therefore be taken as a case-study of how common forms of challenge to the legal order were resolved in a Renaissance state, and how those challenges tended to arise in the first place. The history of the Session strongly suggests that the challenges in Scotland were primarily concerned with meeting the expectations of litigants and administering justice effectively. They do not seem to have been the result of any deliberate remodelling of the legal order designed to intentionally promote central authority. Of course, the foundation of the College of Justice itself might be considered exceptional in this regard, being in some sense the deliberate invention of royal policy. Even here, however, it nevertheless constituted a new embodiment of an existing source of central authority whose exercise had already been strongly developed in the Session during the preceding decades. As we have seen, it also served to reinforce and consolidate existing elements of institutional reform in order to enable the Session to better carry out its role as a law court. Through its embodiment in the Session, therefore, the changing role of central authority in Scotland played a significant part in how a response was formulated within the legal order so as to allow the expectations of litigants to be met by the Renaissance state.

In this regard, it is clear that in the century after 1426 litigants desired judicial institutions which were more regular and flexible than those provided in the medieval legal order, structured as it was around Parliament. The challenge was to arrange the operation of central judicial institutions so that they could achieve this. The inconclusive and halting nature of the fifteenth century developments, often promoted through legislation rather than the organic development of an established judicial body, demonstrates that the challenge did present itself in concrete terms to contemporaries and was recognised as such. At the same time, there was also a distinct preference by litigants for central justice over local, though this could have been as much for the quality of justice available from the newer central institutions as for any intrinsic attraction to central justice. Nevertheless, the long period of experimentation which resulted in the sixteenth century Session does seem to be related in some way to acommodating the role of central

---

[5] J.H. Baker, *The Oxford History of the Laws of England, Volume VI, 1483–1558* (Oxford, 2003), p. 15

authority in meeting the challenge of providing justice. Inevitably, this had constitutional implications. One strand in the development of the Session during the century after 1426, for example, was a subtle shift from a tribunal whose legitimacy derived from its relation to Parliament, and thus the representative Estates, to one whose legitimacy derived essentially from the royal prerogative as exercised in the King's Council. Anachronistic constitutional assumptions in evaluating legitimacy in these terms must of course be avoided. It is also clear that a number of other factors considered in the course of this book largely explain the course of development in question. Nevertheless, there does seem to be an identifiable gravitation in Scotland from the second half of the fifteenth century onwards towards greater reliance on central authority as embodied in the King's Council. In any event, the ultimate success of the fifteenth-century experimentation seems to suggest that reliance upon central authority in one form or another was becoming ever more natural and expedient in Scottish society. The College of Justice is in this respect an important symbol of the new role which central authority was playing in sixteenth century Scotland, as well as a practical vehicle which allowed this role to be exercised.

State and society

All of this has further implications for interpreting developments in governance in Scotland during the same period, and developments in the relationship between state and society. The late-medieval transition to a legal order in which a central court played the dominant role in the administration of justice has always been acknowledged by historians as an important aspect of the development of the early modern state. This is seen in treatments of the development of public order and dispute resolution. These treatments have tended to see a new form of public order based on the rule of law and the prohibition of private violence as achieving a basic primacy in Scotland by the seventeenth century, marked by the termination of feud as a violent form of dispute settlement. However, the precise manner in which a central court affected these developments over a longer period has been left unclear. Studies of the resolution of particular disputes have been carried out, but without being placed in the context of a systematic study of the central court which, after all, almost always played a role in the course of settlement of disputes of any substance. This book has shown how a more balanced impression of the changing course of dispute resolution in sixteenth-century Scotland can be given by incorporating the findings of such systematic study of central justice.

In this respect, the premise of this book has been that the history of the administration of justice should be addressed more systematically in its own terms as primarily the evolution of systems of jurisdiction providing legal remedies so as to do justice. When it is addressed in this way for sixteenth-century Scotland, one conclusion is that the development of central justice would seem to be far more advanced by 1532 than previously supposed in accounts which stress the domination if not monopoly of lawyers, legal culture and a central court only by the early seventeenth century. Some historians have already acknowledged this in the context of arguing that Scottish government generally had undergone a transformation by the end of the sixteenth century. Julian Goodare has stated in this regard that "the momentum for change had begun in the 1530s, with the establishment of the court of session as a college of justice".[6] Nevertheless, his view that "it was in the later sixteenth century that the potential of this development was realized with the dramatic growth of central litigation" must be revised to incorporate recognition of the scope of authority and the breadth and volume of litigation evident in the Session by 1532. The volume of litigation did grow over the course of the sixteenth century, but the role of the Session as a central court was already very established by the 1530s.

From the broader perspective of the relationship between governance and dispute resolution, and between public and private justice, the Session was also clearly playing a central role far earlier than is normally suggested. Central authority and awareness of legal norms were firmly integrated into patterns of dispute resolution in Scotland by the 1530s. Therefore, although "private justice" may have remained prevalent in Scotland into the seventeenth century, the shift towards "public justice" started much earlier than classic accounts of the decline of the Scottish bloodfeud would suggest. Moreover, if Scottish society in the sixteenth century was a "feuding society", it was also most certainly a litigating society. The "justice of the feud" (in Jenny Wormald's phrase) could not have functioned as it did in sixteenth-century Scotland without regard to the availability in the law courts of judicial protection for

[6] J. Goodare, *The Government of Scotland 1560–1625* (Oxford, 2004), p. 172.

legal rights. The breadth of litigation in the Session in the 1530s and the frequency of recourse to its authority outwith litigation remind us that even at this stage legal culture and legal authority informed the settlement of disputes in Scotland in a substantial way. The "justice of the feud" was thus already coloured by the effectiveness of central justice and the suffusion of society by a legal culture which was increasingly ordered around the primacy of central justice. Wormald has pointed to a series of shifts in sixteenth-century Scottish society which "were slowly beginning to create a milieu in which formality, the forms and procedures of the law, the written authenticated record, had an appeal and an authority which would in the end far outweigh the amateur justice of lord and kin".[7] It is a compelling and brilliant analysis and one which acknowledges the sixteenth-century popularity of recourse to a central court and the crucial role of the Session from 1532. However, it too must be revised to incorporate recognition that the integration between public and private justice and the permeation of the culture of settlement by legal expertise and norms was already very advanced by 1532, nearly seven decades before James VI's legislation "anent removeing and extinguischeing of deidlie feids".

Legal rights, law and society

Recognition of the changing role of central authority and the integration of public and private justice also provides an important perspective for assessing how the underlying legal culture of the sixteenth century may have been changing in ways which helped stimulate the abandonment of feud in favour of court action. The place of law, legal rights and legal norms in society generally was shifting to a more central position. In this regard, the most significant change in the sixteenth century could be argued to be a shift towards a culture of vindication of rights, and recognition that endorsement from the legal order was necessary for rights to be secure. From this perspective, the extraordinary importance of the development of a central court and a central jurisdiction governing all lesser jurisdictions can be appreciated more clearly. Dr Wormald does come close to articulating this deeper cultural shift when she writes of the later sixteenth century that "the change thus created was not the result of royal policy imposed from above. It was the result

[7] J. Wormald, "Bloodfeud, Kindred and Government in Early Modern Scotland", *Past and Present* (1980), pp. 54–97 at p. 91.

of a radical, even revolutionary change of attitude and expectation, in a changing world, among that massively influential group, the lairds—the lesser nobility—of sixteenth-century Scotland".[8] The records of the Session suggest, however, that its "supremacy" (as Wormald puts it) was established in its fundamentals by the 1530s, and the primacy of a culture of vindication of rights already taking effect. This analysis helps provide a broader chronological framework for understanding the shift which had occurred by the early seventeenth century and the important argument of Michael Wasser that "increasingly violence came to be futile. What was gained by violence was subsequently lost".[9] In other words, the effectiveness of central justice meant that parties realised that disputes were best pursued in the central courts, and the pressure to settle came to be calibrated in terms of the progress of court actions rather than the violence of the feud, which came to seem ineffective. Society turned towards the formal vindication of rights as the most effective means towards resolving a dispute. This turn is already in evidence in the 1530s.

The nature of legal change

Finally, the nature of legal change more generally in late medieval Scotland is very suggestively exemplified by the history of the Session, in terms of the relations between judicial institutions, remedies, and jurisdiction, and their role in the development of private law. A fundamental theme in exploring the operation of the Session as a law court in this book has been jurisdiction, both in terms of the rules of jurisdiction which were applied, and the range of jurisdiction actually exercised. The way in which the medieval jurisdictional constraints upon the King's Council came to be superseded has been a particular focus of analysis in understanding jurisdictional change. Recent debate about the significance of the foundation of the College of Justice has been dominated by consideration of its jurisdiction as a way of illuminating institutional change, but in charting *jurisdictional change* it has tended to focus on the search for a single defining moment in which the Session finally acquired competence to decide fee and heritage. However,

[8] J. Wormald, "An early modern postscript: the Sandlaw dispute, 1546", in *The Settlement of Disputes in Early Modern Europe*, ed. W. Davies and P. Fouracre (Cambridge, 1986), pp. 191–268 at p. 205.

[9] M.B. Wasser, "Violence and the Central Criminal Courts in Scotland 1603–1638" (University of Columbia, unpublished Ph.D. thesis, 1995), p. 238.

analysing the operation of the Session as a court of law has allowed the question of its jurisdiction in 1532 to be considered for the first time in a much wider context. This has embraced the changing scope of remedies, court procedure and jurisdictional relations between courts as they featured across the legal system as a whole. It is clear that this wider context is crucial to making sense of changes in the jurisdiction of the Session as an individual court. Contested jurisdiction in particular can only be made intelligible in the light of the choice of courts and remedies available and an understanding of the basis for the exercise of jurisdiction by those courts.

The theme of jurisdictional change has been pursued in this book most obviously through the examination of how the Session acquired jurisdiction over fee and heritage. The question was not even asked until it came to be formulated in scholarship of the last two decades by David Sellar and Hector MacQueen. David Sellar saw jurisdictional change as deriving from legislative enactment whilst Hector MacQueen developed a more complex model which suggested a piecemeal expansion of jurisdiction by the Session after 1532, receiving some impulse from the foundation of the College of Justice. Although MacQueen's analysis of how this model applied to fee and heritage has been rejected in earlier chapters, it should be acknowledged that the model itself is highly suggestive and may illuminate other aspects of legal change in the period. However, the interpretations of jurisdictional change built upon the basis of these models have both been rejected in this book. Instead, one of the central arguments advanced through examination of jurisdiction over fee and heritage has been that the Session had already acquired unlimited civil jurisdiction before 1532. This can be seen in the heritage jurisdiction exercised by the Session through the remedy of reduction, and seems consistent with the general tenor of its authority and overall scope of its jurisdiction by 1532.

This argument has been made in detail in the course of the book. However, its main claim might nevertheless seem hard to defend from one perspective in particular. This is that it seems inconsistent with the evidence from the 1530s and 1540s that objections continued to be made to the jurisdiction of the Session through the pleading of exceptions in cases alleged to involve questions of fee and heritage. The fact that they were never accepted does not detract from the fact that they constitute evidence of a view that the fee and heritage bar *might* still fall to be applied. In other words, the conceptual framework within which the fee and heritage restriction made sense continued to be thought valid, at least by some. The answer to this which has been suggested in the course of this book is that the jurisdictional change in question occurred through the gradual substitution for this framework of a new one structured instead around the legal concepts relevant to the remedy of reduction. This brings to mind David Ibbetson's telling observation that "the legal historian has to take into account not simply the rules but also the ideas lying behind the rules, and the doctrinal or conceptual framework joining the rules together".[10]

Ibbetson has noted how such ideas may relate to "essentially neutral questions about legal conceptualization or the way in which legal rules are ordered". He has also drawn attention to how problematic it can be that "these more abstract phenomena... are not identifiable in the way that rules may be".[11] All of this could be stated about the jurisdiction of the Session in the 1530s. However, for the purpose of discussing fee and heritage, it is Ibbetson's analysis of the significance of legal ambiguity which is especially illuminating. He argues that "one aspect of legal ambiguity is especially important, ambiguity stemming from the indeterminacy of the conceptual frameworks referred to above". He points out that "when we are looking at the development of the law through time, one of the principal causes of legal change has been the friction between frameworks, or the shift from one framework to another".[12] In Scotland the years between the early 1500s and the 1540s appear to have witnessed such a shift, as the framework within which procedure by pleadable brieve was understood gave way to a framework structured around the distinctive remedies which could be granted by the Session. By 1532, the legal claims which underlay disputes over contested heritable title were being conceived and ordered in terms of the newer procedural and remedial framework under which they fell within the jurisdiction of the Session.

The mistake would be to try to interpret the newer heritage jurisdiction of the Session in terms of the older structure of remedies and jurisdiction which was presupposed by the jurisdictional limitations upon the late medieval Council. This is why it is futile to search for a particular moment in which fee and heritage jurisdiction was suddenly

---

[10] D. Ibbetson, "What is Legal History a History of?" in A. Lewis and M. Lobban (eds.), *Law and History*, Current Legal Issues 2003, Vol. 6 (Oxford, 2004), pp. 33–40 at p. 35.

[11] Ibbetson, "What is Legal History a History of?", p. 35.

[12] Ibbetson, "What is Legal History a History of?", p. 36.

acquired by the Session. It seems that both the remedial frameworks applicable to heritage disputes were simultaneously valid over an extensive transitional period which was thereby marked by legal ambiguity. By 1532, however, the undoubted competence of the Session to approach heritage disputes in terms of reduction seems to have left the older framework with no useful application. Therefore no cases were remitted to the judge ordinary because of fee and heritage, and as we have seen this seems to have been the case since 1513. This is still consistent with the fact that after 1532 pleaders occasionally pleaded a jurisdictional exception. As David Ibbetson has further noted, "at any moment in time there *might* have been—almost certainly *would* have been—competing frameworks held by different lawyers, perhaps even by the same lawyers, for few of us manage to maintain a harmonious self-consistency all the time."[13]

The fact is that in the 1530s some lawyers pleading before the Session still thought it worth attempting to argue that the Lords of Session were not competent judges in fee and heritage. They might have believed that the older framework still had some application. But the Session judges apparently no longer held such a belief by 1532, which is why we can state that the jurisdiction of the College of Justice in 1532 was unlimited and in principle supreme. The late medieval history of the Session therefore shows how essential it can be to understand jurisdictional change in relation to wider shifts between competing frameworks of jurisdiction and remedies which could require identical legal problems to be characterised, defined and structured differently within each framework. The 1530s and 1540s witnessed the authority of the Session gaining ever greater definition following the foundation of the College of Justice, and the older framework within which its jurisdiction could have been challenged becoming increasingly unintelligible. However, more importantly still for the argument of this book, the older framework already had no practical application by 1532. Once reconstituted as the College of Justice, the Session can therefore be regarded as having become a supreme central civil court. The fundamental place within the legal order of its role as a central court in the seventeenth century and beyond has long been apparent to historians. It is now equally apparent that the role of the Session in the sixteenth century requires much greater attention. A proper

[13] Ibbetson, "What is Legal History a History of?", p. 36.

appreciation of the significance for the development of the Session of the foundation of the College of Justice makes it clear that the legal culture of the sixteenth century must be seen as equally deserving of scholarly attention in order to illuminate the history of both Scots law and of Scottish governance. Moreover, the influence of that legal culture must be seen as well established by 1532. Study of the proceedings of the Session from this point onwards therefore provides an essential basis for understanding both legal and social change in early modern Scotland. By 1532 a "litigating society" was able to draw upon upon a legal culture which was powerfully informed by the adjudication of civil disputes in a supreme central court.

APPENDICES

Appendix 1 (chapter 6)

Fee and Heritage Protests, Exceptions and Remits 1466–1513[1]

A total of 143 protests or exceptions concerning fee and heritage were made, from which 63 remits were made (45 per cent); * indicates where it is not explicitly recorded whether the protest or exception is in relation to fee and heritage, or occasionally whether it relates to the competence of the lords.

Month	Year	Reference	Party or Parties (R signifies a remit)
Nov. 20	1469	*ADA* p. 9	(R) Archibald Ramsay v. Walter Lindsay
May 7	1471	*ADA* p. 10	(R) Abbot etc. of Lindores v. Philip Mowbray
May 15	1471	*ADA* pp. 13,15	(R) William Sinclair v. George Hume
May 15	1471	*ADA* pp. 13,15	(R) Marion Sinclair etc. v. William Sinclair
May 16	1471	*ADA* p. 13	(R) Thomas of Wyntoun v. William of Ruthven
Feb. 20	1472	*ADA* p. 20	(R) John Craig v. Thomas Kinnaird
Feb. 29	1472	*ADA* p. 21	(R) Robert Hamilton v. Alexander Baillie
May 16	1474	*ADA* p. 32	(R) Henry Wemyss v. David Hepburn
July 11	1476	*ADA* p. 48	(R) Andrew Gray v. Patrick of Gordon
July 12	1476	*ADA* p. 48	(R) Laurence of Spens v. Laurence of Crichton
Oct. 7	1478	*ADC* i p. 4	(R) Gilbert McCormack etc. v. Robert Mure
Oct. 8	1478	*ADC* i p. 5	(R) Johne of Petbladdo
Oct. 9	1478	*ADC* i p. 6	(R) Nichol Hostelar
Oct. 9	1478	*ADC* i p. 6	(R) James Auchinlek & Margaret Hostelar
Oct. 15	1478	*ADC* i pp. 11–12	(R) Tutors of Thomas Grandison
Oct. 21	1478	*ADC* i p. 18	(R) Andrew Mowbray v. John of Barton etc.
March 15	1478	*ADC* i p. 22	(R) Arthur Forbes v. John of Wemyss etc.
March 23	1478	*ADC* i p. 25	(R) Margaret Knichtson v. James of Cunningham
March 24	1478	*ADC* i p. 26	(R) Margaret Knichtson v. Laurence Bertram
Oct. 20	1479	*ADA* p. 94	(R) John Newman v. James Crichton
Oct. 26	1479	*ADC* i p. 36	(R) Johne of Houston
March 17	1483	*ADC* ii p. cxvi	(R) Janet Monypenny v. Margaret of Wemyss

[1] This list is of (1) remits because of fee and heritage and (2) isolated protests or exceptions which contested the jurisdiction of the Lords over fee and heritage but which did not lead to a remittance to the judge ordinary. However, in addition, it is assumed that in each case which was remitted to the judge ordinary an exception would have been pled successfully.

(*cont.*)

Month	Year	Reference	Party or Parties (R signifies a remit)
Oct. 15	1483	*ADA* p. *123	(R) William Aysoun v. Duncan Toyschach
Jan. 18	1480	*ADC* i p. 47	(R) John Maxwell v. Robert Charteris
June 21	1480	*ADC* i p. 57	(R) Lord Kilmaurs
June 21	1480	*ADC* i p. 58	(R) John of Porterfield v. Thomas Schethum
June 26	1480	*ADC* i p. 63	(R) John of Wemyss v. John Anderson etc.
June 28	1480	*ADC* i p. 65	(R) Baldred of Blackadder v. James Bonar
June 30	1480	*ADC* i pp. 67–8	(R) Robert Crawford
July 4	1480	*ADC* i p. 73	(R) Alexander Harowar v. Thomas Harowar
July 5	1480	*ADC* i p. 73	(R) Alexander Lauder v. Johne Oliphant
July 12	1480	*ADC* i p. 78	(R) Adam Blackadder v. Thomas Eddington
April 15	1483	*ADC* ii p. cxxxi	(R) John Fleming v. John Semple
Jan. 28	1485	*ADC* i p. *103	(R) William of Stirling
Feb. 3	1488	*ADC* i p. 104	(R) Walter Ogston v. John Abbot
Feb. 7	1488	*ADC* i p. 118	(R) Walter Halliburton v. Umfra Colquhoun
Nov. 4	1490	*ADC* i p. 161	(R) James Livingston v. Cristian Livingston
March 22	1491	*ADC* i p. 188	(R) Alexander Hume v. John Berry
Jan.	1492	*ADC* i p. 263	The King v. John Auchinleck
March 1	1492	*ADC* i p. 216	(R) Umfra Colquhoun v. Jhone Colquhoun
March 5	1492	*ADC* i p. 223	(R) Umfra Colquhoun
March 10	1492	*ADC* i p. 228	(R) Andro Filedare v. James Calder
Oct. 26	1493	*ADC* i p. 318	(R) William Bothwell v. John of Menteith etc.
Oct. 27	1495	*ADC* i p. 405	William Lord Ruthven v. Archibald Preston
Nov. 4	1495	*ADC* i p. 419	(R) Andrew Gourlay v. John Gourlay
Nov. 13	1495	*ADC* i p. 429	(R) Robert Waus v. Archibald Napier
Nov.	1495	*ADC* i p. 424	Michael Balfour v. Alexander Inglis et al.
April	1498	*ADC* ii p. 175	(R) William of Stirling v. James Ogilvy
July 9	1498	*ADC* ii p. 258	(R) James Hamilton v. Robert Hamilton
Jan.	1500	*ADC* ii p. 349	Michael Balfour
Jan.	1500	*ADC* ii p. 350	Thomas Maule
Nov. 14	1500	*ADC* ii p. 434	(R) Marion Sinclare v. David Hume
Nov.	1500	*ADC* ii p. 435	David Stewart
Dec. 4	1500	*ADC* ii p. 464	(R) William Campbell v. John Spark
March 24	1501	*ADC* ii p. 501	(R) John Adamson v. William Frog etc.
July	1501	*ADC* iii p. 35	Alexander Inglis
July	1501	*ADC* iii p. 37	William, earl of Errol
July	1501	*ADC* iii pp. 40–1	Lord Erskin
July	1501	*ADC* iii p. 45	Laird of Wemyss
July	1501	*ADC* iii p. 51	Lord Lindsay
July	1501	*ADC* iii p. 58	Robert Charteris
July	1501	*ADC* iii p. 64	Andro Herring
Feb.	1502	*ADC* iii p. 112	Lord Ross
Feb.	1502	*ADC* iii p. 115	David Kerr
March 3	1502	*ADC* iii p. 123	(R) Jonet Mure v. Alexandir Crombie
July	1502	*ADC* iii p. 146	Lord Erskin
Feb.	1503	*ADC* iii p. 210	Laird of Craigie Ross
Feb.	1503	*ADC* iii p. 303	Earl of Buchan
March 22	1503	CS 5/14 f.58v.	Katherine Maxwell

(*cont.*)

Month	Year	Reference	Party or Parties (R signifies a remit)
March 24	1503	CS 5/14 f.69v.	Alexander Kirkpatrick[2]
March 31	1503	CS 5/14 f.112v.	Sir John Hay of the Snaid[3]
April 4	1503	CS 5/14 p. 156	Alexander Barker*
Nov. 18	1503	CS 5/15 f.42v.	(R) Elizabeth Shaw v. Andrew Mercer
Dec. 12	1503	CS 5/15 f.122r.	Alexander Campbell
Dec. 12	1503	CS 5/15 f.122r.	Laird of Amisfield
Dec. 13	1503	CS 5/15 f.133v.	Lord Oliphant*
Jan. 23	1505	CS 5/16 f.26v.	Lord Lindsay[4]
Feb. 12	1505	CS 5/16 f.74r.	Lord Lindsay*[5]
Feb. 15	1505	CS 5/16 f.83v.	Bishop of Orkney*
Feb. 25	1505	CS 5/16 f.113r.	Alexander Napier[6]
Feb. 28	1505	CS 5/16 f.138	Lord Home*
March 8	1505	CS 5/16 f.178v.	(R) Margaret Johnston v. Alexander Kilpatrik
March 12	1505	CS 5/16 f.202v.	(R) William Turnbull v. John Turnbull
March 7	1505	CS 5/16 f.168v.	Alexander Mure
March 8	1505	CS 5/16 f.177v.	Alexander Kilpatrick
March 15	1505	CS 5/16 f.228v.	David Lindsay
Nov. 26	1505	CS 5/17 f.44v.	Alexander Cramond
Dec. 11	1505	CS 5/17 f.102r.	John Cumming
Dec. 17	1505	CS 5/17 f.140v.	Laird of Gladstone*
Dec. 18	1505	CS 5/17 f.143v.	Sir John Hume
Feb. 10	1505	CS 5/18(1) f.67v.	Archibald, earl of Argyll
Feb. 20	1506	CS 5/18(1) f.108v.	Archibald Dundas
March 4	1506	CS 5/18(1) f.145v.	James Henry
Dec. 16	1506	CS 5/18(2) f.54r.	(R) Alexander Kirkpatrik v. John Hume
Jan. 12	1507	CS 5/18(2) f.85v.	Lord Crichton
Jan. 20	1507	CS 5/18(2) f.116v.	Lord Lindsay*
Jan. 21	1507	CS 5/18(2) f.120v.	David Bruce*
Feb. 8	1507	CS 5/18(2) f.178v.	Laird of Cockpool*
Jan. 10	1507	CS 5/18(2) f.182v.	Sir Robert Dunbedy*
Feb. 12	1507	CS 5/18(2) f.193r.	Alan Borthwick*
Feb. 26	1507	CS 5/18(2) f.227v.	Laird of Mordinton
Feb. 27	1507	CS 5/18(2) f.231v.	Thomas Kilpatrick
March 1	1507	CS 5/18(2) f.237v.	(R) William Dalziel v. John Nisbet
March 2	1507	CS 5/18(2) f.245r.	Robert Crichton
March 3	1507	CS 5/18(2) f.248r.	Janet Hamilton*
March 17	1507	CS 5/18(2) f.322r.	Lord Drummond
March 19	1507	CS 5/18(2) f.333v.	Abbot of Inchaffray
Dec. 12	1507	CS 5/19 f.56r.	John of Ferny

[2] Cf. Nov. 28, 1503, CS 5/15 f.74r.
[3] Cf. Nov. 22, 1503, CS 5/15 f.54r.
[4] Cf. Jan. 19, 1506/7, CS 5/18(2) f.113r.
[5] Cf. Nov. 28, 1505, CS 5/17 f.51r.
[6] Cf. Feb. 20, 1504/5, CS 5/16 f.124r.

(*cont.*)

Month	Year	Reference	Party or Parties (R signifies a remit)
Feb. 10	1508	CS 5/19v f.152r.	James Scrimgeour*
Feb. 18	1508	CS 5/19 f.183v.	(R) William Keith*
Jan. 17	1509	CS 5/20 f.40r.	Thomas Crawford
Jan. 29	1509	CS 5/20 f.69r.	(R) John Hume v. Alexander Kirkpatrick
April 27	1509	CS 5/20 f.173v.	(R) Thomas Forester v. John Robson
May 5	1509	CS 5/20 f.185v.	(R) William Adamson v. Alexander Elphinstone
May 12	1509	CS 5/20 f.203	Burgh Alderman
Nov. 14	1509	CS 5/21 f.22v.	David Menzies
Nov. 16	1509	CS 5/21 f.26v.	Burgh of Dumfries
Nov. 21	1509	CS 5/21 f.33r.	James Baird*
Dec. 10	1509	CS 5/21 f.53v.	Nichol Purdum
Jan. 29	1510	CS 5/21 f.105v.	John Baird
Feb. 14	1510	CS 5/21 f.147r.	Alexander Boswell of Balmehet
March 24	1511	CS 5/22 f.87v.	Robert Calendar
April 7	1511	CS 5/22 f.148v.	John Weir
July 12	1511	CS 5/23 f.33r.	Burgh of Lanark
July 14	1511	CS 5/23 f.35v.	Robert Cunningham v Laird of Rowallen
July 15	1511	CS 5/25 f.43v.	Laird of Pollock
July 23	1511	CS 5/23 f.68v.	(R) John Scrimgeour
Aug. 6	1511	CS 5/25 f.101v.	Huntly v. Laird of Inverugy
Aug. 18	1511	CS 5/25 f.130v.	Alexander Ogilvy
Nov. 18	1512	CS 5/24 f.25v.	William Lyon*
Dec. 15	1512	CS 5/24 f.88v.	George Strachauchin
Dec. 16	1512	CS 5/24 f.93v.	(R) Burgh of Forres v. Abbey of Kinloss
Feb. 21	1513	CS 5/24 f.125r.	James Edmonstone
Feb. 23	1513	CS 5/24 f.135v.	Alexander Ogilvy v. Muriel Calder
Feb. 25	1513	CS 5/24 f.139v.	Alexander Gaderer v. Sir John Campbell
March 1	1513	CS 5/24 f.151v.	(R) Lord Sinclair v. Andro Tullindaff
March 8	1513	CS 5/24 f.184v.	Thomas Brand and William Bothwell
March 10	1513	CS 5/24 f.200r.	John of Drummond
April 21	1513	CS 5/25 f.20v.	Robert Lauder, Laird of Bass
May 10	1513	CS 5/25 f.85v.	Charles Ramsay
May 10	1513	CS 5/25 f.88v.	David Seaton
May 15	1513	CS 5/25 f.88v.	(?R) Sir James Dunbar

Appendix 2 (chapter 6)

Sittings of Council and Auditors 1478–1506[7]

Year	Council[8]	Auditors[9]	Cases[10]	Notes on Council Record[11]
1478	34	25	9	
1479	46	8	4	
1480	32	0	9	
1481	–	4	0	records missing
1482	–	13	1	records missing
1483	13	24	2	8 months-worth of records missing
1484	42	13	1	some gaps in the record
1485	6	0	0	only 1 months-worth of records extant
1486	–	0	0	no records
1487	–	0	0	no records
1488	29	0	2	
1489	15	0	0	
1490	46	0	3	
1491	44	0	3	
1492	62	0	0	
1493	14	16	1	
1494	33	15	0	
1495	33	0	2	
1496			0	There is no reference index which
1497			0	allows the sittings of council
1498			2	to be readily calculated for
1499			0	the period 1496–1500
1500			3	
1501	80		0	
1502	79		1	
1503	48		1	
1504	81		2	
1505	92		0	
1506	81		2	

[7] Beyond 1506 the number of sittings can only be counted by reference to the manuscript record.

[8] Number of days on which council sat, insofar as records survive, calculated from tables in *ADA* and SRO RH 2/1/8 and 2/1/9.

[9] Number of days on which auditors sat, insofar as records survive, calculated from tables in *ADA* and SRO RH 2/1/8 and 2/1/9.

[10] This figure shows the number of cases remitted by council or auditors to the judge ordinary in that calendar year, because of fee and heritage.

[11] These notes relate to known lacunae, and contain information mainly derived from W.M. Gordon, "The Acts of the Scottish Lords of Council: Records and Reports", in *Law Reporting in Britain: Proceedings of the Eleventh British Legal History Conference*, ed. C. Stebbings (London, 1995), pp. 55–57.

Appendix 3 (chapter 7)

Actions involving the pleading of an exception to the jurisdiction of Council and Session over fee and heritage, May 1529–May 1534

Date	NAS reference	Pursuer(s)	Defender(s)
28 July 1529	CS 5/40, f. 74r.	Adam Hopper	Janet Turing & William Adamson
4 Aug. 1529	CS 5/40, f. 81v.	The King	John Crichton & Ninian Seton
12 March 1530	CS 5/41, f. 4	Janet Rowitt	Alison Ruche
19 March 1530	CS 5/41, f. 22v.	Alexander Innes	Lord Oliphant
9 Feb. 1531	CS 5/42, f. 40	Alexander Innes	Alexander Ogilvy
11 Feb. 1531	CS 5/42, f. 46	Archibald Spittal	Finlay Spittal
15 March 1531	CS 5/42, f. 119r.	Helen Rutherford	Mark Kerr
23 Nov. 1531	CS 5/43, f. 92v.	Margaret Inglis	Melchior Cullen
2 Dec. 1532	CS 6/2, f. 19r.	Wigtown	Whithorn
4 July 1533	CS 6/2, f. 219	Thomas Duddingston	Steven Duddingston
13 March 1534	CS 6/4, f. 65r.	The King & Prebendaries of Crieff	William Drummond

BIBLIOGRAPHY

Manuscript sources

National Archives of Scotland

Acts and Decreets of the Lords of Council and Session:
Acta Dominorum Concilii:
CS 5/14–5/43 [13 March 1503–15 May 1532]
Acta Dominorum Concilii et Sessionis:[1]
CS 6/1–6/4 [27 May 1532–20 May 1534]
CS 6/6, 6/8

Edinburgh University Library

Sinclair's Practicks:
Laing MS III 388a
[A provisional text prepared by Dr Athol Murray is available at http://www.stairsociety.org/sinclair.pdf]

Primary printed sources

Acta Dominorum Concilii 1501–1503, ed. J.A. Clyde. Stair Society vol. 8. Edinburgh, 1943.

Acta Dominorum Concilii et Sessionis 1532–1533, ed. I.H. Shearer. Stair Society vol. 14. Edinburgh, 1956.

Acts of the Lords Auditors of Causes and Complaints, ed. T. Thomson. Edinburgh, 1839.

Acts of the Lords of Council in Civil Causes, ed. T. Thomson. Edinburgh, 1839.

Acts of the Lords of Council in Civil Causes Volume II, 1496–1501, ed. G. Neilson and H. Paton. Edinburgh, 1918.

Acts of the Lords of Council Volume III, 1501–1503, ed. A.B. Calderwood. Edinburgh, 1993.

Acts of the Lords of Council in Public Affairs 1501–1554: Selections from the Acta Dominorum Concilii introductory to the Register of the Privy Council of Scotland, ed. R.K. Hannay. Edinburgh, 1932.

The Acts of the Parliaments of Scotland, ed. T. Thomson and C. Innes. 12 vols. Edinburgh, 1814–1875.

The Acts of Sederunt of the Lords of Council and Session; From the Institution of the College of Justice, In May 1532, to January 1553. Edinburgh, 1811.

Anderson A.O., ed. *Scottish Annals from English Chroniclers AD 500 to 1286*. London, 1908.

The Asloan Manuscript, ed. W.A. Craigie. Scottish Text Society. Edinburgh, 1923–1925.

Charters of the Abbey of Inchcolm, ed. D.E. Easson and A. Macdonald. Scottish History Society Third Series 32. Edinburgh, 1938.

The Court Book of the Barony of Carnwath 1523–1542, ed. W.C. Dickinson. Scottish History Society Third Series 29. Edinburgh, 1937.

[1] This nomenclature for the record is modern. The title and binding artifically impose a division in 1532 which was not expressed in this way at the time.

Morison, W.M. *The Decisions of the Court of Session... in the form of a Dictionary*. Edinburgh, 1801–1806.
"Discours particulier D'Escosse, 1559/60", ed. P.G.B. McNeill. In *Miscellany Two*, ed. W.D.H. Sellar, 117–119. Stair Society vol. 35. Edinburgh, 1984.
Early Records of the Burgh of Aberdeen 1317, 1398–1407, ed. W.C. Dickinson. Scottish History Society Third Series 49. Edinburgh, 1957.
Habakkuk Bisset's Rolment of Courtis, vol. 3, ed. P.J. Hamilton-Grierson. Scottish Text Society New Series 18. Edinburgh, 1926.
Keith, Robert. *The History of the Affairs of Church and State from the beginning of the Reformation... to 1568*, ed. J.P. Lawson and C.J. Lyon, 3 vols, Spottiswoode Society. Edinburgh, 1844–1850.
Hope's Major Practicks 1608–1633 Volume I, ed. J. Clyde. Stair Society vol. 3. Edinburgh, 1937.
Letters of James V, 1513–1542, collected and calendered by R.K. Hannay, ed. Denys Hay. Edinburgh, 1954.
Liber Protocollorum M. Cuthberti Simonis, ed. J. Bain and C. Rogers. Grampian Club (1875) vol. 8:1 (English translation), vol. 8:2 (Latin).
Mackenzie, George. *The Institutions of the Law of Scotland.* Edinburgh, 1684.
"The Order of the Holding of the Court of Parliament in Scotland", ed. J.D. Mackie, *Scottish Historical Review* 27 (1948): 191–193.
The Practicks of Sir James Balfour of Pittendreich reproduced from the printed edition of 1754. 2 vols, ed. P.G.B. McNeill. Stair Society vols 21 & 22. Edinburgh, 1962–1963.
Quoniam Attachiamenta, ed. T.D. Fergus. Stair Society vol. 44. Edinburgh, 1996.
The Records of the Parliaments of Scotland to 1707, ed. K.M. Brown et al. St Andrews, 2007 [http://www.rps.ac.uk/].
Regality of Dunfermline Court Book 1531–1538, ed. J.M. Webster and A.A.M. Duncan. Dunfermline, 1953.
Regiam Majestatem and Quoniam Attachiamenta, ed. T.M. Cooper. Stair Society vol. 11. Edinburgh, 1947.
Registrum de Dunfermelyn, ed. C. Innes. Bannatyne Club 74. Edinburgh, 1842.
"Relation of the manner of judicatores of Scotland", ed. J.D. Mackie and W.C. Dickinson, *Scottish Historical Review* 19 (1922): 254–272.
"The Scottish king's household and other fragments", ed. M. Bateson. In *Miscellany of the Scottish History Society (Second Volume)*, 3–43. Scottish History Society First Series 44. Edinburgh, 1904.
The Sheriff Court Book of Fife 1515–1522, ed. W.C. Dickinson. Scottish History Society Third Series 12. Edinburgh, 1928.
Sommerville, J.P., ed. *King James VI and I, Political Writings*. Cambridge, 1994.
A Source Book of Scottish History Volume Two 1424 to 1567, ed. W.C. Dickinson, G. Donaldson, I.A. Milne. Edinburgh, 1953.
Statutes of the Scottish Church, 1225–1559. Being a translation of Concilia Scotiae Ecclesiae Scoticanae Statuta... with Introduction and notes by David Patrick. Scottish History Society vol. 54. Edinburgh, 1907.
Teulet, A. *Relations Politiques de la France et de l'Espagne avec l'Ecosse au XVI[e] Siecle* vol. 1. Paris, 1862.
Theiner, A. *Vetera Monumenta Hibernorum et Scotorum quae ex Vaticani, Neapolis ac Florentiae Tabulariis deprompsit et ordine chronologico disposuit.* Rome, 1864.
Tractatus de legibus et consuetudinibus regnie Anglie, ed. G.D.G. Hall. London, 1965, repr. Oxford, 1993.

Secondary printed sources

Baker, J.H. "The Changing Concept of a Court." In J.H. Baker, *The Legal Profession and the Common Law. Historical Essays*, 154–169. London, 1986.
——. *Introduction to English Legal History*. 4th ed. London, 2002.

——. *The Oxford History of the Laws of England, Volume VI, 1483–1558*. Oxford, 2003.
——. "The superior courts in England, 1450–1800." In *Oberste Gerichtsbarkeit und Zentrale Gewahlt im Europa der Frühen Neuzeit*, ed. Bernhard Diestelkamp, 73–111. Cologne, 1996.
Balfour-Melville, E.W.M. *James I, King of Scots 1406–1437*. London, 1936.
Barrow, G.W.S. *The Kingdom of the Scots: Government, Church and Society from the Eleventh to the Fourteenth Century*. London, 1973.
——. *Kingship and Unity: Scotland 1000–1306*. Edinburgh, 1981.
——. *Robert Bruce and the Community of the Realm of Scotland*. 4th ed. Edinburgh, 2005.
Berman, H.J. *Law and Revolution: the Formation of the Western Legal Tradition*. Harvard, 1983.
Bingham, C. *James V*. London, 1971.
Black, R. "A historical survey of delictual liability in Scotland for personal injuries and death. Part 1. Early History." *The Comparative and International Law Journal of Southern Africa* 8 (1975): 46–70.
Bonney, R. *The European Dynastic States 1494–1660*. Oxford, 1991.
Borthwick, A. "Montrose v. Dundee and the jurisdiction of the Parliament and Council over fee and heritage in the mid-fifteenth century." In *The Scots and Parliament*, ed. C. Jones, 33–53. Edinburgh, 1996.
Borthwick A. and H.L MacQueen. "Three fifteenth-century cases." *Juridical Review* 31 (1986): 123–151.
Brown, A.L. "The Scottish 'establishment' in the later fifteenth century." *Juridical Review* 23 (1978): 89–105.
Brown, J.M., ed. *Scottish Society in the Fifteenth Century*. London, 1977.
Brown, K.M. *Bloodfeud in Scotland 1573–1625: Violence Justice and Politics in an Early Modern Society*. Edinburgh, 1986.
——. *Kingdom or Province? Scotland and the Regal Union, 1603–1715*. London, 1992.
Brown K.M. and R.J. Tanner, eds. *The History of the Scottish Parliament, Volume I. Parliament and Politics in Scotland, 1235–1560*. Edinburgh, 2004.
Brown, K.M. and A.J. Mann, eds. *The History of the Scottish Parliament, Volume II. Parliament and Politics in Scotland 1567–1707*. Edinburgh, 2005.
Brown, M. *James I*. Edinburgh, 1994.
Brundage, J.A. *Medieval Canon Law*. London, 1995.
Brunner, O. *Land and Lordship: Structures of Governance in Medieval Austria*. Transl. from 4th rev. ed. with intro. by H. Kaminsky and J. Van Horn Melton. Philadelphia, 1992.
——. *Land und Herrschaft: Grundfragen der territorialen Verfassungsgeschichte Österreichs im Mittelalter*. 4th ed. Vienna, 1965.
Buckland, W.W. *A Textbook of Roman Law*. 3rd ed. Cambridge, 1963.
Cairns, J.W. "Academic Feud, Bloodfeud, and William Welwood: Legal Education in St Andrews, 1560–1611," *Edinburgh Law Review* 2 (1998): 158–179, 255–287.
——. "Attitudes to Codification and the Scottish Science of Legislation, 1600–1830." *Tulane European and Civil Law Forum* 22 (2007): 1–78.
——. "The civil law tradition in Scottish legal thought." In Carey Miller and Zimmermann, *The Civilian Tradition and Scots Law*, 191–223.
——. "From *Claves Curiae* to Senators of the College of Justice. Changing Rituals and Symbols in Scottish Courts." In *Symbolische Kommunikation vor Gericht in der Frühen Neuzeit*, ed. R. Schulze, 251–268. Berlin, 2006.
——. "Historical introduction." In Reid and R. Zimmermann, *A History of Private Law in Scotland: Volume 1 Introduction and Property*, 14–184.
——. "*Ius Civile* in Scotland, ca. 1600." *Roman Legal Tradition* 2 (2004): 136–170.
——. "Revisiting the Foundation of the College of Justice." In MacQueen, *Miscellany V*, 27–50.
Cairns, J.W., T.D. Fergus, and H.L. MacQueen. "Legal Humanism in Renaissance Scotland." *Journal of Legal History* 11 (1990): 40–69.
Cameron, J.S. *James V: the Personal Rule 1528–1542*. East Linton, 1998.
Carey Miller, D.L. and R. Zimmermann, eds. *The Civilian Tradition and Scots Law*. Berlin, 1997.

Carroll, S. *Blood and Violence in Early Modern France*. Oxford, 2006.

——. "The Peace in the Feud in Sixteenth- and Seventeenth-Century France." 178 *Past and Present* (2003): 74–115.

Cathcart, A. *Kinship and Clientage: Highland Clanship 1451–1609*. Leiden, 2006.

Chorus, J.M.J. "Civilian Elements in European Civil Procedure." In Carey Miller and Zimmermann, *The Civilian Tradition and Scots Law*, 295–305.

Clanchy, M.T. "Law and Love in the Middle Ages." In *Disputes and Settlements*, ed. J. Bossy, 47–67. Cambridge, 1983.

Cooper, T.M. "Freehold in Scots Law." *Juridical Review* 57 (1945): 1–5.

——. "Introduction." In *Regiam Majestatem and Quoniam Attachiamenta*, ed. T.M. Cooper, 1–51. Stair Society vol. 11. Edinburgh, 1947.

Cooper, Lord [Cooper, T.M.]. *Select Scottish Cases of the Thirteenth Century*. Edinburgh, 1944.

Coutts, W. *The Business of the College of Justice in 1600*. Stair Society vol. 50. Edinburgh, 2003.

Davies, R.R. "The Survival of the Bloodfeud in Medieval Wales." *History* (1969): 338–357.

Dawson, J.E.A. *The Politics of Religion in the Age of Mary, Queen of Scots: The Earl of Argyll and the Struggle for Britain and Ireland*. Cambridge, 2002.

——. *Scotland Re-formed 1488–1587*. Edinburgh, 2007.

Dickinson, W.C. "Freehold in Scots Law." *Juridical Review* 57 (1945): 135–151.

——. *Scotland from the Earliest Times to 1603*. Edinburgh, 1961.

——. *Scotland from the Earliest times to 1603*, rev. and ed. A.A.M. Duncan. 3rd ed. Oxford, 1977.

Dilworth, M. *Scottish Monasteries in the Late Middle Ages*. Edinburgh, 1995.

Ditchburn, D. *Scotland and Europe: The Medieval Kingdom and its Contacts with Christendom, 1214–1560*. East Linton, 2001.

Dodd, G. "Sovereignty, Diplomacy and Petitioning: Scotland and the English Parliament in the First Half of the Fourteenth Century." In *England and Scotland in the Fourteenth Century: New Perspectives*, ed. A. King and M. Penman, 172–195. Woodbridge, 2007.

Dodgshon, R.A. *Land and Society in Early Scotland*. Oxford, 1981.

Dolezalek, G. "The Court of Session as a Ius Commune Court—Witnessed by 'Sinclair's Practicks', 1540–1549", in MacQueen, *Miscellany Four*, 51–84.

Donaldson, G. *Scotland: James V to James VII*. Edinburgh, 1965.

Dow, F.D. *Cromwellian Scotland 1651–1660*. Edinburgh, 1979.

Drysdale, T.H. "The Stair Society: the Early Years." In MacQueen, *Miscellany Five*, 243–260.

Duncan, A.A.M. "The Central Courts before 1532." In *An Introduction to Scottish Legal History*, ed. G.C.H. Paton, 321–340. Stair Society vol. 20. Edinburgh, 1958.

——. "The early parliaments of Scotland." *Scottish Historical Review* 45 (1966): 36–58.

——. "*Honi soit qui mal y pense*: David II and Edward III, 1346–52." *Scottish Historical Review* 67 (1988): 113–141.

——. "James I, 1424–1437." *Glasgow University Scottish History Department Occasional Papers*. 2nd ed. Glasgow, 1985.

——. "*Regiam Majestatem*: a Reconsideration." *Juridical Review* 6 (1961): 199–217.

——. *Scotland: The Making of the Kingdom*. Edinburgh, 1975.

Duncan A.A.M. and McDiarmid, M.P. "Some Wrongly Dated Entries in the Acts of the Lords of Council." *Scottish Historical Review* 33 (1954), 86–88.

Easson, D.E. *Gavin Dunbar*. Edinburgh, 1947.

Elton, G.R. *Reformation Europe 1517–1559*. London, 1963.

Engelmann, A. et al. *A History of Continental Civil Procedure*. London, 1928.

Evans, G.R. *Law and Theology in the Middle Ages*. London, 2002.

Ferguson, P.C. *Medieval Papal Representatives in Scotland: Legates, Nuncios, and Judges-Delegate, 1125–1286*. Stair Society vol. 45. Edinburgh, 1997.

Finlay, J. "James Henryson and the Origins of the King's Advocate in Scotland." *Scottish Historical Review* (2000): 17–38.

——. *Men of Law in Pre-Reformation Scotland.* East Linton, 2000.

Ford, J.D. *Law and Opinion in Scotland during the Seventeenth Century.* Oxford, 2007.

——. "The Legal Provisions in the Acts of Union." *Cambridge Law Journal* 66 (2007): 106–141.

Fowler, L. "Forms of Arbitration." in *Proceedings of the Fourth International Congress of Medieval Canon Law*, ed. S. Kuttner, 133–147. Vatican, 1972.

Fowler-Magerl, L. *Ordines iudiciarii and Libelli de ordine iudiciorum (from the middle of the twelfth to the end of the fifteenth century).* Typologie des sources du Moyen Age occidental, fasc. 63 A-III.1. Turnhout, 1994.

Frieda, L. *Catherine de Medici.* London, 2003.

Gibb, A.D. "International Private Law in Scotland in the Sixteenth and Seventeenth Centuries." *Juridical Review* 39 (1927): 369–407.

Gilmour, W.J. "The Development of Arbitration in Scotland." *Arbitration* 41 (1974): 199–202.

Godfrey, A.M. "Arbitration and dispute resolution in sixteenth century Scotland." *Tijdschrift voor Rechtsgeschiedenis* 70 (2002): 109–135.

——. "The Assumption of Jurisdiction: Parliament, the King's Council and the College of Justice in Sixteenth-Century Scotland." *Journal of Legal History* 22 (2001): 21–36.

——. "Civil Procedure, Delay and the Court of Session in Sixteenth Century Scotland." In *The Law's Delay: Essays on Undue Delay in Civil Litigation*, ed. C.H. van Rhee, 107–119. Antwerp, 2004.

——. "Jurisdiction in Heritage and the Foundation of the College of Justice in 1532." In MacQueen, *Miscellany Four*, 9–36.

——. "Jurisdiction over Rights in Land in Later Medieval Scotland." *Juridical Review* (2000): 242–263.

Goodare, J. "The Estates in the Scottish Parliament, 1286–1707." *Parliamentary History* 15 (1996): 11–32.

——. *The Government of Scotland 1560–1625.* Oxford, 2004.

——. "The Scottish parliament and its early modern 'rivals'," *Parliaments, Estates and Representation* 24 (2004): 147–172.

——. "The Scottish parliamentary records 1560–1603." *Historical Research* 72 (1999): 244–67.

——. *State and Society in Early Modern Scotland.* Oxford, 1999.

Gordon, W.M. "The Acts of the Scottish Lords of Council: Records and Reports." In *Law Reporting in Britain*, ed. C. Stebbings, 55–71. London, 1995.

Gouwens, K. and S.E. Reiss, eds. *The Pontificate of Clement VII: History, Politics, Culture.* Aldershot, 2005.

Grant, A. *Independence and Nationhood: Scotland 1306–1469.* London, 1984.

Gray, W.B. "The judicial proceedings of the parliaments of Scotland, 1660–1688." *Juridical Review* 36 (1924): 135–151.

Guenée, B. *States and Rulers in Later Medieval Europe.* Oxford, 1985.

Guide to the National Archives of Scotland. Stair Society Supplementary Series vol. 3. Edinburgh, 1996.

Hamilton-Grierson, P.J. "The Appellate Jurisdiction of the Scottish Parliament." *Scottish Historical Review* 15 (1918): 205–222.

——. "Falsing the Doom." *Scottish Historical Review* 24 (1926): 1–18.

——. "Fencing the Court." 21 *Scottish Historical Review* (1924): 54–62.

Hanawalt, B. "The Power of Word and Symbol: Conflict Resolution in Late Medieval London." In B. Hanawalt, *"Of Good and Ill Repute": Gender and Social Control in Medieval England*, 35–52. Oxford, 1998.

Hannay, R.K. *The College of Justice and other essays*, ed. H.L. MacQueen. Stair Society Supplementary Series vol. 1. Edinburgh, 1990.

——. *The College of Justice*. Edinburgh, 1933. Reprinted in Hannay, *The College of Justice and other essays*, ed. H.L. MacQueen, 1–176.
——. *The Early History of the Scottish Signet*. Edinburgh, 1936. Reprinted in Hannay, *The College of Justice and other essays*, 273–323.
——. "Early Records of Council and Session, 1466–1659." In *An Introductory Survey of the Sources and Literature of Scots Law*, ed. H. McKechnie, 16–24. Stair Society vol. 1. Edinburgh, 1936.
——. "General council and convention of estates." *Scottish Historical Review* 20 (1923): 98–115. Reprinted in Hannay, *The College of Justice and other essays*, 232–272.
——. "General council of estates", *Scottish Historical Review* 20 (1923): 263–284. Reprinted in Hannay, *The College of Justice and other essays*, 251–272.
——. "On the Antecedents of the College of Justice." *The Book of the Old Edinburgh Club* 11 (1922): 87–123. Reprinted in Hannay, *The College of Justice and other essays*, 179–215.
——. "On the Church Lands at the Reformation." *Scottish Historical Review* 16 (1919): 52–72.
——. "On the Foundation of the College of Justice." *Scottish Historical Review* 15 (1918): 30–46.
——. "On 'parliament' and 'general council'." *Scottish Historical Review* 18 (1921): 158–70. Reprinted in Hannay, *The College of Justice and other essays*, 217–230.
——. "Some Questions Regarding Scotland and the Canon Law." *Juridical Review* (1937): 25–34.
——. "A Study in Reformation History." *Scottish Historical Review* 23 (1926): 18–33.
Harding, A. "The medieval brieves of protection and the development of the common law." *Juridical Review* 11 (1966): 115–149.
——. *Medieval Law and the Foundations of the State*. Oxford, 2002.
——. "*Regiam Majestatem* Amongst Medieval Law Books." *Juridical Review* (1984): 97–111.
——. "Rights, Wrongs and Remedies in Late Medieval English and Scots Law." In MacQueen, *Miscellany Four*, 1–8.
Harries, J.D. *Law and Empire in Late Antiquity*. Cambridge, 1999.
Harriss, G.L. "Political Society and the Growth of Government in Late Medieval England." *Past and Present* 138 (1993): 28–57.
——. *Shaping the Nation: England 1360–1461*. The New Oxford History of England. Oxford, 2005.
Helmholz, R.H. *The Oxford History of the Laws of England Volume I: The Canon Law and Ecclesiastical Jurisdiction from 597 to the 1640s*. Oxford, 2004.
Herkless J. and R.K. Hannay. *The Archbishops of St Andrews*, vol. 3. Edinburgh, 1910.
Holdsworth, W. *A History of English Law*. Vol. 14. London 1964.
Honoré, A.M. "Ownership." In *Oxford Essays in Jurisprudence*, ed. A.G. Guest, 107–147. Oxford, 1961.
Hudson, J. "Court Cases and Legal Arguments in England c. 1066–1166." *Transactions of the Royal Historical Society*, 6th series vol. 10 (2000): 91–115.
Hunter, R.L.C. *The Law of Arbitration in Scotland*. 2nd ed. Edinburgh, 2002.
Ibbetson, D. "What is Legal History a History of?" In *Law and History*, Current Legal Issues 2003, Vol. 6, ed. A. Lewis and M. Lobban, 33–40. Oxford, 2004.
Inglis, J.A. *Sir Adam Otterburn of Redhall*. Glasgow, 1935.
Ireland, R.D. "Husband and Wife: Divorce, Nullity of Marriage and Separation." In Paton, *Introduction to Scottish Legal History*, 90–98.
Jackson, C. *Restoration Scotland, 1660–1690: Royalist Politics, Religion and Ideas*. Woodbridge, 2003.
Kaminsky, H. "The Noble Feud in the Later Middle Ages." 177 *Past and Present* (2002): 55–83.
Keen, M.H. *English Society in the Later Middle Ages*. Harmondsworth, 1990.

Knecht, R.J. *Catherine de Medici*. London, 1998.
Le Bras, G. "Canon Law." In *The Legacy of the Middle Ages*, ed. C.G. Crump and E.F. Jacob, 321–361. Oxford, 1926.
Lee, Maurice, Jnr. *The "Inevitable" Union and Other Essays on Early Modern Scotland.* East Linton, 2003.
Luig, K. "The Institutes of National Law in the Seventeenth and Eighteenth Centuries." *Juridical Review* (1972): 193–226.
Lynch, M. *Scotland, A New History*. London, 1991.
——. "Staple Ports." In *The Oxford Companion to Scottish History*, ed. M. Lynch, 590–591. Oxford, 2001.
MacDonald, A.R. *The Burghs and Parliament in Scotland, c. 1550–1651.* Aldershot, 2007.
——. "Deliberative processes in parliament c. 1567–1639: multicameralism and the lords of the articles." *Scottish Historical Review* 81 (2002): 23–51.
Macdougall, N. *James III: A Political Study*. Edinburgh, 1982.
——. *James IV.* Edinburgh, 1989.
Macfarlane, L.J. *William Elphinstone and the Kingdom of Scotland 1431–1514.* Aberdeen, 1985.
Macinnes, A.I. *Clanship, Commerce and the House of Stuart, 1603–1788.* East Linton, 1996.
MacIntosh, G.H. *The Scottish Parliament under Charles II, 1660–1685.* Edinburgh, 2007.
MacLean, A.J. "The 1707 union: Scots law and the house of lords." *Journal of Legal History* 4 (1983): 50–75.
MacQueen, H.L. "The Brieve of Right in Scots Law." *Journal of Legal History* 3 (1982): 52–70.
——. "Canon Law, Custom and Legislation: Law in the Reign of Alexander II." In *The Reign of Alexander II, 1214–49*, ed. R.D. Oram, 221–251. Leiden, 2005.
——. *Common Law and Feudal Society in Medieval Scotland.* Edinburgh, 1993.
——. "Jurisdiction in heritage and the Lords of Council and Session after 1532." In Sellar, *Miscellany Two*, 61–85.
——. "Mackenzie's *Institutions* in Scottish legal history." *Journal of the Law Society of Scotland* (1984): 498–501.
——. ed. *Miscellany Four.* Stair Society vol. 49. Edinburgh, 2002.
——, ed. *Miscellany Five.* Stair Society vol. 52. Edinburgh, 2006.
——. "Pleadable brieves, pleading, and the development of Scots law." *Law and History Review* 4 (1986): 403–422.
——. "Some Notes on Wrang and Unlaw." In MacQueen, *Miscellany Five*, 13–26.
——. "Regiam Majestatem, Scots Law and National Identity." *Scottish Historical Review* (1995). 1–25.
——. "Tears of a legal historian: Scottish feudalism and the *Ius Commune*." *Juridical Review* (2003): 1–28.
——. "Two Visitors in the Session, 1629 and 1636." In MacQueen, *Miscellany Four*, 155–168.
MacQueen, H.L. and W.J. Windram. "Law and courts in the burghs." In *The Scottish Medieval Town*, ed. M. Lynch, M. Spearman and G. Stell, 208–227. Edinburgh, 1988.
MacQueen H.L. and W.D.H. Sellar. "Negligence." In Reid and Zimmermann, *A History of Private Law in Scotland: Volume 1 Introduction and Property*, chap. 17. Also published as "History of Negligence in Scots Law." In *Negligence: the Comparative Legal History of the Law of Torts*, ed. E.J.H. Schrage, 276–277. Comparative Studies in Continental and Anglo-American Legal History vol. 22. Berlin, 2001.
MacQueen, J. "Alexander Mylne, Bishop George Brown, and the Chapter of Dunkeld." In *Humanism and Reform: The Church in Europe, England and Scotland, 1400–1643*, ed. James Kirk, 349–360. Oxford, 1991.

McGladdery, C. *James II*. Edinburgh, 1990.
McKechnie, H. "Judicial Process Upon Brieves." 23rd David Murray Lecture. Glasgow, 1956.
McNeill, P.G.B. "Senators of the College of Justice 1532–1578." *Juridical Review* 23 (1978): 209–215.
McQueen, Alison A.B. "Parliament, the Guardians and John Balliol, 1284–1296." In Brown and Tanner, *The History of the Scottish Parliament, Volume I. Parliament and Politics in Scotland, 1235–1560*, 29–49.
Madden, C. "Royal Treatment of Feudal Casualties in Late Medieval Scotland." *Scottish Historical Review* 55 (1976): 172–194.
Maitland, F.W. *Selected Historical Essays of F.W. Maitland*. ed. H. Cam. Cambridge, 1957.
Martinez-Torrón, Javier. *Anglo-American Law and Canon Law: Canonical Roots of the Common Law Tradition*. Berlin, 1998.
Maxtone Graham, R.M. "Showing the Holding." *Juridical Review* 2 (1957): 251–269.
Meikle, M.M. *A British Frontier? Lairds and Gentlemen in the Eastern Borders, 1540–1603*. East Linton, 2004.
Miscellany One. Stair Society vol. 26. Edinburgh, 1971.
Murray, A.L. "Preface" and "Introduction." In Calderwood, *Acts of the Lords of Council Volume III, 1501–1503*, xiii–xliv.
——. "Exchequer, Council and Session, 1513–1542." In *Stewart Style 1513–1542, Essays on the Court of James V*, ed. J. Hadley Williams, 97–117. East Linton, 1996.
——. "Financing the Royal Household—James V and his Comptrollers." In *The Renaissance and Reformation in Scotland*, ed. I. Cowan and D. Shaw, 41–59. Edinburgh, 1983.
——. "The Scottish Chancery in the Fourteenth and Fifteenth Centuries." In *Écrit et Pouvoir dans les Chancelleries Médiévales: Espace Français, Espace Anglais*, ed. K. Fianu and D.J. Guth, 133–151. Fédération Internationale des Instituts d'Études Médiévales Textes et Études du Moyen Âge 6. Louvain-La-Neuve, 1997.
——. "Sinclair's Practicks." In *Lawmaking and Lawmakers in British History*, ed. A. Harding, 90–104. Royal Historical Society: London, 1980.
——. "Sir John Skene and the exchequer, 1594–1612." In *Miscellany One*, 125–155.
Néve, P., "Recent Work on the Superior Courts of the Ancien Regime in France, Germany and the Low Countries." *The Irish Jurist* (1988): 129–139.
Nicolson, R. "Feudal Developments in Late Medieval Scotland." *Juridical Review* (1973): 1–21.
Nicholson, R. *Scotland: The Later Middle Ages*. Edinburgh, 1974.
Ollivant, S.L. *The Court of the Official in Pre-Reformation Scotland Based on the Surviving Records of the Officials of St Andrews and Edinburgh*. Stair Society vol. 34. Edinburgh, 1982.
Osler, D.J. "The Fantasy Men." *Rechtsgeschichte* 10 (2007): 169–192.
——. "A Survey of the Roman-Dutch Law." In *Iuris Historia: Liber Amicorum Gero Dolezalek*, ed. V. Colli and E. Conte, 405–422. Berkeley, 2008.
——. "The Myth of European Legal History." *Rechtshistorisches Journal* 16 (1997): 393–410.
Parratt, D.R. *The Development and Use of Written Pleadings in Scots Civil Procedure*. Stair Society vol. 48. Edinburgh, 2006.
Paton, G.C.H., ed. *An Introduction to Scottish Legal History*. Stair Society vol. 20. Edinburgh, 1958.
Penman, M. *David II, 1329–71*. East Linton, 2004.
——. "Parliament Lost—Parliament Regained? The Three Estates in the Reign of David II, 1329–71", in Brown and Tanner, *The History of the Scottish Parliament, Volume I. Parliament and Politics in Scotland, 1235–1560*, 74–101.
Phillipson, N. *The Scottish Whigs and the Reform of the Court of Session 1785–1830*. Stair Society vol. 37. Edinburgh, 1990.

Post, J.B. "Courts, Councils and Arbitrators in the Ladbroke Manor Dispute, 1382–1400." In *Medieval Legal Records Edited in Memory of C.A.F. Meekings*, ed. R.F. Hunnisett and J.B. Post, 289–339. London, 1978.
Powell, E. "Arbitration and the Law in England in the Late Middle Ages." *Transactions of the Royal Historical Society* 33 (1983): 49–67.
——. *Kingship, Law, and Society: Criminal Justice in the Reign of Henry V.* Oxford, 1989.
——. "Settlement of Disputes by Arbitration in Fifteenth-Century England." *Law and History Review* 2 (1984): 21–43.
Rait, R.S. *The Parliaments of Scotland.* Glasgow, 1924.
Rawcliffe, C. "That Kindliness Should be Cherished More, and Discord Driven Out: the Settlement of Commercial Disputes by Arbitration in Later Medieval England." In *Enterprise and Individuals in Fifteenth-Century England*, ed. J. Kermode, 99–117. Stroud, 1991.
Reid, K.G.C. *The Law of Property in Scotland.* Edinburgh, 1996.
Reid K.G.C. and R. Zimmermann, eds. *A History of Private Law in Scotland: Volume 1 Introduction and Property*. Oxford, 2000.
Reid, N.H. and G.W.S. Barrow, eds. *The Sheriffs of Scotland: An Interim List to c.1306.* St Andrews, 2002.
Reynolds, S. "The Historiography of the Medieval State." In *Companion to Historiography*, ed. M. Bentley, 117–138. London, 1997.
——. *Kingdoms and Communities in Western Europe 900–1300.* Oxford, 1984.
Ribalta, P.M. "The Impact of Central Institutions." In *Power Elites and State Building*, ed. W. Reinhard, chap. 2. Oxford, 1996.
Richardson H.G. and G.O. Sayles. "The Scottish parliaments of Edward I." *Scottish Historical Review* 25 (1928): 300–317.
Robertson, J.J. "The Canon Law Vehicle of Civilian Influence with Particular Reference to Scotland." In Carey Miller and Zimmermann, *The Civilian Tradition and Scots Law*, 117–133.
Robinson, O.F., T.D. Fergus, and W.M. Gordon. *An Introduction to European Legal History*. 3rd ed. London, 2000.
Rowney, I. "Arbitration in Gentry Disputes of the Later Middle Ages." *History* 67 (1982): 367–376.
Ruffini, Francesco. *L'actio spolii: studio storico-giuridico*. Turin, 1889.
Sanderson, M.H.B. *Cardinal of Scotland: David Beaton, c. 1494–1546.* Edinburgh, 1986
——. *Scottish Rural Society in the Sixteenth Century*. Edinburgh, 1982.
Sellar, W.D.H. "Assistance in Conflict Resolution in Scotland." *Transactions of the Jean Bodin Society* 64 (1997): 267–275.
——. "Celtic law and Scots law: survival and integration." *Scottish Studies* 29 (1989): 1–27.
——. "The Common Law of Scotland and the Common Law of England." In *The British Isles 1100–1500*, ed. R.R. Davies, 82–99. Edinburgh, 1988.
——. "A Historical Perspective." In *The Scottish Legal Tradition*, ed. S. Styles, 29–64. Edinburgh, 1991.
——. ed. *Miscellany Two*. Stair Society 35. Edinburgh, 1984.
——. "The resilience of the Scottish common law." In Carey Miller and Zimmermann, *The Civilian Tradition and Scots Law*, 149–164.
Setton, K.M. *The Papacy and the Levant, 1204–1571.* 4 vols. Philadelphia, 1976–84.
Simpson, J.M. "The advocates as Scottish trade union pioneers." In *The Scottish Tradition: Essays in honour of Ronald Gordon Cant*, ed. G.W.S. Barrow, 164–177. Edinburgh, 1974.
Smith, David B. "The Spiritual Jurisdiction 1560–64." *Records of the Scottish Church History Society* 25 (1995): 1–18. *Sources and Literature of Scots Law*. Stair Society vol. 1. Edinburgh, 1936.
Stein, P.G. "Common Law and Civil Law in historical perspective." *Zeitschrift für Europäisches Privatrecht* 5 (1997): 385–392.

——. "Arbitration under Roman Law." *Arbitration* 41 (1974): 203–206.
——. "The College of Judges of Pavia." *Juridical Review* 64 (1952): 204–213.
——. "The Procedural Models of the Sixteenth Century." *Juridical Review* 27 (1982): 186–197.
——. "Roman Law in Scotland." *Ius Romanum Medii Aevi*, pars v, 13b. Milan 1968. Reprinted in Stein, *The Character and Influence of the Roman Civil Law*, 269–317.
——. *The Character and Influence of the Roman Civil Law*. London, 1988.
——. "The Source of the Romano-canonical Part of *Regiam Majestatem*." *Scottish Historical Review* 48 (1969): 107–123.
Stevenson, D. "The covenanters and the court of session, 1637–1650." *Juridical Review* (1972): 227–247.
——. *Revolution and Counter Revolution 1644–1651*. London, 1979.
——. *The Scottish Revolution 1637–1644*. Newton Abbot, 1973.
Stuart, M.W. *The Scot who was a Frenchman: being the life of John Stewart, duke of Albany, in Scotland, France, and Italy*. London, 1940.
Sutherland, D.W. *The Assize of Novel Disseisin*. Oxford, 1973.
Tanner, R. *The Late Medieval Scottish Parliament: Politics and the Three Estates, 1424–1488*. East Linton, 2001.
——. "The lords of the articles before 1540: a reassessment." *Scottish Historical Review* 79 (2000): 189–212.
Thomas, A. *Princelie Majestie: the Court of James V of Scotland, 1528–1542*. East Linton, 2005.
Thomson, E.E.B. *The Parliament of Scotland, 1690–1702*. London, 1929.
Tompson, R.S. *Islands of the Law: A Legal History of the British Isles*. New York, 2000.
Van Caenegem, R.C. *An Historical Introduction to Private Law*. Cambridge, 1992.
——. "History of European Civil Procedure." In *International Encyclopedia of Comparative Law*, ed. M. Cappelletti, vol. 16, chap. 2. Tübingen, 1973.
Van Rhee, C.H. "Civil Procedure: a European Ius Commune?" *European Review of Private Law* 4 (2000): 589–611.
——. *Litigation and Legislation: Civil Procedure at First Instance in the Great Council for the Netherlands in Malines (1522–1559)*. Brussels, 1997.
——. "The role of exceptions in Continental civil procedure." In *Adventures of the Law: Proceedings of the Sixteenth British Legal History Conference, Dublin, 2003*, ed. P. Brand, K. Costello and W.N. Osborough, 88–105. Dublin, 2005.
Webster, B. *Scotland from the Eleventh Century to 1603*. London, 1975.
Willock, I.D. *The Origins and Development of the Jury in Scotland*. Stair Society vol. 23. Edinburgh, 1966.
Wilson, W.A. *Introductory Essays on Scots Law*. 2nd ed. Edinburgh, 1984.
Wormald, J.M. "Bloodfeud, Kindred and Government in Early Modern Scotland." *Past and Present* 87 (1980): 54–97.
——. *Court, Kirk and Community: Scotland 1470–1625*. London, 1981.
——. "An early modern postscript: the Sandlaw Dispute, 1546." In *The Settlement of Disputes in Early Medieval Europe*, ed. W. Davies and P. Fouracre, 191–268. Cambridge, 1986.
——. *Lords and Men in Scotland: Bonds of Manrent 1442–1603*. Edinburgh, 1985.
Young, J.R. *The Scottish Parliament 1639–1661*. Edinburgh, 1996.
Zmora, Hillay. *State and nobility in early modern Germany*. Cambridge, 1997.
Ziegler, Karl-Heinz. "Arbiter, Arbitrator und amicabilis compositor." *Zeitschrift der Savigny-Stiftung für Rechtsgeschichte (Rom. Abt.)* 84 (1967): 239–276.
Zimmermann, R. *The Law of Obligations: Roman Foundations of the Civilian Tradition*. Oxford, 1996.

Unpublished theses

Borthwick, A.R. "The king, council and councillors in Scotland, c.1430–1460." University of Edinburgh, Ph.D. thesis, 1989.

Cameron, J.S. "Crown-Magnate Relations in the Personal Rule of James V, 1528–1542." University of St Andrews, Ph.D. thesis, 1994.

Chalmers, T.M. "The king's council, patronage, and the governance of Scotland 1460–1513." University of Aberdeen, Ph.D. thesis, 1982.

Emond, W.K. "The Minority of King James V." University of St Andrews, Ph.D. thesis, 1988.

Godfrey, A.M. "The Lords of Council and Session and the Foundation of the College of Justice: a Study in Jurisdiction." University of Edinburgh, Ph.D. thesis, 1998.

Iredell, G.W. "The law, custom and practice of the parliament of Scotland with particular reference to the period 1660–1707." University of London, Ph.D. thesis, 1966.

McNeill, P.G.B. "The Jurisdiction of the Scottish Privy Council 1532–1708." University of Glasgow, Ph.D. thesis, 1961.

McQueen, Alison A.B. "The origins and development of the Scottish parliament, 1249–1329." University of St Andrews, Ph.D. thesis, 2002.

MacQueen, H.L. "Pleadable Brieves and Jurisdiction in Heritage in Later Medieval Scotland." University of Edinburgh, Ph.D thesis, 1985.

O'Brien, I.E. "The Scottish parliament in the fifteenth and sixteenth centuries." University of Glasgow, Ph.D. thesis, 1981.

Wasser, M.B. "Violence and the Central Criminal Courts in Scotland 1603–1638." University of Columbia, Ph.D. thesis, 1995.

INDEX

Medieval Law and Its Practice

ISSN 1873-8176

This peer-reviewed series will publish high-quality monographs and essay collections on all aspects of medieval law. It will accept studies on Roman and canon law, English common law, Continental customary law, and Islamic law. Works may deal with technical aspects of law or with more general social aspects of law and the process of disputing.

1. Miller, W.I. *Audun and the Polar Bear.* Luck, Law, and Largesse in a Medieval Tale of Risky Business. 2008. ISBN 978 90 04 16811 4
2. Lefebvre-Teillard, A. *Autour de l'enfant.* Du droit canonique et romain médiéval au Code Civil de 1804. 2008. ISBN 978 90 04 16937 1
3. Nold, P. *Marriage Advice for a Pope.* John XXII and the Power to Dissolve. 2008. ISBN 978 90 04 17111 4
4. Godfrey, A.M. *Civil Justice in Renaissance Scotland.* The Origins of a Central Court. 2009. ISBN 978 90 04 17466 5